THIRD EDITION

Marketing

ERIC N. BERKOWITZ
UNIVERSITY OF MASSACHUSETTS

ROGER A. KERIN
SOUTHERN METHODIST UNIVERSITY

STEVEN W. HARTLEY
UNIVERSITY OF DENVER

WILLIAM RUDELIUS
UNIVERSITY OF MINNESOTA

IRWIN

HOMEWOOD, IL 60430
BOSTON, MA 02116

© RICHARD D. IRWIN, INC., 1986, 1989, and 1992

EXECUTIVE EDITOR Rob Zwettler
DEVELOPMENTAL EDITOR Andy Winston
PROJECT EDITOR Ethel Shiell
PRODUCTION MANAGER Irene H. Sotiroff
DESIGNER Diane M. Beasley
COMPOSITOR Carlisle Communications, Ltd.
TYPEFACE 10½/12½ Bembo
PRINTER Von Hoffman Press
COVER ILLUSTRATOR Poul Webb

Library of Congress Cataloging-in-Publication Data
Marketing/Eric N. Berkowitz . . . [et al.].—3rd ed.
        p.   cm.
    Rev. ed. of: Marketing/Eric N. Berkowitz, Roger A. Kerin,
William Rudelius.
    Includes bibliographical references and indexes.
    ISBN 0-256-09182-X
    1. Marketing.   I. Berkowitz, Eric N.   II. Berkowitz, Eric N.
Marketing.
HF5415.B44113   1992
658.8—dc20   91–27435

Printed in the United States of America
    2   3   4   5   6   7   8   9   0   VH   8   7   6   5   4   3   2

Preface

Marketing is exciting for students today, not only because of dramatic changes in the marketplace, but also because each student brings experience as a consumer to the classroom. To facilitate an interesting, interactive, and effective classroom experience, a marketing textbook must encourage students to consider their experiences and become active participants in the learning process. Like our first two editions of *Marketing*, this new edition continues the tradition of involving you, the reader, in the dynamic field of marketing, and we are pleased to have this opportunity to share the many elements of the field with you.

Since 1985, over 225,000 students and 1,500 instructors have used *Marketing*. This success and the positive feedback from both groups of users have encouraged us to continue to utilize many of the key features of our textbook and our innovative pedagogical approach. The rapid changes in the marketing discipline have also provided ideas for new material. We believe the combination of the strengths of previous editions and complete, up-to-date information about new developments in marketing provides you with one of the best marketing textbooks available today.

NEW IN THIS EDITION

We have added a chapter titled Ethics and Social Responsibility in Marketing (Chapter 4) to provide a framework for students to address ethical and social responsibility questions about current and future business practices. The chapter also provides exposure to the American Marketing Association's Code of Ethics and introduces the concept of consumer ethics and social responsibility.

To allow students and instructors to analyze contemporary ethical and social responsibility issues, each chapter now ends with a box titled

Ethics and Social Responsibility in the 1990s. These examples are illustrative of the difficult decisions marketing managers face in today's marketplace.

To address the revolution in marketing information collection and use, a new chapter titled Micromarketing, Information Technology, and Forecasting (Chapter 9) expands the material covered in Chapter 7 of the previous edition. This discussion of some of the most exciting changes in marketing keeps students abreast of the impact of new information technologies on marketing research, segmentation, forecasting, and many other marketing tasks.

Many other new marketing topics have also been added. These include green marketing, Japanese-style marketing, the new trademark legislation, brand equity, gray marketing, international trade, and service gap analysis. In addition, we elaborate on trends identified in the first and second editions, such as the move toward "lean" management structures and regional and ethnic segmentation, and analyze new trends such as the declining use of 15-second television ads and the move toward parallel development in the new-product development process.

Twelve of the cases are new or updated. In addition, most of the cases now provide students with an opportunity to perform both quantitative and qualitative analyses of marketing situations. To help students relate to the cases, well-known companies and products are the subjects of the cases.

The author team for this edition has been expanded to allow in-depth coverage of the many diverse topics included in the textbook, and to facilitate author involvement in the production of all instructional resource materials. The newest member of the author team, Professor Steven Hartley, had authored or edited the Services Marketing chapter, the Careers in Marketing Appendix, the Test Bank, the Computer Problem Software, and several video cases in the first and second editions. With this experience and expertise he was a logical addition to our team.

Finally, the package of supplements has been expanded, updated, and integrated to provide every possible learning and teaching tool for students and instructors. New to the package are in-class activities for each chapter, 14 new video cases, a marketing-planning computer software disk, and a collection of *Wall Street Journal* articles.

PEDAGOGICAL FEATURES OF THE THIRD EDITION

As in the first and second editions, we want to involve you in the study of marketing by encouraging you to think about your personal experiences as a consumer and by asking you to take the role of a marketing decision maker. We introduce you to contemporary people and organizations that have made both brilliant and disastrous marketing decisions. These extended examples appear both in the text and in the Marketing Action Memos found throughout the book, which apply marketing principles to actual situations.

Each chapter also integrates recent research related to the marketing discipline. We believe that students must be aware of important research that analyzes and explains marketing concepts and the success or failure of marketing programs. This edition continues to utilize Marketing Research Reports throughout the book to relate research findings to important issues facing marketing managers. Marketing Action Memos and Marketing Research Reports are color-coded to help you identify key topic areas. These areas include: general topics (▭), ethics (▭), and international topics (▭).

The book reinforces major concepts as they are introduced in each chapter to stimulate your understanding of them and foster your ability to apply them appropriately. At the end of every major section, Concept Checks pose two or three questions to test your recall. The Learning Objectives at the beginning of each chapter and the Summary and Key Terms and Concepts at the close provide further reinforcement.

We believe that the use of these unique learning aids lets you learn about, understand, and integrate the many marketing topics covered in our textbook, and allows you to apply them in the constantly changing marketing environment you will encounter as a consumer and a marketing manager.

TEXT ORGANIZATION

Marketing, Third Edition, is divided into six main parts. Part I, Initiating the Marketing Process, looks first at what marketing is and how it identifies and satisfies consumer needs (Chapter 1). Then Chapter 2 provides an overview of the strategic marketing process that occurs in an organization—planning, implementation, and control—which provides a structure for the text. Chapter 3 analyzes the five major environmental factors in our changing marketing environment, while Chapter 4 discusses the significance of ethics and social responsibility in marketing decisions.

Part II, Understanding Buyers and Markets, first describes, in Chapter 5, how ultimate consumers reach buying decisions. Next, because of their important differences from ultimate consumers, industrial and organizational buyers and how they make purchase decisions are covered in Chapter 6.

In Part III, Targeting Marketing Opportunities, the marketing research function is discussed in Chapter 7. The process of segmenting and targeting markets and positioning products appears in Chapter 8. The increasing importance of micromarketing, how today's marketing managers use strategic information systems, and sales forecasting are described in Chapter 9.

Part IV, Satisfying Marketing Opportunities, covers the four Ps—the marketing mix elements. Unlike most competitive textbooks, the product element is divided into the natural chronological sequence of first developing new products (Chapter 10) and then managing the existing products (Chapter 11). Pricing is covered in terms of underlying pricing analysis (Chapter 12), followed by actual price setting (Chapter 13), and the related Appendix A, Financial Aspects of Marketing. Three chapters address the place (distribution) aspects of marketing: Marketing Channels and Wholesaling (Chapter 14), Physical Distribution and Logistics Management (Chapter 15), and Retailing (Chapter 16). Retailing is a separate chapter because of its importance and interest as a career for many of today's students. Promotion is also covered in three chapters. Chapter 17 discusses marketing communications in general and presents an in-depth treatment of sales promotion, an activity that often exceeds advertising in the promotional budgets of many firms but receives minimal coverage in many text-books. Advertising (Chapter 18) and Personal Selling and Sales Management (Chapter 19) complete the coverage of promotional activities.

Part V, Managing the Marketing Process, expands on Chapter 2 to show how the four marketing mix elements are blended to plan (Chapter 20) and implement and control (Chapter 21) marketing programs. Because these topics can become very abstract, both chapters close with a detailed example of how Yoplait yogurt's marketing program is planned, implemented, and controlled.

Part VI, Expanding Marketing Settings, devotes separate chapters to two marketing topics of increasing importance in today's world: International Marketing (Chapter 22) and Marketing of Services (Chapter 23). The part closes with Appendix B, Career Planning in Marketing, which discusses marketing jobs themselves and how to get them.

Cases from actual organizations, a detailed glossary, and three indexes (author; company and product; and subject) complete the book.

As we observe in Chapter 1, we genuinely hope that somewhere in *Marketing* the reader will discover not only the challenge and excitement of marketing, but possibly a career as well.

SUPPLEMENTAL RESOURCE MATERIALS

Developing a comprehensive and integrated package of high-quality instructional supplements was a primary objective for this edition. We have been involved, as authors or supervisors, in the production of all of the supplements that now accompany our text. In addition, all of the supplements that accompanied our first two editions have been updated and revised, while many new supplements have been added to the package. Much attention has been given to providing elements and features in these supplements that were requested by both inexperienced and experienced instructors. As a result, each supplement contains several features not offered with any other marketing text.

Instructor's Manual   The Instructor's Manual includes lecture notes, transparencies and transparency masters, discussions of the ethics and social responsibility examples, and answers to the end-of-chapter Problems and Applications questions. Supplemental Lecture Notes (Marketing Action Memos and Marketing Research Reports) and In-Class Activities are also provided.

Transparency Acetates   A set of 200 four-color overhead transparency acetates is available free to adopters. More than 50 percent of these have been culled from outside the text.

Test Bank   Our Test Bank has been developed to ensure clarity, accuracy, and an appropriate range and level of difficulty. It contains more than 2,000 questions, categorized by chapter, major topic, and subject area within the chapter, and level of learning (definitional, conceptual, or application). The Test Bank includes approximately 10 essay questions, and 75 to 100 multiple choice questions per chapter, making it one of the most comprehensive test packages on the market.

Irwin's Computerized Testing Software   In addition to the printed format, a computerized test bank is available free to adopters. The easy-to-use test bank includes all the questions contained in the printed version. Additional benefits include the ability to:

- Add or delete individual test items
- Personalize individual questions
- Generate several versions of the same exam
- Maintain class files and test scores on disk

Video Case Studies   A unique series of twenty contemporary marketing cases is available on a videotape cassette. Subjects range from the conception and launching of new products to strategies used in designing advertising programs.

Study Guide   Authored by educational consultant, Erica Michaels, the Study Guide enables the student to learn and apply marketing principles instead of simply memorizing facts for an examination. New case problems and five types of exercises are used to accomplish this goal: (1) application exercises, (2) matching terms to definitions, (3) matching concepts to examples, (4) recognition and identification exercises, and (5) chapter recall.

Computer-Problem Software   This software features short cases and problems that allow students to learn about and apply marketing concepts and see the results of marketing decisions on a personal computer.

Marketing Planning Software   The marketing plan software disk is designed to help students use the strategic marketing process introduced in Chapter 2 and discussed in detail in Chapters 20 and 21. The software and accompanying handbook provide a personal and computer-based tool for involving students in the course.

Newsletter/Update   An annual newsletter will update the text with supplemental Marketing Research Reports, Marketing Action Memos, transparency masters, and reprints of pertinent magazine and newspaper articles.

Wall Street Journal **Articles**   A collection of recent *Wall Street Journal* articles with corresponding questions is provided to facilitate class discussion.

DEVELOPMENT OF THIS BOOK

As with any new product, developing a good textbook requires extensive market research and comparative analysis of the competition. We were fortunate in having the developmental resources of Richard D. Irwin to support this effort.

To guide the basic focus of the book, we conducted focus groups, group discussions, and reviews of the manuscript, as well as classroom testing of the manuscript in actual teaching situations. In creating the second edition, we also drew on multiple sources. In addition to another focus group, we commissioned faculty who were using the first edition to keep regular diaries documenting their classroom experiences. We also commissioned instructors who were familiar with other textbooks to do comparative reviews that told us how our book could be improved. The wealth of information that resulted from these reviews enabled us to determine which features of the manuscript were most effective and to revise those that needed more work.

Finally, to write the third edition, a survey of over 150 instructors, including users and nonusers, was conducted to determine the key strengths and weaknesses of the second edition, and faculty from various schools nationwide were commissioned to review our revisions on a chapter-by-chapter basis. Our textbook cases, Test Bank, software, and Study Guide also underwent this painstaking attention and concern for quality.

ACKNOWLEDGMENTS

The preceding section demonstrates the amount of reviewing that went into this project, and we are deeply grateful to the numerous people who have shared their ideas with us. Reviewing a book or supplement takes an incredible amount of energy and attention, and we are glad that the people listed below took the time to do it. Their comments have inspired us to do our best.

Reviewers who contributed to the first and second editions of this book include:

William D. Ash *California State University, Long Beach*

Siva Balasubramanian *University of Iowa*

A. Diane Barlar *University of West Florida*

James Barnes *University of Mississippi*

Thomas Bertsch *James Madison University*

William Brown *University of Nebraska, Omaha*

William G. Browne *Oregon State University*

Stephen Calcich *Norfolk State University*

Gerald Cavallo *Fairfield University*

S. Tamer Cavusgil *Michigan State University*

Clark Compton *University of Missouri, St. Louis*

Ken Crocker *Bowling Green State University*

Joe Cronin *University of Kentucky*

Lowell E. Crow *Western Michigan University*

John H. Cunningham *University of Oregon*

Bill Curtis *University of Nebraska, Lincoln*

Dexter Dalton *St. Louis Community College at Meramec*

Dan Darrow *Ferris State University*

Martin Decatur *Suffolk County Community College*

Francis DeFea *El Camino College*

Bill Dodds *Boston College*

James Donnelly *University of Kentucky*

Roger W. Egerton *Southwestern Oklahoma State University*

Barbara Evans *University of Melbourne (Australia)*

Charles Ford *Arkansas State University*

Donald Fuller *University of Central Florida*

Leslie A. Goldgehn *California State, Hayward*

Kenneth Goodenday *University of Toledo*

James Grimm *Illinois State University*

Richard Hill *University of Illinois*

Al Holden *St. John's University*

Jarrett Hudnall *Stephen F. Austin State University*

Mike Hyman *University of Houston*

Kenneth Jameson *California State University, Dominguez Hills*

James C. Johnson *St. Cloud State University*

Mary Joyce *San Francisco State University*

Herbert Katzenstein *St. John's University*

Roy Klages *State University of New York at Albany*

Priscilla LaBarbera *New York University*

Irene Lange *California State University, Fullerton*

Ed Laube *Macomb Community College*

Karen LeMasters *University of Arizona*

Richard Leventhal *Metropolitan State College*

Lynn Loudenback *New Mexico State University*

Robert Luke *Southwest Missouri State University*

Bart Macchiette *Plymouth State University*

Kenneth Maricle *Virginia Commonwealth University*

Elena Martinez *University of Puerto Rico*

James McAlexander *Iowa State University*

Peter McClure *University of Massachusetts, Boston*

Jim McHugh *St. Louis Community College at Forest Park*

Gary McKinnon *Brigham Young University*

Lee Meadow *Bentley College*

James Meszaros *County College of Morris*

Ron Michaels *Indiana University*

Stephen W. Miller *St. Louis University*

Fred Morgan *Wayne State University*

Donald F. Mulvihill *Virginia Commonwealth University*

Keith Murray *Northeastern University*

Joseph Myslivec *Central Michigan University*

Carl Obermiller *University of Washington*

Allan Palmer *University of North Carolina, Charlotte*

Dennis Pappas *Columbus Technical Institute*

Richard Penn *University of Northern Iowa*

John Penrose *University of Texas, Austin*

William Perttula *San Francisco State University*

Michael Peters *Boston College*

Joe Puri *Florida Atlantic University*

James P. Rakowski *Memphis State University*

Heikki Rinne *Brigham Young University*

Bob Ruekert *University of Minnesota*

Eberhard Scheuing *St. John's University*

Starr Schlobohm *University of New Hampshire*

Stan Scott *Boise State University*

Bob Smiley *Indiana State University*

Allen Smith *Florida Atlantic University*

Robert Swerdlow *Lamar University*

Clint Tankersley *Syracuse University*

Andrew Thacker *California State Polytechnic University, Pomona*

Fred Trawick *University of Alabama at Birmingham*

Thomas Trittipo *Central State University, Oklahoma*

Sue Umashankar *University of Arizona*

Ottilia Voegtli *University of Missouri, St. Louis*

Gerald Waddle *Clemson University*

Randall E. Wade *Rogue Community College*

Harlan Wallingford *Pace University*

James Wilkins *University of Southwestern Louisiana*

Kaylene Williams *University of Delaware*

Wilton Lelund Wilson *Southwest Texas State University*

Robert Witherspoon *Triton College*

Van R. Wood *Texas Tech University*

William R. Wynd *Eastern Washington University*

Reviewers who helped us create this new edition include:

Linda Anglin *Central Michigan University*

Patricia Baconrind *Fort Hays State University*

Siva Balasubramanian *University of Iowa*

James H. Barnes *University of Mississippi*

James Cross, *University of Las Vegas*

John H. Cunningham *University of Oregon*

Linda M. Delene *Western Michigan University*

Paul Dion *Bryant College*

James Gould *Pace University—White Plains Campus*

Marc Goldberg *Portland State University*

Kristine Hovsepian *Ashland University*

Ram Kesavan *University of Detroit*

Gary Law *Cuyahoga Community College*

Richard Leventhal *Metropolitan State College*

Leonard Lindenmuth *State University of New York—Binghamton*

Donald G. Norris *Miami University (OH)*

Dave Olson *North Hennepin Community College*

William S. Piper *The University of Southern Mississippi—Gulf Park*

Gary Poorman *Normandale Community College*

James P. Rakowski *Memphis State University*

Harold S. Sekiguchi *University of Nevada*

Miriam B. Stamps *University of South Florida*

Tom L. Trittipo *Central State University*

Ron Weston *Contra Costa College*

Max White *Southwestern Oklahoma State University*

We were also fortunate to be able to call on the special expertise of educational consultant Erica Michaels, who utilized her extensive experience with undergraduate marketing students to write the Study Guide. In addition, she updated the Glossary and compiled the *Wall Street Journal* articles.

The business community also provided great help in making available cases and information that appear in the text and supplements—much of it for the first time in college materials. Thanks are due to Earl Bakken of Medtronics, Dwight Riskey of Frito-Lay, Inc., Douglas Ziemer of Texas Instruments, and Bob Proscal of Honeywell. We also acknowledge the help of Ed Johnson of Minnesota Color Envelope, Roger K. Thompson of The Olive Garden, Wanda Truxillo of IBM, and James Watkins of Golden Valley Microwave Foods.

Staff support from the University of Massachusetts, the Southern Methodist University, the University of Denver, and the University of Minnesota was essential. We gratefully acknowledge the help of Linda Hoover, Jennifer Kaczmarski, Lucy Toton, Kathy Wamberg, and Elizabeth Wright for their many contributions.

Finally, we acknowledge the professional efforts of the Richard D. Irwin staff. Completion of our book and its many supplements required the attention and commitment of many editorial, production, marketing, and research personnel. Our Homewood-based team included Beth Battram, John Black, Jeff Shelstad, Ethel Shiell, Andy Winston, Rob Zwettler and many others. Our designer, Diane Beasley, has been involved through all three editions! In addition, we were fortunate to have input from a task force of sales representatives who worked to summarize feedback from their customers throughout the United States. The task force included Simon Allen, Frank Chihowski, Jeanne Hantak, Melody Lentsch, Brian Murray, and Art Sotak.

Eric N. Berkowitz
Roger A. Kerin
Steven W. Hartley
William Rudelius

Contents in Brief

Contents

PART II

*Understanding Buyers
and Markets*

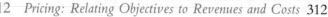

PART V

*Managing the
Marketing Process*

Marketing

Initiating the Marketing Process

People marketing goods, services, and ideas to people. This is the essence of the marketing process, described in Part I, that delivers a standard of living to a nation. Chapter 1 introduces the marketing process by describing the thinking of entrepreneur Jim Watkins as he and his company assume great risks to introduce innovative foods for microwave cooking. Remaining chapters in Part I give a snapshot picture of the marketing process, the environment in which it operates, and its dimensions of ethical and social responsibility. And collectively, the chapters reinforce the importance of people in marketing—how they recognize needs, design products, make ethical choices, and benefit as consumers.

CHAPTER 1

Marketing: A Focus on the Consumer

*A*fter reading this chapter you should be able to:

- Define marketing and explain the importance of (1) discovering and (2) satisfying consumer needs and wants.

- Distinguish between marketing mix elements and environmental factors.

- Describe how today's market orientation era differs from prior eras oriented to production and selling.

- Understand the meaning of ethics and social responsibility and how they relate to the individual, organizations, and society.

- Know what is required for marketing to occur and how it creates utilities for consumers.

Are You Ready for Microwave French Fries . . . as Snacks?

Timing always seems to be a big question for Jim Watkins.

He knows that business success lies in getting the right product to the right market at the right time. Today Watkins's timing problem involves microwave french fries, (opposite page), but he's had other timing problems as well. He seems to make a habit of developing products ahead of their time.

While in college, Watkins spent all of his student-loan money developing a "waterbike," a kind of aquatic motorcycle. It had only one major flaw: when Watkins rode it on its first test, it sank.[1]

Today, about 20 years later, similar designs are skimming across lakes around the country. Watkins's waterbike was simply ahead of its time.

After attending college in the early 1970s, Watkins joined the Pillsbury Company and worked with a team developing a family of 30 new food products to be cooked in microwave ovens.[2] The problem: as shown in Figure 1–1, in 1977 only about 10 percent of American households owned microwave ovens, so sales never took off. It was a case of bad timing all over again.

But Watkins became convinced that the convenience of microwave ovens would soon make them popular with American households. In 1978, he left Pillsbury and started his own business. Watkins named his firm Golden Valley Microwave Foods, Inc. (Golden Valley) and focused it on developing and marketing microwave foods.

Discovering What Consumers Want

Watkins soon concentrated on frozen popcorn and pancakes. He produced them in his own plant so he could control quality. He believed that the secret to success lay not in simply adding new microwave cooking instructions to the labels of existing food products, but in developing food products and the necessary packaging targeted specifically for microwave ovens.

By 1985 half of American households had microwave ovens[3] (see Figure 1–1), and Watkins and Golden Valley developed what they thought was a better microwave popcorn. They accomplished this by following an almost classic textbook approach to marketing: (1) discovering buyers' needs and wants and (2) satisfying them with a quality product.

Watkins's marketing research found two key benefits people wanted in their microwave popcorn: (1) fewer unpopped kernels and (2) good popping results in even low-powered microwave ovens. His research and development (R&D) staff successfully addressed these wants by finding better strains of popcorn and by developing new, patented packages to produce high-quality popped corn regardless of an oven's power. They introduced the Act I brand of microwave frozen popcorn, which was soon followed by the shelf-stable, microwave nonfrozen Act II brand. Both have been huge successes.

Soon Watkins found more than 70 competitors—including giants like the Orville Redenbacher brand—nipping at his heels, so he decided Golden Valley needed another product. Watkins estimated the annual market for microwave french fries to be over $500 million, so he took Golden Valley into the french fries business.[4] Golden Valley put thousands of hours of R&D effort into developing and patenting a "susceptor" package that would crisp and brown each french fry *individually* to provide the quality consumers wanted.

The product was only one element of Golden Valley's marketing dilemma. Its french fries still needed to reach consumers. Vending machines, supermarkets, mass merchandisers, convenience stores, and discount stores were some possible channels to consumers. The difficulty was finding a marketing channel that could display Act II french fries as a convenient consumer snack—and one whose success could help ensure the success of the product.[5]

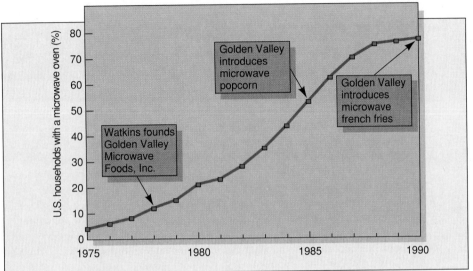

FIGURE 1–1
Percentage of U.S. households with a microwave oven. What potential opportunities and threats does this information provide to Golden Valley Microwave Foods, Inc.? For some insights, see the text

Source: Percentage data provided by International Microwave Power Institute, cited in "The Microwave Boom," *The Wall Street Journal* (March 1, 1990), p. B1. Reprinted by permission of *The Wall Street Journal*, © 1990 Dow Jones & Company, Inc. All Rights Reserved Worldwide.

Microwave French Fries, Marketing, and You

Can Golden Valley get enough consumer sales of its Act II french fries while competing with some firms dozens of times its size? By the time you reach the end of this chapter, you will know the strategy Jim Watkins chose in entering the microwave french fries business.

One key to whether or not Watkins succeeds lies in the subject of this book: marketing. In this chapter and in the rest of the book we'll introduce you to the people, organizations, ideas, activities, and jobs in marketing that have spawned the products and services that have been towering successes, shattering failures, or something in between. The successes we see, buy, and use every day. The failures fade from sight.

Where will Golden Valley be in five years? Prospective buyers will decide. Later in this chapter you can observe some critical marketing decisions made by Watkins. Decide for yourself—along with millions of consumers—whether these decisions were the right ones.

Marketing doesn't happen in a vacuum; it affects all individuals, all organizations, all industries, and all countries. This text seeks not only to teach you marketing concepts, but also to demonstrate its many applications and how it affects our lives. This knowledge should make you a better consumer, help you in your career, and enable you to be a more informed citizen.

In this chapter and the ones that follow, you will feel the excitement of marketing. You will see both successes and disasters. You will be introduced to the dynamic changes that will affect all of us in the 1990s. You will also meet many very human, ordinary men and women whose marketing creativity sometimes achieved brilliant, extraordinary results. And who knows? Somewhere in these pages you may find a career.

FIGURE 1–2
The see-if-you're-really-a-marketing-expert test

Answer the questions below. The correct answers are given later in the chapter.

1 In a nationally televised public hearing, a U.S. senator referred to "Xeroxing some reports." What was the Xerox Corporation's reaction? (*a*) delighted, (*b*) upset, or (*c*) somewhere in between. Why?

2 What is "Polavision"? (*a*) a new breathable contact lens, (*b*) a TV network that competes with Home Box Office, (*c*) special bifocal glasses, (*d*) instant movies, or (*e*) a political newspaper.

3 Right after World War II, International Business Machines Corporation (IBM) commissioned a study to estimate the *total* market for electronic computers. The study's results were (*a*) less than 10, (*b*) 1,000, (*c*) 10,000, (*d*) 100,000, or (*e*) 1 million or more.

4 How should Jim Watkins and tiny Golden Valley try to get early consumer reactions to its new products when it has only a limited budget for consumer studies?

5 To continue needed growth, where should Jim Watkins look for new markets for Golden Valley's present products?

WHAT IS MARKETING?

BEING A MARKETING EXPERT: GOOD NEWS—BAD NEWS

In many respects you are a marketing expert already. But just to test your expertise, try the "marketing expert" questions in Figure 1–2. These questions—some of them easy, others mind boggling—show the diverse problems marketing executives grapple with every day. You'll find the answers in the next few pages.

The Good News: You Already Have Marketing Experience   You are somewhat of an expert because you do many marketing activities every day. You already know many marketing terms, concepts, and principles. For example, would you sell more Sony Walkmans at $500 or $50 each? The answer is $50, of course, so your experience in shopping for products—and maybe even selling them—already gives you great insights into the world of marketing. As a consumer, you've already been involved in thousands of marketing decisions, but mainly on the buying, not the marketing, side.

The Bad News: Surprises about the Obvious   Unfortunately, common sense doesn't always explain some marketing decisions and actions.

    A U.S. senator's reference to "Xeroxing some reports" in a nationally televised public hearing (Question 1, Figure 1–2) sounds like great publicity for the Xerox Corporation, right? But Xerox was upset. After seeing the hearing on TV, a Xerox attorney contacted the senator the next day to remind him of his misuse of the trademarked name *Xerox*. Legally, Xerox is a registered trademark of Xerox Corporation and, as a brand name, should be used only to identify its

Xerox ran this ad to communicate a specific message. What is that message? For the answer and why it is important, see the text.

products and services. With this reminder and other advertisements (like that shown in the accompanying ad), Xerox is trying to protect a precious asset: its own name.

Under American trademark law, if consumers generally start using a brand name as the basic word to describe an entire class of products, then the company loses its exclusive rights to the name. "Xerox" would become "xerox"—just another English word to describe all kinds of photocopying. That fate has already befallen some famous American products such as linoleum, aspirin, cellophane, escalator, and yo-yo.

Today American firms are spending millions of dollars both in advertising and in court cases to protect their important brand names. Examples are Kimberly-Clark's Kleenex and 3M's Scotch tape. Coca-Cola takes dozens of restaurants to court every year for serving another cola drink when the patron asks for a Coca-Cola or even a Coke. Because legal and ethical issues such as the Xerox trademark problem are so central to many marketing decisions, they are addressed throughout the book.

The point here is that although your common sense usually helps you in analyzing marketing problems, sometimes it can mislead you. This book's in-depth study of marketing augments your common sense with an understanding of marketing concepts to help you assess and make marketing decisions more effectively.

MARKETING: USING EXCHANGES TO SATISFY NEEDS

The American Marketing Association, representing marketing professionals in the United States and Canada, states that "**marketing** is the process of planning and executing the conception, pricing, promotion, and distribution of ideas, goods, and services to create exchanges that satisfy individual and organizational objectives."[6] Many people incorrectly believe that marketing is the same thing as advertising or personal selling. This definition shows marketing to be a far broader activity. Further, this definition stresses the importance of beneficial exchanges that satisfy the objectives of both those who buy and those who sell ideas, goods, and services—whether they be individuals or organizations.

To serve both buyers and sellers, marketing seeks (1) to discover the needs and wants of prospective customers and (2) to satisfy them. These prospective customers include both individuals buying for themselves and their households and organizations that buy for their own use (such as manufacturers) or for resale (such as wholesalers and retailers). The key to achieving these two objectives is the idea of **exchange,** which is the trade of things of value between buyer and seller so that each is better off after the trade. This vital concept of exchange in marketing is covered below in more detail.

THE DIVERSE FACTORS INFLUENCING MARKETING ACTIVITIES

Although an organization's marketing activity focuses on assessing and satisfying consumer needs, countless other people, groups, and forces interact to shape the nature of its activities (Figure 1–3). Foremost is the organization itself, whose mission and objectives determine what business it is in and what goals it seeks. Within the organization, top management is responsible for achieving these goals. The marketing department works closely with other departments and employees to help provide the customer-satisfying products required for the organization to survive and prosper.[7]

Figure 1–3 also shows the key people, groups, and forces outside the organization that influence marketing activities. In addition to the customers, two groups with an important stake in the organization's success are the shareholders of a business firm (or often representatives of groups served by a nonprofit organization) and its suppliers. Environmental forces such as social, technological, economic, competitive, and regulatory factors also shape an organization's marketing activities. Finally, an organization's marketing decisions are affected by and in turn often have an important impact on society as a whole.

The organization must strike a continual balance among these individuals and groups, whose objectives sometimes conflict. For example, it is not possible to simultaneously provide the lowest-priced and highest-quality products to customers and pay the highest prices to suppliers, highest wages to employees, and maximum dividends to shareholders.

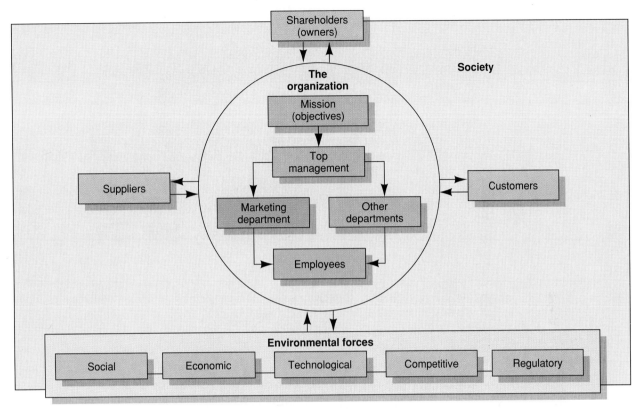

FIGURE 1–3
An organization's marketing department relates to many people, groups, and forces

REQUIREMENTS FOR MARKETING TO OCCUR

For marketing to occur, at least four factors are required: (1) two or more parties (individuals or organizations) with unsatisfied needs, (2) a desire and ability on their part to be satisfied, (3) a way for the parties to communicate, and (4) something to exchange.

Two or More Parties with Unsatisfied Needs   Suppose several years ago you had an unmet need—a desire for a diet, sugar-free soft drink that tasted like Coca-Cola—but you didn't yet know that diet Coke existed. Also unknown to you was that several dozen six-packs of diet Coke were sitting on a shelf at your nearest supermarket, waiting to be bought. This is an example of two parties with unmet needs: you, with a need for a Coke-like diet drink, and your supermarket owner, needing someone to buy the diet Coke.

Desire and Ability to Satisfy These Needs   Both you and the supermarket owner want to satisfy these unmet needs. Furthermore, you have the money to buy the item and the time to get to the supermarket. The store's owner has not only the desire to sell diet Coke but also the ability to do so, since it's stocked on the shelves.

A Way for the Parties to Communicate   The marketing transaction of buying the diet Coke will never occur unless you know the product exists and its location. Similarly, the store owner won't stock diet Coke unless there's a

How does your search for a diet cola show what is needed for marketing to occur? The answer appears in the text.

market of potential consumers near the supermarket who are likely to buy. When you see your supermarket's newspaper ad for half-price off on diet Coke, this communications barrier between you (the buyer) and your supermarket (the seller) is overcome.

Something to Exchange   Marketing occurs when the transaction takes place and both the buyer and seller exchange something of value. In this case, you exchange your money for the supermarket's diet Coke. Both of you have gained something and also given up something, but you are both better off because you have each satisfied your unmet needs. You have the opportunity to drink diet Coke, but you gave up some money; the store gave up the diet Coke but received money, which enables it to remain in business. This exchange process is central to marketing.[8]

CONCEPT CHECK

1 **What is marketing?**

2 **Marketing focuses on _____ and _____ consumer needs.**

3 **What four factors are needed for marketing to occur?**

HOW MARKETING DISCOVERS AND SATISFIES CONSUMER NEEDS

The importance of discovering and satisfying consumer needs is so critical to understanding marketing that we look at each of these two steps in detail below.

DISCOVERING CONSUMER NEEDS

The first objective in marketing is discovering the needs of prospective consumers. Sound simple? Well, it's not. In the abstract, discovering needs looks easy, but when you get down to the specifics of marketing, problems crop up.

Some Product Disasters   With much fanfare, RCA Corporation introduced its SelectaVision Videodisc player to the world in the early 1980s. Polaroid, flushed with the success of its instant still-photography business, introduced Polavision (Question 2, Figure 1–2) as the first instant home movie in 1978. Similarly, Federal Express first hailed its ZapMail, a 2-hour electronic mail service available throughout the United States, in 1984.

All these firms quietly dropped or redirected these products a short time after their introduction, with RCA losing nearly $500 million on its venture, Polaroid losing $170 million, and Federal Express losing $200 million.

These are three of the best-known product disasters in recent U.S. history, but thousands of lesser-known products fail in the marketplace every year. One major reason is that in each case the firm miscalculates consumers' wants and needs for these products. In the RCA Videodisc case, American consumers wanted to record TV programs, something videocassette recorders (VCRs) could do but Videodisc machines could not. They didn't want instant movies as much as they wanted instant still pictures, and Polavision failed in the consumer market. Today, of course, consumers are showing their "electric home movies" on their VCRs. ZapMail failed because of lack of demand, at least partly because major potential customers were buying their own facsimile—or "fax"—machines.

The solution to preventing such product failures seems embarrassingly obvious. First, find out what consumers need and want. Second, produce what they do need and want and don't produce what they don't need and want. This is much more difficult than it sounds.

It's frequently very difficult to get a precise reading on what consumers want and need when they are confronted with revolutionary ideas for new products. Right after World War II, IBM asked one of the most prestigious

RCA's SelectaVision videodisc player was soon replaced by VCRs.

management consulting firms in the United States to estimate the total future market for *all* electronic computers for *all* business, scientific, engineering, and government uses (Question 3, Figure 1–2). The answer was less than 10! Fortunately, key IBM executives disagreed, so IBM started building electronic computers anyway. Where would IBM be today if it had assumed the market estimate was correct? Most of the firms that bought computers five years after the market study had not actually recognized they were prospective buyers because they had no understanding of what computers could do for them: they didn't recognize their own need for faster information processing.

Consumer Needs and Consumer Wants   Should marketing try to satisfy consumer needs or consumer wants? The answer is both! Heated debates rage over this question, and a person's position in the debate usually depends on the definitions of needs and wants and the amount of freedom given to prospective customers to make their own buying decisions.

A *need* occurs when a person feels physiologically deprived of basic necessities like food, clothing, and shelter. A *want* is a felt need that is shaped by a person's knowledge, culture, and personality. So if you feel hungry, you have developed a basic need and desire to eat something. Let's say you then want to eat an apple or a candy bar because, based on your past experience and personality, you know these will satisfy your hunger need. Effective marketing, in the form of creating an awareness of good products at convenient locations, can clearly shape a person's wants.

At issue is whether marketing persuades prospective customers to buy the "wrong" things—say a "bad" candy bar rather than a "good" apple to satisfy hunger pangs. Certainly, marketing tries to influence what we buy. The question that then arises is: At what point do we want government and society to step in to protect consumers? Most Americans would say they want government to protect us from harmful drugs and unsafe cars, but not from candy bars and soft drinks. The issue is not clear-cut, which is why legal and social issues are central to marketing. Because even psychologists and economists still debate the exact meanings of *need* and *want,* we shall avoid the semantic arguments and use the terms interchangeably in the rest of the book.

As shown in Figure 1–4, discovering needs involves looking carefully at prospective customers, whether they are children buying M&M's candy, adults buying Calvin Klein jeans, or firms buying Xerox photocopying machines. A principal activity of a firm's marketing department is to carefully scrutinize the consumers to understand what they need, to study industry trends, to examine competitors' products, and to even analyze the needs of an industrial customers' customers.

What a Market Is   Potential consumers make up a **market,** which is (1) people (2) with the desire and (3) with the ability to buy a specific product. All markets ultimately are people. Even when we say a firm bought a Xerox copier, we mean one or several people in the firm decided to buy it. People who are aware of their unmet needs may have the desire to buy the product, but that alone isn't sufficient. People must also have the ability to buy, such as the authority, time,

FIGURE 1–4
Marketing's first task: discovering consumer needs

and money. As we saw earlier in the definition of marketing, people may buy, or accept, more than just goods or services. For example, they may buy an idea that results in an action, such as having their blood pressure checked annually or turning down their thermostat to save energy.

SATISFYING CONSUMER NEEDS

Marketing doesn't stop with the ideas obtained from discovering consumer needs. Since the organization obviously can't satisfy all consumer needs, it must concentrate its efforts on certain needs of a specific group of potential consumers. This is the **target market,** one or more specific groups of potential consumers toward which an organization directs its marketing program.

The Four Ps: Controllable Marketing Mix Factors   Having selected the target market consumers, the firm must take steps to satisfy their needs. Someone in the organization's marketing department, often the marketing manager, must take action and develop a complete marketing program to reach consumers by pulling a combination of four levers, often called the *four Ps*—a useful short-hand reference to them first published by Professor E. Jerome McCarthy:[9]

- Product: a good, service, or idea to satisfy the consumer's needs.
- Price: what is exchanged for the product.
- Promotion: a means of communication between the seller and buyer.
- Place: a means of getting the product into the consumer's hands.

We'll define each of the four Ps more carefully later in the book, but for now it's important to remember that they are the elements of the marketing mix, or simply the **marketing mix.** These are the marketing manager's controllable factors, the marketing actions of product, price, promotion, and place that he or she can take to solve a marketing problem. The marketing mix elements are called *controllable factors* because they are under the control of the marketing department in an organization.

Red Lobster, Scandinavian Airlines, and Toyota have set world-class standards in satisfying customers. For their strategies, see the text and Marketing Action Memo.

The Uncontrollable, Environmental Factors   There are a host of factors largely beyond the control of the marketing department and its organization. These factors can be placed into five groups (as shown in Figure 1–3): social, technological, economic, competitive, and regulatory forces. Examples are what consumers themselves want and need, changing technology, the state of the economy in terms of whether it is expanding or contracting, actions that competitors take, and government restrictions. These are the **environmental factors** in a marketing decision, the uncontrollable factors involving social, economic, technological, competitive, and regulatory forces. These five forces may serve as accelerators or brakes on marketing, sometimes expanding an organization's marketing opportunities and other times restricting them. These five environmental factors are covered in Chapter 3.

Traditionally, many marketing executives have treated these environmental factors as rigid, absolute constraints that are entirely outside their influence.[10] However, recent studies and marketing successes have shown that a forward-looking, action-oriented firm can often affect some environmental factors. IBM's technical and marketing breakthroughs gave birth to the entire digital electronic computer industry, even though initially consumers were apathetic. Apple did the same for personal computers. After more than a decade of negotiations with Soviet bureaucrats, in 1990 McDonald's opened a 700-seat restaurant in Moscow and served more than 10 million customers its first year. These consumer and political factors might have forestalled productive marketing actions had they been seen as rigid and uncontrollable.

New Standards in Satisfying Customer Needs   The intensity of competition in both domestic and international markets has caused massive restructuring of many American industries and businesses, and the trend will continue. Amer-

---

Marketing Action Memo

MARKETING IN THE 1990s: A NEW VOCABULARY AND MORE INTENSE COMPETITION

Americans are by nature optimistic people: Tomorrow is going to be better than today, and next year's income is going to be better than this year's. But for most of us this rose-colored glasses effect just isn't true. *Business Week* magazine estimates that because of foreign competition, from 1980 to 1990 real income (adjusted for inflation) of American workers not in the export sector fell by 6 percent.

This has "ratcheted up" both domestic and foreign competition for U.S. firms to a new, higher level. This competition has given a new intensity to a business vocabulary for the 1990s: quality, productivity, customer service, moments of truth, and continuous improvement. Here are three examples, from the United States, Europe, and Japan.

■ *Red Lobster seafood restaurant chain.* This sit-down dinner house chain has a simple goal: "Give people what they want, and don't get greedy on pricing." Its legendary concern for quality runs from customer service and sensitivity to the supply of its seafoods. Servers build team spirit and help each other, and the responses from 60,000 customer surveys a year shifted its emphasis from fried to steamed and boiled seafoods.

■ *Scandinavian Airlines (SAS).* When Jan Carlzon became SAS president in 1981, he concluded that customer service and the front-line employees who saw customers were the keys to success. In a year Carlzon notes that 10 million SAS customers see an average of 5 SAS employees for about 15 seconds each—50 million "moments of truth." Carlzon's SAS success lies in empowering the front-line employees to act in those "15 golden seconds," not buck problems up to a manager.

■ *Toyota.* A massive $5 million, five-year study searched for the best carmaker in the world. The clear winner: Japan's Toyota. As *Fortune* magazine observed, "The company simply is tops in quality, productivity, and efficiency. . . . Toyota turns out luxury sedans with Mercedes-like quality using one sixth the labor Mercedes does." Toyota achieves this with its concern for *kaizen,* or "continuous improvement."—permanent dissatisfaction with even exemplary performance.

Sources: Jan Carlzon, *Moments of Truth* (New York: Harper & Row, 1989); Josephine Marcotty, "Red Lobster Casts Its Nets Far and Wide," *Star Tribune* (December 9, 1990), pp. 10, 30; Alex Taylor III, "Why Toyota Keeps Getting Better and Better and Better," *Fortune* (November 19, 1990), pp. 66–79; Alex Taylor III, "New Lessons from Japan's Carmakers," *Fortune* (October 22, 1990), pp. 165–68; "Dispelling the Myths That Are Holding Us Back," *Business Week* (December 17, 1990), pp. 66–78.

---

ican managers are seeking ways to compete more effectively in this new, more intense level of global competition.[11]

For ideas, these managers often look to firms that have been successful and try to understand the reasons for their success. As described in the accompanying Marketing Action Memo, three recent glittering successes are the Red Lobster restaurant chain, Scandinavian Airlines, and Toyota.[12] Some common themes emerge from successful companies like these three: understanding what the customer wants and delivering it, empowering the employees who deal with customers, teamwork and communication, obsession with efficient use of resources and eliminating waste, and continuous improvement. These themes are the blueprints for success in the 1990s and beyond.[13]

FIGURE 1–5
Marketing's second task: satisfying consumer needs

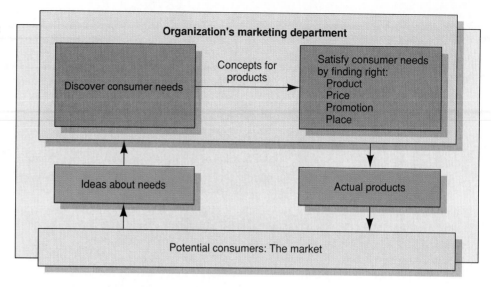

The Marketing Program   After discovering what prospective customers need, the marketing manager must translate the ideas from consumers into some concepts for products the firm might develop (Figure 1–5). These ideas must then be converted into a tangible **marketing program**—a plan that integrates the marketing mix to provide a good, service, or idea to prospective buyers. These prospects then react to the offering favorably (by buying) or unfavorably (by not buying), and the process is repeated. As shown in Figure 1–5, in an effective organization this process is continuous: consumer needs trigger product concepts that are translated into actual products that stimulate further discovery of consumer needs.

A Marketing Program for Golden Valley Microwave Foods   To see the specifics of a marketing program, let's return to the earlier example of Jim Watkins, Golden Valley Microwave Foods, and their microwave french fries.

With Golden Valley's relatively small size, Watkins knew that he and his firm faced a big problem taking on the food giants in the french fries arena. For one thing, it is very expensive to do marketing research to get consumer reactions to Golden Valley's new products. So Watkins deliberately introduces many of his products, like Act II microwave popcorn and french fries, first to distributors stocking vending machines. This gives Golden Valley immediate "test market" results from knowledgeable consumers who buy a package of Act II french fries from a vending machine where they work or go to college and then pop the package into the adjacent microwave oven. Feedback ideas from these consumers permit Golden Valley to fine-tune the product to their tastes (Question 4, Figure 1–2) and to make sure cooking directions are clearly understood and properly used by consumers. For example, with Act II popcorn consumers have a built-in "doneness indicator"—the slowing down of the popping sounds, indicating that the popcorn is completely cooked. This indicator works regardless of the wattage of the microwave oven. However, there is no natural "doneness indicator" for Act II french fries, whose cooking times vary from 1½ minutes for a 1,000-watt microwave oven to 3½ minutes in a 400-watt oven. Hence initial introductions of Act II french fries had to ensure that consumers understood and used this cooking information.

Watkins knew that besides selling Act II french fries through vending machines, he also had to gain space in refrigerated and frozen food sections in "nongrocery retailers" that sell in volume such as club stores like Sam's, Price Club, Costco and Pace. He and Golden Valley Microwave Foods (GVMF) devised two different marketing programs—one directed at vending machine consumers and the other at those who buy at nongrocery retailers. The two programs had these main features:

MARKETING MIX ELEMENT	MARKETING PROGRAM THROUGH VENDING MACHINES	MARKETING PROGRAM THROUGH NONGROCERY RETAILERS
Product	3.18 ounces of *refrigerated* french fries in an Act II package that serves as the cooking unit.	3.18 ounces of *frozen* french fries in an Act II package that serves as the cooking unit.
Price	75¢ for an individual package that you pop in the microwave oven at work or college.	$1.79 for a three-pack to use at home.
Promotion	Sold by GVMF's Vending Division to vending distributors; advertisements directed to the distributors.	Sold by GVMF's Retail Division to large nongrocery chains that advertise in local newspapers.
Place	Consumers buy *refrigerated* Act II french fries in vending machine and pop them in adjacent microwave oven.	Consumers buy *frozen* Act II french fries in the frozen foods section of their nongrocery chain outlet to take home.

And how has the Golden Valley marketing program for its microwave Act II french fries turned out? So far, so good, but it takes time for consumers to accept new products and new technologies. You and millions of consumers like you will be the ultimate test for the success of Golden Valley's Act II french fries.

Current Golden Valley products are shown in the accompanying photo. Besides the traditional Act I and Act II microwave popcorns, the figure shows other flavors (caramel, cheddar cheese, and sour cream & onion) and Act II Lite™—a microwave popcorn for health-conscious consumers, with no cholesterol, 50 percent less fat, and less salt. Other products include Act II pizza pockets, pancakes, waffles, and French toast.

What is not apparent to many consumers is the way Golden Valley has helped revolutionize consumer eating habits with its line of products intended *specifically* for cooking in microwave ovens. First, the high-technology packages

The product line of
Golden Valley
Microwave Foods, Inc.

perform a completely new function—a means of *cooking* the product itself, as well as a means of displaying, holding, and protecting food. Second, to achieve this cooking function with its innovative package, Golden Valley has put millions of dollars into research and development, both to provide tasty microwave food and to protect the consumer. At the temperature needed to cook microwave foods, the cooking package susceptors can give off gases that could potentially migrate into the cooked food or the surrounding air. At significant expense, Golden Valley's R&D labs designed a barrier in the package to eliminate the escape of these gases—something many competitors have not done.

With things going so well, what concerns do Watkins and his firm have? Considerations center on both controllable marketing mix variables and uncontrollable environmental variables. Relating to the former, Golden Valley's phenomenal growth—from annual sales of $8 million to $185 million in seven years—poses serious challenges. For example, how do you grow from 20 to 1,000 employees in seven years and ensure that high-quality products and on-time deliveries are maintained? To continue growing, Watkins knows that he must not only continue to introduce successful new products, but also find new markets. For several years its international division has taken its products to regions where microwave ovens are gaining sales, among them Canada, the Far East, and Western Europe (Question 5, Figure 1–2). This often involves discovering surprises about consumer tastes in these countries; for example, many Western European consumers prefer their popcorn with sugar instead of salt! Still, Watkins keeps his firm focused on the company mission "of developing and producing high-quality microwave-only foods that require significant technological input."[14]

Although Watkins can't anticipate all the uncontrollable factors facing his company, he has taken steps to minimize many threats. Because Golden Valley must ensure continuing supplies of high-quality potatoes, it participated in a joint venture to buy a potato company. To ensure a supply of its company-developed hybrid popcorn, it contracts with farmers in separate growing areas to protect against drought. But there are always hurdles to face. In 1990, microwave cooking gained unfavorable publicity about gases given off in the cooking process and the heater strips used in packages that crisp and brown foods. Golden Valley's sales could be hurt if consumers boycott all microwave foods without realizing that Golden Valley's sandwich packaging materials eliminate these problems.

Jim Watkins remains optimistic and realistic. This is shown by his firm's low overhead and lean operating style. "We make stuff and we sell stuff, and we don't have a lot of nonsense in between. We focus on only one thing—microwave food—and we're *very* competitive."[15] As a reminder of timing lessons from his past, Watkins still keeps a picture of his failed waterbike in his billfold.

CONCEPT CHECK

1 An organization can't satisfy the needs of all consumers, so it must focus on one or more subgroups, which are its _____ .

2 What are the four marketing mix elements that make up the organization's marketing program?

3 What are uncontrollable variables?

HOW MARKETING BECAME SO IMPORTANT

Marketing is a driving force in the modern American economy. To understand why this is so and some related ethical aspects, let us look at (1) the evolution of the market orientation, (2) ethics and social responsibility in marketing, and (3) the breadth and depth of marketing activities.

EVOLUTION OF THE MARKET ORIENTATION

Many market-oriented manufacturing organizations in the United States have experienced four distinct stages in the life of their firms. We can use the Pillsbury Company as an example.

Production Era   Goods were scarce in the early years of the United States, so buyers were willing to accept virtually any goods that were produced and make do with them as best they could. French economist J. B. Say developed his law in the 19th century that described the prevailing business theory of the period: "Production creates its own demand." The central notion was that products would sell themselves, so the major concern of business firms was production, not marketing.[16]

In 1869, Charles Pillsbury founded his company on the basis of high-quality wheat and the accessibility of cheap water power. Robert Keith, a Pillsbury president, described his company at this stage: "We are professional flour

FIGURE 1–6
**Four different
orientations in the
history of American
business**

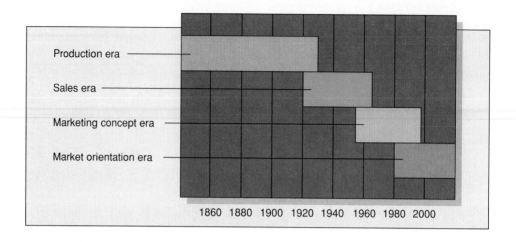

millers. Blessed with a supply of the finest North American wheat, plenty of water power, and excellent milling machinery, we produce flour of the highest quality. Our basic function is to mill quality flour."[17] As shown in Figure 1–6, this production era generally continued in America through the 1920s.

Sales Era   About that time, many firms discovered that they could produce more goods than their regular buyers could consume. Competition became more significant, and the problems of reaching the market became more complex. The usual solution was to hire more salespeople to find new markets and consumers. Pillsbury's philosophy at this stage was summed up simply by Keith: "We must hire salespersons to sell it [the flour] just as we hire accountants to keep our books." The role of the Pillsbury salesforce, in simplified terms, was to find consumers for the goods that the firm found it could produce best, given its existing resources. This sales era continued into the 1950s for Pillsbury and into the 1960s for many other American firms (see Figure 1–6).

The Marketing Concept Era   In the 1960s, marketing became the motivating force in Pillsbury. Since then its policy can be stated as, "We are in the business of satisfying needs and wants of consumers." This is really a brief statement of what has come to be known as the **marketing concept,** the idea is that an organization should (1) strive to satisfy the needs of consumers (2) while also trying to achieve the organization's goals.

The statement of a firm's commitment to satisfying consumer wants and needs that probably launched the marketing concept appeared in a 1952 annual report of General Electric Company[18]: "The concept introduces . . . marketing . . . at the beginning rather than the end of the production cycle and integrates marketing into each phase of the business." This statement had two important points. First, it recognized that sales is just one element of marketing—that marketing includes a much broader range of activities. Second, it changed the point at which marketing ideas are fed into the production cycle from *after* an item is produced to *before* it is designed. Clearly the marketing concept is a focus on the consumer, but the problem for many companies in the 1960s and 1970s was that they didn't implement the marketing concept effectively.

Marketing Research Report

WHAT IS "MARKET ORIENTATION"?

"Customer-driven," "market-driven," "customer-oriented," and "market-oriented" are all terms that have come into vogue in the past decade. The main problem is that there is little agreement about what the terms mean. To try to solve this problem, researchers Ajay K. Kohli and Bernard J. Jaworski interviewed 62 marketing and nonmarketing managers in a variety of industries. They concluded that a "market-oriented" organization has one or more departments (1) actively trying to understand customers' needs and the factors affecting them, (2) sharing this information across departments, and (3) using the information to meet these customer needs.

Each of the three elements of this market orientation deserves elaboration:

1 *Understanding consumer needs.* Managers interviewed stressed that understanding needs goes far beyond listening to what customers *say* they want and need, and involves studying the needs of the customers' customers, competition, regulation, and future needs as well as current needs.

2 *Sharing the information.* Market orientation involves more than just the marketing department—other departments in the organization are involved as well.

3 *Using the information to meet customer needs.* The information must be acted on—translated into a good or service that caters to the current and future needs of customers.

This helps operationalize the term *market orientation,* a concept increasingly important to organizations facing the intense competition of the 1990s.

Source: Adapted from Ajay K. Kohli and Bernard J. Jaworski, "Market Orientation: The Construct, Research Propositions, and Managerial Implications," *Journal of Marketing* (April 1990), pp. 1–18; by permission of the American Marketing Association.

The Market Orientation Era   The 1980s saw many firms such as Red Lobster, Scandinavian Airlines, and Toyota achieve great success in the marketplace by putting huge efforts into implementing the marketing concept, giving their firms what has been called a *market orientation.* As the accompanying Marketing Research Report suggests, an organization that has a **market orientation** has one or more departments (1) actively trying to understand customers' needs and the factors affecting them, (2) sharing this information across departments, and (3) using the information to meet these customer needs.

A key aspect of this market orientation is that understanding consumer needs goes far beyond just talking to customers. Rather, this marketing information or marketing intelligence is gleaned from many sources beyond just the customer, such as observing broad industry trends, studying competitors, understanding the needs of an industrial customer's customers, and looking to likely future needs as well as present ones. Research shows that firms having a demonstrated market orientation are more profitable than those lacking it.[19]

The **consumerism** movement started in the 1960s when American consumers sought to obtain a greater say in the quality of products they bought and the information they received from sellers, in order to increase their influence, power, and rights in dealing with institutions. The movement occurred because the marketing concept was being overlooked by sellers. Although both the marketing concept and consumerism are constant reminders that "the customer is king," with today's competition, firms must also have efficient production and sales operations—carryovers from earlier eras.

ETHICS AND SOCIAL RESPONSIBILITY: BALANCING CONFLICTING GOALS OF DIFFERENT GROUPS

In taking a loan out to buy a new car, should the buyer be told the total interest payments he or she will make over the period of the loan? Should a fast-food restaurant chain use styrofoam boxes to keep their hamburgers warm, thereby contributing to solid-waste problems? Or should a customer always be allowed to return merchandise he or she bought from a store, even if he or she misused the merchandise or didn't read the instructions properly? These questions pose dilemmas for buyers, for sellers, and for society as a whole. They also illustrate the complex ethical and societal issues that marketing decisions can involve.

Ethics   For example, take the issue of honoring a customer's complaint and request to return previously purchased merchandise. Should this request always be honored, even if the buyer didn't follow instructions on the label and misused the merchandise? Of course not. A seller should deal with legitimate complaints fairly to satisfy the customer, but should not honor excessive demands by a complaining customer because the costs of doing so are eventually passed to other customers in the form of higher prices. This marketing issue relates to **ethics,** which are the moral principles and values that govern the actions and decisions of an entire group. Many marketing issues go beyond legal dimensions to include ethical ones.

Social Responsibility   While many difficult ethical issues involve only the buyer and seller, others involve society as a whole. For example, suppose you buy your fast-food hamburger in a styrofoam warming box and put the box in the restaurant's trash can when you finish. Is this just a transaction between you and the restaurant? Not quite! Thrown in a trash dump, the styrofoam hamburger box probably won't degrade for centuries, so society will bear a portion of the cost of your hamburger purchase.

This example illustrates the issue of **social responsibility,** the idea that organizations are part of a larger society and are accountable to society for their actions. So to survive, an organization must balance ethics and social responsibility among the interests of other groups such as its employees, shareholders, and suppliers with those of its customers. American business firms must achieve this balance today under the most intense pressure from competitors throughout the world that they have ever known. Because of the importance of ethical and social responsibility issues in marketing today, they—and related legal and regulatory actions—are discussed throughout this book. In addition, Chapter 4 focuses specifically on issues of ethics and social responsibility.

The well-being of society at large should also be recognized in an organization's marketing decisions.[20] In fact, some marketing experts stress the **societal marketing concept,** the view that an organization should discover and satisfy the needs of its consumers in a way that also provides for society's well-being. Products such as beer in disposable cans and cigarettes have important side effects in terms of dollar and health costs for all of us in society—not just the manufacturer and consumer of the specific product.

This book focuses on **micromarketing,** how an individual organization directs its marketing activities and allocates its resources to benefit its customers.

An overview of this approach appears in Chapter 2. This process contrasts with **macromarketing,** which looks at the aggregate flow of a nation's goods and services to benefit society.[21] Macromarketing addresses broader issues such as whether marketing costs too much, whether advertising is wasteful, and what resource scarcities and pollution side effects result from the marketing system. Macromarketing issues relate directly to the societal marketing concept and are addressed briefly in this book, but the book's main focus is on an organization's marketing activities, or micromarketing.

THE BREADTH AND DEPTH OF MARKETING

Marketing today affects every person and organization. To understand this, let's analyze (1) who markets, (2) what they market, (3) who buys and uses what is marketed, (4) who benefits from these marketing activities, and (5) how they benefit.

Who Markets?   Every organization markets! It's obvious that business firms in manufacturing (Xerox, Heinz, Puma), retailing (Sears, K mart, J. C. Penney), and providing services (Merrill Lynch, National Broadcasting Corporation, Twentieth Century-Fox) market their offerings, as do colleges and universities (to attract good students and faculty members and donations) and government agencies (to encourage Americans to quit smoking or obtain annual health checkups). Individuals such as entertainers or politicians market themselves. Nonprofit organizations (San Francisco Ballet, New York Metropolitan Opera, Museum of Modern Art, your local hospital) also engage in marketing.[22]

Today's Cleveland Clinic is increasingly sensitive to patient needs.

Recent decisions of a world-renowned medical facility, the Cleveland Clinic Foundation, illustrate the diverse marketing-related activities of today's nonprofit organizations. The clinic operates an expanded 1,250-bed hospital in Cleveland and—to respond to growing health care needs in the Southeast— another facility in Fort Lauderdale, Florida. It has programs to serve the specialized needs of low-income and kidney dialysis patients, and it even operates its own 300-room hotel in Cleveland to serve the needs of patients from throughout the United States and the world. To try to improve its patient services, the clinic conducts programs in marketing research, consumer affairs, and physician liaison.

What Is Marketed?   Goods, services, and ideas are marketed. Goods are physical objects, such as toothpaste, cameras, or computers, that satisfy consumer needs. Services are intangible items such as airline trips, financial advice, or telephone calls. Ideas are intangibles such as thoughts about actions or causes. Some of these—such as lawn mowers, dry cleaning, and annual physical examinations—may be bought or accepted by individuals for their own use. Others, such as office copiers and vending machine repair services, are bought by organizations. Finally, the products marketed in today's shrinking globe are increasingly likely to cross a nation's boundaries and involve exports, imports, and international marketing (covered in Chapter 22).

Who Buys and Uses What Is Marketed?   Both individuals and organizations buy and use goods and services that are marketed. **Ultimate consumers** are the people—whether 80 years or 8 months old—who use the goods and services purchased for a household. A household may consist of one person or ten. (The way one or more of the people in the household buys for it is the topic of consumer behavior in Chapter 5.) In contrast, **organizational buyers** are units such as manufacturers, retailers, or government agencies that buy goods and services for their own use or for resale. (Industrial and organizational buyer behavior is covered in Chapter 6.) Although the terms *consumers, buyers,* and *customers* are sometimes used for both ultimate consumers and organizations, there is no consistency on this. In this book you will be able to tell from the example whether the buyers are ultimate consumers, organizations, or both.

Who Benefits?   In our free-enterprise society there are three specific groups that benefit from effective marketing: consumers who buy, organizations that sell, and society as a whole. True competition between products and services in the marketplace ensures that we consumers can obtain (1) the best products and services available (2) at the lowest price. Providing the maximum number of choices leads to the consumer satisfaction and quality of life that we have come to expect from our economic system.

Organizations that provide need-satisfying products with effective marketing programs—for example, McDonald's, IBM, Avon, and Merrill Lynch— have blossomed, but this competition creates problems for the ineffective competitors. For example, Osborne Computers, DeLorean cars, and W. T. Grant retail stores were well-known names a few years back, but may now be unknown to you. Effective marketing actions result in rewards for organizations that serve consumers and in millions of marketing jobs such as those described in Appendix B.

Finally, effective marketing benefits the whole country. It enhances competition, which in turn improves both the quantity of products and services and lowers their prices. This makes the country more competitive in world markets and provides jobs and a higher standard of living for its citizens.

How Do Consumers Benefit?   Marketing creates **utility,** the value to consumers for using the product. This utility is the result of the marketing exchange process. There are four different utilities: form, place, time, and possession. The production of the good or service constitutes *form utility. Place utility* means having the offering available where consumers need it, whereas *time utility* means having it available when needed. *Possession utility* is getting the product to consumers so they can use it.

Thus marketing provides consumers with place, time, and possession utilities by making the good or service available at the right place and right time for the right consumer. Although form utility usually arises in manufacturing activity and could be seen as outside the scope of marketing, an organization's marketing activities influence the product features and packaging. Marketing creates its utilities by bridging space (place utility) and hours (time utility) to provide products (form utility) for consumers to own and use (possession utility).

CONCEPT CHECK

1 Like Pillsbury, many firms have gone through four distinct orientations for their business: starting with the _____ era and ending with today's _____ era.

2 What are the two key characteristics of the marketing concept?

3 What three things are included in this book under the term *product?*

> ### ETHICS AND SOCIAL RESPONSIBILITY IN THE 1990s
>
> **SHOULD PHYSICIANS BE ALLOWED TO SHUT DOWN A COMPETITIVE MEDICAL FACILITY?**
>
> As noted in the chapter, the prestigious Cleveland Clinic opened a medical facility in Fort Lauderdale, Florida, to serve the health-care needs of patients in that area. While local businesses and politicians supported the idea, local physicians were outraged and launched a campaign to keep the Cleveland Clinic from opening.
>
> The reason, according to *The Wall Street Journal,* was the increased competition that the new facility would create for local physicians.[23] In fact, a Cleveland Clinic surgeon who had done 4,000 open-heart operations was denied local hospital privileges.
>
> Should the Cleveland Clinic and other nationally known clinics be encouraged to open new facilities outside their regions? Is this ethical? Does it help or hurt society? Explain your answers.

SUMMARY

1 Our daily exposure to the diverse marketing activities around us has already given us some marketing expertise. Combining this experience with more formal marketing knowledge will enable us to identify and solve important marketing problems.

2 Marketing is the process of planning and executing the conception, pricing, promotion, and distribution of ideas, goods, and services to create exchanges that satisfy individual and organizational objectives. This definition relates to two primary goals of marketing: (*a*) assessing the needs of consumers and (*b*) satisfying them.

3 For marketing to occur, it is necessary to have (*a*) two or more parties with unmet needs, (*b*) a desire and ability to satisfy them, (*c*) communication between the parties, and (*d*) something to exchange.

4 Because an organization doesn't have the resources to satisfy the needs of all consumers, it selects a target market of potential customers—a subset of the entire market—on which to focus its marketing program.

5 Four elements in a marketing program designed to satisfy customer needs are product, price, promotion, and place. These elements are called the *marketing mix,* the *four Ps,* or the *controllable variables* because they are under the general control of the marketing department.

6 Environmental factors, also called *uncontrollable variables,* are largely beyond the organization's control. These include social, technological, economic, competitive, and regulatory forces.

7 In marketing terms, U.S. business history is divided into four periods: the production era, the sales era, the marketing concept era, and the current market orientation era.

8 An organization using a market orientation tries to understand the needs of customers and factors affecting them, share this information within the organization, and use it to meet customer needs.

9 However, customer and organizational needs must be balanced against needs of employees, shareholders, suppliers, and society as a whole. This involves issues of ethics and social responsibility.

10 Most organizations perform marketing activities, whether they are profit-making business firms or nonprofit organizations. They market products, services, and ideas that benefit all consumers, the organization, and the entire nation. Marketing creates utilities that benefit customers.

KEY TERMS AND CONCEPTS

marketing p. 10
exchange p. 10
market p. 14
target market p. 15
marketing mix p. 15
environmental factors p. 16

marketing program p. 18
marketing concept p. 22
market orientation p. 23
consumerism p. 23
ethics p. 24
social responsibility p. 24

societal marketing concept p. 24   ultimate consumers p. 26
micromarketing p. 24   organizational buyers p. 26
macromarketing p. 25   utility p. 27

 CHAPTER PROBLEMS AND APPLICATIONS

1 What consumer wants (or benefits) are met by the following products or stores? (*a*) Carnation Instant Breakfast, (*b*) Adidas running shoes, (*c*) Hertz Rent-A-Car, and (*d*) catalog showroom retail stores.

2 Each of the four products or stores in Question 1 has substitutes. Respective examples are (*a*) a ham and egg breakfast, (*b*) regular tennis shoes, (*c*) taking a bus, and (*d*) a department store. What consumer benefits might these substitutes have in each case that some consumers might value more highly than those products mentioned in Question 1?

3 What are the characteristics (e.g., age, income, education) of the target market customers for the following products or services? (*a*) *National Geographic* magazine, (*b*) *Playboy* magazine, (*c*) New York Giants football team, and (*d*) the U.S. Open tennis tournament.

4 A college in a metropolitan area wishes to increase its evening-school offerings of business-related courses such as marketing, accounting, finance, and management. Who are the target market customers (students) for these courses?

5 What actions involving the four marketing mix elements might be used to reach the target market in Question 4?

6 What environmental factors (uncontrollable variables) must the college in Question 4 consider in designing its marketing program?

7 Polaroid introduced instant still photography, which proved to be a tremendous success. Yet Polavision, its instant movie system, was a total disaster. (*a*) What wants and benefits does each provide to users? (*b*) Which of these do you think contributed to Polavision's failure? (*c*) What research could have been undertaken that might have revealed Polavision's drawbacks?

8 Jim Watkins has chosen to focus the efforts of Golden Valley Microwave Foods, Inc. on just what its name suggests—microwave foods. What are the advantages and disadvantages of this strategy?

9 No firm can rest comfortably on its current product line; it must look for new products. What criteria—some suggested by its company mission statement—should Golden Valley use in deciding what new products to add to its line of microwave foods?

10 Consider the uncontrollable environmental factors that might affect Golden Valley during the coming five years. Which will work in its favor? Which will work against it?

11 Does a firm have the right to "create" wants and try to persuade consumers to buy goods and services they didn't know about earlier? What are examples of "good" and "bad" want creation? Who should decide what is good and bad?

CHAPTER 2

Marketing in the Organization: An Overview

After reading this chapter you should be able to:

- Describe the strategic management process and how it relates to an organization's business (or mission) and objectives.

- Describe the strategic marketing process and its three key phases: planning, implementation, and control.

- Understand how organizations search for new marketing opportunities and select target markets.

- Explain how the marketing mix elements are blended into a cohesive marketing program.

- Describe how marketing control compares actual results with planned objectives and acts on deviations from the plan.

"Big Blue": Trying to Rediscover the Formula

Many believe the advertising campaign was the finest of the 1980s. It was 1981, and IBM had never produced or marketed a personal computer.

So "Big Blue"—the nickname given IBM because of the color of many of its large computers—unveiled the most unlikely of advertising campaigns to announce its new IBM Personal Computer (PC): a little mustachioed man in a black bowler hat. He used an IBM PC not simply to control inventory and move paragraphs (see ads on opposite page) but also to save his "Hat of the Month Club" business.

It was a controversial advertising campaign—some IBM employees were concerned that potential PC buyers might see the ad's Little Tramp—a takeoff on the Charlie Chaplin silent-movie character—as nonprofessional. But the campaign was a smash and did just what it was intended to do: attract attention and inform prospective PC users (the target market) in a nonthreatening way about the benefits of an IBM PC. The result was astounding. IBM's share of the PC market grew from nothing in 1981 to 40 percent in 1985.

By 1986, however, IBM saw its share of the total PC market falling, partly because of IBM "clones" (PCs compatible with IBM PCs). John F. Akers, IBM's new president, declared that IBM had lost touch with its customers and shared their concern that IBM PCs didn't "network" or communicate easily with each other.[1] IBM's answer was a new family of PCs, the Personal System/2 (PS/2), introduced in the late 1980s. The advertising campaign that introduced the PS/2 used the TV characters from *M★A★S★H*—a group of people that IBM hoped American buyers could relate to as they had to the Little Tramp.[2]

By 1990, IBM's ads had the punchline, "How're you going to do it? PS/2 it!" Look at the ads on pages 30 and 49 and think about how computer needs of companies changed between 1981—the introduction of the original IBM PC— and today in the 1990s. How do the ads reflect IBM's new marketing strategy to meet these needs? We'll describe some details of IBM's 1990s marketing strategy for its PS/2 and other computers later in the chapter. IBM's search for a new winning strategy for its computer lines reflects the intense domestic and international competition faced by many U.S. firms in the 1990s.

This chapter gives an overview of how organizations plan, implement, and control successful marketing strategies. In essence, this chapter describes how an organization tries to put the marketing concept into action and become market-oriented in order to serve its customers.

THE STRATEGIC MANAGEMENT PROCESS

Key marketing decisions are made within limits set by the organization. The **strategic management process** involves the steps taken at an organization's corporate and divisional levels to develop long-run master approaches for survival and growth. In contrast, the **strategic marketing process** involves the steps taken at the product and market levels to allocate marketing resources to viable marketing positions and programs.[3] Key steps in each of these two processes are shown in Figure 2–1. For example, the strategic marketing process involves the three phases of planning, implementation, and control. Note that other units in the organization—assumed here to be a manufacturing firm— develop detailed plans based on directions from the strategic management process.

DEFINING THE ORGANIZATION'S BUSINESS (MISSION)

Organizations such as the San Francisco Ballet, Dallas Cowboys, Disneyland, Mayo Clinic, Procter & Gamble, Sears Roebuck, and 3M often ask themselves what "business"—in its broadest sense—they are in. The answer can dramatically narrow or broaden the range of marketing opportunities available.

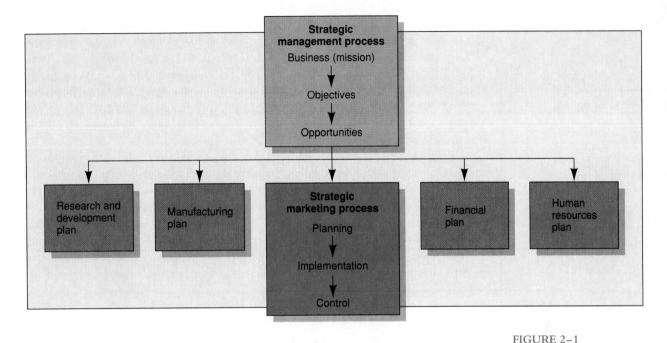

FIGURE 2–1
**Steps in the strategic
management and
strategic marketing
processes**

Railroads may have let other forms of transportation take business away from them because they saw themselves in the railroad business rather than the transportation business.[4] This narrow definition hurt railroads because they failed to design effective marketing strategies to compete with a broad range of modes of transportation, including airlines, trucks, bus lines, and cars.

Focusing the Business with the Three Cs   Business theorists point out that *three Cs*—customers, competitors, and the company itself—interrelate to establish the basic character of an organization's business.[5] An **organization's business (mission)** is a statement about the type of customer it wishes to serve, the specific needs of these customers, and the means or technology by which it will serve these needs. This definition affects the company's growth prospects by establishing guidelines for selecting opportunities in light of customer needs, competitors' actions, the organization's resources, and changes in environmental factors.

Sears's Business   In the 1980s, Sears Roebuck & Company discovered that discounters and specialty stores were winning over more and more of its traditional middle-class customers. This left Sears scrambling to find a market niche. First, it tried promoting itself as a fashion-oriented department store for higher-income customers. Failing at that, Sears then experimented with budget products and finally with "everyday low prices." A Gallup poll showed that Sears failed to convince consumers that its prices and merchandise selection were better than those of its competitors. And in 1990 Wal-Mart passed Sears as the largest retailer in America.[6]

Because of its failed efforts, today Sears is trying to become "itself" again by stressing selection, quality of service and products, reliability, and trust. This definition of its business permits Sears (the company) to seek to adapt to changing consumer tastes (the customer) in light of actions of other catalog and chain-store retailers (the competitors). And it has necessitated an aggressive strategy to sell brand-name products and to subdivide Sears stores into "boutiques" selling lines such as women's apparel, appliances, and electronics even though it had to close its chain of McKids children's apparel stores. Sears has entered the service business in a big way: appliance installation, financial services through Dean Witter, real estate through Coldwell Banker, and even dental and optometry services.[7]

Perhaps Sears's biggest gamble for the 1990s is the development of an interactive computer system linked by telephone to Sears stores, through which consumers can do such varied things as buy products they see advertised, make airline reservations, and get stock quotations, all from their own homes or offices. Sears and IBM invested more than $600 million in the system, called *Prodigy,* before it provided its first sales dollar. Prodigy is targeted at harried, affluent, two-income households who don't want to waste their time waiting in lines or driving around parking lots. Sears obviously runs a diverse set of businesses, but they all tie into its existing, strong distribution system. All of these businesses can also use the Discover credit card, which was Sears's biggest gamble for the 1980s (on which it initially lost $400 million) but has now become a huge success. Today over 38 million shoppers carry the Discover card,

Prodigy is a $600 million joint effort of Sears and IBM.

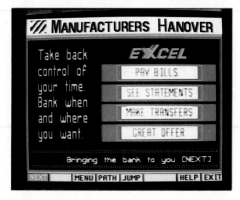

which they can use at 1.2 million stores and restaurants other than Sears—including those of arch-rival Wal-Mart.[8]

SPECIFYING THE ORGANIZATION'S GOALS

An organization must translate the broad statement of its business into the **organization's goals,** specific, measurable objectives it seeks to achieve and by which it can measure its performance. For our purposes, the terms *goals* and *objectives* mean the same thing.

How an Organization's Goals Relate to Its Business   An example of a precise policy statement of an organization's business and goals is that of the Sara Lee Corporation (Figure 2–2). Note that the goals are specific targets that flow directly from the broader statement about Sara Lee Corporation's business. In fact, the business statement is broad enough to cover five business segments that include well-known brand names like Chef Pierre, Jimmy Dean Meats, Sara Lee, Bali, Hanes Hosiery, L'eggs, and Kiwi. Even with this diversity of products and services, Sara Lee Corporation's policy statement about its business and goals gives direction to the entire organization and its business segments.

All organizations, both profit and nonprofit, require some kind of goals. A **business firm** is a privately owned organization that serves its customers in order to earn a profit. In contrast, a **nonprofit organization** is a nongovernmental organization that serves its customers but does not have profit as an organizational goal. Goals of these two different kinds of organizations are discussed separately in the following sections. For simplicity in the rest of the book, however, the terms *firm, company,* and *organization* are used to cover both business and nonprofit operations.

FIGURE 2–2
Mission and goals of Sara Lee Corporation

BUSINESS (MISSION)

Sara Lee Corporation's mission is:

- To be the leading brandname food and package goods company with major market share positions in key consumer markets throughout the world.
- To manufacture and market high-quality, marketing-sensitive products with growth potential.
- To market food products, consumer personnel products, and household and personal care products through common distribution channels.

GOALS

Sara Lee Corporation seeks to maximize our long-term financial performance, enabling us to better serve our stockholders, customers, employees, and the communities in which we do business. Specifically, our goals include:

- To maintain a return on stockholders' equity of at least 20 percent.
- To achieve a real annual growth rate in earnings per share of at least 8 percent.

Sources: *1987 Annual Report* (Chicago: Sara Lee Corporation, 1987), pp. 5–6; and *1990 Annual Report* (Chicago: Sara Lee Corporation, 1990), pp. 1–3.

Goals of Business Firms　Business firms, with some exceptions cited later, must earn profits to survive. **Profit** is the reward to a business firm for the risk it undertakes in offering a product for sale: the money left over after a firm's total expenses are subtracted from its total revenues. As long as profits are earned fairly—and not through collusion, monopoly power, or other unfair business practices—they represent a reward for good performance. Thousands of firms fail every year because they are not run well enough and do not serve consumers thoroughly enough to make profits and continue operations. The profit of a business firm may be expressed in actual money earned during a time period ("an after-tax profit of $5 million") or in terms of the money earned as a percentage of invested capital ("an after-tax profit of 15-percent return on investment [ROI]").

Several different objectives have been identified that business firms can pursue, each of which has some limitations:

- *Profit.* Classic economic theory assumes a firm seeks to maximize long-run profit, achieving as high a financial return on its investment as possible. One difficulty with this is what is meant by *long run*. A year? Five years? Twenty years?
- *Sales revenue.* If profits are acceptable, a firm may elect to maintain or increase its sales level, even though profitability may not be maximized. Increased sales revenue may gain promotions for key executives.
- *Market share.* A firm may choose to maintain or increase its market share, sometimes at the expense of greater profits if industry status or prestige is at stake. **Market share** is the ratio of sales revenue of the firm to the total sales revenue of all firms in the industry, including the firm itself.
- *Unit sales.* Sales revenue may be deceiving because of the effects of inflation, so a firm may choose to maintain or increase the number of units it sells, such as cars, cases of breakfast cereal, or TV sets.
- *Survival.* A firm may choose a safe action with reasonable payoff instead of one with large return that might endanger its future. It must survive today to be in business tomorrow.
- *Social responsibility.* A firm may respond to advocates of corporate responsibility and seek to balance conflicting goals of consumers, employees, and stockholders to promote overall welfare of all these groups, even at the expense of profits.

Whatever its primary goal, a business firm must achieve a profit level that is high enough for it to remain in operation. Satisfactory profits are possible only if consumer needs are identified and satisfied. Procter & Gamble (P&G) is a good example. For its corporate objectives, it seeks a 10 percent after-tax profit (twice the average for U.S. manufacturing firms) and a doubling of the sales revenue from a product every five years. To help achieve these objectives, it uncovers needs and manufactures products that have developed tremendous consumer loyalty in the marketplace. Its high-visibility brands introduced decades ago and still dominant are cases in point: Ivory Soap (introduced in 1879), Crisco (1912), Tide (1947), Pampers (1956), and Crest (1966). The long market lives of these products are proof of their continuing ability to satisfy consumer needs, a basic corporate objective of P&G.

General Electric's
futuristic plastic home
illustrates its search for
growth opportunities in
high technology.

Goals of Nonprofit Organizations   Many private organizations that do not seek profits also exist in the United States. Examples are museums, symphony orchestras, operas, private hospitals, and research institutes. These organizations strive to provide goods or services to consumers with the greatest efficiency and the least cost. The nonprofit organization's survival depends on its meeting the needs of the consumers it serves. Although technically not falling under the definition of "nonprofit organization," government agencies also perform marketing activities in trying to achieve their goal of serving the public good. Such organizations include all levels of federal, state, and local government, as well as special groups such as city schools, state universities, and public hospitals. As discussed later, marketing is an important activity for nonprofit firms and government agencies, just as it is for profit-making businesses.

IDENTIFYING THE ORGANIZATION'S OPPORTUNITIES

To achieve growth, an organization tries to find the right match between the market opportunities in its environment and its own capabilities and resources. Answers to three questions help an organization focus on key opportunities:[9]

1 *What might we do,* in terms of environmental opportunities we foresee?
2 *What do we do best,* in terms of our capabilities, resources, and distinctive competencies?
3 *What must we do,* in terms of achieving success in a market or with a product?

General Electric's Opportunities Search   The search for growth opportunities by General Electric (GE) shows how these questions apply. GE started at the turn of the century with a narrow definition of its business: the generation of electricity. With this definition, GE's focus was on turbines, generators, and transformers. GE initially got into the home appliance business with its General Electric and Hotpoint brand names and into the electric light business to stimulate the demand for electricity. Through the first half of this century these divisions provided tremendous growth for the company.

In the early 1980s GE's performance was lackluster, and it was looking for new business opportunities. In 1981 John F. Welch, Jr., took over as GE's chief executive officer with the charge to get the company moving again. Welch needed to assess where GE stood—an ideal time for a SWOT analysis.

SWOT Analysis   The acronym *SWOT* refers to a simple, effective technique a firm can use to appraise in detail its internal *s*trengths and *w*eaknesses and external *o*pportunities and *t*hreats. The goal of a SWOT analysis is to help a firm identify the strategy-related factors that can have a major effect on it. However, all factors in such an analysis are not of equal value, so the goal is to identify those *critical* factors that can have a major effect on the firm and then build on vital strengths, correct glaring weaknesses, exploit significant opportunities, and avoid disaster-laden threats.[10] That is a big order.

A SWOT analysis of GE's situation in 1981 would have revealed the factors shown in the accompanying Marketing Action Memo. From this kind of analysis, Welch concluded that while GE had many strengths, it had some major problems—bureaucracy, low annual productivity increases, two thirds of revenues coming from slow-growth businesses, and a weakness in global businesses. But he also found that two opportunities that answered the question "What might we do?" were providing services and high-technology products. In terms of "What do we do best?" he believed that GE should find markets that could exploit its technological leadership and avoid competing with low-cost producers in the Far East in small consumer appliances.

In the process Welch answered the third question: "What must we do to achieve success in our businesses?" by providing a strategic focus that stressed growth from GE business sectors that were or could be number 1 or number 2 in market share and profits in their markets. This strategy targeted growth in service and high-technology areas by creating a streamlined organization that sometimes reduced nine layers of management to only four and would not attempt to compete in mass-produced, small consumer appliances. As a result, GE first sold its small-appliance business to Black and Decker and its consumer electronics business (TVs, radios) to a French firm.[11]

This means that American consumers no longer see the GE brand on toasters, mixers, and TV sets, but only on large appliances (dishwashers, refrigerators, and dryers) and light bulbs. And GE is far stronger in industrial segments such as jet engines, aerospace, electrical apparatus, and medical electronics and in services such as insurance and finance. In its high-technology thrust, GE has built an experimental plastic home (see the accompanying picture) in Pittsfield, Massachusetts, with superdurable plastic siding, plastic floors, and plastic windows that save energy in both summer and winter.[12]

An Organization's Distinctive Competency   In assessing organizational opportunities, a firm objectively evaluates its **distinctive competency**—its principal competitive strengths and advantages in terms of marketing, technological, and financial resources. In the strategic management process all three of

Marketing Action Memo

GENERAL ELECTRIC: A "SWOT" TO GET IT MOVING AGAIN

Concerned about its slow growth, in 1981 General Electric (GE) selected John F. Welch, Jr., to head the company and get it moving forward again. A SWOT analysis (described in the text) of GE at that time might have looked as shown below.

LOCATION OF FACTOR	TYPE OF FACTOR	
	FAVORABLE	UNFAVORABLE
Internal	*Strengths:* • Quality products in many consumer and industrial markets • Respected name among buyers of its products • Financial power • Technical leadership in many sectors	*Weaknesses:* • No clear strategic direction • Bureaucracy and many layers of management • Low annual increases in productivity • Two thirds of revenues come from slow-growth businesses • Weak in truly global businesses
External	*Opportunities:* • High-technology and service sectors growing rapidly • International markets growing • U.S. government more lenient in cooperative joint ventures • Company technologies can provide new products for new markets	*Threats:* • Existing markets facing many changes • Foreign firms have lower production costs • Sales gains by competitors in its established markets • Main markets growing slowly

Sources: "To Our Shareholders," *1989 Annual Report* (Fairfield, Conn.: General Electric Co., 1990), pp. 2–7; "Big Changes Are Galvanizing General Electric," *Business Week* (December 18, 1989), pp. 100–102.

these areas must be thoroughly assessed or there may be problems. For example, in reallocating GE's resources to prepare for the 1990s, Welch more than tripled GE's productivity growth to about 6 percent annually, doubled the proportion of its annual revenues coming from high-growth technology and service sectors, and initiated joint ventures with foreign firms like the Tungsram Company of Hungary and Ericsson of Sweden.[13] In this process General Electric, like many other U.S. manufacturing firms, redoubled its efforts not only to increase productivity, but also to improve the quality of the products offered to its customers.

CONCEPT CHECK

1 **What are the three steps in the strategic management process?**

2 **Which is more specific, an organization's business or its goals?**

3 **What is an organization's distinctive competency?**

THE STRATEGIC MARKETING PROCESS: PLANNING PHASE

All approaches to planning will incorporate procedures to find answers to these key questions:

1 Where have we been, where are we now, and where are we headed with our existing plans?
2 Where do we want to go?
3 How do we allocate our resources to get to where we want to go?
4 How do we convert our plans into actions?
5 How do our results compare with our plans, and do deviations require new plans and actions?

This same approach is used in the strategic marketing process, whereby an organization allocates its marketing mix resources to reach its target markets. This process is divided into three phases: planning, implementation, and control (Figure 2–3). This section covers the planning phase; the last two phases are discussed afterward.

FIGURE 2–3
The strategic marketing process

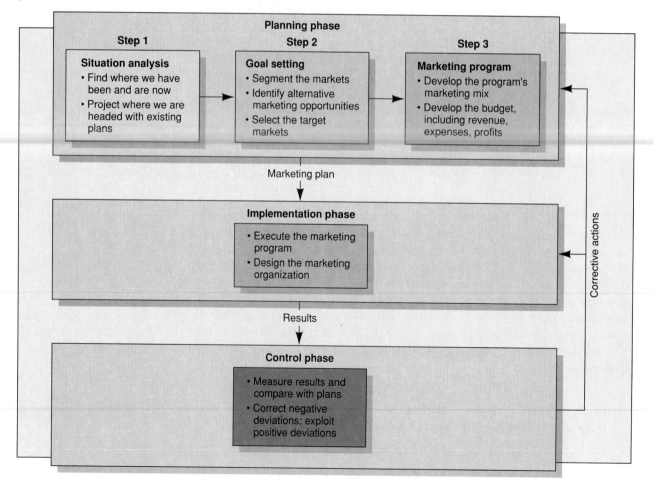

HOW THE PLANNING STEPS TIE TOGETHER

Before details of the planning phase of the strategic marketing process are discussed, it is important to understand how the three steps of the process interrelate. The IBM PC provides an example.

Step 1: Situation Analysis   Suppose it is December 1997 and you are IBM's marketing vice president responsible for marketing its line of PCs. You want to look at the current picture, which is Step 1 (or the situation analysis) in your marketing strategy process. As shown in Part A of Figure 2–4, you have shipped 2 million PCs during 1997, up from 1.5 million in 1993. But competition is heating up, and, with your present product and marketing strategy, you can see unit sales falling to 1 million in 2001.

This is the essence of the **situation analysis**—taking stock of where the firm or product has been recently, where it is now, and where it is likely to end up using present plans. Situation analysis requires that you assess the current strengths and weaknesses of your PC and the markets in which it competes. You then must analyze the factors both inside and outside IBM to project their effect on your future sales. These steps result in your estimate of 1 million units in 2001, a projection neither you nor your boss is very happy about.

Step 2: Goal Setting   Not satisfied with a drop-off in sales for 2001, you set a target of selling 3 million units (Part B of Figure 2–4). This goal isn't pulled out of a hat; **goal setting,** Step 2 in the strategic marketing process, is setting measurable marketing objectives to be achieved. This is the result of a careful analysis of the goals for all of IBM, as well as for your PC division, and assessment of alternative marketing opportunities—in terms of both old and new products *and* old and new markets. This ultimately results in selecting specific target markets to achieve the goal of 3 million units in 2001.

FIGURE 2–4
The planning phase of the strategic marketing process

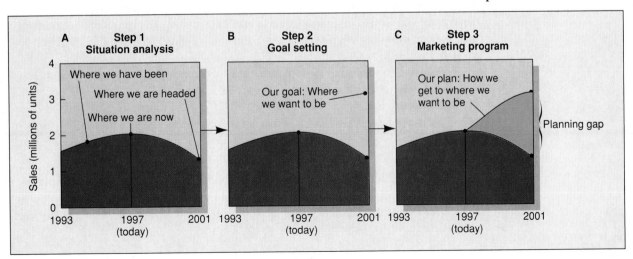

Step 3: Marketing Program The upper line at the right in Part C of Figure 2–4 shows the path you want to follow to sell 3 million units in 2001. The lower one at the right in Part C of Figure 2–4 projects what will happen if you only follow through with current plans. The space between the two lines is often called the **planning gap,** which is the difference between the projection of the path to reach a new goal and the projection of the path of the results of a plan already in place. Your task in Step 3 is to organize IBM's potential resources into a coherent marketing program that uses the four marketing mix elements (product, price, promotion, and place) to reach the targeted goal of 3 million units in 2001.

Plans don't automatically become reality. The implementation and control phases of the strategic marketing process (discussed later) are attempts to convert plans into actions and results.

STEP 1: SITUATION ANALYSIS

There are two steps in the situation analysis of the strategic marketing process.

Finding Where the Organization Has Been and Now Is Discovering where a company has been and is at present involves taking a careful inventory of the strengths and weaknesses of both the markets it serves and the array of competing products in those markets (see Figure 2–4). Two important considerations in this inventory are (1) the industry growth (growth of sales of all the firms competing in that market) and (2) the competitive position of the firm's products relative to those of other businesses in the market.

High profits on a new product soon attract competitors. For example, GE had almost two dozen competitors within two years of introducing its electric carving knife. Similarly, Sony's Walkman, Apple's PC, and Prince's large-head tennis racket stimulated countless high–quality imitators that often leapfrogged the original innovation with improved models.

Projecting Where the Firm Is Headed with Existing Plans When the firm knows where it is now with its present products and markets, it must project future sales and profits on the basis of its existing plans. This requires that the firm assess the impact of both internal and external factors on its products. Both can either constrain or enhance opportunities, as illustrated by IBM's introduction of its PS/2.

Internal factors include departmental objectives and resources, as well as organizational strengths and weaknesses as identified by the SWOT analysis. The marketing manager must consider all of these in assessing the future.

By the mid-1980s IBM's overall market share in PCs had fallen, and it knew action was required. It decided to design a new line of PCs. Internal factors had a major effect on IBM's decision:

- *Departmental goal.* The goal of the department was to develop and market a successful line of new PCs by mid-1987.
- *Resources.* IBM provided almost unlimited financial, technological, and marketing resources to its new PS/2 team.

Sony's Walkman stimulated many high-quality competitors.

- *Strengths.* In designing the PS/2, IBM's special strengths were its name, the strength of its original PC, and its outstanding sales and customer service personnel.
- *Weaknesses.* IBM PCs did not have the ability to "network" or "speak" to each other.

Thus internal factors can have both positive and negative effects on marketing decisions.

External factors in a SWOT analysis cover consumer demand and competitive, economic, political, legal, and technological issues. All these affected IBM's decision to introduce its PS/2:

- *Consumer demand considerations.* IBM research showed that consumers wanted PCs that were fast and user-friendly and could communicate with each other and large systems.
- *Competitive considerations.* Apple, Tandy, Compaq, and other IBM clones were already producing high-quality PCs.
- *Economic considerations.* The dollar was weakening against foreign currencies, especially the Japanese yen, making foreign PCs more expensive for U.S. buyers than American-built PCs.
- *Political and legal considerations.* With the number of IBM clones in existence, a critical issue was whether competitors could legally "clone" its new PS/2.

- *Technological considerations*. Designing a technologically complex PS/2 line of PCs that could network with all sizes of IBM computers was a task that would tax even IBM's resources. Could it be done at a cost that would eventually make the PS/2 profitable?

IBM added up the internal and external factors in the mid–1980s and committed itself to the PS/2 project.

STEP 2: GOAL SETTING

An effective marketing program requires a focus—a specific group of target market customers toward which it is directed. This requires that the marketing manager (1) segment the firm's markets, (2) identify alternative marketing opportunities, and (3) actually select target markets. Note that there is a hierarchy of goals in an organization. For example, marketing objectives must flow directly from goals set by top management in the strategic management process.

Segmenting the Market   The process of **market segmentation** involves aggregating prospective buyers into groups, or segments, that (1) have common needs and (2) will respond similarly to a marketing action. Ideally, each segment can be reached by a specific marketing program targeted to its needs. The Coca-Cola Company now offers four different Coca-Colas to reach market segments that want or don't want sugar and want or don't want caffeine. It also offers new-formula Coca-Cola for those wanting a sweeter taste and Cherry Coke for those wanting that flavor. The decision to target soft drinks to these segments was a major one because, until 1982, the name *Coca-Cola* was never allowed on any drink but the original Coca-Cola—now "Coca-Cola Classic."

Identifying Alternative Market Opportunities   One way for a marketing manager to identify alternative market opportunities is by analyzing various market-product strategies.

As Coca-Cola attempts to increase sales and profits, there are four combinations of present and new markets and products available to it, as shown in Figure 2–5.[14] For example, the Coca-Cola marketing manager can try to use a

FIGURE 2–5
Four market-product strategies: alternative ways to expand marketing opportunities, using Coca-Cola Company products as examples

| | PRODUCTS | |
MARKETS	PRESENT	NEW
Present	**Market penetration** Selling more Coca-Cola to Americans	**Product development** Selling a new product like PowerAde to Americans
New	**Market development** Selling Coca-Cola to the Chinese for the first time	**Diversification** Selling a new product like movies to Europeans

strategy of **market penetration,** which is increasing sales of present products in their existing markets by increasing sales of Coca-Cola to U.S. ultimate consumers. There is no change in the product line, but increased sales are possible through actions such as better advertising, more retail outlets, or lower prices. In fact, Coca-Cola has moved aggressively in all these areas: replacing Pepsi at Burger King fast-food fountains, cosponsoring Super Bowl halftime shows, and staging aggressive price wars in supermarkets.[15]

Market development, which means selling existing products to new markets, has been undertaken by selling Coca-Cola in a new market—such as China, where it is served as a luxury item on silver trays at government functions. Coca-Cola believes opportunities for increased soft-drink sales are greater in international markets than in the United States, and more than three quarters of its profit now comes from abroad.[16]

An expansion strategy using **product development** involves selling a new product to existing markets. Coca-Cola has exploited numerous other new product opportunities by selling new soft drinks to American consumers: Fresca (1966), diet Coke (1982), Cherry Coke (1986), diet Cherry Coke (1986), and PowerAde—a sports drink to compete with Gatorade—(1990).[17]

Diversification involves developing new products and selling them in new markets. This is a potentially high-risk strategy for Coca-Cola because the company has neither previous production experience nor marketing experience on which to draw. In the early 1980s, Coca-Cola acquired Columbia Pictures Industries, a producer of movies and TV programs for U.S. and foreign markets. This acquisition represented diversification strategy far different from selling soft drinks to U.S. consumers. Even Coca-Cola found difficulty in this great a diversification strategy, and in late 1989 sold Columbia Pictures Industries to Sony.

For an explanation of what a product development strategy is and how Coca-Cola uses it with this sports drink, see the text.

Selecting the Target Markets   Having considered a number of alternative marketing opportunities, the organization must select the one or more target markets for which it will develop its marketing program. An important strategic issue for firms to use in selecting target markets is to balance the increased expenses (such as research and development and production) against increased revenues (such as expected sales revenue).

Diet Coke—a sugar-free, caffeinated soft drink—is an example of the difficult choices an organization faces in deciding to introduce a new product. In this case Coca-Cola was especially concerned about **product cannibalism**—a firm's new product gaining sales by stealing them from its other products. Coca-Cola managers were worried that diet Coke would make money at the expense of Tab and not by reaching new customers, and that is exactly what happened. (The even more controversial Coca-Cola decision on new-formula Coca-Cola and Coca-Cola Classic is discussed in Chapter 6.)

STEP 3: THE MARKETING PROGRAM

Selecting the target markets tells the marketing manager which consumers to focus on and what needs to try to satisfy—the *who* aspect of the strategic marketing process. The *how* part involves (1) developing the proper marketing mix and (2) developing the budget. Figure 2–6 shows components of each marketing mix element that are combined to provide a cohesive marketing program.

FIGURE 2–6
Elements of the marketing mix that compose a cohesive marketing program

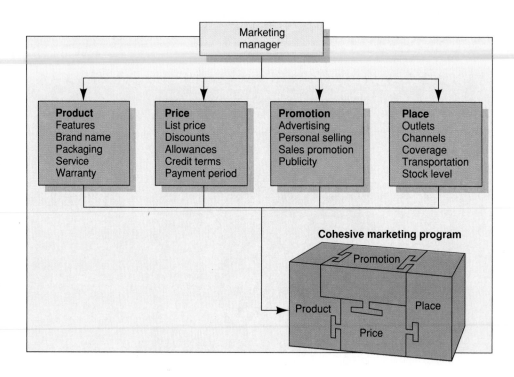

Developing the Marketing Mix   In the 1950s a doting grandfather was babysitting his first grandchild. Called on to change the baby's diapers, he was certain there must be something better than cloth diapers or the poor-quality disposable diapers then on the market. The grandfather, a P&G engineer, did something about this unsatisfied need and convinced the firm to develop a better product. Was the U.S. market large enough to warrant this new product development effort? P&G market researchers estimated that in the United States at that time there were 15 billion diaper changes a year, so the market *was* big enough to justify a closer look.

After several redesigns, many trials with babies, countless interviews with parents, and four trial introductions, a product was found that satisfied consumers' expectations of quality for the price paid. Pampers disposable diapers were the result.

From its introduction in 1956 until the early 1980s, Pampers dominated the disposable diaper market. But in 1982 Kimberly-Clark's Huggies disposable diaper went into national distribution, and P&G's share of the disposable diaper market fell about 17 percent during the next three years (see Figure 2–7).[18]

If you were P&G and lost 17 percent of a $3.5 billion a year market, what would you do? In 1986 P&G's response was to introduce a new, high-absorbency Pampers diaper.

In the 1980s P&G also introduced and promoted its Luvs brand—targeted at the segment wanting a premium diaper. P&G had wanted Luvs, with its superabsorbent gel, to reach a completely new segment of buyers, but—as Figure 2–7 shows—Luvs cannibalized sales of P&G's own Pampers brand.[19]

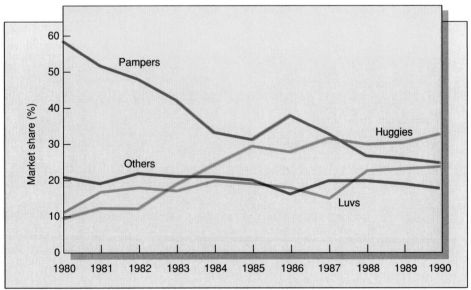

FIGURE 2–7
Market shares in the U.S. disposable diaper market

Sources: Laurie Freeman, "New Diaper Fight," *Advertising Age* (March 5, 1990), p. 4; and Alecia Swasy, "P&G Moves to Revamp Its Pampers," *The Wall Street Journal* (August 9, 1989), p. B1. Reprinted by permission of *The Wall Street Journal*, © 1989 Dow Jones & Company, Inc. All Rights Reserved Worldwide.

Then both P&G's Luvs and Kimberly-Clark's Huggies introduced "gender-specific diapers," with the superabsorbent gel placed differently in the diaper for boys and girls, in 1988 and 1989, respectively. Pampers's market share fell even further.

Pampers counterattacked in 1990 with a new marketing program:

- *Product.* It introduced "Pampers for Boys" and "Pampers for Girls," a thinner, superabsorbent diaper with cuffs to prevent leakage and better-sticking tape fasteners.
- *Price.* It was comparable to the price of the old unisex Pampers.
- *Promotion.* The message was carried to buyers through network TV commercials, magazine and newspaper ads with cents-off coupons, and free samples.
- *Place.* P&G fought for space on retailers' shelves by offering retail allowances of up to $10 per case of diapers, about three times the usual rate.[20]

P&G's diaper war with Kimberly-Clark continues.

Developing the Budget   A P&G marketing executive responsible for introducing the new Pampers had to develop a budget to ensure that revenues would exceed expenses and result in a profit. To project the budget's sales revenue, he first had to answer some key questions:

- What will be the effect of increasing consumer concerns about the need for a biodegradable diaper? (This issue is discussed in Chapter 3.)
- What will Kimberly-Clark's competitive response be?
- If the new Pampers is a success, will it continue to cannibalize sales of P&G's Luvs?

Answering such questions is the first step in developing a realistic budget for the marketing program. The planning phase of the strategic marketing process is discussed in greater detail in Chapter 20.

CONCEPT CHECK

1 What is situation analysis?

2 What is market segmentation?

3 When Coca-Cola decided to produce Fresca and Tab and sell them to its existing customers, which market-product strategy was it following?

THE STRATEGIC MARKETING PROCESS: IMPLEMENTATION PHASE

As shown in Figure 2–3, the result of the tens or hundreds of hours in the planning phase of the strategic marketing process is a **marketing plan**—a written statement identifying the target market, specific marketing goals, the budget, and timing for the marketing program.

Implementation, the second phase of the strategic marketing process, involves carrying out the marketing plan that emerges from the planning phase. Two key elements in the implementation phase are (1) executing the program described in the marketing plan and (2) designing the marketing organization needed.

EXECUTING THE MARKETING PROGRAM

Marketing plans are meaningless pieces of paper without effective execution of those plans.

Marketing Strategies and Marketing Tactics   Effective execution requires attention to detail for both marketing strategies and marketing tactics. A **marketing strategy** is the means by which a marketing goal is to be achieved, characterized by (1) a specified target market and (2) a marketing program to reach it. Although the term *strategy* is often used loosely, it implies both the end sought (target market) and the means to achieve it (marketing program).

To implement a marketing program successfully, hundreds of detailed decisions are often required, such as writing advertising copy or selecting the amount for temporary price reductions. These decisions, called **marketing tactics,** are detailed day-to-day operational decisions essential to the overall success of marketing strategies. Compared with marketing strategies, marketing tactics generally involve actions that must be taken right away. We cannot cover many aspects of marketing tactics in detail in a book of this size, and the emphasis here is on marketing strategy—the strategic marketing process. However, examples of marketing tactics are occasionally described to show the concern for detail present in effective marketing programs.

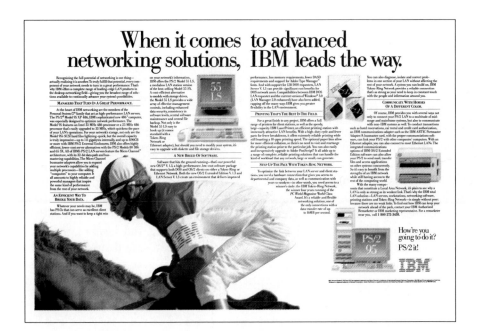

What does this ad suggest about IBM's role in the 1990s? The text on the next page suggests IBM's strategy.

Marketing Strategies for IBM in the 1990s IBM president John F. Akers concluded that IBM's problems in the late 1980s occurred because "IBM took its eye off the ball" and got out of touch with its customers. Akers believed that IBM had persisted in selling computers when customers actually wanted "solutions" on how to get their dozens of computers to "talk" to each other to improve productivity. So IBM in the 1990s has shifted its marketing strategy of selling hardware such as mainframes and PCs to stress "networked computers"—computers and databases linked together to respond better to customer needs.[21] The strategy has returned IBM to what its distinctive competency had traditionally been—"solving customer problems"—as opposed to selling products.

Marketing Tactics for IBM in the 1990s An example of marketing tactics for IBM is its continuous search to find an effective way to communicate its problem-solving capabilities to its customers. The "Little Tramp" advertising campaign (see the ad on page 30) was an unqualified success. When IBM launched its Personal System/2 family of PCs in 1987, its promotional campaign for the PS/2 included a 24-page insert in many business magazines that featured the *M*★*A*★*S*★*H* characters. The advertising campaign was intended to represent "a new generation of IBM teamwork," but the campaign never caught prospective customers' attention like the Little Tramp campaign had.

For its 1990s PS/2 advertising program, IBM devised a catchy tagline that was again at odds with the company's button-down image: "How're you going to do it! PS/2 It!"[22] This series of "PS/2 It!" ads (see pages 30 and 49) translates John Akers's overall customer-oriented strategy into tactical details to help prospective buyers understand how the PS/2 can help solve their problems through "networking." Decisions on marketing tactics such as the details on IBM's advertising campaign follow directly from the higher-level marketing strategy decisions it makes.

DESIGNING THE MARKETING ORGANIZATION

To execute the marketing program effectively, a marketing organization must be developed. In the mid-1980s, General Motors (GM) announced a total reorganization of the company that was prompted by increased competition from Japanese and European imports.

As shown in Figure 2–8, reporting to the president are two group vice presidents—one for small cars (Chevrolet, Pontiac, Saturn, and General Motors of Canada) and the other for large cars (Oldsmobile, Buick, and Cadillac). Under the new organization both the Large Car and Small Car groups are divided into five main departments: R&D (including parts of the old Fisher Body Division), manufacturing and assembly (including parts of the old Assembly Division), marketing, accounting and finance, and human resources. One reason for GM's restructuring is to enable it to respond more quickly to changes in the market.[23] Another reason is the growth in overlapping brands of GM cars that aren't targeted to specific market segments but have similar designs, thus confusing buyers.

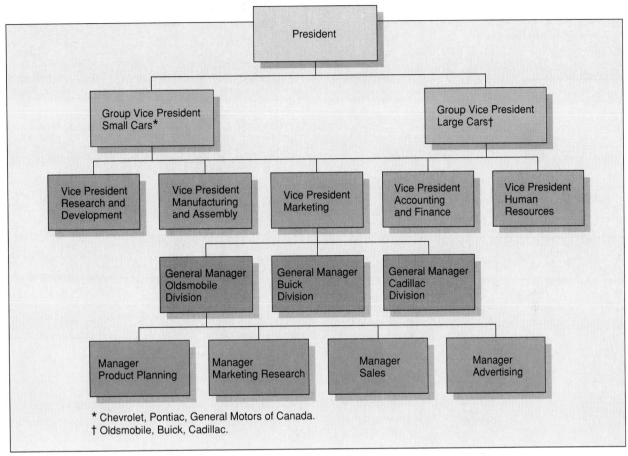

* Chevrolet, Pontiac, General Motors of Canada.
† Oldsmobile, Buick, Cadillac.

FIGURE 2–8
Organization of the automobile operations of General Motors Corporation

THE STRATEGIC MARKETING PROCESS: CONTROL PHASE

The control phase of the strategic marketing process seeks to keep the marketing program moving in the direction set for it (see Figures 2–3 and 2–4). Accomplishing this requires the marketing manager (1) to compare the results of the marketing program with the goals in the written plans to identify deviations and (2) to act on these deviations—correcting negative deviations and exploiting positive ones.

COMPARING RESULTS WITH PLANS TO IDENTIFY DEVIATIONS

In 1985, Eastman Kodak realized that its sales were almost unchanged from 1982 (Figure 2–9). By 1985, technological innovations were redefining the entire

FIGURE 2–9
Evaluation and control of Kodak's marketing program

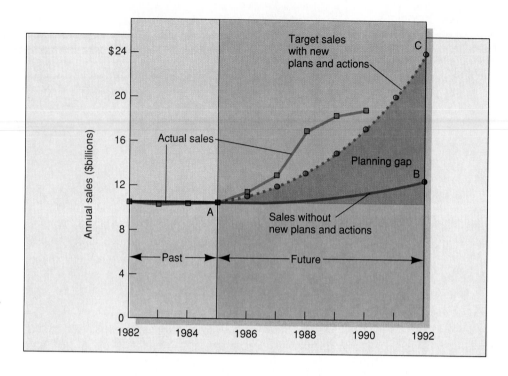

amateur photographic market, and several of Kodak's product lines were faltering. A decreasing market share for instant cameras, declining sales of movie films, and greater competition from Fuji in the traditional film and photographic paper markets necessitated drastic action.

Extending the 1982 to 1985 trend to 1992 would give the sales shown by line AB in Figure 2–9 an unacceptable, low-growth strategy. To equal its late-1970s sales growth, Kodak would have to follow the target sales shown in line AC in Figure 2–9, which could fill in its large, wedge-shaped planning gap. But continued competition could result in sales being far less than the targeted level. This is the essence of evaluation—comparing actual results with planned objectives.

ACTING ON DEVIATIONS

When the evaluation shows that actual performance is not up to expectations, a corrective action is usually needed to adjust and improve the program and help it achieve the planned objective. In contrast, comparing results with plans may sometimes reveal that actual performance is far better than the plan called for. In this case the marketing manager wants to uncover the reason for the good performance and act to exploit it.

In 1985, Kodak's evaluation of its likely performance after 1985 showed that it would need a drastic new action program that involved developing new products and acquiring new businesses. Targeted at consumers were new disposable cameras like the waterproof "Weekend 35," a low-priced "Star" line of 35 mm cameras, faster film, and a complete line of batteries. In addition, to

New Kodak 35 mm
cameras help fill in its
planning gap.

obtain a stronger foothold in the faster-growth pharmaceutical market, in 1988 Kodak bought Sterling Drug, which manufactures consumer products such as Bayer aspirin. Also, pointed at industrial and medical consumers are new 1-hour photoprocessing minilabs, optical-data storage systems, and Kodak's ColorEdge line of color copiers.

This action program helped sales to rise again, thereby putting actual sales after 1985 above the targeted sales (AC) line and helping to close the planning gap shown in Figure 2–9. Kodak's profit has not increased as rapidly as has sales revenue, so Kodak's corrective actions include substantial cost cutting and an attempt to refocus efforts on its basic, "core" product lines.[24] Through these actions Kodak has sought to bring its marketing program under control, which illustrates the final phase in the strategic marketing process.

The implementation and control phases of the strategic marketing process are discussed in greater detail in Chapter 21.

CONCEPT CHECK

1 What is the control phase of the strategic marketing process?

2 How do the objectives set for a marketing program in the planning phase relate to the control phase of the strategic marketing process?

ETHICS AND SOCIAL RESPONSIBILITY IN THE 1990s

WHAT SHOULD POLAROID DO WITH $600 MILLION?

After 14 years of legal battles, on October 12, 1990, a federal judge said that Eastman Kodak should pay the Polaroid Corporation $909.5 million for violating its instant-photography patents. After taxes, Polaroid will be left with about $600 million, about 90 percent of its total profits from 1976 to 1985 when Kodak's violations occurred.[25]

What should Polaroid Chairman I. MacAllister Booth do with the company's $600 million windfall? Suggestions include give it to the employees, give it to the stockholders, put it into improving Polaroid's consumer cameras, start developing industrial products, and give it to charity.

If you were Polaroid chairman Booth, what would you do? Why?

 ## SUMMARY

1 The strategic management process involves the steps taken at an organization's corporate and divisional levels to develop long-run master approaches for survival and growth. Three key steps in this process are (*a*) defining the organization's business (or mission), (*b*) specifying its goals, and (*c*) identifying its opportunities.

2 The strategic marketing process, using objectives and limits set by the strategic management process, involves the steps taken at the product and market levels to allocate marketing resources to viable marketing positions and programs. It has three phases: planning, implementation, and control.

3 The planning phase of the strategic marketing process involves three steps: (*a*) the situation analysis (where are we now, how did we get here, and where are we headed with present plans?), (*b*) goal setting (where do we want to go?), and (*c*) designing a marketing program in the form of a marketing plan that blends the elements of the marketing mix (how do we allocate our marketing resources to get where we want to go?).

4 The task of identifying marketing opportunities can be facilitated by looking at the four combinations of present and new markets and products.

5 The implementation phase of the strategic marketing process involves executing the marketing plan and designing the marketing organization needed.

6 A marketing strategy is the means by which a marketing goal is to be achieved, characterized by (1) a specified target market and (2) a marketing program to reach it. Marketing tactics are detailed, day-to-day operational decisions essential to the overall success of marketing strategies.

7 The control phase of the strategic marketing process involves (*a*) comparing results with the goals established in the marketing plan to identify deviations from plan and (*b*) taking action to correct negative deviations or exploit positive ones.

KEY TERMS AND CONCEPTS

strategic management process p. 32

strategic marketing process p. 32

organization's business (mission) p. 33

organization's goals p. 35

business firm p. 35

nonprofit organization p. 35

profit p. 36

market share p. 36

distinctive competency p. 38

situation analysis p. 41

goal setting p. 41

planning gap p. 42

market segmentation p. 44

market penetration p. 45

market development p. 45

product development p. 45

diversification p. 45

product cannibalism p. 46

marketing plan p. 48

marketing strategy p. 49

marketing tactics p. 49

CHAPTER PROBLEMS AND APPLICATIONS

1 Look again at IBM's PS/2 ads in the chapter. Recognizing that the ads are targeted at businesses, what are (a) good features of the ads and (b) key messages of the ads?

2 How did the three Cs—company, customer, and competitor—lead IBM to conclude it should introduce its new PS/2?

3 Sara Lee Corporation produces a variety of products and services that fall into five divisions: (a) consumer foods, (b) international consumer foods, (c) food service distribution, (d) consumer personal products, and (e) consumer household products. Where are each of these "businesses" included in its business (mission) statement in Figure 2–2?

4 What is the main result of each of the three phases of the strategic marketing process? (a) planning, (b) implementation, and (c) control.

5 Many American liberal arts colleges traditionally have offered an undergraduate degree in liberal arts (the product) to full-time 18-to-22-year-old students (the market). How might such a college use the four market-product expansion strategies shown in Figure 2–5 to compete in the 1990s?

6 Today many Americans are concerned about the volume of their salt intake. Coca-Cola might (a) add salt and no-salt combinations to its existing (b) sugar and no-sugar and (c) caffeine and no-caffeine brands. How many products would Coca-Cola have to offer to hit all these combinations? What are the strengths and weaknesses of such a product strategy?

7 There are both advantages and disadvantages of introducing a new, improved version of an existing brand. What are examples of each for P&G in choosing (a) not to introduce and (b) to introduce new Pampers for Boys and Pampers for Girls disposable diapers?

8 The goal-setting step in the planning phase of the strategic marketing process sets quantified objectives for use in the control phase. What actions are suggested for a marketing manager if measured results are below objectives? Above objectives?

9 Suppose you headed up General Motors today. Develop a simple SWOT analysis for the company based on what you know about its cars and environmental factors.

CHAPTER 3

The Changing Marketing Environment

*A*fter reading this chapter you should be able to:

- Understand how environmental scanning studies social, economic, technological, competitive and regulatory forces.

- Explain how social forces like demographics and culture and economic forces like macroeconomic conditions and consumer income affect marketing.

- Describe how technological changes and their ecological impacts can affect marketing.

- Understand the competitive structures that exist in a market, the role of marketing within each, and key components of competition.

- Explain the major legislation to ensure competition and regulate the elements of the marketing mix.

The Fountain of Youth Has Been Found! It's on Your Supermarket Shelves

What's your cholesterol? How high is your blood pressure? What percentage of your diet is saturated fat? Ten years ago these were absurd questions to pose to a shopper, yet today, the U.S. population is aging. And as society ages, concerns about health and longevity increase. Companies are responding to this demographic and attitudinal shift in the environment by refocusing their advertising of products and developing new food items.

The health craze and concern over food products are real. It is estimated that 30 percent of all U.S. food advertising now includes some health-related message. Kellogg Co. started this trend in 1984, when it advertised its All-Bran cereal as healthful in preventing some types of cancer. This strategy was in response to the National Cancer Institute's report of a relationship between diets high in fiber and reduced levels of colon cancer. Consumers responded as All-Bran sales rose 22 percent.

Others were quick to follow, and oat bran has become an important ingredient for food marketers to emphasize. General Mills, Nabisco, Quaker Oats, and donut chains like Bess Eaton are now making bran products. One consumer survey reported that 74 percent of the Pepsi drinkers would switch to Coke if it contained bran. In 1989 alone, 218 products containing oat bran were introduced.

But environmental change is a two-edged sword, and the environment can change quickly. For oat bran, the change occurred January 18, 1990, when the *New England Journal of Medicine* reported a study that found little cholesterol reduction benefits from bran over other low-fiber foods. Quaker Oats Co., which spent some $20 million dollars to introduce a ready-to-eat oat bran cereal in 1989, found their company stock price dropped $1.625 per share the day the study was published.

The benefits of health claims in the marketing of products is still being played out. Quaker Oats Co. began a series of ads rebutting the study's findings. The Food and Drug Administration is now proposing new regulations regarding the health claims that can be made for a food product.[1]

HOW MARKETING USES ENVIRONMENTAL SCANNING

The change in the age distribution and birth trends in the United States represents an opportunity for companies such as Benetton, Laura Ashley, and even Sears with its line of McDonald's children's clothes.

FIGURE 3–1
**How environmental
scanning reveals
marketing opportunities
and threats**

An organization's very existence often depends on its ability to spot trends in its environment and turn these to its advantage. For each of the three questions below, estimate (1) what percentage of Americans have that characteristic, (2) what type of firm could use this fact as an opportunity, and (3) what type of firm could view it as a threat.

1 What percentage of Americans love Mexican food?
2 What percentage of American women consider themselves overweight?
3 How old is the average American's car?

The percentages, along with some opportunities and threats, are described in the text.

THE MEANING OF ENVIRONMENTAL SCANNING

Like these companies, people in many firms continually acquire information on events occurring outside their organization to identify and interpret potential trends—a process called **environmental scanning.** The objective of environmental scanning is to spot the trends and determine if they pose specific opportunities or threats to the firm, as described in SWOT analysis in Chapter 2. This understanding leads to marketing actions.

Surprisingly, a trend that represents an important opportunity for one firm may be a major threat to another, and vice versa. To understand environmental scanning and its importance, read Figure 3–1 and try to estimate the percentage of Americans with those characteristics and how such facts pose both opportunities and threats for different firms.

Twenty-three percent of all Americans say they love Mexican food. This suggests a marketing opportunity, as seen in the growth of Mexican restaurants (such as Chi-Chi's and Taco Bell), and a threat to more traditional restaurant chains such as McDonald's and Kentucky Fried Chicken. Concerning question 2, nearly 60 percent of American women consider themselves overweight. This figure has led to the boom in diet centers and weight-reduction products. Weight Watchers, owned by H. J. Heinz, had sales over $1.3 billion in 1988, while Nutri/Systems's 1,200 centers had revenues of $232 million. With regard to question 3, the average American owns an eight-year-old car and drives it 8,000 miles a year. The potential replacement demand explains to some extent the importance of the U.S. car market to foreign manufacturers.[2]

AN ENVIRONMENTAL SCAN OF THE 1990s

Every organization exists as part of a larger environment in which continuous changes provide both marketing opportunities and threats. This chapter examines five broad, uncontrollable factors in a company's environment: social, economic, technological, competitive, and regulatory forces. As shown in Figure 3–2, these factors are the environmental forces that affect the marketing activities of a firm.

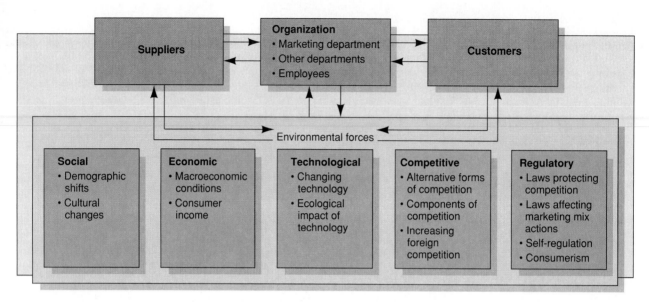

FIGURE 3–2
Environmental forces affecting the organization, as well as its suppliers and customers

A firm conducting an environmental scan of the United States in the 1990s might uncover key trends such as those listed in Figure 3–3 for each of the five environmental forces. Although the list of trends is far from complete, it reveals the breadth of an environmental scan—from identifying changing consumer tastes such as "high-tech and high touch" and the desire for improved product quality and customer service, to technological breakthroughs in biotechnology and competitive challenges in restructuring American corporations. These trends affect all Americans and the businesses and nonprofit organizations that serve them. Trends such as these are covered as the five environmental forces are described in the following pages.

SOCIAL FORCES

The **social forces** of the environment include the characteristics of the population, its income, and its values. Changes in these can have a dramatic impact on marketing strategy.

DEMOGRAPHICS

Describing the distribution of the population according to selected characteristics—where people are, their numbers, and who they are, such as their age, sex, income, and occupation—is referred to as **demographics.**

The Population Trend In 1990, the U.S. population was forecast to be slightly over 250 million people, with a slight but real decline in the number of people under five years of age.[3] This represents a continued graying of America, a significant demographic trend. In 1960, only 9 percent of the population was over age 65; by 1990, this percentage had increased to 12.4.

ENVIRONMENTAL FORCE	TREND IDENTIFIED BY AN ENVIRONMENTAL SCAN
Social	• Growing number and importance of older Americans • Continuing U.S. population shifts to South and West • Desire for "high-tech and high touch": gadgets plus human interaction • Greater desire for product quality and customer service • Greater role for women in jobs and purchase decisions
Economic	• Concern that U.S. budget and trade deficits can trigger inflation • More U.S. firms will look to foreign markets for growth • Continuing decline in real per capita income of Americans • Less consumer acceptance of debt
Technological	• Increased use of massive computer databases and networks • Major breakthroughs in biotechnology and superconductivity • More problems with pollution and solid and nuclear wastes
Competitive	• More employment in small, innovative firms • Downsizing and restructuring of many corporations • Flexible manufacturing will reduce economies of scale • More international competition from Europe and Asia
Regulatory	• Less regulation of U.S. firms competing in international markets • More protection for those owning patents • Greater concern for ethics and social responsibility in business • Renewed emphasis on self-regulation

FIGURE 3–3
An environmental scan of the United States of the 1990s

The composition of America's population is changing (as shown in Figure 3–4) and successful companies must respond to this change. In recent years, a greater marketing attention is being focused on the **mature household.** Such households are headed by people over 50 years old, who represent the fastest-growing age segment in the population. In 1988 this group represented 27.5 percent of the population, but this percentage will climb dramatically to 33.8 percent by the year 2010 and to 38 percent by 2025.[4] People over 50 control 75 percent of the net worth of U.S. households, and the over-50 category includes the period (between ages 55 and 60) when a person's income peaks.

Environmental scanning of this trend has led some companies to already begin responding to this important market. AT&T has developed products aimed at seniors such as emergency dialing mechanisms and amplifiers. The Marriott hotel chain has built high-rise retirement communities. General Foods uses older celebrities in its ads, such as Lena Horne for Post Bran Flakes. Beecham Products USA uses larger type on its product labels. And the demand for anti-aging products and services will grow. Johnson & Johnson, makers of Retin-A (an anti-aging lotion originally designed for treatment of pimples), found that sales of Retin-A rose from $33.5 million in 1987 to $115 million in 1989, when consumers learned of its wrinkle reduction potential.[5]

The Baby Boom   A major reason for the graying of America is that the **baby boomers**—the generation of children born between 1946 and 1964—are growing up. This group accounted for 11.4 percent of the population in 1990, making them important to marketers. It has been estimated that this group will account

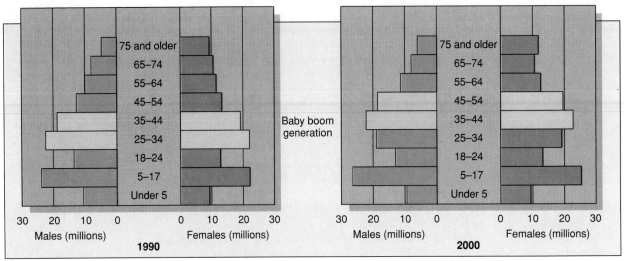

Source: Margaret Ambry, *The Almanac of Consumer Markets* (Chicago: Probus Publishing, 1990), p. 143. Copyright 1990 by American Demographics Books.

FIGURE 3–4
The changing age of Americans

for 56 to 58 percent of the purchases in most consumer categories. As this group ages, their buying behavior will change to reflect greater concern for their children's future and their own retirement.[6] Saving and financial planning will become a more important concern, a trend that led to John Hancock's ad campaign "Real Life, Real Answers." Other companies, such as Club Med and BMW, are refocusing their strategies to a more mature market. Club Med is trying to shed their singles image by promoting family vacations and facilities with day care, and BMW is responding to a more fiscally conservative baby boomer by cutting prices and introducing a lower-priced entry model.[7]

The American Family   Although dramatic changes exist in terms of age and birthrate, marketers are also monitoring a changing American family. In the 1950s, 70 percent of U.S. households consisted of a stay-at-home mother, working father, and one or more children, whereas only 21 percent of today's households do so.[8]

About 50 percent of all first marriages now end in divorce. The majority of divorced people eventually remarry, which has given rise to the **blended family,** one formed by the merging into a single household of two previously separated units. In scanning this environment, Levitz, a furniture retailer, found blended families prefer rectangular tables—his kids on one side, hers on the other.[9]

Geographical Shifts   The major regional shift in the population has been toward Western and Sunbelt states. Figure 3–5 shows that the Mountain region population grew by 22 percent during the 1980s, while the Midwest saw a rather small 1.8 percent increase in the population during the same period. Four states grew by over 30 percent in population in the 1980s: Arizona (36.0 percent), Florida (33.4 percent), Nevada (50.7 percent), and Alaska (37.4 percent).[10]

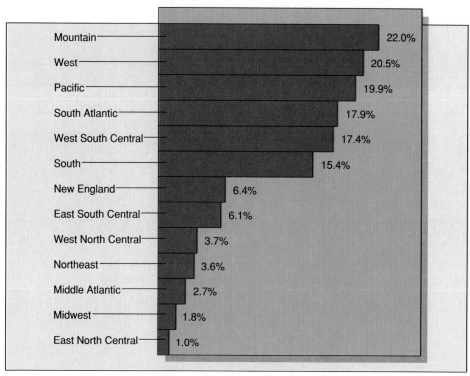

Source: "Snapshots of the Nation," *The Wall Street Journal* (March 9, 1990), p. R13. Reprinted by permission of THE WALL STREET JOURNAL, © 1990 Dow Jones & Company, Inc. All Rights Reserved Worldwide.

FIGURE 3–5
Regional growth in population, 1980–1990

    In recent decades, people have also moved from rural areas to major cities and their suburbs. So marketers focus on population centers, where about three fourths of the population lives. To assist marketers in gathering data on population centers, the government has a three-level classification system that reflects their degree of urbanization. From largest to smallest, these three areas are the consolidated metropolitan statistical area (CMSA), primary metropolitan statistical area (PMSA), and metropolitan statistical area (MSA), as described below:

- *Consolidated metropolitan statistical area (CMSA).* The largest designation in terms of geographical area and market size; is made up of component PMSAs, defined below, that total at least 1 million people.
- *Primary metropolitan statistical area (PMSA).* An area that is part of a larger CMSA that has a total population of 1 million or more. It must also contain counties that conform to the following standards: (1) a total population of at least 100,000, (2) a population that is at least 60 percent urban, and (3) fewer than 50 percent of the resident workers commute to jobs outside the county.
- *Metropolitan statistical area (MSA).* (1) A city having a population of at least 50,000 or (2) an urbanized area with a population in excess of 50,000, with a total metropolitan population of at least 100,000. An MSA may include counties that have close economic and social ties to the central county.

Parents in the "baby boom" generation are concerned about financial planning and providing for their children. What industries will be affected as the "boomers" mature?

Regional Marketing   A new trend within marketing focuses not only on the shifting of consumers geographically, but also on the differences in their product preferences based on where they live. This concept has been referred to as **regional marketing,** which is developing marketing plans to reflect specific area differences in taste preferences, perceived needs, or interests. In Chapter 8, you will learn more about this approach to the market referred to as *geographical segmentation.* The accompanying Marketing Action Memo shows how some companies are beginning to deal with this changing view of a regional America.

Technology has aided marketers to begin to understand the variations of regional preferences. Computerized cash registers have allowed companies to coordinate and analyze a large amount of sales data for geographical units as small as neighborhoods. Scott Paper found that their paper towels had a 47.7 percent share in Chicago, yet only a 2.5 percent share in Los Angeles.[11] And, with more local TV stations coming into being, this focus on regional marketing allows a better targeting of ads and products. Ideally, Scott Paper can now create a specific campaign for their heavy users in Chicago and develop a marketing strategy to encourage new purchases in Los Angeles.

The future of regional marketing depends on the cost of these localized efforts. General Foods, in sponsoring a series of regional events such as a rodeo in Texas and a show at Radio City Music Hall to promote a new Maxwell House coffee, found the costs of specialized events to be two to three times the cost of a single national promotion.[12]

Marketing Action Memo

IS AMERICA THE MELTING POT FOR MARKETING?

*F*or marketers like P&G and Campbell's, thinking that all consumers in America are alike is an obsolete idea. Regional marketing is now being viewed as a possible key to developing successful strategies. For all its supposed homogeneity, many companies are now viewing America as a collection of neighborhoods. Reflecting this perspective, in 1987 Campbell's divided the country and their salesforce into 22 regions. The company discovered that a nacho cheese chowder that New England consumers considered too hot was seen as too bland for Southwestern buyers. Campbell's regionalization approach was considered daring in 1987.

Other companies are now jumping on the regionalization bandwagon. P&G found that vacuum brick-packs of ground coffee were popular in the South. The company repackaged their Folgers brand for those markets and developed a new ad campaign. Folgers sales grew to 32 percent of the market in 1989. Con Agra anticipates marketing catfish as a delicacy in the East and as a traditional food in the Mississippi River region, and auto makers now provide options based on regional preferences of new car buyers.

Regionalism of marketing efforts represents a compromise between the effectiveness of offering unique products based on regional differences and the efficiency of offering the same product across regions. Results to date suggest that regionalism pays off, even with its higher costs.

Sources: "Finding the Right Niche," *Advertising Age* (January 21, 1991), pp. S-1–S-9; Bernie Ward, "Find It, Fill It," *Sky* (September 1989), pp. 74–87; and "Stalking the New Consumer," *Business Week* (August 28, 1989), pp. 54–62.

CULTURE

A second social force, **culture,** incorporates the set of values, ideas, and attitudes of a homogeneous group of people that are transmitted from one generation to the next. Culture includes both material and abstract elements, so monitoring cultural trends is difficult but important for marketing.

The Changing Role of Women   Women's role in the work force has changed significantly in the past few decades. Only 17 million women were in the work force in 1947, but today some 54 million women work, an increase of 210 percent.[13] In 1990, over 60 percent of married women were in the work force, and the number is forecast to be 63 percent by 2000. And of women with children, 65 percent work, a figure that includes 50 percent of mothers with children under one year of age.[14]

One impact of this trend has been seen in the marketing of life insurance. Metropolitan Life, an insurance company, developed a series of print ads aimed at women. Today, Met sales to women represent 42 percent of total sales, versus

This investment ad is
oriented to women.

32 percent in previous years.[15] Advertisements such as that shown above are
being directed to women and placed in publications with female readers. The
higher number of working women has led to changes in the marketing strategies
of many companies. Retailers such as Elizabeth Arden Salons, for instance, have
extended their hours to 8:00 P.M. on Thursday, and they will open early on
request. Both Chrysler and Ford have set up internal committees to study the
women's automobile market.[16]

There is a second important change in the roles of women—increasingly,
they are heading households. In 1970, 21 percent of households were headed by
women. This number will increase to 29 percent by the year 2000.[17] While in the
past women also involuntarily headed households following the death of their
spouses, today this status often reflects a conscious choice. One fourth of females heading households never married, a similar percentage are divorced, an
additional 11 percent are separated from their husbands. As working women's
incomes continue to rise, these women will become even more important to
marketers.

The Changing Role of Men   The changing role of women has affected the
marketing of products to men as well. A cooperative study by Campbell's and
People magazine found that the influence of men on food purchases compared
with that of women has risen from a ratio as low as 10:90 to as much as 50:50
in households where both partners are working.[18] Responding to growing male
influence, Fisher peanuts has changed its advertising strategy. It used to advertise
in *Sports Illustrated* only during major sports events, but now it advertises in the
magazine throughout the year.

Safeway Stores, trying to attract the male shopper, has shifted advertisements to *Newsweek* and *Sports Illustrated* and away from women's publications.

As the roles of men and women change, marketers must become sensitive to the differences of the sexes in terms of how they shop.

Changing Attitudes   Culture also includes attitudes and values. In recent years some major attitudinal changes have occurred toward work and lifestyles. Recent study has shown a decrease in the value of the work ethic and the belief that hard work will pay off. There is a growing sense that the Puritan ethic of "I live to work" may be redefined as "I work to live." Work is seen as a means to an end—recreation, leisure, and entertainment—which has contributed to a growth in sales of products such as videocassette recorders, sports equipment, and easily prepared meals. So as attitudes toward work change, consumers are placing increased importance on quality of life.

There is greater concern for health and well-being as evidenced by the level of sports participation in the United States and increased interest in diet. Sears fitness products, Nike workout clothes, and Lean Cuisine dinners are but a few products developed in response to and profiting from this trend. With the growing concern for nutrition, McDonald's is beginning to post nutritional data about their food in each restaurant. Food-tray liners will also display menu information for the meal by the time of day (e.g., breakfast foods in the morning).[19]

Nike products appeal to health-conscious consumers.

1 Explain the term *regional marketing*.

2 What are the marketing implications of blended families?

3 The work ethic of today may best be stated as "I work _____."

ECONOMIC FORCES

The third component of the environmental scan, the **economy,** pertains to the income, expenditures, and resources that affect the cost of running a business and household. We'll consider two aspects of these economic forces: a macroeconomic view and a microeconomic perspective of individual income.

MACROECONOMIC CONDITIONS

Of particular concern at a societal level is the state of the economy, whether it is inflationary or recessionary. For the consumer the impact of inflation is felt in escalating prices. In 1975 the cost of a Volkswagen Rabbit was $2,599. In 1987, largely because of inflation, the cost of a Golf (the model that replaced the Rabbit) was $10,645, which made it less competitive in the small-car market against the Korean-made Hyundai and Yugoslavian Yugo. A Big Mac at McDonald's was 69 cents in 1975; in 1989 it was averaging $1.60. Inflation reduces the number of items a consumer can buy and affects companies in similar ways.

To manufacture and deliver products, companies borrow money from banks. The rate of interest charged by banks to their largest customers (usually corporations) is called the *prime rate,* which rises during inflationary times and increases the cost of doing business. As the prime rate increases significantly, so does the number of business failures. Within that fact is shown the fate of some large retailers that are no longer in business, such as W.T. Grant (1906 to 1976) and Robert Hall (1940 to 1977), whose demises were somewhat affected by the prime rate. Companies must react to rising interest rates, as auto manufacturers found when the rising price of car loans severely cut demand. A solution was to allow the consumer to extend the payment from 36 to 60 months, so the higher interest charge would not be felt in the size of the monthly payment.

Whereas inflation is a period of rapid price increase, recession is a time of slow economic activity, so businesses decrease production, and unemployment rises. Consumers have less money to spend, so marketers need to focus on the function and value of their products. Department stores such as Woodward & Lothrop in Washington, D.C., and Bloomingdale's in New York find that consumers focus on value during a recession and buy more moderately priced lines than they normally would.

CONSUMER INCOME

The microeconomic trends in terms of consumer income are important issues for marketers. Having a product that meets the needs of consumers may be

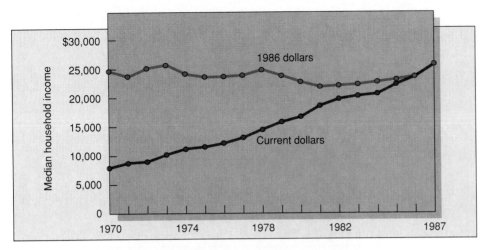

FIGURE 3–6
Trends in median family income from 1970 to 1987

of little value if they are unable to purchase it. A consumer's ability to buy is related to income, which consists of gross, disposable, and discretionary components.

Gross Income   The total amount of money made in one year by a person, household, or family unit is referred to as **gross income.** Figure 3–6 shows the median family income from 1970 to 1987 for households in the United States in terms of current dollars and 1986 dollars (income adjusted for inflation). The figure shows that while the typical U.S. household earned only about $8,700 of income in current dollars in 1970, it earned about $25,986 in 1987. In 1987 dollars, however, income of that typical U.S. household was relatively stable from 1970 to 1987.[20]

In conducting an environmental scan, marketers often focus their efforts on upscale households—those with incomes significantly higher than the typical household. Mazda introduced a $20,000 luxury sedan, the 929, targeted to the baby boomer segment with upscale incomes. Levi Strauss is branching into nondenim clothing. Even Merrill Lynch has put together a mutual fund of companies and products that appeal to baby boomers, called the Fund for Tomorrow.

Disposable Income   The second income component, **disposable income,** is the money a consumer has left after paying taxes to use for food, shelter, and clothing. Thus if taxes rise at a faster rate than does disposable income, consumers must economize. In recent years consumers' allocation of income has shifted. Compared with a decade ago, consumers devote a higher proportion to energy for homes as its cost rises, and the percentage of disposable income spent on food away from home has risen to about one third of the total food budget.[21] The impact of this can be seen in marketing with the growth of family restaurant chains such as Red Lobster and Denny's.

Discretionary Income   The third component of income is **discretionary income,** the money that remains after paying for taxes and necessities. Discre-

As consumers' discretionary income increases, so does the enjoyment of pleasure travel.

Orlando, Florida

tionary income is used for luxury items such as vacations at a Hyatt resort. An obvious problem in defining discretionary versus disposable income is determining what is a luxury and what is a necessity.

The Department of Labor has calculated a budget for a household of four persons. Using these budget amounts, the Census Bureau defines a household as having discretionary income if its spendable income exceeds that of an average, similarly sized family by 30 percent or more. Based on this definition, 31 percent of U.S. households (26 million families) have some discretionary income, and 57 million households have none.[22] The importance of two-income couples is seen by the fact that 46 percent of these couples have discretionary income, as compared with 33 percent of couples in which one spouse works and the other stays at home. Royal Doulton china, Rolex watches, and O'Day yachts all might identify as a possible market the two-person household of professionals, 35 to 54 years old, with incomes over $50,000.[23]

TECHNOLOGICAL FORCES

Our society is in the age of technological change. **Technology,** a major environmental force, refers to inventions or innovations from applied science or engineering research. Each new wave of technological innovation can replace existing products and companies. Do you recognize the items pictured on page 71 and what they have replaced in the last two decades?

THE FUTURE OF TECHNOLOGY

Technological change is the result of research, so it is difficult to predict the timing of new developments. The Battelle Corporation, an internationally rec-

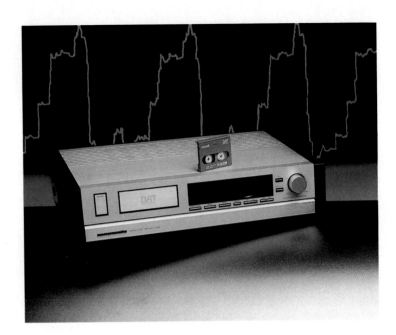

Technology continually
makes products
obsolete.

ognized research and consulting company, has made the following projections regarding technological change to the year 2000[24]:

1 Continued advances in development and refinement of microprocessors
2 Advanced telecommunications systems and techniques
3 Greater use and refinement of robots
4 Improvement in materials technology, resulting in greater strength-to-weight ratios

These trends in technology are seen in today's marketplace. The digital audio-tape player may soon replace the compact-disc player, which has only recently entered the market. Advanced communications systems have spawned a growing industry in cellular radio telephones, and companies compete aggressively to get their phone in every car.

TECHNOLOGY'S IMPACT ON MARKETING

Advanced technology, particularly the development of computers, is having a significant impact on marketing. In the supermarket, computerized checkout scanners allow retailers to monitor which products are selling and at what price level. Hand-held computers are being used by companies like Frito-Lay to allow delivery people to monitor in-store promotions. Also, via computers, salespeople can place orders from their store as well as send a sales report directly to company headquarters. Customer service, an important ingredient in the marketing of services (as discussed in Chapter 23), is also being helped by computer technology. Both Avis and Hertz use hand-held computers to speed up the return of rental cars. Hertz personnel can provide the driver with a receipt while still in the parking lot.[25]

Maps generated by geographic information systems allow companies to make sophisticated marketing decisions.

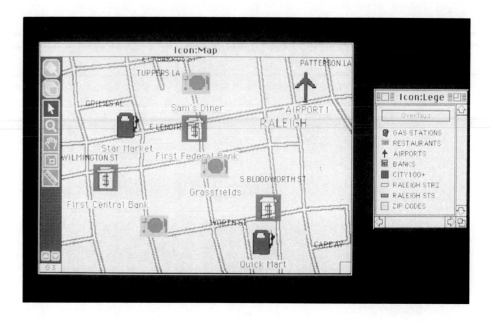

Technology can also help in the development of new products. BMW has developed a Heading Control System that tracks the center stripe and the line on the right side of the road. If a driver gets too close to either, the car's steering self-corrects. Warner Lambert Co., the manufacturer of Trident gum and Rolaids, has developed the first biodegradable plastic by using a starch derived from corn, rice, or wheat. This application can be used in a host of products and will be a potential help in solving the important environmental issue of waste disposal. (This issue is discussed in greater detail in the next section.)[26]

Ultimately, the benefit of technology for marketers will be in allowing them to better understand the consumer. A significant recent development has been the use of electronic maps for a host of marketing problems, from deciding where to locate a new fast-food restaurant to determining the most effective way to route a company's salesforce. Labeled *geographic information systems* (GIS), this technology records different layers of data on the same map. For example, a company can now develop a map of a city with additional information, such as demographics or sales, included in the layout. The fast-food chain Arby's Inc. developed a GIS map to select store locations. Coca-Cola uses GIS to determine the best routing for its delivery trucks. Hubbard Milling's feed division forecast sales in a 12-state area based on a GIS map of animal population and feed consumption of different species. And the Census Bureau is now marketing its TIGER (Topologically Integrated Geographic Encoding and Reference) file, a landmark project in demography. This software will provide a minutely detailed, computerized map of the entire United States, which can be combined with a company's own database on customer sales, traffic routes, and the like.[27] The challenge for marketers in this decade will be to keep pace with the possibilities of computer technology as is discussed in Chapter 9.

Examples of "green" products.

ECOLOGICAL IMPACT OF TECHNOLOGY

Technology has affected society in the development of products and in the ecological balance of the world's resources. **Ecology** refers to the relationship of physical resources in the environment. There is growing recognition that decisions today on use of the earth's resources have long-term consequences to society.

A growing problem in the United States is the disposal of waste. According to the Environmental Protection Agency, half of the nation's waste-disposal sites will be closed by 1995. With landfill space growing increasingly short, there will be increasing consumer pressures on companies to develop and market environmentally sensitive products. This growing environmental concern has even led to specialized magazines such as *Garbage*, which focuses on environmental issues and products.

Other companies are responding as well. Coca-Cola and Pepsi-Cola plan to introduce bottles made from recycled plastic. Procter & Gamble introduced a Spic and Span bottle made of recycled plastics. Webster Industries makes Good Sense trash bags of recycled plastics. Natural Brew coffee filters by Rockline Industries are made without bleach, which can contain dioxins.[28] In many cases the issue of environmental consciousness is being raised to companies by retailers who are in direct contact with customers. Wal-Mart has announced that it will push manufacturers to develop environmentally safe products. The retailer has also promised to highlight those "green" products in ads. The environmental movement is strong also in Canada. Loblaw Cos., a $10 billion Canadian food distributor, has launched a green line of environmentally friendly products. The 100-item green line includes foam plates (no chlorofluorocarbons), motor

Marketing Action Memo

THE BIG ENVIRONMENTAL THREAT: IT'S NOT THE OZONE, IT'S THE BABY!

*C*oncern over the environment is growing. With space in landfills rapidly diminishing, conservation of this space is becoming almost a universal community goal. In every landfill in America there is one item that is disposed of 18 million times annually, accounting for 2 percent of the landfill use. It's not bottles or cans, nor wrappers or containers—it's diapers. Disposable diapers have grown from a small industry of less than $100 million in the mid-1960s to a $3.5 billion industry today. Eighty-five percent of all parents use disposable diapers today for their infants.

Sensing the importance of environmental concerns, however, companies are beginning to respond. Procter & Gamble, the leading maker of disposable diapers, is sponsoring a pilot diaper recycling program in Seattle, and is also spending $20 million on research to develop disposable diapers that will break down in industrial composting systems.

A different tactic is being attempted by American Enviro Products, Inc., of Orange County, California. This firm has developed a biodegradable diaper, called *Bunnies,* that breaks down in 1.5 years (compared to 200 years for the typical disposable diaper). A similar product has been developed by RMed International—a flushable diaper, called TenderSoft, which is 40 percent thinner than conventional disposables.

To some environmentalists, however, degradable diapers are not the answer. The concern ex-

pressed is that the rate such products degrade is still too slow. Also, more than 20 states have considered legislation to ban or tax disposables. In the meantime, who is being helped in the environmental debate? The traditional diaper service, which delivers cloth diapers weekly to homes and picks up the soiled items. The National Association of Diaper Services reports a 38 percent increase in sales, the majority of which are most likely former disposable diaper users.

Sources: "The Green Marketing Revolution," *Advertising Age* (January 29, 1991), special issue; "Turning Pampers into Plant Food," *Business Week* (October 22, 1990), pp. 38–40; Kathleen Deveny, "States Mull Rash of Diaper Regulations," *The Wall Street Journal* (June 15, 1990), pp. B1, B7; "Firm Claims It's Developed 'Flush' Diaper," *The Boston Globe* (January 7, 1990), p. 88; Rose Gutfeld, "Even Environmentalists Still Use Disposable Diapers," *The Wall Street Journal* (January 26, 1989), p. B1; and Mary Ann Galante, "Changing Diapers," *Los Angeles Times* (September 13, 1989), pp. 7, 8.

oil (recycled), and bathroom tissue (recycled paper).[29] The accompanying Marketing Action Memo details how marketers of disposable diapers are becoming more environmentally responsible.

Concern for the environment is reaching the point where companies may have no choice but to respond. While there is much debate from some environmental and industry groups about the need for effectiveness of these measures, it is apparent that the ecological considerations will be important for marketers in the 1990s.[30] This topic is discussed further in Chapter 4.

Rice is a commodity representative of pure competition.

COMPETITIVE FORCES

The fourth component of the environmental scan, **competition,** refers to the alternative firms that could provide a product to satisfy a specific market's needs. There are various forms of competition, and each company must consider its present and potential competitors in designing its marketing strategy.

ALTERNATIVE FORMS OF COMPETITION

There are four basic forms of competition that form a continuum from pure competition to monopolistic competition to oligopoly to monopoly. Chapter 12 contains further discussions on pricing practices under these four forms of competition.

At one end of the continuum is *pure competition,* in which every company has a similar product. Companies that deal in commodities common to agribusiness (for example, wheat, rice, and grain) often are in a pure competition position in which distribution (in the sense of shipping products) is important but other elements of marketing have little impact.

In the second point on the continuum, *monopolistic competition,* the many sellers compete with their products on a substitutable basis. For example, if the price of coffee rises too much, consumers may switch to tea. Coupons or sales are frequently used marketing tactics.

Oligopoly, a common industry structure, occurs when a few companies control the majority of industry sales. For example, in the airline industry over the past few years, 5 carriers (American, Delta, United, Northwest, and USAir) have gained control of 90 percent of all sales.[31] Because there are few sellers, price competition among firms is not desirable because it leads to reduced revenue for all producers.

The final point on the continuum, *monopoly,* occurs when only one firm sells the product. It has been common for producers of goods considered essential to a community: water, electricity, and telephone service. Typically, marketing plays a small role in a monopolistic setting because it is regulated by the state or federal government. Government control usually seeks to ensure price protection for the buyer. The major change in recent years has been the AT&T shift from a monopoly to a monopolistic competitor, with US Sprint and MCI vying for buyers of long-distance phone service. Thus marketing has assumed a more important role at AT&T.

COMPONENTS OF COMPETITION

In developing a marketing program, companies must consider the components that drive competition: entry, bargaining power of buyers and suppliers, existing rivalries, and substitution possibilities.[32] Scanning the environment requires a look at all of them. These relate to a firm's marketing mix decisions and may be used to develop a new entrant, create a barrier to entry, or intensify a fight for market share.

Entry   In considering the competition, a firm must assess the likelihood of new entrants. Additional producers increase industry capacity and tend to lower prices. A company scanning its environment must consider the possible **barriers to entry** for other firms, which are business practices or conditions that make it difficult for new firms to enter the market. Barriers to entry can be in the form of capital requirements, advertising expenditures, product identity, distribution access, or switching costs. The higher the expense of the barrier, the more likely it will deter new entrants. For example, IBM has created a switching cost barrier for companies that may consider Apple Computer equipment because IBM has a different programming language for its machines.

Power of Buyers and Suppliers   A competitive analysis must consider the power of buyers and suppliers. Powerful buyers exist when they are few in number, there are low switching costs, or the product represents a significant share of the buyer's total costs. This last factor leads the buyer to exert significant pressure for price competition. A supplier gains power when the product is critical to the buyer and when it has built up the switching costs.

Existing Competitors and Substitutes   Competitive pressures among existing firms depend on the rate of industry growth. In slow-growth settings, competition is more heated for any possible gains in market share. High fixed costs also create competitive pressures for firms to fill production capacity. For example, hospitals are increasing their advertising in a battle to fill beds, which represent a high fixed cost.

INCREASING FOREIGN COMPETITION

Foreign competition has become a basic ingredient in the environmental scan for most U.S. industries today. The increasing impact of foreign competitors is clearly seen in the U.S. balance of trade—the difference between the monetary value of a nation's exports and imports. In 1971 the United States experienced its first trade deficit since 1888. And in 1987, the U.S. trade deficit exceeded $160 billion annually. The United States is losing some of its market share to the rest of the world in industries such as automobiles[33] and shoes.[34] U.S. firms are turning increasing energies toward competing globally, as seen in Chapter 22 on international marketing.

THE CHANGING FACE OF FOREIGN MARKETS

Whenever U.S. manufacturers considered where significant market opportunities existed, China and other Asian countries were always in the running. However, political changes in Eastern Europe, the reunification of West and East Germany, and the advent of the European Community—1992 (EC-92) have eliminated many trade barriers and created new opportunities. A significant economic and regulatory shift in Europe during 1992 attempts to make the 12 countries indicated in the map function, in a business sense, as one large country (see Figure 3–7). Historical trade barriers, product legislation, and transportation tariffs and requirements will be uniform across these countries. As the accompanying Marketing Action Memo shows, some of these changes are dramatic and others involve more minor details like the composition of jellies and jam.

For many companies, the prospects of these changes suggest a large, potentially profitable mass market, even larger than the United States. As

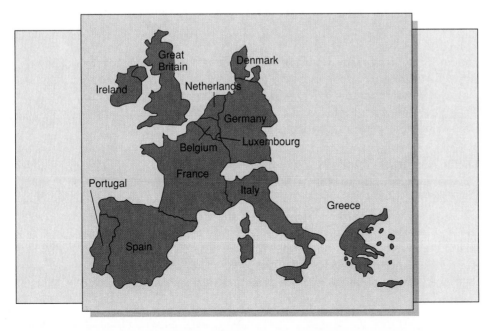

FIGURE 3–7
The 12 member countries of the European Community

Marketing Action Memo

THE UNITED STATES OF EUROPE? REALITY OR MYTH?

*T*he Europe of 1992 presents a dramatic change for U.S. companies to recognize and with which to contend. In some ways, it is likely that marketing in Western Europe will be easier, but it is important to recognize that real differences exist.

To a large extent, marketing in Europe will have to contend with problems similar to those experienced in the past. Effective marketing requires understanding the consumer, and it is at this level where a Pan-Europe approach to marketing must be modified. For example, consider jam. It's probably not a product you've thought a lot about, unless you work for Smucker's or Welch's. Europe 1992 leaves these companies with a sticky problem in marketing jam. The Dutch, for example, even with the passing of new regulations, will continue to spread jam on bread for breakfast. Dutch people like their jam smooth. The French are less fond of smooth jam—they like it lumpy and fruity, and tend to spoon it straight from the jar.

Forget jam, you say. All right, then consider yourself as Maytag, which manufactures washing machines. Ah, Europe 1992—visions of one type of washing machine dance in your head. But it's not so easy. Homemakers in Great Britain prefer washing machines that load from the front, while the French like loading laundry from the top. Germans prefer high spin speeds, Italians want slow spin speeds.

Naming products is no easier, because of language differences. The multiple languages of Europe have always existed and will continue to survive. Consider the problem for Craton Lodge & Knight. This company developed a fruity bitters drink with a made-up name "Pavane." They thought this sounded French and sophisticated. It will be hard to sell this in Europe 1992, though, because the name in German is close to *pavian*, meaning *baboon*.

Changes in Europe will pose significant challenges for marketers. The real challenge will be in understanding which products can transcend cultural differences and which are doomed to be marketing flops.

Sources: John K. Ryans, Jr., and Pradeep A. Rau, *Marketing Strategies for the New Europe: A North American Perspective* (Chicago: American Marketing Association, 1990); Ford S. Worthy, "A New Mass Market Emerges," *Fortune* (Fall 1990), pp. 51–55; Barbara Toman, "Now Comes the Hard Part: Marketing," *The Wall Street Journal Reports* (September 22, 1989), pp. R10, R12; and E. S. Browning, "Sticky Solutions," *The Wall Street Journal Reports* (September 22, 1989), pp. R8, R9.

---

explained in Chapter 22, significant changes in all components of the marketing mix will be required to compete successfully in this new European market. Removal of some trade barriers will open this market to competition, possibly change the ground rules for being profitable, and may make market success for U.S. manufacturers more difficult.[35]

The Pacific Rim   While changes in Europe are dramatic, the Pacific Rim— Asian countries and Australia—is increasingly important to U.S. companies; U.S. exports to this area rose 95 percent between 1985 and 1990. Some 1.7 billion people live on the Asian side of the Pacific Rim, and they represent growing affluence. McKinsey and Co., a consulting firm, estimates that by the year 2000, over 110 million people (not including people in Japan) will have household incomes over $10,000. Within 10 years, about one third of the population will be in their 30s and 40s, a period of peak earning power.[36]

THE NEW LOOK IN AMERICAN CORPORATIONS

Global competition has had two other important effects on corporate America: (1) the restructuring of giant corporations and (2) the birth and growth of many small businesses.

Restructuring Giant Corporations   Although the process known by various names—*downsizing, streamlining,* or **restructuring**—the result is the same: striving for more efficient corporations that can compete globally by selling off unsatisfactory product lines and divisions, closing down unprofitable plants, and often laying off hundreds or thousands of employees.[37] The result is painful for those laid off, and employees still working for the company often find that their jobs are far different, sometimes with one person doing what two did before restructuring. One effect has been a huge reduction in the number of middle managers. Where a decade ago managers had only 2 or 3 people reporting to them, they now often have 8 or 10. The result: far fewer levels from the bottom to the top of corporations, far fewer managers, far different employment opportunities for those entering the work force, and far greater problems for restructured companies in gaining loyalty from their employees.[38]

Restructuring often happens fast. It often involves a *corporate takeover,* or the purchase of a firm by outsiders. The decade of the 1980s was a period of major restructuring among U.S. firms. Among some of the more notable changes, Philip Morris acquired Kraft, Unilever purchased Chesebrough-Pond's, and General Electric spent $6.1 billion to buy RCA. Increasingly, restructuring is occurring on a global level. In 1990, U.S. acquisitions of foreign companies were $10.6 billion, up from $2.4 billion in 1986.[39]

Startup and Growth of Small Businesses   One effect of restructuring on giant corporations is their increased reliance on **outsourcing**—contracting work that formerly was done in-house by employees in marketing research, advertising, public relations, data processing, and training departments to small, outside firms.[40] This has been one factor triggering the major growth in new business startups and in employment in small businesses. Many economists believe that entrepreneurs in these small businesses are the key to U.S. employment growth in the 1990s. Past statistics support this idea: from 1981 to 1985, firms having less than 20 employees added 1.8 million net new jobs to the U.S. economy, whereas firms with 500 or more employees lost a net of about 200,000 jobs.[41]

CONCEPT CHECK

1 What is the difference between a consumer's disposable and discretionary income?

2 In pure competition there are _____ number of sellers.

3 What does restructuring a firm mean?

How Soho won its packaging battle: Zeltzer Seltzer *before* . . . and *after* the legal decision that their original packaging too closely resembled Soho's and was therefore an unfair trade practice.

REGULATORY FORCES

For any organization, the marketing and broader business decisions are constrained, directed, and influenced by regulatory forces. **Regulation** consists of restrictions the state and federal laws place on business with regard to the conduct of its activities. Regulation exists to protect companies as well as consumers. Much of the regulation from the federal and state levels has been passed to ensure competition and fair business practices. For consumers, the focus of legislation is to protect them from unfair trade practices and to ensure their safety.

PROTECTING COMPETITION

Major federal legislation has been passed to encourage free competition, which is deemed desirable because it permits the consumer to determine which competitor will succeed and which will fail. The first such law was the *Sherman Antitrust Act* (1890). Lobbying by farmers in the Midwest against fixed railroad shipping prices led to the passage of this act, which forbids (1) contracts, combinations, or conspiracies in restraint of trade and (2) actual monopolies or attempts to monopolize any part of trade or commerce. Because of vague wording and government inactivity, however, there was only one successful case against a company in the nine years after the act became law, and the Sherman Act was supplemented with the *Clayton Act* (1914). This act forbids certain actions that are likely to lessen competition, although no actual harm has yet occurred.

In the 1930s the federal government had to act again to ensure fair competition. During that time, large chain stores appeared, such as the Great Atlantic & Pacific Tea Company (A&P). Small businesses were threatened, and they lobbied for the *Robinson-Patman Act* (1936). This act makes it unlawful to discriminate in prices charged to different purchasers of the same product, where the effect may substantially lessen competition or help to create a monopoly. Figure 3–8 summarizes some other laws that have been passed to protect competition, as well as for other purposes.

FIGURE 3–8
**Major federal laws
related to marketing**

LAWS TO ENCOURAGE COMPETITION

Celler-Kefauver Antimerger Act (1950) strengthens the Clayton Act to prevent corporate acquisitions that reduced competition.

Hart-Scott-Rodino Act (1976) requires large companies to notify the government of their intent to merge.

PRODUCT-RELATED LAWS

Magnuson-Moss Warranty/FTC Improvement Act (1975) authorizes rules for consumer warranties and class action suits.

1990 Farm Bill sets standards for organic foods and products that use the term *organic*.

PRICING-RELATED LAWS

Automobile Information Disclosure Act (1958) requires manufacturers to post suggested retail prices on the cars.

Fair Credit Reporting Act (1970) requires that a consumer's credit report contain only accurate, relevant, and recent information.

PROMOTION-RELATED LAWS

Truth in Lending Act (1968) makes lenders state the true cost of a loan.

Public Health Cigarette Smoking Act (1969) requires cigarette ads and packages to warn of danger of cigarette smoking.

PLACE-RELATED (DISTRIBUTION) LAWS

Flammable Fabrics Act (1953) prohibits shipment in the United States of any clothing or material that could easily ignite.

PRODUCT-RELATED LEGISLATION

Various federal laws in existence specifically address the product component of the marketing mix. Some are aimed at protecting the company, some at protecting the consumer, and at least one at protecting both.

Company Protection   A company can protect its competitive position in new and novel products under the patent law, which gives inventors the right to exclude others from making, using, or selling products that infringe the patented invention. Polaroid, on the strength of its patents, has successfully driven Kodak out of the color instant photography market. However, U.S. companies estimate the unauthorized use of their patents in foreign countries cost them billions of dollars each year in lost sales revenues.[42]

The federal copyright law is another way for a company to protect its competitive position in a product. The copyright law gives the author of a literary, dramatic, musical, or artistic work the exclusive right to print, perform, or otherwise copy that work. Copyright is secured automatically when the work is created. However, the published work should bear an appropriate copyright notice, including the copyright symbol, the first year of publication, and the name of the copyright owner, and must be registered under the federal copyright law.

Consumer Protection   There are many consumer-oriented federal laws regarding products. One of the oldest is the *Meat Inspection Act* (1906), which provides for meat products to be wholesome, unadulterated, and properly labeled. The *Food, Drug and Cosmetics Act* (1938) is one of the most important of the federal regulatory laws. This act is aimed principally at preventing the adulteration or misbranding of the three categories of products. The various federal consumer protection laws include over 30 amendments and separate laws relating to food, drugs, and cosmetics, such as the *Poison Prevention Packaging Act* (1970) and the *Infant Formula Act* (1980). Various other consumer protection laws have a broader scope, such as the *Fair Packaging and Labeling Act* (1966), the *Child Protection Act* (1966), and the *Consumer Product Safety Act* (1972), which established the Consumer Product Safety Commission to monitor product safety and establish uniform product safety standards. Many of these recent laws came about because of **consumerism,** a grassroots movement started in the 1960s to increase the influence, power, and rights of consumers in dealing with institutions. This movement continues in the 1990s, and is reflected in consumer demands for ecologically safe products and ethical and socially responsible business practices.

Both Company and Consumer Protection   Trademarks are intended to protect both the firm selling a trademarked product and the consumer buying it. A Senate report states that:

> The purposes underlying any trademark statute is twofold. One is to protect the public so that it may be confident that, in purchasing a product bearing a particular trademark which it favorably knows, it will get the product which it asks for and wants to get. Secondly, where the owner of a trademark has spent energy, time and money in presenting to the public the product, he is protected in this investment from misappropriation in pirates and cheats.

This statement was made in connection with another product-related law, the *Lanham Act* (1946), which provides for registration of a company's trademarks. The first user of a trademark in commerce has the exclusive right to use that particular name or symbol in its business. Registration under the Lanham Act provides important advantages to a trademark owner that has used the trademark in interstate or foreign commerce, but it does not confer ownership. A company can lose its trademark if it becomes generic, which means that it has primarily come to be merely a common descriptive word for the product. Coca-Cola, Whopper, and Xerox are registered trademarks, and competitors cannot use these names. Aspirin and escalator are former trademarks that are now generic terms in the United States and can be used by anyone. In 1988, the *Trademark Law Revision Act* resulted in a major change to the Lanham Act—now, a company can secure rights to a name before actual use by declaring an intent to use the name.[43]

REGULATORY CONTROLS ON PRICING

The pricing component of the marketing mix is the focus of regulation from two perspectives: price fixing and price discounting. Although the Sherman Act

These products are identified by protected trademarks. Are any of these trademarks in danger of becoming generic?

did not outlaw price fixing, the courts view this behavior as a *per se illegality* (*per se* means "through or of itself"), which means the courts see price fixing itself as illegal. This per se view has been held since an early court decision in 1897 against the railroads' price fixing agreements.[44]

Certain forms of price discounting are allowed. Quantity discounts are acceptable; that is, buyers can be charged different prices for a product provided there are differences in manufacturing or delivery costs. Promotional allowances or services may be given to buyers on an equal basis proportionate to volume purchased. Also, a firm can meet a competitor's price "in good faith." Legal aspects of pricing are covered in more detail in Chapter 13.

DISTRIBUTION AND THE LAW

The government has four concerns with regard to distribution—earlier referred to as "place" actions in the marketing mix—and the maintenance of competition.[45] The first, *exclusive dealing,* is an arrangement with a buyer to handle only the products of one manufacturer and not those of competitors. This practice is only illegal under the Clayton Act when it substantially lessens competition.

Requirement contracts require a buyer to purchase all or part of its needs for a product from one seller for a period of time. These contracts are not always illegal but depend on the court's interpretation of their impact on distribution.

Exclusive territorial distributorships are a third distribution issue often under regulatory scrutiny. In this situation, a manufacturer grants a distributor the sole rights to sell a product in a specific geographical area. The courts have found few violations with these arrangements.

The fourth distribution strategy is a *tying arrangement,* whereby a seller requires the purchaser of one product to also buy another item in the line. These contracts may be illegal when the seller has such economic power in the tying product that the seller can restrain trade in the tied product. For example, IBM was not allowed to tie lessees of its automatic tabulating machines to the purchase of its tab cards.[46]

Legal aspects of distribution are reviewed in greater detail in Chapter 14.

PROMOTION CONTROLS

Promotion and advertising are aspects of marketing closely monitored by the Federal Trade Commission (FTC), which was established by the *FTC Act of 1914.* The FTC has been concerned with deceptive or misleading advertising and unfair business practices and has the power to (1) issue cease and desist orders and (2) order corrective advertising. In issuing a *cease and desist order,* the FTC orders a company to stop practices it considers unfair. With *corrective advertising,* the FTC can require a company to spend money on advertising to correct previous misleading ads. The enforcement powers of the FTC are so significant that often just an indication of concern from the commission can cause companies to revise their promotion.

CONTROL THROUGH SELF-REGULATION

The government has provided much legislation to create a competitive business climate and protect the consumer. An alternative to government control is **self-regulation,** where an industry attempts to police itself. The four major television networks have used self-regulation to set their own guidelines for TV ads for children's toys. These guidelines have generally worked well. The problem: cable TV and non-network TV have no such guidelines, and their commercials for a Barbie doll make her look almost lifelike, possibly increasing a child's desire for the doll. Critics complain that this double standard on TV commercials amounts to misleading advertising.[47] This example illustrates two problems with self-regulation: noncompliance by members and enforcement. If attempts at self-regulation are too strong, they may violate the Robinson–Patman Act. The best-known self-regulatory group is the Better Business Bureau (BBB). This agency is a voluntary alliance of companies whose goal is to help maintain fair practices. Although the BBB has no legal power, it does try to use "moral suasion" to get members to comply with its ruling.

Recently, the BBB intervened with Carnation Co. regarding their claim for Fancy Feast Gourmet Cat Food. The promotion stated that this brand was the "best-tasting gourmet canned cat foot . . . cats preferred over every other brand." A competitor protested to the BBB and Carnation revised the claim.[48]

CONCEPT CHECK

1 The _____ Act was punitive toward monopolies, whereas the _____ Act was preventive.

2 Explain the Lanham Act.

3 What is a per se illegality?

ETHICS AND SOCIAL RESPONSIBILITY IN THE 1990s

WHAT'S RECYCLED? WHAT'S RECYCLABLE?

Consumer interest in ecology has prompted marketers to promote products and packages that will not harm the environment. Indeed, 31 percent of consumers have bought a product because it was supposed to be ecologically safe. However, the rush by marketers to make environmental claims has not always found favor from governmental bodies. The Federal Trade Commission, Environmental Protection Agency, State's Attorney General, and state Legislature have all expressed concern that some claims are deceptive while others confuse consumers. Companies have countered saying their claims are accurate, although recognizing that specific definitions of terms such as *recycled, biodegradable, photodegradable,* and *recyclable* are subject to interpretation.

Should firms be prohibited from making environmental claims until clearly defined guidelines are established? If yes, should the use of environmental claims be monitored through self-regulation by industry groups like the Better Business Bureau, or by government agencies?

Source: Based on "Green Guidelines Are the Next Step," *Advertising Age* (January 29, 1991), pp. 28, 30; "Suddenly, Green Marketers Are Seeing Red Flags," *Business Week* (February 25, 1991), pp. 74–75; "Agencies Join Rush to Give 'Green' Advice," *The Wall Street Journal* (January 25, 1991), p. B6; and "Datawatch: Environmental Action," *Advertising Age* (December 10, 1990), p. 62.

SUMMARY

1 The population of the United States is aging, and the number of typical families as seen in the 1950s is diminishing. A blended family structure is becoming more common. Baby boomers are an important target market for companies because of their proportion in the population, as well as their high average disposable income. Mature households, those headed by people over age 50, are the fastest-growing segment in America.

2 Recognition of geographical differences in product preferences has given rise to companies developing regional marketing plans.

3 Culture represents abstract values and material possessions. Values are changing toward work, quality of life, and the roles of women and men.

4 Disposable income is the number of dollars left after taxes. Discretionary income is the money consumers have after purchasing their necessities. The median gross income (dollars before taxes) of the U.S. households has been stable since 1970 in real income terms.

5 Growing environmental concern is leading many companies to be more ecologically responsible in their development and marketing of products.

6 The United States is experiencing a deficit balance of trade. While foreign competition affects many industries, 1992 signals the year for 12 European countries to begin acting as a single nation with respect to trade. This restructuring will bring about a major new competitor as well as an important potential market.

7 Global competition has had two major effects on U.S. corporations: (*a*) restructuring them to improve efficiency, and (*b*) stimulating the startup and growth of small businesses.

8 The Sherman Antitrust Act of 1890 made monopolies illegal, whereas the Clayton Act tried to outlaw actions believed to lead to monopolies.

9 A company's brand name or symbol can be protected under the Lanham Act, but if the name becomes generic, the company no longer has sole right to the trademark.

10 Price fixing has been viewed as illegal by the courts. However, price discounting is allowed to meet competition or to account for differences in the cost of manufacture or distribution.

11 There are four aspects of distribution reviewed by courts: exclusive dealing arrangements, requirements contracts, exclusive territorial distributorships, and tying arrangements.

12 The Federal Trade Commission, established in 1914, monitors unfair business practices and deceptive advertising. Two methods used in enforcement are (*a*) cease and desist orders and (*b*) corrective advertising.

13 Self-regulation attempts are common to some industries and organizations such as the Better Business Bureau. However, the effectiveness of self-regulation is coming under greater scrutiny by the courts.

KEY TERMS AND CONCEPTS

environmental scanning p. 59
social forces p. 60
demographics p. 60
mature household p. 61
baby boomers p. 61
blended family p. 62
regional marketing p. 64
culture p. 65
economy p. 68
gross income p. 69
disposable income p. 69

discretionary income p. 69
technology p. 70
ecology p. 73
competition p. 75
barriers to entry p. 76
restructuring p. 79
outsourcing p. 79
regulation p. 80
consumerism p. 82
self-regulation p. 84

CHAPTER PROBLEMS AND APPLICATIONS

1 For many years Gerber's has manufactured baby food in small, single-sized containers. In conducting an environmental scan for the 1990s, identify three trends or factors that might significantly affect this company's future business, and then propose how Gerber's might respond to these changes.

2 Describe the target market for a luxury item such as the Mercedes Benz 190 (the lowest-priced Mercedes). List four magazines in which you would advertise to appeal to this target market.

3 Regional marketing is becoming a strategy used by several companies. What difficulties might Con Agra have with their marketing of catfish as described in the Marketing Action Memo with businesspeople in the United States who travel to different regions of America?

4 The growing concern with the environment was discussed in this chapter. Marketing in an ecologically sensitive manner will be more important to firms. Suggest how the following companies and products might respond to ecological concerns: (*a*) Gillette safety razor division, (*b*) Kentucky Fried Chicken restaurants, and (*c*) Hallmark greeting cards.

5 In recent years in the brewing industry, a couple of large firms that have historically had most of the beer sales (Anheuser–Busch and Miller) have faced competition from many small regional brands. In terms of the continuum of competition, how would you explain this change?

6 When the airline industry became deregulated, how do you think the role of marketing changed? What elements of the marketing mix are more or less important since the 1978 deregulation?

7 The Johnson Company manufactures buttons and pins with slogans and designs. These pins are inexpensive to produce and are sold in retail outlets such as discount stores, hobby shops, and bookstores. Little equipment is needed for a new competitor to enter the market. What strategies should Johnson consider to create effective barriers to entry?

8 For many years Lennox Industries has defined its business as the "manufacturing of heating and air conditioning products." Based on environmental scanning and analysis, how would you redefine Lennox's position? What would you add to the product line?

9 Why would Xerox be concerned about its name becoming generic?

CHAPTER 4

Ethics and Social Responsibility in Marketing

*A*fter reading this chapter you should be able to:

- Appreciate the nature and significance of ethics in marketing.

- Identify factors that influence ethical and unethical marketing decisions.

- Understand the differences between legal and ethical behavior in marketing.

- Distinguish among the different concepts of social responsibility.

- Recognize the importance of ethical and socially responsible consumer behavior.

Know When to Say When

Why would a company spend millions of dollars each year trying to convince people not to abuse its products? Ask Stephen J. Burrows, who launched a national consumer awareness campaign for Anheuser-Busch, the world's largest brewer.

Anheuser-Busch began promoting "Know When to Say When," a campaign for responsible drinking, first with posters in 1983 and two years later with national television commercials. In 1989, the brewery made history in the beer industry by creating a Department of Consumer Awareness and Education, headed by Burrows, with the purpose of managing the company's broad-based responsibility efforts. Other brewers such as A-dolph Coors and Miller Brewing followed Busch and have launched similar efforts designed to encourage safe driving and responsible drinking habits. Such efforts have contributed to a 12 percent decline in fatal drunk-driving accidents since 1982 and a 40 percent drop in teenage drunk-driving deaths during the same period. "These trends convince us that the awareness we've created with 'Know When to Say When' is effective," Mr. Burrows said. "We're going to hit that message louder and with greater frequency."

It appears that Anheuser-Busch means what it says. The company is spending the same amount of money on its "Know When to Say When" campaign as it does on such prominent brands as Michelob, Busch, and Natural Light, or about $30 million. "We are a big part of society's desire to reduce [alcohol] abuse. It's an arena where we can make and have already made a positive contribution," noted Mr. Burrows.

Anheuser-Busch recently unveiled its "Family Talk about Drinking" program aimed at parents. With ads directed at fathers in *Sports Illustrated,* mothers in *Good Housekeeping,* and both in *Newsweek* and *Parent,* parents are invited to call a toll-free number to obtain free guide books to address the topic of underage drinking with their children. They include information on how to be a role model, facts about drinking and driving, and how to encourage positive friendships. Anheuser-Busch doesn't expect to strengthen its already dominant position in the beer industry with the "Family Talk" program because it's not designed to sell beer. Will such efforts for responsibility cause Anheuser-Busch beer sales to decline? That's unlikely, says Burrows, because most people do not abuse alcohol. But if sales did fall off, "that's business that we would gladly lose," he said.

Anheuser-Busch acts on what it views as an ethical obligation to its customers with the "Know When to Say When" campaign. At the same time, the company recognizes its social responsibility to the general public.[1]

This chapter examines the role of ethics and social responsibility in the practice of marketing.

NATURE AND SIGNIFICANCE OF MARKETING ETHICS

Ethics are the moral principles and values that govern the actions and decisions of an individual or group.[2] They serve as guidelines on how to act rightly and justly when faced with moral dilemmas.

ETHICAL/LEGAL FRAMEWORK IN MARKETING

A good starting point for understanding the nature and significance of ethics is the distinction between legality and ethicality of marketing decisions. Figure 4–1 helps to visualize the relationship between laws and ethics.[3] While ethics deal with personal moral principles and values, **laws** are society's values and standards that are enforceable in the courts.[4] This distinction can sometimes lead to the rationalization that if a behavior is within reasonable ethical and legal limits, then it is not really illegal or unethical. But what are the limits?

There are numerous situations where judgment plays a large role in defining ethical and legal boundaries. Consider the following situations. After reading each, assign it to the cell in Figure 4–1 that you think best fits the situation along the ethical–legal continuum.

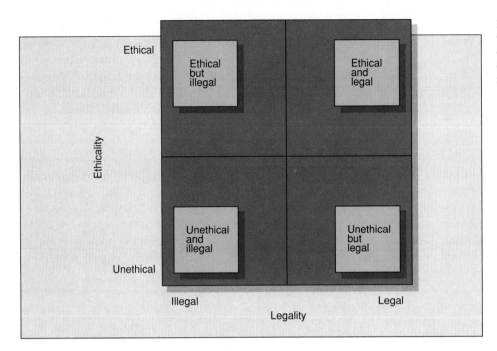

FIGURE 4–1
**Classifying marketing
decisions according to
ethical and legal
relationships**

1 Over 70 percent of the physicians in the Maricopa County Medical Society
   agreed to establish a maximum fee schedule for health services, to curb
   rising medical costs. All physicians were required to adhere to this schedule
   as a condition for membership in the society. The U.S. Supreme Court
   ruled that this agreement to set prices violated the Sherman Act and represented price fixing, which is illegal.[5]

2 A company in California sells a computer program to auto dealers showing
   that car buyers should finance their purchase rather than paying cash. The
   program omits the effect of income taxes and overstates the interest earned
   on savings over the loan period. The finance option always provides a net
   benefit over the cash option. Company employees agree that the program
   does mislead buyers, but say the company will "provide what [car dealers]
   want as long as it is not against the law."[6]

3 R. J. Reynolds Tobacco Company specifically targeted blacks for a new
   brand of cigarette. Public health statistics show that blacks have a high
   incidence of lung cancer and smoking-related illnesses. According to the
   company, it is within the law since cigarettes are legal products.[7]

Did these situations fit neatly into Figure 4–1 as clearly ethical and legal or
unethical and illegal? Probably not. As you read further in this chapter, you will
be asked again to consider these and other ethical dilemmas.

CURRENT STATUS OF ETHICAL BEHAVIOR

There has been a public outcry about the ethical practices of businesspeople.
Public opinion surveys show that 58 percent of U.S. adults rate the ethical
standards of business executives as only "fair" or "poor," 90 percent think

white-collar crime is "very common" or "somewhat common," and 76 percent say the lack of ethics in businesspeople contributes to tumbling societal moral standards.[8] A recent survey of 1,000 senior corporate executives confirms this public perception. Two thirds of these executives think people are "occasionally" unethical in their business dealings, 15 percent believe they are "often" unethical, and 16 percent consider people "seldom" without ethics.[9]

There are at least four possible reasons why the state of perceived ethical business conduct is at its present level.[10] First, there is increased pressure on businesspeople to make decisions in a society characterized by diverse value systems. Consider the ethics of using animals for testing the safety of products. While 60 percent of Americans oppose using animals to test the safety of cosmetics, 43 percent oppose this practice for common medical products such as headache remedies and 20 percent oppose testing to combat life-threatening illnesses like cancer. A few years ago, this issue was rarely, if ever, raised.[11] Second, there is a growing tendency for business decisions to be judged publicly by groups with different values and interests. The decision by R. J. Reynolds Tobacco Company to promote a new brand of cigarette to a segment of the population already at risk for cancer and smoking-related diseases is a case in point. The accompanying Marketing Action Memo details the controversy surrounding this decision and its outcome. Third, the public's expectations of ethical business behavior has increased.[12] Finally, and most disturbing, ethical business conduct may have declined.

CONCEPT CHECK

1   **What are ethics?**

2   **What are four possible reasons for the present state of ethical conduct in the United States?**

UNDERSTANDING ETHICAL BEHAVIOR

Researchers have identified numerous factors that influence ethical behavior.[13] Figure 4–2 presents a framework that shows these factors and their relationships.[14]

SOCIETAL CULTURE AND NORMS

As described in Chapter 3, *culture* refers to the set of values, ideas, and attitudes of a homogeneous group of people that are transmitted from one generation to the next. Culture also affects ethical relationships between individuals, groups, and the institutions and organizations they create. In this way, culture serves as a socializing force that dictates what is morally right and just. This means that moral standards are relative to particular societies. These standards often reflect the laws and regulations that affect social and economic behavior, including marketing practices.

Marketing Action Memo

UPTOWN LEAVES TOWN

Can and should a tobacco marketer target a segment of smokers for a new brand of cigarettes? Of course it can, but should it?

In early 1990, the R. J. Reynolds Tobacco Company canceled a planned market test in Philadelphia of Uptown, a cigarette aimed at black smokers, after scathing attacks by black community leaders, antismoking groups, and the U.S. Secretary of Health & Human Services, Louis Sullivan. According to Mr. Sullivan, "Uptown's message is more disease, more suffering, and more death for a group already bearing more than its share of smoking-related illness and mortality." Statistics from the U.S. Public Health Service show that black men have a 58 percent higher incidence of lung cancer than white men, and blacks lose twice as many years of life as do whites because of smoking-related diseases.

The cost to R. J. Reynolds (RJR) of canceling the market test was $5 to $7 million, based on industry sources. The company's intent ". . . was to market a cigarette among smokers who currently buy competitive products. . . ." A company spokesperson expressed the view that smokers should be given the freedom of choice and that Uptown's withdrawal represented a loss of choice for black smokers and erosion of the free-enterprise system.

The controversy surrounding Uptown represents both an ethical issue and a matter of social responsibility. An editorial in *Advertising Age,* an advertising and business publication, posed the issue succinctly: "Should RJR or other tobacco marketers be effectively barred by the government from designing and promoting cigarette brands meant to appeal to blacks? Or to women? No, not as long as cigarettes are legal." According to Mr. Sullivan, "This is a victory for the citizens of Philadelphia, for minority citizens, and indeed for all Americans—a victory for health." The debate on this issue is likely to be loud and lengthy for some time to come.

Sources: Based on "The Downing of Uptown," *Advertising Age* (January 29, 1990), p. 32; "After Uptown, Are Some Niches Out?" *The Wall Street Journal* (January 22, 1990), pp. B1, B4; "If It's Legal, Cigarette Makers Are Trying It," *Business Week* (February 19, 1990), pp. 52, 54; "Reynolds Kills Uptown," *Advertising Age* (January 22, 1990), p. 1; and "RJR Cancels Test of 'Black' Cigarette," *Marketing News* (February 19, 1990), p. 10.

FIGURE 4–2
A framework for understanding ethical behavior

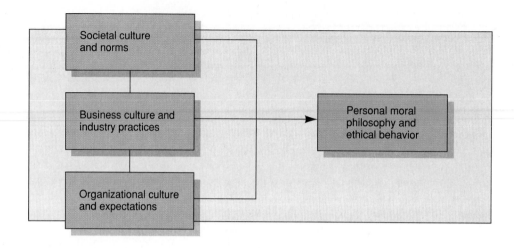

Many of the laws affecting American marketing practices were outlined in Chapter 3. Actions that restrain trade, fix prices, deceive buyers, and result in unsafe products are considered morally wrong in the United States and other countries. However, different cultures view marketing practices differently. Consider the use of another's ideas, copyright, trademark, or patent. These are viewed as intellectual property and unauthorized use is illegal and unethical in the United States. For example, Hallmark Cards, Inc., recently was charged with copying the ideas of a smaller card company without its consent. The courts ruled that Hallmark must stop publishing the cards, buy back existing cards from 21,000 Hallmark stores, and pay damages to the owners of the company.[15]

Outside the United States, however, is another story. U.S. companies estimate that unauthorized use of their copyrights, trademarks, and patents in countries such as Taiwan, Mexico, and Korea cost them $23.8 billion annually. In Korea, for instance, copying is partly rooted in its society's culture. According to a U.S. trade official, many Koreans "have the idea that the thoughts of one man should benefit all," and the Korean government rarely prosecutes infringements.[16] Thinking again about the ethical/legal framework in Figure 4–1, where would you place the practice of using another's trademark if you were in Korea?

BUSINESS CULTURE AND INDUSTRY PRACTICES

Societal culture provides a foundation for understanding moral behavior in business activities. *Business cultures* "comprise the effective rules of the game, the boundaries between competitive and unethical behavior, [and] the codes of conduct in business dealings."[17] The 1980s witnessed numerous instances where business cultures in the brokerage (inside trading), savings and loan (conflicts of interest), and defense (bribery) industries went awry. Business culture affects ethical conduct both in the exchange relationship between sellers and buyers and in the competitive behavior among sellers.

Ethics of Exchange The exchange process is central to the marketing concept. Ethical exchanges between sellers and buyers should result in both parties being better off after a transaction.[18]

Prior to the 1960s, the legal concept of **caveat emptor**—let the buyer beware—was pervasive in the American business culture. As discussed in previous chapters, in 1962 President John F. Kennedy outlined a **Consumer Bill of Rights** that codified the ethics of exchange between buyers and sellers. These were the right (1) to safety, (2) to be informed, (3) to choose, and (4) to be heard.

Consumers expect and often demand that these rights be protected, as have American businesses. However, exceptions exist. A. H. Robins sold the Dalkon Shield, an intrauterine device, that was known to be potentially harmful to women. The company has since established a $2.5 billion fund to compensate women harmed by this device.[19]

The right to be informed means that marketers have an obligation to give consumers complete and accurate information about products and services, but this is not always the case. A study of 175 major banks showed that about 54 percent do not state the interest rate on credit application forms and promotional materials, and 47 percent do not disclose the annual fee for credit cards.[20]

Relating to the third right, today many supermarket chains demand "slotting allowances" from manufacturers, in the form of cash or free goods, to stock new products. This practice could limit the number of new products available to consumers and interfere with their right to choose. One critic of this practice remarked: "If we had had slotting allowances a few years ago, we might not have had granola, herbal tea, or yogurt."[21]

Finally, the right to be heard means that consumers should have access to public-policy makers regarding complaints about products and services. This right was illustrated in the response by Dr. Louis Sullivan, the U.S. Secretary of Health & Human Services, to antismoking interest groups, which contributed to the demise of the Uptown cigarette.

Ethics of Competition Business culture also affects ethical behavior in competition. Two kinds of unethical behavior are most common: (1) industrial espionage and (2) bribery.

Industrial espionage is the clandestine collection of trade secrets or proprietary information about a company's competitors. This practice is most prevalent in high-technology industries such as electronics, specialty chemicals, aerospace, and pharmaceuticals, where technical know-how and secrets separate industry leaders from followers.[22] For example, Hitachi pleaded guilty to stealing confidential IBM documents describing one of its computer systems.[23] But espionage can occur anywhere—even in the ready-to-eat cookie industry! Procter & Gamble charged that competitors photographed its plants and production lines, stole a sample of its cookie dough, and infiltrated a confidential sales presentation to learn about its technology, recipe, and marketing plan. The competitors paid Procter & Gamble $120 million in damages after a lengthy dispute.[24]

The second form of unethical competitive behavior is giving and receiving bribes and kickbacks. Bribes and kickbacks are often disguised as gifts, consultant fees, and favors. This practice is more common in business-to-business and government marketing than in consumer marketing. A 1989 survey of purchasing managers revealed that only 3 percent said they would not accept favors from sellers, compared with 17 percent who would not accept gifts in 1975,[25] and a series of trials in 1990 uncovered widespread bribery in the U.S. Defense Department's awarding of $160 billion in military contracts.[26]

The prevalence of bribery in international marketing prompted legislation to curb this practice. The **Foreign Corrupt Practices Act** makes it a crime for U.S. corporations to bribe an official of a foreign government or political party to obtain or retain business in a foreign country. Since 1980, at least 20 individuals and corporations have been convicted or have pleaded guilty to bribery or related offenses.[27] A recent case involved the Young & Rubicam advertising agency and a conspiracy to make bribes to win the Jamaican Tourist Board advertising account. Read the accompanying Marketing Action Memo and consider the ethical/legal circumstances involved. Where would this situation fit in Figure 4–1 as an (il)legal/(un)ethical behavior in 1981? In 1990?

In general, ethical standards are more likely to be compromised in industries experiencing intense competition and in countries in earlier stages of economic development. A survey of marketing executives in the United States, West Germany, and France revealed that West Germany was perceived as having the most ethical business culture. The United Kingdom was second, followed by the United States, France, and Japan.[28]

CORPORATE CULTURE AND EXPECTATIONS

A third influence on ethical practices is corporate culture. *Corporate culture* reflects the shared values, beliefs, and purpose of employees that affect individual and group behavior. The culture of a company demonstrates itself in the dress ("We don't wear ties"), sayings ("The IBM Way"), and manner of work (team efforts) of employees. Culture is also apparent in the expectations for ethical behavior present in formal codes of ethics and the ethical actions of top management and coworkers.

Codes of Ethics   A **code of ethics** is a formal statement of ethical principles and rules of conduct. It is estimated that 93 percent of major U.S. corporations have some sort of ethics code.[29] These codes of ethics typically cover contributions or payments to government officials and political parties, relations with customers and suppliers, conflicts of interest, and accurate recordkeeping.[30] For example, General Mills provides guidelines for dealing with suppliers, competitors, and customers, and recruits new employees who share these views. However, an ethics code is rarely enough to ensure ethical behavior. Boeing Company, one of the world's largest manufacturers in the aerospace industry, has had an ethics code, ethics advisors, and a corporate office for employees to report infractions since 1964, yet Boeing was recently charged with using inside information to win a government contract and fined $5.2 million.[31]

Marketing Action Memo

A CLOUDY DAY IN JAMAICA

*F*or many, Jamaica means sun and sand, fun and friendly people. For Young & Rubicam, one of the world's largest advertising agencies, Jamaica also meant the Jamaican Tourist Board, a $6 to $8 million account, and the award-winning "Come Back to Jamaica" advertising campaign. But the U.S. Justice Department saw something very different. It saw evidence of bribery, racketeering, perjury, and a conspiracy to violate the Foreign Corrupt Practices Act.

In February 1990, Young & Rubicam pleaded guilty to conspiring to violate the Foreign Corrupt Practices Act and making $132,000 in payments "in furtherance of the conspiracy." The complex charges filed by the Justice Department alleged that the advertising agency paid $900,000 in kickbacks to a Jamaican businessman, who in turn bribed a Jamaican official to award the Jamaican Tourist Board account to Young & Rubicam. The agency faced $7.5 million in fines if the case went to trial and the agency was found guilty. Instead, the agency was fined $500,000 after a plea-bargain agreement. And yes, the agency was fired by the Jamaican Tourist Board.

This case also had a unique legal twist. It so happens that the portion of the Federal Corrupt Practices Act that the agency was charged with violating was voided by Congress in 1988 — seven years after the alleged conspiracy took place. Following the case's resolution, Young & Rubicam asserted in a press release that "if the case were brought today there would have been no charge." What do you think about the legal versus ethical circumstances of this situation?

Sources: Based on "Young & Rubicam Settles Jamaica Case," *The Wall Street Journal* (February 12, 1990), p. B5; "Y&R Plea-Bargains Jamaica Case," *Advertising Age* (February 12, 1990), pp. 1, 56; and "U.S. Sets Trial in Y&R Case," *New York Times* (February 12, 1990), p. C6.

The lack of specificity is one of the major reasons for the violation of ethics codes. Employees must often judge whether a specific behavior is really unethical. The American Marketing Association has addressed this issued by providing a detailed code of ethics, which all members agree to follow. This code is shown in Figure 4–3.

Ethical Behavior of Management and Co-workers   A second reason for violating ethics codes rests in the perceived behavior of top management and co-workers. Observing peers and top management and gauging responses to unethical behavior plays an important role in individual actions. A recent study of business executives reported that 40 percent had been implicitly or explicitly rewarded for engaging in ethically troubling behavior. Moreover, 31 percent of those who refused to engage in unethical behavior were penalized, either through outright punishment or a diminished status in the company.[32] Clearly, ethical dilemmas often bring personal and professional conflict.

PERSONAL MORAL PHILOSOPHY AND ETHICAL BEHAVIOR

Ultimately, ethical choices are based on the personal moral philosophy of the decision maker. Moral philosophy is learned through the process of socialization with friends and family, and by formal education. It is also influenced by the

CODE OF ETHICS

Members of the American Marketing Association (AMA) are committed to ethical professional conduct. They have joined together in subscribing to this Code of Ethics embracing the following topics:

Responsibilities of the Marketer

Marketers must accept responsibility for the consequence of their activities and make every effort to ensure that their decisions, recommendations, and actions function to identify, serve, and satisfy all relevant publics: customers, organizations and society.

Marketers' professional conduct must be guided by:

1 The basic rule of professional ethics: not knowingly to do harm.
2 The adherence to all applicable laws and regulations.
3 The accurate representation of their education, training and experience.
4 The active support, practice and promotion of this Code of Ethics.

Honesty and Fairness

Marketers shall uphold and advance the integrity, honor, and dignity of the marketing profession by:

1 Being honest in serving consumers, clients, employees, suppliers, distributors and the public.
2 Not knowingly participating in conflict of interest without prior notice to all parties involved.
3 Establishing equitable fee schedules including the payment or receipt of usual, customary and/ or legal compensation or marketing exchanges.

Rights and Duties of Parties in the Marketing Exchange Process

Participants in the marketing exchange process should be able to expect that:

1 Products and services offered are safe and fit for their intended uses.
2 Communications about offered products and services are not deceptive.
3 All parties intend to discharge their obligations, financial and otherwise, in good faith.
4 Appropriate internal methods exist for equitable adjustment and/or redress of grievances concerning purchases.

It is understood that the above would include, *but is not limited to,* the following responsibilities of the marketer:

In the area of product development and management

- Disclosure of all substantial risks associated with product or service usage.

FIGURE 4–3
American Marketing Association Code of Ethics

societal, business, and corporate culture in which a person finds himself or herself. Moral philosophies are of two types: (1) moral idealism and (2) utilitarianism.[33]

Moral Idealism   **Moral idealism** is a personal moral philosophy that considers certain individual rights or duties as universal, regardless of the outcome. This philosophy exists in the Consumer Bill of Rights and is favored by moral philosophers and consumer interest groups. For example, the right to know applies to probable defects in an automobile that relate to safety.

This philosophy also applies to ethical duties. For example, Jerome LiCari, Director of Research for the Beech-Nut Nutrition Corporation, advised the Food and Drug Administration that Beech-Nut was selling a blend of synthetic ingredients labeled as 100 percent apple juice. He did so only after his superiors ignored his internal memos. Beech-Nut was subsequently fined $2 million, the company's market share dropped 3 percent, and two executives were indicted. When asked why he acted as he did, LiCari said: "I thought apple juice should be made from apples."[34] LiCari later resigned from Beech-Nut.

- Identification of any product component substitution that might materially change the product or impact on the buyer's purchase decision.
- Identification of extra-cost added features.

In the area of promotions

- Avoidance of false and misleading advertising.
- Rejection of high pressure manipulation, or misleading sales tactics.
- Avoidance of sales promotions that use deception or manipulation.

In the area of distribution

- Not manipulating the availability of a product for purpose of exploitation.
- Not using coercion in the marketing channel.
- Not exerting undue influence over the resellers choice to handle the product.

In the area of pricing

- Not engaging in price fixing.
- Not practicing predatory pricing.
- Disclosing the full price associated with any purchase.

In the area of marketing research

- Prohibiting selling or fund raising under this guise of conducting research.

Source: Reprinted by permission of The American Marketing Association.

- Maintaining research integrity by avoiding misrepresentation and omission of pertinent research data.
- Treating outside clients and suppliers fairly.

Organizational Relationships

Marketers should be aware of how their behavior may influence or impact on the behavior of others in organizational relationships. They should not demand, encourage or apply coercion to obtain unethical behavior in their relationships with others, such as employees, suppliers or customers.

1 Apply confidentiality and anonymity in professional relationships with regard to privileged information.
2 Meet their obligations and responsibilities in contracts and mutual agreements in a timely manner.
3 Avoid taking the work of others, in whole, or in part, and represent this work as their own or directly benefit from it without compensation or consent of the originator or owner.
4 Avoid manipulation to take advantage of situations to maximize personal welfare in a way that unfairly deprives or damages the organization or others.

Any AMA members found to be in violation of any provision of this Code of Ethics may have his or her Association membership suspended or revoked.

FIGURE 4–3
concluded

Utilitarianism   An alternative perspective on moral philosophy is **utilitarianism,** which is a personal moral philosophy that focuses on "the greatest good for the greatest number," by assessing the costs and benefits of the consequences of ethical behavior. If the benefits exceed the costs, then the behavior is ethical. If not, then the behavior is unethical. This philosophy underlies the economic tenets of capitalism,[35] and, not surprisingly, is embraced by many business executives and students.[36]

Utilitarian reasoning was apparent in Nestlé Food Corporation's marketing of Good Start infant formula, sold by Nestlé's Carnation Company. The formula, promoted as hypoallergenic, was designed to prevent or reduce colic caused by an infant's allergic reaction to cow's milk—a condition suffered by 2 percent of babies. However, some severely milk-allergic infants experienced serious side effects after using Good Start, including convulsive vomiting. Physicians and parents charged that the hypoallergenic claim was misleading, and the Food and Drug Administration investigated the matter. A Nestlé vice president defended the claim and product, saying, "I don't understand why our product should work in 100 percent of cases. If we wanted to say it was foolproof, we would have called it allergy-free. We call it hypo-, or less,

Some infants had allergic reactions to Nestlé's Good Start formula, forcing the company to change their labeling on the product.

allergenic.''[37] Nestlé officials seemingly believed that most allergic infants would benefit from Good Start—''the greatest good for the greatest number.'' However, other views prevailed and the claim was dropped from the product label.

An appreciation for the nature of ethics, coupled with a basic understanding of why unethical behavior arises, alerts a person to when and how ethical issues exist in marketing decisions. Ultimately, ethical behavior rests with the individual, but the consequences affect many.

CONCEPT CHECK

1 **What rights are included in the Consumer Bill of Rights?**

2 **What ethical practice is addressed in the Foreign Corrupt Practices Act?**

3 **What is meant by moral idealism?**

UNDERSTANDING SOCIAL RESPONSIBILITY IN MARKETING

As we saw in Chapter 1, the societal marketing concept stresses marketing's social responsibility by not only satisfying the needs of consumers but also providing for society's welfare. **Social responsibility** means that organizations are part of a larger society and are accountable to that society for their actions. Like ethics, agreement on the nature and scope of social responsibility is often difficult to come by, given the diversity of values present in different societal, business, and organizational cultures.

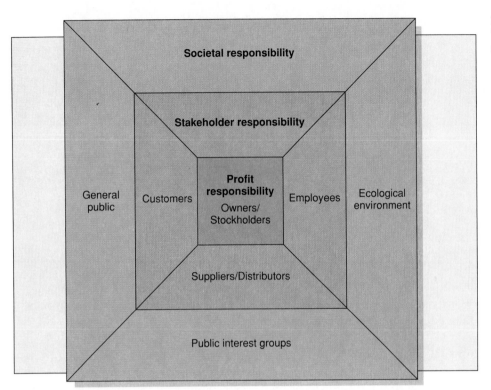

FIGURE 4–4
Three concepts of social responsibility

CONCEPTS OF SOCIAL RESPONSIBILITY

Figure 4–4 shows three concepts of social responsibility: (1) profit responsibility, (2) stakeholder responsibility, and (3) societal responsibility.

Profit Responsibility   *Profit responsibility* holds that companies have a simple duty—to maximize profits for its owners or stockholders. This view is expressed by Nobel Laureate Milton Friedman, who said, "There is one and only one social responsibility of business—to use its resources and engage in activities designed to increase its profits so long as it stays within the rules of the game, which is to say, engages in open and free competition without deception or fraud."[38] Burroughs Wellcome, the maker of AZT, a drug to treat persons afflicted with AIDS, has been charged with adopting this view in its pricing practices. Critics claim that the company's high price for AZT ($8,000 per patient per year) is motivated by a desire to make as much profit as possible, since it is the sole supplier of the drug.[39]

Stakeholder Responsibility   Frequent criticism of the profit view has led to a broader concept of social responsibility. *Stakeholder responsibility* focuses on the obligations an organization has to those who can affect achievement of its objectives. These constituencies include customers, employees, suppliers, and distributors. Source Perrier S.A., the supplier of Perrier bottled water, exercised this responsibility when it recalled 160 million bottles of water in 120 countries after traces of a toxic chemical were found in 13 bottles. The recall cost the

Perrier responsibly responded to its stakeholders when it pulled 160 million bottle of its water from the market at the first hint of quality problems.

company $35 million, and $40 million more was lost in sales. Even though the chemical level was not harmful to humans, Source Perrier's president believed he acted in the best interests of the firm's consumers, distributors, and employees by removing "the least doubt, as minimal as it might be, to weigh on the image of the quality and purity of our product."[40]

NO HARM TO DOLPHINS

Societal Responsibility   An even broader concept of social responsibility has emerged in recent years. *Societal responsibility* refers to obligations that organizations have to the (1) preservation of the ecological environment and (2) general public. Concerns about the environment and public welfare are represented by interest and advocacy groups such as Greenpeace, an international environmental organization.

Chapter 3 detailed the growing importance of ecological issues in marketing. Companies have responded to this concern through what is termed **green marketing**—marketing efforts to produce, promote, and reclaim environmentally sensitive products. Green marketing takes many forms.[41] For example, Shell Oil Company now sells an environmentally cleaner gasoline in the nine U.S. cities with the most severe air-quality problems. H. J. Heinz (Starkist brand), Van Kamp Seafood (Chicken of the Sea brand), and Bumble Bee Seafoods will no longer buy tuna from fishing fleets using techniques that kill or harm dolphins. The aluminum industry recycles 61 percent of aluminum cans for reuse and pays consumers $900 million annually for used cans. These voluntary responses to environmental issues were implemented with little or no additional cost to consumers.

Socially responsible efforts on behalf of the general public are becoming more common. A formal practice is **cause-related marketing** (CRM), which occurs when the charitable contributions of a firm are tied directly to the customer revenues produced through the promotion of one of its products.[42] This definition distinguishes CRM from a firm's standard charitable contributions, which are outright donations. For example, Procter & Gamble raises funds for the Special Olympics when consumers purchase selected company products, and Master Card International linked usage of its card with fund raising for institutions that combat cancer, heart disease, child abuse, drug abuse, and muscular dystrophy. Nestlé and Kimberly Clark jointly instituted a CRM cam-

Special marketing efforts by Nestlé and Kimberly Clark supported the renovation of the Statue of Liberty. This is an example of cause-related marketing.

paign to support renovation of the Statute of Liberty, and Coca-Cola Foods' Minute Maid was linked to the 1992 Olympics. CRM programs incorporate all three concepts of social responsibility by addressing public concerns, satisfying customer needs, and enhancing corporate sales and profits.

THE SOCIAL AUDIT

Converting socially responsible ideas into actions involves careful planning and monitoring of programs. Many companies develop, implement, and evaluate their social responsibility efforts by means of a **social audit,** which is a systematic assessment of a firm's objectives, strategies, and performance in the domain of social responsibility. Frequently, marketing and social responsibility programs are integrated, as is the case with McDonald's.[43] The company's concern for the needs of families with children who are chronically or terminally ill was converted into 129 Ronald McDonald Houses. These facilities, located near treatment centers, enable families to stay together during the child's care. In this case, McDonald's is contributing to the welfare of a portion of its target market.

A social audit consists of five steps:[44]

1 Recognition of a firm's social expectations and the rationale for engaging in social responsibility endeavors
2 Identification of social responsibility causes or programs consistent with the company's mission
3 Determination of organizational objectives and priorities for programs and activities it will undertake
4 Specification of the type and amount of resources necessary to achieve social responsibility objectives
5 Evaluation of social responsibility programs and activities undertaken and assessment of future involvement

Ecological disasters such as the Exxon *Valdez* oil spill in Alaska have moved environmental concerns to the forefront of corporate planning.

Attention to the social audit on environmental matters has increased since 1989, when the Exxon *Valdez* oil tanker spilled 11 million gallons of crude oil in Alaska's Prince William Sound. This spill killed tens of thousands of birds and mammals and fouled a thousand miles of Alaskan coastline. Soon after, the Coalition for Environmentally Responsible Economics drafted guidelines designed to focus attention on environmental concerns and corporate responsibility. These guidelines, called the **Valdez Principles,** encourage companies to (1) eliminate pollutants, minimize hazardous wastes, and conserve nonrenewable resources, (2) market environmentally safe products and services, (3) prepare for accidents and restore damaged environments, (4) provide protection for employees who report environmental hazards, and (5) appoint an environmentalist to their boards of directors, name an executive for environmental affairs, and develop an environmental audit of their global operations to be made available for public inspection.[45]

Development and use of a social audit will depend on the extent to which a company's culture embraces social responsibility as part of its overall mission. 3M is considered an innovator in this regard. The company is investing $150 million in pollution controls for its manufacturing facilities, encourages employees to develop programs that prevent pollution, and now recycles trimmings from its famous Post-it™ pads.[46] Other firms have also taken action to preserve the environment. Read the accompanying Marketing Action Memo to find out why Du Pont is abandoning a profitable $750 million-a-year business as a matter of social responsibility.

TURNING THE TABLE: CONSUMER ETHICS AND SOCIAL RESPONSIBILITY

Consumers also have an obligation to act ethically and responsibly in the exchange process and in the use and disposition of products. Unfortunately, consumer behavior is spotty on both counts.

Marketing Action Memo

PULLING THE PLUG ON A $750 MILLION-A-YEAR BUSINESS

*W*hy would a company abandon a profitable $750 million business? Edgar Woolard, chief executive officer of E. I. du Pont de Nemours & Co. (Du Pont), the world's largest producer of chemicals, probably has been asked this question many times.

Mr. Woolard has announced that Du Pont is making zero pollution a company goal. To make his point, the company will voluntarily suspend all production of chlorofluorcarbons (CFCs) by 2000, or sooner if possible. This decision was made after scientific evidence indicated that CFCs might be seriously depleting the earth's ozone layer. Says Mr. Woolard, "In my opinion it has not been proven that CFCs are harmful to the ozone, but there is a good probability, and we have to deal with that." Du Pont has already invested $170 million in developing substitutes for CFCs, and is prepared to spend $1 billion on the best replacements.

Du Pont's corporate culture is environmentally sensitive partly because this factor is now one of the criteria used to determine managers' compensation reflected in annual raises. Moreover, Mr. Woolard meets monthly with leading environmentalists to discuss how Du Pont might become even more socially responsible. The company voluntarily spends an estimated $50 million annually on environmental projects beyond what the law requires. But the goal of zero pollution will come at a price—Mr. Woolard admits that Du Pont's profits will suffer over the next several years.

Sources: Based on David Kirkpatrick, "Environmentalism: The New Crusade," *Fortune* (February 12, 1990), pp. 44–54; "The Greening of Corporate America," *Business Week* (April 23, 1990), pp. 96–103; and "Business's Green Revolution," *U.S. News & World Report* (February 19, 1990), pp. 45–46.

Unethical practices of consumers are a serious concern to marketers.[47] These practices include filing warranty claims after the claim period; misredeeming coupons; making fraudulent returns of merchandise; providing inaccurate information on credit applications; tampering with utility meters; tapping cable TV lines; recording copyrighted music, videocassettes, and computer software; and submitting phony insurance claims. The cost to marketers in lost sales revenue and prevention expenses is huge. For example, consumers who redeem coupons for unpurchased products or use coupons destined for other products cost manufacturers $500 million each year.[48] The record industry alone loses $1 billion annually due to recording and about 12 percent of VCR owners make illegal copies of videotapes, costing producers millions of dollars in lost revenue.[49] Electrical utilities lose between 1 and 3 percent of yearly revenues due to meter tampering.[50]

Consumer purchase, use, and disposition of environmentally sensitive products relates to consumer social responsibility. Research indicates that consumers are sensitive to ecological issues.[51] However, this research also shows that consumers (1) may be unwilling to sacrifice convenience and pay potentially higher prices to protect the environment and (2) lack the knowledge to make informed decisions dealing with the purchase, use, and disposition of products. For example, PepsiCo Inc. has found that sales of a three-liter soft drink bottle designed to minimize trash does not sell well. Why? The bottle does not fit conveniently into refrigerators. Procter & Gamble Company reports that sales of its concentrated Downy fabric softener, which requires less packaging, have been poor because the concentrate requires mixing with water. Consumers have not responded favorably to the use of paper salad plates and coffee cups designed to replace foam containers at Wendy's International, Inc.[52] Nevertheless, McDonald's has decided to stop using foam containers in an effort to reduce solid waste pollution.

Consumer confusion over which products are environmentally safe is also apparent, given marketers' rush to produce "green products." For example, few consumers realize that nonaerosol "pump" hairsprays are the second-largest cause of air pollution, after drying paint. In California alone, 27 tons of noxious hairspray fumes are expelled every day.[53] And "Biodegradable" claims on a variety of products, including trash bags, have not proven to be accurate, thus leading to buyer confusion.[54] Obviously, consumers will have to be more involved and willing to compromise convenience and sometimes price to become more socially responsible.

Ultimately, marketers and consumers are accountable for ethical and socially responsible behavior. The 1990s will prove to be a testing period for both.

CONCEPT CHECK

1 What is meant by social responsibility?

2 Marketing efforts to produce, promote, and reclaim environmentally sensitive products are called _____ .

3 What is a social audit?

 SUMMARY

1 Ethics are the moral principles and values that govern the actions and decisions of an individual or group. Laws are society's values and standards that are enforceable in the courts. Operating according to the law does not necessarily mean that a practice is ethical.

2 Ethical behavior of businesspeople has come under severe criticism by the public. There are four possible reasons for this criticism: (1) increased pressure on businesspeople to make decisions in a society characterized by diverse value systems, (2) a growing tendency to have business decisions judged publicly by groups with different values and interests, (3) an increase in the public's expectations for ethical behavior, and (4) a possible decline in business ethics.

3 Numerous external factors influence ethical behavior of businesspeople. These include: (1) societal culture and norms, (2) business culture and industry practices, and (3) organizational culture and expectations. Each factor influences the opportunity to engage in ethical or unethical behavior.

4 Ultimately, ethical choices are based on the personal moral philosophy of the decision maker. Two moral philosophies are most prominent: (1) moral idealism and (2) utilitarianism.

5 Social responsibility means that organizations are part of a larger society and are accountable to that society for their actions.

6 There are three concepts of social responsibility: (1) profit responsibility, (2) stakeholder responsibility, and (3) societal responsibility.

7 Growing interest in societal responsibility has resulted in systematic efforts to assess a firm's objectives, strategies, and performance in the domain of social responsibility. This practice is called a social audit.

8 Consumer ethics and social responsibility are as important as business ethics and social responsibility.

KEY TERMS AND CONCEPTS

ethics p. 90
laws p. 90
caveat emptor p. 95
Consumer Bill of Rights p. 95
Foreign Corrupt Practices Act p. 96
code of ethics p. 96
moral idealism p. 98

utilitarianism p. 99
social responsibility p. 100
green marketing p. 102
cause-related marketing p. 102
social audit p. 103
Valdez Principles p. 104

CHAPTER PROBLEMS AND APPLICATIONS

1 What concept of moral philosophy and social responsibility is applicable to the Anheuser-Busch "Know When to Say When" campaign? Why?

2 Five ethical situations were presented in this chapter: (*a*) a medical society's decision to set fee schedules, (*b*) the use of a computer program by auto dealers to arrange financing, (*c*) R. J. Reynolds's introduction of Uptown cigarettes, (*d*) the copying of trademarks and patents in Korea, and (*e*) Young & Rubicam's bribery to get the Jamaican Tourist Board advertising account. Where would each of these situations fit in Figure 4–1?

3 Read again about the Consumer Bill of Rights and the controversy surrounding the planned introduction of Uptown cigarettes by R. J. Reynolds. Which consumer rights are being considered here by public interest groups? By R. J. Reynolds?

4 The American Marketing Association Code of Ethics shown in Figure 4–3 details the rights and duties of parties in the marketing exchange process. How do these rights and duties compare with the Consumer Bill of Rights?

5 Compare and contrast moral idealism and utilitarianism as alternative personal moral philosophies.

6 How would you evaluate Milton Friedman's view of the social responsibility of a firm?

7 The text lists several unethical practices of consumers. Can you name others? Why do you think consumers engage in unethical conduct?

8 Cause-related marketing programs have become popular. Describe two such programs that you are familiar with.

Understanding Buyers and Markets

Understanding people as individual consumers and as members of companies that become organizational buyers is the focus of Part II. Chapter 5 examines the actions people take in purchasing and using products by showing that the behavioral sciences help explain how choices are made or how one brand might be chosen over another. In Chapter 6, Bob Proscal, a product manager for Fiber Optic Products at Honeywell, helps explain how manufacturers, retailers, and government agencies also buy goods and services for their own use or resale. Together these chapters help marketers understand and influence individual, family, and organizational purchases.

CHAPTER 5

Consumer Behavior

*A*fter reading this chapter you should be able to:

- Outline the stages in the consumer decision process.

- Distinguish between three variations of the consumer decision process: routine, limited, and extended problem solving.

- Explain how psychological influences affect consumer behavior, particularly purchase decision processes.

- Identify major sociocultural influences on consumer behavior and their effects on purchase decisions.

- Recognize how marketers can use knowledge of consumer behavior to better understand and influence individual and family purchases.

Know Thy Customer

Successful marketing begins with understanding why and how consumers behave as they do. Consider these examples of how consumer behavior is shaping marketing programs[1]:

- General Motors's Chevrolet Division launched an extensive direct-mail and print advertising campaign to woo women, since they buy 45 percent of new cars and influence 80 percent of all new-car purchases.
- Knowing that 66 percent of grocery purchases are unplanned, innovative supermarkets such as Kroger in Atlanta, Dominick's in Chicago, Von's in Los Angeles, and King's in New Jersey now feature electronic kiosks and video shopping carts to alert shoppers to bargains and "talking shelves" that invite you to stop and buy items.

- Campbell Soup, 7-Eleven, Metropolitan Life Insurance, and Procter & Gamble tailor products, advertising, and sales efforts to fit the unique needs and preferences of regional, ethnic, and racial subcultures in the United States.

This chapter examines **consumer behavior,** the actions a person takes in purchasing and using products and services, including the mental and social processes that precede and follow these actions. This chapter shows how the behavioral sciences help answer questions such as why people choose one product or brand over another, how they make these choices, and how companies use this knowledge to market more effectively to consumers.

CONSUMER PURCHASE DECISION PROCESS

Behind the visible act of making a purchase lies an important decision process that must be investigated. The stages a buyer passes through in making choices about which products and services to buy is the **purchase decision process.** This process has the five stages shown in Figure 5–1: (1) problem recognition, (2) information search, (3) alternative evaluation, (4) purchase decision, and (5) postpurchase behavior.

PROBLEM RECOGNITION

Problem recognition, the initial step in the purchase decision, is perceiving a difference between a person's ideal and actual situations big enough to trigger a decision.[2] This can be as simple as finding an empty milk carton in the refrigerator; noting, as a college freshman, that your high school clothes are not in the style that other students are wearing; or realizing that your stereo system may not be working properly.

In marketing, advertisements or salespeople can activate a consumer's decision process by showing the shortcomings of competing (or currently owned) products. For instance, an advertisement for a compact disc (CD) player could stimulate problem recognition because it emphasizes the sound quality of CD players over that of the conventional stereo system you may now own.

INFORMATION SEARCH

After recognizing a problem, a consumer begins to search for information, the next stage in the purchase decision process. First, you may scan your memory for previous experiences with products or brands.[3] This action is called *internal search.* For frequently purchased products such as shampoo, this may be enough. Or a consumer may undertake an *external search* for information.[4] This is especially needed when past experience or knowledge is insufficient, the risk of

FIGURE 5–1
Purchase decision process

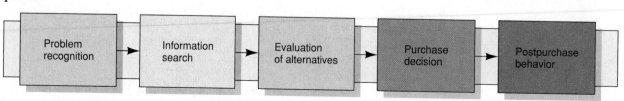

making a wrong purchase decision is high, and the cost of gathering information is low. The primary sources of external information are: (1) *personal sources,* such as relatives and friends whom the consumer trusts; (2) *public sources,* including various product-rating organizations such as *Consumer Reports,* government agencies, and TV "consumer programs"; and (3) *marketer-dominated sources,* such as information from sellers that include advertising, salespeople, and point-of-purchase displays in stores.

Suppose you consider buying an expensive or complex product, such as a CD player. You will probably tap several of these information sources: friends and relatives, CD-player advertisements, and several stores carrying CD players (for demonstrations). You might study the comparative evaluation of single-play model CD players that appeared in *Consumer Reports,* published by a product-testing organization, a portion of which appears in Figure 5–2.

ALTERNATIVE EVALUATION

The information search stage clarifies the problem for the consumer by suggesting criteria to use for the purchase and yielding brand names that might meet the criteria. Based only on the information shown in Figure 5–2, what

FIGURE 5–2
Consumer Reports' evaluation of single-play compact disc players (abridged)

BRAND AND MODEL	PRICE (LIST/ PAID)	BUMP IMMUNITY	DEFECTIVE-DISK IMMUNITY	TRACK-LOCATE SPEED	CONVEN-IENCE AND FEATURES	PROGRAM-MING CAPACITY (SELECTIONS)
JVC XLZ444BK	$330/$260					32
Technics SLP-350	$420/$270					32
Magnavox CDB473BK	$399/$300					20
Sony CDP550	$280/$239					20
Denon DCD-600	$300/$285					15
Onkyo DX2500	$320/$298					16
Realistic CD1500	$250/$180					24
Yamaha CDX510U	$329/$300					24
Nakamichi OMS1a	$329/$315					15
Sharp DX-R750	$280/$180					20

Rating ⬤ ◓ ○ ◑ ⬤
Better ◀ - - - - - - - - - ▶ Worse

Source: *Consumer Reports 1990 Buying Guide Issue* (Mt. Vernon, N.Y.: Consumer Union of United States), pp. 106–7. Also see *Consumer Reports 1991 Buying Guide Issue* (Mt. Vernon, N.Y.: Consumer Union of United States), pp. 46–47.

selection criteria would you use in buying a CD player? Would you use price, track-locate speed, programming capacity, or some combination of these and other criteria?

For some of you, the information provided may be inadequate because it does not contain all the factors you might consider when evaluating CD players. These factors are a consumer's **evaluative criteria,** which represent both the objective attributes of a brand (such as bump immunity) and the subjective ones (such as prestige) you use to compare different products and brands.[5] Firms try to identify and capitalize on both types of criteria; hence Sony emphasizes in its advertising message, "Sony, the one and only," not only the performance characteristics of its products but also the prestige of owning one.

Consumers often have several criteria for evaluating brands. (Didn't you in the exercise above?) Knowing this, companies seek to identify the most important evaluative criteria that consumers use when judging brands. For example, among the evaluative criteria shown in the columns of Figure 5–2, suppose that you use two in considering brands of CD players: (1) a list price under $300 (the first price in column 2 of Figure 5–2) and (2) programming capacity of 20 or more selections (column 7 in Figure 5–2). These criteria establish the brands in your **evoked set**—the group of brands that a consumer would consider acceptable from among all the brands in the product class of which he or she is aware.[6] Your two evaluative criteria result in only three models in your evoked set (Sony, Realistic, and Sharp), which are shaded in Figure 5–2. If these brands don't satisfy you, you can change your evaluative criteria to create a different evoked set of models.

PURCHASE DECISION

Having examined the alternatives in the evoked set, you are almost ready to make a purchase decision. Two choices remain: (1) from whom to buy and (2) when to buy.[7] For a product like a CD player, the information search process probably involved visiting retail stores, seeing different brands in catalogs, or viewing CD player promotions on a home shopping television channel. The choice of which seller to buy from will depend on such considerations as the terms of sale, your past experience buying from the seller, and the return policy. Often a purchase decision involves a simultaneous evaluation of both product attributes and seller characteristics. For example, you might choose the second-most preferred CD player brand at a store with a liberal credit and return policy versus the most preferred brand at a store with more conservative policies.

Deciding when to buy is frequently determined by a number of factors. For instance, you might buy sooner if one of your acceptable brands is on sale or the manufacturer offers a rebate. Other factors such as the store atmosphere, salesperson persuasiveness, and financial circumstances could also affect whether a purchase decision is made or postponed.

For some products, like grocery items, the purchase decision is often characterized by impulse or unplanned buying. The accompanying Marketing Research Report describes both types of buying and the consequences of each. After reading this report, you might consider preparing a shopping list before your next visit to a supermarket.

Marketing Research Report

FORGET THE SHOPPING LIST: FULL SPEED AHEAD!

Probably everyone has purchased an item without thinking about it beforehand. This phenomenon is referred to as *impulse* or *unplanned buying,* and is widespread. It is estimated that half of all retail transactions and two thirds of supermarket purchases are unplanned or bought on impulse.

It is important to distinguish between impulse and unplanned buying. Impulse buying occurs when a consumer experiences a sudden, often powerful and persistent urge to buy something immediately. Consumers sometimes describe this behavior in fanciful or magical terms: "The ice cream was shrieking 'buy me.' " Unplanned buying occurs when a consumer purchases an item different from the one he or she intended to purchase before entering the store. This often happens when one brand is substituted for another (which occurs frequently in grocery shopping).

Impulse buying can have dire consequences. Over 80 percent of people who engage in impulse buying say it leads to disappointment with the purchased item, guilt feelings, and friend and family disapproval. Unplanned buying often increases a consumer's grocery shopping bill. For example, about 75 percent of people who sample a new food in a supermarket buy the product.

Would a shopping list make a difference in the incidence of impulse or unplanned buying? About 31 percent of supermarket shoppers use lists today, compared with 40 percent 10 years ago. Moreover, the typical single shopper without children spends about $.47 per minute during an average supermarket visit of 38 minutes. However, for each minute that exceeds this average caused by browsing, sampling, and making unintended purchases, $1.89 is spent.

Sources: Based on research summarized in James E. Engel, Roger D. Blackwell, and Paul W. Miniard, *Consumer Behavior,* 6th ed. (Hinsdale, Ill.: Dryden Press, 1990), pp. 537–38; Del I. Hawkins, Roger J. Best, and Kenneth A. Coney, *Consumer Behavior: Implications for Marketing Strategy,* 4th ed. (Homewood, Ill.: Richard D. Irwin, 1989), pp. 643–46; and Lawrence Sombe, "Super Marketing," *USA Weekend* (September 8–10, 1989), pp. 4–5.

POSTPURCHASE BEHAVIOR

After buying a product, the consumer compares it with his or her expectations and is either satisfied or dissatisfied. If the consumer is dissatisfied, marketers must decide whether the product was deficient or consumer expectations too high. Product deficiency may require a design change; if expectations are too high, perhaps the company's advertising or the salesperson oversold the product's features.

Sensitivity to a customer's consumption or use experience is extremely important. Studies on automobile purchasing, for instance, show that satisfied buyers tell eight other people about their experience. Dissatisfied buyers complain to 22 people![8] Accordingly, firms like General Electric (GE), Johnson & Johnson, Coca-Cola, and British Airways focus attention on postpurchase behavior to maximize customer satisfaction.[9] These firms, among many others, now provide toll-free telephone numbers, offer liberalized return and refund policies, and engage in staff training to handle complaints, answer questions, and record suggestions. For example, GE operates a database that stores 750,000 answers about 8,500 of its models in 120 product lines to handle 3 million calls annually. Research has shown that such efforts produce positive postpurchase communications among consumers.[10]

Often a consumer is faced with two or more highly attractive alternatives, such as a Sony or a Sharp CD player. If you choose the Sony, you may think, "Should I have purchased the Sharp?" This feeling of postpurchase psychological tension or anxiety is called **cognitive dissonance.** To alleviate it, consumers often attempt to applaud themselves for making the right choice. So after your purchase, you may seek information to confirm your choice by asking friends questions like, "Don't you like my CD player?" or by reading ads of the brand you chose. You might even look for negative information about the brand you didn't buy and decide that the track-locate speed of the Sharp, which was rated "good" in Figure 5–2, was actually a serious deficiency. Firms often use ads or follow-up calls from salespeople in this postpurchase stage to try to convince buyers that they made the right decision. For many years, Buick ran an advertising campaign with the message, "Aren't you really glad you bought a Buick?"

INVOLVEMENT AND PROBLEM-SOLVING VARIATIONS

Sometimes consumers don't engage in the five-step purchase decision process. Instead, they skip or minimize one or more steps depending on the level of **involvement,** the personal, social, and economic significance of the purchase to the consumer.[11] High-involvement purchase occasions typically have at least one of three characteristics—the item to be purchased (1) is expensive, (2) can have serious personal consequences, or (3) could reflect on one's social image. For these occasions, consumers engage in extensive information search, consider many product attributes and brands, form attitudes, and participate in word-of-mouth communication.[12] Low-involvement purchases, such as toothpaste and soap, barely involve most of us, whereas stereo systems and automobiles are very involving. Researchers have identified three general variations in the consumer purchase process based on consumer involvement and product knowledge.[13] Figure 5–3 summarizes some of the important differences between the three problem-solving variations.[14]

Routine Problem Solving   For products such as toothpaste and milk, consumers recognize a problem, make a decision, and spend little effort seeking external information and evaluating alternatives. The purchase process for such items is virtually a habit and typifies low-involvement decision making. Routine problem solving is typically the case for low-priced, frequently purchased products. It is estimated that about 50 percent of all purchase occasions are of this kind.[15]

Limited Problem Solving   In limited problem solving, consumers typically seek some information or rely on a friend to help them evaluate alternatives. In general, several brands might be evaluated using a moderate number of different attributes. You might use limited problem solving in choosing a toaster, a restaurant for dinner, and other purchase situations in which you have little time or effort to spend. Limited problem solving accounts for about 38 percent of purchase occasions.

Extended Problem Solving   In extended problem solving, each of the five stages of the consumer purchase decision process is used in the purchase, including considerable time and effort on external information search and in iden-

CHARACTERISTICS OF PURCHASE DECISION PROCESS	CONSUMER INVOLVEMENT		
	HIGH ← → LOW		
	EXTENDED PROBLEM SOLVING	LIMITED PROBLEM SOLVING	ROUTINE PROBLEM SOLVING
Number of brands examined	Many	Several	One
Number of sellers considered	Many	Several	Few
Number of product attributes evaluated	Many	Moderate	One
Number of external information sources used	Many	Few	None
Time spent searching	Considerable	Little	Minimal

FIGURE 5–3
Comparison of problem-solving variations

tifying and evaluating alternatives. Several brands usually are in the evoked set, and these are evaluated on many attributes. Extended problem solving exists in high-involvement purchase situations for items such as CD players, VCRs, and investments in stocks and bonds. Firms marketing these products put significant effort into informing and educating these consumers. About 12 percent of purchases fall into this category.

SITUATIONAL INFLUENCES

Often the purchase situation will affect the purchase decision process. Five **situational influences** have an impact on your purchase decision process: (1) the purchase task, (2) social surroundings, (3) physical surroundings, (4) temporal effects, and (5) antecedent states.[16] The purchase task is the reason for engaging in the decision in the first place. Information searching and evaluating alternatives may differ depending on whether the purchase is a gift, which often involves the social visibility, or for the buyer's own use. Social surroundings, including the other people present when a purchase decision is made, may also affect what is purchased. Physical surroundings such as decor and music in retail stores may alter how purchase decisions are made. Temporal effects such as time of day or the amount of time available will influence where consumers have breakfast and lunch and what is ordered. Finally, antecedent states, which include the consumer's mood or the amount of cash on hand, can influence purchase behavior and choice.[17]

Figure 5–4 shows the many influences that affect the consumer purchase decision process. The decision to buy a product also involves important psychological and sociocultural influences, the two important topics discussed during the remainder of this chapter. Marketing mix influences are described in Chapters 10 through 21.

CONCEPT CHECK

1 What is the first step in the consumer purchase decision process?

2 The brands a consumer considers buying out of the set of brands in a product class of which the consumer is aware is called the _____ .

3 What is the term for postpurchase anxiety?

FIGURE 5–4
Influences on the consumer purchase decision process

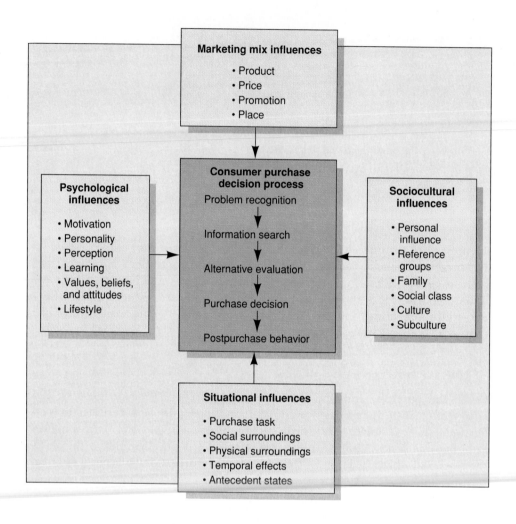

PSYCHOLOGICAL INFLUENCES ON CONSUMER BEHAVIOR

Psychology helps marketers understand why and how consumers behave as they do. In particular, concepts such as motivation and personality; perception; learning; values, beliefs, and attitudes; and lifestyle are useful for interpreting buying processes and directing marketing efforts.

MOTIVATION AND PERSONALITY

Motivation and personality are two familiar psychological concepts that have specific meanings and marketing implications.[18] They are both used frequently to describe why people do some things and not others.

Motivation **Motivation** is the energizing force that causes behavior that satisfies a need. Because consumer needs are the focus of the marketing concept, marketers try to arouse these needs.

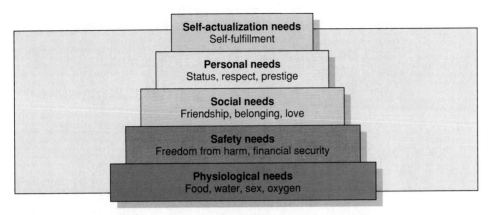

FIGURE 5–5
Hierarchy of needs

An individual's needs are boundless. People possess physiological needs for basics such as water, sex, and food. They also have learned needs, including esteem, achievement, and affection. Psychologists point out that these needs are hierarchical; that is, once physiological needs are met, people seek to satisfy their learned needs. Figure 5–5 shows one need hierarchy and classification scheme that contains five need classes.[19] *Physiological needs* are basic to survival and must be satisfied first. A Burger King advertisement featuring a juicy hamburger attempts to activate the need for food. *Safety needs* involve self-preservation and physical well-being. Smoke detector and burglar alarm manufacturers focus on these needs. *Social needs* are concerned with love and friendship. Dating services and fragrance companies try to arouse these needs. *Personal needs* are represented by the need for achievement, status, prestige, and self-respect. The American Express Gold Card and Brooks Brothers Clothiers appeal to these needs. Sometimes firms try to arouse multiple needs to stimulate problem recognition. Michelin combined security with parental love to promote tire replacement as shown in the advertisement. *Self-actualization needs* involve personal fulfillment. For example, the U.S. Army recruiting program invites you to "Be all that you can be."

Personality **Personality** refers to a person's consistent behaviors or responses to recurring situations. Although numerous personality theories exist, most identify key traits—enduring characteristics within a person or in his or her relationship with others. Such traits include extroversion, compliance, dominance, and aggression, among others. For example, cigarette smokers have been identified as having traits such as aggression and dominance, but not compliance.[20]

Research suggests that compliant people prefer known brand names and use more mouthwash and toilet soaps. In contrast, aggressive types use razors, not electric shavers, and use more cologne and after-shave lotions.[21]

PERCEPTION

One person sees a Cadillac as a mark of achievement; another sees it as ostentatious. This is the result of **perception**—the process by which an individual selects, organizes, and interprets information to create a meaningful picture of the world.

Michelin appeals to
security and parental
love needs in its
advertising.

Selective Perception   Because the average consumer operates in a complex
environment, the human brain attempts to organize and interpret information
with a process called *selective perception,* a filtering of exposure, comprehension,
and retention. *Selective exposure* occurs when people pay attention to messages
that are consistent with their attitudes and beliefs and ignore messages that are
inconsistent. Selective exposure often occurs in the postpurchase stage of the
consumer decision process, when consumers read advertisements for the brand
they just bought. It also occurs when a need exists—you are more likely to "see"
a McDonald's advertisement or the Golden Arches by the road when you are
hungry rather than after you have eaten a pizza.

Selective comprehension involves interpreting information so that it is consistent with your attitudes and beliefs. A marketer's failure to understand this
can have disastrous results. For example, Toro introduced a small, lightweight
snowblower called the Snow Pup. Even though the product worked, sales failed
to meet expectations. Why? Toro later found out that consumers perceived the
name to mean that Snow Pup was a toy or too light to do any serious snow
removal.[22] The accompanying Marketing Action Memo details how the
Eveready Energizer bunny is often "seen" as promoting Duracell—a case of
selective miscomprehension.

Selective retention means that consumers do not remember all the information they see, read, or hear, even minutes after exposure to it. This affects the
internal and external information search stage of the purchase decision process.
This is why furniture and automobile retailers often give consumers product
brochures to take home after they leave the showroom.

Since perception plays such an important role in consumer behavior, it is not
surprising that the topic of subliminal perception is a popular item for discussion.
Subliminal perception means that you see or hear messages without being

Marketing Action Memo

IT KEEPS ON GOING . . . AND GOING . . . AND GOING: THE DURACELL—OR IS IT THE EVEREADY BUNNY?

*H*igh atop the list of favorite and memorable commercials is the mechanical pink bunny powered by Duracell batteries. Or is it Eveready?

Research on the popular pink bunny commercials have uncovered a surprise. In a survey of 4,700 people, 60 percent said the bunny represented the Eveready Energizer brand. But wait—40 percent said the bunny was powered by Duracell! Which brand is it?

A spokesperson for the advertising agency that created the bunny advertisements for Eveready acknowledged that "there's going to be a lag time before people link [the bunny] to the actual product." In the meantime, makers of Duracell, the number-1-selling battery brand, are perfectly happy to be part of the confusion. According to a company spokesperson, "We thank Eveready for helping give us more impact from our advertising budget."

This example is more common than you might think. It has been frequently shown that customers remember a creative ad and the product category,

but perceive the number-1-selling brand's name (Duracell) rather than the name of the challenger—in this case, Eveready.

Sources: Based on Joanne Lipman, "Too Many Think the Bunny Is Duracell's, Not Eveready's," *The Wall Street Journal* (July 31, 1990), pp. B1, B4; Janice Steinberg, "Be Sure to Leave 'Em Laughing," *Advertising Age* (February 5, 1990), p. 52; and "National Agency Report Card," *ADWEEK* (March 12, 1990), pp. 12–15.

---

aware of them. The presence and effect of subliminal perception on behavior is a hotly debated issue, with more popular appeal than scientific support. Indeed, evidence suggests that such messages have limited effects on behavior.[23]

Perceived Risk   Perception plays a major role in the perceived risk in purchasing a product or service. **Perceived risk** represents the anxieties felt because the consumer cannot anticipate the outcomes of a purchase but believes that there may be negative consequences. Examples of possible negative consequences are the size of the financial outlay required to buy the product (Can I afford $200 for those skis?), the risk of physical harm (Is the microwave oven safe?), and the performance of the product (Will the hair coloring work?). A more abstract form is psychosocial (What will my friends say if I wear that sweater?). Perceived risk affects information search because the greater the perceived risk, the more extensive the external search phase is likely to be.

Recognizing the importance of perceived risk, companies develop strategies to reduce the consumer's risk and encourage purchases. These strategies and examples of firms using them include[24]:

- Obtaining seals of approval: the Good Housekeeping seal or Underwriter's Laboratory seal.
- Securing endorsements from influential people: Elizabeth Taylor's Passion line of perfume.
- Providing free trials of the product: sample packages of Duncan Hines Peanut Butter Cookies mailed by P&G.
- Giving extensive usage instructions: Clairol haircoloring.
- Providing warranties and guarantees: Chrysler's 70,000-mile, 7-year warranty for its cars.

LEARNING

Much consumer behavior is learned. Consumers learn which information sources to use for information about products and services, which evaluative criteria to use when assessing alternatives, and, more generally, how to make purchase decisions. **Learning** refers to those behaviors that result from (1) repeated experience and (2) thinking.[25]

Behavioral Learning   *Behavioral learning* is the process of developing automatic responses to a situation built up through repeated exposure to it. Four variables are central to how consumers learn from repeated experience: drive, cue, response, and reinforcement. A *drive* is a need that moves an individual to action. Drives, such as hunger, might be represented by motives. A *cue* is a stimulus or symbol perceived by consumers. A *response* is the action taken by a consumer to satisfy the drive, and a *reinforcement* is the reward. Being hungry (drive), a

Companies use a variety of strategies to reduce consumer-perceived risk.

consumer sees a cue (a billboard), takes action (buys a hamburger), and receives a reward (it tastes great!).

Marketers use two concepts from behavioral learning theory. *Stimulus generalization* occurs when a response elicited by one stimulus (cue) is generalized to another stimulus. Using the same brand name for different products is an application of this concept. *Stimulus discrimination* refers to a person's ability to perceive differences in stimuli. Consumers' tendency to perceive all light beers as being alike led to Budweiser Light commercials that distinguished between many types of "lights" and Bud Light.

Cognitive Learning   Consumers also learn through thinking, reasoning, and mental problem solving without direct experience. This type of learning, called *cognitive learning,* involves making connections between two or more ideas or simply observing the outcomes of others' behaviors and adjusting your own accordingly. Firms also influence this type of learning. Through repetition in advertising, messages such as "Medipren is a headache remedy" attempt to link a brand (Medipren) and an idea (headache remedy) by showing someone using the brand and finding relief.

Brand Loyalty   Learning is also important because it relates to habit formation—the basis of routine problem solving. Furthermore, there is a close link between habits and **brand loyalty,** which is a favorable attitude toward and consistent purchase of a single brand over time. Brand loyalty results from the positive reinforcement of previous actions. So a consumer reduces risk and saves time by consistently purchasing the same brand of shampoo and has favorable results—healthy, shining hair. There is evidence of brand loyalty in many commonly purchased products[26] (Figure 5–6). Note the strong brand loyalty for toothpaste and headache remedies compared with that for garbage bags and batteries.

VALUES, BELIEFS, AND ATTITUDES

Values, beliefs, and attitudes play a central role in consumer decision making and related marketing actions.

Attitude Formation   An **attitude** is a "learned predisposition to respond to an object or class of objects in a consistently favorable or unfavorable way."[27] Attitudes are shaped by our values and beliefs, which are learned. Values vary by

HIGH-LOYALTY PRODUCTS	MEDIUM-LOYALTY PRODUCTS	LOW-LOYALTY PRODUCTS
Cigarettes	Soft drinks	Garbage bags
Toothpaste	Shampoo	Batteries
Headache remedies	Laundry detergent	Gasoline
Coffee	Beer	Underwear

FIGURE 5–6
Brand loyalty of common consumer products

Source: Based on Ronald Alsop, "Brand Loyalty Is Rarely Blind Loyalty," *The Wall Street Journal* (October 19, 1989), p. B1. Reprinted by permission of *The Wall Street Journal,* © 1989 Dow Jones & Company, Inc. All Rights Reserved Worldwide.

Many firms added calcium to their products to create a more favorable attitude.

level of specificity. We speak of American core values, including material well-being and humanitarianism. We also have personal values, such as thriftiness and ambition. Marketers are concerned with both, but focus mostly on personal values. **Values** represent personally or socially preferable modes of conduct or states of existence that are enduring.[28] Personal values affect attitudes by influencing the importance assigned to specific product attributes. Suppose thriftiness is one of your personal values. When you evaluate cars, fuel economy (a product attribute) becomes important. If you believe a specific car has this attribute, you are likely to have a favorable attitude toward it.

Beliefs also play a part in attitude formation. **Beliefs** are a consumer's subjective perception of *how well* a product or brand performs on different attributes. Beliefs are based on personal experience, advertising, and discussions with other people. Beliefs about product attributes are important because, along with personal values, they create the favorable or unfavorable attitude the consumer has toward certain products and services.

Attitude Change   Marketers use three approaches to try to change consumer attitudes toward products and brands, as shown in the examples below.[29]

1 *Changing beliefs about the extent to which a brand has certain attributes:* McDonald's ran an ad to allay consumer concerns about too much cholesterol in its french fries.
2 *Changing the perceived importance of attributes:* 7UP succeeded in building on its positively viewed "no-caffeine" attribute with its "Never had it, never will" slogan to build market share.
3 *Adding new attributes to the product:* P&G added calcium to its Citrus Hill fruit juices hoping consumers would perceive this new product attribute favorably.

LIFESTYLE

Lifestyle is a mode of living that is identified by how people spend their time and resources (activities), what they consider important in their environment (interests), and what they think of themselves and the world around them (opinions).[30] Moreover, lifestyle reflects consumers' **self-concept,** which is the way people see themselves and the way they believe others see them.[31] Hart Schaffner & Marx, a men's clothier, focused a recent promotional campaign on this theme: "The right suit might not help you achieve success. But the wrong suit could limit your chances."

The analysis of consumer lifestyles (also called *psychographics*) has produced many insights into consumers' behavior. For example, lifestyle analysis has proven useful in segmenting and targeting consumers for new and existing products (see Chapter 8).

Lifestyle analysis typically focuses on identifying consumer profiles. The most prominent example of this type of analysis is the Values and Lifestyles (VALS) Program developed by SRI International.[32] The VALS Program has identified eight interconnected categories of adult lifestyles based on a person's self-orientation and resources. Self-orientation describes the patterns of attitudes and activities that help people reinforce their social self-image. Three patterns have been uncovered; they are oriented toward principles, status, and action. A person's resources encompass income, education, self-confidence, health, eagerness to buy, intelligence, and energy level. This dimension is a continuum ranging from minimal to abundant. Figure 5–7 shows the eight lifestyle types and their relationships, and highlights selected demographic and behavioral characteristics of each.

The VALS Program seeks to explain why and how consumers make purchase decisions. For example, *principle-oriented consumers* try to match their behavior with their views of how the world is or should be. These older consumers divide into two categories. Fulfilleds are mature, satisfied, and reflective people who value order, knowledge, and responsibility. Most are well-educated and employed in a profession. Believers, with fewer resources to draw on, are conservative, conventional people with concrete beliefs and strong attachments to family, church, and community. *Status-oriented consumers* are motivated by the actions and opinions of others. These consumers include Achievers, who are successful and career-oriented; value duty, structure, prestige and material rewards; and have abundant resources at their disposal. Strivers, with fewer resources, seek motivation, self-definition, and social approval, and define success in purely financial terms. *Action-oriented consumers* are intensely involved in social and physical activity, enjoy variety, and are risk-takers. Experiencers are young, enthusiastic, impulsive, and rebellious consumers who are still formulating life values and behavior patterns. Makers too are energetic, but focus their attention on practical matters related to family, work, and physical recreation. While Experiencers maintain a vicarious relationship with their surroundings, Makers experience life by working on it—building a house and raising children.

Two consumer types stand apart. Actualizers are successful, sophisticated, active, take-charge people with high self-esteem and abundant resources of all kinds. Image is important to them, not as evidence of power or status, but as an expression of taste, independence, and character. By comparison, Strugglers are poor, often uneducated, and frequently concerned about their well-being. They are the oldest of the VALS consumer types.

Each of these categories exhibit different buying behavior and media preferences. For example, Believers and Makers typically own pick-up trucks and fishing gear; Actualizers are likely to own a foreign luxury car or a home computer. Actualizers, Fulfilleds, and Achievers are most likely to read business magazines. Experiencers read sports magazines.

FIGURE 5–7
VALS 2 psychographic segments

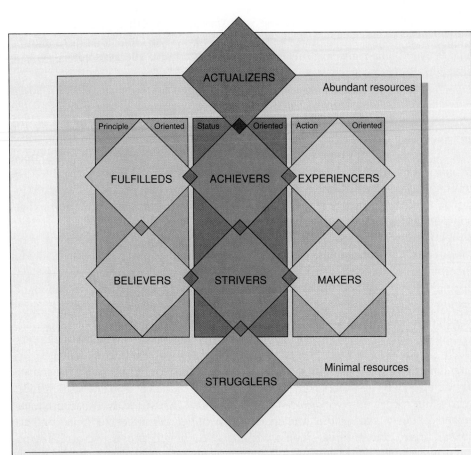

CONSUMER TYPE	PERCENT OF POPULATION	MEDIAN AGE	MEDIAN INCOME	DISTINCTIVE PURCHASE BEHAVIORS
Actualizers	8%	43	$58,000	Possessions reflect a cultivated taste for finer things in life.
Fulfilleds	11	48	38,000	Desire product functionability, value, and durability.
Believers	16	58	21,000	Favor American products and established brands.
Achievers	13	36	50,000	Prefer products that demonstrate success to peers.
Strivers	13	34	25,000	Emulate those with impressive possessions.
Experiencers	12	26	19,000	Avid consumers of clothing, fast food, music, movies, and videos.
Makers	13	30	23,000	Unimpressed by material possessions (except those with a practical purpose).
Strugglers	14	61	9,000	Modest resources limit purchases to urgent needs.

Source: SRI International.

CONCEPT CHECK

1 The problem with the Toro Snow Pup was an example of selective _____ .

2 What three attitude-change approaches are most common?

3 What does *lifestyle* mean?

SOCIOCULTURAL INFLUENCES ON CONSUMER BEHAVIOR

Sociocultural influences, which evolve from a consumer's formal and informal relationships with other people, also exert a significant impact on consumer behavior. These involve personal influence, reference groups, the family, social class, culture, and subculture.

PERSONAL INFLUENCE

A consumer's purchases are often influenced by the views, opinions, or behaviors of others. Two aspects of personal influence are important to marketing: opinion leadership and word-of-mouth activity.

Opinion Leadership   Individuals who exert direct or indirect social influence over others are called **opinion leaders.** Opinion leaders are more likely to be important for products that provide a form of self-expression. Automobiles, clothing, club membership, and PCs are products affected by opinion leaders, but appliances are not.[33]

Identifying, reaching, and influencing opinion leaders is a major challenge for companies. Some firms use sports figures or celebrities as spokespersons to represent their products, such as Bo Jackson for Nike and Lynn Redgrave for Weight Watchers, in the hope that they are opinion leaders. Others promote their products in media believed to reach opinion leaders. Still others use more direct approaches. For example, Ford Motor Company invited executives and professional people to test drive its new Thunderbird.[34] Although only 10 percent said they would purchase the car, 84 percent said they would recommend it to a friend.

Word of Mouth   People influencing each other during their face-to-face conversations is called **word of mouth.** Word of mouth is perhaps the most powerful information source for consumers, because it typically involves friends viewed as trustworthy. When consumers were asked in a recent survey what most influences their buying decisions, 37 percent mentioned a friend's recommendation and 20 percent said advertising.[35]

The power of personal influence has prompted firms to promote positive and retard negative word of mouth.[36] For instance, "teaser" advertising campaigns are run in advance of new product introductions to stimulate conversations. Other techniques such as advertising slogans, music, and humor (California Raisins) also heighten positive word of mouth. On the other hand, rumors about K mart (snake eggs in clothing), McDonald's (worms in ham-

General Mills recognizes Michael Jordan as an opinion leader and features him on its Wheaties cereal box.

burgers), and Corona Extra beer (contaminated beer) have resulted in negative word of mouth, none of which was based on fact. Overcoming or neutralizing negative word of mouth is difficult; however, firms have found that supplying factual information, providing toll-free numbers for consumers to call the company, and giving appropriate product demonstrations have been helpful.

REFERENCE GROUPS

Reference groups are people to whom an individual looks as a basis for self-appraisal or as a source of personal standards. Reference groups affect consumer purchases because they influence the information, attitudes, and aspiration levels that help set a consumer's standards.[37] For example, one of the first questions one asks others when planning to attend a social occasion is "What are you going to wear?" Reference groups have an important influence on the purchase of luxury products but not of necessities—reference groups exert a strong influence on the brand chosen when its use or consumption is highly visible to others.[38]

Consumers have many reference groups, but three groups have clear marketing implications. A *membership group* is one to which a person actually belongs, including fraternities, social clubs, and the family. Such groups are easily identifiable and are targeted by firms selling insurance, insignia products, and charter vacations. An *aspiration group* is one that a person wishes to be a member of or wishes to be identified with, such as a professional society. Firms frequently rely on spokespeople or settings associated with their target market's aspiration group in their advertising. A *dissociative group* is one that a person wishes to maintain a distance from because of differences in values or behaviors. Believing that motorcycle ownership and usage has a "black leather-jacketed biker" stigma, Honda Motor Company has focused its promotional efforts on disassociating its motorcycles from this group.[39]

Marketing Action Memo

TOMORROW'S CONSUMERS TODAY

*W*ho spends $77 billion and influences another $200 billion of purchases per year? Answer: Young people between the ages of 6 and 19.

Youngsters aged 6 to 12 spend $6 billion annually for products ranging from toys to fast food to sports equipment—a fact noted by Toys "R" Us, McDonald's, and Reebok. When not shopping for themselves, they influence what their parents buy, including their own (kids') clothes, video movies, cereals, soft drinks, TVs, and radios in the amount of $50 billion per year.

Teenagers dwarf their younger siblings when it comes to financial muscle and buying enthusiasm. Teens aged 13 to 19 spend $71 billion annually for products like personal care items, cameras, and apparel. They influence another $150 billion in family purchases of VCRs, CD players, personal computers, cars, and food. In fact, research shows that many parents consider their children to be more knowledgeable about these products than they are

themselves! For good measure, teens spend over $33 billion of their parents' money on supermarket items for the family and themselves. Campbell USA, Colgate-Palmolive, Sony, and Polaroid have capitalized on this phenomenon by introducing items attractive to teens.

The buying power and influence of children and teens promises to peak by 2000, when 49 percent of males and 50 percent of females under the age of 17 will hold jobs of some kind. To marketers, the future is now! According to a president of a consumer goods company, "The appeal isn't simply satisfying kids now but also developing them as users of our products so that they'll buy as adults."

Sources: Based on "Family Purse Strings Fall into Young Hands," *The Wall Street Journal* (February 2, 1990), p. B1; Margaret Ambry, *1990 Almanac of Consumer Markets* (New York: American Demographics Press, 1990); " 'SI' Aims for Pint-Sized Good Sports," *USA Weekend* (January 19–21, 1990), p. 16; and Patricia Sellers, "The ABCs of Marketing to Kids," *Fortune* (May 8, 1989), pp. 114–16.

FAMILY INFLUENCE

Family influences on consumer behavior result from three sources: consumer socialization, passage through the family life cycle, and decision making within the family.

Consumer Socialization The process by which people acquire the skills, knowledge, and attitudes necessary to function as consumers is **consumer socialization.** Children learn how to purchase by (1) interacting with adults in purchase situations and (2) their own purchasing and product usage experiences.[40] As children mature into adults, brand preferences emerge that may last a lifetime. Knowledge of this has prompted Sony to introduce "My First Sony," a line of portable audio equipment for children; Time, Inc., to launch *Sports Illustrated for Kids;* and Polaroid to develop the Cool Cam camcorder for children between ages 9 and 14. The accompanying Marketing Action Memo details why marketers are focusing on children as consumers.[41]

Family Life Cycle Consumers act and purchase differently as they go through life. The **family life cycle** concept describes the distinct phases that a family progresses through from formation to retirement, each phase bringing with it identifiable purchasing behaviors.[42] Figure 5–8 illustrates the traditional progression as

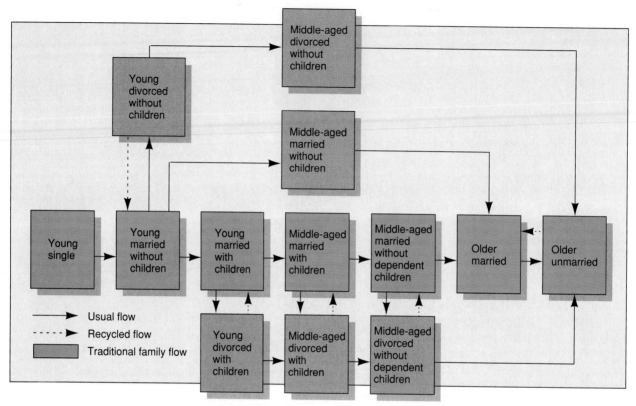

FIGURE 5–8
Modern family life cycle

well as contemporary variations of the family life cycle, including the prevalence of single persons with and without children who will account for almost one third of U.S. households in 1995.

Young singles' buying preferences are for nondurable items, including prepared foods, clothing, personal care products, and entertainment. They comprise about 9 percent of households and represent a target market for recreational travel, automobile, and consumer electronics firms. Young married couples without children are typically more affluent than young singles, because usually both spouses are employed. These couples account for about 10 percent of households and exhibit preferences for furniture, housewares, and gift items for each other. Young marrieds with children represent about 17 percent of households and are driven by the needs of their children. They make up a sizeable market for life insurance, various children's products, and home furnishings. Single parents with children (8 percent of households) are the least financially secure of households with children. Their buying preferences are affected by a limited economic status and tend toward convenience foods, child care services, and personal care items.

Middle-aged married couples with children comprise about 23 percent of households and are typically better off financially than their younger counterparts. They are a significant market for leisure products and home improvement items and represent the fastest-growing family life cycle stage in the 1990s. Middle-aged couples without children account for 20 percent of households and typically have a large amount of discretionary income. These couples buy better home furnishings, status automobiles, and financial services.

Persons in the last two phases—older married and older unmarried—make up 13 percent of households. They are a sizeable market for prescription drugs, medical services, vacation trips, and gifts for younger relatives. These consumers are expected to represent the second-fastest-growing family life cycle stage in the 1990s.

Family Decision Making   A third influence in the decision-making process occurs within the family. Two decision-making styles exist: spouse dominant and joint decision making. With a joint decision-making style, most decisions are made by both husband and wife. Spouse-dominant decisions are those for which either the husband or the wife is responsible. The types of products and services associated with the decision-making styles are shown in Figure 5–9.[43] However, these tendencies are changing with the rise in dual-income families. Today, 43 percent of all food-shopping dollars are spent by male customers, and women influence 80 percent of all new car purchases.[44]

Roles of individual family members in the purchase process are another element of family decision making. Five roles exist: (1) information gatherer, (2) influencer, (3) decision maker, (4) purchaser, and (5) user. Family members assume different roles for different products and services. This knowledge is important to firms. Increasingly, teenagers are the information gatherers, decision makers, and purchasers of grocery items for the family, given the prevalence of working parents and single-parent households. Nabisco, Quaker Oats, Kellogg, and P&G advertise between the rock videos on MTV. Channel One, a daily television news program shown in high schools, features commercials for Head and Shoulders shampoo and Gillette razors.[45]

SOCIAL CLASS

A more subtle influence on consumer behavior than direct contact with others is the social class to which people belong. **Social class** may be defined as the relatively permanent, homogeneous divisions in a society into which people sharing similar values, interests, and behavior can be grouped. A person's occupation, source of income (not level of income), and education determine his or her social class. Figure 5–10 illustrates the seven-category social class structure in the United States. A similar structure exists in Great Britain and Western Europe.[46]

FIGURE 5–9
Influence continuum of spouse in family decision making

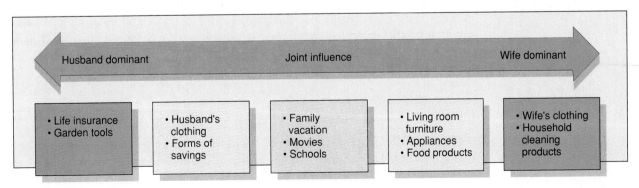

Husband dominant		Joint influence		Wife dominant
• Life insurance • Garden tools	• Husband's clothing • Forms of savings	• Family vacation • Movies • Schools	• Living room furniture • Appliances • Food products	• Wife's clothing • Household cleaning products

FIGURE 5–10
Social class hierarchy in the United States

UPPER AMERICANS (14 percent)

- *Upper-upper class* (0.3%): The "capital S society" world of inherited wealth and aristocratic names.
- *Lower-upper class* (1.2%): The newer social elite, drawn from current professional and corporate leadership.
- *Upper-middle class* (12.5%): The remainder of college-graduate managers and professionals, whose lifestyle centers on private clubs, causes, and the arts.

MIDDLE AMERICANS (70 percent)

- *Middle class* (32%): Average-pay white-collar workers and their blue-collar friends who live on "the better side of town," and try to "do the proper things."
- *Working class* (38%): Average-pay blue-collar workers who lead a "working class lifestyle," whatever their income, educational background, and job.

LOWER AMERICANS (16 percent)

- *Lower class* (9%): Working, not on welfare, but whose living standard is just above poverty.
- *Lower-lower class* (7%): On welfare, visibly poverty stricken, often with no steady employment.

Source: Adapted from Richard P. Coleman, "The Continuing Significance of Social Class in Marketing," *Journal of Consumer Research* (December 1983), pp. 265–80. By permission of The University of Chicago Press.

To some degree, persons within social classes exhibit common attitudes, lifestyles, and buying behaviors. Compared with the middle classes, people in the lower classes have a more short-term time orientation, are more emotional than rational in their reasoning, think in concrete rather than abstract terms, and see fewer personal opportunities. Members of the upper classes focus on achievements and the future and think in abstract or symbolic terms.[47]

Companies use social class as a basis for identifying and reaching particularly good prospects for their products and services. For instance, AT&T has used social class for identifying preferences for different styles of telephones, J. C. Penney has historically appealed to the middle classes, and *New Yorker* magazine reaches the upper classes.[48] In general, people in the upper classes are targeted by companies for items such as financial investments, expensive cars, and evening wear. The middle classes represent a target market for home improvement centers, automobile parts stores, and personal hygiene products. The lower classes are targeted for products such as plastic figurines and scandal tabloids. Firms also recognize differences in media preferences among classes: lower and working classes prefer sports and scandal magazines, middle classes read fashion, romance, and celebrity (*People*) magazines, and upper classes tend to read literary, travel, and news magazines.

CULTURE AND SUBCULTURE

As described in Chapter 3, culture refers to the set of values, ideas, and attitudes that are accepted by a homogeneous group of people and transmitted to the next generation. Thus we often refer to the American culture, the Latin American culture, or the Japanese culture. Cultural underpinnings of American buying patterns were described in Chapter 3; Chapter 22 explores the role of culture in international marketing.

Subgroups within the larger, or national, culture with unique values, ideas, and attitudes are referred to as **subcultures.** Various subcultures exist within the American culture. The three largest racial/ethnic subcultures in the United States are blacks, Hispanics, and Asians. These three groups account for nearly one in four Americans and spend over $500 billion annually for goods and services. Each of these groups exhibit sophisticated social and cultural behaviors that affect their buying patterns.[49]

Black Buying Patterns   Blacks represent the largest racial/ethnic subculture in the United States in terms of population and purchasing power. Consumer research on black buying patterns have focused on similarities and differences with whites.[50] When socioeconomic status differences between blacks and whites are removed, there are more similarities than points of difference, except for brand loyalty. Blacks tend to exhibit higher brand loyalty than whites. However, the tendency for blacks to use a brand name as a dominant attribute for product evaluation declines with a rise in socioeconomic status.

Differences in buying patterns are greater within the black subculture, due to levels of socioeconomic status, than between blacks and whites of similar status. For example, Johnson Products Company, a black-owned firm, markets its hair care products to two segments of blacks—one segment seeks to achieve middle-class status, and the other does not have middle-class aspirations.[51] Furthermore, the typical black family is five years younger than the typical white family. This factor alone accounts for some of the observed differences in preferences for clothing, music, shelter, cars, and many other products, services, and activities.[52] Finally, it must be emphasized that, historically, blacks have been deprived of employment and educational opportunities in the United States. Both factors have resulted in income disparities between blacks and whites, which influence purchase behavior.

Recent research indicates that while blacks are price conscious, they are strongly motivated by quality and choice. They respond more to products and advertising that appeal to their black pride and Afro-American heritage, as well as address their ethnic features and needs regardless of socioeconomic status. On average, blacks are more prone to be television viewers and radio listeners than whites, but a smaller percentage reads newspapers.[53]

Appreciation for the context in which blacks make purchase decisions is a necessary first step in understanding their buying patterns. Current research on black purchase behavior reveals that stereotypes are often misleading, as they also are for the Hispanic and Asian subcultures.

Hispanic Buying Patterns   About 50 percent of Hispanics in the United States are immigrants, and the majority are under the age of 25. Hispanics will surpass blacks as the largest ethnic/racial subculture in the United States by 2010, due in part to migration patterns.

Research on Hispanic buying practices has uncovered several consistent patterns:[54]

1 Hispanics are quality and brand conscious. They are willing to pay a premium price for premium quality and are brand loyal.
2 Hispanics prefer buying American-made products, especially those offered by firms that cater to Hispanic needs.
3 Hispanic buying preferences are strongly influenced by family and peers.
4 Hispanics consider advertising a credible product information source, and about $600 million is spent annually on advertising to them by firms in the United States.
5 Convenience of use is not an important product attribute to Hispanic homemakers with respect to food preparation or consumption, nor is low caffeine in coffee and soft drinks, low fat in dairy products, and low cholesterol in packaged foods.

Despite some consistent buying patterns, marketing to Hispanics has proven to be a challenge for two reasons.[55] First, the Hispanic subculture is diverse and composed of Mexicans, Puerto Ricans, Cubans, and others of Central and South American ancestry. Cultural differences among these nationalities often affect product preferences. For example, Campbell Soup Company sells its Casera line of soups, beans, and sauces using different recipes to appeal to Puerto Ricans on the East Coast and Mexicans in the Southwest. Second, a language barrier exists and commercial messages are frequently misinterpreted when translated into Spanish. Eastern Airlines painfully learned this lesson when the Spanish translation of its "We Earn Our Wings Daily" message implied that passengers often ended up dead.

Sensitivity to the unique needs of Hispanics by firms has paid huge dividends.[56] For example, Metropolitan Life Insurance is the largest insurer of His-

Companies often must address subcultural differences in language and custom.

panics. Goya Foods, dominates the market for ethnic food products sold to Hispanics, and Best Foods's Mazola Corn Oil captures two thirds of the Hispanic market for this product category.

Asian Buying Patterns   About 70 percent of Asians in the United States are immigrants, and most are under the age of 25. Recent U.S. Census figures indicate that Asian-Americans are the fastest-growing racial/ethnic subculture in the United States.[57]

The Asian subculture is composed of Chinese, Japanese, Filipinos, Koreans, Asian-Indians, people from Southeast Asia, and Pacific Islanders. The diversity of the Asian subculture is so great that generalizations about buying patterns of this group are difficult to make. Consumer research on Asian-Americans suggests that individuals and families divide into two groups. "Assimilated" Asian-Americans are conversant in English, highly educated, hold professional and managerial positions, and exhibit buying patterns very much like the typical American consumer. "Nonassimilated" Asian-Americans are recent immigrants and still cling to their native languages and customs.[58]

Studies show that the Asian-American subculture as a whole is characterized by hard work, strong family ties, appreciation for education, and median family incomes exceeding those of white families.[59] Moreover, this subculture is the most entrepreneurial in the United States, as evidenced by the number of Asian-owned businesses.[60] These qualities led Metropolitan Life Insurance to identify Asians as a target for insurance following the company's success in marketing to Hispanics.[61]

Understanding the buying patterns of racial/ethnic subcultures is a necessary first step in marketing to them. When one considers that 38 percent of American children will be black, Hispanic, or Asian by 2010, the long-term consequences of their buying patterns must be understood.[62]

CONCEPT CHECK

1 What are the two primary forms of personal influence?

2 Marketers are concerned with which types of reference groups?

3 What two challenges must marketers overcome when marketing to Hispanics?

ETHICS AND SOCIAL RESPONSIBILITY IN THE 1990s

THE ETHICS OF SUBLIMINAL MESSAGES
Although there is no substantive scientific support for the concept of subliminal perception, it is nevertheless popular. Even if consumers do see or hear messages without being aware of them, would it be ethical for marketers to pursue opportunities to create subliminal messages designed to change buying behavior?

SUMMARY

1 When a consumer buys a product, it is not an act but a process. There are five steps in the purchase decision process: problem recognition, information search, alternative evaluation, purchase decision, and postpurchase behavior.

2 Consumers evaluate alternatives on the basis of attributes. Identifying which attributes are most important to consumers along with understanding consumer beliefs about how a brand performs on those attributes can make the difference between successful and unsuccessful products.

3 Consumer involvement with what is bought affects whether the purchase decision process involves routine, limited, or extended problem solving. Situational influences also affect the process.

4 Perception is important to marketers because of the selectivity of what a consumer sees or hears, comprehends, and retains.

5 Much of the behavior that consumers exhibit is learned. Consumers learn from repeated experience and reasoning. Brand loyalty is a result of learning.

6 Attitudes are learned predispositions to respond to an object or class of objects in a consistently favorable or unfavorable way. Attitudes are based on a person's values and beliefs concerning the attributes of objects.

7 Lifestyle is a mode of living reflected in a person's activities, interests, and opinions of himself or herself and the world. Lifestyle is a manifestation of a person's self-concept.

8 Personal influence takes two forms: opinion leadership and word-of-mouth activity. A specific type of personal influence exists in the form of reference groups.

9 Family influences on consumer behavior result from three sources: consumer socialization, family life cycle, and decision making within the household.

10 Within the United States there are social classes and subcultures that affect a consumer's values and behavior. Marketers must be sensitive to these sociocultural influences when developing a marketing mix.

 ## KEY TERMS AND CONCEPTS

consumer behavior p. 112
purchase decision process p. 112
evaluative criteria p. 114
evoked set p. 114
cognitive dissonance p. 116
involvement p. 116
situational influences p. 117
motivation p. 118
personality p. 119

perception p. 119
subliminal perception p. 121
perceived risk p. 121
learning p. 122
brand loyalty p. 123
attitude p. 123
values p. 124
beliefs p. 124
lifestyle p. 124

CHAPTER PROBLEMS AND APPLICATIONS

1 Think back over your decision of which college to attend and recreate what took place at each stage of the decision process.

2 Review Figure 5–2 in the text, which shows the CD-player attributes identified by *Consumer Reports.* Which attributes are important to you? What other attributes might you consider? Which brand would you prefer?

3 Suppose research at Apple Computer reveals that prospective buyers are anxious about buying PCs for home use. What strategies might you recommend to the company to reduce consumer anxiety?

4 A Porsche salesperson was taking orders on new cars because he was unable to satisfy the demand with the limited number of cars in the showroom and lot. Several persons had backed out of the contract within two weeks of signing the order. What explanation can you give for this behavior, and what remedies would you recommend?

5 Think back about your most recent clothing purchase. How was your purchase affected by your motives, perceptions, learning, attitudes, and lifestyle? What role, if any, was played by your reference group?

6 Which social class would you associate with each of the following items or actions? (*a*) tennis club membership, (*b*) an arrangement of plastic flowers in the kitchen, (*c*) *True Romance* magazine, (*d*) *Smithsonian* magazine, (*e*) formally dressing for dinner frequently, and (*f*) being a member of a bowling team.

7 Assign one or more levels of the hierarchy of needs and the motives described in Figure 5–5 to the following products: (*a*) life insurance, (*b*) cosmetics, (*c*) *The Wall Street Journal,* and (*d*) hamburgers.

8 With which stage in the family life cycle would the purchase of the following products and services be most closely identified? (*a*) bedroom furniture, (*b*) life insurance, (*c*) a Caribbean cruise, (*d*) a house mortgage, and (*e*) children's toys.

9 "The greater the perceived risk in a purchase situation, the more likely that cognitive dissonance will result." Does this statement have any basis given the discussion in the text? Why?

10 Which of the following products would be purchased with a routine problem-solving behavior and which with extended problem-solving behavior? (*a*) razor blades, (*b*) a personal computer, (*c*) a gift for a close personal friend of the opposite sex, and (*d*) a soft drink.

CHAPTER 6

Organizational Markets and Buyer Behavior

---

*A*fter reading this chapter you should be able to:

- Distinguish among industrial, reseller, and government markets.
- Recognize key characteristics of organizational buying that make it different from consumer buying.
- Understand how types of buying situations influence organizational purchasing.
- Describe actions organizations can take to improve their marketing to other organizations.

Fiber Optics: A Serious Light Show

Bob Procsal views light very differently from most people.

As product manager for Fiber Optic Products at Honeywell, MICRO SWITCH Division, Procsal is responsible for fiber optic products (like those in the ad on the opposite page) that sense, modulate, and transmit infrared light for the data communications industry. Converting technology into products and bringing these products to market is part and parcel of his typical day.

Marketing fiber optic technology and products is a challenging assignment. Buyer experience with the technology is limited, even though potential applications are numerous in data communications, computer networks, and industrial automation. Honeywell, MICRO SWITCH Division, and other suppliers such as Hewlett-Packard, Toshiba, Mitsubishi, and ABB HAFO (Sweden) must often convey the benefits of fiber optics technology and specific products through advertising, trade shows, personal selling, and demonstrations. This task often involves communicating with a diverse set of organizational buyers ranging from industrial firms to governmental agencies, throughout the world and in different languages. It also requires knowing which people influence the purchasing decision; what factors they consider important when choosing suppliers and products; and when, where, and how the buying decision is made.

Procsal believes Honeywell, MICRO SWITCH Division, is poised to capture a significant share of the $3 billion fiber optics market in 1992. Ultimate success will depend on continued product development and effective marketing to an ever-growing number of prospective buyers for fiber optic technology in the global marketplace.[1]

The challenge facing Procsal of marketing to organizations is often encountered by both small, start-up corporations and large, well-established companies like Honeywell. Important issues in marketing to organizations are examined in this chapter, which analyzes the types of organizational buyers, key characteristics of organizational buying, and some typical buying decisions. The chapter concludes with how organizations can market to other organizations more effectively.

THE NATURE AND SIZE OF ORGANIZATIONAL MARKETS

Organizational buyers are units such as manufacturers, retailers, and government agencies that buy goods and services for their own use or for resale. For example, all these organizations buy pencils and desks for their own use. However, manufacturers buy raw materials and parts that they reprocess into the finished goods they sell, whereas retailers resell the goods they buy without reprocessing them. Organizational buyers include all the buyers in a nation except the ultimate consumers. These organizational buyers purchase and lease tremendous volumes of capital equipment, raw materials, manufactured parts, supplies, and business services. In fact, because they often buy raw materials and parts, process them, and sell the upgraded product several times before it is purchased by the final organizational buyer or ultimate consumer, the aggregate purchases of organizational buyers in a year are far greater than those by ultimate consumers. Because more than half of all U.S. business school graduates take jobs in firms that sell products or services to other organizations rather than to ultimate consumers,[2] it is important to understand the fundamental aspects of organizational buying behavior.

Organizational buyers are divided into three different markets: (1) industrial, (2) reseller, and (3) government markets.

INDUSTRIAL MARKETS

There are more than 13.6 million firms in the industrial, or business, market (Figure 6–1). These **industrial firms** in some way reprocess a product or service they buy before selling it again to the next buyer. This is certainly true

FIGURE 6–1
Type and number of organizational customers

TYPE OF ORGANIZATION	NUMBER	KIND OF MARKET
Manufacturers	633,000	
Mining	279,000	
Construction	1,829,000	
Farms, forestry, and fisheries	931,000	
Services	6,812,000	Industrial (business) markets— 13,569,000
Finance, insurance, and real estate	2,376,000	
Transportation and public utilities	709,000	
Wholesalers	618,000	
Retailers	2,733,000	Reseller markets— 3,351,000
Government units	83,000	Government markets— 83,000

Source: *Statistical Abstract of the United States,* 110th ed. (Washington, D.C.: U.S. Department of Commerce, 1990).

of a steel mill that converts iron ore into steel. It is also true (if you stretch your imagination) of a firm selling services, such as a bank that takes money from its depositors, reprocesses it, and "sells" it as loans to its borrowers.

The importance of services in the United States today is emphasized by the composition of the industrial markets shown in Figure 6–1. The first four types of industrial firms (manufacturers; mining; construction; and farms, forestry, and fisheries) sell physical products and represent less than half of all the industrial firms, or about 3.7 million. The services market sells diverse services such as legal advice, auto repair, and dry cleaning. Along with finance, insurance, and real estate businesses, and transportation and public utility firms, these service firms represent more than half of all industrial firms, or about 9.9 million. Because of the size and importance of service firms and many not-for-profit organizations (such as the American Red Cross), service marketing is discussed in detail in Chapter 23.

RESELLER MARKETS

Wholesalers and retailers who buy physical products and resell them again without any reprocessing are **resellers.** In the United States there are about 2.7 million retailers and 618,000 wholesalers. In Chapters 14 through 16 we shall see how manufacturers use wholesalers and retailers in their distribution ("place") strategies as channels through which their products reach ultimate consumers. In this chapter we look at these resellers mainly as organizational buyers in terms of (1) how they make their own buying decisions and (2) which products they choose to carry.

GOVERNMENT MARKETS

Government units are the federal, state, and local agencies that buy goods and services for the constituents they serve. There are about 83,000 of these government units in the United States. Their annual purchases vary in size from the

Domtar Gypsum promotes its unique capabilities to industrial buyers.

$25 billion the U.S. government intends to spend for a new telephone system supplied by AT&T and US Sprint Communications to millions or thousands of dollars for local school or sanitation districts.[3]

MEASURING INDUSTRIAL, RESELLER, AND GOVERNMENT MARKETS

Measuring industrial, reseller, and government markets is an important first step for a firm interested in gauging the size of one, two, or all three markets. Fortunately, information is readily available from the federal government to do this. The federal government regularly collects, tabulates, and publishes data on these markets using its **Standard Industrial Classification (SIC) system.**[4] The SIC system groups organizations on the basis of major activity or the major product or service provided, which enables the federal government to publish the number of establishments, number of employees, and sales volumes for each group, designated by a numerical code. Geographic breakdowns are also provided where possible.

The SIC system begins with broad, two-digit categories such as food (SIC code 20), tobacco (SIC code 21), and apparel (SIC code 23). Often each of these two-digit categories is further divided into three-digit and four-digit categories, which represent subindustries within the broader two-digit category. Figure 6–2 presents a detailed breakdown within the food industry to illustrate the classification scheme.

The SIC system permits a firm to find the SIC codes of its present customers and then obtain SIC-coded lists for similar firms that may want the same types of products and services. Also, SIC categories can be monitored to determine the growth in the number of establishments, number of employees, and sales volumes to identify promising marketing opportunities.

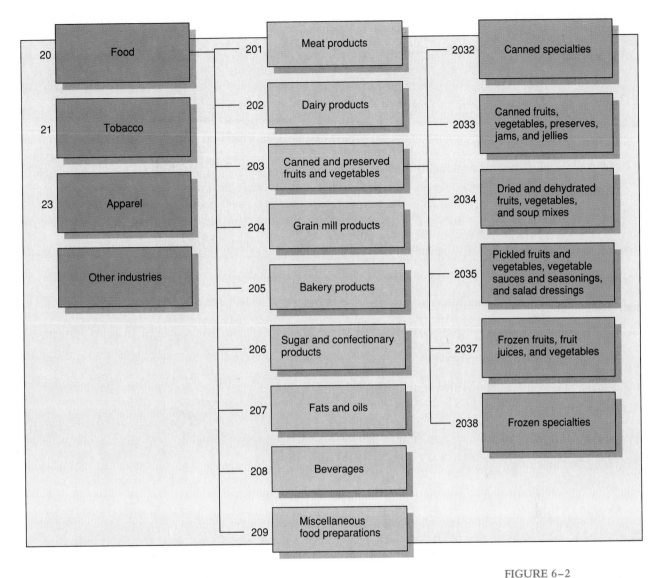

FIGURE 6–2
SIC breakdown for food industries

However, SIC codes have important limitations. The federal government assigns one code to each organization based on its major activity or product, so large firms that engage in many different activities or provide different types of products and services are still given only one SIC code. A second limitation is that four-digit codes are not available for all industries in every geographic area because the federal government will not reveal data when two or fewer organizations exist in an area.

CONCEPT CHECK

1 **What are the three main types of organizational buyers?**

2 **What is the Standard Industrial Classification (SIC) system?**

CHARACTERISTICS OF ORGANIZATIONAL BUYING

Organizations are different from individuals, so buying for an organization is different from buying for yourself or your family.[5] True, in both cases the objective in making the purchase is to solve the buyer's problem—to satisfy a need or want. But unique objectives and policies of an organization put special constraints on how it makes buying decisions. Understanding the characteristics of organizational buying is essential in designing effective marketing programs to reach these buyers.

Organizational buying behavior is the decision-making process that organizations use to establish the need for products and services and identify, evaluate, and choose among alternative brands and suppliers. Some key characteristics of organizational buying behavior are listed in Figure 6–3 and discussed in the following pages.

FIGURE 6–3
Key characteristics of organizational buying behavior

MARKET CHARACTERISTICS

- Demand for industrial products and services is derived.
- Few customers typically exist, and their purchase orders are large.

PRODUCT OR SERVICE CHARACTERISTICS

- Products or services are technical in nature and purchased on the basis of specifications.
- There is a predominance of raw and semifinished goods purchased.
- Heavy emphasis is placed on delivery time, technical assistance, postsale service, and financing assistance.

BUYING PROCESS CHARACTERISTICS

- Technically qualified and professional buyers exist and follow established purchasing policies and procedures.
- Buying objectives and criteria are typically spelled out, as are procedures for evaluating sellers and products (services).
- Multiple buying influences exist, and multiple parties participate in purchase decisions.
- Reciprocal arrangements exist, and negotiation between buyers and sellers is commonplace.

OTHER MARKETING MIX CHARACTERISTICS

- Direct selling to organizational buyers is the rule, and physical distribution is very important.
- Advertising and other forms of promotion are technical in nature.
- Price is often negotiated, evaluated as part of broader seller and product (service) qualities, typically inelastic owing to derived demand, and frequently affected by trade and quantity discounts.

Sources: Adapted from Robert R. Reeder, Edward G. Brierty, and Betty Reeder, *Industrial Marketing,* 2nd ed. (Englewood Cliffs, N.J.: Prentice Hall, 1991), pp. 8–22; Robert W. Eckles, *Business Marketing Management* (Englewood Cliffs, N.J.: Prentice Hall, 1990), pp. 20–26; Frank G. Bingham, Jr., and Barney T. Raffield III, *Business to Business Marketing Management* (Homewood, Ill.: Richard D. Irwin, 1990), pp. 6–14; Michael D. Hutt and Thomas W. Speh, *Business Marketing Management,* 3rd ed. (Hinsdale, Ill.: Dryden Press, 1989), pp. 6–12; and Michael H. Morris, *Industrial and Organizational Marketing* (Columbus, Ohio: Merrill Publishing Company, 1988), pp. 21–28.

DEMAND CHARACTERISTICS

Consumer demand for products and services is affected by their price and availability and by consumers' personal tastes and discretionary income. By comparison, industrial demand is derived.[6] **Derived demand** means that the demand for industrial products and services is driven by, or derived from, demand for consumer products and services. For example, the demand for Weyerhaeuser's pulp and paper products is based on consumer demand for newspapers, Domino's "keep warm" pizza-to-go boxes, Federal Express packages, and disposable diapers. Derived demand is often based on expectations of future consumer demand. For instance, Whirlpool purchases parts for its washers and dryers in anticipation of consumer demand, which is affected by the replacement cycle for these products and by consumer income. Thus forecasting is very important in organizational buying, and it is discussed in Chapter 9.

NUMBER OF POTENTIAL BUYERS

Firms selling consumer products or services often try to reach thousands or millions of individuals or households. For example, your local supermarket or bank probably serves thousands of people, and Quaker Oats tries to reach 80 million American households with its breakfast cereals and probably succeeds in selling to a third or half of these in any given year. In contrast, firms selling to organizations are often restricted to far fewer buyers. Cray Research can sell its supercomputers to fewer than 1,000 organizations throughout the world, and B. F. Goodrich sells its original equipment tires to fewer than 10 car manufacturers.

Consumer needs and wants provide a derived demand for Weyerhaeuser's pulp and paper products.

BUYING OBJECTIVES

Organizations buy products and services for one main reason: to help them achieve their objectives. For business firms the buying objective is usually to increase profits through reducing costs or increasing revenues. Southland Corporation buys automated inventory systems to increase the number of products that can be sold through its 7-Eleven outlets and to keep them fresh. Nissan Motor Company switched its advertising agency because it expects the new agency to devise a more effective ad campaign to help it sell more cars and increase revenues. To improve executive decision making, many firms buy advanced computer systems to process data. The objectives of nonprofit firms and government agencies are usually to meet the needs of the groups they serve. Thus a hospital buys a high-technology diagnostic device to serve its patients better, and the U.S. Department of Labor buys pencils and paper to help run its offices so it can assist American workers. Understanding buying objectives is a necessary first step in marketing to organizations. Recognizing the high costs of energy, Sylvania promotes to prospective buyers cost savings and increased profits made possible by its new fluorescent lights.

BUYING CRITERIA

In making a purchase the buying organization must weigh key buying criteria that apply to the potential supplier and what it wants to sell. **Organizational buying criteria** are the objective attributes of the supplier's products and services and the capabilities of the supplier itself. These criteria serve the same

Sylvania focuses on buyers' objective of reducing costs to improve profits.

purpose as the evaluative criteria used by consumers and described in Chapter 5. Seven of the most commonly used criteria are (1) price, (2) ability to meet the quality specifications required for the item, (3) ability to meet required delivery schedules, (4) technical capability, (5) warranties and claim policies in the event of poor performance, (6) past performance on previous contracts, and (7) production facilities and capacity.[7]

Before reading further, study Figure 6–4 and play the role of an industrial buyer who must purchase a different product for three different firms. Try to select and rank five of the criteria just mentioned as most important in buying (1) paint, (2) desks, and (3) computers for the applications described.

A researcher[8] presented these three buying situations to 170 purchasing managers, who identified the five most important buying criteria for each case as follows:

RANK	CASE 1—PAINT	CASE 2—DESKS	CASE 3—COMPUTERS
1	Quality	Price	Quality
2	Warranties	Quality	Technical capability
3	Delivery	Delivery	Delivery
4	Past performance	Warranties	Production facilities
5	Price	Past performance	Past performance

He observed that, despite the diverse nature of the purchases, three factors in each case were crucial in the choice of a supplier: (1) ability to meet quality standards, (2) ability to deliver the product on time, and (3) performance on previous contracts. He concluded that price is generally the key factor in buying

---

FIGURE 6–4
You be the buyer and choose the buying criteria

Assume that you are the industrial buyer responsible for purchasing each of the items described below:

- *Case 1—paint:* An industrial chemical producer must repaint the interior walls of its manufacturing plant. All the surfaces to be painted are cement and are exposed to severe chemical fumes, which cause paint to deteriorate. It's estimated that the project will require 10 barrels of paint.
- *Case 2—desks:* A large university requires 200 new desks to be used by a large department in a soon-to-be completed university building. The university's policy is to furnish all new offices with metal desks.
- *Case 3—computers:* A large aerospace firm has received a government contract to build two satellites for astronomical research. Each satellite is to have an on-board computer that must stabilize the orbit precisely. The two computers are to be subcontracted, since their electronics and manufacturing tolerances are so complex that only firms with prior experience could guarantee satisfactory performance. The satellites are scheduled to be launched in two years.

There are seven key buying criteria to consider in making each purchase, as outlined in the text. For each of these cases, select the five criteria you consider most critical and rank them from most to least important. To discover which criteria a sample of actual purchasing managers thought were important, see the text.

standard items such as desks. Conversely, when buying more technically complex products such as computers, other criteria are likely to influence the decision and price becomes less important. With many U.S. manufacturers adopting a "just-in-time" (JIT) inventory system that reduces the inventory of production parts to those used within hours or days, on-time delivery is becoming an even more critical buying criterion.[9] Indeed, this buying criterion has assumed special significance in the U.S. automobile industry in recent years. Japanese automakers have long favored this inventory system, and U.S. automakers adopted it as a means to reduce inventory carrying costs and improve productivity. The just-in-time inventory system is discussed further in Chapter 15.

SIZE OF THE ORDER OR PURCHASE

The size of the purchase involved in organizational buying is typically much larger than that in consumer buying. The dollar value of a single purchase made by an organization often runs into the thousands or millions of dollars. For example, Southwest Airlines recently purchased one of Boeing's new 737-500 aircraft for $25 million.[10] With so much money at stake, most organizations place constraints on their buyers in the form of purchasing policies or procedures. Buyers must often get competitive bids from at least three prospective suppliers when the order is above a specific amount, such as $5,000. When the order is above an even higher amount, such as $50,000, it may require the review and approval of a vice president or even the president. Knowing how the size of the order affects buying practices is important in determining who participates in the purchase decision and makes the final decision, and also the length of time required to arrive at a purchase agreement.[11]

BUYER–SELLER INTERACTION

Another distinction between organizational and consumer buying behavior lies in the nature of the interaction between organization buyers and suppliers. Specifically, organizational buying is more likely to involve complex and lengthy negotiations concerning delivery schedules, price, technical specifications, warranties, and claim policies. These negotiations can last as long as five years, as was the case in GE's purchase of a $9.5 million Cray Research supercomputer.[12]

Reciprocal arrangements also exist in organizational buying. **Reciprocity** is an industrial buying practice in which two organizations agree to purchase each other's products and services. For example, GM purchases Borg-Warner transmissions, and Borg-Warner buys trucks and cars from GM.[13] The U.S. Justice Department frowns on reciprocal buying because it restricts the normal operation of the free market. However, the practice exists and can limit the flexibility of organizational buyers in choosing alternative suppliers.

Long-term relationships are also prevalent. As an example, Shanghai Aviation Industrial Corporation, owned by the government of China, announced a $4.5 billion project to build 150 commercial airliners over 10 years. McDonnell Douglas, Boeing, and Europe's Airbus Industry all vied for this lucrative, long-term project, with Boeing getting an initial order valued at $2 billion for delivery of 33 aircraft in 1992. Boeing has sold aircraft to the Chinese government since 1972 and cited this factor as being important in getting the order.[14]

THE BUYING CENTER

For routine purchases with a small dollar value, a single buyer or purchasing manager often makes the purchase decision alone. In many instances, however, several people in the organization participate in the buying process. The individuals in this group, called a **buying center,** share common goals, risks, and knowledge important to a purchase decision. For most large multistore chain resellers, such as Sears, 7-Eleven convenience stores, K mart, Safeway, or Target, the buying center is highly formalized and is called a *buying committee.* However, most industrial firms or government units use informal groups of people or call meetings to arrive at buying decisions.

The importance of the buying center requires that a firm marketing to many industrial firms and government units understand the structure and behavior of these groups. One researcher has suggested four questions to provide guidance in understanding the buying center in these organizations:[15] Which individuals are in the buying center for the product or service? What is the relative influence of each member of the group? What are the buying criteria of each member? How does each member of the group perceive our firm, our products and services, and our salespeople?

To which people in a prospective customer's buying center are these ads targeted—(1) engineering management or (2) design and production engineers? To understand the situation and discover the answer, see the text and Marketing Action Memo.

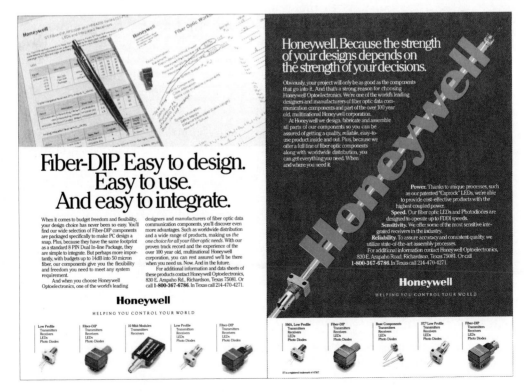

Marketing Action Memo

REACHING DIFFERENT MEMBERS OF A BUYING CENTER WITH CUSTOMIZED ADVERTISEMENTS

*D*ifferent members of a buying center have different buying criteria for choosing suppliers and products. At Honeywell, MICRO SWITCH Division, the marketing staff responsible for fiber optics products develops customized advertisements for each person in a customer's buying center — design engineers, production engineers, engineering management, and purchasing agents. Design and production engineers want new technologies and products that are easy to design, install, and use. Engineering management is concerned with supplier capabilities, including a proven track record and service. Purchasing agents often focus on cost and delivery.

Recognizing that different buying criteria exist, Bob Procsal, product manager for Fiber Optic Products, carefully chooses different messages and media to communicate to each buying center member. For instance, Ad A is directed toward design and production engineers and focuses on some specifics of their buying criteria. Ad B is designed for engineering management and deals at a more general level, with factors such as power, speed, and sensitivity.

Does the added effort and expense of customized advertisements pay off? Yes it does! Inquiries about the company's line of fiber optics products increased 50 percent after this practice was implemented.

Source: Based on an interview with Bob Procsal, Honeywell, MICRO SWITCH Division, March 8, 1990.

Answers to these questions are difficult to come by, particularly when dealing with foreign industrial firms, resellers, and governments. For example, U.S. firms are often frustrated by the fact that Japanese buyers "ask a thousand questions" but give few answers, sometimes rely on third-party individuals to convey views on proposals, are prone to not "talk business," and often say yes to be courteous when they mean no.[16]

People in the Buying Center   The composition of the buying center in a given organization depends on the specific item being bought. Although a buyer or purchasing manager is almost always a member of the buying center, individuals from other functional areas are included depending on what is to be purchased. In buying a million-dollar machine tool, the president (because of the size of the purchase) and the production vice president or manager would probably be members. For key components to be incorporated in a final manufactured product, individuals from R&D, engineering, and quality control are likely to be added. For new word-processing equipment, experienced secretaries who will use the equipment would be members. Still, a major question in penetrating the buying center is finding and reaching the people who will initiate, influence, and actually make the buying decision.[17] The accompanying Marketing Action Memo shows how Honeywell, MICRO SWITCH Division, tailors its advertising to reach slightly different members of the buying centers in its customer organizations.

Roles in the Buying Center   Researchers have identified five specific roles that an individual in a buying center can play.[18] In some purchases the same person may perform two or more of these functions.

- *Users* are the people in the organization who actually use the product or service, such as a secretary who will use a new word processor.
- *Influencers* affect the buying decision, usually by helping define the specifications for what is bought. The information systems manager would be a key influencer in the purchase of a new mainframe computer.
- *Buyers* have formal authority and responsibility to select the supplier and negotiate the terms of the contract. The purchasing manager probably would perform this role in the purchase of a mainframe computer.
- *Deciders* have the formal or informal power to select or approve the supplier that receives the contract. Whereas in routine orders the decider is usually the buyer or purchasing manager, in important technical purchases it is more likely to be someone from R&D, engineering, or quality control. The decider for a key component being incorporated in a final manufactured product might be any of these three people.
- *Gatekeepers* control the flow of information in the buying center. Purchasing personnel, technical experts, and secretaries can all keep salespeople or information from reaching people performing the other four roles.

STAGES IN AN ORGANIZATIONAL BUYING DECISION

As shown in Figure 6–5 (and covered in Chapter 5), the five stages a student might use in buying a CD player also apply to organizational purchases.[19] However, comparing the two right-hand columns in Figure 6–5 reveals some key differences. For example, when a CD player manufacturer buys headphones for its units from a supplier, more individuals are involved, supplier capability becomes more important, and the postpurchase evaluation behavior is more formalized. The headphone-buying decision illustrated is typical of the steps in a purchase made by an organization.[20] Later in the chapter we will analyze more complex purchases made by industrial, reseller, and government organizations.

TYPES OF BUYING SITUATIONS

The number of people in the buying center and the length and complexity of the steps in the buying process largely depend on the specific buying situation. Researchers who have studied organizational buying identify three types of buying situations, which they have termed **buy classes.**[21] These buy classes vary from the routine reorder, or **straight rebuy,** to the completely new purchase, termed **new buy.** In between these extremes is the **modified rebuy.** Some examples will clarify the differences:

- *Straight rebuy:* Here the buyer or purchasing manager reorders an existing product or service from the list of acceptable suppliers, probably without even checking with users or influencers from the engineering, production, or quality-control departments. Office supplies and maintenance services are usually obtained as straight rebuys.

STAGE IN THE BUYING DECISION PROCESS	CONSUMER PURCHASE: CD PLAYER FOR A STUDENT	ORGANIZATIONAL PURCHASE: HEADPHONES FOR A CD PLAYER
Problem recognition	Student doesn't like the sound of the stereo system now owned and desires a CD player.	Marketing research and sales departments observe that competitors are including headphones on their models. The firm decides to include headphones on their own new models, which will be purchased from an outside supplier.
Information search	Student uses past experience, that of friends, ads, and *Consumer Reports* to collect information and uncover alternatives.	Design and production engineers draft specifications for headphones. The purchasing department identifies suppliers of CD player headphones.
Alternative evaluation	Alternative CD players are evaluated on the basis of important attributes desired in a CD player.	Purchasing and engineering personnel visit with suppliers and assess (1) facilities, (2) capacity, (3) quality control, and (4) financial status. They drop any suppliers not satisfactory on these factors.
Purchase decision	A specific brand of CD player is selected, the price is paid, and it is installed in the student's room.	They use (1) quality, (2) price, (3) delivery, and (4) technical capability as key buying criteria to select a supplier. Then they negotiate terms and award a contract.
Postpurchase behavior	Student reevaluates the purchase decision, may return the CD player to the store if it is unsatisfactory, and looks for supportive information to justify the purchase.	They evaluate suppliers using a formal vendor rating system and notify supplier if phones do not meet its quality standard. If problem is not corrected, they drop the firm as a future supplier.

FIGURE 6–5

Comparing the stages in consumer and organizational purchases

- *Modified rebuy:* In this buying situation the users, influencers, or deciders in the buying center want to change the product specifications, price, delivery schedule, or supplier. Although the item purchased is largely the same as with the straight rebuy, the changes usually necessitate enlarging the buying center to include people outside the purchasing department.
- *New buy:* Here the organization is a first-time buyer of the product or service. This involves greater potential risks in the purchase, so the buying center is enlarged to include all those who have a stake in the new buy. The purchase of CD player headphones was a new buy.

The marketing strategies of sellers facing each of these three buying situations can vary greatly because the importance of personnel from functional areas such as purchasing, engineering, production, and R&D often varies with (1) the type of buying situation and (2) the stage of the purchasing process.[22]

Read the accompanying Marketing Research Report and suppose you are a sales representative selling a component part to a manufacturer for use in one of its products. How will your sales task differ depending on the purchase (buy-class) situation?

Marketing Research Report

HOW THE BUYING SITUATION AFFECTS THE BUYING CENTER AND SELLING ACTIONS

*H*ow does the buy-class situation influence the size and behavior of the buying center? Professors Erin Anderson, Wujin Chu, and Barton Weitz looked into the question by asking sales managers about the behavior their salespeople encounter when dealing with their industrial customers. The research findings summarized below illustrate that the buy-class situation affects buying center tendencies in different ways. This research has important implications for industrial selling that are discussed in the text.

	BUY-CLASS SITUATION	
BUYING CENTER DIMENSION	**NEW BUY**	**STRAIGHT/MODIFIED REBUYS**
People involved	Many	Few
Decision time	Long	Short
Problem definition	Uncertain	Well-defined
Buying objective	Good solution	Low price supply
Suppliers considered	New/present	Present
Buying influencer	Technical personnel	Purchasing agent

Source: Erin Anderson, Wujin Chu, and Barton Weitz, "Industrial Purchasing: An Empirical Exploration of the Buy-Class Framework," *Journal of Marketing* (July, 1987), pp. 71–86, by permission of The American Marketing Association.

If it is a new buy for the manufacturer, you should be prepared to act as a consultant to the buyer, work with technical personnel, and expect a long time for a buying decision to be reached. However, if the manufacturer has bought the component part from you before, so it is a straight or modified rebuy, your sales task should emphasize low price and a reliable supply in meetings with the purchasing agent.

CONCEPT CHECK

1 **What are some typical buying criteria that organizations use in making purchase decisions?**

2 **What one department is almost always represented by a person in the buying center?**

3 **What are the three types of buying situations, or buy classes?**

THREE ORGANIZATIONAL NEW BUY DECISIONS

New buy purchase decisions are ones where the most purchasing expertise is needed and where both the benefits of good decisions and penalties of bad ones are likely to be greatest. This means that effective communication among people in the buying center is especially important.[23] Tracing the stages in the buying decisions made by a manufacturer, a reseller, and a government agency highlights some of the similarities and differences of organizational buying. They also illustrate the challenges involved in marketing to organizations.

AN INDUSTRIAL PURCHASE: MACHINE VISION SYSTEMS

Machine vision is becoming widely regarded as one of the keys to the factory of the future.[24] The chief elements of a machine vision system are its optics, light source, camera, video processor, and computer software. Vision systems are mainly used for product inspection. They are also becoming important as one of the chief elements in the information feedback loop of systems that control manufacturing processes. Vision systems, selling in the price range of $5,000, are mostly sold to original equipment manufactures (OEMs) who incorporate them in still larger industrial automation systems, which sell for $50,000 to $100,000.

Finding productive applications for machine vision involves the constant search for technology and designs that satisfy user needs. The buying process for machine vision components and assemblies is frequently a new buy, since many machine vision systems contain elements that require some custom design. Let's track five purchasing stages that the Industrial Automation Division of Texas Instruments (TI) would follow when purchasing components and assemblies for the machine vision systems it produces and installs.[25]

Problem Recognition　TI sales engineers constantly canvass industrial automation equipment users and manufacturers such as American National Can, Ford Motor Company, Grumman Aircraft, and many Japanese firms for leads on upcoming industrial automation projects. They also keep these firms current on TI's technology, products, and services. When a firm needing a machine vision capability identifies a project that would benefit from TI's expertise, TI engineers typically work with the firm to determine the kind of system required to meet the customer's need.

After a contract is won, TI project personnel must often make a **make–buy decision**—an evaluation of whether components and assemblies will be purchased from outside suppliers or built by TI itself. (TI produces many components and assemblies.) When these items are to be purchased from outside suppliers, TI engages in a thorough supplier search and evaluation process.

Information Search　TI employs a sophisticated process for identifying outside suppliers of components and assemblies. For standard items like connectors, printed circuit boards, and components such as resistors and compacitors, the purchasing agent consults TI's computerized, on-line purchasing databank, which contains information on hundreds of suppliers and thousands of products. All products in the databank have been prenegotiated as to price, quality, and delivery time, and many have been assessed using **value analysis**—a sys-

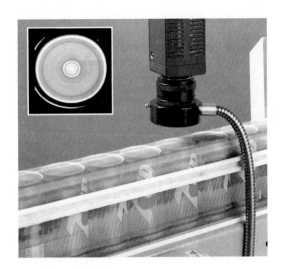

Texas Instruments' machine vision system inspects sealed soft-drink cans at a rate of 1,500 per minute.

tematic appraisal of the design, quality, and performance of a product to reduce purchasing costs.

For one-of-a-kind components or assemblies such as new optics, cameras, and light sources, TI relies on its engineers to keep current on new developments in product technology. This information is often found in technical journals and industry magazines, or at trade shows where suppliers display their most recent innovations. In some instances, supplier representatives might be asked to make presentations to the buying center at TI. Such a group at TI often consists of a project engineer; several design, system, and manufacturing engineers; and a purchasing agent.

Alternative Evaluation TI uses three main buying criteria to select suppliers: price, performance, and delivery. Other important criteria include assurance that a supplier will not go out of business during the contractual period, assurance that the supplier will meet product quality and performance specifications, and service during the contractual period. Typically, two or three suppliers for each standard component and assembly are identified from a **bidders list**—a list of firms believed to be qualified to supply a given item. This list is generated from the company's purchasing databank as well as from engineering inputs. Specific items that are unique or one-of-a-kind may be obtained from a single supplier after careful evaluation by the buying center.

Firms selected from the bidders list are sent a quotation request from the purchasing agent, describing the desired quantity, delivery date(s), and specifications of the components or assemblies. Suppliers are expected to respond to bid requests within 30 days.

Purchase Decision Unlike the short purchase stage in a consumer purchase, the period from supplier selection to order placement to product delivery can take several weeks or even months. Even after bids for components and assemblies are submitted, further negotiation concerning price, performance, and delivery terms is likely. Sometimes conditions related to warranties, indemnities, and payment schedules have to be agreed on.

The purchase decision is further complicated by the fact that two or more suppliers of the same item might be awarded contracts. This practice can occur when large orders are requested. Furthermore, suppliers who are not chosen are informed why their bids were not selected.

Postpurchase Behavior   As in the consumer purchase decision process, postpurchase evaluation occurs in the industrial purchase decision process, but it is formalized and often more sophisticated. All items purchased are examined in a formal product acceptance process. The performance of the supplier is also monitored and recorded. Performance on past contracts determines a supplier's chances of being asked to bid on future purchases, and poor performance may result in a supplier's name being dropped from the bidders list.

A RESELLER PURCHASE: A HOME FOOD DEHYDRATOR

Resellers—wholesalers and retailers—resell the products they purchase without physically changing them. As a result, the stages in their buying decision process differ from those of manufacturers. As an example, let's look at Montgomery Ward's decision to stock a home food dehydrator.

Problem Recognition   Members of Ward's buying committee for electric appliances continually look for appealing new items to stock in its stores and sell through its catalogs. Open to new ideas, the buying committee considered a home food dehydrator, an electric device that dries fresh fruit and vegetables and competes with canning and freezing in home food preservation.

Information Search   Ward's committee assessed the market size to see if a genuine consumer demand exists for food dehydrators. It analyzed how the dehydrators work, their quality, and the chances that unhappy consumers would return these purchased appliances to the store for a refund.

Alternative Evaluation   The buying committee found no home food dehydrators of satisfactory quality that they wanted to sell. Then Wards was approached by a new, start-up firm—Alternative Pioneering Systems—who sells its home food dehydrator under the Harvest Maid brand name. Initial quality-control tests showed that it met Ward's high standards for electric appliances.

A senior buyer on Ward's buying committee checked on the firm itself. He found two young entrepreneurs who had manufactured 500 such dehydrators—a number Wards could sell in a day or two if the product "hit." These entrepreneurs were currently financed on a shoestring through bank loans obtained by using their cars as collateral. The two men had several patents on their device, and it had received the Underwriter's Laboratory approval. The Wards buyer persuaded the two men (1) to seek better financing and (2) to contract out the production of their dehydrators to a larger manufacturer that could produce them in the quantities and with the quality Wards required.

Purchase Decision   Ward's buyer signed a contract with Alternative Pioneering Systems for its Harvest Maid home food dehydrator. At that time no other major chain or catalog store (for example, Sears, Target, J. C. Penney, or K mart) was selling such an appliance. But although Wards had no competition from its major rivals, there was no assurance the dehydrator would sell. On a big gamble, Wards advertised the Harvest Maid dehydrator on the inside front cover of its fall catalog—an extremely valuable advertising space.

Postpurchase Behavior   Ward's buyer and buying committee hit paydirt. The company sold over 20,000 dehydrators in October and November—the peak period for using the appliance—at a retail price of $89. Wards concluded that its decision was a good one and contracted for an expanded Harvest Maid line for the following fall. Today other chains such as Sears and J. C. Penney carry the line.

A GOVERNMENT PURCHASE: APOLLO LUNAR MODULE

Highly technical, first-of-a-kind purchases present special buying problems. This is especially true of the high-performance aircraft, missile, and space systems bought by the U.S. Department of Defense and NASA, but it also applies to technical purchases such as computers, buildings, and mass-transit systems bought by industrial firms and local governments. For example, the price of New Orleans' Super Dome stadium jumped from $35 million to $165 million between ground breaking and completion. Frequently the period between the purchase—or signing the purchase contract—and delivery of the completed system is three to eight years. The lunar module, the element of the Apollo spacecraft that landed on the moon, is an example of a successful government procurement.[26]

Grumman's Lunar Module lands on the moon.

Problem Recognition   For centuries people have dreamed about a visit to the moon, but the United States did not commit to landing an American on the moon until 1961. This commitment marked the problem recognition stage in a decision to procure a system to land a person on the moon and return him or her safely to earth.

Information Search   President Kennedy gave the job of buying a system to NASA, which set to work assessing the technical problems and developing a feasible plan for the landing. Technically, NASA wasn't sure whether the moon landing should be made from an earth orbit or moon orbit. Also, no one was certain whether the moon's surface was solid enough to support the weight of a landing vehicle or even of a person walking on it. Still, NASA decided that the awarding of contracts could not wait until it had definite answers to these questions.

NASA divided the project into pieces, or subsystems, that could be purchased from separate vendors, and also decided which parts of the system it should handle and which it should contract out—its own key make–buy decisions. It divided the Apollo system into several subsystems: the Saturn booster rocket and the command, service, and lunar modules of the Apollo spacecraft.

Alternative Evaluation   NASA engineers and scientists wrote the basic performance specifications for each of these subsystems. They developed buying criteria in order of importance: (1) quality of the contractor's proposed technical design, (2) technical capability demonstrated on past aerospace projects, and (3) price. The first two criteria were critical because many of the specifications were unknown when the contract was awarded and astronauts' lives were at stake. NASA decided to buy 16 lunar modules, counting several early prototypes that would be tested on land and never see space flight.

Purchase Decision   NASA requested technical proposals and price quotations from aerospace firms that had produced successful aircraft or space systems in the past. It awarded the contract to build and test 16 lunar modules to Grumman for a price of $350 million, or about $22 million each.

Postpurchase Behavior   In first-of-a-kind purchases the actual purchase stage is a minor part of the entire process. The years of work start *after* the purchase. Three months after the contract award for the lunar module, Grumman concluded that technical problems had been understated and raised its price to $650 million. Thousands of technical design changes were required, and the contract price grew to $1.6 billion, or $100 million per module—almost five times the initial price. In 1969, astronauts Neil Armstrong and Buzz Aldrin made a successful moon landing in Grumman's lunar module.

Although the success of the Apollo program has not been questioned, its cost overruns have been. The U.S. Congress wants more competition to occur in the production phase of these state-of-the-art systems procurements to both increase quality and lower costs. And since the Challenger space shuttle disaster in 1986, the government is trying to stimulate private business to share more of the risk in space exploration.[27]

1 **What is a make–buy decision?**

2 **What problem did NASA encounter in buying the lunar module that resulted from the lack of precise specifications being available at the time of the contract award?**

MARKETING TO ORGANIZATIONS MORE EFFECTIVELY

The three preceding examples of organizational purchases suggest steps sellers can take to increase their chances of selling products and services to organizations. Firms selling to organizations must learn four key lessons to design and implement successful marketing strategies: (1) understand the organization's needs, (2) get on the right bidders list, (3) find the right people in the buying center, and (4) do the job.

UNDERSTAND THE ORGANIZATION'S NEEDS

As important and obvious as understanding the organization's needs seems, this guideline is violated as often with industrial products as with consumer products. A small firm, I-Point, Inc., devised a temperature-sensitive strip for frozen food packages that would change color when the freezer's temperature got too warm. After spending $12 million developing the product, it found no food companies to buy it.[28] Airplane manufacturers such as Boeing and Lockheed conduct a "chicken test" on jet engines that potential suppliers want to sell them for their new commercial jets. To guarantee that the jet engines will be able to operate after ingesting flocks of birds, engineers buy 20 gross of dead chickens, stuff them into a cannon with a 4-foot diameter barrel, and fire them point-blank into a jet engine running at full throttle—as it would be running on takeoff. Rolls Royce spent several hundred million dollars on a new graphite jet engine. It had only one problem: it failed the chicken test.[29]

In contrast, Caterpillar designed excavators and tractors for small contractors after studying their unique needs.[30] Motorola was chosen over three Japanese competitors to produce the microprocessor for Canon's successful 35 mm camera by not only meeting, but exceeding, Canon's specifications.[31]

GET ON THE RIGHT BIDDER'S LIST

As shown in the accompanying Marketing Research Report, it is critical for a firm to be considered a satisfactory or qualified supplier and to get its name on the bidder's lists of organizations to which it hopes to sell. Ideally, it is desirable to know if the proposed purchase is a new buy or a straight or modified rebuy.[32] If it is a new buy, the organization must get wind of the buyer's need far enough in advance to understand it and offer a product or service to satisfy it. With a straight or modified rebuy the firm knows the need exists and understands what it is, but it can't compete unless its name is on the bidder's list. This is accomplished through sending product samples to be tested and thus qualifying its name for the list.

Marketing Research Report

HOW INDUSTRIAL BUYERS SELECT WINNING BIDDERS

Members of industrial buying centers develop rule-of-thumb guidelines to simplify the complex process of selecting a winning bidder. Researchers Niren Vyas and Arch Woodside interviewed and observed individuals in 18 industrial buying centers with an annual purchase volume of more than $100,000. Some sample decision-making rules that people in these buying centers used in selecting the winning bidder are as follows:

- *Find candidate vendors for the bidder's list.* For straight and modified rebuy products, use existing lists of potential suppliers kept by buyers. For new buys, talk to design engineers and other buyers, draw on past experience, and search trade journals.
- *Qualify (verify) names of satisfactory vendors.* Use distributors when immediate local availability of large numbers of parts in small quantities is essential. Use manufacturers and avoid distributors' margin of profit when a predictable usage pattern exists for a large quantity needed; establish that manufacturers have the capacity, quality, and reasonable transportation costs to fill the order.
- *Invite bids from vendors.* Try to get bids from at least three bidders. Relax criteria, when necessary, to achieve this number. Increase the num-

ber of bids when the size and importance of the purchase warrant it. Tighten criteria when necessary to restrict the number of bidders to six.
- *Evaluate the bids.* Have the purchasing department conduct a commercial evaluation covering price, transportation and tooling costs, delivery schedule, and past performance. Have engineering and production people conduct a technical evaluation to assess the bidder's ability to meet specifications. Drop bidders who are not within 3 percent to 6 percent of the lowest bid price or who do not satisfy technical requirements.
- *Select the winning bidder.* Select two suppliers if the volume and importance of the product warrant it, dividing the contract equally if their prices are within 1 percent of each other or giving a larger contract to the lower bidder. Otherwise select a single supplier. Select the lowest bidder unless past performance justifies choosing the second lowest.

These guidelines help firms that want to sell products to such buyers to develop effective marketing strategies.

Source: Based on Niren Vyas and Arch Woodside, "An Inductive Model of Industrial Supplier Choice Processes," *Journal of Marketing* (Winter 1984), pp. 30–45; by permission of the American Marketing Association.

REACH THE RIGHT PEOPLE IN THE BUYING CENTER

One of the most difficult parts of an industrial salesperson's job is finding the "right" person in the buying center—the decider who really selects the product and supplier or the buyer who actually makes the purchase. A major reason for the success of the Harvest Maid brand of home food dehydrator discussed earlier is that Alternative Pioneering Systems was able to convince the key senior buyer on the Montgomery Ward buying committee that the product was worth stocking and advertising in its catalog. Without that breakthrough, the Harvest Maid food dehydrator might not exist today.

DO THE JOB

Nothing succeeds like success; suppliers to organizations must provide what the customer wants, which leads to repeat orders and success. After G. D. Searle's

A NutraSweet ad directed at prospective users.

chemists discovered a sweetener known as *aspartame,* it marketed the sweetener to Coca-Cola and 60 other manufacturers under the brand name NutraSweet, ringing up $600 million in industrial sales in the process. NutraSweet's low-calorie sweetening ability, coupled with its legitimate claim of "no unpleasant aftertaste," now generates about $900 million in sales each year from industrial customers and the ultimate consumers who buy products, such as Diet Coke, containing NutraSweet.[33]

CONCEPT CHECK

1 **Why is getting on the right bidder's list important to a prospective vendor?**

2 **When Alternative Pioneering Systems finally made its breakthrough in marketing its home food dehydrator, who was the key person in the buying center?**

ETHICS AND SOCIAL RESPONSIBILITY IN THE 1990s

SCRATCHING EACH OTHER'S BACK: THE ETHICS OF RECIPROCITY IN ORGANIZATIONAL BUYING

Reciprocity, the buying practice in which two organizations agree to purchase each other's products and services, is frowned upon by the U.S. Justice Department because it restricts the normal operation of the free market. However, this practice does exist. Do you think reciprocal buying is unethical?

SUMMARY

1   Organizational buyers are divided into three different markets: industrial, reseller, and government. There are about 13.6 million industrial firms, 3.4 million resellers, and 83,000 government units.

2   Measuring industrial, reseller, and government markets is an important first step for firms interested in gauging the size of one, two, or all three markets. The Standard Industrial Classification (SIC) system is a convenient starting point to begin this process.

3   Many aspects of organizational buying behavior are different from consumer buying behavior. Some key differences between the two include demand characteristics, number of potential buyers, buying objectives, buying criteria, size of the order or purchase, buyer–seller interaction, and multiple buying influences within companies.

4   The buying center concept is central to understanding organizational buying behavior. Knowing who composes the buying center and the roles they play in making purchase decisions is important in marketing to organizations. The buying center usually includes a person from the purchasing department and possibly representatives from R&D, engineering, and production, depending on what is being purchased. These people can play one or more of five roles in a purchase decision: user, influencer, buyer, decider, or gatekeeper.

5   The three types of buying situations, or buy classes, are the straight rebuy, the modified rebuy, and the new buy. These form a scale ranging from a routine reorder to a totally new purchase.

6   The stages in an organizational buying decision are the same as those for consumer buying decisions: problem recognition, information search, alternative evaluation, purchase decision, and postpurchase behavior. Examples of organizational purchases described are the purchase of machine vision technology components by an electronics manufacturer (TI), a home food dehydrator by a reseller (Montgomery Ward), and a lunar module by a government unit (NASA).

7   To market more effectively to organizations, a firm must try to understand the organization's needs, get on the right bidders list, reach the right people in the buying center, and do the job properly.

 ## KEY TERMS AND CONCEPTS

organizational buyers p. 140
industrial firms p. 140
resellers p. 141
government units p. 141
Standard Industrial Classification (SIC) system p. 142
organizational buying behavior p. 144
derived demand p. 145
organizational buying criteria p. 146

reciprocity p. 148
buying center p. 149
buy classes p. 151
straight rebuy p. 151
new buy p. 151
modified rebuy p. 151
make–buy decision p. 154
value analysis p. 154
bidder's list p. 155

≡ CHAPTER PROBLEMS AND APPLICATIONS

1 Describe the major differences among industrial firms, resellers, and government units in the United States.

2 Explain how the Standard Industrial Classification (SIC) system might be helpful in understanding industrial, reseller, and government markets, and discuss the limitations inherent in the SIC system.

3 List and discuss the key characteristics of organizational buying that make it different from consumer buying.

4 The importance of buying criteria will often vary according to the type of product purchased. Describe the seven most commonly used buying criteria and how they might rate in importance in the purchase of paint and mainframe computers.

5 What is a buying center? Describe the roles assumed by people in a buying center and what useful questions should be raised to guide any analysis of the structure and behavior of a buying center.

6 Explain the relative influence of the purchasing function and the engineering function in the acquisition of an electronic component part during the first four stages of the organizational buying process in a new buy situation and a straight rebuy situation.

7 Effective marketing is of increasing importance in today's competitive environment. How can firms more effectively market to organizations?

8 A foreign-based producer of apparel for men is interested in the sales volume for such products in the United States. The producer realizes that this is a difficult assignment but has given you a sizable fee to find these data. What information source would you examine first, and what kind of information would be found in this source?

9 A firm that is marketing multimillion-dollar wastewater treatment systems to cities has been unable to sell a new type of system. This setback has occurred even though the firm's systems are cheaper than competitive systems and meet U.S. Environmental Protection Agency (EPA) specifications. To date, the firm's marketing efforts have been directed to city purchasing departments and the various state EPAs to get on approved bidders lists. Talks with city-employed personnel have indicated that the new system is very different from current systems and therefore city sanitary and sewer department engineers, directors of these two departments, and city council members are unfamiliar with the workings of the system. Consulting engineers, hired by cities to work on the engineering and design features of these systems, and paid on a percentage of system cost, are also reluctant to favor the new system. (*a*) What roles do the various individuals play in the purchase process for a wastewater treatment system? (*b*) How could the firm improve the marketing effort behind the new system?

Targeting Marketing Opportunities

Part III describes how people with similar wants and needs become the target of marketing activities. The first step in this process, collecting information about prospective consumers, is discussed in Chapter 7. The information helps marketers focus their efforts on groups with common needs, or market segments. Chapter 8 uses the decisions made by Paul Fireman of Reebok to illustrate how segmentation benefits consumers and companies. Finally, Chapter 9 explains how new information technologies can facilitate information collection and use, and how they can give marketers a competitive advantage.

WHEN KEVIN'S FAMILY LEFT FOR VACATION, THEY FORGOT ONE MINOR DETAIL: KEVIN.
BUT DON'T WORRY...
HE COOKS. HE CLEANS.
HE KICKS SOME BUTT.
FROM JOHN HUGHES
HOME ALONE
A FAMILY COMEDY WITHOUT THE FAMILY.
TWENTIETH CENTURY FOX PRESENTS A JOHN HUGHES PRODUCTION A CHRIS COLUMBUS FILM
HOME ALONE MACAULAY CULKIN JOE PESCI DANIEL STERN JOHN HEARD AND CATHERINE O'HARA MUSIC BY JOHN WILLIAMS
FILM EDITOR RAJA GOSNELL PRODUCTION DESIGNER JOHN MUTO DIRECTOR OF PHOTOGRAPHY JULIO MACAT EXECUTIVE PRODUCERS MARK LEVINSON & SCOTT ROSENFELT AND TARQUIN GOTCH
HUGHES
PG PARENTAL GUIDANCE SUGGESTED
SOME MATERIAL MAY NOT BE SUITABLE FOR CHILDREN
WRITTEN AND PRODUCED BY JOHN HUGHES DIRECTED BY CHRIS COLUMBUS COLOR BY DELUXE
DOLBY STEREO IN SELECTED THEATRES
20th CENTURY FOX
© 1990 TWENTIETH CENTURY FOX

Collecting and Using Marketing Information

After reading this chapter you should be able to:

- Identify five steps a person can follow in reaching a decision, and the significance of each step.
- Explain the four key elements used to define a problem: the objectives, constraints, assumptions, and measures of success.
- Structure a decision into two basic components: the controllable and uncontrollable factors.
- Know three types of information collected to solve a problem: concepts, methods, and data.
- Know how questionnaires, observations, experiments, and panels are used in marketing.
- Understand how marketers identify and implement a solution and evaluate the results.

How Movies Use Marketing Research

As far as plots go, the movies *Who Framed Roger Rabbit, Indiana Jones and the Last Crusade, Star Wars, Home Alone,* and *Fatal Attraction* don't have much in common. But as production and marketing costs of motion pictures skyrocket,[1] all these movies use increasingly sophisticated marketing research and analysis. Some examples of commonly used techniques include:

- *Concept tests of plots:* Concepts for new plots are described to members of the target audience to get their reactions. Used by Columbia Pictures, this concept-testing technique can result in a decision to not produce a film, to alter an element of the plot, or to change casting.[2]

- *Sneak previews of completed films:* These use repeated screenings in "middle America"—cities away from both coasts, such as Dallas, Minneapolis, and St. Louis—to gauge audience reaction by handing out free movie invitations to people 15 to 39 years old.[3] In sneak previews of *Fatal Attraction,* audiences liked everything but the ending, which had Alex (Glenn Close) committing suicide and managing to frame Dan (Michael Douglas) as her murderer by leaving his fingerprints on the knife she used. New scenes were then shot, at an extra cost of $1.3 million, for the ending that regular audiences saw later.[4]
- *Awareness tests before and after the movie's release:* For a movie to be a success, Columbia Pictures believes 60 percent of the target audience should be aware of it on the day it opens. Columbia and other film companies track audience awareness immediately before and after the opening and increase or decrease advertising expenditures depending on the results. Right before the opening of *Indiana Jones and the Temple of Doom,* 90 percent of people polled by Paramount were aware of it and 75 percent intended to see it, so Paramount reduced its advertising.[5]

These examples show how marketing research shapes our movies—from concept tests before production even starts to awareness tests after it is finished. Even the TV and newspaper ads for the movies are tested repeatedly. The chapter also shows how marketing research links to marketing strategy and action.

THE ROLE OF MARKETING RESEARCH

To place marketing research in perspective, we can describe (1) what it is, (2) some of the difficulties in conducting it, and (3) the process marketing executives can use to make effective decisions.

WHAT MARKETING RESEARCH IS AND DOES

Marketing research is the process of defining a marketing problem and opportunity, systematically collecting and analyzing information, and recommending actions to improve an organization's marketing activities.

A Means of Reducing Uncertainty   Assessing the needs and wants of consumers and providing information to help design an organization's marketing program to satisfy them is the role that marketing research performs. This means that marketing research attempts to identify and define both marketing problems and opportunities and to generate and evaluate marketing actions.[6] Although marketing research can provide few answers with complete assurance, it can reduce the uncertainty and increase the likelihood of the success of marketing decisions.[7] It is a great help to the marketing managers who make the final decisions.

Anyone for Juice in a Box?   Suppose in the early 1980s you were asked by a marketing researcher whether you would drink unrefrigerated orange, apple, or cranberry juice that was packaged in a paper carton. Could the aseptic packaging

What are the difficulties faced in asking consumers if they would use a product they've never heard of? To understand some of the problems faced by Ocean Spray marketing researchers when they studied aseptic packaging in the early 1980s, see the text.

technology be moved successfully here from Europe, where refrigeration is less widespread? Would American consumers buy fresh juice in boxes stored on a retailer's shelf at room temperature? The answers to these kinds of questions asked by Ocean Spray's marketing researchers resulted in advertisements to address such concerns that led to Ocean Spray's very successful national introduction of aseptic packaging.

WHY GOOD MARKETING RESEARCH IS DIFFICULT

The dilemmas faced by marketing researchers at Ocean Spray when trying to assess consumers' willingness to buy juices sold in aseptic packages illustrate why good marketing research requires great care—especially because of the inherent difficulties in asking consumers questions.[8]

- Do consumers really know whether they are likely to buy a particular product that they probably have never thought about before? Can they really assess its advantages and disadvantages on the spur of the moment?
- Even if they know the answer, will they reveal it? When personal or status questions are involved, will people give honest answers?
- Will their actual purchase behavior be the same as their stated interest or intentions? Will they buy the same brand they say they will? To appear progressive, consumers often overstate their likelihood of buying a new product.

When people know they are being measured, the very measurement process itself can significantly affect their answers and behaviors. A task of marketing research is to overcome these difficulties to provide useful information.

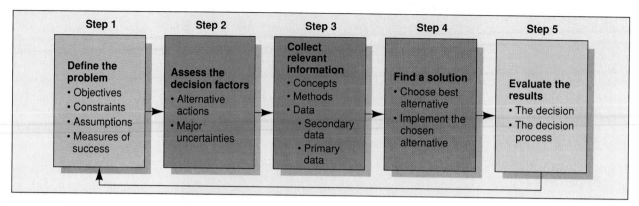

FIGURE 7–1
Five-step approach to
making decisions

STEPS IN MAKING EFFECTIVE DECISIONS

A **decision** is a conscious choice from among two or more alternatives. All of
us make many such decisions daily. At work we choose from alternative ways
to accomplish an assigned task. At college we choose from alternative courses.
As consumers we choose from alternative brands. No magic formula guarantees
correct decisions all the time.

Managers and researchers have tried to improve the outcomes of decisions
by using more formal, systematic approaches to *decision making*, the act of consciously choosing from alternatives. People who do not use some kind of
system—and many do not—may make poor decisions. The systematic approach
to making decisions (or problem solving) described in this chapter uses five steps
and is shown in Figure 7–1. This five-step approach provides a mental checklist
for making any decision—either business or personal. For example, suppose you
are the product manager for Ocean Spray cranberry juice. You might outline
one of your typical decisions in this way:

- *Define the problem:* Choose an advertising medium to introduce aseptically
  packaged cranberry juice nationally in the U.S. market.
- *Assess the decision factors:* Consider (1) alternative media and (2) uncontrollable factors that might affect the decision.
- *Collect relevant information:* Obtain the information pertinent to selecting an
  advertising medium.
- *Find a solution:* Select the best advertising medium from among the alternatives studied and put it into action.
- *Evaluate the results:* Assess whether the advertising medium chosen was
  successful and why.

Although Ocean Spray's marketing research and actions led the way, other U.S.
firms soon adopted aseptic packages, and today Americans use more than $600
million worth of aseptic cartons annually.

CONCEPT CHECK

1 What is marketing research?

2 What are the problems in collecting marketing research data from consumers when they know they are being measured?

STEP 1: DEFINE THE PROBLEM

Toy designers at Fisher-Price Toys, the nation's top marketer of infant and preschool toys, had a problem some years back: they developed toys they thought kids would like, but how could they be certain? To research the problem, Fisher-Price got six children, aged 3 to 4, to make twice-a-week visits to play at its state licensed nursery school in East Aurora, New York.[9] However, the children soon lost their jobs: Fisher-Price changes its toy testers every six weeks to ensure that one group's way-out ideas don't lead to changes the nation's toy users don't want.

Fisher-Price's toy testing shows how to define the problem and its four key elements: objectives, constraints, assumptions, and measures of success. For example, the original model of a classic Fisher-Price toy, the chatter telephone, was simply a wooden phone with a dial that rang a bell. Observers noted, however, that the children kept grabbing the receiver like a handle to pull the phone along behind them, so a designer added wheels, a noisemaker, and eyes that bobbed up and down on an experimental version of the toy.

OBJECTIVES

Objectives are the goals the decision maker seeks to achieve in solving a problem. Typical marketing objectives are increasing revenues and profits, discovering what consumers are aware of and want, and finding out why a product isn't selling well. For Fisher-Price the immediate objective was to decide whether to market the old or new chatter telephone.

CONSTRAINTS

The **constraints** in a decision are the restrictions placed on potential solutions by the nature and importance of the problem. Common constraints in marketing problems are limitations on the time and money available to solve the problem. Thus Fisher-Price might set two constraints on its decision to select either the old or new version of the chatter telephone: the decision must be made in 10 weeks, and no research budget is available beyond that needed for collecting data in its nursery school.

In problem solving, there are human constraints as well: a person's mind can have "tunnel vision" that unnecessarily restricts the search for alternatives. Then the task is to uncover new alternatives that may lead to a solution. As an example of redefining a problem, solve these two puzzles, paying attention to what thoughts go through your mind[10]:

1 Connect the nine dots to the right using four straight lines without lifting your pen from the paper or retracing a line.
2 Arrange the six matches to the left in a pattern that gives four equilateral triangles of the same size. (If you've forgotten your geometry, an equilateral triangle is a triangle with three sides of equal length.)

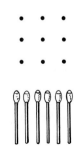

The solutions appear in Figure 7–2 along with some suggestions for opening your mind and finding creative solutions to problems—techniques that marketing people looking for new products or original advertising copy often use.

FIGURE 7–2
Solutions to the dot and match problems

The solutions to the dot and match problems are shown below, along with the tricks a person's mind plays that may prevent solving the problem.

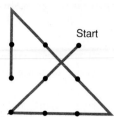

Start

The dot problem
Solution is to extend the lines beyond the dots. Most people make the implicit assumption that they cannot do this.

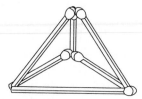

The match problem
Solution is to build a pyramid in three dimensions. Most people incorrectly assume that the matches must lie on a flat surface.

Experts say that people can do a number of things to open up their minds and overcome implicit constraints or assumptions that inhibit solutions:

1 Recast or restate the problem.
2 Make the problem more explicit by writing it down or stating it aloud to a friend or co-worker (including the objectives, constraints, assumptions, and measures of success).
3 Leave it for a while to "simmer on the back burner" before attacking it afresh.

Source: Based on Martin Scheerer, "Problem Solving," *Scientific American* (April 1963), pp. 118–28. Copyright © 1963 by Scientific American, Inc. All rights reserved.

ASSUMPTIONS

Assumptions are the conjectures about factors or situations that simplify the problem enough to allow it to be solved within the existing constraints. If more money or time becomes available, sometimes the assumptions themselves are investigated. For example, the product manager for the Fisher-Price chatter telephone might make these assumptions: (1) the children in the Fisher-Price nursery school are typical of all American children and (2) an indication of their preference is the amount of time spent playing with each toy when other toys are also available.

MEASURES OF SUCCESS

Effective decision makers specify **measures of success**, which are criteria or standards used in evaluating proposed solutions to the problem. For the Fisher-Price problem, if a measure of success were the total time children spend playing with each of the two designs, the results of observing them would lead to clearcut actions as follows:

OUTCOME OF DATA COLLECTION	MARKETING ACTION
Children spend more time playing with old design.	Continue with old design; don't introduce new design.
Children spend more time playing with new design.	Introduce new design; drop old design.

One test of whether marketing research should be undertaken is if different outcomes will lead to different marketing actions. If all the research outcomes lead to the same action—such as top management sticking with the older design regardless of what the observed children like—the research is useless and a waste of money.

In this case research results showed that kids liked the new design, so Fisher-Price introduced its noise-making pull-toy telephone, which has become a toy classic and sold millions.

Most marketing researchers would agree with philosopher John Dewey's observation that "a problem well-defined is half-solved," but they know that defining a problem is an incredibly difficult, although essential, task. For example, if the objectives are too broad, the problem may not be researchable. If they are too narrow, the value of the research results may be seriously lessened. This is why marketing researchers spend so much time in defining a marketing problem precisely and writing a formal proposal describing the research to be done.

STEP 2: ASSESS THE DECISION FACTORS

Decision factors are the different sets of variables—the alternatives and uncertainties—that combine to give the outcome of a decision. These two sets of variables differ by the degree of control that the decision maker can exert over them. **Alternatives** are the factors over which the decision maker has control. **Uncertainties** are the uncontrollable factors that the decision maker cannot influence. In Step 2 of this approach the decision maker faces the problem of identifying in detail (1) the principal alternatives that can be considered reasonable approaches to solving the problem and (2) the major uncertainties that can affect a particular alternative and result in its being a good or a poor solution to the problem.

ALTERNATIVES: THE CONTROLLABLE DECISION FACTORS

Experienced marketing managers insist on searching for more than a single alternative solution to a problem because the new alternatives may lead to better solutions. One widely used method is to start the problem statement with, "In what ways can we . . . ?" For example:

- In what ways can we put our Xerox copier to new uses?
- In what ways can we put our old pipelines to new uses?
- In what ways can we put the needs of college students for socializing and washing their clothes together to start a business?

With respect to the first question, the Xerox Corporation probably exists today because although its early plain-paper photocopier was a disaster for its intended use, it did make copies that could be used in offset printing. Discovering this fact, the executives at Xerox used revenues from this application to perfect and sell the Xerox plain-paper copier. They had temporarily redefined their task to discover and produce a copier for a different application.[11]

The blend of pub atmosphere with laundromat services led to the success of Duds 'N Suds.

In one giant leap of creativity, Williams Companies moved from the petroleum business into the telecommunications business. How? By running fiber optics telecommunications cables through 1,000 miles of unused petroleum pipeline. Today it is the fourth-largest marketer of long-distance telecommunications—in competition with AT&T, MCI, and US Sprint.[12]

To develop new alternatives, creative people often blend unusual elements into a winning combination that doesn't occur to the average person. An Iowa State University student observed that today's college students want a comfortable social atmosphere and also have to do their own laundry. The result: Duds 'N Suds, a chain of laundromat-pubs located near almost 100 college campuses across the United States.

Talking to customers, trading ideas with co-workers, holding formal brainstorming sessions, and learning from competitors are efficient ways to search for alternative ideas for improving marketing mix actions. Using these techniques to uncover new product ideas is discussed in Chapter 10.

UNCERTAINTIES: THE UNCONTROLLABLE DECISION FACTORS

Well-chosen alternatives can go haywire because of uncertainties, which can relate to factors within the firm or can involve consumers, competitors, national or international affairs, or even the weather.

Creative minds at Booz, Allen & Hamilton's research division slaved over what they were sure was a great new product idea: bubble gum a child could eat. But they could never lick two key uncertainties. First, tests with kids showed that until they got the knack of blowing bubbles, they would dribble the sticky stuff down their chins. This consumer uncertainty was also tied to a technical one: the research division found that foaming agents safe to eat made poor bubbles.

Even the weather can be a critical marketing uncertainty. Booz, Allen & Hamilton's research lab developed a temporary hair coloring the consumer applied by inserting a solid block of hair dye into a specially designed comb. It was a disaster. Researchers subsequently discovered that when people perspired on hot days, any extra dye applied to their hair ran down their foreheads and necks. One of the company's executives explained, "It just didn't occur to us to look at this under conditions where people perspire."[13]

1 What are examples of constraints in solving a problem?

2 What does "measure of success" mean?

3 What is the difference between uncertainties and alternatives?

STEP 3: COLLECT RELEVANT INFORMATION

Collecting enough relevant information to make a rational, informed decision sometimes simply means using your knowledge to decide immediately. At other times it entails collecting an enormous amount of information at great expense.

Defined broadly, three kinds of information used to solve marketing problems are concepts, methods, and data. To understand the abstract topic of information, assume you are the marketing vice president for Scripto and are struggling to find a new writing instrument to introduce into the market.

CONCEPTS

One valuable type of concept, a **hypothesis**, is a conjecture about the relationship of two or more factors or what might happen in the future. Hypotheses that lead to marketing actions can come from many sources: theoretical reasoning, marketing studies, technical breakthroughs, informal conversations, and even educated guesses.

For example, as the marketing vice president of Scripto, you can marshal the following facts:

- More than 1 billion ballpoint disposable stick pens are sold in the United States annually.
- Stick pens are the most widely used writing instruments by students and teenagers. Your competitor Eraser Mate has introduced an erasable ink pen with refills that is widely used by students.

From this information, you can develop a hypothesis: there is a substantial demand—especially among students and teenagers—for a disposable, erasable pen. A **new product concept** is a tentative description of a product or service a firm might offer for sale. A "disposable, erasable pen" is a new product concept that Scripto wanted to consider.

METHODS

Methods are the approaches that can be used to solve part or all of a problem. For example, as marketing vice president of Scripto you face a number of methodological questions, including:

- How do you ask students about the price they might pay for the proposed pen?
- How do you phrase a question to determine whether they would buy the product if it were available?
- How do you forecast expected sales after the new product is introduced?

Millions of other people have asked exactly these same questions about millions of other products and services.

How can you find and use the methodologies that other marketing researchers have found successful? Information on useful methods is available in tradebooks, textbooks, and handbooks that relate to marketing and marketing research.[14] Some periodicals and technical journals such as the *Journal of Marketing* and the *Journal of Marketing Research* summarize methods and techniques valuable in addressing marketing problems. Of course, as the Scripto marketing vice president you must apply the methods that have worked for others to your particular problems with your new pen. Special methods vital to marketing are (1) sampling and (2) statistical inference.

Sampling   Marketing researchers often select a group of distributors, customers, or prospects, ask them questions, and treat their answers as typical of all those in whom they are interested. There are two ways of sampling, or selecting representative elements from a population: probability and nonprobability sampling. **Probability sampling** involves using precise rules to select the sample such that each element of the population has a specific known chance of being selected. For example, if a college wants to know how last year's 1,000 graduates are doing, it can put their names in a bowl and randomly select 50 names of graduates to contact. The chance of being selected—50/1,000 or 0.05—is known in advance, and all graduates have an equal chance of being contacted.

These journals describe methods that help solve marketing problems.

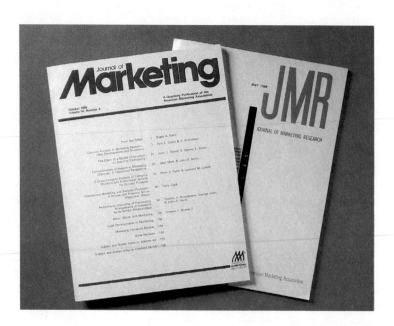

This procedure helps select a sample (the 50 graduates) that is representative of the entire population (the 1,000 graduates) and allows conclusions to be drawn about the entire population.

When time and budget are limited, researchers may opt for **nonprobability sampling** and use arbitrary judgments to select the sample so that the chance of selecting a particular element may be unknown or 0. If the college decides arbitrarily to select the 50 graduates from last year's class who live closest to the college, many members of the class have been arbitrarily eliminated. This has introduced a bias that makes it dangerous to draw conclusions about the population from this geographically restricted sample.

Statistical Inference The method of **statistical inference** involves drawing conclusions about a *population* (the "universe" of all people, stores, or salespeople about which they wish to generalize) from a *sample* (some elements of the universe) taken from that population.

To draw accurate inferences about the population, the sample elements should be representative of that universe. If the sample is not typical, bias can be introduced, resulting in bad marketing decisions. For example, had Scripto selected a nonrepresentative sample of people who said they didn't like the Eraser Mate pen, it probably would have dropped the idea of introducing its own competing pen. As things turned out, Scripto went on to collect secondary and primary data—topics discussed next—that verified and refined its new product concept and it introduced its very successful Scripto Erasable Pen.

SECONDARY DATA

Figure 7–3 shows how the different kinds of marketing information fit together. **Data,** the facts and figures pertinent to the problem, are divided into two main parts: secondary data and primary data. **Secondary data** are facts and figures that have already been recorded before the project at hand, whereas **primary data** are facts and figures that are newly collected for the project.

Internal Secondary Data Data that have already been collected and exist inside the business firm or other organization are internal secondary data. These include financial statements (like the firm's balance sheet and income statement), research reports, customer letters, sales reports on customer calls, and customer lists.

External Secondary Data Published data from outside the firm are external secondary data. Probably the best known are U.S. Census Bureau reports. The *U.S. Census of Population* is published every 10 years and provides detailed information on American households, such as number of people per household, their ages, their sex, household income, and education of the head of the household. These are basic sources of information used by manufacturers and retailers to identify characteristics and trends of ultimate consumers.

Other census reports are vital to business firms selling products and services to organizations. The *U.S. Census of Manufactures,* published about every five years, lists the number and size of manufacturing firms by industry group

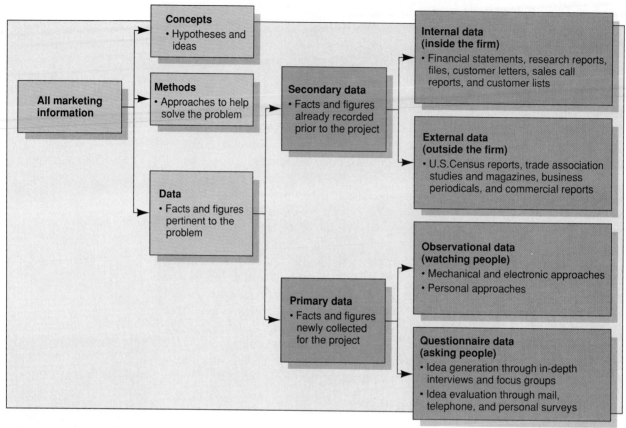

FIGURE 7–3
Types of marketing information

(the Standard Industrial Classifications described in Chapter 6). The *U.S. Census of Retail Trade,* also published about every five years, provides comparable detailed information on retailers.

In addition, trade associations, universities, and business periodicals provide detailed data of value to marketing researchers. A number of commercial organizations also serve the research needs of consumer goods manufacturers. The best known is the A. C. Nielsen Company's Nielsen Television Ratings, discussed later in the chapter. *Sales and Marketing Management* magazine publishes four special issues each year that provide useful data for firms selling both consumer and industrial products; sample data from the magazine appear in Chapter 9. Databases and specialized data services can be accessed by a telephone link from a personal computer on a marketer's desk—topics covered in Chapter 9.

Advantages and Disadvantages of Secondary Data   A general rule among marketing people is to use secondary data first and then collect primary data. Two important advantages of secondary data are (1) the tremendous time savings if the data have already been collected and published and (2) the low cost (for example, most census reports are available for only a few dollars each). Furthermore, a greater level of detail is often available through secondary data.

Because the U.S. Census Bureau can require business establishments to report information about themselves, industry data usually are more complete than if a private organization attempted to collect them.

However, these advantages must be weighed against some significant disadvantages. First, the secondary data may be out of date. If you are working on a project and you use 1980 *U.S. Census of Population* data, by 1991 — when you need it — the data would have been already 11 years old. And published data from the 1990 Census of Population taken in April 1990 don't appear until 1992.

Second, the definitions or categories might not be quite right for your project. For example, suppose you are interested in the age group from 13 to 16, but many census data age statistics appear only from the 10 to 14 and 15 to 19 age groupings. Finally, because the data are collected for another purpose, they may not be specific enough for your needs as a marketing researcher. In such cases it may be necessary to collect primary data.

CONCEPT CHECK

1 What are methods?

2 What is the difference between secondary and primary data?

3 What are some advantages and disadvantages of *U.S. Census of Population* data?

PRIMARY DATA

There are really only two ways to collect primary data, the original data for a marketing study: (1) by observing people and (2) by asking them questions.

Observational Data   Facts and figures obtained by watching, either mechanically or in person, how people actually behave is the way marketing researchers collect **observational data**. National TV ratings, such as those of the A.C. Nielsen Company shown in Figure 7–4, are an example of mechanical observational data collected by a "people meter," which is attached to TV sets in 4,000 homes across the country. The people meter is a small box wired to every TV set in the household. When a household member watches TV, he or she is supposed to push a button on the box and to push it again when he or she stops watching. All information is sent automatically through phone lines to Nielsen each night. The people meter is supposed to measure who in the household is watching what program on every TV set owned. The Nielsen TV ratings in Figure 7–4 are the percentage of people-meter households whose TV sets are tuned to the program.

A Nielsen "people meter" collects information about a household's TV viewing.

The people meter's limitations — as with all observational data collected mechanically — relate to how its measurements are taken. Critics of people meters aren't so sure the devices are measuring what they are supposed to. They are concerned that many household members, especially teenagers and the elderly, will find it annoying to hit the button every time they start or stop watching TV. A "passive people meter" now on the drawing board is intended to address some of these problems and is discussed in Chapter 9.[15]

FIGURE 7-4
Nielsen ratings of the top 10 regularly scheduled national television shows for April 15–21, 1991

RANK	PROGRAM	NETWORK	NIELSEN RATING
1	Cheers	NBC	18.8
2	60 Minutes	CBS	18.6
3	Roseanne	ABC	18.3
4	STAT	ABC	17.1
5	Murphy Brown	CBS	16.3
6	Funniest Home Videos	ABC	15.8
7	Designing Women	CBS	15.6
8	Funniest People	ABC	15.4
9	A Different World (tie)	NBC	15.1
9	Empty Nest (tie)	NBC	15.1

Source: Nielsen Media Research.

Nielsen ratings report the percentage of the 88.6 million American households with TV that are watching a specific program. Precision in Nielsen ratings is critical because 1 percentage point change can mean gaining or losing up to $50 million during the main viewing season because advertisers pay rates based on the size of audience for a TV program. Programs that have consistently low ratings—less than 9 percent or 10 percent—often can't get advertisers and are dropped from the air.[16]

Personal observational data, which are collected by having a person watch a marketing activity, are also a type of primary data. For example, Procter & Gamble observes how consumers bake cakes in its Duncan Hines kitchens to see if the baking instructions on the cake mix box are understood and followed correctly. Chrysler watches how drivers sit behind the wheel of a car to see if they can turn or push the radio and air conditioner knobs conveniently.

Personal observation is both useful and flexible, but it can be costly and unreliable when different observers report different conclusions in watching the same event. Also, although observation can reveal *what* people do, it cannot easily determine *why* they do it, such as why they are buying or not buying a product. This is a principal reason for using questionnaires.

Questionnaire Data   **Questionnaire data** are facts and figures obtained by asking people about their attitudes, awareness, intentions, and behaviors. Because so many questions might be asked in questionnaires, it is essential that the researcher concentrate on those directly related to the marketing problem at hand. Many marketing researchers divide questionnaire data used for hypothesis generation from those used for hypothesis evaluation.

Marketing studies for *hypothesis generation* seek to uncover hypotheses that can be evaluated in later research. Hamburger Helper didn't fare too well with consumers when General Mills introduced it. Initial instructions called for cooking a half pound of hamburger separately from the noodles or potatoes, which were later mixed with the hamburger. *Individual interviews* (a single researcher asking questions of one respondent) showed that consumers (1) didn't think it

Focus groups enable a moderator to obtain information from 6 to 10 people at the same time.

contained enough meat and (2) didn't want the hassle of cooking in two different pots. So the Hamburger Helper product manager changed the recipe to call for a full pound of meat and to allow users to prepare it in one dish; this converted a potential failure into a success.[17]

Focus groups are informal sessions in which six to ten past, present, or prospective customers are directed by a discussion leader, or moderator, to identify what they do and don't like about the firm's products and its competitors' products, how they use the products, and special needs they have that the products don't address. Often tape recorded and done in special interviewing rooms with a two-way mirror, these groups enable marketing researchers and managers to hear and watch consumer reactions. The informality and peer support in an effective focus group uncover ideas that are often difficult to obtain with individual interviews. General Motors' Buick Division used a series of focus groups to help develop the features and ads for the Regal two-door, six-passenger coupe. The focus groups revealed that customers wanted a *real* back seat, four-wheel independent suspension, and regular—*not* oversized—bumpers.[18]

In hypothesis evaluation the marketing researcher tests ideas discovered in the idea generation stage to help the marketing manager recommend marketing actions. This test usually is a mail, telephone, or personal survey of a large sample of past, present, or prospective consumers. In choosing between the three alternatives, the marketing researcher has to make important trade-offs (as shown in Figure 7–5) to balance cost against the expected quality of information obtained. The figure shows that personal interview surveys have a major advantage of enabling the interviewer to be flexible in asking probing questions or getting reactions to visual materials. In contrast, mail surveys usually have the lower cost per completed survey. Telephone surveys lie between the other two technologies in terms of flexibility and cost.

FIGURE 7–5

Comparison of mail, telephone, and personal interview surveys

BASIS OF COMPARISON	MAIL SURVEYS	TELEPHONE SURVEYS	PERSONAL INTERVIEW SURVEYS
Cost per completed survey	Usually the least expensive, assuming adequate return rate	Moderately expensive, assuming reasonable completion rate	Most expensive because of interviewer's time and travel expenses
Ability to probe and ask complex questions	Little, since self-administered format must be short and simple	Some, since interviewer can probe and elaborate on questions to a degree	Much, since interviewer can show visual materials, gain rapport, and probe
Opportunity for interviewer to bias results	None, since form is completed without interviewer	Some because of voice inflection of interviewer	Significant because of voice and facial expressions of interviewer
Anonymity given respondent	Complete, since no signature is required	Some because of telephone contact	Little because of face-to-face contact

Suppose tonight after school you open a letter from your state legislator and see a questionnaire that includes the two questions shown here:

QUESTION	YES	NO
Environment		
1 Do you think that our state should enact Gestapo-type laws that would reward citizens for spying on and reporting on other citizens for such offenses as air or water pollution?	☐	☐
University autonomy		
2 Would you agree that administrators of state-supported educational institutions should be discharged for pampering revolutionaries?	☐	☐

He is looking for a "no" answer to the first question and a "yes" to the second. He is "stacking the deck," using leading questions. Reporting statistical results of such biased questions would give a very distorted picture of the constituents' actual opinions. Hence the proper phrasing of a question is vital in uncovering useful marketing information.

Figure 7–6 shows a number of different formats for questions taken from a Wendy's survey that assessed fast-food restaurant preferences among present and prospective consumers. Question 1 is an example of an *open-end question,* which the respondent can answer in his or her own words. In contrast, questions in which the respondent simply checks an answer are *closed-end* or *fixed alternative questions.* Question 2 is an example of the simplest fixed alternative question, a *dichotomous question* that allows only a "yes" or "no" answer.

A fixed alternative question with three or more choices uses a *scale.* Question 5 is an example of a question that uses a *semantic differential scale,* a seven-point scale in which the opposite ends have one- or two-word adjectives that have opposite meanings. For example, depending on how clean the respondent feels that Wendy's is, he or she would check the left-hand space on the scale, the right-hand space, or one of the five intervening points. Question 6 uses a *Likert scale,* in which the respondent is asked to indicate the extent to which he or she agrees or disagrees with a statement.

The questionnaire in Figure 7–6 is an excerpt of a precisely worded survey that provides valuable information to the marketing researcher at Wendy's. Questions 1 to 8 inform him or her about the likes and dislikes in eating out, frequency of eating out at fast-food restaurants generally and at Wendy's specifically, and sources of information used in making decisions about fast-food restaurants. Question 9 gives details about the personal characteristics of the respondent or the respondent's household, which can be used in trying to segment the fast-food market, a topic discussed in Chapter 9.

Figure 7–7 shows typical problems to guard against in wording questions to obtain meaningful answers from respondents (see page 186). For example, in a question of whether you eat at fast-food restaurants regularly, the word *regularly* is ambiguous. Two people might answer "yes" to the question, but one might mean "once a day" while the other means "once or twice a year." Both answers appear as "yes" to the researcher who tabulates them, but they suggest that dramatically different marketing actions be directed to each of these two prospective consumers. Therefore it is essential that marketing research questions be worded precisely so that all respondents interpret the same question similarly.

Interviews and surveys of distributors—retailers and wholesalers in the marketing channel—are also very important for manufacturers. A reason given for the success of many Japanese consumer products in the U.S. market, such as Sony Walkmans and Toyota automobiles, is the stress that Japanese marketers place on obtaining accurate information from their distributors.[19]

Ethical Aspects of Collecting Questionnaire Data   Obtaining marketing research data through telephone and personal interviews is increasingly difficult. Not only do some consumers, retailers, and wholesalers feel they have been bombarded by too many questionnaires, but they are increasingly suspicious of interviewers who claim to be collecting marketing research data but instead are creating an opportunity to get a foot in the door—often both literally and figuratively—and start a sales presentation. This unethical practice has been condemned by legitimate marketing research organizations, which are working to stop such abuses.

Professional marketing researchers also have to make ethical decisions in collecting and using survey data. Examples of potential conflicts include covering up the problems caused by nonrespondents or poor samples, compromising the reliability of a study to complete it, or reporting only part of the data so the client will like the results. Using formal statements on ethical policies and instituting rewards and punishments can improve ethical behavior in marketing research.[20]

Panels and Experiments   Two special ways that observations and questionnaires are sometimes used are panels and experiments.

Marketing researchers often want to know if consumers are changing their behavior over time, and so they take successive measurements of the same

FIGURE 7–6
Sample questions from Wendy's survey

1 What things are most important to you when you decide to eat out and go to a restaurant?

_____

_____

_____

_____

_____

_____

2 Have you eaten fast-food restaurant food in the past three months?
☐ Yes ☐ No

3 If "yes" to Question 2, how often do you eat there?
☐ Once a week or more   ☐ Two or three times a month
☐ Once a month or less

4 How important is it to you that a fast-food restaurant satisfy you on the following characteristics? Check the box that describes your feelings.

CHARAC-TERISTIC	VERY IMPOR-TANT	SOME-WHAT IMPOR-TANT	IMPOR-TANT	UN-IMPOR-TANT	SOME-WHAT UNIMPOR-TANT	VERY UNIMPOR-TANT
Taste of food	☐	☐	☐	☐	☐	☐
Cleanliness	☐	☐	☐	☐	☐	☐
Price	☐	☐	☐	☐	☐	☐
Variety on menu	☐	☐	☐	☐	☐	☐

5 Check the space on the scale below that describes how you feel about Wendy's on the characteristics shown.

CHARACTERISTIC	CHECK THE SPACE DESCRIBING HOW WENDY'S IS		
Taste of food	Tasty __ __ __ __ __ __ __	Not tasty
Cleanliness	Clean __ __ __ __ __ __ __	Dirty
Price	Inexpensive __ __ __ __ __ __ __	Expensive
Variety on menu	Wide __ __ __ __ __ __ __	Narrow

Source: Adapted from a questionnaire developed by Carol Scott and Robert A. Hansen.

people. A **panel** is a sample of consumers or stores from which researchers take a series of measurements. For example, in this way a consumer's switching from one brand of breakfast cereal to another can be measured. Nielsen's national TV ratings are developed from its people-meter households that make up a panel and are measured repeatedly through time.

An **experiment** involves obtaining data by manipulating factors under tightly controlled conditions to test cause and effect. The interest is in whether changing one of the conditions (a cause) will change the behavior of what is studied (the effect). Both the causal conditions and the resulting behavior are variables. Two types of causal conditions can occur: (1) experimental and (2) extraneous independent variables. An **experimental independent variable** (or

FIGURE 7–6 *(concluded)*

6 Check the box that describes your agreement with the statement.

STATEMENT	STRONGLY AGREE	AGREE	DON'T KNOW	DISAGREE	STRONGLY DISAGREE
Adults like to take their families to fast-food restaurants.	☐	☐	☐	☐	☐
Our children have a say in where the family eats.	☐	☐	☐	☐	☐

7 How important is this information about fast-food restaurants?

SOURCE OF INFORMATION	VERY IMPORTANT SOURCE	SOMEWHAT IMPORTANT SOURCE	NOT AN IMPORTANT SOURCE
Television	☐	☐	☐
Newspapers	☐	☐	☐
Billboards	☐	☐	☐
Mail	☐	☐	☐

8 In the past three months, how often have you eaten at each of these three fast-food restaurants?

RESTAURANT	ONCE A WEEK OR MORE	TWO OR THREE TIMES A MONTH	ONCE A MONTH OR LESS
Burger King	☐	☐	☐
McDonald's	☐	☐	☐
Wendy's	☐	☐	☐

9 Please answer the following questions about you and your household.
  a Are you ☐ Male ☐ Female
  b Are you ☐ Single ☐ Married ☐ Other (widowed, divorced)
  c How many children under age 18 live in your home?
    ☐ 0 ☐ 1 ☐ 2 ☐ 3 ☐ 4 ☐ 5 or more
  d What is your age?
    ☐ 24 or less ☐ 25–39 ☐ 40 or over
  e What is your approximate total annual household income?
    ☐ Less than $15,000 ☐ $15,000–$30,000 ☐ More than $30,000

simply, the experimental variable) is the causal condition manipulated or controlled by the experimenter. In contrast, an **extraneous independent variable** (or simply, the extraneous variable) is the causal condition that is a result of outside factors that the experimenter cannot control. Such a variable might change the behavior of what is studied.

The change in the behavior of what is studied is called the **dependent variable**. The experimenter tries to arrange a change in the independent variable and then measure the accompanying change, or absence of it, in the dependent variable.

In marketing experiments the experimental independent variables are often one or more of the marketing mix variables, such as the product features, price,

FIGURE 7–7
Typical problems in wording questions

PROBLEM	SAMPLE QUESTION	EXPLANATION
Leading question	Why do you like Wendy's fresh meat hamburgers better than those of competitors made with frozen meat?	Consumer is led to make statement favoring Wendy's hamburgers.
Ambiguous question	Do you eat at fast-food restaurants regularly? ☐ Yes ☐ No	What is meant by word *regularly*—once a day, once a month, or what?
Unanswerable question	What was the occasion for your eating your first hamburger?	Who can remember the answer? Does it matter?
Two questions in one	Do you eat Wendy's hamburgers and chili? ☐ Yes ☐ No	How do you answer if you eat Wendy's hamburgers but not chili?
Nonexhaustive question	Where do you live? ☐ At home ☐ In dormitory	What do you check if you live in an apartment?
Nonmutually exclusive answers	What is your age? ☐ Under 20 ☐ 20–40 ☐ 40 and over	What answer does a 40-year-old check?

or advertising used. The ideal dependent variable usually is a change in purchases of an individual, household, or entire organization. If actual purchases cannot be used as a dependent variable, factors that are believed to be highly related to purchases, such as preferences in a taste test or intentions to buy, are used.

A potential difficulty with experiments is that extraneous independent variables can distort the results of an experiment and affect the dependent variable. A researcher's task is to identify the effect of the experimental variable of interest on the dependent variable when the effects of extraneous variables in an experiment might hide it. The Coke taste test experiment described in the next sections illustrates some of the potential dangers of marketing experiments.

Advantages and Disadvantages of Primary Data   Compared with secondary data, primary data have the advantage of being more timely and specific to the problem being studied. The main disadvantages are that primary data are usually far more costly and time consuming to collect than secondary data.

CONCEPT CHECK

1 A mail questionnaire asks you, "Do you eat pizza?" What kind of question is this?

2 Does a mail, telephone, or personal interview survey provide the greatest flexibility for asking probing questions?

3 What is the difference between an independent and dependent variable?

Coca-Cola's marketing dilemma: Who's taking market share from whom? For Coca-Cola's puzzling problem and the lessons it hopes it has learned, see the text.

STEP 4: FIND A SOLUTION

Mark Twain once observed, "Collecting data is like collecting garbage. You've got to know what you're going to do with the stuff before you collect it." The purpose of Step 4 is to analyze the collected data effectively to keep it from having the value of garbage. This requires using the data to find the alternative that best meets the measure of success the decision maker specified in defining the problem, and then to put that alternative into effect. Coca-Cola's continuing decisions on its "new Coke" illustrate both Steps 4 and 5 of the decision-making process discussed in this chapter.

CHOOSE THE BEST ALTERNATIVE: THE PROBLEM'S SOLUTION

The **solution** is simply the best alternative that has been identified to solve the problem. We recognize the best alternative by finding the one that best meets the measure of success established in defining the problem (Step 1). Through the early 1980s the Coca-Cola Company had a terrible dilemma: its old reliable "Formula 7X," that had been the backbone of the company for a century, was losing market share to arch-rival Pepsi-Cola. Blind taste tests (the actual brand hidden from the taster) showed that cola drinkers preferred the sweeter Pepsi to the crisper taste of the original Coke. Because of this, Coca-Cola conducted a $4 million, three-year study involving over 190,000 taste tests around the United States in search of a new formulation for Coke that consumers would prefer to the original 7X Formula and to Pepsi. Thus the company's measure of success evolved: the new formula that would be most preferred to the original 7X formula. So Coca-Cola marketing executives developed a new, sweeter formula for Coke, which became "new" Coke. The result: in blind taste tests consumers preferred the new to the old Coke formula 53 percent to 47 percent. Coca-Cola executives thought they had found the solution to their competitive problem with Pepsi.[21]

IMPLEMENT THE CHOSEN ALTERNATIVE

Identifying the best alternative—the potential solution—to the problem isn't enough. The difficulty is that no one may get around to putting the solution into effect. Someone must "make something happen"—see that the solution gets implemented.

In the case of Coke, company executives decided to replace the 7X formula with the new sweeter-tasting formula using the marketing program shown under the title "the original 1985 strategy" in the accompanying Marketing Action Memo. The company introduced the new formula amid much fanfare, thereby implementing a marketing program to put what it believed was the best alternative into effect.

This was one of the most carefully planned brand transitions in history, a marketing program to replace an existing successful brand with a new, expected-to-be-more-successful brand. Coca-Cola spent tens of millions of dollars in developing and marketing its new sweeter cola. Management experience and judgment were paired with the available marketing research. The marketing program was planned and implemented in excruciating detail.

In terms of Step 4, Coca-Cola had developed the marketing plan for its new cola very carefully and then worked hard to implement it. However, as is often the case with new products, things didn't work out quite as expected. That is the reason for evaluation, the final step in the decision process.

STEP 5: EVALUATE THE RESULTS

Evaluating results is a continuing way of life for effective marketing managers. There are really two aspects of this evaluation process:

- *Evaluate the decision itself:* This involves comparing actual results with plans and the measure of success defined in Step 1. If results don't achieve what is targeted, the next step is taking appropriate corrective action—the evaluation activity described in Chapter 2.
- *Evaluate the decision process used:* This involves changing the activities in one or more of the steps used in reaching a decision, such as altering the methods used to define the problem, collect the data, or implement the plan.

A careful look at the new Coke marketing program can reveal how marketing managers learn lessons from unpleasant results and try to move a marketing program forward.

EVALUATION OF THE DECISION ITSELF: THE NEW COKE STRATEGY

For the three months following the introduction of new Coke, Coca-Cola's Atlanta headquarters was bombarded by 1,500 phone calls daily from angry Coke drinkers asking the company to return to 7X (the original Coke formu-

Marketing Action Memo

COCA-COLA'S MARKETING STRATEGY FOR THE SAME SWEETER COLA—SIX YEARS APART

*W*hat marketing lessons has the Coca-Cola Company learned about marketing its sweeter-tasting cola after its 1985 fiasco? One major lesson: the original 1985 new product introduction avoid- ed a direct confrontation with Pepsi, whereas the 1991 strategy puts Coke II in a head-to-head fight with its arch-rival. The table below compares the two strategies:

MARKETING MIX ELEMENT	ORIGINAL 1985 STRATEGY	"QUICK-FIX" 1985 STRATEGY	1991 STRATEGY
Product	Introduce a sweeter-tasting cola under the Coca-Cola brand name. Drop the old 7X formula. Retain original packaging design.	Name the new, sweeter cola "Coke" and package it using a red and white design. Bring back the 7X formula as "Coca-Cola Classic."	Relaunch new Coke as "Coke II." Put splashes of blue on the can—to go head-to-head against Pepsi. Continue offering Coca-Cola Classic.
Price	After initial "cents-off" deals, set same price as competitors.	Same.	Same.
Promotion	Introduce the sweeter formula as "responding to consumer preferences." Target promotions at consumers and distributors.	Reintroduce the 7X formula as "bowing to the desires of the American public." Advertise both products heavily.	Use advertising that stresses Coke II gives a "real cola taste" with the sweetness of Pepsi.
Place	Phase the new Coca-Cola into distribution. Phase out 7X line.	Distribute both new Coke and Coca-Cola Classic.	Distribute both Coke II and Coca-Cola Classic.

Sources: Michael J. McCarthy, "New Coke Gets a New Look, New Chance," *The Wall Street Journal* (March 7, 1990), pp. B1, B7; and Thomas More, "He Put the Kick Back into Coke," *Fortune* (October 26, 1987), pp. 46–56.

lation). On July 10, 1985, in front of TV cameras, the head of the company announced the return of 7X as "Coca-Cola Classic" and retained the new formulation as simply "Coke." The feedback loop in Figure 7–1 reflects this action: in the evaluation process (Step 5) the company redefined its problem and went back to Step 1 to initiate a new marketing program.

The column in the Marketing Action Memo headed "Quick-Fix 1985 Strategy" summarizes these actions. But by offering both Coca-Cola Classic and new Coke, the company ran the danger of the two brands cannibalizing each other rather than taking market share from Pepsi—the original reason for the new formula and marketing program.

While the 1985 quick-fix strategy bought time for the Coca-Cola Company, it didn't solve its most fundamental quandary: what should it do with the two brands now? As the company's marketing strategists labored over this question, one thing became evident: the original 1985 new Coke launch had

" CHEESEBURGER AND A COKE,... IS THAT THE NEW COKE OR THE OLD COKE
OR THE NEW OLD COKE OR THE OLD NEW COKE OR THE OLD OLD....?"

inadvertently positioned new Coke against the original Coke formula in the minds of cola drinkers across the country! It had *not* done what it was intended to do—position the new Coke against Pepsi.

Market-share information also highlights why the problem of new Coke won't disappear quietly. Figure 7–8 shows that at the start of 1990, Coca-Cola Classic was outselling new Coke 19 to 1. The declining market share of new Coke is critical because in the $40 billion U.S. soft-drink market, a decline of 1 percent in market share represents $400 million in lost sales. And Coca-Cola's taste tests still showed that its new Coke was a stronger competitor to Pepsi than Coca-Cola Classic.

Both the soft-drink industry and Coca-Cola executives still believe that new Coke's sweeter taste wins over Pepsi in blind taste tests. As a result, this process of continuing evaluation has given rise to the company's new strategy: give a new life to new Coke and take great care to position it against Pepsi, not Coca-Cola Classic!

To bring this about, in a 1991 test market Coca-Cola gave new Coke a new name—Coke II—and a new package to compete directly with Pepsi ("1991 strategy" column in the Marketing Action Memo). Whether the Coke II name and the red and white packaging with a trace of blue—the Pepsi colors—will increase new Coke II's share of the $40 billion soft-drink market is up to consumers across America.[22]

EVALUATION OF THE DECISION PROCESS: THE NEW COKE STRATEGY

Postmortems of the decision process itself help to avoid repeating the same error over and over. In the case of new Coke, the Coca-Cola Company has learned several lessons. First, marketing research lessons include the need to use a well-

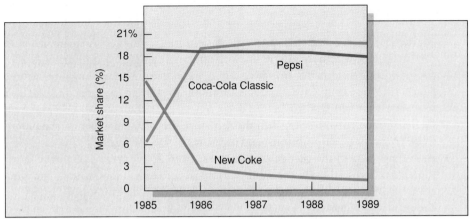

FIGURE 7–8
Market shares since the 1985 introduction of new Coke

Source: Wheat, First Securities Inc., as cited in Michael J. McCarthy, "New Coke Gets a New Look, New Chance," *The Wall Street Journal* (March 7, 1990), p. B1. Reprinted by permission of *The Wall Street Journal,* © 1990 Dow Jones & Company, Inc. All Rights Reserved Worldwide.

known brand name like Coke in taste experiments and to explain to participants that in choosing a new cola formula, the company would drop the original Coke formula.[23]

Perhaps equally important, the decision process must keep in mind the objectives of the marketing program, in this case taking market share away from Pepsi. In the original 1985 new Coke launch, the company accidentally wound up competing with itself because of the accompanying bad publicity. Future new product introductions by the company should take care that the decision process recognizes the need to avoid cannibalizing its own products.

CONCEPT CHECK

1 **Why can't a marketing manager's decision making stop with selecting the best alternative to solve a problem?**

2 **What two factors should be evaluated after reaching a decision?**

ETHICS AND SOCIAL RESPONSIBILITY IN THE 1990s

HOW MUCH SHOULD YOU TELL YOUR CLIENT?

As a marketing researcher, you mail out 1,000 questionnaires for a client to find out what American consumers want when they buy a new 35 mm camera. You get back only 50 completed questionnaires, and you are concerned that the returns may give a biased picture of what these camera buyers want. What kind of bias may be present? Should you tell your client about your concerns or just tabulate the data and write your final report?

SUMMARY

1 Marketing research is the process of defining a marketing problem and opportunity, systematically collecting and analyzing information, and recommending actions to improve an organization's marketing activities. Marketing research assists in decision making. The chapter uses a five-step sequence that can lead to better decisions.

2 Defining the problem, Step 1 in the sequence, involves identifying the objectives, constraints, assumptions, and measures of success related to the problem.

3 Assessing two kinds of decision factors, Step 2, requires specifying both the alternatives (the controllable variables) and the uncertainties (the uncontrollable variables) that interact to lead to the outcome—good or bad—of the decision.

4 Collecting relevant information, Step 3, includes considering pertinent concepts, methods, and data.

5 Secondary data have been recorded prior to the project and include those internal and external to the organization.

6 Primary data are collected specifically for the project and are obtained by either observing or questioning people. In the latter case ideas are often generated through individual interviews and focus groups. Ideas are often evaluated using large-scale mail, telephone, or personal interview surveys.

7 Experiments manipulate a situation to measure the effect of an independent variable (cause) on the dependent variable (result or effect). With panels, repeated measurements are taken from the sample units—such as consumers or stores.

8 Finding the solution to a problem is Step 4. It involves both selecting the alternative that best meets the measures of success specified in Step 1 and also developing and executing a plan to put the chosen alternative into effect.

9 Step 5 in the sequence involves evaluating both the decision itself and the process used to reach it and helps the decision maker learn lessons that can be used in the future.

KEY TERMS AND CONCEPTS

marketing research p. 168	nonprobability sampling p. 177
decision p. 170	statistical inference p. 177
objectives p. 171	data p. 177
constraints p. 171	secondary data p. 177
assumptions p. 172	primary data p. 177
measures of success p. 172	observational data p. 179
decision factors p. 173	questionnaire data p. 180
alternatives p. 173	panel p. 183
uncertainties p. 173	experiment p. 184
hypothesis p. 175	experimental independent variable p. 184
new product concept p. 175	extraneous independent variable p. 185
methods p. 175	dependent variable p. 185
probability sampling p. 176	solution p. 187

CHAPTER PROBLEMS AND APPLICATIONS

1 Before the people meter, Nielsen obtained national TV ratings by using "audimeters" attached to TV sets in 1,170 American households. These devices measured (1) if the TV set was turned on and (2) if so, to which channel. What are the limitations of this mechanical observation method?

2 Before the people meter, Nielsen obtained ratings of local TV stations by having households fill out diary questionnaires. These gave information on (1) who was watching TV and (2) what program. What are the limitations of this questionnaire method?

3 For the two questions in the legislator's questionnaire shown in the chapter, (a) what is the factual issue for which opinions are sought and (b) how has the legislator managed to bias the question to get the answer he wants?

4 Rework Question 1 in the legislator's questionnaire to make it an unbiased question in the form of (a) an open-end question and (b) a Likert scale question.

5 Suppose Fisher-Price wants to run an experimental and control group experiment to evaluate a proposed chatter telephone design. It has two different groups of children on which to run an experiment for one week each. The control group has the old toy telephone, whereas the experimental group is exposed to the newly designed pull toy with wheels, a noisemaker, and bobbing eyes. The dependent variable is the average number of minutes during the two-hour play period that one of the children is playing with the toy, and the results are as follows:

ACTIVITY	EXPERIMENTAL GROUP	CONTROL GROUP
Experimental variable	New design	Old design
After measurement	62 minutes	13 minutes

Should Fisher-Price introduce the new design? Why?

6 A rich aunt has decided to set you up in a business of your own choosing. To her delight, you decide on a service business—giving flying lessons in ultralight planes to your fellow college students. Some questions from the first draft of a mail questionnaire you plan to use are shown below. In terms of Figure 7–7, (a) identify the problem with each question and (b) correct it. NOTE: Some questions may have more than one problem.

a Have you ever flown in commercial airliners and in ultralight planes?
  ☐ Yes ☐ No

b Why do you think ultralights are so much safer than hang gliders?

_____

c When did you first know you like to fly?
  ☐ Under 10 ☐ 10 to 20 ☐ 21 to 30 ☐ Over 30

d How much did you spend on recreational activities last year?
  ☐ $100 or less   ☐ $401 to $800   ☐ $1,201 to $1,600
  ☐ $101 to $400   ☐ $801 to $1,201 ☐ $1,600 or more

e How much would you pay for ultralight flying lessons? _____

f Would you sign up for a class that met regularly? ☐ Yes ☐ No

7 As owner of a chain of supermarkets, you get the idea that you could sell more fresh strawberries by leaving them individually out on a tray and letting customers then fill their own pint or quart box with strawberries. (a) Describe an experiment to test this idea. (b) What are some possible measures of success?

8 Suppose on a rainy night you are driving on a two-lane highway at 50 miles per hour. As you come over the crest of the hill, you see that a car 100 yards ahead of you has plowed into a tank truck, obstructing your lane. You are afraid that too much braking will cause a bad skid, so your main choices are to steer into the left lane or into the right shoulder. Further, you can't tell if traffic is coming toward you. Apply the five steps of the decision sequence to address this problem.

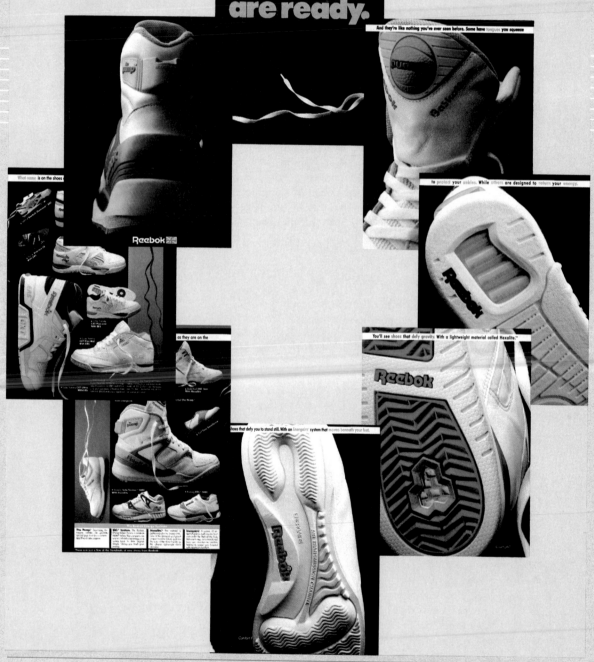

Welcome to the 90's. Your shoes are ready.

And they're like nothing you've ever seen before. Some have tongues you squeeze

to protect your ankles. While others are designed to return your energy.

You'll see shoes that defy gravity. With a lightweight material called Hexalite.™

shoes that defy you to stand still. With an Energaire™ system that moves beneath your feet.

Reebok

CHAPTER 8

Market Segmentation, Targeting, and Positioning

After reading this chapter you should be able to:

- Explain what market segmentation is, when to use it, and the five steps used in segmentation.

- Recognize the different factors used to segment consumer and industrial markets.

- Understand the significance of heavy, medium, and light users and nonusers in targeting markets.

- Develop a market-product grid to use in segmenting and targeting a market.

- Interpret a cross tabulation to analyze market segments.

- Understand how marketing managers position products in the marketplace.

Reebok: Changing Forever (?) What You Put on Your Feet

As you read this you just might be wearing a shoe pictured in the accompanying ad. This is possible because of a very unlikely occurrence in 1979.

That's the year when Paul Fireman, a camping equipment distributor, wandered through an international trade fair and saw Reebok's custom track shoes. He bought the U.S. license from the British manufacturer and started producing top-of-the-line running shoes. Sales hit $1.5 million in 1981, but Fireman saw that the running boom had peaked and he needed other opportunities. This realization put him a giant step ahead of Nike, which kept churning out running shoes that were piling up in warehouses.[1]

In a brilliant marketing decision, Fireman introduced the first soft-leather aerobic-dance shoe—the Reebok "Freestyle"—in 1982. The flamboyant colors of these Reebok designer sneakers captured the attention of aerobic-dance instructors and students alike. This color strategy still helps the sneakers get good display space in stores and attracts a lot of consumer attention.

Today known as Reebok International, Ltd., the firm successively introduced tennis shoes, children's shoes ("Weeboks"), and basketball shoes in 1984 and walking shoes in 1986. For those who don't want to buy four different pairs of shoes to run, play tennis, shoot baskets, and walk in, Reebok introduced—of course—"cross-trainers" in 1988. This was soon followed by the $170 Reebok "Pump," a high-tech, high-top basketball sneaker with its own built-in air compressor located in the toe of the shoe. The Pump outsold Nike's competitive shoe (which has air pumped into it with a separate device) by 20 to 1. Both Reebok and Nike are moving aggressively into the European sport-shoe markets in the 1990s.[2]

The Reebok strategy, making shoes designed to satisfy needs of different customers, illustrates successful market segmentation, the main topic of this chapter. It also helps explain why Reebok's sales grew by more than 100,000 percent—from $1.5 million to over $1.8 billion—in the decade from 1981 to 1991.

After discussing why markets need to be segmented, this chapter covers the steps a firm uses in segmenting and targeting a market and then positioning its offering in the marketplace.

WHY SEGMENT MARKETS?

A business firm segments its markets so it can respond more effectively to the wants of groups of prospective buyers and thus increase its sales and profits. Nonprofit organizations also segment the clients they serve to satisfy client needs more effectively while achieving the organization's goals. Let's use the dilemma of sneaker buyers finding their ideal Reebok shoes to describe (1) what market segmentation is and (2) when it is necessary to segment markets.

WHAT MARKET SEGMENTATION MEANS

People have different needs and wants, even though it would be easier for marketers if they didn't. **Market segmentation** involves aggregating prospective buyers into groups that (1) have common needs and (2) will respond similarly to a marketing action. The groups that result from this process are **market segments,** a relatively homogeneous collection of prospective buyers.

The existence of different market segments has caused firms to use a marketing strategy of **product differentiation,** a strategy that has come to have two different but related meanings. In its broadest sense, product differentiation involves a firm's using different marketing mix activities, such as product features and advertising, to help consumers perceive the product as being different and better than competing products. The perceived differences may involve physical features or nonphysical ones, such as image or price.[3]

In a narrower sense, product differentiation involves a firm's selling two or more products with different features targeted to different market segments. A firm can get into trouble when its different products blend together in consumers' minds and don't reach distinct market segments successfully. The Reebok example discussed next shows both how a manufacturer has succeeded in using a product differentiation strategy to offer different products targeted to separate market segments and also how its success is forcing new efforts to separate two groups of its shoes in consumers' minds.

Segmentation: Linking Needs to Actions   The definition of market segmentation first stresses the importance of aggregating—or grouping—people or organizations in a market according to the similarity of their needs and the benefits they are looking for in making a purchase. Second, such needs and benefits must be related to specific, tangible marketing actions the firm can take. These actions may involve separate products or other aspects of the marketing mix such as price, advertising or personal selling activities, or distribution strategies—the four Ps.

The process of segmenting a market and selecting specific segments as targets is the link between the various buyers' needs and the organization's marketing program (Figure 8–1). Market segmentation is only a means to an end: in an economist's terms, it relates supply (the organization's actions) to demand (customer needs). A basic test of the usefulness of the segmentation process is whether it leads to tangible marketing actions.

Using Market-Product Grids   A **market-product grid** is a framework to relate the segments of a market to products offered or potential marketing actions by the firm. The grid in Figure 8–2 shows different markets of sneaker users as rows in the grid, while the columns show the different shoe products (or marketing actions) chosen by Reebok.

The darker-shaded cells in Figure 8–2, labeled P, represent the primary market segment that Reebok targeted when it introduced each shoe. The lightly shaded cells labeled S represent the secondary market segments that also started buying the shoe. In some cases, Reebok discovered that large numbers of people in a segment not originally targeted for a style of shoe bought the shoe. In fact, as many as 75 to 80 percent of the running shoes and aerobic-dance shoes are bought by nonathletes represented by the (1) comfort- and style-conscious and (2) walker segments shown in Figure 8–2—although walkers may object to being labeled "nonathletes." When this trend became apparent to Reebok in 1986, it introduced its walking shoes targeted directly at the walker segment.

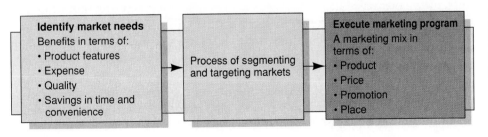

FIGURE 8–1
Market segmentation links market needs to an organization's marketing program

MARKET SEGMENT		PRODUCT (Kind of shoes)						
GENERAL	GROUP WITH NEED	RUNNING (1981)	AEROBIC (1982)	TENNIS (1984)	BASKET-BALL (1984)	WALKING (1986)	CROSS-TRAINERS (1988)	CHILDREN'S (1984)
Performance-concious consumers (athletes)	Runners	P					P	
	Aerobic dancers		P				P	
	Tennis players			P			P	
	Basketball players				P		P	
Fashion-concious consumers (nonathletes)	Comfort - and style-conscious	S	S	S	S	S	S	
	Walkers	S	S	S	S	P	P	
	Children							P

Key: P = primary market; S = secondary market

FIGURE 8–2
Market-product grid showing how seven different styles of Reebok shoes reach segments of customers with different needs

Figure 8–2 also introduces one of the potential dangers of market segmentation for a firm: subdividing an entire market into two or more segments, thereby increasing the competition from other firms that focus their efforts on a single segment. Notice that Reebok's strategy is to reach both the performance (athletes) and fashion (nonathletes) segments. In the 1990s Reebok finds itself trying to clarify its vague identity among consumers who see Nike as a "performance shoe" and L.A. Gear as a "fashion shoe." In trying to compete in both markets, Reebok runs the danger of being first in neither.[4] To be more responsive to both markets, in 1990 Reebok divided its U.S. operations into two separate units: "Technology," targeted at athletes, performance-oriented consumers, and children; and "Lifestyle," targeted at style-conscious consumers.

WHEN TO SEGMENT MARKETS

A business firm goes to the trouble and expense of segmenting its markets when this increases its sales revenue, profit, and ROI. When its expenses more than offset the potentially increased revenues from segmentation, it should not attempt to segment its market. The specific situations that illustrate this point are the cases of (1) one product and multiple market segments and (2) multiple products and multiple market segments.

One Product and Multiple Market Segments   When a firm produces only a single product or service and attempts to sell it to two or more market segments, it avoids the extra cost of developing and producing additional versions of the product, which often entail extremely high research, engineering, and manufacturing expenses. In this case the incremental costs of taking the product into new product segments are typically those of a separate promotional campaign or a new channel of distribution. Although these expenses can be high, they are rarely as large as those for developing an entirely new product.

Movies and magazines are single products frequently directed to two or more distinct market segments. Movie companies often run different TV commercials featuring different aspects of a newly released film (love, or drama, or spectacular scenery) that are targeted to different market segments. As shown in the margin at right, Street and Smith's official yearbook, *College Football,* uses different covers in different regions of the United States, featuring a college football star from that region. *Time* magazine now publishes more than 200 different U.S. editions and also over 100 international editions, each targeted at its own geographic and demographic segments and its own mix of advertisements. Although multiple TV commercials for movies and separate covers or advertisements for magazines are expensive, they are minor compared with the costs of producing an entirely new movie or magazine for another market segment. Even Procter & Gamble is now marketing its Crest toothpaste with different advertising campaigns targeted at six different market segments, including children, Hispanics, and senior citizens.[5]

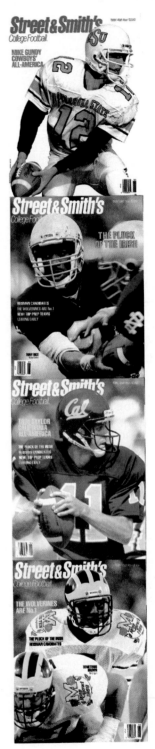

Multiple Products and Multiple Market Segments   Reebok's seven different styles of shoes, each targeted at a different type of user, are an example of multiple products aimed at multiple markets. Manufacturing seven styles of shoes is clearly more expensive than producing one but seems worthwhile if it serves customers' needs better, doesn't reduce quality or increase price, and adds to the sales revenues and profits.

Product differentiation is generally an effective strategy, as in the Reebok example. But it can be carried too far. For example, in some cases American auto manufacturers have offered so many models and options to try to reach diverse market segments that sales revenue and profits have suffered in competition with imports.

The three basic elements that distinguish one model of car from another are (1) frames, (2) engines and drive trains, and (3) name plates. Adding other options in the form of various (4) body styles, (5) transmissions, (6) interiors, and (7) colors results in an incredible number of options. Perhaps the extreme case occurred in 1982 when Ford Thunderbird had exactly 69,120 options compared with 32 (including colors) on the 1982 Honda Accord (Figure 8–3). Some experts estimate the proliferation of these options has added an average of $1,000 to the sticker price of American cars—giving American consumers another reason to buy the lower-priced Japanese imports. Japanese manufacturers have done extensive marketing research on American consumers and have selected a combination of options to meet the most typical needs.[6]

American car manufacturers are concluding that the costs of developing, producing, and servicing dozens of slightly different products probably outweigh the premium that consumers are willing to pay for the wider array of choices and are simplifying their product lines. For example, Ford's Thunderbird now has fewer options, and its sales brochures stress "preferred equipment

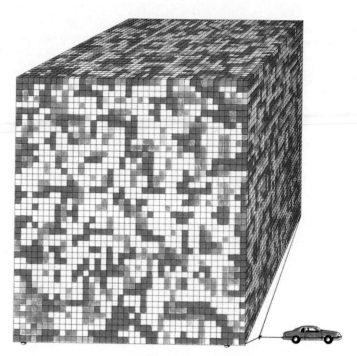

Honda Accord: 32 option combinations   **Ford Thunderbird:** 69,120 option combinations

Source: James Cook, "Where's the Niche?" *Forbes* (September 24, 1984), p. 54. © Forbes Inc., 1984.

FIGURE 8–3

Product differentiation running wild; the number of options available on a 1982 Ford Thunderbird compared with those on a Honda Accord

packages" to simplify buying decisions for customers. GM, too, is trying to reduce the number of options and models it offers: by 1992 it plans to eliminate 43 of the 175 models it offered in 1990.[7] Although there are fewer choices, this provides two benefits to consumers: (1) lower prices through higher volume production of fewer models and (2) higher quality because of the ability to debug fewer basic designs.

CONCEPT CHECK

1 Market segmentation involves dividing a market into distinct groups that have two key characteristics. What are they?

2 What is product differentiation?

3 The process of segmenting and targeting markets is a bridge between what two marketing activities?

STEPS IN SEGMENTING AND TARGETING MARKETS

The process of segmenting a market and then selecting and reaching the target segments is divided into the five steps discussed in this section. Segmenting a market is not a science—it requires large doses of common sense and managerial judgment.[8]

Market segmentation and target markets can be abstract topics, so put on your entrepreneur's hat to experience the process. Suppose you own a Wendy's fast-food restaurant next to a large urban university that offers both day and evening classes. Your restaurant specializes in the Wendy's basics: hamburgers, french fries, Frosty milkshakes, and chili. Even though you are part of a chain and have some restrictions on menu and decor, you are free to set your hours of business and to undertake local advertising. How can market segmentation help?

FORM PROSPECTIVE BUYERS INTO SEGMENTS

Grouping prospective buyers into meaningful segments involves meeting some specific criteria for segmentation and finding specific variables to segment the consumer or industrial market being analyzed.[9]

Criteria to Use in Forming the Segments   A marketing manager should develop segments for a market that meet five principal criteria (Figure 8–4):

- *Potential for increased profit and ROI:* The best segmentation approach is the one that maximizes the opportunity for future profit and ROI. If this potential is maximized through no segmentation, don't segment. For nonprofit organizations, the analogous criterion is the potential for serving client users more effectively.
- *Similarity of needs of potential buyers within a segment:* Potential buyers within a segment should be similar in terms of a marketing activity, such as product features sought or advertising media used.
- *Difference of needs of buyers among segments:* If the needs of the various segments aren't appreciably different, combine them into fewer segments. A different segment usually requires a different marketing action that in turn means greater costs. If increased revenues don't offset extra costs, combine segments and reduce the number of marketing actions.
- *Feasibility of a marketing action to reach a segment:* Reaching a segment requires a simple but effective marketing action. If no such action exists, don't segment.
- *Simplicity and cost of assigning potential buyers to segments:* A marketing manager must be able to put a market segmentation plan into effect. This means being able to recognize the characteristics of potential buyers and assign them to a segment.

FIGURE 8–4
The process of segmenting and targeting markets connects the firm's marketing actions to its identification of marketing needs

Ways to Segment Consumer Markets   Figure 8–5 shows a number of variables that can be used to segment consumer markets. They are divided into two general categories: customer characteristics and buying situation. Some examples of how certain characteristics can be used to segment specific markets include the following:

- *Region* (a geographical customer characteristic): Campbell's found that its new canned nacho cheese sauce, which could be heated and poured directly onto nacho chips, was too hot for Americans in the East and not hot enough for those in the West and Southwest. The result: today Campbell's plants in Texas and California produce a hotter nacho cheese sauce to serve their regions than that produced in the other plants.
- *Family size* (a demographic customer characteristic): More than half of all U.S. households have only one or two persons in them, so Campbell's packages meals with only one or two servings —from Great Starts breakfasts to L'Orient dinners. Because these smaller households often have smaller kitchens, GE downsized its microwave oven, restyled it to hang under a kitchen cabinet, and moved into the number 2 position in microwaves. However, GE also offers extra large refrigerators for growing families at the beginning of their family life cycle.[10]
- *Lifestyle* (a psychographic customer characteristic): Psychographic variables are consumer activities, interests, and opinions. Knowing that a specific consumer segment is liberal politically, likes science fiction, and likes to take chances is of value in designing movies and TV commercials.
- *Benefits offered* (a situation characteristic): Important benefits offered to different customers are often a useful way to segment markets because they can lead directly to specific marketing actions, such as a new product or ad campaign.[11] For example, some consumers want or need a more healthy lifestyle. The H. J. Heinz Company's Weight Watchers unit has achieved great success with its diet centers; it recently extended its line of low-calorie foods by developing a mayonnaise without cholesterol. What may become the hottest new appliance of the 1990s is MicroFridge Inc.'s combination microwave/refrigerator/freezer aimed at college dorm students.[12]

MicroFridge: the "All-Everything Appliance" for a student's dorm room.

FIGURE 8–5
Segmentation variables and breakdowns for consumer markets

MAIN DIMENSION	SEGMENTATION VARIABLE	TYPICAL BREAKDOWNS
CUSTOMER CHARACTERISTICS		
Geographic	Region	Pacific; Mountain; West North Central; West South Central; East North Central; East South Central; South Atlantic; Middle Atlantic; New England
	City or metropolitan statistical area (MSA) size	Under 5,000; 5,000 to 19,999; 20,000 to 49,999; 50,000 to 99,999; 100,000 to 249,999; 250,000 to 499,999; 500,000 to 999,999; 1,000,000 to 3,999,999; 4,000,000 or over
	Density	Urban; suburban; rural
	Climate	Northern; Southern
Demographic	Age	Infant, under 6; 6 to 11; 12 to 17; 18 to 24; 25 to 34; 35 to 49; 50 to 64; 65 or over
	Sex	Male; female
	Family size	1 to 2; 3 to 4; 5 or over
	Stage of family life cycle	Young single; young married, no children; young married, youngest child under 6; young married, youngest child 6 or older; older married, with children; older married, no children under 18; older single; other older married, no children under 18
	Ages of children	No child under 18; youngest child 6 to 17; youngest child under 6
	Children under 18	0; 1; more than 1
	Income	Under $5,000; $5,000 to $14,999; $15,000 to $24,999; $25,000 to $34,999; $35,000 to $49,999; $50,000 or over
	Education	Grade school or less; some high school; high school graduate; some college; college graduate
	Race	Asian; black; Hispanic; white; other
	Home ownership	Own home; rent home
Psychographic	Personality	Gregarious; compulsive; extroverted; aggressive; ambitious
	Lifestyle	Use of one's time; values and importance; beliefs
BUYING SITUATIONS		
Benefits sought	Product features	Situation specific; general
	Needs	Quality; service; economy
Usage	Rate of use	Light user; medium user; heavy user
	User states	Nonuser; ex-user; prospect; first-time user; regular user
Awareness and intentions	Readiness to buy	Unaware; aware; informed; interested; intending to buy
	Brand familiarity	Insistence; preference; recognition; nonrecognition; rejection
Buying condition	Type of buying activity	Minimum effort buying; comparison buying; special effort buying
	Kind of store	Convenience; wide breadth; specialty

- **Usage rate** (which refers to quantity consumed or patronage—store visits—during a specific period, and varies significantly among different customer groups): Airlines have developed frequent-flyer programs to encourage passengers to use the same airline repeatedly—a technique sometimes called "frequency marketing," which focuses on usage rate.[13] This usage rate is often stated as the **80/20 rule**, a concept that suggests that 80 percent of a firm's sales are obtained from 20 percent of its customers.

The percentages in the 80/20 rule are not really fixed at exactly 80 percent and 20 percent, but rather suggest that a small fraction of customers provides a large fraction of a firm's sales. For example, Simmons Market Research Bureau, Inc., periodically surveys about 20,000 adults 18 years of age and older to discover how the products and services they buy and the media they watch relate to their demographic characteristics. Figure 8–6 shows the results of a question Simmons asks about the respondent's frequency of use (or patronage) of "fast-food, drive-in, family, and steak house restaurants."

As shown in the right column of Figure 8–6, the importance of the segment increases as we move up the table. Among nonusers of these restaurants, prospects (who *might become* users) are more important than nonprospects (who are *never likely* to become users). Moving up the rows to the users, it seems logical that light users of these restaurants (1 to 5 times per month) are important but less so than medium users (6 to 13 times per month), who in turn are a less important segment than the critical group—the heavy users (14 or more times per month). The "Actual Consumption" column in Figure 8–6 tells how much of the total monthly sales of these restaurants are accounted for by the heavy, medium, and light users. For example, the 36,769,000 American adults who go to these restaurants 14 or more times in a typical month represent about 44.8 percent of the sales revenues.

FIGURE 8–6
Patronage (use) of fast-food, drive-in, family, and steak house restaurants

USER OR NONUSER	SPECIFIC SEGMENT	ADULTS, 18 AND OVER		ACTUAL CONSUMPTION (%)	USAGE INDEX PER PERSON*	IMPORTANCE OF SEGMENT
		NUMBER (1,000s)	PERCENT			
Users	Heavy users (14+ per month)	36,769	20.3%	44.8%	522	High
	Medium users (6–13 per month)	51,309	28.4	40.4	337	
	Light users (1–5 per month)	63,371	35.0	14.8	100	
Total users		151,449	83.7	100.0	283	
Nonusers	Prospects	?	?	0	0	
	Nonprospects	?	?	0	0	Low
Total nonusers		29,682	16.3	0	0	
Total	Users and nonusers	181,131	100.0%	100.0%	—	—

* Where monthly consumption of a light user equals 100.

Source: *Simmonds 1990 Study of Media and Markets: Restaurants, Stores, and Grocery Shopping—P-11* (New York: Simmonds Market Research Bureau, Inc., 1990), pp. 0001–0003.

The "Usage Index per Person" column in Figure 8–6 emphasizes the importance of the heavy user group even more. Giving the light users (1 to 5 restaurant visits per month) an index of 100, the heavy users have an index of 522. In other words, for every $1.00 spent by a light user in one of these restaurants in a month, each heavy user spends $5.22. This is the reason for the emphasis in almost all marketing strategies on effective ways to reach these heavy users. Thus as a Wendy's restaurant owner you want to keep the heavy-user segment constantly in mind. Fortunately, many college students fall into the heavy-user segment for fast-food restaurants.

As part of the Simmons survey, restaurant patrons were asked if each restaurant was (1) the sole restaurant they went to, (2) the primary one, or (3) one of several secondary ones. This national information, shown in Figure 8–7, might give you, as a Wendy's owner, some ideas in developing your local strategy. The Wendy's bar in Figure 8–7 shows that your sole (0.3 percent), primary (17.2 percent), and secondary (11.5 percent) user segments are somewhat behind Burger King and far behind McDonald's, so a natural strategy is to look at these two competitors and devise a marketing program to win customers from them.

The "nonusers" part of your own bar in Figure 8–7 also provides ideas. It shows that 16.4 percent of adult Americans don't go to these restaurants in a typical month (also shown in Figure 8–6) and are really nonprospects—unlikely to ever patronize your restaurant. But the 54.6 percent of the Wendy's bar shown as prospects may be worth detailed thought. These adults use the product category (fast-food, drive-in, family, and steak house restaurants) but *do not* go to Wendy's. New menu items or new promotional strategies might succeed in converting these "prospects" to "users." One key conclusion emerges about usage: in market segmentation studies, some measure of usage or revenues derived from various segments is central to the analysis.

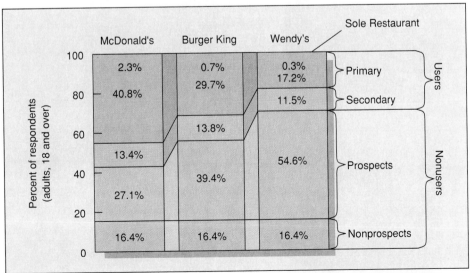

FIGURE 8–7
Comparison of various kinds of users and nonusers for McDonald's, Burger King, and Wendy's restaurants

Source: *Simmons 1990 Study of Media and Markets: Restaurants, Stores, and Grocery Shopping—P-11* (New York: Simmons Market Research Bureau, Inc., 1990), p. 0001.

In determining one or two variables to segment the market for your Wendy's restaurant, very broadly we find two main markets: students and nonstudents. To segment the students, we could try a variety of demographic variables, such as age, sex, year in school, or college major; or psychographic variables, such as personality characteristics, attitudes, or interests. But none of these variables really meets the five criteria listed previously—particularly the fourth criterion about leading to a feasible marketing action to reach the various segments. Four student segments that *do* meet these criteria include the following:

- Students living in dormitories (college residence halls, sororities, fraternities).
- Students living near the college in apartments.
- Day commuter students living outside the area.
- Night commuter students living outside the area.

These segmentation variables are really a combination of where the student lives and the time he or she is on campus (and near your restaurant). For nonstudents who might be customers, similar variables might be used:

- Faculty and staff members at the university.
- People who live in the area but aren't connected with the university.
- People who work in the area but aren't connected with the university.

People in each of these segments aren't quite as similar as those in the students', which makes them harder to reach with a marketing program or action. Think

In serving needs of diverse industrial customers, Xerox uses different segmentation variables than manufacturers of consumer products.

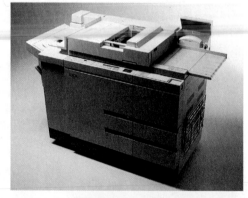

about (1) whether the needs of all these segments are different and (2) how various advertising media can be used to reach these groups effectively.

Ways to Segment Industrial Markets Variables for segmenting industrial markets are shown in Figure 8–8. A product manager at Xerox responsible for a line of photocopiers might use a number of these segmentation variables, as follows:

- *Location:* Firms located in a metropolitan statistical area (MSA) might receive a personal sales call, whereas those outside the MSA might be contacted by telephone.
- *SIC code:* Firms categorized by the Standard Industrial Classification (SIC) code as manufacturers might have different photocopying needs than do retailers or lawyers.
- *Number of employees:* The size of the firm is related to the volume of photocopying done, for a given industry or SIC, so larger firms in terms of employment might require larger machines than do smaller firms.

FORM PRODUCTS TO BE SOLD INTO GROUPS

As important as grouping customers into segments is finding a means of grouping the products you're selling into meaningful categories. If the firm has only one product or service, this isn't a problem, but when it has dozens or hundreds,

FIGURE 8–8
Segmentation variables and breakdowns for industrial markets

MAIN DIMENSION	SEGMENTATION VARIABLE	TYPICAL BREAKDOWNS
CUSTOMER CHARACTERISTICS		
Geographical	Region	Pacific; Mountain; West North Central; West South Central; East North Central; East South Central; South Atlantic; Middle Atlantic; New England
	Location	In MSA; not in MSA
Demographic	SIC code	2-digit; 3-digit; 4-digit categories
	Number of employees	1 to 19; 20 to 99; 100 to 249; 250 or over
	Number of production workers	1 to 19; 20 to 99; 100 to 249; 250 or over
	Annual sales volume	Less than $1 million; $1 million to $10 million; $10 million to $100 million; over $100 million
	Number of establishments	With 1 to 19 employees; with 20 or more employees
BUYING SITUATIONS		
Nature of good	Kind	Product or service
	Where used	Installation; component of final product; supplies
	Application	Office use; limited production use; heavy production use
Buying condition	Purchase location	Centralized; decentralized
	Who buys	Individual buyer; group
	Type of buy	New buy; modified rebuy; straight rebuy

these must be grouped in some way so buyers can relate to them. This is why department stores and supermarkets are organized into product groups, with the departments or aisles containing related merchandise. Likewise manufacturers have product lines that are the groupings they use in the catalogs sent to customers.

What are the groupings for your restaurant? It could be the item purchased, such as a Frosty, chili, hamburgers, and french fries, but this is where judgment—the qualitative aspect of marketing—comes in. Students really buy an eating experience, or a meal that satisfies a need at a particular time of day, so the product grouping can be defined by meal or time of day as breakfast, lunch, between-meal snack, dinner, and after-dinner snack. These groupings are more closely related to the way purchases are actually made and permit you to market the entire meal, not just your french fries or Frosties.

DEVELOP A MARKET-PRODUCT GRID AND ESTIMATE SIZE OF MARKETS

Developing a market-product grid means labeling the markets (or horizontal rows) and products (or vertical columns), as shown in Figure 8–9. In addition, the size of the market in each cell, or the market-product combination, must be estimated. For your restaurant this involves estimating the number of, or sales revenue obtained from, each kind of meal that can reasonably be expected to be sold to each market segment. This is a form of the usage rate analysis discussed earlier in the chapter.

The market sizes in Figure 8–9 may be simple "guesstimates" if you don't have time for formal marketing research (as discussed in Chapter 7). But even such crude estimates of the size of specific markets using a market-product grid are far better than the usual estimates of the entire market.

FIGURE 8–9
Selecting a target market for your fast-food restaurant next to a metropolitan college (target market is shaded)

MARKETS	BREAKFAST	LUNCH	BETWEEN-MEAL SNACK	DINNER	AFTER-DINNER SNACK
STUDENT					
Dormitory	0	S	L	0	L
Apartment	S	L	L	S	S
Day commuter	0	L	M	S	0
Night commuter	0	0	S	L	M
NONSTUDENT					
Faculty or staff	0	L	S	S	0
Live in area	0	S	M	M	S
Work in area	S	L	0	S	0

PRODUCTS: MEALS

Key: L, Large market; M, medium market; S, small market; 0, no market.

SELECT TARGET MARKETS

A firm must take care to choose its target market segments carefully. If it picks too narrow a group of segments, it may fail to reach the volume of sales and profits it needs. If it selects too broad a group of segments, it may spread its marketing efforts so thin that the extra expenses more than offset the increased sales and profits.

Criteria to Use in Picking the Target Segments   There are two different kinds of criteria present in the market segmentation process: (1) those to use in dividing the market into segments (discussed earlier) and (2) those to use in actually picking the target segments (Figure 8–4). Even experienced marketing executives often confuse these two different sets of criteria. The five criteria to use in actually selecting the target segments apply to your Wendy's restaurant this way:

- *Size:* The estimated size of the market in the segment is an important factor in deciding whether it's worth going after. There is really no market for breakfasts among dormitory students (Figure 8–9), so why devote any marketing effort toward reaching a small or nonexistent market?
- *Expected growth:* Although the size of the market in the segment may be small now, perhaps it is growing significantly or is expected to grow in the future. Night commuters may not look important now, but with the decline in traditional day students in many colleges, the evening adult education programs are expected to expand in the future. Thus the future market among night commuters is probably more encouraging than the current picture shown in Figure 8–9.
- *Competitive position:* Is there a lot of competition in the segment now or is there likely to be in the future? The less the competition, the more attractive the segment is. For example, if the college dormitories announce a new policy of "no meals on weekends," this segment is suddenly more promising for your restaurant.

Packaged foods targeted at market segments with special tastes.

- *Cost of reaching the segment:* A segment that is inaccessible to a firm's marketing actions should not be pursued. For example, the few nonstudents who live in the area may not be economically reachable with ads in newspapers or other media. As a result, do not waste money trying to advertise to them.
- *Compatibility with the organization's objectives and resources:* If your restaurant doesn't have the cooking equipment to make breakfasts and has a policy against spending more money on restaurant equipment, then don't try to reach the breakfast segment.

As is often the case in marketing decisions, a particular segment may appear attractive according to some criteria and very unattractive according to others.

Choose the Segments   Ultimately a marketing executive has to use these criteria to choose the segments for special marketing efforts. As shown in Figure 8–9, let's assume you've written off the breakfast market for two reasons: market size and (in)compatibility with your objectives and resources. In terms of competitive position and cost of reaching the segment, you choose to focus on the four student segments and not the three nonstudent segments (although you're certainly not going to turn away business from the nonstudent segments). This combination of market-product segments—your target market—is shaded in Figure 8–9.

TAKE MARKETING ACTIONS TO REACH TARGET MARKETS

The purpose of developing a market-product grid is to trigger marketing actions to increase revenues and profits. This means that someone must develop and execute an action plan.

Your Wendy's Segmentation Strategy   With your Wendy's restaurant you've already reached one significant decision: there is a limited market for breakfast, so you won't open for business until 10:30 A.M. In fact, Wendy's attempt at a breakfast menu was a disaster and was discontinued in 1986. Wendy's evaluates

Wendy's original menu.

possible new menu items continuously, not only to compete with McDonald's (and its new pizza) but with a complex array of outlets that sell reheatable packaged foods—such as supermarkets, convenience stores, and gas stations.[14]

Another essential decision is where and what meals to advertise to reach specific market segments. An ad in the student newspaper could reach all the student segments, but you might consider this "shotgun approach" too expensive and want a more focused "rifle approach" to reach smaller segments. If you choose three segments for special actions (Figure 8–10), advertising actions to reach them might include:

- *Day commuters* (an entire market segment): Run ads inside commuter buses and put flyers under the windshield wipers of cars in parking lots used by day commuters. These ads and flyers promote all the meals at your restaurant to a single segment of students—a horizontal cut through the market-product grid.
- *Between-meals snacks* (directed to all four student markets): To promote eating during this downtime for your restaurant, offer "Ten percent off all purchases between 2:00 and 4:30 P.M. during winter quarter." This ad promotes a single meal to all four student segments—a vertical cut through the market-product grid.
- *Dinners to night commuters:* The most focused of all three campaigns, this ad promotes a single meal to a single student segment. The campaign might consist of a windshield flyer offering a free Frosty with the coupon when the person buys a hamburger and french fries.

Depending on how your advertising actions work, you can repeat, modify, or drop them and design new campaigns for other segments you feel warrant the effort. This example of advertising your Wendy's restaurant is just a small piece of a complete marketing program using all the elements of the marketing mix.

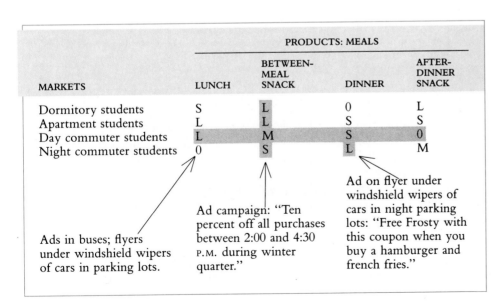

FIGURE 8–10
Advertising actions to reach specific student segments

MARKETS	LUNCH	BETWEEN-MEAL SNACK	DINNER	AFTER-DINNER SNACK
Dormitory students	S	L	0	L
Apartment students	L	L	S	S
Day commuter students	L	M	S	0
Night commuter students	0	S	L	M

PRODUCTS: MEALS

Ads in buses; flyers under windshield wipers of cars in parking lots.

Ad campaign: "Ten percent off all purchases between 2:00 and 4:30 P.M. during winter quarter."

Ad on flyer under windshield wipers of cars in night parking lots: "Free Frosty with this coupon when you buy a hamburger and french fries."

Marketing Action Memo

HOW APPLE SEGMENTS ITS MARKETS

*W*hen John Sculley moved from Pepsi-Cola to become president of Apple Computer in 1983, he took over the company that some computer industry wags called "Camp Runamok," because it had no coherent product line that was directed at identifiable market segments.

Sculley took immediate action to avoid potential disaster and set about targeting his firm's computers at specific market segments. Because the market-product grid shifts as a firm's strategy changes, the one shown here is based on the product line that existed in 1991. Apple's recent market-product analysis has given it a coherent strategy to compete with IBM. Uses for these products range from word and data processing to sophisticated applications involving multicomputer networks, desktop publishing, and scientific work stations. Camp Runamok is back on track.

MARKET		PRODUCT						
		Apple II	Macintosh					
			Classic	SE/30	Portable	LC	IIsi & IIci	IIfx
Home		■			■			
School	Students/teachers	■	■			■		
	Administration		■				■	
College/ university	Students/faculty			■			■	■
	Administration			■		■	■	
Business	Clerical					■		
	Managerial				■	■		
	Technical						■	■

Sources: *No Matter Which One You Choose, a Macintosh Is a Macintosh Is a Macintosh* (Cupertino, Calif.: Apple Computer Company, November 1990), pp. 1–4; John Battelle, "IIfx, A/UX Impress Opening-Day Crowds," *MacWEEK* (March 27, 1990), pp. 1, 10; and Bradley Johnson, "New Mac Ups Power," *Advertising Age* (March 12, 1990), p. 2.

Apple's Segmentation Strategy   Steven Jobs and Stephen Wozniak didn't realize they were developing today's multibillion-dollar PC industry when they invented the Apple II in a garage in 1976. Under Jobs's inspirational leadership through the early 1980s, Apple was run with a focus on products and little concern for markets. Apple's control of its brainy, creative young engineers was likened to "Boy Scouts without adult supervision."[15] When IBM entered the PC market in 1981, Apple lost significant market share, and many experts predicted it wouldn't survive.

Enter John Sculley, who in 1983 moved to Apple's presidency from Pepsi-Cola. Sculley, as shown in the Marketing Action Memo, formalized and gave cohesiveness to Apple's market segmentation strategy and targeted specific Ap-

Apple's line of
Macintosh computers
are targeted at the needs
of different market
segments.

ple machines to particular market segments. As in most segmentation situations, a single Apple product does not fit into an exclusive market niche. Rather, there is overlap among products in the product line and also among the markets to which they are directed. But a market segmentation strategy enables Apple to offer different products to meet the needs of the different market segments.

In talking to PC users, Sculley reached some key conclusions that redirected Apple's segmentation strategy. First, he concluded that the popularity of cheap, imported PCs meant that Apple could not count on significant revenues from individual households (the "home" market segment), so he reduced efforts to reach that segment. Next, he concluded that Apple must penetrate the business market, which meant designing Apple products that would network easily with competitive computers. Apple's Macintosh line succeeded in penetrating the business market. But as the line caught on, Apple raised prices on its Macintosh line and alienated prospective buyers. In 1990 the company cut prices and added new Macintosh products, including the "Classic" at an astounding $999 price. Production could not keep up with demand for the Classic.

Sculley knows that he must continue to introduce new products to serve the needs of diverse segments. On the Apple drawing board for the early 1990s: a 6-pound portable, notebook-size computer, another that can recognize handwriting, and a system for electronic games that combines a computer and compact-disk player.[16]

Segmentation Strategies of Small Firms   Many startup firms attribute their success to finding a specialized market segment, or niche, in which their small size is not a major disadvantage relative to their giant competitors. Some have used this initial niche strategy to become large firms today. For example, An Wang built today's giant Wang Laboratories by initially focusing on the networking of computer work stations years before it became fashionable. Similarly, Sirjang Lal Tandon successfully targeted Tandon Corporation's efforts toward specialized niches within the computer disk drive and PC markets.[17] Tiny Sorrell Ridge has had remarkable success with its line of no–sugar, all-natural fruit spreads targeted at consumers who desire natural foods.[18]

CONCEPT CHECK	
	1 **What are some of the variables used to segment consumer markets?**
	2 **What are some criteria used to decide which segments to choose for targets?**
	3 **Why is usage rate important in segmentation studies?**

ANALYZING MARKET SEGMENTS USING CROSS TABULATIONS

To do a more precise market segmentation analysis of your Wendy's restaurant, suppose you survey fast-food patrons throughout the metropolitan area where your restaurant is located, using the questionnaire shown in Figure 7–6. You want to use this information as best you can to study the market's segments and develop your strategy. Probably the most widely used approach today in marketing is to develop and interpret cross tabulations of data obtained by questionnaires.

DEVELOPING CROSS TABULATIONS

A **cross tabulation,** or "cross tab," is a method of presenting and relating data having two or more variables. It is used to analyze and discover relationships in the data. Two important aspects of cross tabulations are deciding which of two variables to pair together to help understand the situation and forming the resulting cross tabulations.

Pairing the Questions   Marketers pair two questions to understand marketing relationships and to find effective marketing actions. The Wendy's questionnaire in Figure 7–6 gives many questions that might be paired to understand the fast-food business better and help reach a decision about marketing actions to increase revenues. For example, if you want to study your hypothesis that as the age of the head of household increases, patronage of fast-food restaurants declines, you can cross tabulate Questions 9*d* and 3.

Forming Cross Tabulations   Using the answers to Question 3 as the column headings and the answers to Question 9*d* as the row headings gives a cross tabulation, as shown in Figure 8–11, using the answers 586 respondents gave to both questions. The figure shows two forms of the cross tabulation:

- The raw data or answers to the specific questions are shown in Figure 8–11, A. For example, this cross tab shows that 144 households whose head was 24 years or younger ate at fast-food restaurants once a week or more.
- Answers on a percentage basis, with the percentages running horizontally, are shown in Figure 8–11, B. Of the 215 households headed by someone 24 years or younger, 67.0 percent ate at a fast-food restaurant at least once a week and only 8.8 percent ate there once a month or less.

Two other forms of cross tabulation using the raw data shown in Figure 8–11, A, are as described in Problem 7 at the end of the chapter.

INTERPRETING CROSS TABULATIONS

A careful analysis of Figure 8–11 shows that patronage of fast-food restaurants is related to the age of the head of the household. Note that as the age of the head of the household increases, fast-food restaurant patronage declines, as shown by highlighted numbers on diagonal lines in Figure 8–11. This means that if you want to reach the heavy user segment, you should direct your marketing efforts to the segment that is 24 years old or younger.

As discussed earlier in the chapter, there are various ways to segment a consumer market besides according to age. For example, you could make subsequent cross tabulations to analyze patronage related to where students live and the meals they eat to obtain more precise information for the market-product grid in Figure 8–11.

A, ABSOLUTE FREQUENCIES

AGE OF HEAD OF HOUSEHOLD (YEARS)	FREQUENCY			
	ONCE A WEEK OR MORE	2 OR 3 TIMES A MONTH	ONCE A MONTH OR LESS	TOTAL
24 or less	144	52	19	215
25 to 39	46	58	29	133
40 or over	82	69	87	238
Total	272	179	135	586

B, ROW PERCENTAGES: RUNNING PERCENTAGES HORIZONTALLY

AGE OF HEAD OF HOUSEHOLD (YEARS)	FREQUENCY			
	ONCE A WEEK OR MORE	2 OR 3 TIMES A MONTH	ONCE A MONTH OR LESS	TOTAL
24 or less	67.0%	24.2%	8.8%	100.0%
25 to 39	34.6	43.6	21.8	100.0
40 or over	34.4	29.0	36.6	100.0
Total	46.4%	30.6%	23.0%	100.0%

FIGURE 8–11
Two forms of a cross tabulation relating age of head of household to fast-food restaurant patronage

VALUE OF CROSS TABULATIONS

Probably the most widely used technique for organizing and presenting marketing data, cross tabulations have some important advantages.[19] The simple format permits direct interpretation and an easy means of communicating data to management. They have great flexibility and can be used to summarize experimental, observational, and questionnaire data. Also, cross tabulations may be easily generated by today's personal computers.

Cross tabulations also have some disadvantages. For example, they can be misleading if the percentages are based on too small a number of observations. Also, cross tabulations can hide some relations because each typically only shows two or three variables. Balancing both advantages and disadvantages, more marketing decisions are probably made using cross tabulations than any other method of analyzing data.

The ultimate value of cross tabulations to a marketing manager lies in obtaining a better understanding of the wants and needs of buyers and targeting key segments. This enables a marketing manager to "position" the offering in the minds of buyers, the topic discussed next.

POSITIONING THE PRODUCT

When a company offers a product commercially, a decision critical to its long-term success is how to position it in the market on introduction. **Product positioning** refers to the place an offering occupies in consumers' minds on important attributes relative to competitive offerings.

TWO APPROACHES TO PRODUCT POSITIONING

There are several approaches to positioning a new product in the market. Head-to-head positioning involves competing directly with competitors on similar product attributes in the same target market. Using this strategy, Dollar competes directly with Avis and Hertz, and Volvo pits its turbo-charged cars against Porsche (see the accompanying advertisement). When Wendy's saw McDonald's temporarily cut its quarter-pound cheeseburger price to 99 cents, it responded with a head-to-head strategy by offering a junior bacon cheeseburger for 99 cents.

Differentiation positioning involves seeking a less competitive, smaller market niche in which to locate a brand. Curtis Mathes has promoted its television sets for the quality market with the slogan, "The most expensive television sets money can buy." McDonald's, trying to appeal to the health-conscious segment, introduced its low-fat McLean Deluxe hamburger to avoid direct competition with Wendy's and Burger King.[20] Companies also follow a differentiation positioning strategy among brands within their own product line to try to minimize cannibalization of a brand's sales or shares (which occurs when a company's new brand steals sales from other products in its line).

PRODUCT POSITIONING USING PERCEPTUAL MAPS

A key to positioning a product effectively is the perceptions of consumers.[21] In determining a brand's position and the preferences of consumers, companies obtain three types of data from consumers:

1 Evaluations of the important attributes for a product class.
2 Judgments of existing brands with the important attributes.
3 Ratings of an "ideal" brand's attributes.

From these data, it is possible to develop a **perceptual map**, a means of displaying or graphing in two dimensions the location of products or brands in the minds of consumers. The example illustrates how a manager can use perceptual maps to see how consumers perceive competing products or brands and then take actions to try to change the product offering and the image it projects to consumers.

As mentioned in Chapter 2, by the 1980s GM was concerned that the image of its five main models of U.S. cars—Chevrolet, Pontiac, Oldsmobile, Buick, and Cadillac—had so blurred in the minds of American consumers that they could not distinguish one brand from another. In fact, GM's Cadillac is still trying to overcome bad image problems from its 1981 decision to sell the Cimarron, an "economy" Cadillac that consumers saw as a thinly veiled Chevrolet Cavalier.[22]

So in 1982 GM interviewed consumers and developed the perceptual map shown in Figure 8–12, A. Note that the two dimensions on the perceptual map are (1) low price versus high price and (2) family/conservative versus personal/expressive appeal. Figure 8–12, A, shows that GM indeed had a problem. Although there was some variation in the vertical dimension (consumers' perception of price), there was little difference in the horizontal dimension (family/conservative appeal versus personal/expressive appeal). In 1986 GM set new goals for where it wanted its models to be when its small car Saturn would be introduced (which turned out to be 1990). This involves **repositioning** the models, or changing the place an offering occupies in a consumer's mind relative to competitive offerings. Note the repositioning changes intended for two of its models from 1982 to 1990:

1 Oldsmobile was to be increased slightly in price and repositioned as a more personal/expressive car.
2 Pontiac was to be reduced slightly in price and to be made a more personal/expressive car to move it further away from Chevrolet.

To fill in a glaring gap in its brands, in 1990 GM positioned its new low-price, import-fighter Saturn, as shown in Figure 8–12, B.[23] To convert these perceptual maps to actions, GM changed some of its basic designs and the advertising used to describe its models to prospective buyers. Today, things have not worked out as GM intended. It has had difficulty repositioning its five main models to separate them in consumers' minds, especially the three middle brands—Buick, Oldsmobile, and Pontiac—for which about 80 percent of the models vary only slightly in price and engineering.[24]

But GM is experiencing successes, too. The quality of GM cars has improved significantly, as indicated by its Cadillac Division's receiving the coveted

FIGURE 8–12
The General Motors strategy to reposition its major car brands, including its 1990 Saturn introduction

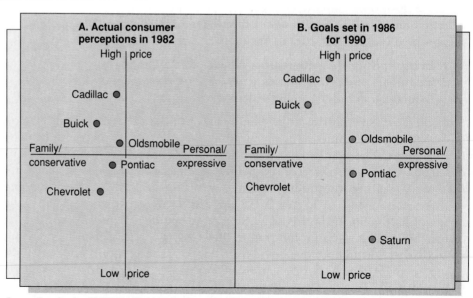

Sources: Jesse Snyder, "4 GM Car Divisions Are Repositioned in an Effort to Help Sales," *Automotive News* (September 15, 1986), pp. 1, 49; and Joseph B. White, "GM Puts Low Price on Saturn to Sell in Small-Car Field," *The Wall Street Journal* (October 5, 1990), pp. B1, B6.

Malcom Baldrige award in 1990 for quality in manufacturing and customer service.[25] In 1991 it launched a new-product blitz by introducing redesigned versions of nine brands that represent one third of its U.S. car sales.[26] Some of the intervening steps in GM's positioning strategy are explained in a case in the back of this text.

1 What is cross tabulation?

2 What are some advantages of cross tabulations?

3 Why do marketers use perceptual maps in product positioning decisions?

ETHICS AND SOCIAL RESPONSIBILITY IN THE 1990s

CAN HEAD-TO-HEAD POSITIONING OF A NEW MEDICATION RAISE PATIENTS' COSTS WITHOUT ANY BENEFITS?

The worldwide market for thrombolytics—a medicine to break up blood clots in heart-attack victims—is $600 million a year. The pharmaceutical firm that introduced TPA (for *tissue plasminogen activator*) to compete in the thrombolytics market used high-pressure marketing and a head-to-head positioning strategy to convince doctors they should prescribe TPA rather than the traditional streptokivase. The price: $2,500 per treatment for TPA versus $220 for the older treatment.

Subsequent research showed no difference in the effectiveness of the two medicines. Researchers say U.S. doctors often accept and prescribe the latest drugs because (1) they "are enamored of new technologies," (2) they fear malpractice suits, and (3) cost is not a primary concern in the United States, in contrast to Canada and Europe.

A U.S. Senate committee is looking into what *Time* magazine calls these "overzealous marketing practices in the drug industry."[27] What do you believe should be done?

 SUMMARY

1 Market segmentation is aggregating prospective buyers into groups that have common needs and will respond similarly to a marketing action.

2 A straightforward approach to segmenting, targeting, and reaching a market involves five steps: (*a*) form prospective buyers into segments, by characteristics such as their needs, (*b*) form products to be sold into groups, (*c*) develop a market-product grid and estimate size of markets, (*d*) select target markets, and (*e*) take marketing actions to reach the target markets.

3 Marketing variables often are used to represent customer needs in the market segmentation process. For consumer markets, typical customer

variables are region, metropolitan statistical area, age, income, benefits sought, and usage rate. For industrial markets, comparable variables are geographical location, size of firm, and Standard Industrial Classification (SIC) code.

4 Usage rate is an important factor in a market segmentation study. Users are often divided into heavy, medium, and light users.

5 Nonusers are often divided into prospects and nonprospects. Nonusers of a firm's brand may be important because they are prospects — users of some other brand in the product class that may be convinced to change brands.

6 Criteria used (*a*) to segment markets and (*b*) to choose target segments are related but different. The former includes potential to increase profits, similarity of needs of buyers within a segment, difference of needs among segments, and feasibility of a resulting marketing action. The latter includes market size, expected growth, the competitive position of the firm's offering in the segment, and the cost of reaching the segment.

7 A market-product grid is a useful way to display what products can be directed at which market segments, but the grid must lead to marketing actions for the segmentation process to be worthwhile.

8 Cross tabulations are widely used today in market segmentation studies to identify needs of various customer segments and the actions to reach them.

9 A company can position a product head-to-head against the competition or seek a differentiated position. A concern with positioning is often to avoid cannibalization of the existing product line. In positioning, a firm often uses consumer judgments in the form of perceptual maps to locate its product relative to competing ones.

KEY TERMS AND CONCEPTS

market segmentation p. 196
market segments p. 196
product differentiation p. 196
market-product grid p. 197
usage rate p. 204

80/20 rule p. 204
cross tabulation p. 214
product positioning p. 216
perceptual map p. 217
repositioning p. 218

CHAPTER PROBLEMS AND APPLICATIONS

1 What variables might be used to segment these consumer markets? (*a*) lawn mowers, (*b*) frozen dinners, (*c*) dry breakfast cereals, and (*d*) soft drinks.

2 What variables might be used to segment these industrial markets? (*a*) industrial sweepers, (*b*) photocopiers, (*c*) computerized production control systems, and (*d*) car rental agencies.

3 In Figure 8–10 the dormitory market segment includes students living in college-owned residence halls, sororities, and fraternities. What market needs are common to these students that justify combining them into a single segment in studying the market for your Wendy's restaurant?

4 You may disagree with the estimates of market size given for the rows in the market-product grid in Figure 8–10. Estimate the market size and give a brief justification for these market segments: (*a*) dormitory students, (*b*) day commuters, and (*c*) people who work in the area.

5 Suppose you want to increase revenues from your fast-food restaurant shown in Figure 8–10 even further. What advertising actions might you take to increase revenues from (*a*) dormitory students, (*b*) dinners, and (*c*) after-dinner snacks from night commuters?

6 Look back at Figure 7–6. Which questions would you pair to form a cross tabulation to uncover the following relationships? (*a*) frequency of fast-food restaurant patronage and restaurant characteristics important to the customer, (*b*) age of the head of household and source of information used about fast-food restaurants, (*c*) frequency of patronage of Wendy's and source of information used about fast-food restaurants, and (*d*) how much children have to say about where the family eats and number of children in the household.

7 Look back at Figure 8–11, A. (*a*) Run the percentages vertically and tell what they mean. (*b*) Express all numbers in the table as a percentage of the total number of people sampled (586) and tell what the percentages mean.

8 In Figure 8–11, (*a*) what might be other names for the three patronage levels shown in the columns? (*b*) Which is likely to be of special interest to Wendy's and why?

9 Using GM's 1990 positioning goals that it set in 1986 (Figure 8–12, B) as a reference, (*a*) what product design changes would it have to make to reposition the Oldsmobile and Pontiac lines on the family/conservative versus personal/expressive dimension, (*b*) why did it position Saturn where it did, and (*c*) where might it seek to position a new-car entry to be more competitive in the 1990s?

CHAPTER 9

Micromarketing, Information Technology, and Forecasting

*A*fter reading this chapter you should be able to:

- Define and explain the use and importance of micromarketing.

- Describe three kinds of information systems used by today's marketers.

- Describe the factors that have made micromarketing both necessary and possible.

- Recognize structured and unstructured marketing decisions and their impact on data used in information systems.

- Recognize the top-down and buildup approaches to forecasting sales.

- Use the lost-horse and linear trend extrapolation methods to make a simple forecast.

Micromarketing: Putting Consumers and Retailers under a Microscope

Outside Atlanta, Georgia sits an A&P supermarket where Michael J. McCarthy and his family shop. To Mike's surprise, Market Metrics—a small marketing research company in Lancaster, Pennsylvania—knows a lot more about his supermarket than Mike does himself. For example, using detailed data captured in a variety of ways—from supermarket scanners to site visits—Market Metrics knows that the supermarket:

- Has 10 checkouts, all with scanners.
- Contains 33,900 square feet of selling space.
- Averages weekly sales of $350,000.
- Has 20 end-of-aisle displays.

- Devotes 150 feet of space to both upright freezers and health and beauty products.
- Sells to 14,372 people, whose average household income is $42,912.
- Is the third-ranked supermarket in its nine-county trading area (its 9 percent market share trails two Krogers with shares of 22 percent and 13 percent, respectively).
- Serves a trading area in which 26 percent of the people in it are under 15 years of age.

Combining this information about the A&P store—and 30,000 other supermarkets across the United States—with the consumption patterns of hundreds of supermarket items and the demographic characteristics of households in a store's trading area enables Market Metrics to tell grocery manufacturers what will sell well in a particular store. In Mike McCarthy's A&P store, for example, Market Metrics says baby food, baking mixes, dry dinner mixes, and laundry supplies will sell especially well, but artificial sweeteners, pet food, film, foil, breakfast food, and yogurt won't.[1]

Welcome to the era of micromarketing! In this context micromarketing has a far narrower meaning than that mentioned in Chapter 1. Here, the term **micromarketing**—sometimes called *database marketing*—means combining demographic, media, and consumption profiles of households with buyer profiles of stores and products in order to target buyers in a neighborhood or for a specific product. Micromarketing extends the concept of market segmentation described in the last chapter to marketing actions undreamed of a decade ago. For example, when using geographic market segmentation, consumer-product firms have found that it isn't good enough to focus on a region, state, or even a city; they are now narrowing the shopper target to a bull's-eye no larger than a neighborhood or a single store.[2] And increasingly, micromarketing is able to target an individual household or specific person in that household.[3]

The result: a revolution in marketing information collection and use that will continue to restructure and redefine marketing activities of American firms and consumers into the 21st century. This chapter first describes the strategic role of information systems in the 1990s and then covers what has made micromarketing both necessary and possible, how information technology is used in marketing, and sales forecasting.

STRATEGIC ROLE OF INFORMATION TECHNOLOGY IN THE 1990s

Since the advent of computers after World War II and personal computers in the 1980s, management perceptions of the value and use of information have changed significantly. Even the terms are changing: while a decade ago managers talked about *manufacturing information systems* and *marketing information systems,* the lines of separation among the various departments in a firm are increasingly blurred. So today, all generally fall under the broader term of **information technology**, which involves designing and managing a computer and communication system to satisfy an organization's requirements for information processing and access.

Let us look at the evolution of the collection and use of information over the past decades to understand where we are headed and what it means for marketing in the 1990s.

1950s AND 1960s: MANAGEMENT INFORMATION SYSTEMS

Initially in the 1950s and 1960s, management used computers to automate the basic business processes of the firm—processes such as customer orders, payroll, and inventory control. These activities evolved into **management information systems** (MIS), which are computerized methods of processing predefined transactions to produce fixed-format reports on schedule.[4] As shown in Figure 9–1, the main function of management information systems are transaction processing through automating basic processes like customer orders and payroll. Until recently, virtually all the data in these management information systems were entered into the systems by having in-house data-entry clerks keyboard the data. Today's widely used management information systems produce detailed reports for marketing managers and top management on what customers are buying or sales volume by geographic area and product line.

1970s AND 1980s: MANAGEMENT SUPPORT SYSTEMS

As databases became more widespread and computers moved onto managers' desks in the 1970s and 1980s, information systems became more sophisticated. As shown in Figure 9–1, **management support systems** (MSS), which are computerized methods of providing managers with the ability to query and analyze information in on-line databases, developed. Market Metrics' management support system was described in the example that opened the chapter. When Borden Inc., which produces Classico pasta sauce, sought to increase its sales, it asked Market Metrics to list the best stores for Classico consumers— metropolitan households with at least $35,000 annual income and interested in gourmet-style pasta sauces. Querying its database, Market Metrics told Borden, among other things, that while Classico would sell well in about 75 to 80 percent of West Coast stores, in rural areas the estimate was 50 percent or less—and which stores should put Classico on their shelves.[5]

	USE OF INFORMATION SYSTEM		
Function of information system	Automating basic processes	Satisfying information needs	Developing competitive strategy
Transaction processing	Management information systems (MIS)		Strategic information systems (SIS)
Query and analysis		Management support systems (MSS)	

FIGURE 9–1
Three kinds of information systems that comprise today's information technology

Source: Adapted from Charles Wiseman, *Strategic Information Systems* (Homewood, Ill.: Richard D. Irwin, 1988), p. 95.

1990s AND BEYOND: STRATEGIC INFORMATION SYSTEMS

Information as a Strategic Weapon   Starting in the mid-1980s, business information took on a new dimension. Business strategists became increasingly convinced that information could and would become a strategic weapon by which an innovative firm could attain a sustainable competitive advantage.[6] This gave rise to what today are called **strategic information systems,** computerized methods of achieving long-run advantage by querying and analyzing on-line databases linking customers and suppliers through remote devices and telecommunications. As implied in Figure 9–1, just as an MSS includes MIS capability, so strategic information systems (SIS) include both MSS and MIS. All three kinds of information systems comprise what is today called "information technology."

Information technology in the form of an SIS can provide a sustainable competitive advantage in a number of ways: building barriers to entry, increasing switching costs (the expense of changing from one supplier to another), and locking customers into essential information and databases.[7] As the electronic and data links among firms get tighter, the likelihood of a sustainable competitive advantage for the firm controlling the SIS increases.

American Airlines uses its SABRE reservation system to obtain a marketing advantage.

SABRE as a Sustainable Competitive Advantage   SABRE, a computerized travel reservation system pioneered by American Airlines, completely transformed marketing and distribution in the airline business.[8] During several years in the 1980s SABRE contributed more to American's annual profit than its airline business did. Among the reasons for SABRE'S early importance was a programming "bias" toward American Airlines's flights. For example, "an independent [travel] agent who subscribed to SABRE knew, when requesting a listing of flights from New York to Los Angeles with stops in between, that the first items to appear on the screen might show neither the most direct way nor the least expensive way, but for sure they would show the American way."[9] In 1985 the Civil Aeronautics Board issued a ruling prohibiting bias on screen displays. So ways that SABRE contributes revenues to American Airlines today include:

- Other airlines pay for each of their flights booked on SABRE.
- Hotels and car rental firms receive reservations made on SABRE.
- Travel agents lease SABRE terminals.

During one recent year SABRE accounted for 10 percent of all hotel reservations, 20 percent of all car rentals, and 45 percent of all airline reservations made through travel agents. Along with United Airlines' Apollo computerized reservation system, the two airlines in the past decade have used their SIS capabilities to virtually preempt the major channels of ticket distribution—thereby providing huge strategic marketing advantages. Such advantages for SABRE include:[10]

- *Barriers to entry*—It could cost competing airlines hundreds of millions of dollars to develop and implement a system comparable to SABRE—a near-impossible task in today's deregulated airline structure.

- *Increasing switching costs*—While a travel agency might change computerized airline reservation systems with a 30-day notice, the cost of retraining reservation clerks makes such a plan very costly and likely to be error prone.
- *Competitive intelligence*—SABRE not only permits American to utilize countless sales reports by travel agency and geographic market areas, but it can blunt competitors' fare reductions or scheduling changes because they must be entered *in advance* on the SABRE system.
- *Innovative marketing strategies*—To promote customer loyalty, American introduced "Advantage," the industry's first frequent-flier program, which was possible only through SABRE's capability for customer tracking.

Further, almost 100 "yield managers" working in American Airlines' Dallas headquarters use SABRE's query and analysis capability to balance fare prices, fare travel restrictions, and seat availability to try to maximize revenues.

In the 1990s many firms are looking for similar ways to use their information technology to achieve a sustainable competitive advantage over other firms in their industry. Examples throughout the chapter will illustrate how they are trying to achieve this.

CONCEPT CHECK

1 **What is micromarketing?**

2 **Identify and compare the three kinds of information systems that are in use by marketers today.**

3 **How has SABRE provided a sustainable competitive advantage for American Airlines?**

MICROMARKETING: THE REVOLUTION ARRIVES

As shown in Figure 9–2, micromarketing forces today's marketing manager to be increasingly aware of many complex factors. To comprehend further how micromarketing has revolutionized today's market segmentation and marketing mix actions, it is necessary to analyze (1) what has made micromarketing necessary and (2) what has made micromarketing possible.

WHAT MAKES MICROMARKETING NECESSARY: THE CAUSES

Two sources of marketing problems have helped trigger the rise of micromarketing: (1) more demanding consumers and (2) excessive business costs.

More Demanding Consumers   As mentioned in Chapter 3, today's consumers are constantly changing. But Box 1 in Figure 9–2 notes that one common factor remains: consumers are far more demanding than they were even five years ago. Research studies show that consumers:

FIGURE 9–2
Complex factors influence marketing managers as they develop micromarketing strategies

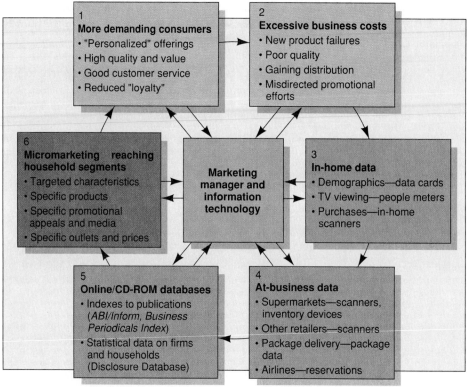

Note: Blue boxes show consumer and business factors that have made micromarketing necessary, while green boxes show the data and collection methods that have made micromarketing possible.

- *Want "personalized" offerings*—Consumers increasingly seek the combination of product and services that are tailored to their unique wants and needs. For example, ten days after specifying their unique wants in a new car order, Japanese consumers buying a Toyota will have their built-to-order car.
- *Desire high quality and value*—Consumers are willing to pay a premium for quality, the characteristics of which Americans rank from top to bottom as: reliability, durability, ease of maintenance, ease of use, a known or trusted brand name, and (last) low price.[11]
- *Require "caring" customer service*—Effective customer service means having the seller's representatives treat customers like they want to be treated. For IBM this means an electronic customer support system that automatically diagnoses potential trouble to alert IBM service people, who sometimes show up on a customer's doorstep *before* the glitch appears on the customer's IBM equipment.[12]
- *Reduced loyalty to sellers*—For today's consumer, the issue is not that a product, brand, or store served their needs last year but whether it will serve their needs today. Sellers have discovered that defecting customers exact a terrible price in lost revenues. Figure 9–3 shows that reducing customer defections by 5 percent increases profit from 30 percent to 85 percent, depending on the business. IBM estimates that if it can improve satisfaction 1 percent for worldwide customers of its AS/400 minicomputers, it will increase revenues by over $200 million in the next five years.[13]

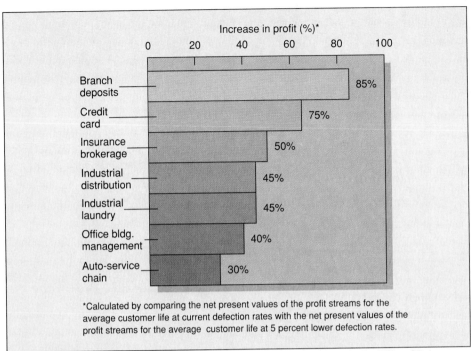

Source: Frederick F. Reickheld and W. Earl Sasser, Jr., "Zero Defections: Quality Comes to Services," *Harvard Business Review* (September–October 1990), p. 110.

FIGURE 9–3
The impact on profit of reducing customer defections by 5 percent

Excessive Business Costs   Box 2 in Figure 9–2 identifies some of the key sources of excessive business costs that have driven today's manufacturers and retailers to use micromarketing. Poor quality can lead directly to new product failures (discussed in greater detail in Chapter 10), customer defections, and billions of dollars in lost revenues and profit.[14] After extensive research, the American Society of Quality Control carefully defines **quality** as the totality of features and characteristics of a product or service that bear on its ability to satisfy stated or implied needs.[15] Surveys of top executives of U.S. firms show that they feel improving product and service quality is the most critical challenge facing them in the coming years. In fact, Ford Motor Company's statement of its Guiding Principles starts by declaring, "Quality comes first; to achieve customer satisfaction, the quality of our products and services must be our number one priority."

Most experts believe that the dominant factor in the success of Japan's products in world markets is the country's concern for quality.[16] This preoccupation with quality in Japan is traced to W. Edwards Deming, an American consultant, whose simple chain of events linking quality, markets, and jobs (Figure 9–4) has altered Japanese production and quality control efforts over the past four decades. Japan's prestigious Deming Award is given annually to Japanese firms achieving outstanding performance on quality.

In the late 1980s the U.S. introduced the Malcolm Baldrige National Quality Award, which is patterned after the Deming Award. Recent Baldrige Award winners such as Federal Express and IBM's plant that manufactures the AS/400 minicomputers have met rigid standards for both product and service quality.

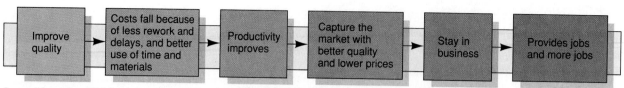

Source: Adapted from W. Edwards Deming, *Out of Crisis* (Cambridge, Mass.: MIT Center for Advanced Engineering Study, 1986).

FIGURE 9–4

The Deming chain reaction linking quality, markets, and jobs

For example, Federal Express has its own internal Service Quality Indicator (SQI), a list of critical points that determine success or failure on a daily basis. These measuring points for Federal Express's quality of customer service and the "trouble indicators" include:

- *Late delivery*—There's trouble if delivery occurs after the specified hour, worse if it's after the specified day.
- *Proof of delivery*—Trouble appears if no customer signature appears on the delivery form—a delivery considered a failure by SQI standards.
- *Request for adjustment*—A customer request for a billing adjustment causes the delivery to be considered a failure by SQI standards.
- *Failure to pick up, damage, or loss*—All these are considered failures by SQI standards—with a heavy SQI penalty for their occurrence.

Federal Express delivers 1.5 million packages a day. With company bonuses tied to SQI performance, employees know that the company takes the quality of its customer service very seriously.[17]

Gaining distribution on retailers' shelves is increasingly costly and, as will be discussed in Chapter 10, may actually require manufacturers to pay for retail shelf space for new products. The cost of retail distribution has triggered micromarketing strategies because both retailers and manufacturers now have computerized records telling them how much revenue retail shelf space should and actually does generate. Products not meeting sales targets are dropped.

In past years, large grocery-product manufacturers spent tens or hundreds of millions of dollars annually on radio, TV, and magazine advertisements. Much of this was wasted because consumers have become increasingly blasé about these messages, many of which are no longer penetrating the consumers' consciousness. The result: these grocery-product firms have cut back substantially on national advertising campaigns and instead use micromarketing strategies to choose advertising media that are far less expensive and more effective in targeting the specific customers they want to reach—thereby saving millions of advertising dollars.

WHAT MAKES MICROMARKETING POSSIBLE: THE TECHNOLOGY OF INFORMATION

Marketing data have little value by themselves: they are simply facts or statistics. To translate data to information—data organized in a fashion that leads to marketing actions—the data must be unbiased, timely, pertinent to the problem, accessible, and organized and presented in a way that helps the marketing man-

For its ScanAmerica service, Arbitron has household members use a data scan wand to scan the Universal Product Codes of items purchased.

ager make decisions that lead to marketing actions. This section covers key sources of information that have been revolutionized by technological breakthroughs in collecting, organizing, and presenting marketing data (1) in a consumer's home, (2) in various kinds of business firms, (3) by combining all of these data sources, and (4) through on-line databases.

In-Home Data   To develop micromarketing strategies, as shown in Box 3 in Figure 9–2, marketing managers need incredible amounts of raw data about consumers and their households—their demographics and lifestyles, TV viewing habits, use of other promotional media (such as magazines, newspapers, and coupons), and their purchases. Historically there have been two especially severe problems in collecting these data: (1) the cost and (2) the potential bias in the data collected. Breakthroughs in technology in the past decade have addressed both issues. Recently invented credit cards (discussed later in the chapter) now contain detailed data on a consumer's demographics, lifestyle, and household. In-home optical scanners used by services like Arbitron can record purchases not captured by, say, supermarket scanners. Data on TV viewing and use of other promotional media like coupons and direct mail are captured electronically and inexpensively with little intrusion on the consumer's activities. It is important to avoid intruding on a consumer to avoid having the measurement process alter the consumer's normal marketing behavior. This concern is the reason Nielsen will soon replace today's people meters with "passive people meters," tentatively named Smart Sense. If Smart Sense works as planned, its image-recognition computerized camera will automatically record who in the household is watching TV without the intrusion of their having to push buttons to register their TV viewing behavior.

At-Business Data   Business firms themselves (Box 4, Figure 9–2) collect huge volumes of detailed data for micromarketing purposes. All of us have seen our supermarket checkout clerks use electronic optical scanners that "read" the Universal Product Code (UPC) on our purchased items to record on our sales slip. Over 95 percent of all U.S. supermarkets with annual sales over $2 million now use scanners, whose detailed data now enable supermarkets and manufacturers to track performance weekly by store, product category, and brand level.[18] Other retailers such as department stores, mass merchandisers, and clothing stores are increasingly using scanners to track purchases.

Other businesses use electronic tracking of purchases, inventories, and reservations to facilitate their micromarketing actions. The SABRE computer system used by American Airlines, described earlier in the chapter, tracks airline, hotel, and rental car reservations. Federal Express delivery people use hand–held "Super Trackers" that scan UPC codes and double as data–input keyboards, to collect real–time data that permit the location of packages to be identified throughout their trips. Frito-Lay's sales representatives use hand–held computers to track the inventories of their snacks in the stores; then they walk to their truck to input these data into a larger computer that prints the customer's invoice and sends the data back to company headquarters.[19] And available now at your computer store: "notepad computers" that enable you to write directly on the screen with a special stylus in order to read and manipulate hand-written letters, numbers, and drawings while working on a personal computer. State Farm Insurance is developing these so that a claims adjuster for auto damages can mark the damaged auto part on an exploded-view diagram and let the notepad calculate the cost of repair.[20]

Single-Source Data: Putting It All Together   In the late 1980s new marketing data services emerged that offered **single-source data,** information provided by a single firm on household demographics and lifestyle, purchases, TV viewing behavior, and responses to promotions like coupons and free samples. The significant advantage of single-source data is the ability of one service to collect, analyze, and interrelate all this information. BehaviorScan, offered by Informa-

Ten thousand Frito-Lay sales representatives use their hand-held computers to track snack inventories on store shelves. Here one representative attaches his computer to a printer in his truck to generate a sales invoice for the store.

tion Resources, Inc., tracks about 75,000 households in 27 U.S. market areas. Campbell Soup's Swanson frozen dinners used the information from a single-source data service to shift a TV ad campaign from a serious to light theme and increase sales of Swanson dinners 14 percent.[21]

On-Line and CD-ROM Databases With your own personal computer, a modem, and some communications software, you can access about 5,000 on-line databases (Box 5, Figure 9–2).[22] Hence on-line databases are no longer restricted to huge corporations and reference librarians. As shown in Figure 9–5, information in on-line databases divides into two general categories: (1) indexes to articles in publications, which are accessed through key word searches, and (2) statistical and directory data on households, products, and companies. When desired, this information can be transferred to the user's own computer. Because of the cost of the telecommunications link to these on-line databases, many libraries obtain CD-ROM (compact disc, read-only memory) optical discs that are read by a laser on special drives attached to microcomputers. Often updated monthly, one CD-ROM disc can contain the same amount of information as an entire 20-volume encyclopedia.

FIGURE 9–5

Examples of information in on-line databases (probably available through your college or public library)

KIND OF INFORMATION	NAME	DESCRIPTION
Index to journals and periodicals	ABI/Inform*	Covers over 800 publications on business and management topics
	Business Periodicals Index*	Covers 345 journals and trade publications on business and management topics
	National Newspaper Index	Covers stories in newspapers like the *New York Times* and *The Wall Street Journal,* plus newswire services
Statistical and directory data on households, products, and companies	Disclosure Database*†	Gives data on over 12,000 publicly traded corporations required to file U.S. Security and Exchange Commission reports
	D & B Dun's Financial Records	Gives financial data on over 650,000 public and private companies in the United States
	County and City Data Book*	Gives social/economic statistics on U.S. geographic areas from U.S. Census Bureau and 15 other federal agencies

*Also available on CD-ROM.
†Called "Compact D" on CD-ROM.

Source: Judy Wells and Nancy Herther, business reference librarians, University of Minnesota Libraries.

CONCEPT CHECK

1 What are the factors that have made micromarketing (*a*) necessary and (*b*) possible?

2 What is the formal definition of "quality" and its significance to American business today?

3 What is single-source data?

USING INFORMATION TECHNOLOGY IN MARKETING

Let's look at (1) when information technology is needed in marketing, (2) key elements in an information system, and (3) an actual information system being used.

WHEN INFORMATION TECHNOLOGY IS NEEDED IN MARKETING

Not every firm needs information technology to help it make marketing decisions. The need for it is largely determined by (1) the value versus the cost of marketing information and (2) the kinds of decisions a marketing manager makes and how they relate to the information included in the information system.

Trade-Offs: Value versus Cost of Marketing Data   Information and data can be valuable commodities, but they can also be very expensive. As mentioned earlier, the facts and figures that make up marketing information have no value by themselves. Their value comes from being organized and interpreted to help the decision maker reach better decisions.

In practice, a marketing manager (1) sets the priority of the data from most valuable to least valuable in solving a problem, (2) assesses the cost of collecting each kind of data, and (3) stops collecting more data on the list when the cost of

Using an information system to make better marketing decisions.

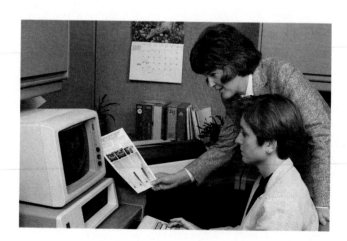

collection outweighs their value in improving the decisions. Although these are very difficult guidelines to apply, they stress an important issue: the value of the data must be balanced against their cost of collection and use. Great care is needed to use information technology that is user-friendly and that assists marketing managers reach decisions.

Kinds of Decisions a Marketing Manager Makes A marketing manager makes two distinctly different kinds of decisions. One type is *structured decisions,* routine and repetitive decisions for which standard solutions exist. A product manager for a grocery products manufacturer may plan dozens of sales promotions (coupons and deals) over a five-year period. For these structured decisions the manager can access the information system to determine what will be the impact on case sales of moving the promotion up two weeks or changing a coupon's price allowance.

In contrast, *unstructured decisions* are complex decisions for which there are no cut-and-dried solutions. For example, a department store manager may ask for an assessment of the impact on sales of changing the department's location within the store. The accompanying Marketing Research Report points out that marketing managers rely more heavily on their own past experience in making these unstructured decisions, as opposed to structured ones.

One-time and special reports don't go into an information system. Only the cost-effective, repetitive information is typically included and becomes the database used with pertinent models to provide the standardized, periodic reports produced by the information system. In the Marketing Research Report, four of the kinds of information shown would clearly go in an information system: diary panel data (item 2), the company's weekly sales report (item 3), store audit data (item 4), and season of sales year (item 7). Other kinds of information might go into an information system if the data were collected repeatedly in the same format.

KEY ELEMENTS IN AN INFORMATION SYSTEM

All three kinds of information systems described earlier are used by today's marketing managers seeking user-friendly systems to assist them in their decisions. As shown in Figure 9–6, today's strategic information system that helps a marketing manager develop micromarketing strategies contains five key elements:

1 *Input devices*—These means of collecting marketing data include in-store and in-home scanners, people meters, and purchase/reservation workstations.
2 *Databases*—The marketing data collected by the input devices are stored in diverse databases containing data on households, products, retailers, media, and promotions.
3 *Models*—The models provide hypotheses about the relationships among the data contained in the databases to enable the decision maker to organize, interpret, and communicate the resulting information in order to reach marketing decisions.[23]

Marketing Research Report

INFORMATION FOR MARKETING DECISIONS: WHAT GOES INTO AN INFORMATION SYSTEM?

*H*ow important is past experience when marketing managers make structured versus unstructured decisions? What information do they use for these two kinds of decision? What might go into an information system?

Researchers W. Steven Perkins and Ram C. Rao sought answers to these questions by having experienced marketing managers rate different kinds of information they would need for two different marketing decisions: (1) the scheduling of consumer promotions (a structured decision) and (2) introducing new products (an unstructured decision).

The researchers found that past experience is especially important for marketing managers making unstructured decisions such as introducing new products, but not as important for structured decisions. The researchers used a 10-point scale to evaluate the importance of different kinds of information (where 0 = very unimportant and 10 = very important). As shown in the figure, there are significant differences in the kinds of information managers want for scheduling consumer promotions compared to introducing new products.

Look carefully at the eight kinds of information in the figure. Which ones are repetitive information that might go into an information system? For the answer, see the text.

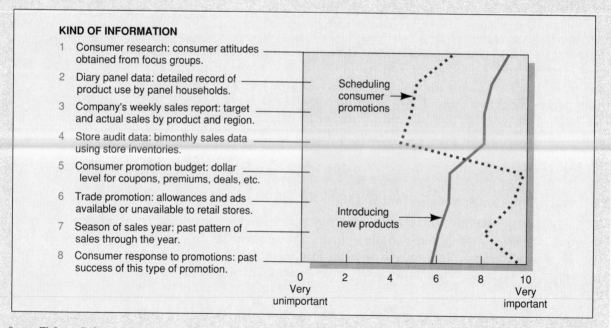

KIND OF INFORMATION

1. Consumer research: consumer attitudes obtained from focus groups.
2. Diary panel data: detailed record of product use by panel households.
3. Company's weekly sales report: target and actual sales by product and region.
4. Store audit data: bimonthly sales data using store inventories.
5. Consumer promotion budget: dollar level for coupons, premiums, deals, etc.
6. Trade promotion: allowances and ads available or unavailable to retail stores.
7. Season of sales year: past pattern of sales through the year.
8. Consumer response to promotions: past success of this type of promotion.

Source: W. Steven Perkins and Ram C. Rao, "The Role of Experience in Information Use and Decision Making by Marketing Managers," *Journal of Marketing Research* (February 1990), pp. 1–10.

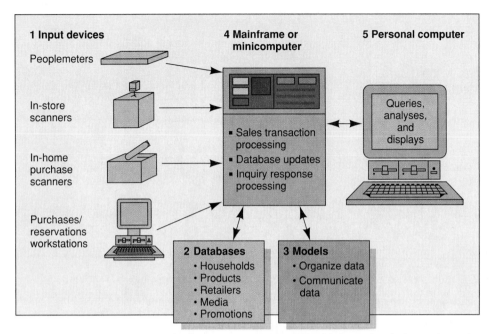

FIGURE 9–6
Strategic information system for use in today's micromarketing decisions

Note that this system captures marketing data from many sources using an array of devices; updates databases; and responds to the marketing manager's queries.

4 *Mainframe or minicomputer*—This is today's main means of collecting, processing, and updating the data coming from the input devices, databases, and models. Coming off the drawing boards to replace these older computers are systems of networked microcomputers.[24]

5 *Personal computer*—The PC on the marketing manager's desk serves as an input and output device and a means of querying the system to obtain and analyze the data it contains.[25]

An information system like this permits a marketing manager to reach decisions using **sensitivity analysis**, asking "what if" questions to determine how changes in a factor like price or advertising affect marketing results like sales revenues or profits.

DAHL'S SUPERMARKET: AN SIS FOR 2001 . . . OR 1995!

A trip to a supermarket in Des Moines, Iowa, may give you a crystal-ball glimpse of what the future holds for tomorrow's micromarketing managers using a state-of-the-art strategic information system to reach decisions. Suppose you've moved to Des Moines, have just joined the Vision Value Club, and walk into the Dahl's Foods supermarket.[26] On a step-by-step basis here's what you will see and how it impacts the SIS for the supermarket and grocery product manufacturers:

1 As a card-carrying member of the Vision Value Club, you have a plastic "smart card," which doubles as a Visa and cash card and contains a computer chip detailing your demographic background (address, age, family,

What may lie in your future: press a touch-sensitive screen at your supermarket checkout counter to receive coupons or recipes while your bill is tallied. On this screen, red numbers and a check mark show that an item is discounted.

pets, etc.). It's also a modern version of trading stamps—it remembers how many "points" you've earned toward premiums ranging from toys to camcorders.

2 You walk into Dahl's and pick up a list of that month's discounts. At the checkout lane, a split-screen monitor displays a running total of your purchases along with promotional minivideos. On Pampers disposable diapers, for example, the monitor tells you that the product is 50 cents off and it's worth 200 points toward Value Club premiums. The touch-sensitive screen (see the accompanying photo) allows you to obtain instant coupons from a small laser printer. You will never have to clip another coupon for supermarket products.

3 The monitor shows a preliminary bill of $118.75. Discounts bring it down to $107.81, a 10 percent savings. And you've picked up 650 more points, almost enough for a new toaster. You put the purchases on your card, and Dahl's automatically deducts $107.81 from your checking account.

4 Your purchases are tallied by Dahl's computer and added to its database of Value Club members. The marketing company that is a partner in the program analyzes the database and learns that you are one of 5,000 customers with children under age 2. Dahl's and Procter & Gamble design a marketing program for your group. The store sends you a mailer with an offer for 75 cents off and a free gallon of milk for every large package of Pampers you purchase.

5 You believe that's a pretty good deal, so you return to the store to use your electronic Pampers "coupon" and get the free milk with the diapers. While there, you buy a few more things as well. You add 216 points to your Value Club balance. Only 125 more to go until you've earned that toaster.

Analyzing the data from their promotion, the Procter & Gamble's marketers find that only 25 percent of their target customers responded. Unlike you, apparently most of the other 5,000 people targeted with the Pampers electronic coupon didn't think 75 cents off an $11 dollar bag of diapers and a free gallon of milk was worth coming to the store. Next time, the marketers decide they'll give people a $1.25 coupon.

Marketing Action Memo

OPERATION DESERT STORM: AN SIS ON 3 × 5 CARDS

*F*ew Americans would argue that the Persian Gulf War involved the United States's most strategic decisions in 1991. So was the U.S. general who was responsible for providing the food, water, shelter, clothing, and equipment for a half million American and Allied troops in the war hunkered down with his computer-based strategic information system?

Not a chance. Desert Storm's Lieutenant General William "Gus" Pagonis had a decidedly low-tech approach: "I use 3 × 5 cards," he said.

Although backed up by an incredible array of information systems, Pagonis used what he calls "centralized command/decentralized execution." Pagonis needed methods of getting the essential information and avoiding unnecessary detail—just like any head of a large organization. Two examples:

- *Oral reports*—Every morning of Desert Storm Pagonis held a 30-minute meeting for his 40 top

officers. Everyone stood to make them stick to the topic. No meeting exceeded 30 minutes.
- *Written reports*—To control verbose army reports, Pagonis hit on the 3 × 5 cards that keep the background of the problem and request for action under clear focus. He handled 100 cards a day, usually responding to them within 12 hours with direct messages like "O.K." and "psm" (please see me).

When a major tried to sneak a 5 × 8 card into the system, Pagonis rejected it. His system works. "Nobody could have done the job better," observed Allied commander General H. Norman Schwarzkopf.

Source: "Half Audie Murphy, Half Jack Welch," *Business Week* (March 4, 1991), pp. 42–43; Benjamin Weiser, "In Logistics, Desert Storm Victory Is Only Half the Battle," *Washington Post* (March 5, 1991), p. A16.

While only experimental in 1991, some version of this supermarket and SIS is expected to be operating in the mid-1990s—a long time before the 21st century.

INFORMATION AND "BACKWARD MARKETING RESEARCH" IN SMALL BUSINESS

This discussion on information and information systems may suggest that small businesses won't be able to compete in the future because they can't afford costly information systems, but this is untrue for two reasons. First, the advent of personal computers and on-line databases makes huge volumes of data accessible to even small businesses. Second, data and elaborate information systems are not ends in themselves but the means to another end—making better decisions. The accompanying Marketing Action Memo describes how key logistics decisions for Operation Desert Storm were reduced to 3 × 5 cards—an incredibly efficient decision process, backed up by an SIS.

Many small businesses exist precisely because of their micromarketing capabilities: they understand and meet the needs of their special niche of customers far better than large businesses can ever do. Also, they are experts in "backward marketing research" and in finding useful, inexpensive marketing data. Backward marketing research involves identifying possible marketing actions that might be taken and "working backwards" to specify the marketing data needed. For example, Phil Kelly quit Chicago's Marshall Field's department store and opened his chain of Mallards men's clothing stores. Using only his own time and tenacity he got the bulk of the data needed from published sources at *no cost*. Four years after startup, Mallards had five stores and almost $5 million in annual sales.[27]

1 **What is the difference between structured and unstructured decisions for a marketing manager?**

2 **How does sensitivity analysis show up in the decision described for the Dahl's Foods/Procter & Gamble's SIS?**

MARKET AND SALES FORECASTING

Forecasting or estimating the actual size of a market is critical both in micromarketing decisions and more traditional marketing decisions. This is because overestimating the size of a market may mean wasting research and development, manufacturing, and marketing dollars on new products that fail. Underestimating it may mean missing the chance to introduce successful new products. We will discuss (1) some basic forecasting terms, (2) two major approaches to forecasting, and (3) specific forecasting techniques.

BASIC FORECASTING TERMS

Unfortunately there are no standard definitions for some forecasting concepts, so it's necessary to take care in defining the terms used.

Market or Industry Potential   The term **market potential,** or **industry potential,** refers to the maximum total sales of a product by all firms to a segment under specified environmental conditions and marketing efforts of the firms. For example, the market potential for cake mix sales to U.S. consumers in 1998 might be 12 million cases—what Pillsbury, Betty Crocker, Duncan Hines, and other cake mix producers would sell to American consumers under the assumptions that (1) past patterns of dessert consumption continue and (2) the same level of promotional effort continues relative to other desserts. If one of these assumptions proves false, the estimate of market potential will be wrong. For example, if American consumers suddenly become more concerned about eating refined sugar and shift their dessert preferences from cakes to fresh fruits, the estimate of market potential will be too high.

Sales or Company Forecast   What one firm expects to sell under specified conditions for the uncontrollable and controllable factors that affect the forecast is the **sales forecast,** or **company forecast.** For example, Duncan Hines might

A competitor's marketing actions can affect the sales forecast for a cake mix brand.

develop its sales forecast of 4 million cases of cake mix for U.S. consumers in 1998, assuming past dessert preferences continue and the same relative level of advertising expenditures between it, Pillsbury, and Betty Crocker. If Betty Crocker suddenly cuts its advertising in half, Duncan Hines's old sales forecast will probably be too low.

With both market potential estimates and sales forecasts, it is necessary to specify some significant details: the product involved (all cake mixes, only white cake mixes, or only Bundt cake mixes); the time period involved (month, quarter, or year); the segment involved (United States, Southwest region, upper-income buyer, or single-person households); controllable marketing mix factors (price and level of advertising support); uncontrollable factors (consumer tastes and actions of competitors); and the units of measurement (number of cases sold or total sales revenues).

TWO BASIC APPROACHES TO FORECASTING

A marketing manager rarely wants a single number for an annual forecast, such as 5,000 units or $75 million in sales revenue. Rather, the manager wants this total subdivided into elements the manager works with, such as sales by product line or sales to a market segment. The two basic approaches to sales forecasting are (1) subdividing the total sales forecast (top-down forecast) or (2) building the total sales forecast by summing up the components (buildup forecast).

Top-Down Forecast   A **top-down forecast** involves subdividing an aggregate forecast into its principal components. A shoe manufacturer can use a top-down forecast to estimate the percentage of its total shoe sales in a state and develop state-by-state forecasts for shoe sales for the coming year. The "Survey of Buying Power" published annually by *Sales and Marketing Management* magazine is a widely used source of such top-down forecasting information.

For example, as shown in Figure 9–7, the state of New York has 7.24 percent of the U.S. population, 8.20 percent of the U.S. effective buying income, and 7.11 percent of the U.S. retail sales. If the shoe manufacturer wanted to use a single factor related to expected shoe sales, it would choose the factor

1989 Regional State Summaries of...					
Population		Effective buying income		Retail sales	
Region State	1989 Total Population (Thousands)	% of U.S.	1989 Total EBI ($000)	% of U.S.	1989 Total Retail Sales ($000)	% of U.S.
MIDDLE ATLANTIC	**37,958.0**	**15.1928**	**565,304,970**	**17.1957**	**265,013,099**	**15.3891**
New Jersey	7,789.8	3.1179	138,379,390	4.2092	60,971,615	3.5406
New York	18,078.2	7.2359	269,608,653	8.2011	122,452,786	7.1108
Pennsylvania	12,090.0	4.8390	157,316,927	4.7854	81,588,698	4.7377

Source: Adapted from "1990 Survey of Buying Power," Part I, *Sales and Marketing Management* (August 13, 1990), pp. B-2, B-3, B-5.

FIGURE 9–7
U.S. population, effective buying income, and retail sales for selected states, 1989

that has been most closely related to shoe sales historically, in this case the percentage of U.S. retail sales. The top-down forecast would then be that 7.11 percent of the firm's sales would be made in the state of New York.

Sometimes multiple factors are considered, such as the *buying power index* (BPI) developed by *Sales and Marketing Management* magazine that gives weights of 0.2, 0.5, and 0.3, respectively, to the three previously mentioned factors, as follows:

$$\begin{aligned} \text{BPI} &= (0.2 \times \text{Percent of population}) + (0.5 \times \text{Percent of effective buying income}) + (0.3 \times \text{Percent of retail sales}) \\ &= (0.2 \times 7.2359) + (0.5 \times 8.2011) + (0.3 \times 7.1108) \\ &= 1.4472 + 4.1006 + 2.1332 \\ &= 7.681 = 7.68\% \end{aligned}$$

Thus the BPI forecasts 7.68 percent of the firm's shoe sales will occur in New York—significantly higher than if retail sales alone were used for the forecast. The forecast can be converted into dollars by using *Sales and Marketing Management* magazine's "Survey of Buying Power," Part II (in an annual October issue), which gives retail sales of various lines of merchandise such as footwear.

Buildup Forecast A **buildup forecast** involves summing the sales forecasts of each of the components to arrive at the total forecast. It is a widely used method when there are identifiable components such as products, product lines, or market segments in the forecasting problem.

Figure 9–8 shows how GE's aerospace department uses the buildup approach to develop a sales forecast involving three broad categories of projects or products: (1) work currently under contract that can be forecast precisely, (2) follow-up work that is likely to result from current contracts, and (3) new business that results from GE's proposals for new business, which is difficult to forecast. Each of these three forecasts is the sum of a number of individual products or projects, which for simplicity are not shown. In turn, forecasts for each of the three kinds of business can be summed to give the total sales forecast for the entire department.

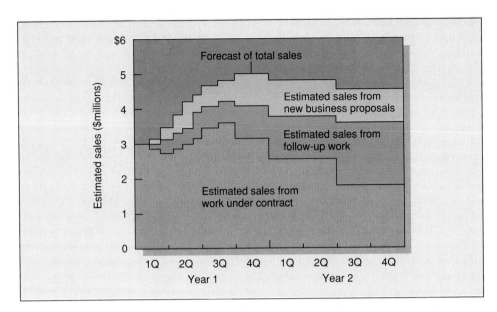

FIGURE 9–8
Buildup approach to a two-year sales forecast for General Electric's Aerospace Vehicle Department

SPECIFIC SALES FORECASTING TECHNIQUES

Broadly speaking, three main sales forecasting techniques are available that can lead to the forecasts used in the top-down or buildup approaches. Ordered from least costly in terms of both time and money to most costly, these are (1) judgments of the decision maker, (2) surveys of knowledgeable groups, and (3) statistical methods.

Judgments of the Decision Maker   Probably 99.9 percent of all sales forecasts are judgments of the person who must act on the results of the forecast—the individual decision maker. An example is the forecasts of likely sales, and hence the quantity to order, for the 8,500 items stocked in a typical supermarket that must be forecast by the stock clerk or manager. A **direct forecast** involves estimating the value to be forecast without any intervening steps. Examples appear in your daily life: How many quarts of milk should I buy? How much time should I allow to drive to the game? How much money should I get out of the instant cash machine? Your mind may go through some intervening steps but so quickly you're unaware of it.

So in estimating the amount of money to get from the instant cash machine, you probably made some unconscious (or conscious) intervening estimates (such as counting the cash in your billfold or the special events you need cash for) to obtain your direct estimate. Lost-horse forecasting does this in a more structured way. A **lost-horse forecast** involves starting with the last known value of the item being forecast, listing the factors that could affect the forecast, assessing whether they have a positive or negative impact, and making the final forecast. The technique gets its name from how you'd find a lost horse: go to where it was last seen, put yourself in its shoes, consider those factors which could affect where you might go (to the pond if you're thirsty, the hayfield if you're hungry, and so on), and go there. For example, a product manager for Wilson's tennis rackets in 1992 who needed to make a sales forecast through 1998 would start with the known value of 1992 sales and list the positive factors (more tennis courts, more TV publicity) and the negative ones (competition from other sports, high prices of graphite and ceramic rackets) to arrive at the final series of annual sales forecasts.

Surveys of Knowledgeable Groups   If you wonder what your firm's sales will be next year, ask people who are likely to know something about future sales. Four common groups that are surveyed to develop sales forecasts are prospective buyers, the firm's salesforce, its executives, and experts.

A **survey of buyers' intentions forecast** involves asking prospective customers whether they are likely to buy the product during some future time period. For industrial products with few prospective buyers who are able and willing to predict their future buying behavior, this can be effective. For example, there are probably only a few hundred customers in the entire world for Cray Research's supercomputers, so Cray simply surveys these prospects to develop its sales forecasts.

A **salesforce survey forecast** involves asking the firm's salespeople to estimate sales during a coming period. Because these people are in contact with customers and are likely to know what customers like and dislike, there is logic to this approach. However, salespeople can be unreliable forecasters—painting too rosy a picture if they are enthusiastic about a new product and too grim a forecast if their sales quota is based on it.

A **jury of executive opinion forecast** involves asking knowledgeable executives inside the firm—such as vice presidents of marketing, research and development, finance, and production—about likely sales during a coming period. Although this approach is fast and includes judgments from diverse functional areas, it can be biased by a dominant executive whose judgments are deferred to by the others.

A **survey of experts forecast** involves asking experts on a topic to make a judgment about some future event. A **Delphi forecast** is an example of a survey of experts and involves polling people knowledgeable about the forecast topic (often by mail) to obtain a sequence of anonymous estimates. Now used regularly by more than 100 large corporations, the Delphi forecast gets its name from the ancient Greek oracle at Delphi who was supposed to see into the future. A major advantage of Delphi forecasting is that the anonymous expert does not have to defend his or her views or feel obliged to agree with a supervisor's estimate.

A **technological forecast** involves estimating when scientific breakthroughs will occur. By what year do you think the following events will occur?

- Development of automated language translators.
- Production of 20 percent of the world's food by ocean farming.
- Growth of new organs and limbs through biochemical stimulation.
- Widespread use of telepathy and ESP in communications.

In 1963 experts used the Delphi method to estimate the year by which these and other events shown in Figure 9–9 would occur. Some of the projections look

BREAKTHROUGH	PROJECTED YEAR★		
	OPINION OF 25% OF PANEL	OPINION OF 50% OF PANEL	OPINION OF 75% OF PANEL
Economical desalination of sea-water	1964	1970	1980
Automated language translators	1968	1972	1976
Reliable weather forecasts	1972	1975	1988
Economical ocean-floor mining (other than offshore drilling)	1980	1989	2000
Limited weather control	1987	1990	2000
Production of 20 percent of the world's food by ocean farming	2000	2000	2017
Growth of new organs and limbs through biochemical stimulation	1995	2007	2040
Use of drugs to raise intelligence levels	1984	2012	2050
Use of telepathy and ESP in communications	2040	3000	3000

★Projecting the most rapid breakthrough in this area.

FIGURE 9–9
Projected years for scientific breakthroughs according to a 1963 Delphi technological forecast

good, but the figure shows even experts have bad days at their crystal ball. Limited degree of weather control by 1995, anyone?

Statistical Methods   The best-known statistical method of forecasting is **trend extrapolation,** which involves extending a pattern observed in past data into the future. When the pattern is described with a straight line, it is *linear trend extrapolation.* Suppose that in early 1981 you were a sales forecaster for the Xerox Corporation and had actual sales revenues running from 1974 to 1980 (Figure 9–10). Using linear trend extrapolation, you draw a line to fit the past data and project it into the future to give the forecast values shown for 1981 to 1994.

If in 1992 you want to compare your forecasts with actual results, you are in for a surprise—illustrating the strength and weakness of trend extrapolation. Trend extrapolation assumes that the underlying relationships in the past will continue into the future, which is the basis of the method's key strength: simplicity. If this assumption proves correct, you have an accurate forecast. However, if this proves wrong, the forecast is likely to be wrong. In this case your forecasts from 1981 through 1987 were too low. Xerox's aggressive new product development and marketing in the 1980s helped alter the factors underlying the linear trend extrapolation and caused the forecast to be too low.

In practice, marketing managers often use several of the forecasting techniques to estimate the size of markets important to them. Also, they often do three separate forecasts based on different sets of assumptions: (1) "best case" with optimistic assumptions, (2) "worst case" with pessimistic ones, and (3) "most likely case" with most reasonable assumptions.

FIGURE 9–10
Linear trend extrapolation of sales revenues of Xerox, made at the start of 1981

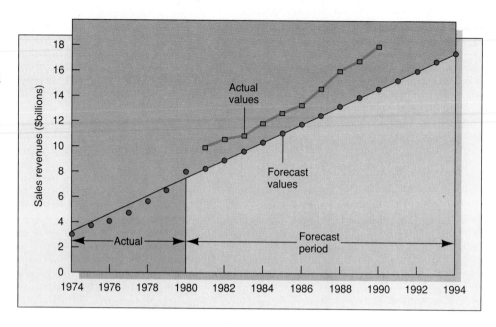

CONCEPT CHECK

1 What is the difference between the top-down and buildup approaches to forecasting sales?

2 How do you make a lost-horse forecast?

3 What is linear trend extrapolation?

ETHICS AND SOCIAL RESPONSIBILITY IN THE 1990s

HOW PRIVATE SHOULD MICROMARKETING DATA ON HOUSEHOLDS BE?

Lotus Development Corporation developed what many consider an ideal product for micromarketers: a massive, relatively inexpensive database permitting users to specify the kind of customers they were targeting and then receive the names and addresses (but not phone numbers, incomes, or credit history) of thousands of individual households.

This is the kind of household information direct marketers have routinely sold to each other for decades. Priced at $695 and offered in a CD-ROM format that was accessible to microcomputer users, Marketplace: Households would have substantially lowered the cost and increased the precision of micromarketers in their direct marketing efforts in many different industries. In response to a public outcry over invasion of privacy, Lotus announced it was dropping Marketplace: Households in early 1991.[28]

What are the advantages and disadvantages (1) to households in the database and (2) to micromarketers using the database? Was Lotus right when it dropped Marketplace: Households?

SUMMARY

1 Micromarketing involves combining demographic, media, and consumption profiles of households with buyer profiles of stores and products in order to target buyers in a neighborhood or for a specific product. It represents a revolutionary extension of market segmentation.

2 Information and information technology are increasingly seen as a means for a firm to obtain a sustainable competitive advantage. Three kinds of information systems operating today are management information systems, management support systems, and strategic information systems.

3 Micromarketing has been made necessary by more demanding consumers and excessive business and marketing costs. Quality and customer service are essential for American businesses to be competitive in today's international markets.

4 Micromarketing has been made possible by breakthroughs in the technology of information often collected electronically in-home, at-business, through single-source data services, and in on-line and CD-ROM databases.

5 Managers generally make two kinds of decisions—structured and unstructured—and must balance the value versus the cost of information.

6 Today's strategic information system used for micromarketing has five key elements: input devices, databases, models, mainframe or minicomputer, and the personal computer on a manager's desk.

7 Two basic approaches to forecasting sales are the top-down and buildup methods. Three forecasting techniques are judgments of individuals, surveys of groups, and statistical methods.

8 Individual judgments are the most widely used forecasting methods. Two common examples are direct and lost-horse forecasts.

9 Asking questions of groups of people who are knowledgeable about likely future sales is another frequently used method of forecasting. Four such groups are prospective buyers, the salesforce, executives, and experts.

10 Statistical forecasting methods, such as trend extrapolation, extend a pattern observed in past data into the future.

KEY TERMS AND CONCEPTS

micromarketing p. 224
information technology p. 224
management information systems p. 225
management support systems p. 225
strategic information systems p. 226
quality p. 229
single-source data 232
sensitivity analysis p. 237
market potential p. 240
industry potential p. 240
sales forecast p. 240
company forecast p. 240
top-down forecast p. 241

buildup forecast p. 242
direct forecast p. 243
lost-horse forecast p. 243
survey of buyers' intentions forecast p. 244
salesforce survey forecast p. 244
jury of executive opinion forecast p. 244
survey of experts forecast p. 244
Delphi forecast p. 244
technological forecast p. 244
trend extrapolation p. 245

≡ CHAPTER PROBLEMS AND APPLICATIONS

1 The chapter described two ways of electronically collecting information on a household's purchases: a scanner at the retailer's sales counter and an in-home scanner. How do these compare in terms of (*a*) quantity of a household's purchases measured and (*b*) possible bias reflected by consumers knowing they are being measured?

2 You walk up to the supermarket checkout counter with six cartons of yogurt you want to buy. (*a*) Describe circumstances under which the checkout procedure with electronic scanner (*1*) will measure all six items and (*2*) could miss the six items. (*b*) What problems do missing sales data cause for micromarketers?

3 Compare the planned Nielsen passive people meter ("Smart Sense") with the original people meter described in Chapter 7 in terms of (*a*) quality of information of TV viewing and (*b*) ability to get households to participate in the Nielsen TV panel.

4 Aim toothpaste runs an in-store experiment evaluating a coupon along with (*a*) in-store ads in half the stores and (*b*) no in-store ads in the other half of the stores.[29] The results of the Aim experiment are as follows, where a sales index of 100 indicates average store sales in the weeks before the experiment.

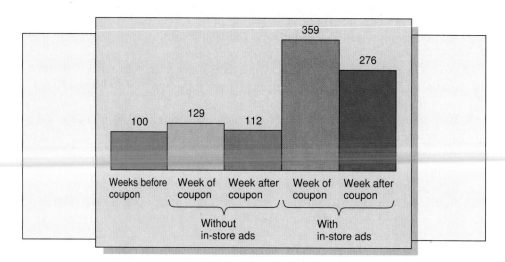

(*a*) What measures of success are appropriate? (*b*) What are your conclusions and recommendations? (*c*) How can micromarketers use experiments like this?

5 Another field experiment with coupons and in-store advertising for Wisk detergent is run. The index of sales is as follows:

	WEEKS BEFORE COUPON	WEEK OF COUPON	WEEK AFTER COUPON
Without in-store ads	100	144	108
With in-store ads	100	268	203

What are your conclusions and recommendations?

6 In designing an information system, the format in which information is presented to a harried marketing manager is often vital. (*a*) If you were a marketing manager and interrogated your information system, would you rather see the results shown in Question 4 or Question 5? (*b*) What are one or two strengths and weaknesses of each format?

7 Suppose you are associate dean of your college's business school responsible for scheduling courses for the school year. (*a*) What repetitive information would you include in your information system to help schedule classes? (*b*) What special, one-time information might affect your schedule? (*c*) What standardized output reports do you have to provide? When?

8 What is the impact of a strategic information system like that used by Dahl's Foods supermarket on (*a*) product quality and (*b*) service quality for households that shop at the supermarket?

9 Suppose you are to make a sales forecast using a top-down approach to estimate the percentage of a manufacturer's total U.S. sales going to each of the 50 states. You plan to use only a single factor—percentage of U.S. population, percentage of effective buying income, or percentage of retail sales. Which of the three factors would you use if your sales forecast were for each of the following manufacturers, and why? (*a*) Morton salt, (*b*) Christian Dior dresses, and (*c*) Columbia records.

10 Which of the following variables would linear trend extrapolation be more accurate for? (*a*) Annual population of the United States or (*b*) annual sales of cars produced in the United States by General Motors. Why?

Satisfying Marketing Opportunities

Part IV covers the unique combination of product, price, place, and promotion that results in an offering for potential customers. How products are developed and managed is the focus of Chapters 10 and 11. Pricing is covered in Chapters 12 and 13 and Appendix A. Three chapters address the place (distribution) element, which includes the retailing successes of Sam Walton, founder of Wal-Mart Stores. Finally, three promotion chapters cover topics ranging from Procter & Gamble's promotional standards to using Bo Jackson and Snoopy in attention-getting ads.

Developing New Products

- Understand the ways in which consumer and industrial products can be classified.
- Recommend strategies for marketing the different types of consumer products.
- Explain the implications of alternative ways of viewing "newness" in new products.
- Understand the purposes of each step of the new product process.
- Analyze the factors contributing to a product's success or failure.

How Much Is a Closer Shave Worth? Try Ten Years and $200 Million!

Gillette spent ten years and $200 million on research and development alone to produce its new Sensor razor, and the company plans to spend another $175 million in promotion to introduce its Sensor in 19 countries. In this chapter and the next we'll explore the product aspect of the marketing mix. It is often expensive, difficult, and challenging. A look at the Sensor shows why.

In developing its new razor, Gillette had a number of employees wait to shave until after they came to work in the morning. A microscopic camera mounted on the Sensor razors they used there measured the whiskers. Cut whiskers were also collected and measured. According to Gillette, a close-up view of a man's face looks like a street with a lot of potholes and bumps. Existing razors are like cars without shock absorbers driving over these roads. The Sensor razor (which has 19 patents) is revolutionary because it is not just a razor handle and a blade head that pivots. Its twin blades each have tiny springs welded to them. The blades can move independently up, down, and sideways. Wherever there is a whisker, the Sensor can go. A prototype of the Sensor was first developed in 1979; designing and perfecting the complex production line cost Gillette $150 million dollars and several years.

What does the new Sensor mean for Gillette? Many industry analysts believe Gillette has bet the company on this new product introduction.[1]

Will customers buy it? That question is the ultimate test for any new product. Early indications are that the Sensor is a big success, but Gillette must keep this potential success going.[2]

As you will learn in this chapter, the odds of a new product being successful are not great. In understanding new products, think of the Sensor's challenge and cost to Gillette. For a firm to develop a successful new product it requires razor-sharp marketing.

The essence of marketing is in developing products such as a new, technologically advanced razor to meet consumer needs. A **product** is a good, service, or idea consisting of a bundle of tangible and intangible attributes that satisfies consumers and is received in exchange for money or some other unit of value. Tangible attributes include physical characteristics such as color or sweetness, and intangible attributes include becoming healthier or wealthier. Hence a product includes the breakfast cereal you eat, the accountant who fills out your tax return, or the American Red Cross, which provides you self-satisfaction when you donate your blood. In many instances we exchange money to obtain the product, whereas in other instances we exchange our time and other valuables, such as our blood.

The life of a company often depends on how it conceives, produces, and markets new products. In this chapter we discuss the decisions involved in developing and marketing a new product. Chapter 11 covers the process of managing existing products.

THE VARIATIONS OF PRODUCTS

A product varies in terms of whether it is a consumer or industrial good. For most organizations the product decision is not made in isolation because companies often offer a range of products. To better appreciate the product decision, let's first define some terms pertaining to products.

PRODUCT LINE AND PRODUCT MIX

A **product line** is a group of products that are closely related because they satisfy a class of needs, are used together, are sold to the same customer group, are distributed through the same type of outlets, or fall within a given price range.[3] Polaroid has two major product lines consisting of cameras and film;

Some items in Adidas's broadening product line.

Adidas's product lines are shoes and clothing; the Mayo Clinic's product lines consist of inpatient hospital care, outpatient physician services, and medical research. Each product line has its own marketing strategy.

Within each product line is the *product item,* a specific product as noted by a unique brand, size, or price. For example, Downy softener for clothes comes in 12-ounce and 22-ounce sizes; each size is considered a separate item and assigned a distinct ordering code, or *stock keeping unit (SKU).*

The third way to look at products is by the **product mix,** or the number of product lines offered by a company. Cray Research has a single product line consisting of supercomputers, which are sold mostly to governments and large-businesses. American Brands, Inc., however, has many product lines consisting of cigarettes (Pall Mall), sporting equipment (Titleist golf balls), distilled beverages (Jim Beam liquors), and even services (Pinkerton security).

CLASSIFYING PRODUCTS

Both the federal government and companies classify products but for different purposes. The government's classification method helps it collect information on industrial activity. Companies classify products to help develop similar marketing strategies for the wide range of products offered. Two major ways to classify products are by degree of product tangibility and by type of user.

Degree of Tangibility   Classification by degree of tangibility divides products into one of three categories.[4] First is a *nondurable good,* an item consumed in one or a few uses, such as food products and fuel. A *durable good* is one that usually lasts over an extended number of uses, such as appliances, automobiles, and stereo equipment. *Services* are defined as activities, benefits, or satisfactions offered for sale, such as marketing research, health care, and education. As noted in Chapter 1, services are intangible. According to this classification, government data indicate that the United States is becoming a service economy.

This classification method also provides direction for marketing actions. Nondurable products such as Wrigley's gum are purchased frequently and at relatively low cost. Advertising is important to remind consumers of the item's existence, and wide distribution in retail outlets is essential. A consumer wanting Wrigley's Spearmint Gum would most likely purchase another brand of spearmint gum if Wrigley's were not available. Durable products, however, generally cost more than nondurable goods and last longer, so consumers usually deliberate longer before purchasing them. Therefore personal selling is an important component in durable-product marketing because it assists in answering consumer questions and concerns.

Marketing is increasingly being used with services. Services are intangibles, so a major goal in marketing is to make the benefits of purchasing the product real to consumers. Thus Northwest Airlines shows the fun of a Florida vacation or the joy of seeing grandparents. People who provide the service are often the key to its success in the market because consumers often evaluate the product by the service provider they meet—the Hertz reservation clerk, the receptionist at the university admissions office, or the nurse in the doctor's office.

Type of User   The second major type of product classification is according to the user. **Consumer goods** are products purchased by the ultimate consumer, whereas **industrial goods** are products used in the production of other products for ultimate consumers. In many instances the differences are distinct: Oil of Olay face moisturizer and Bass shoes are clearly consumer products, whereas DEC computers and high-tension steel springs are industrial goods used in producing other products or services.

There are difficulties, however, with this classification because some products can be considered both consumer and industrial items. A Macintosh computer can be sold to consumers as a final product or to industrial firms for office use. Each classification results in different marketing actions. Viewed as a consumer product, the Macintosh would be sold through computer stores like ComputerLand. As an industrial product, the Macintosh might be sold by a salesperson offering discounts for multiple purchases. Classifying by the type of user focuses on the market and the user's purchase behavior, which determine the marketing mix strategy.

CLASSIFYING CONSUMER AND INDUSTRIAL GOODS

Because the buyer is the key to marketing, consumer and industrial product classifications are discussed in greater detail.

Shoes are an example of a consumer good.

CLASSIFICATION OF CONSUMER GOODS

Convenience, shopping, specialty, and unsought products are the four types of consumer goods. They differ in terms of (1) effort the consumer spends on the decision, (2) attributes used in purchase, and (3) frequency of purchase.

Convenience goods are items that the consumer purchases frequently, conveniently, and with a minimum of shopping effort. **Shopping goods** are items for which the consumer compares several alternatives on criteria, such as price, quality, or style. **Specialty goods** are items, such as Waterford crystal, that a consumer makes a special effort to search out and buy. **Unsought goods** are items that the consumer either does not know about or knows about but does not initially want. Figure 10–1 shows how the classification of a consumer product into one of these four types results in different aspects of the marketing mix being stressed. Different degrees of brand loyalty and amounts of shopping effort are displayed by the consumer for a product in each of the four classes.

The manner in which a consumer good is classified depends on the individual. One person may view a camera as a shopping good and visit several stores before deciding on a brand, whereas a friend may view cameras as a specialty good and will only buy a Nikon.

The product classification of a consumer good can change the longer a product is on the market. When first introduced, the Litton microwave oven was unique, a specialty good. Now there are several competing brands on the market, and microwaves are a shopping good for many consumers.

The Waterford brand of crystal is a specialty good.

CLASSIFICATION OF INDUSTRIAL GOODS

A major characteristic of industrial goods is that sales of items are often the result of *derived demand;* that is, sales of industrial products frequently result (or are derived) from the sale of consumer goods. For example, if consumer demand for Fords (a consumer product) increases, the firm may increase its demand for paint spraying equipment (an industrial product). Industrial goods are classified not only on the attributes the consumer uses, but also on how the item is to be used. Thus industrial products may be classified as production or support goods.

Production Goods   Items used in the manufacturing process that become part of the final product are **production goods.** These include raw materials such as grain or lumber, as well as component parts. For example, a company that manufactures door hinges used by GM in its car doors is producing a component part. As noted in Chapter 6, the marketing of production goods is based on factors such as price, quality, delivery, and service. Marketers of these products tend to sell directly to industrial users.

Support Goods   The second class of industrial goods is **support goods,** which are items used to assist in producing other goods and services. Support goods include installations, accessory equipment, supplies, and services.

- *Installations* consist of buildings and fixed equipment. Because a significant amount of capital is required to purchase installations, the industrial buyer

BASIS OF COMPARISON	TYPE OF CONSUMER GOOD			
	CONVENIENCE	SHOPPING	SPECIALTY	UNSOUGHT
Product	Toothpaste, cake mix, hand soap, laundry detergent	Cameras, TVs, briefcases, clothing	Rolls Royce cars, Rolex watches	Burial insurance, thesaurus
Price	Relatively inexpensive	Fairly expensive	Usually very expensive	Varies
Place (distribution)	Widespread; many outlets	Large number of selective outlets	Very limited	Often limited
Promotion	Price, availability, and awareness stressed	Differentiation from competitors stressed	Uniqueness of brand and status stressed	Awareness is essential
Brand loyalty of consumers	Aware of brand, but will accept substitutes	Prefer specific brands, but will accept substitutes	Very brand loyal; will not accept substitutes	Will accept substitutes
Purchase behavior of consumers	Frequent purchases; little time and effort spent shopping; routine decision	Infrequent purchases; comparison shopping; uses decision time	Infrequenct purchases; extensive time spent to decide and get the item	Very infrequent purchases, some comparison shopping

FIGURE 10–1
Classification of consumer goods

deals directly with construction companies and manufacturers through sales representatives. The pricing of installations is often by competitive bidding.

- *Accessory equipment* includes tools and office equipment and is usually purchased in small-order sizes by buyers. As a result, instead of dealing directly with buyers, sellers of industrial accessories use distributors to contact a large number of buyers.
- *Supplies* are similar to consumer convenience goods and consist of products such as stationery, paper clips, and brooms. These are purchased with little effort, using the straight rebuy decision sequence discussed in Chapter 6. Price and delivery are key factors considered by the buyers of supplies.
- *Services* are intangible activities to assist the industrial buyer. This category can include maintenance and repair services and advisory services such as tax or legal counsel. The reputation of the seller of services is a major factor in marketing these industrial goods.

CONCEPT CHECK

1 Explain the difference between product mix and product line.

2 To which type of good (industrial or consumer) does the term *derived demand* generally apply?

3 A limited problem-solving approach is common to which type of consumer good?

NEW PRODUCTS AND WHY THEY FAIL

New products are the lifeblood of a company and keep it growing. The importance placed on the sale of new products is increasing for many companies, but the financial risks are large. The number of new products introduced each year is huge, but varies from industry to industry. In 1990 alone, the number of new pet foods increased 27 percent over the previous year, while new fruit and vegetable products increased 52 percent. Because many companies report product development costs increasing between 10 and 20 percent annually, in some product categories the number of new product introductions is decreasing. In the soup category, for example, there were 26 percent fewer new product introductions in 1990 than in 1989.[5] A study of only industrial firms found that 15 percent of current sales were from products introduced within the last five years.[6] Before discussing how new products reach the stage of commercialization when they are available to the consumer, we'll begin by looking at *what* a new product is.

WHAT IS A NEW PRODUCT?

The term *new* is difficult to define. Does changing the color of a laundry detergent mean it is a new product, as a compact camcorder would be considered new? There are several ways to view the newness of a product.

Newness Compared with Existing Products If a product is functionally different from existing offerings, it can be defined as new. The microwave oven and automobile were once functionally new, but for most products the innovation is more a modification of an old product than a dramatic functional change.

Newness in Legal Terms The Federal Trade Commission advised that the term *new* be limited to use with a product up to six months after it enters regular distribution.[7] The difficulty with this suggestion is in the interpretation of the term *regular distribution*.

Microwave cooking: a discontinuous innovation that has revolutionized some consumption patterns.

Newness from the Company's Perspective Companies generally view a new product as either a revised item or a completely new innovation. With a revised product the modifications can be either major or minor. Major revisions in 35 mm cameras are the automatic focus capability of Canon's EOS (for electrical optical system) and the talking ability of Minolta's camera. A minor revision is the self-contained lens protector of Pentax's 35 mm camera. A completely new product might be a technological breakthrough (such as the cellular car telephone) or a product new to the company but offered by competing firms.

Rather than viewing a product as new for a specified period (such as six months), companies often use an objective measure such as sales, market share, or percentage of sales potential. When a product is introduced to the market, a large advertising expenditure is often required to inform potential buyers. If a company considers a product new for only six months, advertising expenditures may be reduced prematurely.

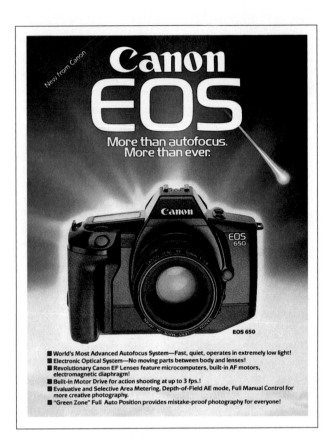

The autofocus feature makes this 35 mm camera a new product.

Newness from the Consumer's Perspective   A fourth way to define new products is in terms of their effects on consumption.[8] This approach classifies new products according to the degree of learning required by the consumer, as shown in Figure 10–2.

With a *continuous innovation*, no new behaviors must be learned. One of the hottest continuous new product introductions of 1990 was Nintendo's Game Boy, a palm-sized device with a tiny screen and game controls. This product allowed video-game players to enjoy their hobby without being tied to the television set. In 1990 alone, 3.5 million units were sold along with 12 million pieces of Game Boy software.[9] For Nintendo game players, no new behaviors were required to be learned to use the Game Boy. When minimal consumer education is required, marketing depends on generating awareness and having strong distribution in appropriate outlets.

The *dynamically continuous innovation* is represented by the Reebok Pump inflatable athletic shoe. As noted in Chapter 8, this new product has an inflatable cushion that the athlete pumps up until the shoe conforms to the shape of the foot. Although a slight change in behavior is needed, radically new behavior is not required by the consumer to wear a pair of Pumps. People know how to put on shoes as well as how to operate a pump; it was inflating the shoe that was a novel concept.

	Low	Degree of change behavior and learning needed by consumer	High
BASIS OF COMPARISON	**CONTINUOUS INNOVATION**	**DYNAMICALLY CONTINUOUS INNOVATION**	**DISCONTINUOUS INNOVATION**
Definition	Requires no new learning by consumers	Disrupts consumer's normal routine but does not require totally new learning	Establishes new consumption patterns among consumers
Examples	Sensor and New Improved Tide	Electric toothbrush, compact disc player, and automatic flash units for cameras	VCR, microwave oven, and home computer
Marketing emphasis	Generate awareness among consumers and obtain widespread distribution	Advertise benefits to consumers, stressing point of differentiation and consumer advantage	Educate consumers through product trial and personal selling

FIGURE 10–2
Consumption effects define newness

A *discontinuous innovation* involves making the consumer establish entirely new consumption patterns. In marketing these new products, a significant amount of time must often be spent initially educating the consumer on how to use the product, such as cooking with a microwave oven or operating a personal computer.

WHY PRODUCTS FAIL

Thousands of product failures that occur every year cost American businesses billions of dollars. Some estimates place new product failure rates as high as 80 percent.[10] To learn marketing lessons from these failures, we can analyze why new products fail and then study several failures in detail. As we go through the new product process later in the chapter, we can identify ways such failures might have been avoided—admitting that hindsight is clearer than foresight.

Recently introduced new consumer products.

Reasons for New Product Failures   Many factors contribute to new product failures or are symptoms of them: incompatibility with the firm's objectives and capabilities, competition that is too tough, lack of top management support, and lack of money. However, six factors, often present in combination, are far more fundamental:

1 *Too small a target market*: The market is too small to warrant the R&D, production, and marketing expenses to reach it. In 1990 Kodak discontinued its Ultralife lithium battery. Seen as a major breakthrough in 1987 because of its 10-year shelf life, the battery was touted as lasting twice as long as an alkaline battery. Yet the product was only available in the nine-volt size, which accounts for less than 10 percent of the batteries sold in the United States.[11]

2 *Insignificant point of difference*: Computerized home-banking services have been a technology promoted as the new way to bank, yet consumers see little benefit or need to go home after work and juggle their money between accounts. While the monthly costs of the services have been as low as $10–$12, consumers have not seen the value.[12]

3 *Poor product quality*: R. J. Reynolds developed the smokeless cigarette at an estimated cost of almost $1 billion. But after five months of test marketing in 1989, the product was killed. The reason was best stated by one employee of a 7–Eleven store in Phoenix, Arizona: "They're terrible. They're nasty. They're beyond nasty."[13]

4 *No access to market*: Manufacturers of potentially better products can't communicate this to prospective buyers or gain retail shelf space. Dozens of useful computer software programs can't get the attention of prospective buyers or space in computer stores.

5 *Bad timing*: The product is introduced too soon, too late, or at a time when consumer tastes are shifting dramatically. Miller Brewing Co. launched Matilda Bay wine coolers in September 1987, just after the peak summer season. Another bad-timing factor was that the product was introduced just as the wine cooler market began to peak in sales.[14]

6 *Poor execution of the marketing mix*: Coca-Cola thought its Minute Maid Squeeze-Fresh frozen orange juice concentrate in a squeeze bottle was a hit. The idea was that consumers could make one glass of juice at a time, and the concentrate stayed fresh in the refrigerator for over a month. After two test markets, the product was finished. Consumers loved the idea, but the product was messy to use, and consumers didn't know how much concentrate to mix.[15]

A Look at Some Failures   Before reading further, study the product failures described in Figure 10–3 and try to identify which of the six reasons is the most likely explanation for their failure. The three examples are discussed in greater detail below.

General Electric's high-tech refrigerators with rotary compressors have hurt the company's reputation for innovation and may cost GE up to $350 million to repair—an expensive mistake. Product quality was the problem. The

FIGURE 10–3
Why did these new products fail?

As explained in detail in the text, new products often fail because of one or a combination of six reasons: (1) too small a target market, (2) insignificant point of difference, (3) poor product quality, (4) no access to market, (5) bad timing, and (6) poor execution of the marketing mix.

Look at the three products described below, and try to give the reason that they failed in the marketplace:

- GE's high-tech line of refrigerators that used a rotary compressor.
- Del Monte's Barbecue Ketchup that contained finely chopped onions and was aimed at the heavy ketchup-eating segment.
- Mennen's Real deodorant, a cream-like antiperspirant developed for women, that was applied like a roll-on.

Compare your insights with those in the text.

compressor had a serious design flaw that made the refrigerator fail. GE is stuck honoring its five-year warranty. And while the company has replaced over one million compressors, it can't locate over 200,000 units with the same problem.[16]

Del Monte aimed its Barbecue Ketchup to the heavy ketchup-using segment—children and teenagers. The problem is that most consumers in this segment hate onions, so the product's difference—onions mixed with regular ketchup—worked against it. As a result, the target market was too small. The product was subsequently reintroduced as a gourmet sauce for meat cooked on outdoor grills.

Poor execution of the marketing mix hurt Real, Mennen's deodorant. The product was introduced with a $14 million advertising campaign. One problem, though, was that customers found that if they twisted the dispenser too hard, too

Marketing Research Report

WINNER OR LOSER: IS NEW PRODUCT SUCCESS JUST LUCK?

*W*hat makes some products winners and others losers? Knowing this answer is a key to a new product strategy. Two Canadian professors, R. G. Cooper and E. J. Kleinschmidt, studied 203 new products—winners and losers in the marketplace—to find the answer. Having reviewed previous research in this area, the researchers identified 10 factors reported to lead to success.

To determine whether these factors really differed between winners and losers, they conducted

personal interviews with the managers most knowledgeable about 203 products in 125 firms. Figure 10–4 shows the managers' answers about where winners and losers differ. Study the figure. For the conclusions the researchers reached from this information, see the text.

Source: R. G. Cooper and E. J. Kleinschmidt, "New Products—What Separates Winners from Losers?" *Journal of Product Innovation Management* (September 1987), pp. 169–84. Copyright © 1987 by Elsevier Science Publishing Co., Inc.

FACTORS	DIFFERENCE (success)–(failure)	IMPORTANCE OF DIFFERENCE	MEAN VALUES ON SCALE FROM 0 TO 10		
Existence and quality of "protocol"	2.68	Very important	Failure 5.44 / Success 8.12		
Product advantage	2.32	Very important	F 4.93 / S 7.25		
Effectiveness of pre-hardware activities	1.67	Important	F 3.13 / S 4.80		
Effectiveness of technological activities in new product process	1.51	Important	F 4.06 / S 5.57		
Synergy with firm's marketing strengths	1.30	Important	F 5.00 / S 6.30		
Synergy with firm's technology strengths	1.29	Important	F 5.86 / S 7.15		
Effectiveness of marketing activities in new product process	1.12	Important	F 2.53 / S 3.65		
Top management support	0.92	Important	F 5.37 / S 6.29		
Market potential	0.91	Important	F 5.61 / S 6.52		
Market competitiveness	–0.24	Not important	F 6.44 / S 6.20		

Scale: 0 (Very unimportant) — 2 — 4 — 6 — 8 — 10 (Very important)

FIGURE 10–4
Factors that separate new product winners from losers

much cream came out, creating an instant mess. Also, the name Real gave little indication of the product or its benefits. Where is Real today? It's not completely dead, because Mennen plans to rename and reintroduce the product.[17]

As shown in the accompanying Marketing Research Report, often a combination of factors separate successful from unsuccessful products. The greatest differences between those products that succeed and those that don't are in having a real product advantage and having a precise *protocol*—a statement that identifies a well-defined target market before product development begins; specifies customers' needs, wants, and preferences; and carefully states what the product would be and do. Figure 10–4 shows that many of the factors that are necessary for success involve marketing activities that occur before the product—or hardware—actually undergoes production.[18]

Developing successful new products may sometimes involve luck, but more often it involves having a product that really meets a need and has significant points of difference over competitive products. The likelihood of success is improved by paying attention to the early steps of the new product process described in the next section of the text.

1 From a consumer's viewpoint, what kind of innovation would an improved electric toothbrush be?

2 What does "insignificant point of difference" mean as a reason for new product failure?

THE NEW PRODUCT PROCESS

In September 1987, after several years of R&D, Canon introduced a new camera, the EOS. This new camera contains two microprocessors that control the focusing, light exposure, and shutter speed. This technology has set the standard among the generation of "smart" cameras.[19] There were several steps that had to be taken before this product was ready for market. Figure 10–5 shows the seven stages of the **new product process,** the sequence of activities a firm uses to identify business opportunities and convert them to a salable good or service. This sequence begins with new product strategy development and ends with commercialization.[20]

NEW PRODUCT STRATEGY DEVELOPMENT

For companies, **new product strategy development** involves defining the role for a new product in terms of the firm's overall corporate objectives. This step in the new product process has been added by many companies recently to provide a needed focus for ideas and concepts developed in later stages. 3M, for example, has a corporate objective that a quarter of a division's sales must come from products introduced within the past five years.[21] Hershey Foods Corporation has a goal of developing at least one successful new product a year.[22]

Objectives: Identify Markets and Strategic Rules   During this step the company uses the environmental scanning process described in Chapter 3 to identify trends that pose either opportunities or threats. Relevant company strengths and

FIGURE 10–5
Stages in the new product process

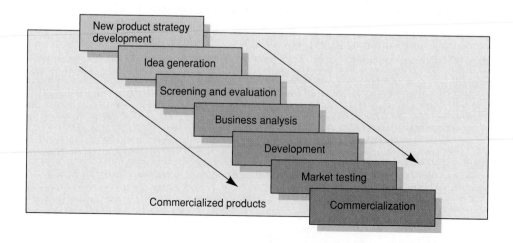

weaknesses are also identified. The outcome of new product strategy development is not new product ideas, but markets for which new products will be developed and strategic roles new products might serve—the vital protocol activity explained earlier in the discussion of the Marketing Research Report on new product winners and losers.

Proactive and Reactive New Product Strategies   New product strategies can be generally classified as either proactive or reactive. Proactive strategies lead to an allocation of resources to identify and seize opportunities. These approaches involve future-oriented R&D, consumer research, entrepreneurial development, or acquisition.[23] In a proactive approach to developing new products many companies scan the international marketplace to uncover opportunities. Hershey Foods, for example, developed its successful Symphony candy bar by modeling the creamier, smoother-tasting chocolate found in Europe. American brewers have recently introduced dry beers like Anheuser-Busch Dry, a new-product concept pioneered by leading Japanese brewers like Sapporo.

In response to the proactive new product approach being taken by many companies, there is one consulting company, Intersweep, that goes through foreign grocery stores to uncover possible new product ideas for U.S. companies. General Electric (GE) encourages its researchers to transfer technologies from one department to others. For example, GE applied its technology used in a medical diagnostic tool for imaging the human body to a device for examining jet engines for wear.[24]

Reactive strategies involve taking a defensive approach by responding to a competitor's actions. Mazda, General Motors, and Chrysler introduced their mini-vans in the late 1980s. Chrysler, the firm that had first introduced this type of vehicle, later redesigned its popular product with a different dashboard, grille, and bucket seats. A small number of Japanese and Korean firms, like Nissan, have taken almost 10 percent of the U.S. soup market with inexpensive, dry soups made from long, thin ramen noodles. In late 1989, Campbell's reacted with its own version of compressed noodle soup that is made by adding boiling water.[25] Some companies even mirror a competitor's new product with a "me-too" copy. Anheuser-Busch introduced Busch Cold Filtered Draft beer in response to Miller's successful introduction of genuine draft.[26] Other firms might take a leapfrog approach. For example, Minolta developed the first autofocus camera, but Canon has extended the technology to improve on Minolta's original product.

In a recent survey, Booz, Allen & Hamilton, Inc., a national consulting firm, asked responding firms what strategic role was served by their most successful recent product. These roles, shown in Figure 10–6, help define the direction of new product development and divide into externally and internally driven factors, which lead to the proactive and reactive strategies just described.

IDEA GENERATION

Developing a pool of concepts as candidates for new products, or **idea generation**, must build on the previous stage's results. New product ideas are generated by consumers, employees, basic R&D, and competitors.

FIGURE 10–6
**Strategic roles of most
successful new products**

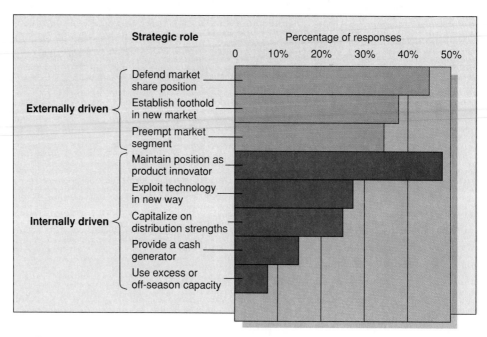

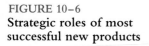

Customer Suggestions   Personal interviews, an important form of marketing research discussed in Chapter 7, was used by Techsonic Industries, an Alabama company that makes depth finders for fishing enthusiasts. Although Japanese competitors make more sophisticated products, speaking to 25 sports-enthusiast groups helped Techsonic discover that these potential customers wanted a gauge that could be read in bright sunlight.[27] Proctor & Gamble, in its environmental scan of Japanese consumers, detected a very strong concern among Japanese parents with keeping their babies clean. In fact, market research showed that Japanese consumers changed their babies' diapers far more frequently than American parents. In response to this market difference P&G developed Ultra Pampers, a more absorbent diaper that makes frequent changing less necessary. Today, Ultra Pampers is the market leader in Japan.[28]

Companies often analyze consumer complaints or problems to discover new product opportunities. They also pose complaints to a sample of consumers, who are asked to suggest products with such deficiencies, in order to identify new product opportunities.[29] Listening to growing concerns about cholesterol and fat in its food, McDonald's is testing an all-vegetable-oil mixture and eliminating beef tallow from its frying process for french fries. It is also reformulating its shakes with a low-fat mixture, and has introduced a low-fat hamburger.[30] Guardsman Elevator Company, a firm that services elevators, has developed a product to prevent vandals from riding on top of elevators. The company developed an infrared technology to trigger an alarm and shut off elevator power whenever anyone gets on top of an elevator. The company forecasts a market potential of 400,000 units.[31]

Employee and Co-Worker Suggestions   Employees may be encouraged to suggest new product ideas through suggestion boxes or contests. The federal government has a Beneficial Suggestion Program awarding employees a cash percentage of the cost savings gained from their ideas. The idea for General Mills's $150 million-a-year Nature Valley Granola Bars came when one of its marketing managers observed co-workers bringing granola to work in plastic bags.

Paul Breedlove, a Texas Instruments (TI) engineer, discussed with some co-workers an idea for a hand-held calculator that could talk. They just laughed, so he did some more work on the idea and eventually sold them on it. The company still refused to fund the idea because it was "too wild," but Breedlove and his believing co-workers got $25,000 from a special fund TI uses to finance long shots. Breedlove's concept came to market as Speak & Spell, a microprocessor that helps children learn to spell. Its success spawned a family of new products such as Speak & Math and Speak & Read, largely because of the commitment by TI to generate a pool of alternative new product ideas.

3M, a leader in product innovation, has a 15 percent rule that allows anyone in the company to spend up to fifteen percent of the workweek on anything he or she wants to. In addition, the company has developed grants of up to $50,000 to carry a concept past the idea stage. This approach allowed one employee, Sanford Cobb, to develop a lighting technology with a potential for millions of dollars in future sales.[32]

Research and Development Breakthroughs   Another source of new products is a firm's basic research, but the costs are great. Toray Industries, Inc., of Japan relies on basic research to help its position as a leading international management giant. In 1966 one of its researchers was testing uses for a monomer—a basic chemical building block that he had discovered. A colleague suggested turning it into acrylic fiber by charring or carbonizing it. The resulting monomer was far stronger and stiffer than similar fibers. Toray used this product to become the world's number one supplier of carbon fibers for everything from tennis rackets to aircraft parts. Monsanto has invested $1 billion in biotechnology research. Its first commercial product is BGH (Bovine Growth Hormone), which boosts the milk production of cows.[33]

Competitive Products   New product ideas can also be found by analyzing the competition. A six-person intelligence team from the Marriott Corporation spent six months traveling around the country staying at economy hotels. The team assessed the competition's strengths and weaknesses on everything from the soundproof qualities of the rooms to the softness of the towels. Marriott then budgeted $500 million for a new economy hotel chain, Fairfield Inns. Opened in 1987, its occupancy rate exceeds the industry average.[34]

SCREENING AND EVALUATION

The third stage of the new product process is **screening and evaluation**, which involves internal and external evaluations of the new product ideas to eliminate those that warrant no further effort.

Internal Approach   Internally, the firm evaluates the technical feasibility of the proposal and whether the idea meets the new product strategy objectives defined in Step 1. In 1957 Earl Bakken, founder of Medtronic, built the first external

FIGURE 10–7 **A weighted point system Medtronic uses to try to spot a winning new medical product**

GENERAL FACTOR	SPECIFIC FACTOR	SCALE	TOTAL POINTS
Size of target market	Incidence of malady	Undefinable — 10,000s — 1,000,000s ✓ — 100,000,000s (0 5 10 15 20)	12
	Product usage	One per many patients — One per patient ✓ (0 5)	5
	Cost effective for health care system	No — Yes ✓ (0 5 10)	7
	Application of product	Other — Spine ✓ — Brain — Brain/Heart — Heart (0 5 10 15 20)	3
Significant point of difference	Treatment evaluation	Similar to existing approaches — Better than existing approaches — Clearly superior to existing approaches ✓ (0 5 10)	10
	Clearness of function	Questioned or uncertain — Direct cause and effect ✓ (0 5 10)	8
Product quality	Restore natural physiology	Partial ✓ — Total (0 5 10 15 20)	6
	Restore viability	Partial — Full ✓ (0 5 10 15 20)	13
	Characteristic of product	Capital equipment → External → Permanently worn → Implantable → Totally implanted ✓ (0 5 10 15 20)	20
	Mode of operation	Chemical ✓ — Mechanical — Electrical mechanical — Electrical (0 5 10 15 20)	7
	Product development team	Physician only — Engineer only — Physician and engineer ✓ — Physician with engineering training (0 5 10)	6
Access to market	Physician users know Medtronic name?	No — Some (50%) — Yes (all) ✓ (0 5 10)	10
	Inventor's ability, willingness to be champion	Not well known Not willing to promote ✓ — Well known Willing to promote (0 5 10 15 20)	8
Timing	Technologies in place	No — Partially ✓ — Yes (0 5 10)	6
	Entrepreneur in place	No — Partially ✓ — Yes (0 5 10)	4
	Social acceptance	Negative — Positive ✓ (0 5 10)	8
Miscellaneous	Gut feel about success	Uncertain — Good chance — Positive ✓ — Highly positive (0 5 10 15 20)	12
Total			145

Source: Earl Bakken and Medtronic, Inc.

portable heart pacemaker. Working with a team of scientists, Medtronic later built the first implantable pacemaker—a device enabling bedridden people suffering from heart problems to regain their normal, productive lives.

For internal screening and evaluation in its search for new products, Medtronic has developed the *weighted point system* shown in Figure 10–7, which establishes screening criteria and assigns weights to each one used to evaluate new product ideas. The 17 specific factors in the figure are grouped into five of the categories cited earlier for new product failures. (The sixth category, poor execution of the marketing mix, enters the new product process later.) Medtronic believes that a score of at least 120 is needed on the "hurdle" in the point system to find a winning new product.

Medtronic and other high-technology medical firms are trying to perfect an implantable drug dispenser. A hypothetical evaluation for it appears in Figure 10–7. Note that in developing state-of-the-art products, technological factors as well as marketing ones carry important weights in the screening criteria.

External Approach   Concept tests are external evaluations that consist of preliminary testing of the new product idea (rather than the actual product) with consumers. Concept tests usually rely on written descriptions of the product but may be augmented with sketches, mock-ups, or promotional literature.[35] Several key questions are asked during concept testing: How does the customer perceive the product? Who would use it? How would it be used?

Frito-Lay spent a year interviewing 10,000 consumers about the concept of a multigrain snack chip. The company experimented with 50 different shapes before settling on a thin, rectangular chip with ridges and a slightly salty, nutty flavor. The product, called Sun Chips, appeared on the market in 1991.[36]

A year's worth of consumer interviews went into the development of Sun Chips.

1 **What step in the new product process has been added in recent years?**

2 **What are four sources of new product ideas?**

3 **What is a weighted point system, as used internally by a firm in the new product process?**

BUSINESS ANALYSIS

Business analysis involves specifying the features of the product and the marketing strategy needed to commercialize it and making necessary financial projections. This is the last checkpoint before significant capital is invested in creating a prototype of the product. Economic analysis, marketing strategy review, and legal examination of the proposed product are conducted at this stage. It is at this point that the product is analyzed relative to its existing synergies with the firm's marketing and technological strengths, two criteria noted in Figure 10–4.

The marketing strategy review studies the new product idea in relation to the marketing program to support it. The proposed product is assessed to determine whether it will help or hurt sales of existing products. Likewise, the product is examined to assess whether it can be sold through existing channels or if new outlets will be needed.

After the product's important features are defined, economic considerations focus on several issues, starting with costs of R&D, production, and marketing. For financial projections, the firm must also forecast the possible revenues from future product sales and forecast market shares. Airwick's new product criteria requires a product to be both a specialty and a noncommodity household item. The company also wants a new idea to have potential revenues of $30 to $100 million annually. Investments are expected to be recouped within two years. These requirements have led the company to discard ideas like plant care items, toilet bowl cleaners, and a fire extinguisher—all in the business analysis stage.[37] In this stage the firm also estimates how many units of the product must be sold to cover the costs of production and projects a return on investment to determine the profitability.

As an important aspect of the business analysis, the proposed new product is studied to determine whether it can be protected with a patent. An attractive new product proposal is one in which the technology can be patented or not easily copied.[38]

DEVELOPMENT

Product ideas that survive the business analysis proceed to actual **development**, turning the idea on paper into a prototype. This results in a demonstrable, producible product in hand. Outsiders seldom understand the technical complexities of the development stage, which involves not only manufacturing the product but also performing laboratory and consumer tests to ensure that it meets the standards set. Design of the product becomes an important element.

Liquid Tide, introduced by P&G, looks like a simple modification of its original Tide detergent. However, P&G sees this product as a technological breakthrough: the first detergent without phosphates that cleans as well as existing phosphate detergents.

To achieve this breakthrough, P&G spent 400,000 hours and combined technologies from its laboratories in three countries. The new ingredient in Liquid Tide that helps suspend the dirt in wash water came out of the P&G research lab in Cincinnati. The cleaning agents in the product came from P&G scientists in Japan. Cleaning agent technology is especially advanced in Japan because consumers there wash clothes in colder water (about 70° F) than consumers in the United States (95° F) and Europe (160° F). P&G scientists thought that Liquid Tide also needed water-softening ingredients to make the cleaning agents work better. For this technology it turned to P&G's lab in Belgium, whose experience was based on European water, which has more than twice the mineral content of U.S. wash water.[39]

The prototype product is tested in the laboratory to see if it achieves the physical standards set for it. Prototypes of disposable consumer goods are also subjected to consumer tests, often in-home placements of the product to see if consumers actually perceive it as a better product after they use it. In a blind test consumers preferred Liquid Tide nine to one over the detergent of their own choice tested in their washers. In developing the new Air 180 athletic shoe, Nike

Liquid Tide—a breakthrough using technologies from Belgium, Japan, and the United States.

had 186 runners from Alaska to the Virgin Islands test the product. They were asked to run a minimum of 45 miles a week and tell how the shoes held up.[40]

MARKET TESTING

The **market testing** stage of the new product process involves exposing actual products to prospective consumers under realistic purchase conditions to see if they will buy. Often a product is developed, tested, refined, and then tested again to get consumer reactions through either test marketing or purchase laboratories.

Test Marketing   Test marketing involves offering a product for sale on a limited basis in a defined area. This test is done to determine whether consumers will actually buy the product and to try different ways of marketing it.[41] Only about a third of the products test marketed do well enough to go on to the next phase. These market tests are usually conducted in cities that are viewed as being representative of U.S. consumers. Figure 10–8 shows the cities commonly used for two different types of market tests. *Standard markets* are those test sites where companies sell a new product through normal distribution channels and monitor the results. *Selected controlled markets*, sometimes referred to as *forced distribution markets*, are those in which the total test is conducted by an outside agency. An outside testing service conducts the test by paying retailers for shelf space, and thus guaranteeing the most popular test markets distribution.

In examining the commercial viability of the new product, companies measure sales in the test area, often with *store audits*. These audits, conducted by groups such as the A.C. Nielsen Company, measure the sales in grocery stores and the number of cases ordered by a store from the wholesaler. This gives the company an indication of potential sales volume and market share in the test

FIGURE 10–8
The most popular test markets

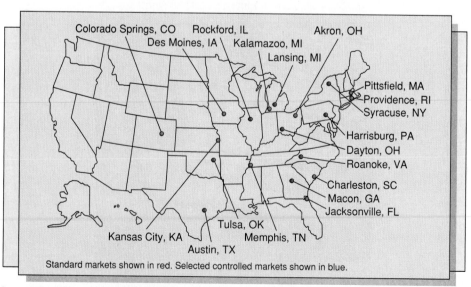

Standard markets shown in red. Selected controlled markets shown in blue.

Source: "The Nation's Most Popular Test Markets," *Sales & Marketing Management* (March 1989), pp. 65–69. Reprinted by permission of Sales & Marketing Management, Copyright © 1989.

area. Although test markets have not been able to predict exact future sales or share, they do help a company with an idea of relative product performance and the likelihood of having a loser or a winner.[42]

Market tests are also used to check other elements of the marketing mix besides the product itself, such as price, level of advertising support, and distribution. In test marketing its new compact drink dispenser for small and medium offices, Coca-Cola analyzed both the distribution channel and the advertising. During the market test, Coca-Cola discovered that office managers are the people who decide whether machines are installed in break rooms. In Atlanta, the company tested a direct-mail campaign to office managers where customers could call a toll-free number or send in a response card. The direct-mail program received twice the projected response. Coca-Cola introduced the dispenser, called BreakMate, in 1990.[43] In industrial marketing, market tests are often used to gain a record of product performance. This experience can then be used as part of the sales presentation when the product is offered elsewhere.

There is no required time period for an appropriate market test. In the brewing industry, Coors tested its Herman Joseph brew for about three years, while Anheuser-Busch recently moved its Michelob Dry brand from market test to national distribution in three months. After a quick four-city market test, the company feared competition from G. Heileman and Ashai, a Japanese brewer.[44]

There are difficulties with test marketing, a primary one being how well the results can be projected. Representativenesss of the test market to the target market for the product is very important. Market tests also are expensive because production lines must be set up, as well as promotion and sales programs. Costs can run from $250,000 to $1 million, depending on the size of the city and the cost of buying media time or space to advertise the product.[45]

Market tests also reveal plans to competitors, sometimes enabling them to get a product into national distribution first. When a product can be easily copied by a competitor, test marketing may not be used. Although Hunt-Wesson got its Prima Salsa Tomato Sauce into the test market first, Chesebrough-Pond's Ragu Extra Thick & Zesty beat it into national introduction. Publications such as *Advertising Age* regularly list products being tested and the location of the test market. Companies also instruct their salespeople to look for new competing products in test markets and report their existence to headquarters.

The disadvantages of test markets have led some consumer goods firms to shorten them, simplify them, or drop them entirely. *Controlled distribution minimarkets* are market tests run in smaller test areas that electronically monitor product purchases at checkout counters more carefully, and they can reduce market test costs by 60 percent to 80 percent. Playtex chose to skip test marketing entirely in the introduction of its Jhirmack shampoo. The company felt the brand name was strong enough to gain national distribution. Skipping test marketing can, however, prove costly. In order to beat the competition, Colgate-Palmolive rushed its Fab 1 Shot laundry detergent into full-scale commercialization without test marketing. The product is a prepackaged amount of laundry detergent that eliminates the need for measuring. The problem: consumers couldn't use a reduced amount for smaller loads, which led to lost sales for the product.

Playtex was successful
with Jhirmack shampoo
without test marketing.

Purchase Laboratories   Because of the limitations of test markets, one of the best assessment techniques for a new product launch is the purchase laboratory, in which competing test brands are displayed.[46] These purchase labs are usually run in shopping malls, where consumers are questioned to identify who uses the product class being tested. Willing participants are questioned on usage, reasons for purchase, and important product attributes. Consumers are also shown advertising for the new brand along with competitors' advertising and are given money to buy or not buy a package of the product (or the competitors') from a mock grocery shelf. Consumers who purchase the test brand are interviewed later for their reactions.[47] Based on these reactions, the company may decide to proceed to the last stage of the new product process.

Market testing is a valuable step in the new product process, but not all products can be judged in this way. Testing a service beyond the concept level is very difficult because the service is intangible and consumers can't see what they are buying. Similarly, market testing of expensive consumer products such as cars or VCRs or costly industrial products like jet engines or computers is impractical.

COMMERCIALIZATION

Finally, the product is brought to the point of **commercialization—**positioning and launching it in full-scale production and sales. Because of the many steps involved in developing a new product, bringing a new concept to this stage involves many delays and significant expense. The cost of commercialization has increased for many consumer product companies as retailers have begun to require special payments. Because space is limited in many stores, particularly supermarkets, many retailers require manufacturers to pay a **slotting fee,** a payment a manufacturer makes to place a new item on a retailer's shelf. A recent study in the grocery industry found that manufacturers paid an average of $5.1 million dollars to get a new product on store shelves.[48]

Getting the new product to market does not guarantee success. The cost of failure can be far more than merely sales the new product failed to make. For example, if a new grocery product does not achieve a predetermined sales target,

Marketing Research Report

FACING PRODUCT DISASTERS: THE CASES OF PINTO AND EXTRA STRENGTH TYLENOL

As products and their distribution systems become more complex, chances for problems increase. What happens when a product has a problem, the public finds out about it, and the company must either redesign or recall it? Can sales of the product ever recover? Professors Marc G. Weinberger and Jean Romeo examined the history of four such products, including the Ford Pinto and Extra Strength Tylenol, discussed here. The Pinto and Tylenol cases have opposite outcomes.

FORD PINTO

Introduced in 1970, Ford's Pinto became one of the company's best-selling compact cars. The gas tank, however, was located only seven inches from the rear bumper, making it susceptible to fires in rear-end collisions. Much publicity occurred about deaths from crashes involving the Pinto. In August 1977, *Mother Jones* magazine published a story about Pinto fires and deaths, to be followed by the "60 Minutes" television show in June 1978. Pinto's share of the compact car market fell from 40 percent to 32 percent after the magazine article and to 23 percent after the television story. Although Ford recalled the car and modified the gas-tank placement, sales and market share continued to fall. Eventually, Pinto production was dropped.

EXTRA STRENGTH TYLENOL

In the case of Tylenol, a deranged person, not the company, was the source of the disaster. Tylenol was a strong brand in the analgesic market, with 37 percent market share in 1982. Then, in September 1982, seven Chicagoans died after each took an Extra Strength Tylenol capsule tainted with cyanide. Johnson & Johnson, the manufacturer, halted production and all promotion. The company, although not at fault, at huge cost recalled 22 million bottles, launched a major repackaging effort, and began a major public relations campaign. One year after the incident, Extra Strength Tylenol's market share had fallen from 37 to 30 percent. Four years after the production stoppage, the brand's market share was back to its pre-disaster level.

Better testing of the Pinto prototype could have avoided Ford's product disaster. Although little can be done to protect society completely from deranged people, the tampering with the Extra Strength Tylenol packages led directly to industry and government packaging actions (discussed further in Chapter 11).

Source: Marc G. Weinberger and Jean B. Romeo, "The Impact of Negative Product News," *Business Horizons* (January–February 1989), pp. 44–50. Copyright 1989 by the Foundation for the School of Business at Indiana University. Used with permission.

some retailers require a **failure fee**, a penalty payment by a manufacturer to compensate the retailer for sales its valuable shelf space never made.[49] Product problems that can or do cost people's lives are potential nightmares for many firms. The Marketing Research Report describes the Pinto and Extra Strength Tylenol disasters, after which the Pinto disappeared from the marketplace and the Tylenol brands managed to survive after an initial sales plummet.

Lag from Idea to New Product The time from idea generation to commercialization can be lengthy: 32 years for the heart pacemaker, 55 years for the zipper, 18 years for minute rice. Companies generally proceed carefully because, at this last stage, commercialization, production, and marketing expenses are greatest. To minimize the financial risk of a market failure of a new product introduction, many grocery product manufacturers use *regional rollouts,* introducing the product sequentially into geographical areas of the United States to allow production levels and marketing activities to build up gradually.

In recent years, companies have begun to recognize that speed is important in bringing a new product to market. A recent study by McKinsey & Company, a management consulting firm, has shown that high-tech products that come to market late but on budget will earn 33 percent less profit over five years. Yet those products that come out on time (and 50 percent over budget) will earn only 4 percent less profit.[50] Over the past several years IBM, for example, has built several lap top computer prototypes. The company, however, has had to kill the products before commercialization because competitors offered better, more advanced machines to the market before IBM. As a result some companies—such as NEC, Honda, Fuji, and Xerox—have moved away from the development approach that uses the sequence of stages described in this chapter. A new trend, termed *parallel development* (the simultaneous development of both the product and the production process), is being tried. With this approach, multidisciplinary *venture teams* of marketing, manufacturing, and R&D personnel stay with the product from conception to production. The results are significant. While AT&T used to take two years to bring a new phone design to the stage of commercialization, its new 4200 model required less than a year. Honda has cut car development from five years to three, while Hewlett-Packard has reduced the development time for computer printers from 54 months to

FIGURE 10–9
Marketing information and methods used in the new product process

STAGE OF PROCESS	PURPOSE OF STAGE	MARKETING INFORMATION AND METHODS USED
New product strategy development	Identify new product niches to reach in light of company objectives	Company objectives; assessment of firm's current strengths and weaknesses in terms of market and product
Idea generation	Develop concepts for possible products	Ideas from employees and co-workers, consumers, R&D, and competitors; methods of brainstorming and focus groups
Screening and evaluation	Separate good product ideas from bad ones inexpensively	Screening criteria, concept tests, and weighted point systems
Business analysis	Identify the product's features and its marketing strategy, and make financial projections	Product's key features, anticipated marketing mix strategy; economic, marketing, production, legal, and profitability analyses
Development	Create the prototype product, and test it in the laboratory and on consumers	Laboratory and consumer tests on product prototypes
Market testing	Test product and marketing strategy in the marketplace on a limited scale	Test markets, controlled distribution minimarkets, purchase laboratories
Commercialization	Position and offer product in the marketplace	Perceptual maps, product positioning, regional rollouts

22.[51] Early reports indicate that involving these multidisciplinary teams early in the product development process also leads to increased success rates for the new products introduced.[52]

How the New Product Process Reduces Failures   Figure 10–9 identifies the purpose of each stage of the new product process and the kinds of marketing information and methods used. Firms that follow the seven stages in the new product process reduce risks and have a better chance of averting new product failures. A look at Figure 10–9 suggests information that might help avoid some new product failures. Although using the new product process does not guarantee successful products, it does increase a firm's success rate.

CONCEPT CHECK

1 How does the development stage of the new product process involve testing the product inside and outside the firm?

2 What is a test market?

3 What is commercialization of a new product?

ETHICS AND SOCIAL RESPONSIBILITY IN THE 1990s

BOTTLED WATER: WHERE DOES SELF-REGULATION STOP AND FEDERAL REGULATION START?

Many industries stress "self-regulation"—having firms in the industry set and abide by guidelines to protect both consumers and fair competition. This has been the case with the $2 billion-a-year bottled mineral water industry. But rain clouds are on the horizon. Look at these claims for the reason:

- Artesia Waters, Inc. describes its product as "100 percent pure sparkling Texas Natural Water."
- Lithia Springs Water Company describes its "world's finest" bottled mineral water as "naturally pure." The firm also recommends its Love Water brand as an "invigorator" before bedtime.[53]

What benefits are these brands giving you? Do you think you are getting something better than tap water?

A recent U.S. Food and Drug Administration (FDA) report revealed that Artesia Waters mineral water is heavily processed and comes from the same underground source that San Antonio uses for its municipal water supply, and Lithia Springs water, like 31 percent of the brands the FDA studied, was tainted with bacteria. If consumers believe their bottled water comes from far-off natural sources, they are often wrong.

What should be done? Should the industry rely on self-regulation or turn to greater regulation by the FDA?

SUMMARY

1 A product is a good, service, or idea consisting of a bundle of tangible and intangible attributes that satisfies consumers and is received in exchange for money or some other unit of value. A company's product decisions involve the product item, product line, and range of its product mix.

2 Products can be classified by tangibility and by user. By degree of tangibility, products divide into nondurable goods, durable goods, and services. By user, the major distinctions are consumer or industrial goods. Consumer goods consist of convenience, shopping, and specialty products. Industrial goods are for either production or support.

3 There are several ways to define a new product, such as the degree of distinction from existing products, a time base specified by the FTC, a company perspective, or effect on a consumer's usage pattern.

4 In terms of its effect on a consumer's use of a product, a discontinuous innovation represents the greatest change and a continuous innovation the least. A dynamically continuous innovation is disruptive but not totally new.

5 The failure of a new product is usually attributable to one of six reasons: too small a target market, insignificant point of difference, poor product quality, no access to market, poor timing, and poor execution of the marketing mix.

6 The new product process consists of seven stages. Objectives for new products are determined in the first stage, new product strategy development; this is followed by idea generation, screening and evaluation, business analysis, development, market testing, and commercialization.

7 Ideas for new products come from several sources, including consumers, employees, R&D laboratories, and competitors.

8 Screening and evaluation are often done internally using a weighted point system or externally using concept tests.

9 Business analysis involves defining the features of the new product, a marketing strategy to introduce it, and a financial forecast.

10 Development involves not only producing a prototype product but also testing it in the lab and on consumers to see that it meets the standards set for it.

11 In market testing new products, companies often rely on market tests to see that consumers will actually buy the product when it's offered for sale and that other marketing mix factors are working. Products surviving this stage are commercialized—taken to market.

 KEY TERMS AND CONCEPTS

product p. 254   **industrial goods** p. 256
product line p. 254   **convenience goods** p. 257
product mix p. 255   **shopping goods** p. 257
consumer goods p. 256   **specialty goods** p. 257

CHAPTER PROBLEMS AND APPLICATIONS

1 Products can be classified as either consumer or industrial goods. How would you classify the following products? (*a*) Johnson's baby shampoo, (*b*) a Black & Decker two-speed drill, and (*c*) an arc welder.

2 Are products like Nature Valley Granola bars and Eddie Bauer hiking boots convenience, shopping, specialty, or unsought goods?

3 Based on your answer to Problem 2, how would the marketing actions differ for each product and the classification to which you assigned it?

4 In terms of the behavioral effect on consumers, how would the PC, such as a Macintosh or IBM PS/2, be classified? In light of this classification, what actions would you suggest to the manufacturers of these products to increase their sales in the market?

5 Several alternative definitions were presented for a new product. How would a company's marketing strategy be affected if it used (*a*) the legal definition or (*b*) a behavioral definition?

6 In terms of the weighted point system used to screen new product ideas at Medtronic (Figure 10–7), what is the significance of the following factors: incidence of malady, treatment evaluation, restoration of natural physiology, and physicians' knowledge of Medtronic name? What are the advantages and disadvantages of such a system?

7 Test marketing and purchase laboratories are two approaches for assessing the potential commercial success of a new product. Based on the strengths and weaknesses of each approach, what methods would you suggest for the following items? (*a*) A new, improved ketchup, (*b*) a three-dimensional television system that took the company ten years to develop, and (*c*) a new children's toy on which the company holds a patent.

8 Look back at Figure 10–6, which outlines the roles for new products. If a company followed the role of defending market share position, what type of positioning strategy might be implemented?

9 Concept testing is an important step in the new product process. Outline the concept tests for (*a*) an electrically powered car and (*b*) a new loan payment system for automobiles that is based on a variable rate interest. What are the differences in developing concept tests for products as opposed to services?

CHAPTER 11

Managing the Product

*A*fter reading this chapter you should be able to:

- Explain the product life cycle concept and relate a marketing strategy to each stage.

- Recognize the differences in product life cycles for various products and their implications for marketing decisions.

- Understand alternative approaches to managing a product's life cycle.

- Identify the attributes of a successful brand name.

- Explain the rationale for alternative brand name strategies employed by companies.

- Understand the benefits of packaging and warranties in the marketing of a product.

The Procrastinator's Dream—It's Only One *Word*

What can you have in your home, on your boat, in your office? What are people using to order pizzas from Pizza Delight in New York or hamburgers from McDonald's in Houston? Still can't guess? Here's one more clue—it's the same thing the President of the United States uses for the hotline to Moscow. It's not the phone, or even overnight mail, it's the technology that has led to the new phrase of business, "Fax it!"—a facsimile machine.

In 1983, sales of fax machines were under 50,000 units, yet a look at Figure 11–1 shows the dramatic growth that has occurred since fax machine sales accelerated in 1987. Facsimile machines, or faxes as they are often called, can transmit words and graphics over phone lines. Although

FIGURE 11–1
The exploding life cycle of fax machines

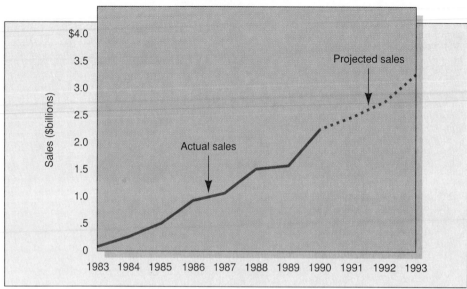

Sources: Data derived from "FAX's Future Fracas," *Dallas Times Herald* (August 17, 1990), pp. B1, B3; Frederick H. Katayama, "Who's Fueling the Fax Frenzy," *Fortune* (October 23, 1989), pp. 151–56; "Fax Boom Continues," *Purchasing* (October 26, 1989), p. 72; and "It's a Fax, Fax, Fax World," *Business Week* (March 21, 1988), p. 136.

speed and reproduction clarity vary by the type of machine, technological advances during the past decade have reduced the early-1980s machine weighing 300 pounds to a portable unit of under 10 pounds that is also three times faster in transmission and reception of information.

The projections for the early 1990s show continued strong growth in fax sales at the expense of other services. For many years the last-minute memo to the office or a customer had to be sent by overnight mail via the post office or companies like Federal Express. In fact, saying "Fed Ex this" became the term for sending something by overnight delivery. Yet the development of new products often means that as a new product enters the market, it affects the sales of the existing alternatives. Federal Express has lost about 20,000 documents a day, which represents $200,000 per day in sales, to this new technology. As one Federal Express executive said, "We can't compete with fax because it delivers within minutes." One industry analyst has estimated that fax technology could steal approximately 30 percent of Federal Express's overnight letter delivery business. Western Union's telex business has been all but killed. To stave off the loss, some overnight delivery services, like DHL, are offering new services that combine fax with their other capabilities. DHL's NetExpress service uses the company's courier service and adds fax delivery (as opposed to its earlier air delivery) at competitive prices.

Where will it end? Well, the end may not be in sight. After all, we have only had a couple of National Fax Day celebrations. On January 10, 1989, the first such day did occur, highlighting the opening of 5,500 public fax stations around the country. Contributing to fax's popularity is the fact that prices are dropping rapidly, from the early days of thousands of dollars per machine to today's prices of under $300.[1] Who knows, a fax may soon be a standard feature in a car. But one question still remains—what excuse can a good procrastinator use now?

The development process of new products, discussed in Chapter 10, is expensive and often time consuming, but the results can lead to commercialization—a product for the marketplace. This chapter covers the marketing of a product when it enters the market, the life of a product, the brand name, and package design. Consumers first see new products at the commercialization stage but these products don't always live forever.

PRODUCT LIFE CYCLE

Products, like people, have been viewed as having a life cycle. The **product life cycle** concept describes the stages a new product goes through in the marketplace: introduction, growth, maturity, and decline (Figure 11–2).[2] There are two curves shown in this figure: total industry sales revenue and total industry profit, which represent the sum of sales revenue and profit of all firms producing the product. The reasons for the changes in each curve and the marketing decisions involved are discussed in the following pages.

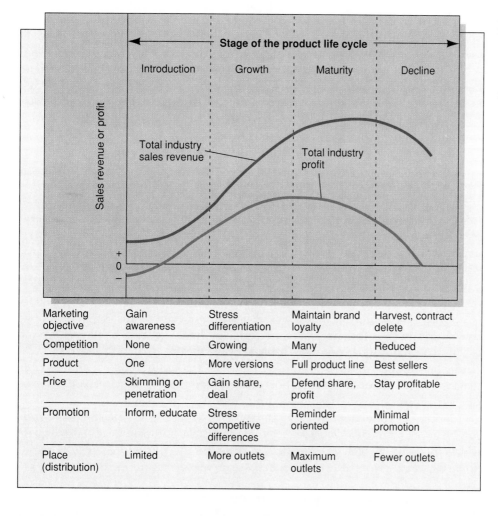

FIGURE 11–2
How stages of the product life cycle relate to a firm's marketing objectives and marketing mix actions

	Introduction	Growth	Maturity	Decline
Marketing objective	Gain awareness	Stress differentiation	Maintain brand loyalty	Harvest, contract delete
Competition	None	Growing	Many	Reduced
Product	One	More versions	Full product line	Best sellers
Price	Skimming or penetration	Gain share, deal	Defend share, profit	Stay profitable
Promotion	Inform, educate	Stress competitive differences	Reminder oriented	Minimal promotion
Place (distribution)	Limited	More outlets	Maximum outlets	Fewer outlets

FIGURE 11–3
Product life cycle for windsurfers (a.k.a. sailboards) in the United Kingdom

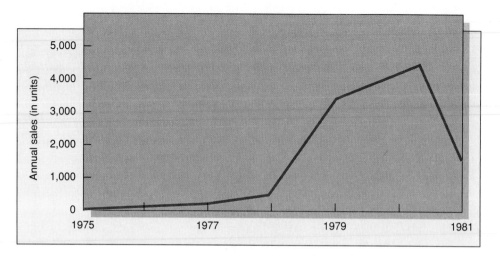

INTRODUCTION STAGE

The introduction stage of the product life cycle occurs when the product first enters the market, sales grow slowly, and profit is little. Look at Figure 11–3, which shows the product life cycle for sailboards for windsurfing, after they were introduced into the United Kingdom. Sales grew slowly until 1978. The lack of profit is often a result of the large investment costs of product development and a shift of industry profit from negative to positive during the introductory stage. The marketing objective for a company at this stage is to promote consumer awareness and gain trial—the initial purchase of a product by a consumer.

In order to gain awareness among consumers in the introduction stage, *USA Today,* in the early 1980s, provided large discounts for bulk orders to hotels and airlines. These organizations then distributed the newspaper free to customers. In the introduction stage there are no competitors with the same product, and heavy promotional expenditures are often made to build *primary demand,* or a desire for the product class (such as food processors or potatoes) rather than for a specific brand. To induce primary demand, early sailboard companies such as Mistral offered free lessons with every board purchase. Demand for a specific brand is referred to as *selective demand* and occurs later in the life cycle.

Other marketing mix variables also are important at this stage. Gaining distribution outlets for the product is often difficult because retailers may be hesitant to carry a new product. Moreover, in this stage a company often restricts the number of variations of the product to ensure control of product quality. For example, the first sailboards were designed to be stable and easy to use. Variations on board design occurred later.

During introduction, pricing can be either high or low. A high initial price may be used as part of a *skimming* strategy to help the company recover the costs of development, as well as capitalize on the price insensitivity of early buyers. However, high prices also tend to make competitors more eager to enter the

USA Today used special discounts to help generate customer awareness.

market because they see the opportunity for profit. To discourage competitive entry, a company can price low, referred to as *penetration pricing*. This pricing strategy also helps build market share, but a company must closely monitor costs. These and other pricing techniques are covered in depth in Chapter 13.

GROWTH STAGE

The second stage of the product life cycle, growth, is characterized by rapid increases in sales, and it is in this stage that competitors appear. For example, Figure 11–3 shows the dramatic increase in sales of sailboards from 1978 to 1979. The number of companies selling sailboards was also increasing: from one in 1975 to eight in 1979. The change in the number of competitors in the fax industry has been equally dramatic. In 1983 there were just seven manufacturers and nine brands. By 1990 there were some 25 manufacturers and 60 possible brands from which to choose.[3]

The result is that industry profit usually peaks during the growth stage. The emphasis of advertising shifts to selective demand, in which product benefits are compared with those of competitors' offerings.

Products in the growth stage have an increase in sales because of new people trying the product and a growing proportion of *repeat purchasers*—people who tried the product, were satisfied, and buy again. As a product moves through the life cycle, the ratio of repeat to trial purchases grows. Failure to achieve substantial repeat purchasers usually means an early death for a product. Alberto-Culver introduced Mr. Culver's Sparklers, which were solid air fresheners that looked like stained glass. The problem was there were almost no repeat purchasers because buyers treated the product like cheap window decorations, left them there, and didn't buy new ones.

At the growth stage changes start to appear in the product. To help differentiate the brand from those of competitors, an improved version or new features may be added to the original design. Variations on the early, stable sailboard appeared in 1977. Racing sailboards were introduced, which had different sail sizes and board lengths. Also, in 1980, "fun" boards, a third version, were offered for wave jumping. In a service business new features can also be added. Mobile phones are in the growth stage, with many new competitors entering the market. To differentiate itself from other competitors, Metrophone offers new subscribers free long distance calling on weekends, while NYNEX Mobile offers a free phone message service to new subscribers.[4]

In the growth stage it is important to gain as much distribution for the product as required. In the retail store, for example, this often means that competing companies fight for shelf space. The retail battle in the fax industry is intense. In 1986, at the early stages of the life cycle, only 11 percent of office machine dealers carried this equipment. Now more than 60 percent of these dealers carry fax equipment and the fight is on for which brands will be represented.[5]

MATURITY STAGE

The third stage, maturity, is characterized by a leveling off of total industry sales revenue. Also, marginal competitors begin to leave the market. Most consumers who would buy the product are either repeat purchasers of the item or have tried and abandoned it. As you can see in Figure 11–2, there is a slight sales increase in the maturity stage, as the last buyers enter the market. Profit declines because there is fierce price competition among many sellers and the cost of gaining each new buyer at this stage is greater than the resulting revenue.

Figure 11–3 shows the flattening of sales of sailboards from 1979 to 1980, when the product was in its maturity stage in the United Kingdom. Retail prices fell by 40 percent the five years up to 1980 as the number of competitors grew. The marketing objective for a company is to maintain its existing buyers because few new customers are available to replace any who are lost.

Promotional expenses in the maturity stage often are directed toward contests or games to keep people using the product, and price competition continues through cents-off coupons. Companies are often hurt when distribution outlets drop the mature product in favor of other new products in the introductory or growth stage. A major factor in a company's strategy is to reduce overall marketing costs by improving its promotional and distribution efficiency.[6]

Microwave ovens are an example of a product now in the mature stage of the life cycle. In 1980, 15 percent of all U.S. homes had this kitchen appliance, but today, 75 to 80 percent of all American homes have them.[7]

DECLINE STAGE

The decline stage is the beginning of the end and occurs when sales and profits are steadily dropping. Frequently a product enters this stage not because of any wrong strategy of the company but because of environmental changes. New technology led to video cameras, which pushed 8 mm movie cameras into decline. The Salk vaccine for polio reduced the need for iron lung machines and moved their manufacturers into decline. Advertising support for a product in this stage diminishes. The decline stage is often the most difficult for a company to address. Dropping a product is an emotional decision in that many individuals have committed time and effort to its early successes in the product life cycle. Products in decline, however, tend to consume a disproportionate share of management time and financial resources relative to their worth. To handle a declining product, a company follows one of three strategies.

Deletion   The most drastic action, deletion, is dropping the product from the line. Studies have shown that few companies that delete a product have specified policies to meet customer obligations, but customer objections to a product deletion are common.[8]

Harvesting   A second strategy, harvesting, is when a company retains the product but reduces support costs. The product continues to be offered, but salespeople do not allocate time in selling, nor are advertising dollars spent. The purpose of harvesting is to maintain the ability to meet customer requests.

Contracting   Some companies operate on a scale that makes it financially unwise for them to carry a product after sales decline below a certain level. However, this same sales level might be profitable for a smaller company, and the larger firm may contract with a smaller company to manufacture the product. In this way its production budget is freed for more profitable items, but the item is still available to customers. An alternative to contracting manufacturing is to contract the marketing. Some companies find that their manufacturing efficiencies allow them to continue producing the product but require others to sell it.

SOME DIMENSIONS OF THE PRODUCT LIFE CYCLE

Some important aspects of product life cycles are (1) their length, (2) the shape of their curves, and (3) how they vary with different levels of the products. Look at the photos on page 290 and think about where the three products are in their life cycles and why.

Length of the Product Life Cycle   There is no exact time that a product takes to move through its life cycle. If a company introduces products that are similar to others in its line, rough estimates can be made, but several factors can affect the length of a product's life. Credit alters a product's life cycle by making it available to more consumers sooner than if purchases were only by cash, and mass communication informs the market of a new product introduction at a quicker rate. Technological advances and company experience can also move products quickly through their life cycles. In the United Kingdom, it took five years after stable sailboards were introduced until new technology and design led to racing boards. And in only three years, technology led to the introduction of fun boards.

Look at each of the three products and (1) estimate where the products are in their life cycles and (2) decide which products they displaced or are being displaced by. The text gives the answers, along with explanations of factors affecting product life cycles.

EpiLady: removes hair without cutting.

The Cuisinart performs numerous kitchen tasks.

Ninja Turtles adorn many products.

Where are these products in their life cycles?

The Shape of the Product Life Cycle   The product life cycle curve shown in Figure 11–2 might be referred to as a *generalized life cycle,* but not all products have the same shape to their curve.[9] In fact, there are several different life cycle curves, each type suggesting different marketing strategies.[10] Figure 11–4 shows the shape of life cycle curves for four different types of products: high learning, low learning, fashion, and fad products.

A *high learning product* is one for which significant education of the customer is required and there is an extended introductory period (Figure 11–4, A). Products such as home computers have this type of life cycle curve because consumers have to understand the benefits of purchasing the product or be

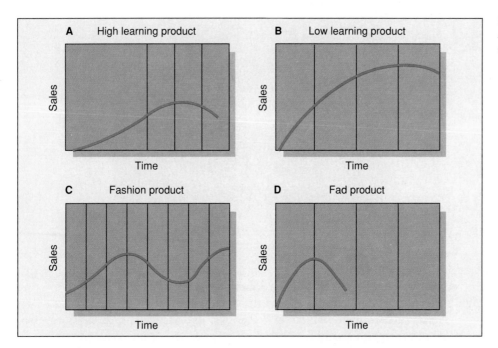

FIGURE 11–4
Alternative product life cycles

educated in a new way of performing a familiar task. Microwave ovens, for example, necessitate that the consumer learn a new way of cooking and alter familiar recipes. And, Cuisinarts in the late growth stage come with detailed manuals.

One of the most recent introductions of a high learning product was introduced by a company called Epi Products, run by three sisters. In 1986, these businesspeople introduced Epilady, a hand-held appliance that removes leg hair at its root. By 1989, Epilady achieved sales of 3.5 million units. The product was aimed at replacing the traditional razors or creams that many women have used for the removal of unwanted leg hair. Because the product is different than a razor, and somewhat painful to use, the company distributed the item through department stores. This approach allowed salesclerks to demonstrate how to use the item, which is necessary for a high learning product. (The company used video displays in smaller stores to explain the Epilady.) Massive promotion also accompanied the introduction. Additionally, the company added a toll free 800 number to answer customer questions. But Epilady demonstrated the reality of the product life cycle—as sales rose dramatically in the growth stage, competitors entered. Remington and other manufacturers sold lower-priced versions of the product. By late 1990, Epi Products had filed for bankruptcy.[11]

In contrast, for a *low learning product,* sales begin immediately because little learning is required by the consumer and the benefits of purchase are readily understood (Figure 11–4, B).[12] This product often can be easily imitated by competitors, so the marketing strategy is to gain strong distributor outlets at the beginning. In this way, as competitors rapidly enter, the best retail outlets already have the innovator's product. It is also important to have the manufacturing capacity to meet demand.

A new consumer fad?

A *fashion product* (Figure 11–4, C), for example, such as hemline lengths on skirts or lapel widths on sports jackets, is introduced, declines, and then seems to return. Life cycles for fashion products most often appear in women's and men's clothing styles. The length of the cycles may be years or decades.

A *fad,* such as wall walkers or toe socks, experiences rapid sales on introduction and then an equally rapid decline (Figure 11–4, D). One entrepreneur, hoping to create a worldwide fad, has paid for exclusive rights to the Great Wall of China. He plans to sell rubble from the Wall mounted on a little wooden base. Some companies make fads their primary business. Creative Programming, Inc., produces novelty videotapes. In 1988 they introduced "Video Baby" for $19.95, which they promote as letting you have the full, rich experience of parenthood, without the mess and inconvenience of the real thing. The company also sells "Video Dog" and "Video Cat" and says more are on the way.[13]

Following Coca-Cola's 1985 New Coke experience, two entrepreneurs introduced their Jolt Cola, with "all the sugar and twice the caffeine" of competing colas. Their marketing task was to move Jolt from being simply a fad in the minds of consumers to being a permanent entry in the very competitive cola market.

The Product Level: Class, Form, and Brand   The product life cycle shown in Figure 11–2 is a total industry curve. Yet, in managing a product it is important to often distinguish among the multiple life cycles (industry, class, and form) that may exist. **Product class** refers to the entire product category or industry, such as the total cigarette industry shown in Figure 11–5, A. **Product form** pertains to variations within the class. For example, in the cigarette industry there are filter and nonfilter product forms (Figure 11–5, A). A final type of life cycle curve can represent the brand, such as the four brands of cigarettes in Figure 11–5, B. During the period shown, sales of the Marlboro brand were growing and the Kent and L&M brands were in the decline stage of the product life cycle as cigarette smokers shifted from nonfiltered to filtered cigarettes or quit smoking entirely. Today many companies offer both nonfiltered and filtered cigarettes.

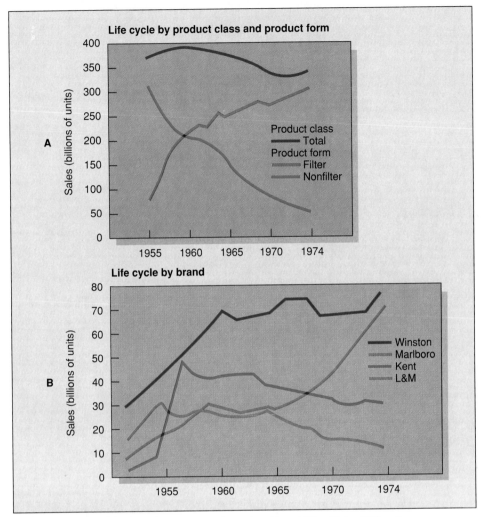

FIGURE 11–5
Life cycles of product form and product class

Source: Redrawn from Richard N. Cardozo, *Product Policy* (Reading, Mass.: Addison-Wesley, 1979), p. 6.

The Life Cycle and Consumers   The life cycle of a product depends on sales to consumers. Not all consumers rush to buy a product in the introductory stage, and the shapes of the life cycle curves indicate that most sales occur after the product has been on the market for some time. In essence, a product diffuses, or spreads, through the population, a concept called the *diffusion of innovation.*

Some people are attracted to a product early, others buy it only after they see their friends with the item. Figure 11–6 shows the consumer population divided into five categories of product adopters based on when they adopt a new product. Brief profiles accompany each category. For any product to be successful, it must be purchased by innovators and early adopters. This is why manufacturers of new pharmaceuticals try to gain adoption by leading hospitals,

FIGURE 11–6
Five categories and profiles of product adopters

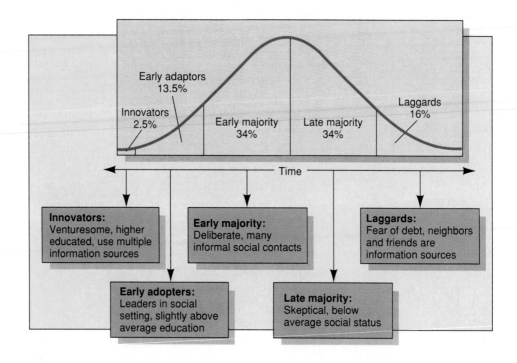

clinics, and physicians that are widely respected in the medical field. Once accepted by innovators and early adopters, the adoption of new products moves on to the early majority, late majority, and laggard categories.

Several factors affect whether a consumer will adopt a new product or not. Common reasons for resisting a product in the introduction stage are usage barriers (the product is not compatible with existing habits), value barriers (the product provides no incentive to change), and risk barriers, which can be either physical, psychological, economic, or social. Among the psychological barriers that exist are cultural differences or image. Look at the accompanying Marketing Research Report and try to match up the reasons why certain products have had differing results in gaining consumer acceptance.

Recognizing the concept of the product life cycle helps a marketing manager to remember that a product may need continual adjustments to prevent sales declines and to formulate a marketing strategy to stimulate sales. Failure to recognize the life cycle concept often has dramatic consequences. In the 1960s, airline passenger miles increased by 15 percent a year, and airline companies ordered dozens of new wide-body jets such as the Boeing 747 and McDonnell Douglas DC-10. By the mid-1970s these same planes were standing empty on the runways, because airline officials had just extrapolated past trends on passenger usage and failed to see that smaller, more fuel-efficient planes would replace the 747 and DC-10 jets on shorter domestic flights.[14] Today, even though some new models are being produced, these wide-body jets are in the mature or declining stage of their product life cycle.

Marketing Research Report

ARE YOU A DIFFUSION EXPERT? TAKE THE BARRIER TEST

*L*isted below are several products that have been relatively slow to gain widespread diffusion through the population. Try to match up the example with the barrier that has caused the problem. Then read on in this report to learn the analysis of these diffusion problems by Professors S. Ram and Jagdish N. Sheth.

INNOVATION	BARRIER LETTER	BARRIER
Tofu (an inexpensive protein substitute)	_____	a. Tradition
RCA videodisc player (which plays movies on a disc similar to an album)	_____	b. Economic risk
Industrial machine tools from India	_____	c. Usage
Cranberry sauce as a year-round food item	_____	d. Value
		e. Image

Moving a product through the life cycle means getting customers to adopt it in the introductory stage. For tofu, a protein substitute that can be mixed with other foods for taste and texture, success has been slow. The problem is one of usage (*c*). Few people have recipes for this item. Also, with the increasing usage of pre-prepared foods even cooking skills are changing.

The RCA videodisc player was introduced at about the same time as videocassette recorders, and was seen as an alternative technology to that being offered by Sony's VCRs. Although the quality of the picture was good and the players were less expensive than VCRs, the problem was still one of value (*d*)—the videodisc player could not record movies.

Industrial tools from India face a difficult image problem (*e*) in trying to be commercially successful in the United States. While the tools themselves are of a high quality, not many Americans have an image of India as a technologically sophisticated country.

Finally, there is the cranberry sauce marketed by such cooperatives as Ocean Spray. Sales for this product are strong during one time of the year, Thanksgiving, but this advantage of tradition (*a*) is also cranberry sauce's greatest barrier in getting consumers to think of it as a year-round food item.

Solutions to these barriers exist, but require creative marketing. For tofu, the product must be made easier to use. For the videodisc player, little hope exists since the technology has been quickly replaced by VCRs. For Indian manufacturers, image advertising is necessary to educate the potential buyers (in this case, industrial consumers) about the real India. And finally, Ocean Spray must continue to look for and publicize alternative ways to use cranberries in drinks, mixes, and dishes.

Source: S. Ram and Jagdish N. Sheth, "Consumer Resistance to Innovations: The Marketing Problem and Its Solutions," *Journal of Consumer Marketing* (Spring 1989), pp. 5–14.

CONCEPT CHECK

1 Advertising plays a major role in the _____ stage of the product life cycle, and _____ plays a major role in maturity.

2 How do high learning and low learning products differ?

3 What does the life cycle for a fashion product look like?

MANAGING THE PRODUCT'S LIFE CYCLE

An important task for a firm is to manage its products through the successive stages of their life cycles. This section discusses the role of the product manager who is usually responsible for this and analyzes three ways to manage a product through its life cycle: modifying the product, modifying the market, and repositioning the product.

ROLE OF A PRODUCT MANAGER

The product manager (sometimes called *brand manager*) manages the marketing efforts for a close-knit family of products or brands. Introduced by P&G in 1927, the product manager style of marketing organization is used by consumer goods firms such as General Foods and Frito-Lay and by industrial firms such as Intel and Hewlett-Packard. All product managers are responsible for managing existing products through the stages of the life cycle, and some are also responsible for developing new products. The product manager's marketing responsibilities include developing and executing a marketing program for the product line described in an annual marketing plan and approving ad copy, media selection, and package design. The role of product managers in planning, implementing, and controlling marketing strategy is covered in depth in Chapters 20 and 21.

MODIFYING THE PRODUCT

Product modification involves altering a product's characteristic, such as its quality, performance, or appearance, to try to increase and extend the product's sales. Johnson Controls Inc., a battery manufacturer for companies like Sears, has developed a backup battery. Backup batteries are similar to traditional car batteries, except that they have been modified to have reserve power. With this kind of battery, if you find it dead because you left the lights on, you simply switch a lever on the battery and initiate its backup power.[15] Another kind of product modification is Black & Decker's changing the angle on its Philips screwdriver to prevent the tip from slipping out of the screw.[16]

New features, packages, or scents can be used to change a product's characteristics and give the sense of a revised product. Procter & Gamble revamped Pert shampoo with a new formula that combined a shampoo and hair conditioner in one application. Prior to the modification, Pert was in the decline stage of the life cycle with only 2 percent of the market. After reformulation, PertPlus became the top-selling shampoo in the United States, with 12 percent market share in an industry with over 1,000 competitors.[17]

A modified shampoo led to a market leader.

MODIFYING THE MARKET

With **marketing modification** strategies, a company tries to increase a product's use among existing customers, create new use situations, or find new customers.

Increasing Use   Promoting more frequent usage has been a strategy of Woolite, a laundry soap. Originally intended for the hand washing of woolen material, Woolite now promotes itself for use with all fine clothing items.

Creating New Use Situation   Finding new uses for an existing product has been the major strategy in extending the life of Arm & Hammer Baking Soda. This product, originally intended as a baking ingredient, is now being promoted as toothpaste; a deodorizer for cat litter, carpeting, and refrigerators; and a fire extinguisher.

Finding New Users   To prevent sales declines in wall-to-wall carpeting, carpet manufacturers found new user groups such as schools and hospitals. To expand company sales, Nautilus, a manufacturer of fitness equipment for gyms, entered the home market in 1988. Commercial accounts represented 95 percent of the company's sales in 1987, but the home market has a $1 to $5 billion sales potential. U.S. sales of video games plummeted from $3 billion in 1982 to $100 million in 1985. But they rebounded to $3 billion in 1990 by targeting improved games, such as Nintendo, at two new segments: (1) 8- to 14-year-olds, most of whom can't remember the old games, and (2) adults who want more sophisticated games.[18]

REPOSITIONING THE PRODUCT

Often a company decides to reposition its product or product line in an attempt to prevent sales decline. *Product repositioning* is changing the place a product occupies in a consumer's mind relative to competitive products. A firm can reposition a product by changing one or more of the four marketing mix elements. Four factors that trigger a repositioning action are discussed below.

Reacting to a Competitor's Position   One reason to reposition a product is because a competitor's entrenched position is adversely affecting sales and market share. Coca-Cola recently repositioned New Coke, after watching its market share slide from a high of 15 percent in 1985 to less than 2 percent in 1989. The new brand, called Coke II, has been reformulated to be sweeter, like rival Pepsi-Cola. Test-marketed during 1990 in Spokane, Washington, early signs of this repositioning strategy have led the company to expand testing to other cities.[19]

Reaching a New Market   Dannon Yogurt introduced Yop, a liquid yogurt, in France. The product flopped because the French were not interested in another dairy product. When Dannon repositioned Yop as a soft drink for the health-conscious French consumer, sales soared.[20]

Repositioning can involve more than changing advertising copy. The New Balance Company changed its product's position as a running shoe for the serious runner to a shoe for the mass market. The distribution strategy was altered from selling only through specialty running stores to selling through discount and department stores as well.

Marketing Action Memo

CHOLESTEROL, FAT, WORMS—ARE THESE YOUR WORRIES? TRY THE OTHER WHITE MEAT!

*W*orms, fat, high cholesterol—these are all concerns expressed about pork. So much so that the consumption of pork started to drop along with beef, as shown in the figure below. By 1986, annual consumption had fallen to 59 pounds per person, from a high of 68 pounds in 1968. As shown in the chart, beef too had fallen, while poultry experienced a strong resurgence tied to consumers' concerns about health. The drop was serious enough for the National Pork Producers Council to recognize the need for change.

The result was a call to a Chicago advertising agency, which decided on the need for a repositioning strategy in light of the trend in the marketplace. Analyzing the product led to the discovery of some important advantages. Improved breeding and feeding had led to the development of a pork less fatty than that of 20 years earlier. Furthermore, pork is significantly cheaper than most cuts of beef. The new image campaign was simple—"Pork: The Other White Meat." At first glance, hog producers were horrified. They had tried for years to associate pork as a meat-and-potatoes type of food; now, the repositioning strategy was leading pork into the chicken coop. The new advertisements for

pork also contained recipes on how to prepare it stylishly and in a nutritional fashion. And in a bid for the ultimate form of consumer acceptance, the Pork Council worked with McDonald's to test a McRib pork sandwich on its menu.

Is it working? Well, one look at the graph and the results are clear. While beef continues its decline, pork consumption is inching up. And as one cattle rancher from Nebraska put it, "No doubt about it, the hog guys beat us bad. . . ."

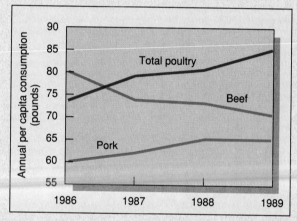

Source: Data for figure from United States Department of Agriculture.

Source: Joshua Levine, "Cluck, Cluck, Oink," *Forbes* (April 16, 1990), pp. 126–27. Copyright © 1990 Forbes, Inc.

Catching a Rising Trend   Changing consumer trends can also lead to repositioning. From 1986 to 1989 annual per-capita consumption of beef fell almost 10 pounds, while consumption of poultry rose almost 13 pounds. For many years the National Pork Producers Council positioned their product as being similar to beef. Noticing the trend toward poultry, a dramatic repositioning campaign was begun and is described in the accompanying Marketing Action Memo.

Changing the Value Offered   In repositioning a product, a company can decide to change the value it offers buyers and trade up or down. **Trading up** involves adding value to the product (or line) through additional features or higher-quality materials. BMW built its reputation in the United States with small, sporty sedans that sell for $20,000 to $35,000. BMW then traded up with a new model, 750sci, which costs $67,000. The car is targeted at the Mercedes Benz buyer, who is 45 to 55 years old and has an income above $150,000.[21] A department store can trade up by adding a designer clothes section to the store.

Trading down involves reducing the number of features, quality, or price. Epilady adapted a trading down strategy to appeal to the mass market by producing a $55 unit with few features compared to its deluxe unit with multiple speeds, priced at $89.

CONCEPT CHECK

1 How does a product manager help manage a product's life cycle?

2 What does "creating new use situations" mean in managing a product's life cycle?

3 Explain the difference between trading up and trading down in repositioning.

BRANDING

A basic decision in marketing products is **branding,** in which an organization uses a name, phrase, design, symbols, or combination of these to identify its products and distinguish them from those of competitors. A **brand name** is any word, "device" (design, sound, shape, or color), or combination of these used to distinguish a seller's goods or services. Some brand names can be spoken, such as a Big Mac hamburger. Other brand names cannot be spoken, such as the rainbow-colored apple (the *logotype* or *logo*) that Apple Computer puts on its machines and in its ads. A **trade name** is a commercial, legal name under which a company does business. The Campbell Soup Company is the trade name of that firm.

A **trademark** identifies that a firm has legally registered its brand name or trade name so the firm has its exclusive use, thereby preventing others from using it. In the United States, 680,000 trademarks are registered with the U.S. Patent and Trademark Office. As discussed in Chapter 3, trademarks are protected under the Lanham Act. A well-known trademark can help a company advertise its offerings to customers and develop their brand loyalty. Figure 11–7 shows examples of well-known trademarks.

Because a good trademark can help sell a product, *product counterfeiting,* which involves low-cost copies of popular brands not manufactured by the original producer, has been a growing problem. Counterfeit products can steal sales from the original manufacturer or hurt the company's reputation. Counterfeiting losses to U.S. companies were estimated to be $40 billion in 1990.[22] To protect against counterfeiting, the federal government passed the Trademark Counterfeiting Act, which makes counterfeiting a federal offense with offenders subject to prison sentences, damage payments, and seizure of counterfeit merchandise.

FIGURE 11–7
Examples of well-known trademarks

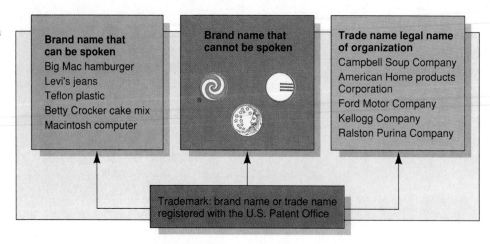

Brand name that can be spoken	Brand name that cannot be spoken	Trade name legal name of organization
Big Mac hamburger		Campbell Soup Company
Levi's jeans		American Home products Corporation
Teflon plastic		Ford Motor Company
Betty Crocker cake mix		Kellogg Company
Macintosh computer		Ralston Purina Company

Trademark: brand name or trade name registered with the U.S. Patent Office

THE VALUE OF BRANDING

Branding policy is important not only for manufacturers but also for retailers and consumers. Retailers value branding because consumers shop at stores that carry their desired brands. Some retailers have created their own store brands to further enhance loyalty from their customers. Sears exclusively offers the Kenmore brand for its appliance line and Craftsman as the brand for tools.

A good brand name is of such importance to a company that it has led to a concept called **brand equity,** the added value a given brand name gives to a product beyond the functional benefits provided. This value has two distinct advantages. First, brand equity provides a competitive advantage, such as the Sunkist label that implies quality fruit. A second advantage of brand equity is its ability to endure environmental changes. GI Joe, a popular brand name of military action figures, was dropped by Hasbro Toys after the Vietnam War made these items unpopular. Hasbro later restored the name on a new line of toy soldiers and sales now top $200 million annually.[23]

Consumers, however, may benefit most from branding. Recognizing competing products by distinct trademarks allows them to be more efficient shoppers. Consumers can recognize and avoid products with which they are dissatisfied, while becoming loyal to other, more satisfying brands. As discussed in Chapter 5, brand loyalty often eases consumers' decision making by eliminating the need for an external search. Also, the expense of establishing a brand on the marketplace means that some brands are reintroduced years after they apparently died.

LICENSING

The value of brand equity is evident in the strategy of licensing. **Licensing** is a contractual agreement whereby a company allows another firm to use its brand name, patent, trade secret, or other property for a royalty or a fee. Licensing can be very profitable to a licensor, and a licensee. Playboy has earned over $260 million licensing its name for merchandise ranging from shoes in the United States to wallpaper in Europe and cooking classes in Brazil. Murjani has sold over $500 million of clothing bearing the Coca-Cola logo.[24]

Simple names can be very effective.

A relatively unique brand name license occurred in 1990 with the hit movie *Teenage Mutant Ninja Turtles*. Over 100 manufacturers paid over $500 million to put the name and the creatures on posters, pizzas, action figures, and clothing.[25] The life cycle of these turtles best falls into the category of a fad (Figure 11–4, D), and they are approaching the decline stage. Fads tend to replace other fads, like wall walkers or pet rocks. Licensing allows a company to enter new markets without engaging in the expensive product development approach. It does require a brand name that has important value to the consumer, however.

PICKING A GOOD BRAND NAME

We take brand names such as Dial, Sanyo, Porsche, and Danskin for granted, but it is often a difficult and expensive process to pick a good name. Four criteria are mentioned most often in selecting a good brand name.[26]

The name should suggest the product benefits. For example, Accutron (watches), Easy Off (oven cleaner), Glass Plus (glass cleaner), Cling-Free (antistatic cloth for drying clothes), and Tidy Bowl (toilet bowl cleaner) all clearly describe the value of purchasing the product.

The name should be memorable, distinctive, and positive. In the car industry, when a competitor has a memorable name, others quickly imitate. In the 1960s Ford named a car the Mustang. Soon there were Pintos, Colts, Mavericks, and Broncos. The Thunderbird stimulated the Phoenix, Eagle, Sunbird, and Firebird.

The name should fit the company or product image. Sharp is a name that can apply to audio and video equipment. NCR (the National Cash Register Company) has had difficulty extending its name to its line of computers. Excedrin is a scientific-sounding name, good for an analgesic. Anacin, however, is perceived negatively because of its prefix meaning "not." The name *Apple* is considered a stroke of genius. When Apple Computer was created, there wasn't any PC market. The name was friendly, safe, and trustworthy. Name experts believe the name PCjr helped kill IBM's home computer because it sounded too much like a toy. Read the accompanying Marketing Action Memo to find out why Nissan Motor Corporation USA never introduced the

Marketing Action Memo

WHAT'S IN A NAME? A LOT!

*W*ould you buy a Nissan Bluebird sedan or a Nissan Fair Lady sportscar? Probably not. However, these names appeared on the Nissan Stanza and Nissan 300ZX before Nissan Motor Corporation USA changed them. According to a company spokesperson, "Fair Lady [didn't] evoke performance-oriented images. You could even say it's wimpy." Bluebird had "a very feminine, almost weak connotation."

Picking brand names is tricky, particularly when firms attempt to use names in different countries. For example, a popular perfume in the Soviet Union called Red Kremlin flopped in the United States. Similarly, American consumers would not be crazy about the Japanese citrus-based beverage called Pocarisweat, or the Japanese coffee creamer called Creap, or the French soft drink Pschitt.

Even names with considerable brand equity are not easily transportable to other products. For example, when the A.1 name for steak sauce was put in a poultry sauce line, the line failed. "We forgot A.1 meant steak to people," said a company spokesperson.

These examples illustrate that a name has meaning for consumers, and should be carefully assessed before applying it to a product. Finding good names that are not already registered with the U.S. Patent and Trademark Office is often a challenging assignment with much at stake.

Sources: Based on Judann Dagnoli, "Beware Line Extensions," *Advertising Age* (October 29, 1990), p. 50; Christopher Burns, "By Any Other Name . . ." *Dallas Times Herald* (April 30, 1990), p. A7; and "No Brand Like an Old Brand," *Forbes* (June 11, 1990), pp. 179–80.

Nissan Fair Lady sportscar in the United States, and why product image is important in branding.

The name should have no legal restrictions. Daniel Yankelovich, who founded one of the first large marketing research firms, was informed he could no longer use his name—at least for any marketing research ventures. After he sold his firm to Saatchi & Saatchi Co., a London-based advertising company, Mr. Yankelovich started a new company using his name in the firm's name, along with some products the firm was selling. A federal court ruled he did not have unrestricted use of his name. A similar problem befell New York's Taylor wine family. They found that they could no longer use the family name for promoting wines after selling Taylor Wine Co. to Coca-Cola Co.[27]

Additionally, it has been suggested that the name should be simple (such as Bold laundry detergent, Sure deodorant, and Bic pens), and should be emotional (such as Joy and My Sin perfumes). In the development of names for international use, having a nonmeaningful brand name has been considered a benefit. A name such as Exxon does not have any prior impressions or undesirable images among a diverse world population of different languages and cultures.[28]

BRANDING STRATEGIES

In deciding to brand a product, companies have several possible strategies, including manufacturer branding, reseller branding, or mixed branding approaches.

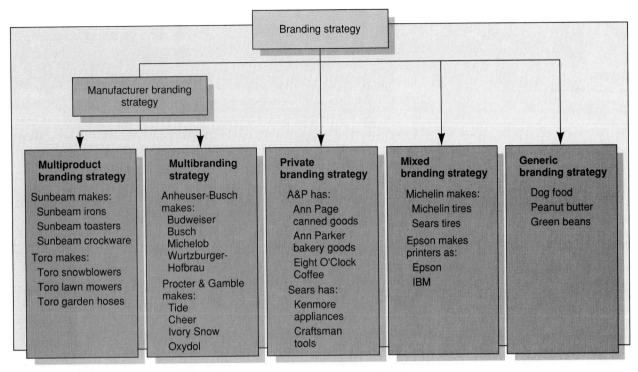

FIGURE 11–8
**Alternative branding
strategies**

Manufacturer Branding   With **manufacturer branding,** the producer dictates the brand name using either a multiproduct or multibrand approach. **Multiproduct branding** is when a company uses one name for all its products. This approach is often referred to as a *blanket* or *family* branding strategy (Figure 11–8).

There are several advantages to this approach. Capitalizing again on brand equity, consumers who have had a good experience with the product will carry this favorable attitude to other items with the same name. Mattel's most enduring brand-name toy is the Barbie doll, introduced in 1959. The company, along with Ralston Purina, has a cereal called Breakfast with Barbie and plans to use the name on girl-sized costumes, bed sheets, and eventually children's clothing and beauty products.[29] This is an example of a *line extension,* because the new products are seen as extending an existing line rather than starting a completely new one. This approach can also result in lower advertising costs because the same name is used on all products within the line, raising the level of brand awareness.

In recent years there has been an increasing trend toward *brand extensions,* applying the same brand name to related products within the same category.[30] Dr. Scholl's, the maker of foot pads and remedies, has extended its name to a broader line of foot products, including shoes and socks. Campbell Soup Co. uses its name on a line of cooking utensils, with the familiar red and white packaging.[31] Procter & Gamble extended the Pringles brand of potato chips to frozen french fries and to dips for their chips.[32]

However, there are some risks to the multiproduct branding approach. Poor performance of one item may have a negative impact on similarly named items in the line. Also, too many uses for one brand name can dilute the image of a product line.

An alternative manufacturer's branding strategy, **multibranding,** involves giving each product a distinct name. Multibranding is a useful strategy when each brand is intended for a different marketing segment. P&G makes Camay soap for those concerned with soft skin, Safeguard for those who want deodorant protection, and Lava for those who desire a strong cleaner. Competing internationally, P&G even uses multiple brand names for the same product. PertPlus shampoo is sold as Rejoice in Hong Kong, PertPlus in the Middle East, and Vidal Sassoon in the United Kingdom. However, international branding strategies do differ. In Japan, where corporate names are important, P&G markets the company's name prominently with the brand name of the product.[33]

Compared with the multiproduct approach, promotional costs tend to be higher with multibranding. The company must generate awareness among consumers and retailers for each new brand name without the benefit of any previous impressions. The advantages of this approach are that each brand is unique to each market segment and there is no risk that a product failure will affect other products in the line.

Private Branding   A company uses **private branding,** often called *private labeling* or *reseller branding,* when it manufactures products but sells them under the brand name of a wholesaler or retailer. Radio Shack, Sears, and K mart are large retailers that have their own brand names.

Matsushita of Japan manufactures VCRs for Magnavox, GE, Sylvania, Philco, J. C. Penney, and Curtis Mathes. The advantage to the manufacturer is that promotional costs are shifted to the retailer or other company, and the manufacturer can often sell more units through others than by themselves.[34] There is a risk, though, because the manufacturer's sales depend heavily on the efforts of others.

Mixed Branding   A compromise between manufacturer and private branding is **mixed branding** where a firm markets products under its own name and that of a reseller, because the segment attracted to the reseller is different from their own market. Sanyo and Toshiba manufacture television sets for Sears, as well as for themselves. This process is similar to Michelin's, which manufactures tires for Sears as well as under its own name. A new development in mixed branding strategy has been explored by Polaroid. It is allowing Minolta, a competing camera company, to sell the Spectra Pro instant camera as the Minolta Instant Pro. Minolta has a very strong brand name in cameras, and Polaroid believes the Minolta name will lend positive identification to the high-end camera market.[35]

Generic Branding   An alternative branding approach is the **generic brand,** which is a no-brand product such as dog food, peanut butter, or green beans. There is no identification other than a description of the contents. The major appeal is that the price is up to one-third less than that of branded items. In 1990, generic brands accounted for only .7 percent of total grocery sales. The limited appeal of generics has been attributed to low inflation, the importance of brand name, and greater promotional efforts for brand-name items.[36] Consumers who use generics see these products as being as good as brand-name items, and in light of what they expect, users of these products are relatively pleased with their purchases.[37]

PACKAGING

The **packaging** component of a product refers to any container in which it is offered for sale and on which information is communicated. To a great extent, the customer's first exposure to the product is the package, and it is an expensive and important part of the marketing strategy. A grocery product package is especially important because packaging designers using eye cameras have discovered that a typical consumer's eye sweep of a grocery shelf is a mere 2.3 seconds.[38] Today's packaging costs exceed $50 billion and are also substantial for the consumer: an estimated 10 cents of every dollar spent by a consumer goes to packaging.[39]

BENEFITS OF PACKAGING

Despite the cost, packaging is essential because packages provide important benefits for the manufacturer, retailer, and ultimate consumer.

Communication Benefits   A major benefit of packaging is the information on it conveyed to the consumer, such as directions on how to use the product and the composition of the product, which is needed to satisfy legal requirements of product disclosure.[40] Other information consists of seals and symbols, either government-required or commercial seals of approval (such as the Good House-keeping seal).[41]

Functional Benefits   Packaging often plays an important functional role, such as convenience, protection, or storage. Quaker State has changed its oil containers to eliminate the need for a separate spout, and Borden has changed the

New packaging for traditional products.

shape of its Elmer's Wonder Bond adhesive to prevent clogging of the spout. To increase convenience, Colgate and Check-Up brands of toothpaste are now sold in pump dispensers.

The convenience dimension of packaging is becoming increasingly important. A Richard Simmons salad dressing is being sold in a pump-top bottle, while microwave popcorn has been a major market success.[42]

Consumer protection is becoming a growing function of packaging. In 1982 a mentally ill person put cyanide into several bottles of Tylenol, which resulted in several deaths. Since that time, the development of tamper-resistant packaging has become important. Companies such as the one that produces Skippy peanut butter have turned to safety seals or pop tops, which reveal previous opening. The concern among many is that no package is truly tamper resistant. The federal government now has a law that carries maximum penalties of life imprisonment and $250,000 fines for tampering.[43]

Another functional value of packaging is in extending storage and *shelf life* (the time a product can be stored before it spoils). New technology allows products requiring refrigeration to be packaged in paper-sealed containers, which dramatically increases their shelf life. Called *aseptic* or germ-free packaging, it allows milk to stay fresh for five years without refrigeration.

Perceptual Benefits   A third component of packaging is the perception created in the consumer's mind. Just Born Inc., a candy manufacturer of such brands as Jelly Joes and Mike and Ike Treats, discovered the importance of this component of packaging. For many years the brands were sold in old-fashioned black and white packages, but in the late 1980s the packaging was changed to four color, with animated grape and cherry characters. Sales increased 25 percent. Procter & Gamble, the manufacturer of Clearasil acne cream, changes the packaging every year. This redesign gives it the appearance of a new cream, which is important to the target market of teenagers who purchase the product.[44]

A package can connote status, economy, or even product quality. Equally fresh potato chips were wrapped in two different types of bags: wax paper and polyvinyl. Consumers rated the chips in the polyvinyl as crisper and even tastier, even though the chips were identical.[45]

Did the new package designs for these candies help or hurt sales? For the answer, see the text.

In the past, the color of packages was selected subjectively. For example, the famous Campbell's soup can was the inspiration of a company executive who liked Cornell University's red and white football uniforms. Today, there is greater recognition that color affects consumers' perceptions. When the color of the can of Barrelhead Sugar-Free Root Beer changed to beige from blue, consumers said it tasted more like old-fashioned root beer.[46] And Owens-Corning judged the pink color of its fiber insulation to be so important that the color was given trademark status by the courts.[47]

TRENDS IN PACKAGING

Companies are seeing packaging as a way to increase sales of existing brands. Valvoline Motor Oil Co. tested 40 variations for its packaging of motor oil before deciding to increase the size and add more color to the label. American Home Products made the packaging for Wheatena cereal more modern and saw sales increase by 25 percent in test markets. But redesigns are not without expense—some packaging changes can cost upwards of $300,000, because of alterations in production equipment. There can also be other risks. Coors redesigned the label of their beer to say "Original Draft" instead of "Banquet Beer." Customers thought the taste had changed, so the company was forced to go back to the original label.[48]

There are two different trends in packaging that are major factors in the 1990s. One trend involves environmental sensitivity. Because of the growing concern about solid waste disposal, recyclable material and biodegradable alternatives for packaging are two approaches receiving a great deal of attention. Lever Brothers Co. is trying to address these concerns with a test of a "bag-in-box" package for their Wisk laundry detergent. Procter & Gamble uses recycled cardboard in 70 percent of its paper packaging, and is packaging Tide, Cheer, Era, and Dash detergents in jugs that contain 25 percent recycled plastic. Spic and Span liquid cleaner is to be packaged in 100 percent recycled material, and a similar approach is planned by Heinz for their ketchup bottle.[49]

The need for environmentally friendly packaging is becoming increasingly clear. The aseptic package that was considered by a panel of food technologists in 1989 to be the best technological achievement of the past 50 years is now being outlawed in some states. The design of the box is said to make recycling difficult.[50] Figure 11–9 shows that progress is being made on the environmental issue.

A second trend that will gain greater attention in the 1990s relates to the health and safety concerns of packaging materials. During the 1980s, there was a growing trend in the use of microwavable packaging for convenience. Recent studies by the Food and Drug Administration, however, suggest that the heating of some packages can lead to potentially cancer-causing agents seeping into food products. The major concern has been related to packaging that contains heat susceptors, thin metalicized plastic film strips that help brown microwavable food. Companies like Du Pont, 3M, and Raytheon are working to develop alternatives in anticipation of regulatory changes regarding packaging.[51]

FIGURE 11–9
The challenging concerns of environmentally sensitive packaging

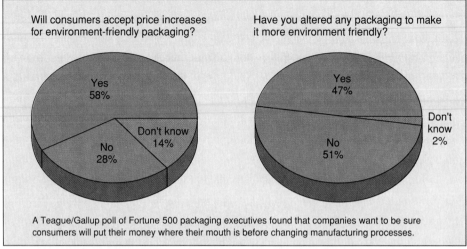

Will consumers accept price increases for environment-friendly packaging?

Yes 58%

No 28%

Don't know 14%

Have you altered any packaging to make it more environment friendly?

Yes 47%

No 51%

Don't know 2%

A Teague/Gallup poll of Fortune 500 packaging executives found that companies want to be sure consumers will put their money where their mouth is before changing manufacturing processes.

Source: *Marketing News* (March 19, 1990), p. 16, by permission of The American Marketing Association.

PRODUCT WARRANTY

A final component for product consideration is the **warranty,** which is a statement indicating the liability of the manufacturer for product deficiencies. There are various degrees of product warranties with different implications for manufacturers and customers.

THE VARIATIONS OF A WARRANTY

Some companies offer *express warranties,* which are written statements of liabilities. In recent years the government has required greater disclosure on express warranties to indicate whether the warranty is a limited-coverage or full-coverage alternative. A *limited-coverage warranty* specifically states the bounds of coverage and, more important, areas of noncoverage, whereas a *full warranty* has no limits of noncoverage. Peugeot is a company that boldly touts its warranty coverage. The Magnuson-Moss Warranty/FTC Improvement Act (1975) regulates the content of consumer warranties and so has strengthened consumer rights with regard to warranties.

With greater frequency, manufacturers are being held to *implied warranties,* which assign responsibility for product deficiencies to the manufacturer. Studies show that warranties are important and affect a consumer's product evaluation. Brands that have limited warranties tend to receive less positive evaluations compared with full-warranty items.[52]

THE GROWING IMPORTANCE OF WARRANTIES

Warranties are important in light of increasing product liability claims. In the early part of this century the courts protected companies, but the trend now is toward "strict liability" rulings, where a manufacturer is liable for any product defect, whether it followed reasonable research standards or not. This issue is hotly contested by companies and consumer advocates.

Warranties represent much more to the buyer than just protection from negative consequences—they can hold a significant marketing advantage for the producer. Sears has built a strong reputation for its Craftsman tool line with a simple warranty: if you break a tool, it's replaced with no questions asked. Zippo has an equally simple guarantee: "If it ever fails, we'll fix it free."

1 How does a generic brand differ from a private brand?

2 Explain the role of packaging in terms of perception.

3 What is the difference between an expressed and an implied warranty?

ETHICS AND SOCIAL RESPONSIBILITY IN THE 1990s

CONSUMERS ARE PAYING MORE FOR LESS IN DOWNSIZED PACKAGES

For more than 30 years, Starkist put 6.5 ounces of tuna into its regular-sized can. Today, Starkist puts 6.125 ounces of tuna into its can but charges the same price. Colgate-Palmolive's Ajax king-size laundry detergent package has remained the same size, but the contents have been cut from 61 ounces to 55 ounces and the package price increased from $2.59 to $2.79. Procter & Gamble has cut the number of Pampers disposable diapers in its packages from 88 to 80 while leaving the price the same. Other companies such as Quaker Oats, Hershey Foods, Gerber Products, and Ragu Foods have allegedly engaged in similar practices, according to Robert Adams, the attorney general of New York.

Consumer advocates charge that "downsizing" packages while maintaining or increasing prices is a subtle and unannounced way of taking advantage of consumers' buying habits. Manufacturers argue that this practice is a way of keeping prices from rising beyond psychological barriers for their products.

Is downsizing an unethical practice if manufacturers do not inform consumers that the package contents are less than they were previously?

Sources: Based on John B. Hinge, "Critics Call Cuts in Package Size Deceptive Move," *The Wall Street Journal* (February 5, 1991), pp. B1, B8; and Judann Dagnoli, "State AGs Attack Downsized Brand," *Advertising Age* (February 18, 1991), pp. 1, 46.

 ## SUMMARY

1 Products have a finite life cycle consisting of four stages: introduction, growth, maturity, and decline. The marketing objectives for each stage differ.

2 In the introductory stage the need is to establish primary demand, whereas the growth stage requires selective demand strategies. In the maturity stage the need is to maintain market share; the decline stage necessitates a deleting, harvesting, or contracting strategy.

3 There are various shapes to the product life cycle. High learning products have a long introductory period, and low learning products rapidly enter the growth stage. There are also different curves for fashions and fads. Different product life cycle curves can exist for the product class, product form, and brand.

4 In managing a product's life cycle, changes can be made in the product itself or in the target market. Product modification approaches include changes in the quality, performance, or appearance. Market modification approaches entail increasing a product's use among existing customers, creating new use situations, or finding new users.

5 Product repositioning can be done by modifying the product, as well as through changes in advertising, pricing, or distribution.

6 Branding enables a firm to distinguish its product in the marketplace from those of its competitors. A good brand name should suggest the product benefits; be memorable; fit the company or product image; be free of legal restrictions; and be simple and emotional. In international marketing, non-meaningful brand names avoid cultural problems and undesirable images.

7 Licensing of a brand name is being used by more companies. The company allows the name to be used without having to manufacture the product.

8 Manufacturers can follow one of three branding strategies: a manufacturer's brand, a reseller brand, or a mixed brand approach. With a manufacturer's branding approach, the company can use the same brand name for all products in the line (multiproduct, or family, branding) or can give products different brands (multibranding).

9 A reseller, or private, brand is used when a firm manufactures a product but sells it under the brand name of a wholesaler or retailer. A generic brand is a product with no identification of manufacturer or reseller that is offered on the basis of price appeal.

10 Packaging provides communication, functional, and perceptual benefits. The two emerging trends in packaging are greater concerns regarding the environmental impact and the safety of packaging materials.

11 The warranty, a statement of a manufacturer's liability for product deficiencies, is an important aspect of a manufacturer's product strategy.

≡ KEY TERMS AND CONCEPTS

CHAPTER PROBLEMS AND APPLICATIONS

1 Several years ago, Apple Computer was one of the first to mass market PCs. IBM, the giant, had no competing product, but within a short time it announced its PC model. Steven Jobs, the founder of Apple, is said to have exclaimed, "We're glad to see IBM is entering the market." According to the product life cycle, is there any rationale for this statement?

2 Several manufacturers of aseptic packaging (paper containers) have formed a trade association to advertise its merits. What is the rationale for competitors collectively advertising in the early stages of a product's life?

3 Listed below are three different products in various stages of the product life cycle. What marketing strategies would you suggest to these companies? (*a*) GTE cellular telephone company—growth stage, (*b*) Mountain Stream tap-water purifying systems—introductory stage, and (*c*) hand-held manual can openers—decline stage.

4 In many communities the birth rate has dropped substantially, adversely affecting hospitals' pediatric medicine departments. Although pediatrics as a specialty is declining, hospitals still need a complete service mix. As the chief executive of a hospital, what decline strategies would you suggest?

5 It has often been suggested that products are intentionally made to break down or wear out. Is this strategy a planned product modification approach?

6 The product manager of GE is reviewing the penetration of trash compactors in American homes. After more than a decade in existence, this product is in relatively few homes. What problems account for this poor penetration? What is the shape of the trash compactor life cycle?

7 Several alternative product life cycles were reviewed in this chapter. Why is it important for a company to realize what type of life cycle curve may represent its product?

8 For several years Ferrari has been known as the manufacturer of expensive luxury automobiles. The company plans to attract the major segment of the car-buying market who purchase medium-priced automobiles. As Ferrari considers this trading-down strategy, what branding strategy would you recommend? What are the trade-offs to consider with your strategy?

9 The nature of product warranties has changed as the federal court system reassesses the meaning of warranties. How does the regulatory trend toward warranties affect product development?

CHAPTER 12

Pricing: Relating Objectives to Revenues and Costs

*A*fter reading this chapter you should be able to:

- Identify the elements that make up a price.

- Recognize the constraints on a firm's pricing latitude and the objectives a firm has in setting prices.

- Explain what a demand curve is and how it affects a firm's total and marginal revenue.

- Recognize what price elasticity of demand means to a manager facing a pricing decision.

- Explain the role of costs in pricing decisions.

- Calculate a break-even point for various combinations of price, fixed cost, and variable cost.

Potato Chip Economics at Frito-Lay

Remember back in 1989, when the bag price of Lay's® and Ruffles® brand potato chips went up a dime in most parts of the country and they were hard to find in your favorite store? What you experienced was Potato Chip Economics 101 as taught by Frito-Lay, the world's premier marketer of snack chips.

A drought in the Red River Valley of North Dakota caused a potato shortage and a rise in raw potato prices. Fewer potatoes at a higher cost spelled trouble for Doug Boyle, director of Potato Chip Brands at Frito-Lay. He knew that American consumers, who devour over a billion pounds of potato chips each year, would demand their Lay's® and Ruffles® potato chips. Potato costs would pinch his profit margin and a limited potato supply would affect how many chips Frito-Lay could sell. What should be done?

Discussion among company executives resulted in a two-pronged response. First, the bag price on Lay's® and Ruffles® brand potato chips would increase 10 cents to cover higher potato costs and provide an acceptable profit margin on fewer bags sold. Second, potato chip promotional activities were reduced.

"What we attempted to do was manage demand for potato chips by using price and other tools at our disposal," noted Dwight Riskey, vice president of Marketing Research and New Business. Did the response work? According to Mr. Riskey, demand and supply were synchronized during the shortage. Once the shortage passed, Frito-Lay resumed its promotions for potato chips and reduced the bag price by a dime to the original.[1]

This chapter and Chapter 13 cover important factors organizations use in developing prices. The role of price in marketing strategy and a step-by-step procedure organizations use to set prices for products and services are discussed. Relevant concepts from economics and accounting show how each assists the marketing executive in developing the price component in the marketing mix.

NATURE AND IMPORTANCE OF PRICE

The price paid for goods and services goes by many names. You pay *tuition* for your education, *rent* for an apartment, *interest* on a bank credit card, and a *premium* for car insurance. Your dentist or physician charges you a *fee*, a professional or social organization charges *dues*, and transportation companies charge a *fare*. In business a consultant may require a *retainer* for services rendered, an executive is given a *salary*, a salesperson receives a *commission*, and a worker is paid a *wage*. Of course, what you pay for clothes or a haircut is termed a *price*.

WHAT IS A PRICE?

These examples highlight the many varied ways that price plays a part in our daily lives. From a marketing viewpoint, **price** is the money or other considerations (including other goods and services) exchanged for the ownership or use of a good or service. For example, Shell Oil recently exchanged 1 million pest control devices for sugar from a Caribbean country, and Wilkinson Sword exchanged some of its knives for advertising used to promote its razor blades. Consumers exchange trading stamps such as S&H Green Stamps for a variety of products. This practice of exchanging goods and services for other goods and services rather than for money is called **barter.** These transactions account for $5 billion annually in domestic and international trade.[2]

For most products and services, money is exchanged, although the amount is not always the same as the list or quoted price. Suppose you decide to buy two identical Jaguar XJ220 models that are initially scheduled for a 1992 European introduction.[3] The XJ220s will have V-6 turbo-charged engines and accelerate from 0 to 100 mph in eight seconds. The list price is $586,593 for each. As a quantity discount for buying two Jaguars, you get $7,000 off the list price for each. You are required to put down a deposit of $79,950. However, you agree to pay half down and the other half when the cars are delivered, which results in a financing fee of $3,000 per car. You are allowed $1,000 for your only trade—your 1982 Honda—amounting to $500 off the price of each car.

Applying the "price equation" (as shown in Figure 12–1) to your purchase, your price per car is:

Price = List price − Discounts and allowances + Extra fees

$$= \$586{,}593 \; - \; (\$7{,}000 \; + \; \$500) \qquad + \; \$3{,}000$$

$$= \$582{,}093$$

Are you still interested? Perhaps you might look at the Porsche 959 or Ferrari F40 to compare prices. Figure 12–1 also illustrates how the price equation applies to a variety of different products and services.

PRICE AS AN INDICATOR OF VALUE

From a consumer's standpoint, price is often used to indicate value when it is paired with the perceived benefits of a product or service. Specifically, **value** can be defined as the ratio of perceived benefits to price (Value = Perceived benefits/Price).[4] This relationship shows that for a given price, as perceived benefits increase, value increases. Also, for a given price, value decreases when perceived benefits decrease. Creative marketers engage in **value-pricing,** the practice of

FIGURE 12–1
The price of four different purchases

ITEM PURCHASED	PRICE EQUATION					
	PRICE	=	LIST PRICE	−	DISCOUNTS AND ALLOWANCES	+ EXTRA FEES
New car bought by an individual	Final price	=	List price	−	Quantity discount Cash discount Trade-ins	+ Financing charges Special accessories
Term in college bought by a student	Tuition	=	Published tuition	−	Scholarship Other financial aid Discounts for number of credits taken	+ Special activity fees
Bank loan obtained by a small business	Principal and interest	=	Amount of loan sought	−	Allowance for collateral	+ Premium for uncertain creditworthiness
Merchandise bought from a wholesaler by a retailer	Invoice price	=	List price	−	Quantity discount Cash discount Season discount Functional or trade discount	+ Penalty for late payment

simultaneously increasing product and service benefits and decreasing price.[5] U.S. carmakers have struggled to overcome this latter relationship in their battle with Japanese automobile producers.

For some products, price influences the perception of overall quality, and ultimately value, to consumers.[6] For example, in a survey of home furnishing buyers, 84 percent agreed with the statement: "The higher the price, the higher the quality." For computer software it has been shown that consumers believe a low price implies poor quality.[7]

Consumer value assessments are often comparative. Here value involves the judgment by a consumer of the worth and desirability of a product or service relative to substitutes that satisfy the same need.[8] In this instance a "reference value" emerges, which involves comparing the costs and benefits of substitute items. For example, although Equal, a sugar substitute with NutraSweet, might be more expensive than sugar, some consumers "value" it more highly than sugar because Equal contains no calories.

How consumers make value assessments is not fully understood. Nevertheless, companies consider this factor when making price decisions, as will be shown in Chapter 13.

PRICE IN THE MARKETING MIX

Pricing is also a critical decision made by a marketing executive, because price has a direct effect on a firm's profits. This is apparent from a firm's **profit equation:**

Profit = Total revenue − Total cost

or

Profit = (Unit price × Quantity sold) − Total cost

What makes this relationship even more important is that price affects the quantity sold, as illustrated with demand curves later in this chapter. Furthermore, since the quantity sold sometimes affects a firm's costs because of efficiency of production, price also indirectly affects costs. So pricing decisions influence both total revenue and total cost, which makes pricing one of the most important decisions marketing executives face.[9]

The importance of price in the marketing mix necessitates an understanding of six major steps involved in the process organizations go through in setting prices (Figure 12–2):

- Identify pricing constraints and objectives.
- Estimate demand and revenue.
- Determine cost, volume, and profit relationships.
- Select an approximate price level.
- Set list or quoted price.
- Make special adjustments to list or quoted price.

The first three steps are covered in this chapter and the last three in Chapter 13.

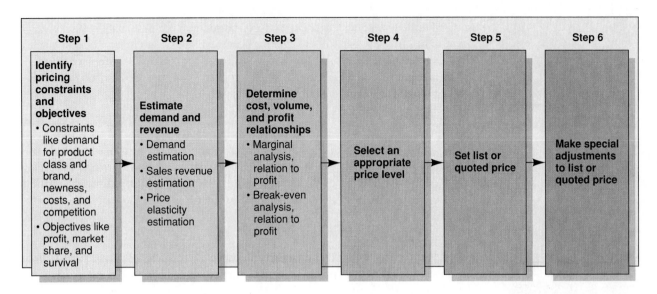

FIGURE 12–2
Steps in setting price

STEP 1: IDENTIFYING PRICING CONSTRAINTS AND OBJECTIVES

To define a problem, Chapter 7 showed that it is important to consider both the objectives and constraints that narrow the range of alternatives available to solve it. These same principles apply in solving a pricing problem. Let's first review the pricing constraints so that we can better understand the nature of pricing alternatives.

IDENTIFYING PRICING CONSTRAINTS

Factors that limit the latitude of prices a firm may set are **pricing constraints.** Consumer demand for the product clearly affects the price that can be charged. Other constraints on price are set by factors within the organization: newness of the product, whether it is part of a product line, and cost of and flexibility in changing a price. Competitive factors such as the nature of competition and prices set by competitors also restrict the latitude of an organization's ability to set price. Legal and regulatory constraints on pricing are discussed in Chapter 13.

Demand for the Product Class, Product, and Brand   The number of potential buyers for the product class (such as cars), product (sports cars), and brand (Jaguar XJ220) clearly affects the price a seller can charge. So does whether the item is a luxury—like a Jaguar—or a necessity—like bread and a roof over your head. The nature of demand is discussed later in the chapter.

Newness of the Product: Stage in the Product Life Cycle   The newer a product and the earlier it is in its life cycle, the higher is the price that can usually be charged. When NutraSweet was introduced in 1983, it was the only nonartificial sugar substitute that was safe to use, contained few calories, and was sweeter than sugar. The newness of the product coupled with patent protection meant that a premium price could be charged. However, once its patent expired in 1991, numerous rivals emerged, which affected the pricing latitude for NutraSweet and often caused price reductions.[10]

Single Product versus a Product Line   When Sony introduced its CD player, not only was it unique and in the introductory stage of its product life cycle but also it was the *only* CD player Sony sold, so the firm had great latitude in setting a price. Now, with a line of CD player products, the price of individual models has to be consistent with the others based on features provided and meaningful price differentials.

Interior of MGM Grand Air airplane.

Cost of Producing and Marketing the Product   In the long run, a firm's price must cover all the costs of producing and marketing a product. If the price doesn't cover the cost, the firm will fail, so in the long run a firm's costs set a floor under its price. Regent Air and McClain Airlines painfully learned this lesson. Both airlines provided luxury transcontinental air service for one-way airfares as high as $1,000. Unfortunately, the total cost of providing this red-carpet service exceeded the total revenue and both companies failed. Another luxury airline, MGM Grand Air, has been more successful in balancing the total revenue–total cost relationship and recorded a profit in its second year of operation.[11]

Cost of Changing Prices and Time Period They Apply   If the U.S. Air Force asks Pratt & Whitney (P&W) to provide spare jet engines to power the B-1B bomber, P&W can easily set a new price for the engines to reflect its latest information, since only one buyer has to be informed. But if Sears or L.L. Bean decides that sweater prices are too low in its winter catalogs after thousands of catalogs have been mailed to customers, it has a big problem. It can't easily inform thousands of potential buyers that the price has changed, so Sears or L.L. Bean must consider the cost of changing prices and the time period for which they apply in developing the price list for its catalog items.

Type of Competitive Markets   The seller's price is constrained by the type of market in which it competes. Economists generally delineate four types of competitive markets: pure monopoly, oligopoly, monopolistic competition, and pure competition. Figure 12–3 shows that the type of competition dramatically influences the latitude of price competition and in turn the nature of product differentiation and extent of advertising. A firm must recognize the general type of competitive market it is in to understand the latitude of both its price and nonprice strategies. For example:

- *Pure monopoly:* Pacific Power & Light, an electric power company, receives approval from the state utility commission for the rates it can charge California consumers. In most areas of the state it is the only source of electricity for consumers and runs public-service ads to show them how to conserve electricity.

	TYPE OF COMPETITIVE MARKET			
STRATEGIES AVAILABLE	PURE MONOPOLY (One seller who sets the price for a unique product)	OLIGOPOLY (Few sellers who are sensitive to each other's prices)	MONOPOLISTIC COMPETITION (Many sellers who compete on nonprice factors)	PURE COMPETITION (Many sellers who follow the market price for identical, commodity products)
Price competition	None: sole seller sets price	Some: price leader or follower of competitors	Some: compete over range of prices	Almost none: market sets price
Product differentiation	None: no other producers	Various: depends on industry	Some: differentiate products from competitors'	None: products are identical
Extent of advertising	Little: purpose is to increase demand for product class	Some: purpose is to inform but avoid price competition	Much: purpose is to differentiate firm's products from competitors'	Little: purpose is to inform prospects that seller's products are available

FIGURE 12–3

Pricing, product, and advertising strategies available to firms in four types of competitive markets

- *Oligopoly:* The few sellers of aluminum (Reynolds, Alcoa) or American-built, mainframe computers try to avoid price competition because it can lead to disastrous price wars in which all lose money. Yet firms in such industries stay aware of a competitor's price cuts or increases and may follow suit. The products can be undifferentiated (aluminum) or differentiated (mainframe computers), and informative advertising that avoids head-to-head price competition is used.
- *Monopolistic competition:* Dozens of regional, private brands of peanut butter compete with national brands like Skippy and Jif. Both price competition (regional, private brands being lower than national brands) and nonprice competition (product features and advertising) exist.
- *Pure competition:* Hundreds of local grain elevators sell corn whose price per bushel is set by the marketplace. Within strains, the corn is identical, so advertising only informs buyers that the seller's corn is available.

Competitors' Prices   A firm must know or anticipate what specific price its present and potential competitors now or will charge. When the NutraSweet Company planned the market introduction of Simplesse® all natural fat substitute, it had to consider the price of fat replacements already available as well as potential competitors such as Procter & Gamble's Olestra and a fat substitute product being developed by Kraft General Foods, Inc.[12]

Simplesse® and the Simplesse symbol are trademarks of The Simplesse Company.

IDENTIFYING PRICING OBJECTIVES

Expectations that specify the role of price in an organization's marketing and strategic plans are **pricing objectives.** To the extent possible, these organizational pricing objectives are also carried to lower levels in the organization, such as in setting objectives for marketing managers responsible for an individual brand.[13] Chapter 2 discussed six broad objectives that an organization may pursue, which tie in directly to the organization's pricing policies.

Profit   Three different objectives relate to a firm's profit, usually measured in terms of return on investment (ROI) or return on assets. One objective is *managing for long-run profits,* which is followed by many Japanese firms that are willing to forgo immediate profit in cars, TV sets, or computers to develop quality products that can penetrate competitive markets in the future. A *maximizing current profit* objective, such as during this quarter or year, is common in many firms because the targets can be set and performance measured quickly. American firms are sometimes criticized for this short-run orientation. A *target return* objective involves a firm like Du Pont or Exxon setting a goal (such as 20 percent) for pretax ROI. These three profit objectives have different implications for a firm's pricing objectives.

Sales   Given that a firm's profit is high enough for it to remain in business, its objectives may be to increase sales revenue. The hope is that the increase in sales revenue will in turn lead to increases in market share and profit. Cutting price on one product in a firm's line may increase its sales revenue but reduce those of related products. Objectives related to sales revenue or unit sales have the advantage of being translated easily into meaningful targets for marketing managers responsible for a product line or brand—far more easily than with an ROI target, for example.

Market Share   Market share is the ratio of the firm's sales revenues or unit sales to those of the industry (competitors plus the firm itself). Companies often pursue a market share objective when industry sales are flat or declining and they want to get a larger share. Anheuser-Busch has adopted this objective in the brewing industry. According to August A. Busch III, the company's chief executive officer, "We want 50 percent of the [beer] market in the mid-1990s."[14] As described in the accompanying Marketing Action Memo, Anheuser-Busch announced a price-cutting strategy to meet the competition and bolster its market share. Although increased market share is a primary goal of some firms, others see it as a means to other ends: increasing sales and profits.

General Motors uses low-interest financing and rebates to increase unit sales.

Unit Volume   Many firms use unit volume, the quantity produced or sold, as a pricing objective. These firms often sell multiple products at very different prices and are sensitive to matching production capacity with unit volume. Using unit volume as an objective, however, can sometimes be misleading from a profit standpoint. Volume can be increased by employing sales incentives (such as lowering prices, giving rebates, or offering lower interest rates). By doing this the company chooses to lower profits in the short run to quickly sell their product. This was the case in 1990 when General Motors, in an attempt to clear out older models, offered low-interest car loans and rebates. Although profits declined temporarily, they satisfied their objective of increasing volume to make room for the new model-year cars.

Survival   In some instances, profits, sales, and market share are less important objectives of the firm than mere survival. Pan Am Airlines has struggled to

Marketing Action Memo

DON'T DISCOUNT THE KING WHEN IT COMES TO MARKET SHARE

*B*eer consumption in the United States has gone flat in recent years, due to changing drinking habits. As a result, some major brewers have begun to compete for a larger market share through new products and increased promotion. Others, such as Miller Brewing and Coors, initiated a price discounting program to grab market share from Stroh's and Heileman.

However, Miller and Coors "went after the elk and deer, and shot the elephant," said an industry analyst. The elephant? Anheuser-Busch, the king of beers with a 43.2 percent market share, saw its sales and market share suffer due to price cutting by Miller and Coors. "We cannot permit a further slowing in our volume," an Anheuser-Busch spokesperson said, adding that the company will take "appropriate competitive pricing actions to support our long-term market share growth strategy."

Anheuser-Busch avoided price cutting in the past and relied on promotion and new products to build market share. But August A. Busch III, the CEO of Anheuser-Busch, conceded that his company would play the price game. He said, "We don't want to start a blood bath, but whatever the competition wants to do, we'll do. Everyone understands that market share is key in a mature industry."

Aggressive pricing can build market share. Miller increased its share through price discounting, as did Coors. Who lost share? Stroh's and Heileman. Who reigns supreme? Anheuser-Busch. Because of its competitors, Anheuser-Busch now uses price discounting to preserve market share and, where possible, increase it with the ultimate objective of achieving a 50 percent share of the U.S. beer market.

Sources: Based on Patricia Sellers, "Busch Fights to Have It All," *Fortune* (January 15, 1990), pp. 81–88; "Bud Puts Stress on Promotions, Trims TV Ads," *The Wall Street Journal* (February 20, 1990), pp. B1, B6; "Anheuser-Busch, Slugging It Out, Plans Beer Price Cuts," *The Wall Street Journal* (October 26, 1989), pp. B1, B6; and "A Warning Shot from the King of Beers," *Business Week* (December 18, 1989), p. 124.

attract passengers with low fares, no-penalty advance-booking policies, and aggressive promotions to improve the firm's cash flow. This pricing objective has helped Pan Am to stay alive in the competitive airline industry.[15]

Social Responsibility A firm may forgo higher profit on sales and follow a pricing objective that recognizes its obligations to customers and society in general. Medtronics followed this pricing policy when it introduced the world's first heart pacemaker. Gerber supplies a specially formulated product free of charge to children who cannot tolerate foods based on cow's milk.[16] Government agencies, which set many prices for services they offer, use social responsibility as a primary pricing objective. As a result, in the arid South and Southwest the federal government sells water to users at a price that is only about 19 percent of the total cost of providing it.[17]

CONCEPT CHECK

1 What do you have to do to the list price to determine the final price?

2 How does the type of competitive market a firm is in affect its latitude in setting price?

STEP 2: ESTIMATING DEMAND AND REVENUE

Basic to setting a product's price is the extent of customer demand for it. Understanding demand requires a look at how both economists and business-people view it.

FUNDAMENTALS IN ESTIMATING DEMAND AND REVENUE

Newsweek recently conducted a pricing experiment at newsstands in 11 cities throughout the United States.[18] Houston newsstand buyers paid $2.25. In Fort Worth, New York, Los Angeles, San Francisco, and Atlanta, newsstand buyers paid the regular $2.00 price. In San Diego, the price was $1.50. The price in Minneapolis–St. Paul, New Orleans, and Detroit was only $1.00. By comparison, the regular newsstand price for *Time* and *U.S. News and World Report*, *Newsweek*'s competitors, was $1.95. Why did *Newsweek* conduct the experiment? According to a *Newsweek* executive, "We want to figure out what the demand curve for our magazine at the newsstand is." And you thought that demand curves only existed to confuse you on a test in basic economics!

The Demand Curve   A **demand curve** shows a maximum number of products consumers will buy at a given price. Demand curve D_1 in Figure 12–4 shows the newsstand demand for *Newsweek* under present conditions. Note that as price falls, people buy more. But price is not the complete story in estimating demand. Economists stress three other key factors:

1 *Consumer tastes:* As we saw in Chapter 3, these depend on many factors such as demographics, culture, and technology. Because consumer tastes can change quickly, up-to-date marketing research is essential.

FIGURE 12–4
Illustrative demand curves for *Newsweek* magazine

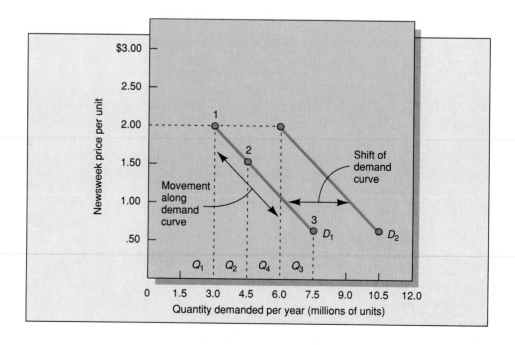

2 *Price and availability of other products:* As the price of close substitute products falls (*Time* for *Newsweek*) and their availability increases, the demand for a product declines.

3 *Consumer income:* In general, as real consumer income (allowing for inflation) increases, demand for a product also increases.

The first of these two factors influences what consumers *want* to buy, and the third affects what they *can* buy. Along with price, these are often called **demand factors,** or factors that determine consumers' willingness and ability to pay for goods and services.

Movement Along versus Shift of a Demand Curve   Demand curve D_1 in Figure 12–4 shows that as the price is lowered from \$2 to \$1.50, the quantity demanded increases from 3 million to 4.5 million units per year. This is an example of a movement along a demand curve and assumes that other factors (consumer tastes, price and availability of substitutes, and consumer income) remain unchanged.

What if some of these factors change? For example, if advertising causes more people to want *Newsweek,* newsstand distribution is increased, and consumer incomes double, then the demand increases. This is shown in Figure 12–4 as a shift of the demand curve to the right, from D_1 to D_2. This means that more *Newsweek* magazines are wanted for a given price: at a price of \$2, the demand is 6 million units per year (Q_4) on D_2 rather than 3 million units per year (Q_1) on D_1.

FUNDAMENTALS IN ESTIMATING REVENUE

While economists may talk about "demand curves," marketing executives are more likely to speak in terms of "revenues generated." Demand curves lead directly to three related revenue concepts critical to pricing decisions: **total revenue, average revenue,** and **marginal revenue** (Figure 12–5).

FIGURE 12–5
**Fundamental revenue
concepts**

Total revenue (TR) is the total money received from the sale of a product. If:

   TR = Total revenue

   P = Unit price of the product

   Q = Quantity of the product sold

then:

   TR = P × Q

Average revenue (AR) is the average amount of money received for selling one unit of the product, or simply the price of that unit. Average revenue is the total revenue divided by the quantity sold:

$$AR = \frac{TR}{Q} = P$$

Marginal revenue (MR) is the change in total revenue obtained by selling one additional unit:

$$MR = \frac{\text{Change in TR}}{\text{1 unit increase in Q}} = \frac{\Delta TR}{\Delta Q}$$

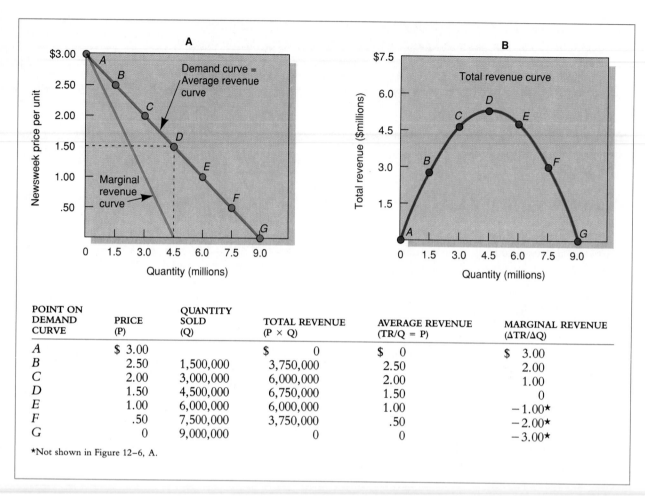

POINT ON DEMAND CURVE	PRICE (P)	QUANTITY SOLD (Q)	TOTAL REVENUE (P × Q)	AVERAGE REVENUE (TR/Q = P)	MARGINAL REVENUE (ΔTR/ΔQ)
A	$ 3.00		$ 0	$ 0	$ 3.00
B	2.50	1,500,000	3,750,000	2.50	2.00
C	2.00	3,000,000	6,000,000	2.00	1.00
D	1.50	4,500,000	6,750,000	1.50	0
E	1.00	6,000,000	6,000,000	1.00	−1.00★
F	.50	7,500,000	3,750,000	.50	−2.00★
G	0	9,000,000	0	0	−3.00★

*Not shown in Figure 12–6, A.

FIGURE 12–6
How a downward-sloping demand curve affects total, average, and marginal revenue

Demand Curves and Revenue   Figure 12–6, A, again shows the demand curve for *Newsweek,* but it is now extended to intersect both the price and quantity axes. The demand curve shows that as price is reduced, the quantity of *Newsweek* magazines sold throughout the United States increases. This relationship holds whether the price is reduced from $3 to $2.50 on the demand curve or is reduced from $1 to $0 on the curve. In the former case the market demands no *Newsweek* magazines, whereas in the latter case 9 million could be given away at $0 per unit.

It is likely that if *Newsweek* was given away, more than 9 million would be demanded. This fact illustrates two important points. First, it can be dangerous to extend a demand curve beyond the range of prices for which it really applies. Second, most demand curves are rounded (or convex) to the origin, thereby avoiding an unrealistic picture of what demand looks like when a straight-line curve intersects either the price axis or the quantity axis.

Figure 12–6, B, shows the total revenue curve for *Newsweek* calculated from the demand curve shown in Figure 12–6, A. The total revenue curve is developed by simply multiplying the unit price times the quantity for each of the points on the demand curve. Total revenue starts at $0 (point *A*), reaches a maximum of $6,750,000 at point *D,* and returns to $0 at point G. This shows that as price is reduced in the *A*-to-*D* segment of the curve, total revenues are increased. However, cutting price in the *D*-to-*G* segment results in a decline in total revenue.

Marginal revenue, which is the slope of the total revenue curve, is positive but decreasing when the price lies in the range from $3 to above $1.50 per unit. But below $1.50 per unit, marginal revenue is actually negative, so the extra quantity of magazines sold is more than offset by the decrease in the price per unit.

For any downward-sloping, straight-line demand curve, the marginal revenue curve always falls at a rate twice as fast as the demand curve. As shown in Figure 12–6, A, the marginal revenue becomes $0 per unit at a quantity sold of 4.5 million units—the very point at which total revenue is maximum (see Figure 12–6, B). Because a rational marketing manager would never operate in the region of the demand curve in which marginal revenue is negative, only the positive portion is shown in typical graphs of demand curves.

What price did *Newsweek* select after conducting its experiment? They kept the price at $2.00. However, through expanded newsstand distribution and more aggressive advertising, *Newsweek* was later able to shift its demand curve to the right and charge a price of $2.50 without affecting its newsstand volume.

Price Elasticity of Demand   With a downward-sloping demand curve, we have been concerned with the responsiveness of demand to price changes. This can be conveniently measured by **price elasticity of demand,** or the percentage change in quantity demanded relative to a percentage change in price. Price elasticity of demand (E) is expressed as follows:

$$E = \frac{\text{Percentage change in quantity demanded}}{\text{Percentage change in price}}$$

Because quantity demanded usually decreases as price increases, price elasticity of demand is usually a negative number. However, for the sake of simplicity and by convention, elasticity figures are shown as positive numbers.

Price elasticity of demand assumes three forms: elastic demand, inelastic demand, and unitary demand elasticity. *Elastic demand* exists when a small percentage decrease in price produces a larger percentage increase in quantity demanded. Price elasticity is greater than 1 with elastic demand. *Inelastic demand* exists when a small percentage decrease in price produces a smaller percentage increase in quantity demanded. With inelastic demand, price elasticity is less than 1. *Unitary demand* exists when the percentage change in price is identical to the percentage change in quantity demanded. In this instance, price elasticity is equal to 1.

Price elasticity of demand is determined by a number of factors. First, the more substitutes a product or service has, the more likely it is to be price elastic. For example, butter has many possible substitutes in a meal and is price elastic, but gasoline has almost no substitutes and is price inelastic. Second, products and services considered to be necessities are price inelastic. For example, open-heart surgery is price inelastic, whereas airline tickets for a vacation are price

Snack foods evidence elastic demand, whereas fruits and vegetables evidence inelastic demand.

elastic. Third, items that require a large cash outlay compared with a person's disposable income are price elastic. Accordingly, cars and yachts are price elastic; books and movie tickets are price inelastic.

Price elasticity is important to marketing managers because of its relationship to total revenue. For example, with elastic demand, total revenue increases when price decreases, but decreases when price increases. With inelastic demand, total revenue increases when price increases and decreases when price decreases. Finally, with unitary demand total revenue is unaffected by a slight price change.

Because of this relationship between price elasticity and a firm's total revenue, it is important that marketing managers recognize that price elasticity of demand is not the same over all possible prices of a product. Figure 12–6, B, illustrates this point using the *Newsweek* demand curve shown in Figure 12–6, A. As the price decreases from $2.50 to $2, total revenue increases, indicating an elastic demand. However, when the price decreases from $1 to 50 cents, total revenue declines, indicating an inelastic demand. Unitary demand elasticity exists at a price of $1.50.

Price Elasticities for Brands and Product Classes　Marketing executives also recognize that the price elasticity of demand is not always the same for product classes (such as stereo receivers) and brands within a product class (such as Sony and Marantz). For example, marketing experiments on brands of cola, coffee, and snack and specialty foods generally show elasticities of 1.5 to 2.5, indicating they are price elastic. By comparison, entire product classes of fruits and vegetables have elasticities of about 0.8 —they are price inelastic.[19]

Recently, the price elasticity of demand for cigarettes has become a hotly debated public health issue and a matter of social responsibility. Research generally shows that cigarettes are price inelastic.[20] However, price elasticity differs

Marketing Action Memo

PRICE ELASTICITY UP IN SMOKE

*T*oday, 30 percent of men and 24 percent of women in the United States smoke, and about 25 percent of all regular cigarette smokers are expected to die of smoking-related diseases. These statistics have prompted the U.S. Surgeon General's Office to explore innovative programs and initiatives to discourage smoking.

One of the more notable considerations in the fight against smoking is the use of economic incentives based on research focusing on the *price elasticity of demand for cigarettes*. This research shows that price elasticity for cigarettes varies by age. For persons 12–17 years old, a 10 percent increase in cigarette prices results in a 14 percent decline in smoking (price elasticity = 1.40), which indicates that this age group is *price elastic*. For persons 26–35 years old, cigarette consumption typically declines about 5 percent when prices rise 10 percent (price elasticity = .5). This age group is *price inelastic*.

According to the Surgeon General's report: "The principal message of this body of research on price elasticity of demand is that an increase in the price of cigarettes appears to curtail smoking, particularly the initiation of smoking by teenagers." In practical terms, this means that progressively higher excise taxes on cigarettes, which increase the price of cigarettes, could reduce the incidence of smoking, at least among teenagers and possibly the poor.

Pricing in the cigarette industry is a hotly contested issue, as is the matter of price elasticity. For example, several producers have introduced low-priced brands that are about half the price of existing brands. This action has drawn heavy fire from smoking foes. According to the executive director of the Coalition on Smoking and Health: "Bringing out a cigarette that sells for far less than the standard price is a blatant effort to attract young smokers who are extraordinarily price sensitive, and other poorer individuals."

Tobacco marketers take strong exception to such criticism. Whatever the outcome of this heated exchange, few would disagree that price elasticity of demand will play a central role in this public health debate.

Sources: Based on "Tobacco Suit Exposes Ways Cigarette Firms Keep Profits Fat," *The Wall Street Journal* (March 5, 1990), pp. A1, A6; *Reducing the Health Consequences of Smoking: 25 Years of Progress. A Report of the Surgeon General* (Washington, D.C.: U.S. Department of Health and Human Services, 1989); "Elasticity, It's Wonderful," *Fortune* (February 13, 1989), pp. 123–24; *The Health Consequences of Smoking: Nicotine Addiction. A Report of the Surgeon General* (Washington, D.C.: U.S. Department of Health and Human Services, 1988); M. Gonzales and B. Edmonson, "The Smoking Class," *American Demographics* (November 1988), pp. 34–37, 58–59; and "Cigarette Smokers Will Quit—at a Price," *Business Week* (June 18, 1990), p. 20.

by the age of the smoker, as described in the accompanying Marketing Action Memo. As shown, price elasticity is not only a relevant concept for marketing managers, it is also important for public policy affecting pricing practices.

CONCEPT CHECK

1 What is the difference between a movement along and a shift of a demand curve?

2 What does it mean if a product has a price elasticity of demand that is greater than 1?

STEP 3: DETERMINING COST, VOLUME, AND PROFIT RELATIONSHIPS

The profit equation described at the beginning of the chapter showed that Profit = Total revenue − Total cost. Therefore, understanding the role and behavior of costs is critical for all marketing decisions, particularly pricing decisions. Four cost concepts are important in pricing decisions: **total cost, fixed cost, variable cost,** and **marginal cost** (Figure 12–7).

MARGINAL ANALYSIS AND PROFIT MAXIMIZATION

A basic idea in business, economics, and indeed everyday life is marginal analysis. In personal terms, marginal analysis means that people will continue to do something as long as the incremental return exceeds the incremental cost. This same idea holds true in marketing and pricing decisions. In this setting, **marginal analysis** means that as long as revenue received from the sale of an additional product (marginal revenue) is greater than the additional cost of producing and selling it (marginal cost), a firm will expand its output of that product.[21]

Marginal analysis is central to the concept of maximizing profits. In Figure 12–8, A, marginal revenue and marginal cost are graphed. Marginal cost starts out high at lower quantity levels, decreases to a minimum through production and marketing efficiencies, and then rises again due to the inefficiencies of overworked labor and equipment. Marginal revenue follows a downward slope. In Figure 12–8, B, total cost and total revenue curves corresponding to the marginal cost and marginal revenue curves are graphed. Total cost initially rises as quantity increases but increases at the slowest rate at the quantity where marginal cost is lowest. The total revenue curve increases to a maximum and then starts to decline, as shown in Figure 12–6, B.

FIGURE 12–7
Fundamental cost concepts

Total cost (TC) is the total expense incurred by a firm in producing and marketing the product. Total cost is the sum of fixed cost and variable cost.

Fixed cost (FC) is the sum of the expenses of the firm that are stable and do not change with the quantity of product that is produced and sold. Examples of fixed costs are rent on the building, executive salaries, and insurance.

Variable cost (VC) is the sum of the expenses of the firm that vary directly with the quantity of product that is produced and sold. For example, as the quantity sold doubles, the variable cost doubles. Examples are the direct labor and direct materials used in producing the product and the sales commissions that are tied directly to the quantity sold. As mentioned above:

$$TC = FC + VC$$

Variable cost expressed on a per unit basis is called *unit variable cost (UVC)*.

Marginal cost (MC) is the change in total cost that results from producing and marketing one additional unit:

$$MC = \frac{\text{Change in TC}}{\text{1 unit increase in Q}} = \frac{\Delta TC}{\Delta Q}$$

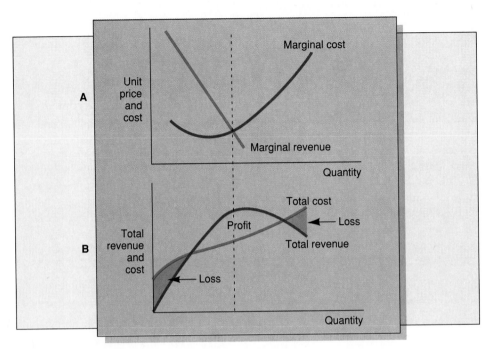

FIGURE 12–8
**Profit maximization
pricing**

The message of marginal analysis, then, is to operate up to the quantity and price level where marginal revenue equals marginal cost (MR = MC). Up to the output quantity at which MR = MC, each increase in total revenue resulting from selling one additional unit exceeds the increase in the total cost of producing and marketing that unit. Beyond the point at which MR = MC, however, the increase in total revenue from selling one more unit is less than the cost of producing and marketing that unit. At the quantity at which MR = MC, the total revenue curve lies farthest above the total cost curve and they are parallel. The debut of General Motors' Saturn provides an illustration of marginal analysis, as described in the accompanying Marketing Action Memo.

BREAK-EVEN ANALYSIS

Marketing managers often employ a simpler approach for looking at cost, volume, and profit relationships, which is also based on the profit equation.[22] **Break-even analysis** is a technique that analyzes the relationship between total revenue and total cost to determine profitability at various levels of output. The **break-even point** (BEP) is the quantity at which total revenue and total cost are equal and beyond which profit occurs. In terms of the definitions in Figure 12–7:

$$\text{BEP}_{\text{Quantity}} = \frac{\text{Fixed cost}}{\text{Unit price} - \text{Unit variable cost}}$$

Calculating a Break-Even Point   Consider, for example, a corn farmer who wishes to identify how many bushels of corn he must sell to cover his fixed cost at a given price. Suppose the farmer had a fixed cost (FC) of $2,000 (for real

Marketing Action Memo

MARGINAL ANALYSIS AND GM'S SATURN

*I*t was a beautiful October day in 1990 when General Motors' Saturn rolled off the assembly line in Spring Hill, Tennessee. After spending almost $3.5 billion over eight years on technical development, manufacturing facilities, and consumer research, the Saturn debuted with fanfare and high expectations. But a question remained. Would Saturn be a marketing *and* a financial success? According to an auto industry analyst, "The car will be a marketing success but a financial flop." How can this happen? The answer lies in marginal analysis and cost, volume, and profit relationships.

Manufacturing plans for Saturn indicate that 120,000 cars will be built with a single production shift in 1991. In 1992, with a second production shift added, 240,000 cars will be built. However, for Saturn to be a financial success, a production volume of 500,000 cars will be necessary. For this to happen, a sizable incremental increase in manu-

facturing facilities will be necessary, thus adding to total costs.

At the same time, Saturn sales must meet expectations that, given its price and features, are comparable to Honda and Toyota (two main competitors), and a $100 million advertising expense. Failing to achieve total revenue expectations will further reduce the likelihood of Saturn being a financial success.

Will Saturn fall prey to marginal analysis? A tally of total revenue and total cost through the 1990s will tell the tale.

Source: Based on "Here Comes GM's Saturn," *Business Week* (April 9, 1990), pp. 56–61; "GM's Saturn Enters Crucial Period," *Advertising Age* (March 5, 1990), p. 16; "GM's Plan for Saturn, to Beat Small Imports, Trails Original Goals," *The Wall Street Journal* (July 9, 1990), pp. A1, A12; and "Introduction of GM Saturn Cars Is Hurt by Output Troubles at Automated Plant," *The Wall Street Journal* (December 4, 1990), p. A3.

estate taxes, interest on a bank loan, and other fixed expenses) and a unit variable cost (UVC) of $1 per bushel (for labor, corn seed, herbicides, and pesticides). If the price (P) is $2 per bushel, his break-even quantity is 2,000 bushels:

$$\text{BEP}_{\text{Quantity}} = \frac{\text{FC}}{\text{P} - \text{UVC}} = \frac{\$2,000}{\$2 - \$1} = 2,000 \text{ bushels}$$

FIGURE 12–9
Calculating a break-even point

Figure 12–9 shows that the break-even quantity at a price of $2 per bushel is 2,000 bushels, since at this quantity total revenue equals total cost. At less than

QUANTITY SOLD (Q)	PRICE PER BUSHEL (P)	TOTAL REVENUE (TR) (P × Q)	UNIT VARIABLE COST (UVC)	TOTAL VARIABLE COSTS (TVC) (UVC × Q)	FIXED COST (FC)	TOTAL COST (TC) (TVC + FC)	PROFIT (TR − TC)
0	$2	$ 0	$1	$ 0	$2,000	$2,000	− $2,000
1,000	2	2,000	1	1,000	2,000	3,000	− 1,000
2,000	2	4,000	1	2,000	2,000	4,000	0
3,000	2	6,000	1	3,000	2,000	5,000	1,000
4,000	2	8,000	1	4,000	2,000	6,000	2,000
5,000	2	10,000	1	5,000	2,000	7,000	3,000
6,000	2	12,000	1	6,000	2,000	8,000	4,000

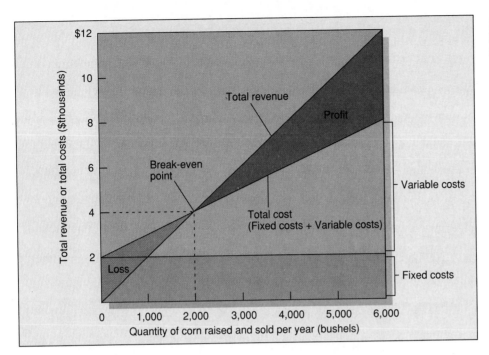

FIGURE 12–10
Break-even analysis chart

2,000 bushels the farmer incurs a loss, and at more than 2,000 bushels he makes a profit. Figure 12–10 shows a graphic presentation of the break-even analysis, called a **break-even chart.**

Applications of Break-Even Analysis   Because of its simplicity, break-even analysis is used extensively in marketing, most frequently to study the impact on profit of changes in price, fixed cost, and variable cost. The mechanics of break-even analysis are the basis of the widely used electronic spreadsheets offered by computer programs such as Lotus 1-2-3 that permit managers to answer hypothetical "what if . . ." questions about the effect of changes in price and cost on their profit.

   Although use of electronic spreadsheets in pricing is covered in Chapter 13, an example here will show the power of break-even analysis. As described in Figure 12–11, if an electronic calculator manufacturer automates its production, thereby increasing fixed cost and reducing variable cost by substituting machines for workers, this increases the break-even point from 333,333 to 500,000 units per year.

   But what about the impact of the higher level of fixed cost on profit? Remember, profit at any output quantity is given by:

Profit = Total revenue − Total cost

$$= (P \times Q) - [FC + (UVC \times Q)]$$

So profit at 1 million units of sales before automation is:

Profit = $(P \times Q) - [FC + (UVC \times Q)]$

$$= (\$10 \times 1,000,000) - [\$1,000,000 + (\$7 \times 1,000,000)]$$

$$= \$10,000,000 - \$8,000,000$$

$$= \$2,000,000$$

FIGURE 12–11
The cost trade-off: fixed versus variable costs

Executives in virtually every mass-production industry—from locomotives and cars to electronic calculators and breakfast cereals—are searching for ways to increase quality and reduce production costs to remain competitive in world markets. Increasingly they are substituting robots, automation, and computer-controlled manufacturing systems for blue- and white-collar workers.

To understand the implications of this on the break-even point and profit, consider this example of an electronic calculator manufacturer:

BEFORE AUTOMATION		AFTER AUTOMATION	
P = $10 per unit		P = $10 per unit	
FC = $1,000,000		FC = $4,000,000	
UVC = $7 per unit		UVC = $2 per unit	

$$BEP_{Quantity} = \frac{FC}{P - UVC} \qquad\qquad BEP_{Quantity} = \frac{FC}{P - UVC}$$

$$= \frac{\$1,000,000}{\$10 - \$7} \qquad\qquad\qquad = \frac{\$4,000,000}{\$10 - \$2}$$

$$= 333,333 \text{ units} \qquad\qquad\qquad\quad = 500,000 \text{ units}$$

The automation increases the fixed cost and increases the break-even quantity from 333,333 to 500,000 units per year. So if annual sales fall within this range, the calculator manufacturer will incur a loss with the automated plant, whereas it would have made a profit it if had not automated.

But what about its potential profit if it sells 1 million units a year? Look carefully at the two break-even charts below and see the text to check your conclusions:

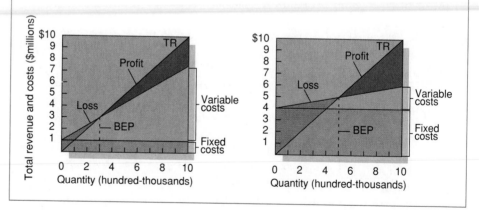

After automation, profit is:

$$\text{Profit} = (P \times Q) - [FC + (UVC \times Q)]$$

$$= (\$10 \times 1,000,000) - [\$4,000,000 + (\$2 \times 1,000,000)]$$

$$= \$10,000,000 - \$6,000,000$$

$$= \$4,000,000$$

Automation, by adding to fixed cost, increases profit by $2 million at 1 million units of sales. Thus as the quantity sold increases for the automated plant, the potential increase or leverage on profit is tremendous. This is why with large production and sales volumes, automated plants for GM cars or Texas Instruments calculators produce large profits. Also, firms in other industries, such as airline, railroad, and hotel and motel industries, that require a high fixed cost can reap large profits when they go even slightly beyond the break-even point.

CONCEPT CHECK

1 **What is the difference between fixed cost and variable cost?**

2 **What is a break-even point?**

ETHICS AND SOCIAL RESPONSIBILITY IN THE 1990s

PRICE DISCOUNTING OF COLLEGE TUITIONS

Figure 12–1 detailed how the price equation applies to college tuition. Recently, about 20 elite colleges and universities were investigated by the U.S. Justice Department because it believed that these institutions had violated the Sherman Anti-Trust Act. Allegedly, officials of these institutions would communicate with one another concerning the amount of financial aid a prospective student would be offered by each school. If a student was accepted for admission at two or more of these institutions and qualified for financial aid, officials from the schools would agree on the amount of financial aid to be awarded to the student. Therefore, when a prospective student received a letter of acceptance from each school, the financial aid amount from each institution would be identical.

The supposed intent of this practice was to reduce price competition. Under this practice, a student would presumably base his or her school choice on the merits of the school and not solely tuition, which has increased 10 percent annually in recent years.

Putting aside the legality of this practice, is this conduct ethical and did these colleges and universities behave in a socially responsible fashion?

Sources: Based on Gary Putka, "Colleges Cancel Aid Meetings under Scrutiny," *The Wall Street Journal* (March 12, 1991), pp. B1, B4; and Kent B. Monroe, *Pricing: Making Profitable Decisions,* 2nd ed. (New York: McGraw-Hill, 1990), pp. 444–45.

SUMMARY

1 Price is the money or other considerations exchanged for the ownership or use of a product or service. Although price typically includes money, the amount exchanged is often different from the list or quoted price because of allowances and extra fees.

2 Consumers use price as an indicator of value when it is paired with the perceived benefits of a good or service. Sometimes price influences consumer perceptions of quality itself and at other times consumers make value assessments by comparing the costs and benefits of substitute items.

3 Pricing constraints such as demand, product newness, costs, competitors, other products sold by the firm, and the type of competitive market restrict a firm's pricing latitude.

4 Pricing objectives, which specify the role of price in a firm's marketing strategy, may include pricing for profit, sales revenue, market share, unit sales, survival, or some socially responsible price level.

5 A demand curve shows the maximum number of products consumers will buy at a given price and for a given set of (*a*) consumer tastes, (*b*) price and availability of other products, and (*c*) consumer income. When any of these change, there is a shift of the demand curve.

6 Price elasticity of demand measures the sensitivity of units sold to a change in price. When demand is elastic, a reduction in price is more than offset by an increase in units sold, so that total revenue increases.

7 It is necessary to consider cost behavior when making pricing decisions. Important cost concepts include total cost, variable cost, fixed cost, and marginal cost.

8 Break-even analysis shows the relationship between total revenue and total cost at various quantities of output for given conditions of price, fixed cost, and variable cost. The break-even point is where total revenue and total cost are equal.

KEY TERMS AND CONCEPTS

price p. 314

barter p. 314

value p. 315

value-pricing p. 315

profit equation p. 316

pricing constraints p. 317

pricing objectives p. 319

demand curve p. 322

demand factors p. 323

total revenue p. 323

average revenue p. 323

marginal revenue p. 323

price elasticity of demand p. 325

total cost p. 328

fixed cost p. 328

variable cost p. 328

marginal cost p. 328

marginal analysis p. 328

break-even analysis p. 329

break-even point p. 329

break-even chart p. 331

CHAPTER PROBLEMS AND APPLICATIONS

1 How would the price equation apply to the purchase price of (*a*) gasoline, (*b*) an airline ticket, and (*c*) a checking account?

2 When the telephone industry was deregulated and AT&T (the Bell System) lost its virtual monopolistic position, the company experienced an immediate change in its pricing practices for telephones and long-distance phone rates because of a barrage of new competitors entering the market. How might this different competitive environment bring about new or different pricing constraints for AT&T?

3 What would be your response to the statement, "Profit maximization is the only legitimate pricing objective for the firm"?

4 How is a downward-sloping demand curve related to total revenue and marginal revenue?

5 A marketing executive once said, "If the price elasticity of demand for your product is inelastic, then your price is probably too low." What is this executive saying in terms of the economic principles discussed in this chapter?

6 A marketing manager reduced the price on a brand of cereal by 10 percent and observed a 25 percent increase in quantity sold. The manager then thought that if the price were reduced by another 20 percent, a 50 percent increase in quantity sold would occur. What would be your response to the marketing manager's reasoning?

7 A student theater group at a university has developed a demand schedule that shows the relationship between ticket prices and demand based on a student survey, as follows:

TICKET PRICE	NUMBER OF STUDENTS WHO WOULD BUY
$1	300
2	250
3	200
4	150
5	100

a. Graph the demand curve and the total revenue curve based on these data. What ticket price might be set based on this analysis?

b. What other factors should be considered before the final price is set?

8 Touché Toiletries, Inc., has developed an addition to its Lizardman Cologne line tentatively branded Ode d'Toade Cologne. Unit variable costs are 45 cents for a 3-ounce bottle, and heavy advertising expenditures in the first year would result in total fixed costs of $900,000. Ode d'Toade Cologne is priced at $7.50 for a 3-ounce bottle. How many bottles of Ode d'Toade must be sold to break even?

9 Suppose that marketing executives for Touché Toiletries reduced the price to $6.50 for a 3-ounce bottle of Ode d'Toade and the fixed costs were $1,100,000. Suppose further that the unit variable cost remained at 45 cents for a 3-ounce bottle. (*a*) How many bottles must be sold to break even? (*b*) What dollar profit level would Ode d'Toade achieve if 200,000 bottles were sold?

10 Executives of Random Recordings, Inc., produced an album entitled *Sunshine/Moonshine* by the Starshine Sisters Band. The cost and price information was as follows:

Album cover	$1.00 per album
Songwriter's royalties	0.30 per album
Recording artists' royalties	0.70 per album
Direct material and labor costs to produce the album	1.00 per album
Fixed cost of producing an album (advertising, studio fee, etc.)	100,000.00
Selling price	7.00 per album

a. Prepare a chart like that in Figure 12–10 showing total cost, fixed cost, and total revenue for album quantity sold levels starting at 10,000 albums through 100,000 albums at 10,000 album intervals, that is, 10,000, 20,000, 30,000, and so on.

b. What is the break-even point for the album?

CHAPTER 13

Pricing: Arriving at the Final Price

After reading this chapter you should be able to:

- Understand how to establish the initial "approximate price level" using demand-based, cost-based, profit-based, and competition-based methods.

- Identify the major factors considered in deriving a final list or quoted price from the approximate price level.

- Describe adjustments made to the approximate price level based on geography, discounts, and allowances.

- Prepare basic financial analyses useful in evaluating alternative prices and arriving at the final sales price.

- Describe the principal laws and regulations affecting pricing practices.

Arriving at 75,000 Prices—Every Day!

What has an average life span of six days, is a member of a family of 225,000, and resides in an electronic environment? A computer virus? No. An American Airlines fare on one of its 16,000 routes in the United States? Yes!

Airfare pricing is one of the most complex tasks in airline marketing. On an average day, over 200,000 fares are changed in the airline industry. American Airlines alone changes more than 75,000 fares daily. Each pricing decision made by American Airlines considers the company's costs, competitor behavior, profit goals, and customers' traveling preferences. With an average of 14 fares for each route, American Airlines seeks to maximize passenger revenues by selling the right seats (mix of full fares and discount fares) to the right customers (business travelers versus pleasure travelers) at the right place (trip origin and destination) at the right prices. These pricing decisions would be impossible without sophisticated computer technology and knowledgeable pricing analysts. Is American Airlines successful? American is one of the largest, most profitable airlines in the world.[1]

The American Airlines experience documents how factors related to demand, cost, competition, and the company affect prices for a single firm and an entire industry. It also shows the relationship between art, science, and technology in pricing decisions.

This chapter describes how companies select an appropriate price level, highlights important considerations in setting a list or quoted price, and identifies various price adjustments that can be made to prices set by the firm—the last three steps an organization uses in setting price (Figure 13–1). In addition, an overview of legal and regulatory aspects of pricing is provided.

STEP 4: SELECT AN APPROXIMATE PRICE LEVEL

A key to a marketing manager's setting a final price for a product is to find an "approximate price level" to use as a reasonable starting point. Four common approaches to helping find this approximate price level are (1) demand-based, (2) cost-based, (3) profit-based, and (4) competition-based methods (Figure 13–2). Although these methods are discussed separately below, some of them overlap, and an effective marketing manager will consider several in searching for an approximate price level.

DEMAND-BASED METHODS

Demand-based methods of finding a price level weigh factors underlying expected customer tastes and preferences more heavily than such factors as cost, profit, and competition.

FIGURE 13–1
Steps in setting price

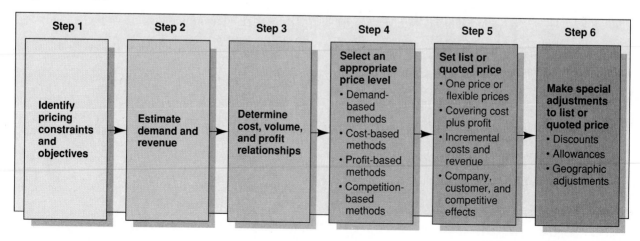

Skimming Pricing   A firm introducing a new or innovative product can use **skimming pricing,** setting the highest initial price that customers really desiring the product are willing to pay. These customers are not very price sensitive because they weigh the new product's price, quality, and ability to satisfy their needs against the same characteristics of substitutes. As the demand of these customers is satisfied, the firm lowers the price to attract another, more price-sensitive segment. Thus skimming pricing gets its name from skimming successive layers of "cream," or customer segments, as prices are lowered in a series of steps.

The initial pricing of VCRs at more than $1,500 and the Trivial Pursuit game at $39.95 are examples of skimming pricing. Within three years after their introductions, both products were often priced at less than half their initial prices. Sometimes minor modifications are made in the product when it is offered at a lower price to a new segment; publishing hardback bestselling novels in paperback is an example. Skimming pricing is an effective strategy when (1) enough prospective customers are willing to buy the product immediately at the high initial price to make these sales profitable, (2) the high initial

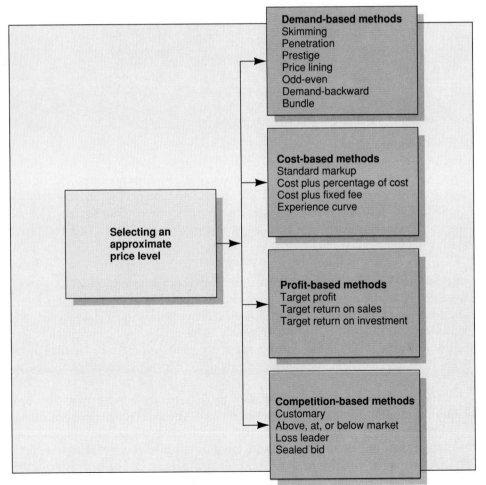

FIGURE 13–2
Four methods of selecting an approximate price level

Trivial Pursuit was
priced high on
introduction and
subsequently priced
lower to reach a broader
audience.

price will not attract competitors, (3) lowering price has only a minor effect on increasing the sales volume and reducing the unit costs, and (4) customers interpret the high price as signifying high quality. These four conditions are most likely to exist when the new product is protected by patents or copyrights or its uniqueness is understood and appreciated by customers. StarSignal, a small California firm, has adopted a skimming strategy for its $26,000 fax machine, which prints color documents.[2]

Penetration Pricing   Setting a low initial price on a new product to appeal immediately to the mass market is **penetration pricing,** the exact opposite of skimming pricing. IBM consciously chose a penetration strategy when in 1990 it introduced a line of high-powered personal computers for business and scientific purposes. Pricing the computers at roughly half of what competitors were charging, a company spokesperson said, "We've priced these things to go."[3]

The conditions favoring penetration pricing are the reverse of those supporting skimming pricing: (1) many segments of the market are price sensitive, (2) a low initial price discourages competitors from entering the market, and (3) unit production and marketing costs fall dramatically as production volumes increase. Thus the firm using penetration pricing may (1) maintain the initial price for a time to gain profit loss from its low introductory level or (2) lower the price further, counting on the new volume to generate the necessary profit.

Prestige pricing is commonly used for perfumes.

In some situations penetration pricing may follow skimming pricing. A company might initially price a product high to attract price-insensitive consumers and recoup initial research and development costs and introductory promotional expenditures. Once this is done, penetration pricing is used to appeal to a broader segment of the population and increase market share. The move from skimming to penetration pricing for VCRs and the Trivial Pursuit game is an example of a successful transition.[4]

Prestige Pricing   As noted in Chapter 12, consumers may use price as a measure of the quality or prestige of an item so that as price is lowered beyond some point, demand for the item actually falls. **Prestige pricing** involves setting a high price so that status-conscious consumers will be attracted to the product and buy it (Figure 13–3, A). The demand curve slopes downward and to the right between points A and B but turns back to the left between points B and C, since demand is actually reduced between points B and C. From A to B buyers see the lowering of price as a bargain and buy more; from B to C they become dubious about the quality and prestige and buy less. A marketing manager's pricing strategy here is to stay above price P_0 (the initial price). Heublein, Inc., successfully repositioned its Popov brand of vodka to make it a prestige brand. It increased price by 8 percent, which led to a 1 percent decline in market share but a whopping 30 percent increase in profit.[5]

Rolls Royce cars, diamonds, perfumes, fine china, and crystal have an element of prestige pricing appeal in them and may sell worse at lower prices than at higher ones. Bijan's in New York City has offered a five-piece set of crocodile luggage for $55,000 or a bulletproof, mink-lined raincoat for the executive who has everything else for $14,000.

FIGURE 13–3
Demand curves for two types of demand-based methods

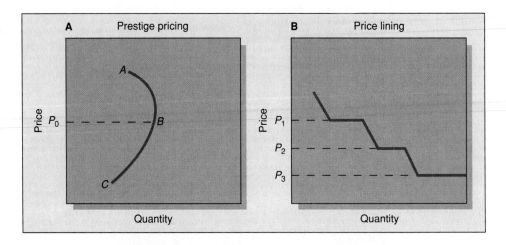

Price Lining   Often a firm that is selling not just a single product but a line of products may price them at a number of different specific pricing points, which is called **price lining.** For example, a department store manager may price a line of women's dresses at $59, $79, and $99. As shown in Figure 13–3, B, this assumes that demand is elastic at each of these price points but inelastic between these price points. In some instances all the items might be purchased for the same cost and then marked up at different percentages to achieve these price points based on color, style, and expected demand. In other instances manufac-

Marketing Research Report

THE MAGICAL NUMBER 9

*W*hen was the last time you saw an item priced at $.99, $19.99, or $199.99? Have you ever wondered whether this practice stimulates demand?

The common practice of listing a price ending in 9 or 99 has been the subject of recent research, which has produced interesting results. For example, in a study of food products it was found that there was a 10 percent increase in sales when items had a price ending in 9 rather than another number such as 0, 1, or 7. This research suggests that it would be more appropriate to price an item at, say, $.79 rather than $.78 because sales will be the same at both prices and a seller would lose one cent on every item purchased.

Why does this happen? Research on price perception suggests that consumers have a tendency to view items with prices ending in 9 as low-priced.

Furthermore, consumers typically exhibit a downward bias of 3.5 percent below the actual price when remembering prices ending in 9. The downward bias is even more pronounced when 9 price-endings are compared with even-endings such as zero. In this situation, consumers are likely to remember the odd-ending price to be 5.1 percent lower than the even-ending price!

Do these findings mean that odd-ending prices should always be used? Not necessarily. Sometimes consumers interpret these prices as meaning lower quality.

Sources: Based on Robert C. Blattberg and Scott A. Neslin, *Sales Promotion: Concepts, Methods, and Strategies* (Englewood Cliffs, N.J.: Prentice Hall, 1990), pp. 349–50; Robert M. Schindler and Alan R. Wiman, "Effects of Odd Pricing on Price Recall," *Journal of Business Research* (November 1989), pp. 165–78; and Kent B. Monroe, *Pricing: Making Profitable Decisions*, 2nd ed. (New York: McGraw-Hill, 1990).

Retailers use odd–even
pricing to attract
customers.

turers design products for different price points and retailers apply approximately the same markup percentages to achieve the three or four different price points offered to consumers. Sellers often feel that a limited number (such as three or four) price points is preferable to 8 or 10 different ones, which may only confuse prospective buyers.[6]

Odd-Even Pricing Sears offers a Craftsman radial saw for $499.99; J. C. Penney prices a five-piece living room set at $2,499; and K mart sells Windex glass cleaner on sale for 99 cents. Why not simply price these items at $500, $2,500, and $1, respectively? These retailers are using **odd-even pricing,** which involves setting prices a few dollars or cents under an even number. The presumption is that consumers see the Sears radial saw as priced at "something over $400" rather than "about $500." In theory demand increases if the price drops from $500 to $499.99. But does this occur in actual practice? Read the accompanying Marketing Research Report to find out if and why this happens.

Demand-Backward Pricing Manufacturers sometimes estimate the price that consumers would be willing to pay for a relatively expensive item such as a shopping good. They then work backward through the margins that may have to be paid to retailers and wholesalers to determine what price they can charge wholesalers for the product. This **demand-backward pricing** results in the manufacturer deliberately adjusting the quality of the component parts in the product to achieve the target price. In the 1980s a small manufacturer, Alternative Pioneering Systems, concluded that a home food dehydrator offered for less than $100 would have a sizable market. It then designed the product so that its price to wholesalers plus the wholesale and retail margins would result in a final consumer purchase price of $99.95—an example of the successful use of demand-backward pricing.

Bundle Pricing   A frequently used demand-oriented pricing practice is **bundle pricing**—the marketing of two or more products in a single "package" price. For example, American Airlines offers vacation packages that include airfare, car rental, and lodging. AT&T sells computer hardware, software, and maintenance contracts together. Bundle pricing is based on the idea that consumers value the package more than the individual items. This is due to benefits received from not having to make separate purchases and enhanced satisfaction from one item given the presence of another. Moreover, bundle pricing often provides a lower total cost to buyers and lower marketing costs to sellers.[7]

| CONCEPT CHECK | 1 What are the circumstances in pricing a new product that might support skimming or penetration pricing? |
| | 2 What is odd-even pricing? |

COST-BASED METHODS

In cost-based methods the price setter stresses the supply or cost side of the pricing problem, not the demand side. Price is set by looking at the production and marketing costs and then adding enough to cover direct expenses, overhead, and profit.

Standard Markup Pricing   Managers of supermarkets and other retail stores have such a large number of products that estimating the demand for each product as a means of setting price is impossible. Therefore they use **standard markup pricing,** which entails adding a fixed percentage to the cost of all items in a specific product class. This percentage markup varies depending on the type of retail store (such as furniture, clothing, or grocery) and on the product involved. High-volume products usually have smaller markups than do low-volume products. Supermarkets such as Kroger, Safeway, and Jewel have different markups for staple items and discretionary items. The markup on staple items like sugar, flour, and dairy products varies from 10 percent to 23 percent, whereas markups on discretionary items like snack foods and candy ranges from 27 percent to 47 percent. These markups must cover all expenses of the store, pay for overhead costs, and contribute something to profits. For supermarkets these markups, which may appear very large, result in only a 1 percent profit on sales revenue if the store is operating efficiently. By comparison, consider the markups on snacks and beverages purchased at your local movie theater. As shown in the Marketing Action Memo, markups for these products can be as large as 87 percent! An explanation of how to compute a markup, along with operating statement data and other ratios, is given in Appendix A to this chapter.

Marketing Action Memo

MUNCHIE MARKUPS AT THE MOVIES

Snacks and beverages purchased at movie theaters are big business. It is estimated that $850 million is spent annually for these goodies, which in turn account for 75 percent of a theater's profits. The average American spends $2.93 for snacks and beverages each time he or she visits a movie theater in addition to the average admission price of $5.00.

There is a decided preference for certain items and snack assortments: 42 percent of patrons buy popcorn and soft drinks; 17 percent buy soft drinks only; 12 percent buy popcorn only; 12 percent buy popcorn, soft drinks, and candy; 8 percent buy candy only; 7 percent buy soft drinks and candy; and 2 percent buy popcorn and candy.

But the real news is not what moviegoers buy or how much they spend. The real news and the best news of all is how delicious the markups are for various movie munchies. A soft drink that costs the theater 10 cents will typically sell for 75 cents, a markup of 87 percent. A candy bar that costs a theater 35 cents will sell for $1, a markup of 65 percent. A tub of popcorn that costs the theater 30

cents will be sold for $2, a markup of 85 percent. Enjoy the movies and munch on those markups!

Sources: "Coming Soon to a Theater Near You: Recession," *Business Week* (December 3, 1990), pp. 127–28; "Pulling Them In with Beer, Pizza, and Celluloid," *Adweek's Marketing Week* (March 5, 1990), p. 23; "Those Peculiar Candies That Star at the Movies," *Forbes* (May 19, 1986), pp. 174, 176; and "Our Reel-Life Snacks," *USA Weekend* (March 14–16, 1986), p. 26.

their sales for
chase without
for delivery of

Experience Cu
on the learnin
services declin
producing and
enough that th
example, if the
doubles, then
percent of the
100th unit. Th
cost $85, the 2
costs with expe
and U.S. firms
have decreased
from $1,000 to
priced as low a

PROFIT-BA

A price setter
profit-based m
volume of prof
ment.

Target Profit
volume of pro
framing store
typical framed

- Variable
- Fixed cos

Figure 13–4 shows the way standard markups combine to establish the selling price of the manufacturer to the wholesaler, the wholesaler to the retailer, and the retailer to the ultimate consumer. For example, the markups on a home appliance (for simplicity, sold to consumers for exactly $100) can increase as the product gets closer to the ultimate consumers; that is, the manufacturer has a 15 percent markup on its selling price, the wholesaler 20 percent, and the retailer 40 percent.

These larger markups later in the channel reflect the fact that as the product gets closer to the ultimate consumer, the seller has a smaller volume of the product and must provide a greater number of services or amount of individual attention to the buyer. The manufacturer gets $48 for selling the appliance to the wholesaler, who gets $60 from the retailer, who gets $100 from the ultimate consumer. As noted in the discussion of demand-backward pricing, if the manufacturer targets the price to the ultimate consumer at $100, it must verify that this includes adequate markups for the retailer, wholesaler, and itself.

Cost plus Percentage-of-Cost Pricing   Some manufacturing, architectural, and construction firms use a variation of standard markup pricing. In **cost plus percentage-of-cost pricing,** they add a fixed percentage to the production or

FIGURE 13–4
Markups of th
manufacturer
wholesaler, ar
on a home ap
sold to the cc
$100

- Demand is insensitive to price up to $60 per unit.
- A target profit of $7,000 is sought at an annual volume of 1,000 units (framed pictures).

The price can be calculated as follows:

$$\text{Profit} = \text{Total revenue} - \text{Total cost}$$

$$\text{Profit} = (P \times Q) - [FC + (UVC \times Q)]$$

$$\$7,000 = (P \times 1,000) - [\$26,000 + (\$22 \times 1,000)]$$

$$\$7,000 = 1,000P - (\$26,000 + \$22,000)$$

$$1,000P = \$7,000 + \$48,000$$

$$P = \$55$$

Note that a critical assumption is that this higher average price of a framed picture will not cause the demand to fall.

Target Return-on-Sales Pricing A difficulty with target profit pricing is that although it is simple and the target involves only a specific dollar volume, there is no benchmark of sales or investment used to show how much of the firm's effort is needed to achieve the target. Firms like supermarket chains often use **target return-on-sales pricing** to set typical prices that will give the firm a profit that is a specified percentage, say 1 percent, of the sales volume. Suppose the owner decides to use target return-on-sales pricing for the frame shop and makes the same first three assumptions shown previously. The owner now sets a target of 20 percent return on sales at an annual volume of 1,250 units. This gives:

$$\text{Target return on sales} = \frac{\text{Target profit}}{\text{Total revenue}}$$

$$20\% = \frac{TR - TC}{TR}$$

$$0.20 = \frac{P \times Q - [FC + (UVC \times Q)]}{TR}$$

$$0.20 = \frac{P \times 1,250 - [\$26,000 + (\$22 \times 1,250)]}{P \times 1,250}$$

$$P = \$53.50$$

So at a price of $53.50 per unit and an annual quantity of 1,250 frames:

$$TR = P \times Q = \$53.50 \times 1,250 = \$66,875$$

$$TC = FC + (UVC \times Q) = 26,000 + (22 \times 1,250) = \$53,500$$

$$\text{Profit} = TR - TC = \$66,875 - \$53,500 = \$13,375$$

As a check:

$$\text{Target return on sales} = \frac{\text{Target profit}}{\text{Total revenue}} = \frac{\$13,375}{\$66,875} = 20\%$$

Target Return-on-Investment Pricing Firms like GM set annual return-on-investment (ROI) targets such as ROI of 20 percent. **Target return-on-investment pricing** is a method of setting prices to achieve this target.

Suppose the store owner sets a target ROI of 10 percent, which is twice that achieved the previous year. She considers raising the average price of a framed picture to $54 or $58 — up from last year's average of $50. To do this, she might improve product quality by offering better frames and higher quality matting, which will increase the cost but also probably will offset the decreased revenue from the lower number of units that can be sold next year.

To handle this wide variety of assumptions, today's managers use computerized spreadsheets to project operating statements based on a diverse set of assumptions. Figure 13–5 shows a computerized spreadsheet that results from software programs such as Lotus 1-2-3. The assumptions are shown at the top and the projected results at the bottom. A previous year's operating statement results are shown in the column headed "Last year," and the assumptions and spreadsheet results for four different sets of assumptions are shown in columns A, B, C, and D.

In choosing a price or another action using spreadsheet results, the decision maker must (1) study the results of the computer simulation projections and (2) assess the realism of the assumptions underlying each set of projections. For example, the store owner sees from the bottom row of Figure 13–5 that all four spreadsheet simulations exceed the after-tax target ROI of 10 percent. But after more thought she judges it to be more realistic to set an average price of $58 per unit, allow the unit variable cost to increase by 20 percent to account for more expensive framing and matting, and settle for the same unit sales as the 1,000 units sold last year. She selects simulation D in this computerized spreadsheet approach to target ROI pricing and has a goal of 14 percent after-tax ROI. Of course, these same calculations can be done by hand, but this is far more time consuming.

FIGURE 13–5
Results of computer spreadsheet simulation to select price to achieve a target return on investment

ASSUMPTIONS OR RESULTS	FINANCIAL ELEMENT	LAST YEAR	SIMULATION			
			A	B	C	D
Assumptions	Price per unit (P)	$50	$54	$54	$58	$58
	Units sold (Q)	1,000	1,200	1,100	1,100	1,000
	Change in unit variable cost (UVC)	0%	+10%	+10%	+20%	+20%
	Unit variable cost	$22.00	$24.20	$24.20	$26.40	$26.40
	Total expenses	$8,000	Same	Same	Same	Same
	Owner's salary	$18,000	Same	Same	Same	Same
	Investment	$20,000	Same	Same	Same	Same
	State and federal taxes	50%	Same	Same	Same	Same
Spreadsheet simulation results	Net sales (P × Q)	$50,000	$64,800	$59,400	$63,800	$58,000
	Less: COGS (Q × UVC)	22,000	29,040	26,620	29,040	26,400
	Gross margin	$28,000	$35,760	$32,780	$34,760	$31,600
	Less: total expenses	8,000	8,000	8,000	8,000	8,000
	Less: owner's salary	18,000	18,000	18,000	18,000	18,000
	Net profit before taxes	$ 2,000	$ 9,760	$ 6,780	$ 8,760	$ 5,600
	Less: taxes	1,000	4,880	3,390	4,380	2,800
	Net profit after taxes	$ 1,000	$ 4,880	$ 3,390	$ 4,380	$ 2,800
	Investment	$20,000	$20,000	$20,000	$20,000	$20,000
	Return on investment	5.0%	24.4%	17.0%	21.9%	14.0%

COMPETITION-BASED METHODS

Rather than emphasize demand, cost, or profit factors, a price setter can stress what competitors or "the market" is doing.

Customary Pricing   For some products where tradition, a standardized channel of distribution, or other competitive factors dictate the price, **customary pricing** is used. For example, candy bars offered through standard vending machines have a customary price of 50 cents, and a significant departure from this price may result in a loss of sales for the manufacturer. Hershey typically has changed the amount of chocolate in its candy bars depending on the price of raw chocolate rather than vary its customary retail price, so it can continue selling through vending machines.

Above-, At-, or Below-Market Pricing   For most products it is difficult to identify a specific market price for a product or product class. Still, marketing managers often have a subjective feel for the competitors' price or market price. Using this benchmark, they then may deliberately choose a strategy of **above-, at-, or below-market pricing.**

Among watch manufacturers, Rolex takes pride in emphasizing that it makes one of the most expensive watches you can buy—a clear example of above-market pricing. Manufacturers of national brands of clothing such as Hart Schaffner & Marx and Christian Dior and retailers like Neiman-Marcus deliberately set premium prices for their products.

Large mass-merchandise chains such as Sears and Montgomery Ward generally use at-market pricing.[10] These chains often establish the going market price in the minds of their competitors. Similarly, Revlon and Cluett Peabody & Company (the maker of Arrow shirts) generally price their products "at market." They also provide a reference price for competitors that use above- and below-market pricing.

In contrast, a number of firms use a strategy of below-market pricing. Manufacturers of all generic products and retailers who offer their own private brands of products ranging from peanut butter to shampoo deliberately set prices for these products about 8 percent to 10 percent below the prices of nationally branded competitive products such as Skippy peanut butter, Vidal Sassoon shampoo, or Crest toothpaste. One Price Clothing Stores, Inc., a discount chain with more than 100 stores, is probably the ultimate in both low price and simplicity: all of its women's sportswear, blouses, and skirts are priced at $6! The clothes are not imperfects or seconds; instead, One Price buys surplus production from more than 600 manufacturers of clothes intended to have a retail price three to four times its $6 price.[11]

Loss-Leader Pricing   For a special promotion many retail stores deliberately sell a product below its customary price to attract attention to it. For example, Pechin's, a legendary supermarket 50 miles south of Pittsburgh, prices rib steaks at $2.29 a pound, which is below its cost. The purpose of this **loss-leader pricing** is not to increase sales of the rib steaks but to attract customers in hopes

Christian Dior uses an above-market pricing strategy.

they will buy other products as well, particularly the discretionary items carrying large markups. This tactic works for Pechin's, which has five times the sales of a typical supermarket.[12]

Sealed-Bid Pricing   When the U.S. Department of Commerce wants to buy a million number 2 wooden pencils or the U.S. Army wants to buy 100,000 mess kits, it would probably use **sealed-bid pricing.** This involves the buying agency widely publicizing specifications for the items to inform prospective manufacturers, who are invited to submit a bid that includes a specific price for the quantity ordered. The bid must be submitted by a specific time to a specific buying agency at a specific location. Several days later the bids are opened in public and read aloud, and the lowest qualified bidder is awarded the contract.

CONCEPT CHECK

1 What is standard markup pricing?

2 What profit-based pricing method should a manager use if he or she wants to reflect the percentage of the firm's resources used in obtaining the profit?

3 What is the purpose of loss-leader pricing when used by a retail firm?

STEP 5: SET THE LIST OR QUOTED PRICE

The first four steps in setting price covered in Chapter 12 and this chapter result in an approximate price level for the product that appears reasonable. But it still remains for the manager to set a specific list or quoted price in light of all relevant factors.

ONE-PRICE VERSUS FLEXIBLE-PRICE POLICY

A seller must decide whether to follow a one-price or flexible-price policy. A **one-price policy** is setting the same price for similar customers who buy the same product and quantities under the same conditions. In contrast, a **flexible-price policy** is offering the same product and quantities to similar customers, but at different prices. As noted at the end of this chapter, there are legal constraints under the Robinson-Patman Act to prevent carrying a flexible-price policy to the extreme of price discrimination.

Prices paid by an ultimate consumer illustrate the differences in these two policies, although the same principles apply to manufacturers and wholesalers as well. When you buy a Coca-Cola for 50 cents from a vending machine or a Wilson Sting tennis racket from a discount store, you are offered the product at a single price. You can buy it or not, but there is no variation in the price under the seller's one-price policy. But with a car or a house the seller generally uses a flexible-price policy, and you might negotiate a purchase at a price that lies within a range of prices. Flexible prices give sellers greater discretion in setting the final price in light of demand, cost, and competitive factors.

Deregulation of the airline, communications (telephone), trucking, and banking industries has promoted flexible pricing. As one example, Figure 13–6 shows four airline fares a person can be charged for a seat on a flight from Dallas–Fort Worth to each of three other cities.

PRICING TO COVER COST PLUS PROFIT

Unless you are the federal government or some other nonprofit organization, in the long run prices you set must cover all costs and contribute some profit or you'll go out of business. This may not be true in the short run or may not even apply to prices of specific products in a product line. Prices of rib steak, as loss leaders in a supermarket, don't cover costs but are used because customers buy other high-margin products to offset this loss. Gillette safety razors and Barbie dolls may be priced below cost to stimulate sales of Gillette blades and Barbie's clothes, on which highly profitable margins exist. Many firms no longer exist because in the long run their revenues couldn't cover their costs and provide adequate profit.

BALANCING INCREMENTAL COSTS AND REVENUES

When a price is changed or new advertising or selling programs are planned, their effect on the quantity sold must be considered. This assessment, called *marginal analysis* (Chapter 12), involves a continuing, concise trade-off of incremental costs against incremental revenues.

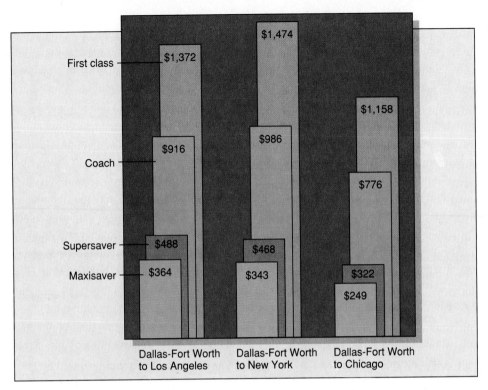

FIGURE 13–6
**Flexible pricing in the
airline industry—
round-trip ticket prices
offered according to
four different levels of
air travel
accommodations**

Do marketing and business managers really use marginal analysis? Yes, they do, but they often don't use phrases like *marginal revenue, marginal cost,* and *elasticity of demand.*

Think about these managerial questions:

- How many extra units do we have to sell to pay for that $1,000 advertisement?
- How much savings on unit variable cost do we have to get to keep the break-even point the same if we invest in a $10,000 labor-saving machine?
- Should we hire three more salespeople or not?

All these questions are a form of managerial or incremental analysis, even though these exact words are not used.

Figure 13–7 shows the power—and some limitations—of marginal analysis applied to a marketing decision. Note that the frame store owner must either conclude that a simple advertising campaign will more than pay for itself in additional sales or not undertake the campaign. The decision could also have been made to increase the average price of a framed picture to cover the cost of the campaign, but the principle still applies: expected incremental revenues from pricing and other marketing actions must more than offset incremental costs.

The example in Figure 13–7 shows both the main advantage and difficulty of marginal analysis. The advantage is its common-sense usefulness, and the difficulty is obtaining the necessary data to make decisions. The owner can measure the cost quite easily, but the incremental revenue generated by the ads is difficult to measure. She could partly solve this problem by offering $2 off the purchase price with use of a coupon printed in the ad to see which sales resulted from the ad.

FIGURE 13–7
The power of marginal analysis in real-world decisions

Suppose the owner of a picture framing store is considering buying a series of magazine ads to reach her up-scale target market. The cost of the ads is $1,000, the average price of a framed picture is $50, and the unit variable cost (materials plus labor) is $30.

This is a direct application of marginal analysis that an astute manager uses to estimate the incremental revenue or incremental number of units that must be obtained to at least cover the incremental cost. In this example the number of extra picture frames that must be sold is obtained as follows:

$$\text{Incremental number of frames} = \frac{\text{Extra fixed cost}}{\text{Price} - \text{Unit variable cost}}$$

$$= \frac{\$1,000 \text{ of advertising}}{\$50 - \$30}$$

$$= 50 \text{ frames}$$

So unless there are some other benefits of the ads, such as long-term goodwill, she should only buy the ads if she expects they will increase picture frame sales by at least 50 units.

COMPANY, CUSTOMER, AND COMPETITIVE EFFECTS

As the final list or quoted price is set, the effects on the company, customers, and competitors must be assessed.

Company Effects   For a firm with several products, a decision on the price of a single product must also consider the impact on the demand for other products in the line. IBM has an enviable record of assessing the impact of a price change in a mainframe computer on the substitutes (its other mainframe computers) and complements (its peripheral equipment) in its product line. In contrast, GM has often struggled in its attempts to position its cars by price points. For example, GM recently had to adjust the price of its Allante luxury car relative to the ZR-1 Corvette, and is still tinkering with the price of the new Saturn model relative to other cars in its product line, such as Geo.[13]

Customer Effects   In setting price, retailers weigh factors heavily that satisfy the perceptions or expectations of ultimate consumers, such as the customary prices for a variety of consumer products. Retailers have found that they should not price their store brands 20 to 25 percent below manufacturers' brands. When they do, consumers often view the lower price as signaling lower quality and don't buy.[14] Manufacturers and wholesalers must choose prices that result in profit for resellers in the channel to gain their cooperation and support. Toro failed to do this on its lines of lawn mowers and snow throwers. Toro decided to augment its traditional hardware outlet distribution by also selling through big discounters such as K mart and Target. To do so, it set prices for the discounters substantially below those for its traditional hardware outlets. Many unhappy hardware stores abandoned Toro products in favor of mowers and snow throwers from other manufacturers.

Competitive Effects   A manager's pricing decision is immediately apparent to most competitors, who may retaliate with price changes of their own. Therefore, a manager who sets a final list or quoted price must anticipate potential price responses from competitors. Regardless of whether a firm is a price leader or follower, it wants to avoid cutthroat price wars in which no firm in the industry makes a satisfactory profit. This is the case in the residential long-distance telephone industry, where AT&T, MCI, US Sprint, and ITT compete head-to-head for customers. Each time AT&T lowers its per-minute charge by a penny and competitors match the price, it gives up $1 billion in revenues.[15]

STEP 6: MAKE SPECIAL ADJUSTMENTS TO THE LIST OR QUOTED PRICE

When you pay 50 cents for a bag of M&Ms in a vending machine or receive a quoted price of $5,000 from a contractor to build a new kitchen, the pricing sequence ends with the last step just described: setting the list or quoted price. But when you are a manufacturer of M&M candies or gas grills and sell your product to dozens or hundreds of wholesalers and retailers in your channel of distribution, you may need to make a variety of special adjustments to the list or quoted price. Wholesalers also must adjust list or quoted prices they set for retailers. Three special adjustments to the list or quoted price are (1) discounts, (2) allowances, and (3) geographical adjustments (Figure 13–8).

DISCOUNTS

Discounts are reductions from list price that a seller gives a buyer as a reward for some activity of the buyer that is favorable to the seller. Four kinds of discounts are especially important in marketing strategy: (1) quantity, (2) seasonal, (3) trade (functional), and (4) cash discounts.

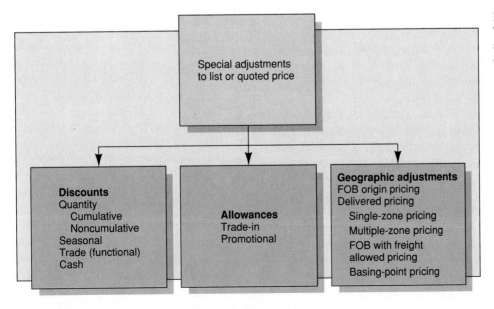

FIGURE 13–8
Three special adjustments to list or quoted price

Quantity Discounts   To encourage customers to buy larger quantities of a product, firms at all levels in the channel of distribution offer **quantity discounts,** which are reductions in unit costs for a larger order.[16] For example, an instant photocopying service might set a price of 10 cents a copy for copies 1 to 25, 9 cents a copy for 26 to 100, and 8 cents a copy for 101 or more. Because the photocopying service gets more of the buyer's business and has longer production runs that reduce its order-handling costs, it is willing to pass on some of the cost savings in the form of quantity discounts to the buyer.

Quantity discounts are of two general kinds: noncumulative and cumulative. *Noncumulative quantity discounts* are based on the size of an individual purchase order. They encourage large individual purchase orders, not a series of orders. This discount is used by Federal Express to encourage companies to ship a large number of packages at one time. *Cumulative quantity discounts* apply to the accumulation of purchases of a product over a given time period, typically a year. Cumulative quantity discounts encourage repeat buying by a single customer to a far greater degree than do noncumulative quantity discounts. A recent decision by Burger King to replace Pepsi-Cola with Coca-Cola in its outlets was based on the cumulative quantity discounts offered by Coca-Cola on its syrup.[17]

Seasonal Discounts   To encourage buyers to stock inventory earlier than their normal demand would require, manufacturers often use seasonal discounts. A firm like Toro that manufactures lawn mowers and snow throwers offers seasonal discounts to encourage wholesalers and retailers to stock up on lawn mowers in January and February and on snow throwers in July and August—five or six months before the seasonal demand by ultimate consumers. This enables Toro to smooth out seasonal manufacturing peaks and troughs, thereby contributing to more efficient production. It also rewards wholesalers and retailers for the risk they accept in assuming increased inventory carrying costs and having supplies in stock at the time they are wanted by customers.

Trade (Functional) Discounts   To reward wholesalers and retailers for marketing functions they will perform in the future, a manufacturer often gives trade, or functional, discounts. These reductions off the list or base price are offered to resellers in the channel of distribution on the basis of (1) where they are in the channel and (2) the marketing activities they are expected to perform in the future.

Suppose a manufacturer quotes price in the following form: list price—$100 less 30/10/5. The first number in the percentage sequence always refers to the retail end of the channel, and the last number always refers to the wholesaler or jobber closest to the manufacturer in the channel. The trade discounts are simply subtracted one at a time. This price quote shows $100 in the manufacturer's suggested retail price; 30 percent of the suggested retail price is available to the retailer to cover costs and provide a profit of $30 ($100 × 0.3 = $30); wholesalers closest to the retailer in the channel get 10 percent of their selling price ($70 × 0.1 = $7); and the final group of wholesalers in the channel (probably jobbers) that are closest to the manufacturer get 5 percent of their

USUALLY THE BEST COSTS A LITTLE MORE
BUT RIGHT NOW IT COSTS A LITTLE LESS

Regular Price	$1149.95
Pre-season Savings	$ 200.00
Sale Price	**$ 949.95**

2-YEAR LIMITED WARRANTY TORO LAST

Model 56125

**COMPACT, ECONOMICAL RIDER
FOR AVERAGE SIZE YARDS**

• Dependable 7 hp Tecumseh engine
• Key-Lectric® starting; five forward speeds
• 25" Whirlwind® deck
• Optional Easy Empty® Catcher

It may seem early to buy a riding mower, but to save $200 you're right on time. During our Toro pre-season rider sale we're taking $200 off the regular price. But you better hurry. Once it's time to mow the lawn, this sale will be over.

Ask us about our Toro-sponsored consumer-credit programs. We make it easy to step up to a Toro.

TORO   Haven't you done without a Toro long enough?®

Toro uses seasonal discounts to stimulate consumer demand.

selling price ($63 × 0.05 = $3.15). Thus starting with the manufacturer's retail price and subtracting the three trade discounts shows that the manufacturer's selling price to the wholesaler or jobber closest to it is $59.85 (Figure 13–9).

Traditional trade discounts have been established in various product lines such as hardware, food, and pharmaceutical items. Although the manufacturer may suggest the trade discounts shown in the example just cited, the sellers are free to alter the discount schedule depending on their competitive situation.

Cash Discounts   To encourage retailers to pay their bills quickly, manufacturers offer them cash discounts. Suppose a retailer receives a bill quoted as $1,000, 2/10 net 30. This means that the bill for the product is $1,000, but the retailer can

FIGURE 13–9
The structure of trade discounts

Terms	List price less 30/10/5	
	Manufacturer's suggested retail price	$100.00
Subtract	Retail discount, 30 percent of manufacturer's suggested retail price	30.00
Yields	Retail cost or wholesaler sales price	$ 70.00
Subtract	Wholesaler discount, 10 percent of wholesaler sales price	7.00
Yields	Wholesaler cost or jobber sales price	$ 63.00
Subtract	Jobber discount, 5 percent of jobber sales price	3.15
Yields	Jobber cost, or manufacturer's sales price	$ 59.85

Discounts for cash as opposed to credit have become popular.

take a 2 percent discount ($1,000 × 0.02 = $20) if payment is made within 10 days and send a check for $980. If the payment cannot be made within 10 days, the total amount of $1,000 is due within 30 days. It is usually understood by the buyer that an interest charge will be added after the first 30 days of free credit.

Naive buyers may think that the 2 percent discount offered is not substantial. What this means is that the buyer pays 2 percent on the total amount to be able to use that amount an extra 20 days—from day 11 to day 30. In a 360-day business year, this is an effective annual interest rate of 36 percent (2% × 360/20 = 36%). Because the effective interest rate is so high, firms that cannot take advantage of a 2/10 net 30 cash discount often try to borrow money from their local banks at rates far lower than the 36 percent they must pay by not taking advantage of the cash discount.

Retailers provide cash discounts to consumers as well to eliminate the cost of credit granted to consumers.[18] These discounts take the form of discount-for-cash policies. For example, Breuners, a furniture dealer in California, offers a 5 percent discount for cash, 4 Day Tire Stores advertise a 2 percent discount, and gasoline stations offer a "cents-off" discount for cash, as opposed to credit card, purchases.

ALLOWANCES

Allowances—like discounts—are reductions from list or quoted prices to buyers for performing some activity.

Trade-In Allowances   A new car dealer can offer a substantial reduction in the list price of that new Mazda Miata by offering you a trade-in allowance of $500 for your 1980 Chevrolet. A trade-in allowance is a price reduction given when a used product is part of the payment on a new product. Trade-ins are an effective way to lower the price a buyer has to pay without formally reducing the list price.

Promotional Allowances   Sellers in the channel of distribution can qualify for **promotional allowances** for undertaking certain advertising or selling activities to promote a product. Various types of allowances include an actual cash payment or an extra amount of "free goods" (as with a free case of pizzas to a retailer for every dozen cases purchased).[19] Frequently a portion of these savings is passed on to the consumer, as shown in the accompanying Marketing Action Memo.

GEOGRAPHICAL ADJUSTMENTS

Geographical adjustments are made by manufacturers or even wholesalers to list or quoted price to reflect the cost of transportation of the products from seller to buyer. The two general methods for quoting prices related to transportation costs are (1) FOB origin pricing and (2) uniform delivered pricing.

FOB Origin Pricing   FOB means "free on board" some vehicle at some location, which means the seller pays the cost of loading the product onto the vehicle that is used (such as a barge, railroad car, or truck). **FOB origin pricing** usually involves the seller's naming the location of this loading as the seller's factory or warehouse (such as "FOB Detroit" or "FOB factory"). The title to the goods passes to the buyer at the point of loading, so the buyer becomes responsible for picking the specific mode of transportation, for all the transportation costs, and for subsequent handling of the product. Buyers farthest from the seller face the big disadvantage of paying the higher transportation costs.

Uniform Delivered Pricing   When a **uniform delivered pricing** method is used, the price the seller quotes includes all transportation costs. It is quoted in a contract as "FOB buyer's location," and the seller selects the mode of transportation, pays the freight charges, and is responsible for any damage that may occur, since the seller retains title to the goods until delivered to the buyer. Although they go by various names, four kinds of delivered pricing methods are (1) single-zone pricing, (2) multiple-zone pricing, (3) FOB with freight-allowed pricing, and (4) basing-point pricing.

In *single-zone pricing* all buyers pay the same delivered price for the products, regardless of their distance from the seller. This method is also called *postage stamp pricing* because it is the way that U.S. postal rates are set for first-class mail. So although a store offering free delivery in a metropolitan area has lower transportation costs for goods shipped to customers nearer the store than for those shipped to distant ones, customers pay the same delivered price.

In *multiple-zone pricing* a firm divides its selling territory into geographic areas, or zones. The delivered price to all buyers within any one zone is the same, but prices across zones vary depending on the transportation cost to the

Marketing Action Memo

SECRETS BEHIND THE PRICE SPECIALS

Do you ever wonder what goes on behind the scene when your local supermarket features specials on its products? In a New York City supermarket, whose advertisement is shown here, the price specials reflect the allowances that the manufacturer gave the supermarket to push the product. The retailer usually pays $1.15 for a can of Bumble Bee white tuna ($55.43 ÷ 48 = $1.15), but the allowance reduced the cost per can to 96 cents. In this instance the retailer had a 3-cent retail markup on the product (99-cent retail price in ad—96-cent cost). Similar calculations apply to the other examples.

The use of discounts and allowances is very common. It is estimated that $8 billion a year is spent on price adjustments, and the figure is growing. A decade ago, 20 percent to 30 percent of sales carried allowances and discounts, which averaged 6 percent to 8 percent of manufacturers' list price. Today about 60 percent of manufacturers' sales carry price adjustments, which average about 12 percent of their list price. Allowances of various kinds amount to 44 percent of typical marketing budgets for manufacturers.

Bristol-Myers, which sells deodorants, analgesics, and cough and cold remedies, estimates that 63 percent to 68 percent of its sales to retailers carry allowances.

Sources: Based on "Want Shelf Space at the Supermarket? Ante Up," *Business Week* (August 7, 1989), pp. 60–61; Joanne Lipman, "Firms Bid to Cut Sales Coupons, Other Incentives," *The Wall Street Journal* (February 3, 1987), p. 37; and Monci Jo Williams, "The No-Win Game of Price Promotions," *Fortune* (July 11, 1983), pp. 92–102; © 1983 Time Inc. All rights reserved.

---

zone and the level of competition and demand within the zone. The U.S. postal system uses multiple-zone pricing for mailing packages. This system is also used in setting prices on long distance phone calls.

With *FOB with freight-allowed pricing,* also called *freight absorption pricing,* the price is quoted by the seller as "FOB plant—freight allowed." The buyer is allowed to deduct freight expenses from the list price of the goods, so the seller agrees to pay, or "absorbs," the transportation costs.

Basing-point pricing involves selecting one or more geographical locations (basing point) from which the list price for products plus freight expenses are charged to the buyer. For example, a company might designate St. Louis as the basing point and charge all buyers a list price of $100 plus freight from St. Louis to their location. Basing-point pricing methods have been used in the steel, cement, and lumber industries where freight expenses are a significant part of the total cost to the buyer and products are largely undifferentiated.

LEGAL AND REGULATORY ASPECTS OF PRICING

Arriving at a final price is clearly a complex process. The task is further complicated by legal and regulatory restrictions. Chapter 3 described the regulatory environment of companies. Here we elaborate on the specific laws and regulations affecting pricing decisions. Five pricing practices have received the most scrutiny: (1) price-fixing, (2) price discrimination, (3) deceptive pricing, (4) geographical pricing, and (5) predatory pricing.[20]

Price-Fixing   A conspiracy among firms to set prices for a product is termed **price-fixing.** Price-fixing is illegal per se under the Sherman Act (*per se* means in and of itself). When two or more competitors explicitly or implicitly set prices, this practice is called *horizontal price-fixing.* For example, a federal grand jury once indicted Saks Fifth Avenue and I. Magnin, two retailers, on charges of conspiring to fix prices on women's clothing.[21]

Vertical *price-fixing* involves controlling agreements between independent buyers and sellers (a manufacturer and a retailer) whereby sellers are required to not sell products below a minimum retail price. This practice, called *resale price maintenance,* was declared illegal per se in 1975 under provisions of the Consumer Goods Pricing Act.[22]

It is important to recognize that a manufacturer's "suggested retail price" is not illegal per se. The issue of legality only arises when manufacturers enforce such a practice by coercion. Furthermore, there appears to be a movement toward a "rule of reason" in pricing cases.[23] This rule holds that circumstances surrounding a practice must be considered before making a judgment about its legality. The rule of reason perspective is the direct opposite of the per se rule, which holds that a practice is illegal in and of itself.

Price Discrimination   The Clayton Act as amended by the Robinson-Patman Act prohibits **price discrimination**—the practice of charging different prices to different buyers for goods of like grade and quality.[24] However, not all price differences are illegal; only those which substantially lessen competition or create a monopoly are deemed unlawful. Moreover, "goods" is narrowly defined and does not include discrimination in services.

A unique feature of the Robinson-Patman Act is that it allows for price differentials to different customers under the following conditions:

1 When price differences charged to different customers do not exceed the differences in the cost of manufacture, sale, or delivery resulting from differing methods or quantities in which such goods are sold or delivered to buyers. This condition is called the *cost justification defense.*

2 Price differences resulting from meeting changing market conditions, avoiding obsolescence of seasonal merchandise including perishables or closing out sales.

3 When price differences are quoted to selected buyers in good faith to meet competitors' prices and are not intended to injure competition. This condition is called the *meet the competition defense.*

The Robinson–Patman Act also covers promotional allowances. To legally offer promotional allowances to buyers, the seller must do so on a proportionally equal basis to all buyers distributing the seller's products. In general, the rule of reason applies frequently in price discrimination cases and is often applied to cases involving flexible pricing practices of firms.

Deceptive Pricing   Price deals that mislead consumers fall into the category of deceptive pricing. Deceptive pricing is outlawed by the Federal Trade Commission Act. The FTC monitors such practices and has published a regulation titled "Guides Against Deceptive Pricing" designed to help businesspeople avoid a charge of deception. The five most common deceptive pricing practices are described in Figure 13–10. As you read about these practices it should be clear that laws cannot be passed and enforced to protect consumers and competitors against all of these practices, so it is essential to rely on the ethical standards of those making and publicizing pricing decisions.

Geographical Pricing   FOB origin pricing is legal, as are FOB freight-allowed pricing practices, providing no conspiracy to set prices exists. Basing-point pricing can be viewed as illegal under the Robinson–Patman Act and the Federal Trade Commission Act if there is clear-cut evidence of a conspiracy to set prices. In general, geographical pricing practices have been immune from legal and regulatory restrictions, except in those instances in which a conspiracy to lessen

FIGURE 13–10
Five most common deceptive pricing practices

- *Bait and switch:* A deceptive practice exists when a firm offers a very low price on a product (the bait) to attract customers to a store. Once in the store, the customer is persuaded to purchase a higher-priced item (the switch) using a variety of tricks, including (1) downgrading the promoted item and (2) not having the item in stock or refusing to take orders for the item.
- *Bargains conditional on other purchases:* This practice may exist when a buyer is offered "1-Cent Sales," "Buy 1, Get 1 Free," and "Get 2 for the Price of 1." Such pricing is legal only if the first items are sold at the regular price, not a price inflated for the offer. Substituting lower-quality items on either the first or second purchase is also considered deceptive.
- *Comparable value comparisons:* Advertising such as "Retail Value $100.00, Our Price $85.00," is deceptive if a verified and substantial number of stores in the market area did not price the item at $100.
- *Comparisons with suggested prices:* A claim that a price is below a manufacturer's suggested or list price may be deceptive if few or no sales occur at that price in a retailer's market area.
- *Former price comparisons:* When a seller represents a price as reduced, the item must have been offered in good faith at a higher price for a substantial previous period. Setting a high price for the purpose of establishing a reference for a price reduction is deceptive.

competition exists under the Sherman Act or price discrimination exists under the Robinson-Patman Act.

Predatory Pricing **Predatory pricing** is the practice of charging a very low price for a product with the intent of driving competitors out of business. Once competitors have been driven out, the firm raises its prices. This practice is illegal under the Sherman Act and the Federal Trade Commission Act. Proving the presence of this practice has been difficult and expensive, because it must be shown that the predator explicitly attempted to destroy a competitor and the predatory price was below the defendant's average cost. However, in 1990, Brown & Williamson, the third-largest U.S. cigarette marketer, was charged with engaging in predatory pricing and was ordered to pay Liggett & Myers, the maker of Chesterfield cigarettes, $148.8 million in damages.[25]

CONCEPT CHECK

1 Why would a seller choose a flexible-price policy over a one-price policy?

2 If a firm wished to encourage repeat purchases by a buyer throughout a year, would a cumulative or noncumulative quantity discount be a better strategy?

3 Which pricing practices are covered by the Sherman Act?

ETHICS AND SOCIAL RESPONSIBILITY IN THE 1990s

THE PRICE OF LIFE

What price should be charged for a product that will treat acquired immune deficiency syndrome (AIDS)? Executives at Burroughs Wellcome Company had to make this determination when the company received approval from the Food and Drug Administration to market Retrovir,® a drug found to be effective in the treatment of AIDS.

The initial cost for a one-year patient supply of Retrovir® was $8,000. According to a company official, the high price was due to the "uncertain market for the drug, the possible advent of new therapies, and profit margins customarily generated by new medicines." (The estimated research and development cost of the drug was between $80 and $100 million.) A critic countered, saying, "Burroughs Wellcome has an obligation to give up a significant amount of money to allow people to get access."

What ethical and social responsibility does Burroughs Wellcome have in connection with the pricing of Retrovir®?

Sources: Based on Brian O'Reilly, "The Inside Story of the AIDS Drug," *Fortune* (November 5, 1990), pp. 112–29; "Profiting from Disease," *The Economist* (January 27, 1990), pp. 17–18; and "AZT Maker Expected to Reap Big Gain," *The New York Times* (August 19, 1989), p. 8.

SUMMARY

1 Four general methods of finding an approximate price level for a product or service are demand-based, cost-based, profit-based, and competition-based pricing methods.

2 Demand-based pricing methods stress consumer demand and revenue implications of pricing and include seven types: skimming, penetration, prestige, price lining, odd-even, demand-backward pricing, and bundle pricing.

3 Cost-based pricing methods emphasize the cost aspects of pricing and include four types: standard markup, cost plus percentage-of-cost, cost plus fixed-fee, and experience curve pricing.

4 Profit-based pricing methods focus on a balance between revenues and costs to set a price and include three types: target profit, target return-on-sales, and target return-on-investment pricing.

5 Competition-based pricing methods stress what competitors or the marketplace are doing and include four types: customary; above-, at-, or below-market; loss-leader; and sealed-bid pricing.

6 Given an approximate price level for a product, a manager must set a list or quoted price by considering factors such as one-price versus a flexible-price policy; pricing to cover cost plus profit in the long run; balancing incremental costs and revenues; and the effects of the proposed price on the company, customer, and competitors.

7 List or quoted price is often modified through discounts, allowances, and geographical adjustments.

8 Legal and regulatory issues in pricing focus on price-fixing, price discrimination, deceptive pricing, geographical pricing, and predatory pricing.

KEY TERMS AND CONCEPTS

skimming pricing p. 339
penetration pricing p. 340
prestige pricing p. 341
price lining p. 342
odd-even pricing p. 343
demand-backward pricing p. 343
bundle pricing p. 344
standard markup pricing p. 344
cost plus percentage-of-cost
  pricing p. 345
cost plus fixed-fee pricing p. 346
experience curve pricing p. 347
target profit pricing p. 347
target return-on-sales pricing p. 348
target return-on-investment
  pricing p. 348

customary pricing p. 350
above-, at-, or below-market
  pricing p. 350
loss-leader pricing p. 350
sealed-bid pricing p. 351
one-price policy p. 352
flexible-price policy p. 352
quantity discounts p. 356
promotional allowances p. 359
FOB origin pricing p. 359
uniform delivered pricing p. 359
basing-point pricing p. 360
price-fixing p. 361
price discrimination p. 361
predatory pricing p. 363

CHAPTER PROBLEMS AND APPLICATIONS

1 Under what conditions would a camera manufacturer adopt a skimming price approach for a new product? A penetration approach?

2 What are some similarities and differences between skimming pricing, prestige pricing, and above-market pricing?

3 A producer of microwave ovens has adopted an experience curve pricing approach for its new model. The firm believes it can reduce the cost of producing the model by 20 percent each time volume doubles. The cost to produce the first unit was $1,000. What would be the approximate cost of the 4,096th unit?

4 The Hesper Corporation is a leading manufacturer of high-quality upholstered sofas. Current plans call for an increase of $600,000 in the advertising budget. If the firm sells its sofas for an average price of $850 and the unit variable costs are $550, then what dollar sales increase will be necessary to cover the additional advertising?

5 Suppose executives estimate that the unit variable cost for their VCR is $100, the fixed cost related to the product is $10 million annually, and the target volume for next year is 100,000 recorders. What sales price will be necessary to achieve a target profit of $1 million?

6 A manufacturer of motor oil has a trade discount policy whereby the manufacturer's suggested retail price is $30 per case with the terms of 40/20/10. The manufacturer sells its products through jobbers, who sell to wholesalers, who sell to gasoline stations. What will the manufacturer's sale price be?

7 What are the effective annual interest rates for the following cash discount terms? (*a*) 1/10 net 30, (*b*) 2/10 net 30, and (*c*) 2/10 net 60.

8 Suppose a manufacturer of exercise equipment sets a suggested price to the consumer of $395 for a particular piece of equipment to be competitive with similar equipment. The manufacturer sells its equipment to a sporting goods wholesaler who receives a 25 percent markup and a retailer who receives a 50 percent markup. What demand-based pricing method is being used, and at what price will the manufacturer sell the equipment to the wholesaler?

9 A furniture manufacturer located in North Carolina operates at a freight cost disadvantage relative to competitors in the Midwest and West. What methods of quoting prices could this firm adopt to make it more competitive in these states?

10 Is there any truth in the statement, "Geographical pricing schemes will always be unfair to some buyers"? Why or why not?

Financial Aspects of Marketing

Basic concepts from accounting and finance provide valuable tools for marketing executives. This appendix describes an actual company's use of accounting and financial concepts and illustrates how they assist the owner in making marketing decisions.

The Caplow Company

An accomplished artist and calligrapher, Jane Westerlund, decided to apply some of her experience to the picture framing business in Minneapolis. She bought an existing retail frame store, The Caplow Company, from a friend who owned the business and wanted to retire. She avoided the do-it-yourself end of the framing business and chose two kinds of business activities: (1) cutting the frame, mats, and glass for customers who brought in their own pictures or prints to be framed and (2) selling prints and posters that she had purchased from wholesalers.

To understand how accounting, finance, and marketing relate to each other, let's analyze (1) the operating statement for her frame shop, (2) some general ratios of interest that are derived from the operating statement, and (3) some ratios that pertain specifically to her pricing decisions.

THE OPERATING STATEMENT

The operating statement (also called an *income statement* or *profit-and-loss statement*) summarizes the profitability of a business firm for a specific time period, usually a month, quarter, or year. The title of the operating statement for The Caplow Company shows it is for a one-year period (Figure A–1). The purpose of an operating statement is to show the profit of the firm and the revenues and expenses that led to that profit. This information tells the owner or manager what has happened in the past and suggests actions to improve future profitability.

The left side of Figure A–1 shows that there are three key elements to all operating statements: (1) sales of the firm's goods and services, (2) costs incurred in making and selling the goods and services, and (3) profit or loss, which is the difference between sales and costs.

THE CAPLOW COMPANY
Operating Statement
For the Year Ending December 31, 1993

Sales	Gross sales			$80,500
	Less: Returns and allowances			500
	Net sales			80,000
Costs	Cost of goods sold:			
	Beginning inventory at cost		$ 6,000	
	Purchases at billed cost	$21,000		
	Less: Purchase discounts	300		
	Purchases at net cost	20,700		
	Plus freight-in	100		
	Net cost of delivered purchases		20,800	
	Direct labor (framing)		14,200	
	Cost of goods available for sale		41,000	
	Less: Ending inventory at cost		5,000	
	Cost of goods sold			36,000
	Gross margin (gross profit)			44,000
	Expenses:			
	Selling expenses:			
	Sales salaries	2,000		
	Advertising expense	3,000		
	Total selling expense		5,000	
	Administrative expenses:			
	Owner's salary	18,000		
	Bookkeeper's salary	1,200		
	Office supplies	300		
	Total administrative expense		19,500	
	General expenses:			
	Depreciation expense	1,000		
	Interest expense	500		
	Rent expense	2,100		
	Utility expenses (heat, electricity)	3,000		
	Repairs and maintenance	2,300		
	Insurance	2,000		
	Social security taxes	2,200		
	Total general expense		13,100	
	Total expenses			37,600
Profit or loss	Profit before taxes			6,400

Sales Elements The sales element of Figure A–1 has four terms that need explanation:

- *Gross sales* are the total amount billed to customers. Dissatisfied customers or errors may reduce the gross sales through returns or allowances.
- *Returns* occur when a customer gives the item purchased back to the seller, who either refunds the purchase price or allows the customer a credit on subsequent purchases. In any event the seller now owns the item again.

- *Allowances* are given when a customer is dissatisfied with the item purchased and the seller reduces the original purchase price. Unlike returns, in the case of allowances the buyer owns the item.
- *Net sales* are simply gross sales minus returns and allowances.

The operating statement for The Caplow Company shows that:

Gross sales	$80,500
Less: Returns and allowances	500
Net sales	$80,000

The low level of returns and allowances shows the shop generally has done a good job in satisfying customers, which is essential in building the repeat business necessary for success.

Cost Elements   The *cost of goods sold* is the total cost of the products sold during the period. This item varies according to the kind of business. A retail store purchases finished goods and resells them to customers without reworking them in any way. In contrast, a manufacturing firm combines raw and semifinished materials and parts, uses labor and overhead to rework these into finished goods, and then sells them to customers. All these activities are reflected in the cost of goods sold item on a manufacturer's operating statement. Note that the frame shop has some features of a pure retailer (prints and posters it buys that are resold without alteration) and a pure manufacturer (assembling the raw materials of molding, matting, and glass to form a completed frame).

Some terms that relate to cost of goods sold need clarification:

- *Inventory* is the physical material that is purchased from suppliers, may or may not be reworked, and is available for sale to customers. In the frame shop inventory includes molding, matting, glass, prints, and posters.
- *Purchase discounts* are reductions in the original billed price for reasons like prompt payment of the bill or the quantity bought.
- *Direct labor* is the cost of the labor used in producing the finished product. For the frame shop this is the cost of producing the completed frames from the molding, matting, and glass.
- *Gross margin (gross profit)* is the money remaining to manage the business, sell the products or services, and give some profit. Gross margin is net sales minus cost of goods sold.

The two right-hand columns in Figure A–1 between "Net sales" and "Gross margin" calculate the cost of goods sold:

Net sales		$80,000
Cost of goods sold		
Beginning inventory at cost	$ 6,000	
Net cost of delivered purchases	20,800	
Direct labor (framing)	14,200	
Cost of goods available for sale	41,000	
Less: ending inventory at cost	5,000	
Cost of goods sold		36,000
Gross margin (gross profit)		$44,000

This section considers the beginning and ending inventories, the net cost of purchases delivered during the year, and the cost of the direct labor going into making the frames. Subtracting the $36,000 cost of goods sold from the $80,000 net sales gives the $44,000 gross margin.

Three major categories of expenses are shown in Figure A–1 below the gross margin:

- *Selling expenses* are the costs of selling the product or service produced by the firm. For The Caplow Company there are two such selling expenses: sales salaries of part-time employees waiting on customers and the advertising expense of simple newspaper ads and direct-mail ads sent to customers.
- *Administrative expenses* are the costs of managing the business and for The Caplow Company include three expenses: the owner's salary, a part-time bookkeeper's salary, and office supplies expense.
- *General expenses* are miscellaneous costs not covered elsewhere; for the frame shop these include seven items: depreciation expense (on her equipment), interest expense, rent expense, utility expenses, repairs and maintenance expense, insurance expense, and social security taxes.

As shown in Figure A–1, selling, administrative, and general expenses total $37,600 for The Caplow Company.

Profit Element   What the company has earned, the *profit before taxes,* is found by subtracting cost of goods sold and expenses from net sales. For The Caplow Company, Figure A–1 shows that profit before taxes is $6,400.

GENERAL OPERATING RATIOS TO ANALYZE OPERATIONS

Looking only at the elements of Caplow's operating statement that extend to the right-hand column highlights the firm's performance on some important dimensions. Using operating ratios such as *expense-to-sales ratios* for expressing basic expense or profit elements as a percentage of net sales gives further insights:

ELEMENT IN OPERATING STATEMENT	DOLLAR VALUE	PERCENTAGE OF NET SALES
Gross sales	$80,500	
Less: Returns and allowances	500	
Net sales	80,000	100%
Less: Cost of goods sold	36,000	45
Gross margin	44,000	55
Less: Total expenses	37,600	47
Profit (or loss) before taxes	6,400	8%

Westerlund can use this information to compare her firm's performance from one time period to the next. To do so, it is especially important that she keep the same definitions for each element of her operating statement, also a significant factor in using the electronic spreadsheets discussed in Chapter 13. Performance comparisons between periods are more difficult if she changes definitions for the accounting elements in the operating statement.

She can use either the dollar values or the operating ratios (the value of the element of the operating statement divided by net sales) to analyze the firm's performance. However, the operating ratios are more valuable than the dollar values for two reasons: (1) the simplicity of working with percentages rather than dollars and (2) the availability of operating ratios of typical firms in the same industry, which are published by Dun & Bradstreet and trade associations. Thus Westerlund can compare her firm's performance not only with that of *other* frame shops but also with that of *small* frame shops that have annual net sales, for example, of under $100,000. In this way she can identify where her operations are better or worse than other similar firms. For example, if trade association data showed a typical frame shop of her size had a ratio of cost of goods sold to net sales of 37 percent, compared with her 45 percent, she might consider steps to reduce this cost through purchase discounts, reducing inbound freight charges, finding lower cost suppliers, and so on.

RATIOS TO USE IN SETTING AND EVALUATING PRICE

Using The Caplow Company as an example, we can study four ratios that relate closely to setting a price: (1) markup, (2) markdown, (3) stockturns, and (4) return on investment. These terms are defined in Figure A–2 and explained below.

Markup   Both markup and gross margin refer to the amount added to the cost of goods sold to arrive at the selling price, and they may be expressed either in dollar or percentage terms. However, the term *markup* is more commonly used in setting retail prices. Suppose the average price Westerlund charges for a

FIGURE A–2
How to calculate selling price, markup, markdown, stockturn, and return on investment

NAME OF FINANCIAL ELEMENT OR RATIO	WHAT IT MEASURES	EQUATION
Selling price ($)	Price customer sees	Cost of goods sold (COGS) + Markup
Markup ($)	Dollars added to COGS to arrive at selling price	Selling price − COGS
Markup on selling price (%)	Relates markup to selling price	$\dfrac{\text{Markup}}{\text{Selling price}} \times 100 = \dfrac{\text{Selling price} - \text{COGS}}{\text{Selling price}} \times 100$
Markup on cost (%)	Relates markup to cost	$\dfrac{\text{Markup}}{\text{COGS}} \times 100 = \dfrac{\text{Selling price} - \text{COGS}}{\text{COGS}}$
Markdown (%)	Ability of firm to sell its products at initial selling price	$\dfrac{\text{Markdowns} + \text{Allowances}}{\text{Net sales}} \times 100$
Stockturn rate	Ability of firm to move its inventory quickly	$\dfrac{\text{COGS}}{\text{Average inventory at cost}}$ or $\dfrac{\text{Net sales}}{\text{Average inventory at selling price}}$
Return on investment (%)	Profit performance of firm compared with money invested in it	$\dfrac{\text{Net profit after taxes}}{\text{Investment}} \times 100$

framed picture is \$80. Then in terms of the first two definitions in Figure A–2 and the earlier information from the operating statement:

ELEMENT OF PRICE	DOLLAR VALUE
Cost of goods sold	\$36
Markup (or gross margin)	44
Selling price	\$80

The third definition in Figure A–2 gives the percentage markup on selling price:

$$\text{Markup on selling price (\%)} = \frac{\text{Markup}}{\text{Selling price}} \times 100$$

$$= \frac{44}{80} \times 100$$

$$= 55\%$$

And the percentage markup on cost is obtained as follows:

$$\text{Markup on cost (\%)} = \frac{\text{Markup}}{\text{Cost of goods sold}} \times 100$$

$$= \frac{44}{36} \times 100$$

$$= 122.2\%$$

Inexperienced retail clerks sometimes fail to distinguish between the two definitions of markup, which (as the above calculations show) can represent a tremendous difference, so it is essential to know whether the base is cost or selling price. Marketers generally use selling price as the base for talking about "markups" unless they specifically state they are using cost as a base.

Retailers and wholesalers that rely heavily on markup pricing (discussed in Chapter 13) often use standardized tables that convert markup on selling price to markup on cost, and vice versa. The two equations below show how to convert one to the other:

$$\text{Markup on selling price (\%)} = \frac{\text{Markup on cost (\%)}}{100\% + \text{Markup on cost (\%)}} \times 100$$

$$\text{Markup on cost (\%)} = \frac{\text{Markup on selling price (\%)}}{100\% - \text{Markup on selling price (\%)}} \times 100$$

Using the data from The Caplow Company gives:

$$\text{Markup on selling price (\%)} = \frac{\text{Markup on cost (\%)}}{100\% + \text{Markup on cost (\%)}} \times 100$$

$$= \frac{122.2}{100 + 122.2} \times 100$$

$$= 55\%$$

$$\text{Markup on cost (\%)} = \frac{\text{Markup on selling price (\%)}}{100\% - \text{Markup on selling price (\%)}} \times 100$$

$$= \frac{55}{100 - 55} \times 100$$

$$= 122.2\%$$

The use of an incorrect markup base is shown in Westerlund's business. A markup of 122.2 percent on her cost of goods sold for a typical frame she sells gives 122.2% × $36 = $44 of markup. Added to the $36 cost of goods sold, this gives her selling price of $80 for the framed picture. However, a new clerk working for her who erroneously priced the framed picture at 55 percent of cost of goods sold set the final price at $55.80 ($36 of cost of goods sold plus 55% × $36 = $19.80). The error, if repeated, can be disastrous: frames would be accidentally sold at $55.80, or $24.20 below the intended selling price of $80.

Markdown   A markdown is a reduction in a retail price that is necessary if the item will not sell at the full selling price to which it has been marked up. The item might not sell for a variety of reasons: the selling price was set too high or the item is out of style or has become soiled or damaged. The seller "takes a markdown" by lowering the price to sell it, thereby converting it to cash to buy future inventory that will sell faster.

The markdown ratio cannot be calculated directly from the operating statement. As shown in the fifth item of Figure A–2, the numerator of the markdown ratio is the total dollar amounts of both markdowns and allowances. Both markdowns and allowances are reductions in the prices of goods that are purchased by customers. Returns are often available for resale and are not included in calculating the markdown ratio.

Suppose The Caplow Company had $300 in customer allowances and $700 in markdowns on the prints and posters that are stocked and available for sale. Since the frames are custom made for individual customers, there is little reason for a markdown there. Caplow's markdown ratio is then:

$$\text{Markdown} = \frac{\text{Markdowns + Allowances}}{\text{Net sales}} \times 100$$

$$= \frac{\$700 + \$300}{\$80,000} \times 100$$

$$= 1.25\%$$

Other kinds of retailers often have markdown ratios several times this amount. For example, women's dress stores have markdowns of about 25 percent, and menswear stores have markdowns of about 1 percent.

Stockturn Rate   A business firm is anxious to have its inventory move quickly, or "turn over." Stockturn rate, or simply stockturns, measures this inventory movement. For a retailer a slow stockturn rate may show it is buying merchandise customers don't want, so this is a critical measure of performance. When a firm sells only a single product, one convenient way to measure stockturn rate is simply to divide its cost of goods sold by average inventory at cost. The sixth item in Figure A–2 shows how to calculate stockturn rate using information in the operating statement:

$$\text{Stockturn rate} = \frac{\text{Cost of goods sold}}{\text{Average inventory at cost}}$$

The dollar amount of average inventory at cost is calculated by adding the beginning and ending inventories for the year and dividing by 2 to get the average. From Caplow's operating statement, we have:

$$\text{Stockturn rate} = \frac{\text{Cost of goods sold}}{\text{Average inventory at cost}}$$

$$= \frac{\text{Cost of goods sold}}{\dfrac{\text{Beginning inventory} + \text{Ending inventory}}{2}}$$

$$= \frac{\$36,000}{\dfrac{\$6,000 + \$5,000}{2}}$$

$$= \frac{\$36,000}{\$5,500}$$

$$= 6.5 \text{ stockturns per year}$$

What is considered a "good stockturn" varies by the kind of industry. For example, supermarkets have limited shelf space for thousands of new products from manufacturers each year, so they watch stockturn carefully by product line. The stockturn rate in supermarkets for breakfast foods is about 17 times per year, for pet food is about 22 times, and for paper products is about 25 times per year.

Return on Investment   A better measure of the performance of a firm than the amount of profit it makes in a year is its ROI, which is the ratio of net income to the investment used to earn that net income. To calculate ROI, it is necessary to subtract income taxes from profit before taxes to obtain net income, then divide this figure by the investment that can be found on a firm's balance sheet (another accounting statement that shows the firm's assets, liabilities, and net worth). While financial and accounting experts have many definitions for "investment," an often-used definition is "total assets."

For our purposes, let's assume that Westerlund has total assets (investment) of $20,000 in The Caplow Company, which covers inventory, store fixtures, and framing equipment. If she pays $1,000 in income taxes, her store's net income is $5,400, so her ROI is given by the seventh item in Figure A–2:

$$\text{Return on investment} = \text{Net income/investment} \times 100$$

$$= \$5,400/\$20,000 \times 100$$

$$= 27\%$$

If Westerlund wants to improve her ROI next year, the strategies she might take are found in this alternative equation for ROI:

$$\text{ROI} = \text{Net sales/investment} \times \text{Net income/net sales}$$

$$= \text{Investment turnover} \times \text{Profit margin}$$

This equation suggests that The Caplow Company's ROI can be improved by raising turnover or increasing profit margin. Increasing stockturns will accomplish the former, whereas lowering cost of goods sold to net sales will cause the latter.

CHAPTER 14

Marketing Channels and Wholesaling

---

*A*fter reading this chapter you should be able to:

- Explain what is meant by a marketing channel of distribution and why intermediaries are needed.

- Recognize differences between marketing channels for consumer and industrial products and services.

- Describe the types and functions of firms that perform wholesaling activities.

- Distinguish among traditional marketing channels and different types of vertical marketing systems.

- Describe factors considered by marketing executives when selecting and managing a marketing channel.

Why You Can't Find a Saturn in a Chevrolet Showroom

Why are General Motors, Honda, Toyota, and Nissan spending millions of dollars developing entirely new distribution and dealer networks when each already has hundreds of dealers? The answer: Honda, Toyota, and Nissan can't entice young, upscale, American buyers of European cars such as Mercedes Benz, Porsche, BMW, and Audi into the showrooms of their existing dealers. But General Motors is another matter—car industry research reveals that 42 percent of all new-car shoppers don't even consider a General Motors car, let alone a GM dealer!

Licensing new dealers and not selling through existing ones is occurring because target market buyers do not shop at each of these manufacturers' showrooms. Honda led the way for this practice in 1986, when it used separate dealerships for the

Acura Legend. Commented a Honda executive, "People looking for those [expensive European] cars don't come to a Honda dealer for that sort of merchandise, and I don't expect they ever will." In 1989, Nissan started using a new dealer distribution network for Infiniti, and Toyota did the same for its new luxury car, the Lexus. General Motors' subsidiary Saturn Corporation followed in 1990, with the goal of selling 80 percent of its cars to drivers who otherwise would have not bought a GM product.

The new dealer distribution efforts reflect automaker strategies to reach different target markets and better satisfy buyer wants. For example, R. G. (Skip) LeFauve, Saturn's president, said that each Saturn dealer will tailor its sales and service facilities to handle the ways buyers select and purchase their cars and have their cars serviced.[1]

Distribution is critical not only for cars but also for the marketing success of such diverse products as magazines, PCs, snack foods, beverages, record albums, health care services, and cosmetics. Similarly, distribution is so important in marketing private and business airplanes that Cessna Aircraft considers its dealers to be the firm's greatest asset.

This chapter focuses on marketing channels of distribution and why they are an important component in the marketing mix. It then shows how such channels benefit consumers and the sequence of firms that make up a marketing channel. Finally, it describes factors that influence the choice and management of marketing channels, including channel conflict and legal restrictions.

NATURE AND IMPORTANCE OF MARKETING CHANNELS

Reaching prospective buyers, either directly or indirectly, is a prerequisite for successful marketing. At the same time buyers benefit from distribution systems used by firms.

DEFINING MARKETING CHANNELS OF DISTRIBUTION

You see the results of distribution every day. You may have purchased Lay's Potato Chips at the 7-Eleven store, your lunch at McDonald's, and Levi jeans at Sears. Each of these items was brought to you by a marketing channel of distribution, or simply a **marketing channel,** which consists of individuals and firms involved in the process of making a product or service available for use or consumption by consumers or industrial users.

Marketing channels can be compared to a pipeline through which water flows from a source to terminus. Marketing channels make possible the flow of goods from a producer, through intermediaries, to a buyer. Intermediaries go by various names (Figure 14–1) and perform various functions. Some intermediaries actually purchase items from the seller, store them, and resell them to buyers. For example, Sunshine Biscuits produces cookies and sells them to food wholesalers. The wholesalers then sell the cookies to supermarkets and grocery stores, which in turn sell them to consumers. Other intermediaries such as brokers and agents represent sellers but do not actually take title to products—

FIGURE 14–1
Terms used for marketing intermediaries

TERM	MEANING
Middleman	Any intermediary between manufacturer and end-user markets
Agent or broker	Any intermediary with legal authority to act on behalf of the manufacturer
Wholesaler	An intermediary who sells to other intermediaries, usually to retailers; usually applies to consumer markets
Retailer	An intermediary who sells to consumers
Distributor	An imprecise term, usually used to describe intermediaries who perform a variety of distribution functions, including selling, maintaining inventories, extending credit, and so on; a more common term in industrial markets but may also be used to refer to wholesalers
Dealer	An even more imprecise term that can mean the same as distributor, retailer, wholesaler, and so forth

Source: Adapted from Frederick E. Webster, Jr., *Marketing for Managers* (New York: Harper & Row, 1974), p. 191. Copyright © 1974 by Frederick E. Webster, Jr. Reprinted by permission of Harper Collins Publishers.

their role is to bring a seller and buyer together. Century 21 real estate agents are examples of this type of intermediary. The importance of intermediaries is made even clearer when we consider the functions they perform and the benefits they create for buyers.

RATIONALE FOR INTERMEDIARIES

Few consumers appreciate the value of intermediaries; however, producers recognize that intermediaries make selling goods and services more efficient because they minimize the number of sales contacts necessary to reach a target market. Figure 14–2 shows a simple example of how this comes about in the personal computer industry. Without a retail intermediary (such as Computer-Land), IBM, Apple, Compaq, and Epson would each have to make four contacts to reach the four buyers shown who are in the target market. However, each producer has to make only one contact when ComputerLand acts as an intermediary. Equally important from a macromarketing perspective, the total number of industry transactions is reduced from 16 to 8, which reduces producer cost and hence benefits the consumer. This simple example also illustrates why computer manufacturers constantly compete with each other to gain access to computer retailers such as ComputerLand, Businessland, and MicroAge.[2]

Functions Performed by Intermediaries   Intermediaries make possible the flow of products from producers to buyers by performing three basic functions (Figure 14–3). Most prominently, intermediaries perform a transactional function that involves buying, selling, and risk taking because they stock merchandise

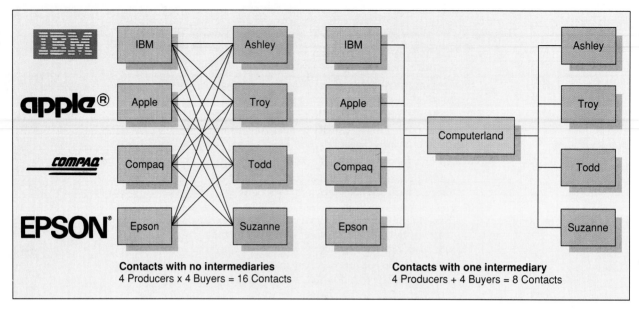

Contacts with no intermediaries
4 Producers x 4 Buyers = 16 Contacts

Contacts with one intermediary
4 Producers + 4 Buyers = 8 Contacts

FIGURE 14–2
**How intermediaries
minimize transactions**

in anticipation of sales. Intermediaries perform a logistical function evident in the gathering, storing, and dispersing of products (see Chapter 15 on physical distribution). Finally, intermediaries perform facilitating functions, which assist producers in making goods and services more attractive to buyers.

All three groups of functions must be performed in a marketing channel even though each channel member may not participate in all three. Channel members often negotiate about which specific functions they will perform. Sometimes conflict results, and a breakdown in relationships among channel members occurs. This happened in 1991 when PepsiCo, Inc. terminated its marketing and distribution arrangement with its bottler in France, citing poor performance. However, because all channel functions must be performed, PepsiCo can eliminate this intermediary but not the functions it performs. So PepsiCo will either have to find another bottler or set up its own bottling operation to perform the channel functions.[3]

Utilities Created by Intermediaries   Consumers also benefit from intermediaries. Having the goods and services you want, when you want them, where you want them, and in the form you want them is the ideal result of marketing channels. In more specific terms, marketing channels help create the four utilities described in Chapter 1: time, place, form, and possession. Time utility refers to having a product or service when you want it. For example, Federal Express provides next-morning delivery. Place utility means having a product or service available where consumers want it, such as having a Gulf gas station located on a long stretch of lonely highway. Form utility involves enhancing a product or service to make it more appealing to buyers, for example, tailoring services provided by the men's shop in Foley's Department Store in Houston. Possession utility entails efforts by intermediaries to help buyers take possession of a product or service, such as having airline tickets delivered by a travel agency.

TYPE OF FUNCTION	DESCRIPTION
Transactional functions	*Buying:* Purchasing products for resale or as an agent for supply of a product *Selling:* Contacting potential customers, promoting products, and soliciting orders *Risk taking:* Assuming business risks in the ownership of inventory that can become obsolete or deteriorate
Logistical functions	*Assorting:* Creating product assortments from several sources to serve customers *Storing:* Assembling and protecting products at a convenient location to offer better customer service *Sorting:* Purchasing in large quantities and breaking into smaller amounts desired by customers *Transporting:* Physically moving a product to customers
Facilitating functions	*Financing:* Extending credit to customers *Grading:* Inspecting, testing, or judging products and assigning them quality grades *Marketing information and research:* Providing information to customers and suppliers, including competitive conditions and trends

FIGURE 14–3
Marketing channel functions performed by intermediaries

Source: Based on Frederick E. Webster, Jr., *Industrial Marketing Strategy* (New York: John Wiley & Sons, 1979), pp. 162–63.

CONCEPT CHECK

1 **What is meant by a marketing channel?**

2 **What are the three basic functions performed by intermediaries?**

3 **What utilities are created by intermediaries?**

CHANNEL STRUCTURE AND ORGANIZATION

A product can take many routes on its journey from a producer to buyers, and marketers search for the most efficient route from the many alternatives available.

MARKETING CHANNELS FOR CONSUMER GOODS AND SERVICES

Figure 14–4 shows the four most common marketing channels for consumer goods and services. It also shows the number of levels in each marketing channel, as evidenced by the number of intermediaries between a producer and ultimate buyers. As the number of intermediaries between a producer and buyer increases, the channel is viewed as increasing in length. Thus the producer → wholesaler → retailer → consumer channel is longer than the producer → consumer channel.

Marketing
intermediaries create
utilities for customers.

Channel A represents a **direct channel,** because a producer and ultimate consumers deal directly with each other. Many products and services are distributed this way. A number of insurance companies sell their financial services using a direct channel and branch sales offices and World Book Educational Products sells its encyclopedias door-to-door. Schwan's Sales Enterprises of Marshall, Minnesota, markets a full line of frozen foods in 49 states and parts of Canada using door-to-door salespeople who sell from refrigerated trucks. Because there are no intermediaries with a direct channel, the producer must perform all channel functions.

The remaining three channel forms are **indirect channels,** because intermediaries are inserted between the producer and consumers and perform numerous channel functions.

Channel B, with a retailer added, is most common when a retailer is large and can buy in large quantities from a producer or when the cost of inventory makes it too expensive to use a wholesaler. Manufacturers such as GM, Ford, and Chrysler use this channel, and a local car dealer acts as a retailer. Why is there no wholesaler? So many variations exist in the product that it would be impossible for a wholesaler to stock all the models required to satisfy buyers; in addition, the cost of maintaining an inventory would be too high. However, large retailers such as Sears, 7-Eleven, Safeway, and J. C. Penney buy in sufficient quantities to make it cost effective for a producer to deal with only a retail intermediary.

Adding a wholesaler in Channel C is most common for low-cost, low-unit value items that are frequently purchased by consumers, such as candy, confectionary items, and magazines. For example, Mars sells its line of candies to wholesalers in case quantities; then they can break down (sort) the cases so that individual retailers can order in boxes or much smaller quantities.

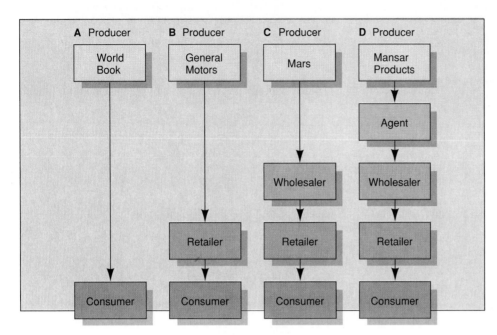

FIGURE 14–4
Common marketing channels for consumer goods and services

Channel D, the most indirect channel, is used when there are many small manufacturers and many small retailers and an agent is used to help coordinate a large supply of the product. Mansar Products, Ltd., is a Belgian producer of specialty jewelry that uses agents to sell to wholesalers in the United States, which then sell to many small retailers.

MARKETING CHANNELS FOR INDUSTRIAL GOODS AND SERVICES

The four most common channels for industrial goods and services are shown in Figure 14–5.[4] In contrast with channels for consumer products, industrial channels typically are shorter and rely on one intermediary or none at all because industrial users are fewer in number, tend to be more concentrated geographically, and buy in larger quantities (see Chapter 6).

Channel A, represented by IBM's large, mainframe computer business, is a direct channel. Firms using this channel maintain their own salesforce and are responsible for all channel functions. This channel arrangement is employed when buyers are large and well defined, the sales effort requires extensive negotiations, and the products are of high unit value and require hands-on expertise in terms of installation or use.[5]

Channels B, C, and D are indirect channels with one or more intermediaries to reach industrial users. In Channel B an **industrial distributor** performs a variety of marketing channel functions, including selling, stocking, and delivering a full product assortment and financing.[6] In many ways, industrial distributors are like wholesalers in consumer channels. Ingersoll-Rand, for example, uses industrial distributors to sell its line of pneumatic tools.

FIGURE 14–5
**Common marketing
channels for industrial
goods and services**

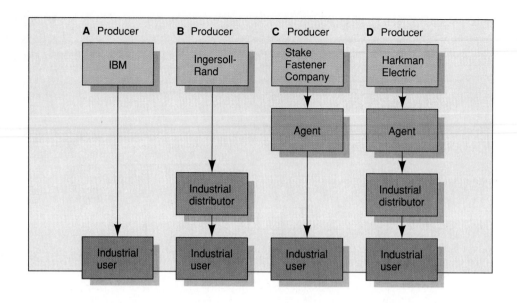

Channel C introduces a second intermediary, an *agent,* who serves primarily as the independent selling arm of producers and represents a producer to industrial users. For example, Stake Fastener Company, a California-based producer of industrial fasteners, has an agent call on industrial users rather than employing its own salesforce.

Channel D is the longest channel and includes both agents and distributors. For instance, Harkman Electric, a small Texas-based producer of electric products, uses agents to call on distributors who sell to industrial users.

MULTIPLE CHANNELS AND STRATEGIC ALLIANCES

In some situations producers use **dual distribution,** an arrangement whereby a firm reaches different buyers by employing two or more different types of channels for the same basic product.[7] For example, GE sells its large appliances directly to home and apartment builders but uses retail stores to sell to consumers. In some instances, firms use multiple channels when a multibrand strategy is employed (see Chapter 11). Hallmark sells its Hallmark greeting cards through Hallmark stores and select department stores, and its Ambassador brand of cards through discount and drugstore chains. In other instances, a firm will distribute modified products through different channels. Zoecon Corporation sells its insect control chemicals to professional pest-control operators such as Orkin and Terminex. A modified compound is sold to the Boyle-Midway Division of American Home Products for use in its Black-Flag Roach Ender brand.

A recent innovation in marketing channels is the use of **strategic channel alliances,** whereby one firm's marketing channel is used to sell another firm's products. These alliances are very popular in international marketing, where the creation of marketing channel relationships is expensive and time consuming.[8] For example, General Mills recently signed a pact with Nestlé S.A. whereby General Mills's cereals will be sold and distributed by Nestlé in Europe. General

Motors distributes the Swedish Saab through its dealers in Canada. And Kraft General Foods uses the distribution system of Ajinomoto, a major Japanese food company, to market its Maxwell House coffee in Japan.

These examples illustrate the creative routes to the marketplace available through dual distribution and strategic channel alliances. They also show how innovative firms can reach more buyers and increase sales volume.

DIRECT MARKETING CHANNELS

Increasingly, many firms are using direct marketing to reach buyers. **Direct marketing** allows consumers to buy products by interacting with various advertising media without a face-to-face meeting with a salesperson.[9] Direct marketing includes mail-order selling, direct-mail sales, catalog sales, telemarketing, video-text, and televised home shopping (for example, the Home Shopping Network).

Some firms sell products almost entirely through direct marketing. These firms include L. L. Bean (apparel) and Sharper Image (expensive gifts and novelties). Manufacturers such as Nestlé and Sunkist, in addition to using traditional channels composed of wholesalers and retailers, employ direct marketing through catalogs and telemarketing to reach more buyers.[10] At the same time, retailers such as Sears and J. C. Penney use direct marketing techniques to augment conventional store merchandising activities. Some experts believe that direct marketing will account for as much as 20 percent of all retail transactions in the United States in the 1990s.[11] Direct marketing is covered in greater depth in Chapter 16.

A CLOSER LOOK AT WHOLESALING INTERMEDIARIES

Channel structures for consumer and industrial products assume various forms based on the number and type of intermediaries. Knowledge of the roles played by these intermediaries is important for understanding how channels operate in practice.

The terms *wholesaler, agent,* and *retailer* have been used in a general fashion consistent with the meanings given in Figure 14–1. However, on closer inspection a variety of specific types of intermediaries emerges. Figure 14–6 shows a common classification of intermediaries that engage in wholesaling activities—those activities involved in selling products and services to those who are buying for the purposes of resale or business use. Intermediaries engaged in retailing activities are discussed in detail in Chapter 16. Figure 14–7 describes the functions performed by major types of independent wholesalers.

Merchant Wholesalers   Merchant wholesalers are independently owned firms that take title to the merchandise they handle. They go by various names, including industrial distributor (described earlier). About 80 percent of the firms engaged in wholesaling activities are merchant wholesalers.

Merchant wholesalers are classified as either full-service or limited-service wholesalers, depending on the number of functions performed. Two major types of full-service wholesalers exist. **General merchandise** (or *full-line*) **wholesalers** carry a broad assortment of merchandise and perform all channel

FIGURE 14–6
Types of wholesaling intermediaries

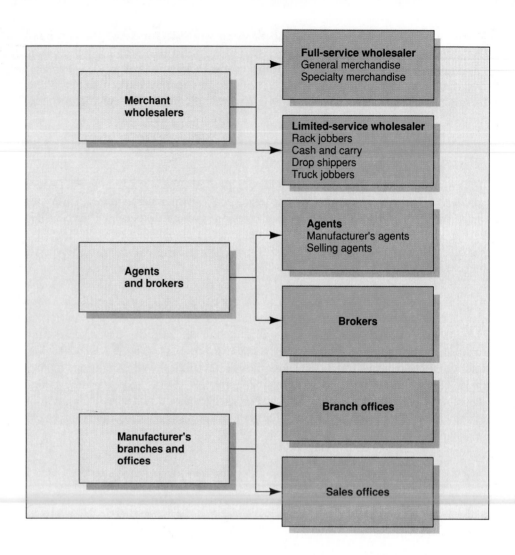

functions. This type of wholesaler is most prevalent in the hardware, drug, and clothing industries. However, these wholesalers do not maintain much depth of assortment within specific product lines. **Specialty merchandise** (or *limited-line*) **wholesalers** offer a relatively narrow range of products but have an extensive assortment within the product lines carried. They perform all channel functions and are found in the health foods, automotive parts, and seafood industries.

Four major types of limited-service wholesalers exist. **Rack jobbers** furnish the racks or shelves that display merchandise in retail stores, perform all channel functions, and sell on consignment to retailers, which means they retain the title to the products displayed and bill retailers only for the merchandise sold. Familiar products such as hosiery, toys, housewares, and health and beauty aids are sold by rack jobbers. **Cash and carry wholesalers** take title to merchandise but sell only to buyers who call on them, pay cash for merchandise, and furnish their own transportation for merchandise. They carry a limited product assortment and do not make deliveries, extend credit, or supply market

MERCHANT WHOLESALERS

FUNCTIONS PERFORMED	FULL SERVICE		LIMITED SERVICE				AGENTS AND BROKERS		
	GENERAL MERCHAN-DISE	SPECIALTY MERCHAN-DISE	RACK JOBBERS	CASH AND CARRY	DROP SHIPPERS	TRUCK JOBBERS	MANUFAC-TURER'S AGENTS	SELLING AGENTS	BROKERS
TRANSACTIONAL FUNCTIONS									
Buying ★									
Sales calls on customers									
Risk taking (taking title to products)									
LOGISTICAL FUNCTIONS									
Creates product assortments									
Stores products (maintains inventory)									
Sorts products									
Transports products									
FACILITATING FUNCTIONS									
Provides financing (credit)									
Provides market information and research									
Grading									

★ Key: ●, Yes; ●, sometimes; ●, no.

Sources: Adapted from Louis W. Stern, Adel I. El-Ansary, and James R. Brown, *Management in Marketing Channels* (Englewood Cliffs, N.J.: Prentice Hall, 1989), pp. 99–108; Kenneth G. Hardy and Allan J. Magrath, *Marketing Channel Management* (Glenview, Ill.: Scott, Foresman, 1988), pp. 3–5, 310–34; and Bert Rosenbloom, *Marketing Channels,* 3rd ed. (Hinsdale, Ill.: Dryden Press, 1987), pp. 44–47.

FIGURE 14–7
Functions performed by independent wholesaler types

information. This wholesaler is common in electric supplies, office supplies, hardware products, and groceries. **Drop shippers,** or *desk jobbers,* are wholesalers who own the merchandise they sell but do not physically handle, stock, or deliver it. They simply solicit orders from retailers and other wholesalers and have the merchandise shipped directly from a producer to a buyer. Drop shippers are used for bulky products such as coal, lumber, and chemicals, which are sold in extremely large quantities. **Truck jobbers** are small wholesalers who have a small warehouse from which they stock their trucks for distribution to retailers. They usually handle limited assortments of fast-moving or perishable items that are sold for cash directly from trucks in their original packages. Truck jobbers handle products like bakery items, dairy products, meat, and tobacco.

Agents and Brokers   Unlike merchant wholesalers, agents and brokers do not take title to merchandise and typically provide fewer channel functions. They make their profit from commissions or fees paid for their services, whereas merchant wholesalers make their profit from the sale of the merchandise they own.[12]

Manufacturer's agents and selling agents are the two major types of agents used by producers. **Manufacturer's agents,** or *manufacturer's representatives,* work for several producers and carry noncompetitive, complementary merchandise in an exclusive territory.[13] Manufacturer's agents act as a producer's sales arm in a territory and are principally responsible for the transactional channel functions, primarily selling. They are used extensively in the automotive supply, footwear, and fabricated steel industries. However, Swank Jewelry, Japanese computer firms, and Apple have used manufacturer's agents as well. By comparison, **selling agents** represent a single producer and are responsible for the entire marketing function of that producer. They design promotional plans, set prices, determine distribution policies, and make recommendations on product strategy. Selling agents are used by small producers in the textile, apparel, food, and home furnishing industries.

Brokers are independent firms or individuals whose principal function is to bring buyers and sellers together to make sales. Brokers, unlike agents, usually have no continuous relationship with the buyer or seller but negotiate a contract between two parties and then move on to another task. Brokers are used extensively by producers of seasonal products (such as fruits and vegetables) and in the real estate industry.

A unique broker that acts in many ways like a manufacturer's agent is a food broker, representing buyers and sellers in the grocery industry. Food brokers differ from conventional brokers because they act on behalf of producers on a permanent basis and receive a commission for their services. For example, Nabisco uses food brokers to sell its candies, margarine, and Planters peanuts, but it sells its line of cookies and crackers directly to retail stores. Do agents and brokers make a difference in a product's success? The accompanying Marketing Action Memo describes how Mr. Coffee used both manufacturer's agents and brokers to become the leader in the electric-drip coffee maker market.

Manufacturer's Branches and Offices   Unlike merchant wholesalers, agents and brokers, manufacturer's branches and offices are wholly owned extensions of the producer that perform wholesaling activities. Producers will assume wholesaling functions when there are no intermediaries to perform these activities, customers are few in number and geographically concentrated, or orders are large or require significant attention. Wholesaling activities performed by producers are conducted by means of a branch office or sales office. A *manufacturer's branch office* carries a producer's inventory, performs the functions of a full-service wholesaler, and is an alternative to a merchant wholesaler. A *manufacturer's sales office* does not carry inventory, typically performs only a sales function, and serves as an alternative to agents and brokers.

Marketing Action Memo

MR. COFFEE + AGENTS + BROKERS = SUCCESS

*V*incent Marotta hated the way coffee tasted, but he was convinced that its poor taste was caused not by bad coffee but the machines that brewed it. In 1972, he developed the prototype for what is now known as Mr. Coffee, the first electric-drip coffee maker. By 1990 over 50 million Mr. Coffees had been sold, as well as billions of coffee filters. Was Mr. Coffee's success only a result of a high-quality product that satisfied a need, and of effective advertising using Joe DiMaggio as its spokesperson? Not quite. Distribution played an integral role.

Mr. Coffee and its filters were sold by manufacturer's agents who called on appliance and mass merchandise stores. In time, however, it became apparent that Mr. Coffee users found it inconvenient to visit appliance and mass merchandise stores to buy replacement filters. These customers would benefit by having filters in the stores where they bought their coffee, namely, in the 168,000 retail food outlets throughout the United States. Therefore, a national network of food brokers was hired to sell Mr. Coffee filters to supermarkets and grocery stores. The result? It is estimated that about 75 percent of Mr. Coffee's filter sales come from retail food outlets.

In 1989, the company introduced the Ice Tea Pot by Mr. Coffee, using its network of manufacturer's agents to call on appliance and mass merchandise stores. Filters are again sold by food brokers to retail food outlets.

Sources: Based on an interview with Mr. James Yurak, executive vice president, Mr. Coffee, June 1, 1990; "After a Little Reheating, Mr. Coffee Is Just Fine," *Business Week* (August 20, 1990), p. 77; "The Yankee Clipper Returns to 'Pitch' in Mr. Coffee Lineup," *The Wall Street Journal* (August 22, 1990), p. B3; and "DiMaggio a Sure Bet in Day of Pete Rose," *Dallas Times Herald* (August 30, 1990), p. A19.

VERTICAL MARKETING SYSTEMS

The traditional marketing channels described so far represent a loosely knit network of independent producers and intermediaries brought together to distribute goods and services. However, new channel arrangements are emerging to improve efficiency in performing channel functions and achieving greater marketing impact. For example, **vertical marketing systems** are professionally managed and centrally coordinated marketing channels designed to achieve channel economies and maximum marketing impact.[14] Figure 14–8 depicts the major types of vertical marketing systems: corporate, contractual, and administered.

Corporate Systems   The combination of successive stages of production and distribution under a single ownership is a *corporate vertical marketing system.* For example, a producer might own the intermediary at the next level down in the channel. This practice, called *forward integration,* is exemplified by Polo/Ralph

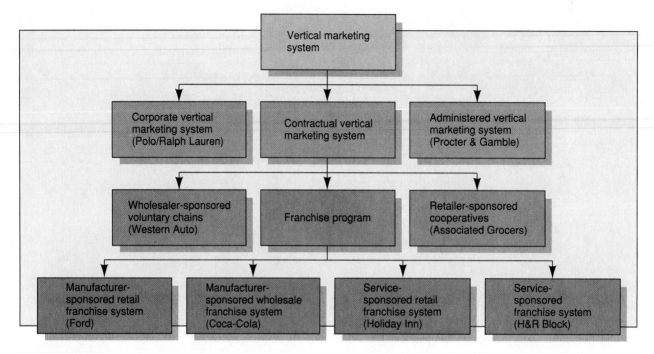

FIGURE 14–8
**Types of vertical
marketing systems**

Lauren, which manufactures clothing and also owns apparel shops.[15] Other
examples of forward integration include Goodyear, Singer, Sherwin Williams,
and the building materials division of Boise Cascade. Alternatively, a retailer
might own a manufacturing operation, a practice called *backward integration.* For
example, Kroger supermarkets operate manufacturing facilities that produce
everything from aspirin to cottage cheese, for sale under the Kroger label.

Contractual Systems Under a *contractual vertical marketing system,* independent
production and distribution firms integrate their efforts on a contractual basis to
obtain greater functional economies and marketing impact than they could
achieve alone. Contractual systems are the most popular among the three types
of vertical marketing systems and are estimated to account for about 40 percent
of all retail sales.

Three variations of contractual systems exist. *Wholesaler-sponsored voluntary
chains* involve a wholesaler that develops a contractual relationship with small,
independent retailers to standardize and coordinate buying practices, merchandising programs, and inventory management efforts. With the organization of
a large number of independent retailers, economies of scale and volume discounts can be achieved to compete with chain stores. Western Auto, IGA, and
Ben Franklin stores represent wholesaler-sponsored voluntary chains. *Retailer-
sponsored cooperatives* exist when small, independent retailers form an organization that operates a wholesale facility cooperatively. Member retailers then concentrate their buying power through the wholesaler and plan collaborative

Western Auto is an example of a wholesaler-sponsored voluntary chain.

promotional and pricing activities. Examples of retailer-sponsored cooperatives include Associated Grocers and Certified Grocers.

The most visible variation of contractual systems is **franchising,** a contractual arrangement between a parent company (a franchisor) and an individual or firm (a franchisee) that allows the franchise to operate a certain type of business under an established name and according to specific rules. Franchises generate almost $700 billion in sales through about 535,000 outlets annually in the United States.[16] Four types of franchise arrangements are most popular.[17] Manufacturer-sponsored retail franchise systems are most prominent in the automobile industry, where a manufacturer such as Ford licenses dealers to sell its cars subject to various sales and service conditions. Manufacturer-sponsored wholesale systems are evident in the soft drink industry, where Pepsi-Cola licenses wholesalers (bottlers) who purchase concentrate from Pepsi-Cola and then carbonate, bottle, promote, and distribute its products to supermarkets and restaurants. Service-sponsored retail franchise systems are provided by firms that have designed a unique approach for performing a service and wish to profit by selling the franchise to others. Holiday Inn, Avis, and McDonald's represent this franchising approach. Service-sponsored franchise systems exist when franchisors license individuals or firms to dispense a service under a trade name and specific guidelines. Examples include Snelling and Snelling, Inc., employment services, and H&R Block tax services. Service-sponsored franchise arrangements are expected to be the fastest-growing type of franchise in the 1990s.[18] Franchising is discussed further in Chapter 16.

Administered Systems In comparison, *administered vertical marketing systems* achieve coordination at successive stages of production and distribution by the

H&R Block represents a successful service-sponsored franchise system.

size and influence of one channel member rather than through ownership. P&G, given its broad product assortment ranging from disposable diapers to detergents, is able to obtain excellent cooperation from supermarkets in displaying, promoting, and pricing its products. Sears gains numerous concessions from manufacturers in terms of product specifications, price levels, and promotional support.

<table>
<tr><td>CONCEPT CHECK</td><td>1 What is the difference between a direct and an indirect channel?</td></tr>
<tr><td></td><td>2 Why are channels for industrial products typically shorter than channels for consumer products?</td></tr>
<tr><td></td><td>3 What is the principal distinction between a corporate vertical marketing system and an administered vertical marketing system?</td></tr>
</table>

CHANNEL CHOICE AND MANAGEMENT

Marketing channels not only link a producer to its buyers, but also provide the means through which a firm implements various elements of its marketing strategy.[19] Therefore, choosing a marketing channel is a critical decision.

Marketing Action Memo

MARKETING CHANNELS FOR MICROCOMPUTERS INTO THE 21ST CENTURY

*T*he 1990s will witness major changes in marketing channels for microcomputers. Some will be carryover effects from the 1980s.

Apple computer has pruned its dealer network and IBM has closed its computer retail stores. ComputerLand and Businessland, two large chain retailers, are stocking Asian-manufactured computers. New retailing forms have emerged, called *value-added resellers* (VARs). VARs, which provide already assembled (turnkey) or customized computer systems for special applications to business, have captured market share from computer stores that sell only computers.

Intense competition, a refocus away from consumer users to business users, and increased user sophistication and knowledge about microcomputers have revolutionized the choice and management of marketing channels. The dominant channel at each stage of the product life cycle for microcomputers into the 21st century is shown below.

For Apple and IBM, the 21st century may already be here: they are experimenting now with selling their microcomputers through some mass merchandisers, and CompuAdd Corporation has established a chain of 84 no-frills retail stores that cater to the microcomputer bargain hunter. As for

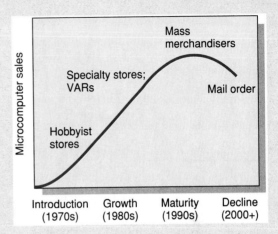

mail order, Dell Computer Corporation pioneered and is now the leader in this marketing channel, which Tandy Corporation has also begun using to reach customers who don't shop its Radio Shack stores.

Sources: Based on Jim Bartimo, "Mass Market Transforms PC Retailing," *The Wall Street Journal* (December 18, 1990), p. B1; Brenton R. Schlender, "Who's Ahead in the Computer Wars," *Fortune* (February 12, 1990), pp. 58–66; "Can Dell, CompuAdd Broaden Niches?" *The Wall Street Journal* (February 5, 1990), p. B1; "What's in a Name? A Lot, Says Tandy," *Business Week* (February 27, 1989), p. 109; Kate Bertrand, "The Channel Challenge," *Business Marketing* (May 1988), pp. 42–50; "IBM Tests Selling Its PCs within Department Stores," *The Wall Street Journal* (November 21, 1988), p. B1.

FACTORS AFFECTING CHANNEL CHOICE AND MANAGEMENT

The final choice of a marketing channel by a producer depends on a number of factors that often interact with each other. The accompanying Marketing Action Memo illustrates how numerous factors combine to alter marketing channels for microcomputers.

Environmental Factors The changing environment described in Chapter 3 has an important effect on the choice and management of a marketing channel. For example, the Fuller Brush Company, which is a name synonymous with door-to-door selling, now uses catalogs and has opened retail stores in some cities.[20] Rising employment among women, resulting in fewer being at home during working hours, prompted this action. Deregulation of the financial services industry led Merrill Lynch to reconsider its direct selling effort and examine indirect channels and intermediaries (for example, retail stores such as Sears) for the many investment services it provides.[21] Advances in the technology of growing, transporting, and storing perishable cut flowers has allowed Kroger to eliminate flower wholesalers and buy direct from flower growers around the world. Today, Kroger's annual cut-flower sales exceed $100 million, making it the largest flower retailer in the United States.[22] Technological advances have also made it possible to market microcomputers that require less training for users. This advance has enabled the broadened distribution of these products.

Consumer Factors   Consumer characteristics have a direct bearing on the choice and management of a marketing channel. Determining which channel is most appropriate is based on answers to fundamental questions such as: Who are potential customers? Where do they buy? When do they buy? How do they buy? What do they buy? These answers also indicate the type of intermediary best suited to reaching target buyers. For example, Ricoh Company, Ltd., studied the serious (as opposed to recreational) camera user and concluded that a change in marketing channels was necessary. The company terminated its contract with a wholesaler who sold to mass merchandise stores and began using manufacturer's agents who sold to photo specialty stores. These stores agreed to stock and display Ricoh's full line and promote it prominently, and sales volume tripled within 18 months.[23] Similarly, increased user sophistication and unique needs have spurred changes in the microcomputer marketing channel.

Product Factors   In general, highly sophisticated products such as large, scientific computers, unstandardized products such as custom-built machinery, and products of high unit value are distributed directly to buyers. Unsophisticated, standardized products with low unit value, such as table salt, are typically distributed through indirect channels. A product's stage in the life cycle also affects marketing channels, as shown earlier in the Marketing Action Memo on microcomputers.

Technology helped Kroger become the nation's largest flower retailer.

Company Factors   A firm's financial, human, or technological capabilities affect channel choice. For example, firms that are unable to employ a salesforce might use manufacturer's agents or selling agents to reach wholesalers or buyers. If a firm has multiple products for a particular target market, it might use a direct channel, whereas firms with a limited product line might use intermediaries of various types to reach buyers. The role of company factors is evident in the distribution of correctable typewriter ribbons.[24] IBM distributes its ribbons directly through its own salesforce, which sells and services IBM office products. However, Burroughs, Frankel, Eaton Allen Corporation, Liquid Paper, and General Ribbon use indirect channels partially because of more limited resources and a narrower product line. They reach buyers through wholesalers, office supply dealers, and typewriter machine dealers.

Company factors also apply to intermediaries. For example, microcomputer hardware and software producers wishing to reach business users might look to retailers such as Micro Age, which has its own salesforce that calls on businesses.

CHANNEL DESIGN CONSIDERATIONS

Recognizing that numerous routes to buyers exist and also recognizing the factors just described, marketing executives typically consider three questions when choosing a marketing channel and intermediaries:

1 Which channel and intermediaries will provide the best coverage of the target market?
2 Which channel and intermediaries will best satisfy the buying requirements of the target market?
3 Which channel and intermediaries will be the most profitable?

Target Market Coverage   Achieving the best coverage of the target market requires attention to the density and type of intermediaries to be used at the retail level of distribution. Three degrees of distribution density exist: intensive, exclusive, and selective. **Intensive distribution** means that a firm tries to place its products and services in as many outlets as possible. Intensive distribution is usually chosen for convenience products or services; for example, chewing gum, automatic teller machines, and cigarettes. Increasingly, medical services are distributed in this fashion.

Exclusive distribution is the extreme opposite of intensive distribution because only one retail outlet in a specified geographical area carries the firm's product. Exclusive distribution is typically chosen for specialty products or services; for example, automobiles, some women's fragrances, men's suits, and yachts. Sometimes manufacturers sign exclusive distribution agreements with retail chain stores. Next, Inc., originally sold its innovative computer system only through Businessland outlets but has since broadened its distribution.

Selective distribution lies between these two extremes and means that a firm selects a few retail outlets in a specific area to carry its products. This is the most common form of distribution intensity and is usually associated with shopping goods or services such as Rolex watches, Ben Hogan golf clubs, and Henredon furniture.

The type or availability of a retail outlet will also influence whether a target market is reached. For example, GM, Toyota, Nissan, and Honda have established new dealers for their new cars to reach different target markets, as described in the beginning of the chapter. The L'eggs division of the Hanes Corporation distributes fashionable white pantyhose to nurses through catalogs because supermarkets and department stores do not typically carry these items.[25]

Satisfying Buyer Requirements   A second consideration in channel design is gaining access to channels and intermediaries that satisfy at least some of the interests buyers might want fulfilled when they purchase a firm's products or services. These interests fall into four categories: (1) information, (2) convenience, (3) variety, and (4) attendant services.

Information is an important requirement when buyers have limited knowledge or desire specific data about a product or service. Properly chosen intermediaries communicate with buyers through in-store displays, demonstrations, and personal selling. Computer stores have grown in popularity as a source for small computers because they provide such information. Similarly, direct sales firms such as Amway, Avon, and Tupperware have been able to identify the unique information needs of Japanese women and successfully communicate the benefits of their products and method of selling. Amway is the seventh-fastest growing firm in Japan, and Avon records almost $300 million in Japanese sales each year through direct selling.[26]

Convenience has multiple meanings for buyers, such as proximity or driving time to a retail outlet. For example, 7-Eleven stores with over 6,000 outlets nationwide satisfy this interest for buyers, and candy, tobacco, and snack food firms benefit by gaining display space in these stores. For other consumers, convenience means a minimum of time and hassle. The rapid growth of Jiffy Lube and Minut-Lube, which promise to change engine oil and filters in less than 10 minutes, appeal to this aspect of convenience.[27]

Variety reflects buyers' interest in having numerous competing and complementary items from which to choose. Variety is evident in both the breadth and depth of products and brands carried by intermediaries, which enhances their attraction to buyers. Thus a manufacturer of men's ties would seek distribution through stores that offer a full line of men's clothing.

Consumer desire to reduce time and hassle has prompted growth of Jiffy Lube.

Attendant services provided by intermediaries are an important buying requirement for products such as appliances that require delivery, installation, and credit. Therefore Whirlpool seeks dealers that provide such services.

Profitability   The third consideration in designing a channel is profitability, which is determined by the margins earned (revenues minus cost) for each channel member and for the channel as a whole. Channel cost is the critical dimension of profitability. These costs include distribution, advertising, and selling expenses associated with different types of marketing channels. The extent to which channel members share these costs determines the margins received by each member and by the channel as a whole.

CHANNEL RELATIONSHIPS: CONFLICT, COOPERATION, AND LAW

Unfortunately, because channels consist of independent individuals and firms, there is always potential for disagreements concerning who performs which channel functions, how profits are allocated, which products and services will be provided by whom, and who makes critical channel-related decisions. These channel conflicts necessitate measures for dealing with them. Sometimes they result in legal action.

Conflict in Marketing Channels   Channel conflict arises when one channel member believes another channel member is engaged in behavior that prevents it from achieving its goals.[28] Two types of conflict occur in marketing channels: vertical conflict and horizontal conflict.

Vertical conflict occurs between different levels in a marketing channel; for example, between a manufacturer and a wholesaler or retailer or between a wholesaler and a retailer. Three sources of vertical conflict are most common. First, conflict arises when a channel member bypasses another member and sells or buys products direct. This conflict emerged when Wal-Mart elected to purchase products direct from manufacturers rather than through manufacturer's agents, as described in the accompanying Marketing Action Memo. Second, disagreements over how profit margins are distributed among channel members produce conflict. This happened when Businessland and Compaq Computer Corporation disagreed over how price discounts were applied in the sale of Compaq's products. Compaq Computer stopped selling to Businessland for 13 months, until the issue was resolved.[29] A third conflict situation arises when manufacturers believe wholesalers or retailers are not giving their products adequate attention. For example, H. J. Heinz Company found itself in a conflict situation with its supermarkets in Great Britain when supermarkets promoted and displayed private brands at the expense of Heinz brands.[30]

Horizontal conflict occurs between intermediaries at the same level in a marketing channel, such as between two or more retailers (Target and K mart) or two or more wholesalers that handle the same manufacturer's brands. Two sources of horizontal conflict are most common. First, horizontal conflict arises when a manufacturer increases its distribution coverage in a geographical area. For example, a franchised Cadillac dealer in Chicago might complain to GM that another franchised Cadillac dealer has located too close to its dealership.

Marketing Action Memo

WAL-MART STORES' "DITCH THE REP" POLICY MEANS WAR!

*W*hat do Thomas Jefferson and Benjamin Franklin have to do with marketing channels? Just ask the Organization of Manufacturers Representatives (OMR). According to OMR, these founding fathers symbolize free enterprise. People dressed like them picketed Wal-Mart Stores to protest the company's practice of dealing with manufacturers directly instead of buying products through independent manufacturer's representatives, or "reps." This action followed a full-page ad in *The Wall Street Journal* describing OMR's complaint.

OMR was concerned that if Wal-Mart stops dealing with reps, first other large retailers like Target, Sears, and J. C. Penney and then midsize retailers will do likewise. An OMR spokesperson noted, "The functions a rep performs would have to be performed by somebody. A lot of those functions would have to be performed by the retailers themselves. Those that aren't would have to be performed by manufacturers." The final result, according to OMR, is that expenses to retailers and consumers would increase. Moreover, manufacturer's reps would lose business, and according to Joseph B. Mittelman, chairman of OMR, "We're standing up and fighting."

What was intended as a battle became only a skirmish. Wal-Mart buys directly from manufacturers when volume shipments warrant it, and buys from reps when it is economically prudent to do so. In short, as a large U.S. retailer, Wal-Mart has the buying power and customer franchises to determine from whom and how it buys.

"IF WE HAD THOUGHT ONE PERSON SHOULD TELL EVERYBODY ELSE HOW TO DO BUSINESS, WE WOULD HAVE DONE THINGS DIFFERENTLY."

Sources: Telephone interview with Jane Arend, public relations coordinator, Wal-Mart, May 30, 1990; "Sales Representatives' Group to Stage Protest at Wal-Mart," *Dallas Times Herald* (July 2, 1987), p. C2; "Independent Sales Reps Launch Wal-Mart Fight," *Dallas Morning News* (January 4, 1987), p. 5Hff; "Wal-Mart Faces a Fight over Purchasing Policy," *The Wall Street Journal* (December 11, 1986); and telephone interview with George W. Brown, OMR executive director, July 10, 1987.

Second, dual distribution causes conflict when different types of retailers carry the same brands. For instance, Revlon's Charlie perfume can be found in drugstores, department stores, and discount stores, which may lead to complaints by any one of the retailers.

Securing Cooperation in Marketing Channels   Conflict can have destructive effects on the workings of a marketing channel, so it is necessary to secure cooperation among channel members. One means is through a **channel captain,** a channel member that coordinates, directs, and supports other channel members. Channel captains can be producers, wholesalers, or retailers. P&G assumes this role because it has a strong consumer following in brands such as Crest, Tide, and Pampers. Therefore, it can set policies or terms that supermarkets will follow. McKesson–Robbins, a drug wholesaler, is a channel captain because it coordinates and supports the product flow from numerous small drug manufacturers to more than 20,000 drugstores and nearly 6,000 hospitals nationwide. Wal-Mart and K mart are retail channel captains because of their strong consumer image, number of outlets, and purchasing volume.

A firm becomes a channel captain because it is typically the channel member with the greatest power to influence the behavior of other members.[31] Power can take four forms. First, economic power arises from the ability of a firm to reward or influence other members given its strong financial position or customer franchise. IBM and Toys "R" Us have such economic power. Expertise is a second source of power over other channel members. For example, American Hospital Supply helps its customers (hospitals) manage inventory and streamline order processing for hundreds of medical supplies. Third, identification with a particular channel member may also create power for that channel member. For instance, retailers may compete to carry the Ralph Lauren line, or clothing manufacturers may compete to be carried by Neiman-Marcus or Bloomingdale's. In both instances the desire to be associated with a channel member gives that firm power over others. Finally, power can arise from the legitimate right of one channel member to dictate the behavior of other members. This situation would occur under contractual vertical marketing systems where a franchisor could legitimately direct how a franchisee behaves. Other means for securing cooperation in marketing channels rest in the different variations of vertical marketing systems.

Legal Considerations   Conflict in marketing channels is typically resolved through negotiation or the exercise of power by channel members. Sometimes conflict produces legal action. Therefore knowledge of legal restrictions affecting channel strategies and practices is important. Some restrictions were described in Chapter 13, namely vertical price-fixing and price discrimination. However, other legal considerations unique to marketing channels warrant attention.[32]

In general, suppliers can select whomever they want as channel intermediaries and may refuse to deal with whomever they choose. This right was established in the case of the *United States* vs. *Colgate and Company* in 1919. However, the Federal Trade Commission and the Justice Department monitor channel practices that restrain competition, create monopolies, or otherwise represent unfair methods of competition under the Sherman Act (1890) and the Clayton Act (1914). Six practices have received the most attention (Figure 14–9).

Dual distribution, although not illegal, can be viewed as anticompetitive in some situations. The most common situation arises when a manufacturer distributes through its own vertically integrated channel in competition with independent wholesalers and retailers that also sell its products. If the manufacturer's behavior is viewed as an attempt to lessen competition by eliminating wholesalers or retailers, then such action would violate both the Sherman and Clayton Acts.

FIGURE 14–9
Channel strategies and practices affected by legal restrictions

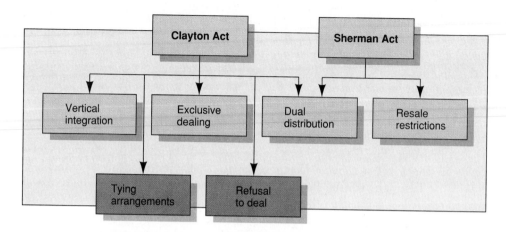

Vertical integration is viewed in a similar light. Although not illegal, this practice is sometimes subject to legal action under the Clayton Act if it has the potential to lessen competition or foster monopoly.

The Clayton Act specifically prohibits exclusive dealing and tying arrangements when they lessen competition or create monopolies. *Exclusive dealing* exists when a supplier requires channel members to sell only its products or restricts distributors from selling directly competitive products. *Tying arrangements* occur when a supplier requires a distributor purchasing some products to buy others from the supplier. These arrangements often arise in franchising. They are illegal if the tied products could be purchased at fair market values from other suppliers at desired quality standards of the franchiser. Full-line forcing is a special kind of tying arrangement. This practice involves a supplier requiring that a channel member carry its full line of products in order to sell a specific item in the supplier's line.

Even though a supplier has a legal right to choose intermediaries to carry and represent its products, a *refusal to deal* with existing channel members may be illegal under the Clayton Act. For example, an attempt to coerce an intermediary to perform in a certain way by refusing to deal with that firm would be illegal.

Resale restrictions refer to a supplier's attempt to stipulate to whom distributors may resell the supplier's products and in what specific geographical areas or territories they may be sold. These practices have been prosecuted under the Sherman Act. Today, however, the courts apply the "rule of reason" in such cases and consider whether such restrictions have a "demonstrable economic effect."[33]

CONCEPT CHECK

1   What are the three degrees of distribution density?

2   What are the three questions marketing executives consider when choosing a marketing channel and intermediaries?

3   What is meant by "exclusive dealing?"

ETHICS AND SOCIAL RESPONSIBILITY IN THE 1990s

THE ETHICS AND RESPONSIBILITY OF CHANNEL POWER

How firms acquire and use power in marketing channels has often prompted legal restrictions. Nevertheless, power gained through the economic strength, expertise, identification with others, and legitimate rights of channel members can be used in numerous ways.

Recently, some supermarket chains have demanded slotting allowances from manufacturers, paid in the form of money or free goods, to stock and display products. The allowances, which can range from $100 for a single store to upwards of $25,000 for a supermarket chain, have been labeled "ransom" and "extortional allowances." Supermarket operators see these allowances as a reasonable cost of handling business for manufacturers.

Is the practice of charging slotting allowances unethical behavior?

Sources: Based on Lois Therrien, "Want Shelf Space at Supermarkets? Ante Up," *Business Week* (August 7, 1989), pp. 60–61; Christine Donahue, "Conflict in the Aisles," *Adweek's Marketing Week* (September 4, 1989), pp. 20–21; and Alan Radding, "Egghead Loads Up on Software Slotting," *Advertising Age* (July 24, 1989), p. 70.

 ## SUMMARY

1 A marketing channel consists of individuals and firms involved in the process of making a product or service available for use by consumers or industrial users.

2 Intermediaries make possible the flow of products and services from producers to buyers by performing transactional, logistical, and facilitating functions. At the same time, intermediaries create time, place, form, and possession utility for consumers.

3 Channel structure describes the route taken by products and services from producers to buyers. Direct channels represent the shortest route because producers interact directly with buyers. Indirect channels include intermediaries between producers and buyers.

4 In general, marketing channels for consumer products and services contain more intermediaries than do channels for industrial products and services. In some situations, producers use multiple channels and strategic channel alliances for reaching buyers.

5 Numerous types of wholesalers can exist within a marketing channel. The principal distinction between the various types of wholesalers lies in whether they take title to the items they sell and the channel functions they perform.

6 Vertical marketing systems are professionally managed and centrally coordinated marketing channels designed to achieve channel function economies and marketing impact. A vertical marketing system may be one of three types: corporate, administered, or contractual.

7 Marketing managers consider environmental, consumer, product, and company factors when choosing and managing marketing channels.

8 Channel design considerations are based on the target market coverage sought by producers, the buyer requirements to be satisfied, and the profitability of the channel. Target market coverage comes about through one of three levels of distribution density: intensive, exclusive, and selective distribution. Buyer requirements are evident in the amount of information, convenience, variety, and service sought by consumers. Profitability relates to the margins obtained by each channel member and the channel as a whole.

9 Conflicts in marketing channels are inevitable. Vertical conflict occurs between different levels in a channel. Horizontal conflict occurs between intermediaries at the same level in the channel.

10 Legal issues in the management of marketing channels typically arise from six practices: dual distribution, vertical integration, exclusive dealing, tying arrangements, refusal to deal, and resale restrictions.

 ## KEY TERMS AND CONCEPTS

marketing channel p. 376
direct channel p. 380
indirect channels p. 380
industrial distributor p. 381
dual distribution p. 382
strategic channel alliances p. 382
direct marketing p. 383
general merchandise
  wholesalers p. 383
specialty merchandise
  wholesalers p. 384
rack jobbers p. 384

cash and carry wholesalers p. 384
drop shippers p. 385
truck jobbers p. 385
manufacturer's agents p. 386
selling agents p. 386
brokers p. 386
vertical marketing systems p. 387
franchising p. 389
intensive distribution p. 393
exclusive distribution p. 393
selective distribution p. 393
channel captain p. 396

 ## CHAPTER PROBLEMS AND APPLICATIONS

1 In what ways do marketing channels play an instrumental role in implementing a producer's marketing strategy?

2 A distributor for Celanese Chemical Company stores large quantities of chemicals, blends these chemicals to satisfy requests of customers, and delivers the blends to a customer's warehouse within 24 hours of receiving an order. What utilities does this distributor provide?

3 Suppose the president of a carpet manufacturing firm has asked you to look into the possibility of bypassing the firm's wholesalers (who sell to carpet, department, and furniture stores) and selling directly to these stores. What caution would you voice on this matter, and what type of information would you gather before making this decision?

4 What type of channel conflict is likely to be caused by dual distribution, and what type of conflict can be reduced by direct distribution? Why?

5 Suppose a Swedish-based manufacturer of home entertainment equipment such as stereos and VCRs is interested in designing a marketing channel in the United States to sell these products. What advice would you give the company? Be specific.

6 How does the channel captain idea differ among corporate, administered, and contractual vertical marketing systems with particular reference to the use of the different forms of power available to firms?

7 Suppose 10 firms in an industry wished to reach 10,000 potential customers by selling to them directly. How many sales contacts would be required in this industry if each firm called on each customer? How many sales contacts would be required if an intermediary were placed between the firms and potential customers?

8 Comment on this statement: "The only distinction among merchant wholesalers and agents and brokers is that merchant wholesalers take title to the products they sell."

9 How do specialty, shopping, and convenience goods generally relate to intensive, selective, and exclusive distribution? Give a brand name that is an example of each goods–distribution matchup.

10 Look again at the chapter opening example. Do you think the new dealer networks developed by GM, Nissan, Toyota, and Honda will be successful? Why or why not?

CHAPTER 15

Physical Distribution and Logistics Management

*A*fter reading this chapter you should be able to:

- Explain what physical distribution and logistics management are and how they relate to the marketing mix.

- Recognize the growing importance of customer service in successful marketing.

- Explain how logistics costs are balanced with customer service factors to reach a logistics decision.

- Describe the various transportation and warehousing options available to logistics managers.

- Understand reasons for holding inventory and newer philosophies that are intended to reduce inventory costs.

Distribution: Often the Key to a Satisfied Customer

Andy Warhol was right about people being famous for 15 minutes sometime in their life, at least in your case. Your 15 minutes come when you discover you've won $3,000,000 in Lotto America!

With check in hand you see a magazine ad for a BMW 850i and decide it's time to trade in your tired '68 Volkswagen Beetle. You head for your nearest BMW dealer, assuming your new BMW will be available. But how does it arrive in the dealer's showroom on time and in good condition when it's built in a German factory 6,000 miles away? Not only does your BMW have to meet all of its train, ship, and truck departures, but it also must not have dents, scratches, or broken rear-view mirrors. You're not about to put $73,600 on the table for a banged-up car.

Your BMW 850i probably rode by rail and ship to "NEAT"—the North East Auto–Marine Terminal (shown on the chapter opening page), which is operated by the New York–New Jersey Port Authority and leads all U.S. ports in handling imported foreign cars.[1] NEAT can handle up to 5,000 vehicles a day and operates an automated system that can dewax and wash 100 cars an hour. When a BMW, Peugot, or Mazda receives a scratch or dent during its ocean voyage, NEAT personnel do reworking and touch-up painting with a paint-mixing system that matches the damaged car's color precisely. A conveyor will deliver your BMW to the NEAT distribution area, where it is loaded on a truck for delivery to your dealer.

This complex movement of BMWs from manufacturer to showroom can be a disaster for a dealer—especially if ads in national magazines bring potential buyers into a showroom that has no new models because of a breakdown in the distribution system.

Retail products that aren't in the right place at the right time for sale to consumers who may have already decided to buy them illustrate the critical nature of the movement and storage of products in a firm's marketing program. The best-laid product and promotional strategies of a firm may be hurt or destroyed by poor physical distribution of the products it wishes to sell. This chapter examines the physical distribution process that moves products from the producer to buyer and how a firm tries to balance distribution costs against the need for effective customer service. It also presents an overview of the tools that are used in the movement and storage system.

MEANING OF PHYSICAL DISTRIBUTION AND LOGISTICS MANAGEMENT

Physical distribution is the part of marketing that addresses how products are moved and stored. A physical distribution channel includes intermediaries often not considered to be part of the marketing channel described in Chapter 14, such as transportation companies, public warehouses, and insurance companies that support the movement and storage of products. These agents, who do not take title to (actually own) the goods they handle, are referred to as *facilitators* because their main function is to facilitate the movement of goods.

INCREASING IMPORTANCE OF PHYSICAL DISTRIBUTION

Beginning in the 1950s, American business firms started placing more importance on their physical distribution systems. Several factors account for this trend. Soaring fuel prices meant it cost far more to move products than it had previously, and high interest rates drove up the cost of carrying inventory. More intense competition for U.S. firms, both domestically and internationally, caused them to search for new ways to reduce costs and improve efficiencies.

Stacking containers two high doubles a train's capacity and leads to significant efficiencies in a logistics system.

Because retail inventory philosophy changed so that retailers stocked less and wholesalers and manufacturers stocked more, and manufacturers' product lines proliferated to reach new segments, the demands for an efficient physical distribution system increased. Finally, improved computer technology permitted more sophisticated tracking of the thousands of items manufacturers produce and send through their distribution channels.

TWO VIEWS OF PHYSICAL MOVEMENT AND STORAGE ACTIVITIES

Marketing managers generally agree that physical distribution involves the movement and storage of goods. Beyond that they have different views on what physical distribution and physical distribution management really are. For our purposes, **physical distribution management** is organizing the movement and storage of finished goods to the customer. This traditional marketing view of physical distribution management looks at only the outbound flow of finished products from the manufacturer to the customer. It fails to consider activities involving the inbound flow of raw materials and parts that often have a great impact on the success of the marketing program. Marketers justify this narrow view of physical movements by concentrating on activities that they influence while leaving responsibility for the earliest movement and storage activities involving materials supply to the manufacturing, traffic, or purchasing department.

A more comprehensive view of all these physical movement and storage activities is **logistics management,** which involves the coordination of the movement and storage of raw materials, parts, and finished goods to achieve a

FIGURE 15–1
Relation of physical distribution and logistics to a manufacturing firm's operations

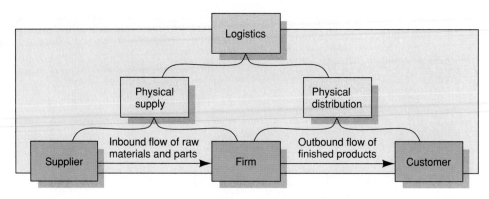

given service level while minimizing the total logistics cost of these activities.[2] This concept includes *both* physical supply and physical distribution, that is, both inbound and outbound activities. On a practical level, there is no consistent use of physical distribution terms generally, and many people use them loosely. The term *logistics management,* or *logistics,* is used in this chapter.

Figure 15–1 shows the relation of physical supply, physical distribution, and logistics to the operations of a manufacturing firm. This chart shows how the firm receives its physical supply in the form of raw materials and parts from its suppliers, converts these to finished products in its plant, and then provides physical distribution of these finished products to its customers. The concepts of physical supply, physical distribution, and logistics also apply to nonmanufacturing firms, such as retailers and wholesalers, for which the inbound activities include the finished goods that are resold to customers without physical modification.

HOW MOVEMENT AND STORAGE ACTIVITIES VARY AMONG FIRMS

The importance of movement and storage activities varies greatly by industry, but can exceed 15 percent of sales when both inbound and outbound movements are considered. However, for firms that don't physically move or store many items, these costs will be minor. For example, insurance companies and banks deal mainly with distributing paperwork, and most of their inbound materials are supplies.

At the other end of the spectrum are firms that produce many products from diverse raw materials at spatially separated plants and distribute the products to wide geographic markets. For large consumer food companies like Procter & Gamble, which are competing in the national market, the massiveness of their logistics problems becomes apparent. P&G produces more than 80 brands, all needing different raw materials, that are nationally distributed; the system has to move all the raw materials to the manufacturing plants and then all the finished products (brands) to the marketplace. The size of P&G's logistics

Product perishability makes logistics very important to the food industry.

problems can be reduced by working closely with its distributors, which is why it now has more than a dozen of its own employees working near Wal-Mart's national headquarters in Arkansas.[3]

Most firms lie between these extreme examples. The importance of logistics to a firm can be placed on a scale from very low to very high, generally based on these key factors that reflect the amount of movement and storage needed for the system to function:

- Number, weight, volume, and perishability of raw materials and final products.
- Number of material supply points.
- Number of material processing points.
- Number of product consumption points.

As the number of any of these factors increases, the complexity and cost of the logistics system generally increases as well.

The average outbound logistical costs for manufacturing companies is 7.5 cents on each dollar of sales. For manufacturers of consumer goods, logistics costs are about 7.0 cents on each dollar of sales, and for industrial goods they are about 9.0 cents per dollar of sales.[4] Figure 15–2 shows that transportation is the largest component and takes 2.9 cents of each dollar of sales.

RELATION TO MARKETING STRATEGY

Bernard LaLonde, a prominent distribution expert, has remarked, "American management's philosophy has been: 'If you're smart enough to make it, aggressive enough to sell it—then any dummy can get it there!' Now we're paying for [that philosophy]."[5]

FIGURE 15–2
Breakdown of the 7.5 cents of each sales dollar used for outbound logistical (distribution) activities for manufacturing firms

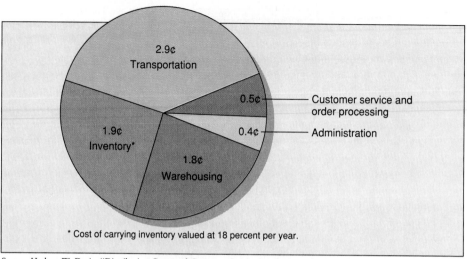

* Cost of carrying inventory valued at 18 percent per year.

Source: Herbert W. Davis, "Distribution Costs and Customer Service Levels: How Do You Compare in 1989?" in *Proceedings of the Council of Logistics Management* (1989), pp. 49–57.

What this means is that the best-laid marketing strategies can fail if the logistics system doesn't support them—a product cannot be purchased if it is not available when the consumer attempts to buy it (like your BMW 850i). Or suppose Procter & Gamble attempts to boost trial for its Crest tartar-control toothpaste using a massive coupon campaign. If consumers attempting to redeem the coupons found that the product was out of stock because of a lack of field inventory, it is doubtful that they would save the coupons and try to redeem them later. If they did, trial would still have been delayed, along with the real key to the new product success: repeat buys. So a good product, attractively priced and effectively promoted, could be destroyed through poor logistics.

Product Factors   Some of the logistical factors that interact with product decisions are physical product characteristics, packaging, and product differentiation. Physical product characteristics that affect the movement and storage of the product include the weight/bulk relationship, the weight/value relationship, and the risk associated with buying the product. For example, since a product such as coal is of low value compared with its weight, transportation costs could erode any profits from sales. To reduce these costs, a drop shipper is used who takes title but not the physical possession of the goods and arranges for the coal to move directly from the mine to the customer, thereby avoiding the transportation to and from the drop shipper. The important point is that physical product characteristics often dictate logistical actions.

Packaging is an area where both product and promotional factors interact with logistics. The marketer may view the interior package as a point-of-purchase device at retail but not consider its logistical implications. For instance, does the package provide adequate protection? Does the product's package al-

The weight, bulk, size, perishability, and strength of the product and package determine how the logistics system transports and stores it.

low it to be easily placed in an exterior package (such as a carton)? Do any factors such as unique shapes make handling, stacking, or filling of the package difficult? How many cartons can be placed in a vehicle? Various departments within a firm must coordinate efforts to ensure that a package desirable from a marketing standpoint is logistically acceptable.

A product can be differentiated through customer service and on-time delivery, especially if it is a mature product with many nearly identical competitors and low brand loyalty. The 1990s will see increasing emphasis on finding ways for logistics management to be used as part of a company's competitive strategy in increasing customer service and on-time delivery while reducing logistical costs.[6]

Pricing Factors   Pricing interacts with logistics in several ways. Terms of transfer of the product's title and responsibility for transfer are determined by the specific geographic pricing system used. Some of these methods build transportation costs into the quoted price of the product.

Pricing discounts also may have logistical implications. A quantity discount is used to encourage buyers to purchase large quantities and to reward them for holding inventory. When these pricing discounts are combined with volume transportation discounts, buyers can gain even larger savings.

Promotional Factors   Promotion interacts with logistics in the areas of advertising, sales promotion, and personal selling. Advertising and promotional campaigns must be planned and coordinated with the logistics system to ensure product availability at the appropriate time. Distribution must be synchronized with sales to ensure timely and efficient handling of orders. Trade promotions and contests or incentives for the salesforce also may create irregular demand that logistics will have to deal with efficiently.

Place Factors   Many intermediaries in marketing channels got their start because of logistical problems that existing intermediaries couldn't solve to the consumers' satisfaction. For example, careful attention to movement and storage of food products helped to make Cub Foods (a Midwestern chain) superwarehouses a retailing innovation copied across the country. A Cub Foods store has sales of about six times the weekly sales of a conventional supermarket. Its high-volume, low-price strategy is possible because of basic logistical decisions: taking some shipments directly from manufacturers, obtaining quantity discounts from them, and storing and displaying merchandise in the original cartons stacked to the store's 24-foot ceilings.[7]

CONCEPT CHECK	1 What is the broader logistics management view of physical distribution?
	2 Why is logistics more important to a consumer good manufacturer than to a bank?
	3 How does logistics interact with the product element of the marketing mix?

OBJECTIVES OF THE LOGISTICS SYSTEM

The definition of logistics management presented previously contains four key words or phrases: coordination, movement and storage, total logistics cost, and service level. As just discussed, there is a need to coordinate activities among functional departments, including marketing. *Movement and storage* refers to the continuous flow of physical goods into and out of the firm, much like a pipeline for a manufacturing firm. Parts, supplies, and raw materials flow into it so it can produce the product and have finished goods flow out to be distributed through the marketing channel. The total logistics cost and service aspects of the definition will be explored in more detail.

TOTAL LOGISTICS COST CONCEPT

Logistics attempts to minimize the total cost of moving and storing the goods a firm uses and produces. There are many individual cost elements present in a logistics system, so **total logistics cost** includes expenses associated with transportation, materials handling and warehousing, inventory, stockouts (being out of inventory), and order processing. Often as one of these costs decreases, another increases. For example, as inventory levels (and costs) rise, stockouts probably drop, so the net impact of both must be assessed. By considering all relevant costs as part of a logistics system, this effect can be determined, as shown in Figure 15–3. As the number of warehouses increases, inventory costs rise and transportation costs fall because more overall inventory is warehoused,

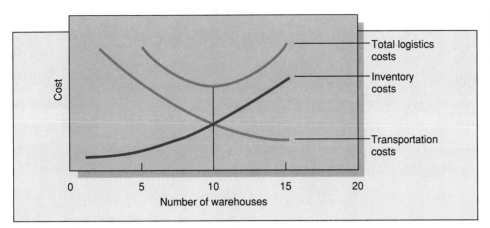

FIGURE 15–3
**How logistics costs vary
with number of
warehouses used**

but it is transported in bulk closer to customers. The net effect is to minimize the total costs of the logistics system shown in Figure 15–3 by having 10 warehouses. This means the total cost curve is minimized at a point where neither of the two individual cost elements is at a minimum but the overall system is.

CUSTOMER SERVICE CONCEPT

If logistics is a pipeline, the end of it—or *output*—is the service delivered to customers. The increasing importance of customer service has been covered earlier, especially in Chapter 9. In terms of logistics, **customer service** is the ability of a logistics system to satisfy users in terms of time, dependability, communications, and convenience.[8]

It would be simple to cut the total costs of a logistics system if customer service could be ignored, but competition prevents this. A firm's goal is to provide adequate customer service while controlling the associated costs. Unrealistically high customer service could lead to runaway costs, whereas minimum customer service could antagonize customers and destroy the firm's competitive position. Thus a balance or trade-off between total logistics cost and customer service is required, as suggested in Figure 15–4.

A renewed focus on customers has propelled the changes in the role and importance of customer service jobs. Companies now see customer service as a strategic tool for increasing customer satisfaction and sales, not merely as an expense. For example, in 1990 3M completed a survey about customer service among 18,000 European customers in 16 countries, with personal interviews conducted in 13 languages. The survey revealed surprising agreement in all countries about the importance of customer service and stressed factors like condition of product delivered, on-time delivery, quick delivery after order placement, and effective handling of problems.[9]

Time   Time in a logistics setting refers to **lead time** for an item, which means the lag from ordering an item until it is received in stock. This is sometimes also referred to as **order cycle time** or **replenishment time.** The

FIGURE 15–4

Logistics managers balance total logistics cost factors against customer service factors

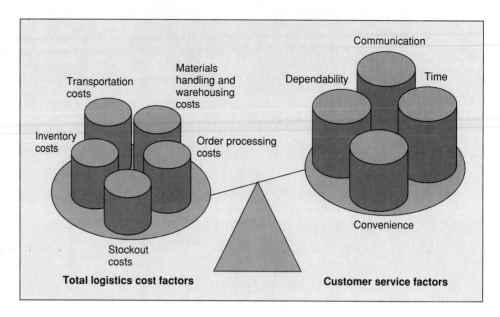

various elements that make up the typical order cycle for businesses include recognition of the need to order, order transmittal, processing, preparation, and transportation.

These issues may not seem important to consumers unless desired items are out of stock. However, in buying products such as cars and some furniture brands, where specific orders are placed with manufacturers, the consumer may directly face lead-time issues. Although effective customer service seeks to reduce lead times, achieving this goal often increases associated costs.

Dependability   Dependability is the consistency, or reliability, of replenishment. It can be broken into three elements: consistent lead time (the period from order placement to delivery), safe delivery, and correct delivery. Studies indicate that dependability is a key element in customer service.[10] Consistent service allows planning (such as appropriate inventory levels), whereas inconsistencies thwart this planning. Customers may be willing to accept longer lead times if they know about it in advance and can adjust their operations. Surprise delays may shut down a production line, and early deliveries may cause special problems for storing the extra inventory.

Communication   Communication is a two-way link between buyer and seller that helps in monitoring service. Each party can try to resolve problems if it is aware of them at an early stage. Status reports on orders are a typical area where communication is important. Clear, timely communication is essential to achieve effective customer service.

Convenience   Since different customers have different service needs, a customer service system should be flexible to accommodate these needs. For example, if an important customer requires deliveries before 7A.M., this must be

A key reason for Wal-Mart's low prices is its highly efficient logistics system, which includes close cooperation with its major suppliers.

done. Convenience levels may be established for separate groups of customers based on their potential profitability to the seller. A growing customer that already accounts for 30 percent of a firm's sales volume requires good service, whereas another customer that provides only 1 percent of sales may not warrant the higher, more costly levels of service.

Service Situation   Customer service is highly situational. A manufacturer like Apple Computer or Westinghouse will probably include all the service elements that have been discussed. However, a retailer like Sears or K mart usually focuses on communication and convenience (specifically, location, hours open, and credit policy) because order cycle time and dependability have little significance in dealing with a retailer's customers but are important when the retailer deals with suppliers.

COST–SERVICE TRADE-OFFS

Costs set an upper limit on the amount of customer service a firm should provide. The same service levels may be obtained with different combinations of resources (such as low-cost transportation with warehouses versus high-cost transportation without them). For example, IBM has begun closing 120 parts warehouses because Federal Express (the overnight air service) now inventories high-priced parts for IBM's computer workstations. The inventories kept at Federal's sorting hubs in Memphis, Oakland, and Newark mean that its high-cost overnight transportation is being substituted for IBM's higher-cost parts warehouses scattered across the United States. The result: better service for IBM customers at a lower cost.[11] Many distribution and logistics experts believe that this IBM–Federal Express kind of relationship will be more common in the future as manufacturers (like IBM) use third-party logistics firms (like Federal Express) to serve customers more efficiently.[12]

The cooperation between Wal-Mart and Procter & Gamble described earlier in the chapter is a success story for customer service: Wal-Mart maintains smaller inventories of P&G's Pampers diapers and has reduced its stockouts, and P&G has increased its proportion of on-time deliveries from 94 percent to 99.6

FIGURE 15–5
Examples of customer service standards

TYPE OF FIRM	CUSTOMER SERVICE STANDARD
Wholesaler	At least 98% of orders filled accurately
Manufacturer	Order cycle time of no more than 5 days
Retailer	Returns accepted within 30 days
Airline	At least 90% of arrivals on time
Trucker	A maximum of 5% loss and damage per year
Restaurant	Lunch served within 5 minutes of order

percent.[13] Studies indicate that service costs grow at an increasing rate. One firm found that to increase on-time delivery from a 95 percent rate to a 100 percent rate tripled costs because of the extra tracking of orders, inventory, and deliveries that was required. Higher levels of service require tactics such as more inventory to cut stockouts, more expensive transportation to improve speed and lessen damage, possibly more warehouses, and double or triple checking of orders to ensure correctness. These actions all add to costs, so judgments have to be made about the proper levels of customer service.

CUSTOMER SERVICE STANDARDS

Firms operating effective logistics systems usually develop a set of written customer service standards. These serve as objectives and provide a benchmark against which results can be measured for control purposes. In developing these standards, the place to start is with the customers. What are their service needs? What do competitors offer them? Are the customers willing to pay a bit more for better service? After these questions are answered, realistic standards can be set and an ongoing measurement program established to monitor results. Typical standards relate to time, reliability, stock-out levels, and loss and damage. They must be quantifiable and measurable, as shown in Figure 15–5.

During the control process, deviations from standards must be noted and investigated. For example, a high loss and damage record may indicate a need for a more expensive mode of transport, a different carrier, or better protective packaging. These will result in some added costs but improve service and decrease costs of loss and damage.

CONCEPT CHECK

1 What is the trade-off between total cost and customer service in a logistics system?

2 In what ways do key customer service factors differ between a manufacturer and a retailer?

MAJOR LOGISTICS FUNCTIONS

As mentioned earlier, a business firm can adopt a logistics strategy varying between basic and advanced, depending on the extent to which it adopts the concept. Four key elements in a logistics system described in the following sections include: (1) transportation, (2) warehousing and materials handling, (3) order processing, and (4) inventory management.

TRANSPORTATION

Transportation provides the movement of goods necessary in a logistics system. There are five basic modes of transportation: railroads, motor carriers, air carriers, pipelines, and water carriers. In addition, there are modal combinations involving two or more of the five basic modes. All can be evaluated on six basic service criteria:

- *Cost:* Charges for transportation.
- *Time:* Speed of transit.
- *Capability:* What can be realistically carried with this mode.
- *Dependability:* Reliability of service regarding time, loss, and damage.
- *Accessibility:* Convenience of the mode's routes (such as pipeline availability).
- *Frequency:* Scheduling.

Figure 15–6 summarizes service advantages and disadvantages of the modes of transportation available.

The process of picking a mode of transportation involves making trade-offs among these often-conflicting service criteria. In a decision about moving a specific product from the point of origin to a specific destination, the modes can then be evaluated on each criterion. Typically, in the final decision, the user will

MODE	RELATIVE ADVANTAGES	RELATIVE DISADVANTAGES
Rail	Full capability Extensive routes Low cost	Some reliability, damage problems Not always complete pickup and delivery Sometimes slow
Truck	Complete pickup and delivery Extensive routes Fairly fast	Size and weight restrictions Higher cost More weather sensitive
Air	Fast Low damage Frequent departures	High cost Limited capabilities
Pipeline	Low cost Very reliable	Limited routes (accessibility) Slow
Water	Low cost Huge capacities	Slow Limited routes and schedules More weather sensitive

FIGURE 15–6

Advantages and disadvantages of five modes of transportation

likely strike a balance between cost and the level of customer service required. One criterion, such as cost or time, may assume such great importance for a particular product that several alternative modes of transportation are ruled out.

Railroads   Railroads today usually carry heavy, bulky items over fairly long distances. Their predominant cargos are coal, ores, and grain. They can carry larger shipments than trucks (in terms of total weight per vehicle) at reasonable cost, and their routes are more extensive than those of either water carriers or pipelines.

  Railroads still dominate the five modes of transportation in terms of ton-miles carried. A ton-mile is a standard transport measure that reflects both weight carried and distance moved, or one ton of cargo moved one mile. So five tons moved 100 miles is 500 ton-miles. But railroads have lost higher valued traffic to other modes and now account for only about 10 percent of freight dollars. Railroads dominate other modes in bulky, lower-value products. The 1970s was a decade of turbulence for many railroads, with many bankruptcies and reorganizations. The Conrail (Consolidated Rail Corporation) system is a result of the bankruptcy of several railroads in the Northeastern United States. It was formerly owned by the federal government, but was sold to investors in

Railroads dominate shipping of bulky, lower-value products.

1987 through a common stock offering. Several mergers also occurred in the 1980s, creating a national system dominated by a half-dozen large regional railroads.[14] The Staggers Rail Act of 1980 enacted deregulation provisions allowing the railroads more operating freedom such as giving rail shippers more flexible rates and long-term contracts covering a series of shipments, as opposed to having to treat each individual shipment as a separate transaction.

Today's railroads have improved their service and are using more sophisticated equipment than a decade ago. Service innovations include unit trains, run-through trains, and minitrains. A *unit train* is a train dedicated to one commodity (often coal), using permanently coupled cars that run a continuous loop from shipper to receiver and back, thereby gaining important loading, movement, and reloading efficiencies. A *run-through train* carries more than one commodity but makes no stops. *Minitrains* are shorter trains that run on more frequent schedules and often help implement a just-in-time inventory system (described later in the chapter).

Motor Carriers   The motor carrier, or trucking, industry is composed of many small firms, as opposed to railroading. There are about 40,000 for-hire, regulated, interstate motor trucking companies in the United States today. In addition, there are many more independent truckers and private carriage operations owned by firms that transport their own products in their own trucks.[15] The congressional deregulation of trucking in 1980 led to severe financial problems for many truckers, but afforded shippers more service options and latitude in negotiating rates.

The biggest advantage of motor carriage is the complete door-to-door service. Trucks can go almost anywhere there is a road; however, they cannot carry all items because of size and weight restrictions. They typically carry higher-valued items than do railroads, often items that are packaged. Trucks carry only about a quarter of all ton-mile traffic but about three quarters of the total dollar value of traffic.

Trucks are often faster than rail, especially for shorter distances, but are more sensitive to bad-weather interruptions. Rates are generally higher than rail, although extreme price-cutting has appeared in some segments of the industry as a result of the increased competition fostered by trucking deregulation. This has enabled Procter & Gamble to reduce the unit cost of getting its products to its customers and has been an important factor in its decision to reduce the number of production sites from 12 to 9 for laundry granules and from 7 to 3 for shortening and oil.[16]

Air Carriers   Most of the general public's interest in air carriers, or airlines, centers around passenger traffic, but shippers look at their freight operations. Air freight is costly, but its speed may create savings in lower inventory levels to offset the cost. The items that can be carried are limited by space constraints and are usually valuable and lightweight, such as perishable flowers, clothing, and electronic parts. The items have to be delivered to an airport and picked up at the destination, although this service is available from specialized firms. Products moved in containers are especially amenable to this mode of shipment. The 1980s deregulation that significantly affected other modes of transportation has

Different modes offer different advantages; trucks give door-to-door service; pipelines and barges are inexpensive; and ships carry bulk.

hit airlines hard: more than 200 airlines have disappeared or merged into today's five largest U.S. airlines (American, United, Delta, USAir, and Northwest).[17]

Pipelines   Usual cargos for long-distance commercial pipelines are crude oil and its products and natural gas. Pipelines are an inexpensive, automated mode and are very reliable. Routes are fixed and tend to be concentrated regionally. The speed is slow, but operation is continuous. Currently pipelines are second to railroads in ton-miles carried domestically.

Water Carriers   Several forms exist within the water transportation mode. Domestically, the major options are the river systems (barges) and the St. Lawrence Seaway. The ships and barges are large and tend to haul bulky items of low value (such as coal and iron ore). Rates are low, but so is transit speed. Technological innovations have enabled some of the Great Lakes ships to carry huge cargos. Water transportation is available only to firms shipping certain

Marketing Action Memo

FLY-BY-NIGHT IDEA + CUSTOMER SERVICE + KISS = FEDERAL EXPRESS

*A*rmed with one of his college term papers, which got a C− grade, Frederick W. Smith didn't build a better mousetrap and wait for the world to beat a path to his door. Instead, he set out to show the world that with his simple new innovation *he* could beat a path to everybody else's door.

He gave the name *Federal Express* to his door-to-door flying parcel service that uses garish orange, white, and purple jets. And he advertised "absolutely, positively overnight" delivery for his small-parcel service—limited to 70 pounds, the weight one person can carry. "I figured we had to be enormously reliable," says Smith, "since our service is frequently used for expensive spare parts, live organs, or other emergency shipments."

But Federal Express isn't your typical fly-by-night outfit. After all, Smith *did* write his term paper at Yale, and he *did* use a family trust of $4 million to get started—and Federal Express *did* lose $29 million in its first 26 months of operation.

What Smith had was a good idea, a good understanding of customer service, and the tenacity and resources to stick with it. First, Smith reasoned, he had to own his own jet aircraft so *all* parcels could be picked up early in the evening, flown to a single sorting center (Memphis), and rerouted to their final destination before dawn. That's part of Fred Smith's KISS ("Keep it simple, stupid") principle.

As the business has grown, it's not as simple as it used to be. Today Federal Express operates the largest cargo fleet of aircraft in the free world, including 20 Boeing 747s and 24 DC 10s.

Always looking for a better idea, in 1989 Federal Express started a new, lower-priced delivery service called Fed Ex Standard Overnight. The new overnight service offers delivery of documents and packages by the following afternoon at a price lower than that charged for the current service that promises delivery by 10:30 A.M. This offering further segments the overnight delivery market by providing—you guessed it—a customer service at lower price to those customers who don't need morning delivery.

Sources: Based on Bryan M. Iwamoto, "Night Moves," *Express Magazine* (Winter 1990), pp. 21–23; Rick Christie, "When It Doesn't Have to Be There Fast," *The Wall Street Journal* (June 28, 1989), p. B1; Roy Rowan, "Business Triumphs of the Seventies," *Fortune* (December 1979), pp. 34.

---

commodities that have access to the river systems, the Great Lakes, intercoastal or coastal waterways, or ocean ports. Most overseas traffic moves on ships.

Package and Express Companies   Several alternatives exist for moving small packages and letters. In addition to the government post offices, package services such as United Parcel Service (UPS) specialize in parcels under 70 pounds and provide pickup and delivery. Express companies such as Federal Express (see the accompanying Marketing Action Memo) and Purolator Courier offer fast movement of small packages. Pickup and delivery are provided, and next-morning delivery is guaranteed. Since these services are generally high cost, they are usually reserved for vital and lightweight shipments. Emery Air Freight, which merged with Purolator in 1987, concentrates in air-expressing the over 70-pound packages and is trying to take advantage of the popularity of just-in-time inventory systems (discussed later in the chapter) to serve customers in this large-package segment.

Freight Forwarders   Firms that accumulate small shipments into larger lots and then hire a carrier to move them, usually at reduced rates, are **freight forwarders,** or freight consolidators. Since per-pound rates for large shipments are lower than for small shipments, the forwarder's profit comes from the rate differential between large and small lots. Some of these firms specialize in air freight and others in surface freight.

The main advantage of using a freight forwarder is service. Pickup and delivery are provided, and the forwarders generally give more attention to small shipments (which they consolidate) than do carriers.

Intermodal Transportation   Sometimes it is possible to use **intermodal transportation,** which involves coordinating or combining different transportation modes to get the best features of each, while minimizing the shortcomings. The most popular coordination approach is truck-rail, also referred to as *piggyback* or *trailer on flatcar* (TOFC). Other intermodal arrangements involve some form of water transport. The basic idea in TOFC is to achieve the door-to-door capabilities of truck, along with the long-haul economies of rail. Trucks pick up shipments and proceed to railyards, where the trailers are disconnected, loaded onto flatcars, and travel by rail to a destination point. The trailers then are unloaded, hooked up to a power unit (tractor), and driven away. TOFC rates are now competitive, spurring a growth in this traffic. Packaged goods and some agricultural shipments are often carried by TOFC.

All the intermodal approaches share one theme: use of some form of container moved by truck for part of the distance. TOFC uses a truck trailer as a container, whereas the water plans generally employ conventional containers. They can be easily stacked and sorted and provide added product protection. Expensive handling equipment is required for these containers and is available only at certain locations. Containerization has also given a major push to export shipments.

CONCEPT CHECK

1. What are some new kinds of train service offered by railroads to compete more effectively with other modes of transportation?

2. What is intermodal transportation?

WAREHOUSING AND MATERIALS HANDLING

Warehouses not only allow firms to hold their stock in decentralized locations but are also used for sorting, consolidation, product-recall programs, product "aging" (for example, wine and tobacco), "mixing" (or blending) of items, and for tax reasons, such as state inventory taxes. Warehouses are second to transportation in cost significance for logistics systems.

Warehouses may be an integral part of customer service policy, as when a firm has warehouses within 500 miles of all customers to provide rapid resupply. Unfortunately, overall inventory levels will likely rise as well, resulting in higher costs, so a trade-off between costs and customer service must be made.

Warehousing presents several managerial issues: (1) the number, type, and location of warehouses needed and (2) ownership arrangements. The first of these decisions is based on the location of a company's markets, sources of inbound goods, and transportation routes and rates. Volumes moving in each direction must be considered, and a balance struck between the total costs incurred and the benefits received from having a warehouse in a particular place.

Once the number, type, and location of warehouses is determined, then ownership issues can be addressed. Public and private warehouses are the major options and will be discussed next, along with several types of warehouses that provide specific benefits.

Public Warehouses   Space and inventory-support services are provided by **public warehouses** on a rental basis. Because renters pay for only the amount of space and inventory-support services they require for manufacturers requiring limited warehouse usage this is less expensive than owning and operating their own warehouses. Public warehouses also are flexible because they can be

Warehouse space is a key to costomer service.

Private warehouses often stock a large, stable volume of goods.

used only when the space is required (for example, seasonally) or to fulfill some task such as a product recall. Public warehouses entail no fixed costs, long-term commitment, or ownership risks and are managed by people who know the warehouse business.

Many situations lend themselves to the use of public warehouses, as when new geographical markets (or test markets) are entered and product demand is uncertain. Vehicle load transportation rates (for larger shipments) can also be used if added space is available. They're also beneficial for firms that don't have the money or expertise to run their own warehouse. Over 10,000 public warehouses are available in the United States. Some of these concentrate on specific types of goods (such as farm products or frozen food), whereas others serve general storage needs.

Private Warehouses   An alternative to renting warehouse space is owning it. Private warehouses are owned and operated by a firm in the channel of distribution, such as the manufacturer or retailer. The owner of a warehouse is responsible for its management and operation, including hiring, labor and union negotiations, investment in handling equipment, insurance, and utility bills. A concern with private warehouses is their adaptability—specialized warehouses may not be attractive for resale, which could be important if market conditions necessitate relocating the inventory to be warehoused.

In private warehousing both fixed and variable costs are present. In comparing the costs with those of public warehousing, a break-even analysis can be used. To cover the fixed costs, a high level of use is necessary. Private warehousing is cheaper in the long run if it is used extensively, although the adaptability and real estate risks remain. An operational benefit of private warehousing is control over operations. Products not amenable to public warehousing include hazardous materials, sterile materials, or products such as fine wine that require long aging. Conditions that generally favor private warehousing include

Marketing Action Memo

WAL-MART: WHERE WAREHOUSE LOCATION MATTERS

Chairman Sam Walton's Wal-Mart chain has grown from a small cluster of stores in Arkansas to a 35-state chain of more than 1,400 discount department stores, over 120 Sam's Wholesale Clubs, and 3 hypermarkets. Wal-Mart has over $25 billion in annual sales.

Sam Walton gives much of the credit for growth in sales and profitability to the Wal-Mart version of hub-and-spoke distribution marketing. Like most retailers, Wal-Mart endorses the first three guidelines to retail success—location, location, and location—but then comes the surprise: Wal-Mart is primarily concerned with *warehouse* location. As reported in *Forbes* magazine: "Other retailers built warehouses to serve existing outlets, but Walton went at it the other way around. He started with a giant warehouse, then spotted stores all around it."

Today, some 77 percent of store needs are fulfilled from 13 distribution centers. All centers are highly automated, with online receipt of orders from store registers and automatic inventory control. Re-ordering is often done online from 200 vendors such as Procter & Gamble, using the same stock number as its suppliers to avoid reticketing each arriving shipping container. It is rare that store orders take more than 36 to 48 hours to fulfil.

The distribution system is being fine-tuned constantly, although distribution costs now stand at a remarkably low 2 cents on the dollar—believed to be less than half the standard for the industry. Supplying its growing number of stores is a continuing test for Wal-Mart's distribution system.

Sources: "Stalking the New Consumer," *Business Week* (August 28, 1989), pp. 54–62; "Wal-Mart Credits Deep Discounts to Hub-and-Spoke Planning," *Marketing News* (June 20, 1986), p. 18; Thomas C. Hayes, "Hypermarkets Catching On in U.S.," *International Herald Tribune* (February 6–7, 1988), pp. 9, 11; and "Here Come the 'Malls without Walls'," *Time* (February 8, 1988), p. 50.

a large, stable volume of stock moving through the warehouse, adequate financial resources, available managerial expertise, and a definite need for control of warehousing operations or some specific capabilities.

A **distribution center** is a warehouse that emphasizes speed and efficient product flow to hold goods for short periods of time and move them out as soon as possible. This contrasts with more traditional warehouses that often hold goods for extended periods of time. Distribution centers usually are one story (although it may be a high one) to avoid elevators, and are strategically located for transportation access, often near interstate highways. They may serve as consolidation points for other warehouses within the system. The tremendous success of rural retailing chains such as Wal-Mart stores and Duckwell-Alco stores is due to sophisticated distribution centers that serve their retail outlets.[18] In fact, as noted in the accompanying Marketing Action Memo, one key to Wal-Mart's low retail prices is its efficient network of warehouse distribution centers, which serves its retail stores within a 400-mile radius.[19]

The major benefit of distribution centers is improved customer service. They receive orders from customers and fill them quickly from local stocks. They are also entwined with production by receiving and consolidating shipments of materials and perhaps providing some production capabilities such as blending or final assembly to meet customer needs as close to the consumption point as possible.

Materials handling
through automation.

Materials Handling   Materials handling, which involves moving goods over short distances into, within, and out of warehouses and manufacturing plants, is a key part of warehouse operations. The two major problems with this activity are high labor costs and high rates of loss and damage. Every time an item is handled, there is a chance for loss or damage. Common materials handling equipment includes forklifts, cranes, and conveyors.

Recently, materials handling in warehouses has been automated by using computers to reduce the cost of holding, moving, and recording the inventories of stores. This automation in warehouses replaces trucks and operators with robotic equipment that places goods into storage and retrieves them under direction of a computerized control system. Fewer than 10 people can operate the warehouse from a control center. Records are immediately updated to yield precise inventory data, and productivity is greatly enhanced. The warehouse can have a higher ceiling, since the equipment can safely reach greater heights. The best applications for this technology are warehouses that handle high-turnover items of similar shape, such as packaged foods and cosmetics. This is why firms such as General Mills, Revlon, and Frito-Lay use automated warehouses. However, a risk to using automated warehouses is their inflexibility. If needs change significantly, it may be impossible to adapt or—worse yet—move the facility.

ORDER PROCESSING

There are several stages in the processing of an order. An order request starts the process, which is followed by entering the order, notifying production or a warehouse to prepare an order, checking inventory, possibly creating a back-order, (an order for an out-of-stock item), checking credit, preparing all paperwork that follows the order, and possibly sending a confirmation of the order to the customer. This information transfer within the firm is facilitated by an accurate computerized information system. Data from this system can be used for other purposes, such as product planning, market planning, customer analysis, and other marketing research activities. Many firms have invested heavily in these systems to integrate logistics into their other marketing activities.

INVENTORY MANAGEMENT

The major problem in managing inventory is maintaining the delicate balance between too little and too much of it. Too little may result in poor service, stockouts, brand switching, and loss of market share; too much leads to higher costs because of the money tied up in the inventory and the chance that it may become obsolete.

Different departments within the firm may have directly opposing views on inventory. Marketing and production managers may favor higher levels to improve customer service and aid in long production runs, whereas financial managers may be worried about the increased cost.

Inventory management received renewed attention in the 1980s because of an increased emphasis on increasing profit through effective cost reduction. Estimates of average U.S. inventory costs usually range from 10 percent to 35 percent of the inventory's value. However, detailed studies indicate the costs may be at the high end of this range.

Reasons for Inventory   Traditionally, carrying inventory has been justified on several grounds: (1) to offer a buffer against variations in supply and demand, often caused by poor forecasting, (2) to provide better customer service, (3) to promote production efficiencies, (4) to provide a hedge against price increases by suppliers, (5) to promote purchasing and transportation discounts, and (6) to protect the firm from contingencies such as strikes and shortages.

Inventory Costs   Specific inventory costs are often hard to detect because they are spread throughout the firm and in diverse locations such as production lines and decentralized warehouses. A typical general set of inventory costs includes:

- *Capital costs:* The opportunity costs resulting from tying up funds in inventory instead of using them in other, more profitable investments; these are related to interest rates.
- *Inventory service costs:* Items such as insurance and taxes that are present in many states.
- *Storage costs:* Warehousing space and materials handling.
- *Risk costs:* Possible loss, damage, pilferage, perishability, and obsolescence.

Storage costs, risk costs, and some service costs vary according to the characteristics of the item inventoried. Capital costs are always present and are proportional to the *value* of the item and prevailing interest rates. Controlling inventory costs requires accurate forecasts of future demand.

Newer Inventory Strategies   Several methods exist for improving inventory management. Increasingly important is the **just-in-time (JIT) concept,** which is an inventory supply system that operates with very lean inventories to hold down costs and requires fast, on-time delivery. In this system that is used extensively by Japanese manufacturers, when parts are needed for production, they arrive from suppliers "just in time."[20]

Proponents cite several advantages to JIT. First, there are the financial advantages that come from lower inventory levels and/or faster inventory turn-

Just-in-time inventory management is gaining importance in U.S. manufacturing.

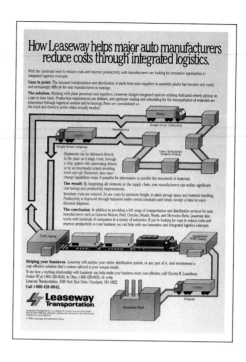

over. Second, the Japanese experience suggests that JIT yields better reliability in production scheduling and product quality. Smaller, more frequent shipments to manufacturers seem to lead to better quality.

For JIT to work properly, suppliers must be able to provide fast, reliable deliveries, or there will be a production disruption for the buyer. So with JIT the supplier incurs more responsibility and risk for inventory, quality products, and on-time delivery than with former systems. Ideally, to reduce these risks, the suppliers are near the user. This is often the case in Japan, where many suppliers are purposely located near the manufacturers. Although the United States doesn't lend itself as readily to such location strategies, certain industries, such as the automotive industry, have located many facilities quite close together in the Midwest. It's not surprising that many of the U.S. JIT users are located there. The accompanying Marketing Action Memo on JIT describes how General Motors uses JIT systems in producing some of its cars.

In summary, a well-managed logistics system that delivers high levels of customer service is a valuable marketing tool. Instead of being just another expense, it can serve to generate sales and possibly to allow premium prices to be obtained because of the value provided to customers. With increased global competition in many industries, improved logistics performance—especially customer service—is a means for a firm to gain a competitive advantage.

CONCEPT CHECK

1 What are the basic trade-offs between the modes of transportation?

2 What are the advantages of using public warehouses? Private warehouses?

3 What are the strengths and weaknesses of a just-in-time system?

Marketing Action Memo

HOW GENERAL MOTORS USES JUST-IN-TIME SYSTEMS

Just-in-time (JIT) inventory systems require reliable replenishment of supplies to prevent a production shutdown, since these systems run with very low inventories of raw materials and parts. Ideally, suppliers should be located near the production plant to improve the reliability of delivery.

General Motors (GM) requires overnight delivery to implement a JIT system at its Oldsmobile assembly plant in Lansing, Michigan. Various parts are consolidated in a shipment that comes from Kalamazoo, 118 miles away, and are delivered during the night for the next day's production. Thus Oldsmobile production at this facility can operate with only a day's inventory of those parts. What GM needs is reliable, overnight deliveries of these items at a reasonable cost. It found this in the form of Conrail's Minitrain, a shorter-than-normal train that makes no stops between Kalamazoo and Lansing. The Minitrain leaves Kalamazoo at 6 P.M. When the production workers arrive at the Lansing plant at 6 A.M. the next morning, the parts are in the factory and available for use that day.

In 1990 GM's Buick Le Sabre was the only U.S. car to place in the "top 10" in owner satisfaction based on problems owners reported in the first three months after purchase. At least part of the reason for the high quality is that the Buick Le Sabre plant shifted to a just-in-time system in 1985. GM sent evaluation teams to suppliers and placed orders with about 600 suppliers on how many parts to ship, at what time of day, and in what order, so they match needs of cars coming down the assembly line. About 80 suppliers have been dropped because they couldn't meet the exacting quality standards or on-time delivery goals. With sometimes only an hour's supply of some parts on hand, defects or late delivery can shut down the production line.

JIT savings can be tremendous: GM estimates that it saved $1 billion over a two-year period by reducing its average inventory by $30 billion.

Sources: Based on Wendy Zellner, "Buick City: The Factory That's Getting Things Right," *Business Week* (October 22, 1990), p. 87; Marybeth Pallas, "GM's Evaluation Procedure," *Harvard Business Review* (July–August, 1989), p. 130; "Freight Transportation: A Revitalized Industry Emerges," *Forbes* (August 1, 1983), pp. Ad1–12; Jeremy Main, "The Trouble with Managing Japanese Style," *Fortune* (April 2, 1984), pp. 50–56.

ETHICS AND SOCIAL RESPONSIBILITY IN THE 1990s

HOW DO NEW SUPPLIERS GET ORDERS FROM JIT MANUFACTURERS?

For decades American businesses operated on the principle of obtaining frequent competitive bids from several suppliers before awarding a contract to the lowest-price bidder that could meet the bid specifications. The rationale: the frequent continuing competition among bidders ensured low prices and high quality for the buyer.

JIT has changed much of that. Now long-term strategic alliances between a buyer and seller are designed to provide continuous supplies over extended periods of time—often months or years. This often restricts the ability of new small firms to compete effectively with existing suppliers for contracts awarded by JIT manufacturers.

What are the benefits and costs to society of such long-term alliances? What should a new small vendor do to be able to compete for contracts from JIT buyers?

SUMMARY

1 A comprehensive definition of physical distribution activities, called *business logistics,* includes both inbound and outbound activities.

2 The importance of logistical activities varies among firms. Production activities generally create a more complex system, as do the width of the product line and number of geographic markets served.

3 Although some marketers may pay little attention to logistics, they do so at their own peril. Logistics directly affects the success of the marketing program and all areas of the marketing mix.

4 The total cost concept suggests that a system of costs is present. The individual elements can be balanced against one another to minimize total costs.

5 Cost minimization is irrelevant without specifying an acceptable service level that must be maintained. The importance of customer service varies among industries, but many of them are becoming more aware of its importance.

6 Although key customer service factors depend on the service situation, important elements of the customer service program are likely to be time-related dependability, communications, and convenience.

7 The five modes of transportation (railroads, motor carriers, air carriers, pipelines, and water carriers) offer shippers different service benefits. Better service often costs more, although it may result in savings in other areas of the logistics system.

8 A variety of warehousing arrangements exists to serve various needs. Public warehouses are rented as needed, so they provide flexibility. Two important developments in private (owned) warehousing are the distribution center concept and automated warehousing.

9 Inventory management is critical, since too much inventory greatly increases costs and too little may result in stockouts. Various methods are available to manage inventory. A currently popular approach is the just-in-time concept, which attempts to minimize inventory in the system.

KEY TERMS AND CONCEPTS

physical distribution
  management p. 405
logistics management p. 405
total logistics cost p. 410
customer service p. 411
lead time p. 411
order cycle time p. 411

replenishment time p. 411
intermodal transportation p. 420
freight forwarders p. 420
public warehouses p. 421
distribution center p. 423
materials handling p. 424
just-in-time (JIT) concept p. 425

CHAPTER PROBLEMS AND APPLICATIONS

1 List several companies whose logistical activities are unimportant. Also list several whose focus is only on the inbound or outbound side.

2 Give an example of how logistical activities might affect trade promotion strategies.

3 What are some types of business in which order processing may be among the paramount success factors?

4 What behavioral problems might arise to negate the logistics concept within the firm?

5 What customer service factors would be vital to buyers in the following types of companies? *(a)* manufacturing, *(b)* retailing, *(c)* hospitals, and *(d)* construction.

6 Name come cases when extremely high service levels (for example, 99 percent) would be warranted.

7 What mode of transportation would be the best for the following products? *(a)* farm machinery, *(b)* liquid ammonia, *(c)* wheat, and *(d)* coal.

8 Assume you work for a Chicago firm expanding to California. You are uncertain whether to rent or buy needed warehouse space. You have a forecast you feel is reliable that indicates you will have enough sales volume to justify owning a warehouse. Make a list of *specific fixed* and *variable* costs that you will have to cover if you choose this option.

9 The auto industry is a heavy user of the just-in-time concept. Why? What other industries would be good candidates for its application? What do they have in common?

CHAPTER 16

Retailing

*A*fter reading this chapter you should be able to:

- Identify retailers in terms of the utilities they provide.
- Explain the alternative ways to classify retail outlets.
- Classify retailers in terms of the retail positioning matrix.
- Develop retailing mix strategies over the life cycle of a retail store.
- Explain the impact of computers on retail methods and store operations.

Want to See the Future of Retailing? Just Go to Bentonville, Arkansas!

Imagine investing $1,000 in a new company in 1970 and having that decision make you worth $500,000 today! Would you risk it on a company located in Bentonville, Arkansas? A company that said its strategy was to locate enormous discount stores in smaller-sized communities like Ocoee, Florida, Harrison, Arkansas, or Garland, Texas? Well, the insightful student of retailing may have decided to go along with Sam Walton, the founder of Wal-Mart Stores (see facing page). Wal-Mart has been designated as the retailer of the decade, and according to *Fortune* magazine, is one of America's most admired corporations. In 1989, Wal-Mart's continued success led to its reporting a $1 billion net income. The company started by Sam Walton in 1962 now operates over 1,300 Wal-Mart stores and adds 150 Wal-Mart outlets every year.

What is the secret of Wal-Mart's success? Sam's first rule is customer service. By satellite transmission he talks to all store managers and urges them to be aggressive with their hospitality. In addition, the stores are supported by an immense and sophisticated merchandising program. Its advanced computer system handles credit card transactions, inventory analysis, and distribution tracking. The company also operates 14 distribution centers, where it orders directly from manufacturers and operates its own fleet of trucks. Laser scanners move goods through miles of conveyor belts to the appropriate loading dock.

Ultimately, though, if you want the secret of Wal-Mart's success, you just might ask Sam Walton. He won't hide the truth—it's Wal-Mart's people and how they relate to their customers. Sam's plan for being the number one retailer is to get every employee to believe the Wal-Mart pledge: "From this day forward, I solemnly promise and declare that every customer that comes within 10 feet of me, I will smile, look them in the eye, and greet them, so help me, Sam."[1]

Retailing involves customer service, technology, effective merchandising, and is always very competitive. This chapter will begin to outline the variations and the range of decisions involved in this highly visible component of the marketing distribution channel.

Where do your customers shop? If you're selling books, cosmetics, or auto accessories, what retail outlet should you use? If you're thinking of opening a store, what type should it be? How much will you charge for the record albums you plan to sell? These are difficult and important questions that are an integral part of retailing. In the channel of distribution, retailing is where the customer meets the product. It is through retailing that exchange (a central aspect of marketing) occurs. **Retailing** includes all activities involved in selling, renting, and providing services to ultimate customers for personal, nonbusiness use.

SELLING SOAP THE HIGH-TECH WAY

SCANNERS TRACK SUDSY SALES AND MONITOR THE SUPPLY ON THE SHELVES.

STORES BEAM ORDERS VIA SATELLITE TO AN IBM COMPUTER AT HEADQUARTERS.

SUDSY INC. SCHEDULES SHIPPING TO SATISFY WAL-MART'S NEEDS.

CARTONS OF SUDSY MOVE ON CONVEYORS INTO ONE OF WAL-MART'S 6,537 TRUCKS.

WITHIN 36 HOURS OF THE STORE'S ORDER, THE NEW SUDSY GOES ON SALE.

WAL-MART USES ITS SATELLITE TO TELL MANAGERS ABOUT A DISCOUNT ON SUDSY.

Source: John Huey, "Will Wal-Mart Take Over the World," *Fortune* (January 30, 1989), p. 54.

THE VALUE OF RETAILING

Retailing is an important marketing activity. Not only do producers and consumers meet in a retailing outlet, but retailing also provides multiple values to the consumer and the economy as a whole. To consumers, these values are in the form of services provided, or utilities. Retailing's economic value is represented by the people employed in retailing, as well as by the total amount of money exchanged in retail sales.

CONSUMER UTILITIES OFFERED BY RETAILING

The utilities provided by intermediaries are of major value to retailers. Time, place, possession, and form utilities are offered by most retailers in varying degrees, but one utility is often stressed more than others. Look at Figure 16–1 to see how well you can match the retailer with the utility being stressed in the description.

FIGURE 16–1
Which company best represents which utilities?

Amway	Since 1959, Amway has grown to 750,000 representatives who sell soap and related products. Although relatively new, Amway alone accounts for about one sixth of all direct sales in the United States. Amway products are not sold in stores.
Staples	Begun in 1986, these stores carry over 5,000 office product items in a warehouse-type setting. Customers stroll down aisles with grocery carts picking up pens, paper, fax machines, or even office furniture. Almost anything needed to set up an office can be found at Staples, for 20 percent to 75 percent off of manufacturers' suggested prices. Staples gives club members a deeper discount on selected items. The stores accept cash or credit cards.
Legal Sea Foods	Opened in the 1970s with one restaurant, Legal Sea Foods now has four locations. Known for high-quality, fresh fish, Legal's has become a popular Boston eating establishment. It will also sell you fresh, uncooked fish. The staff will cut, fillet, or trim anything from octopus to shark to meet your needs.
Toys "R" Us	A distinctive toy store with a backwards *R*, this company is what every kid dreams about. Walking into a Toys "R" Us store is like living under the Christmas tree. Unlike most stores, which reduce their space allotted to toys after the Christmas season, everything is always available at Toys "R" Us.

MATCH THEM UP

Time	Place	Possession	Form
___	___	___	___

Marketing Research Report

BROWSERS: ARE THEY REALLY IMPORTANT TO RETAILERS?

Two of the overlooked utilities of retailing are entertainment and recreation. Many consumers go to stores just to relax. Coupled with these utilities, retail outlets also provide information utility, since stores assist people in learning about new products. But are the people who browse through stores different from those who don't? Also, are browsers important to retailers? Are they more interested in the products they look at than nonbrowsers? Do they have more information about products than nonbrowsers? Are they opinion leaders for other potential buyers?

To answer these questions, Professors Peter Bloch, Nancy Ridgeway, and Daniel L. Sherrell conducted a study. They surveyed 712 people about their browsing behavior, by asking people to report how often they visited clothing and computer stores just to look around, rather than to make a purchase. From these data, the professors classified people as either heavy browsers (who go to a store more than once a month just to look), light browsers (who go once a month or less to look), and nonbrowsers.

Do these three types of people differ? The table shows the results for browsers of clothing and computers. Mean scores are shown on three measures—involvement, knowledge, and opinion leadership. The higher the mean score, the more involvement, knowledge, or opinion leadership is expressed by that group. The results show that nonbrowsers were least involved in the product,

Mean scores of browser segments on scales

CLOTHING	NON-BROWSERS	LIGHT BROWSERS	HEAVY BROWSERS
Involvement	3.56	5.46	6.89
Product knowledge	5.08	6.80	7.66
Opinion leadership	2.64	3.43	3.85
COMPUTERS			
Involvement	4.11	6.95	8.00
Product knowledge	4.63	7.62	8.88
Opinion leadership	2.48	3.86	4.44

least knowledgeable, and least likely to serve as opinion leaders for others. Heavy browsers were the most involved, knowledgeable, and likely to be opinion leaders. These findings were true for both clothing and computer stores.

As a retailer, it is important to recognize that the person in the store who is "just looking" may be valuable. This person considers the products to be important, is seeking information about them, and may ultimately influence others about what to buy and where. From the survey's results, it is clear that the two overlooked utilities of entertainment and information are important to successful retailing.

Source: Peter Bloch, Nancy Ridgeway, and Daniel L. Sherrell, "Extending the Concept of Shopping: An Investigation of Browsing Activity," *Journal of the Academy of Marketing Science* (Winter 1989), pp. 13–22. Copyright The Academy of Marketing Science.

Having 750,000 representatives, as Amway does, puts the company's products close to the consumer-place utility. Taking cash, credit cards, and giving member discounts (i.e., making an item easy to purchase) is all part of the possession utility as offered by Staples. Form utility, production or alteration of a product, is offered by Legal Sea Foods as it cuts and fillets a shark to the customer's specifications. Finding toy shelves stocked in May is the time utility dreamed about by every child who enters Toys "R" Us.

Shopping malls sponsor antique shows, and department stores often offer guest speakers or fashion shows, both of which provide entertainment to pro-

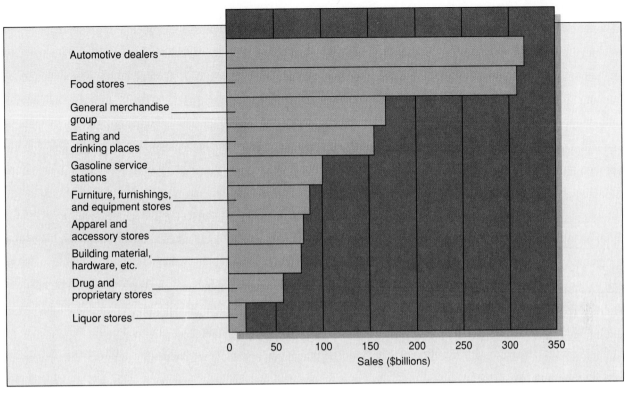

Automotive dealers

Food stores

General merchandise group

Eating and drinking places

Gasoline service stations

Furniture, furnishings, and equipment stores

Apparel and accessory stores

Building material, hardware, etc.

Drug and proprietary stores

Liquor stores

0   50   100   150   200   250   300   350

Sales ($billions)

FIGURE 16–2
Retail sales, by type of business

spective customers. Many consumers find shopping a wonderful form of recreation and entertainment that is composed of several of the four basic utilities. The accompanying Marketing Research Report describes three segments: those that browse (heavy and light), those that don't, and how they differ.

As we discuss retailing, consider the importance of browsers, particularly the heavy segment. These people are far more involved with products, and as extremely knowledgeable consumers, they are important people for others to turn to for information. Put heavy browsers in Wal-Mart's clothing department and they might never go home.

THE ECONOMIC IMPACT OF RETAILING

Retailing provides values to the individual consumer and is important to the economy as a whole. The 50 largest retailers in the United States account for $325 billion of sales and employ over 3.76 million people.[2] Food stores, automobile dealers, and general merchandise outlets such as department stores are significant contributors to the U.S. economy (Figure 16–2).

The magnitude of retailing sales is hard to imagine; the sales of the five largest retailing chains in the United States are more than many countries' gross national product (GNP). Sears's $50 billion of sales in 1988 far surpassed the GNP of Egypt for that same year, and Safeway, K mart, and J. C. Penney have sales in excess of the GNPs of both the Sudan and Burma (Figure 16–3).

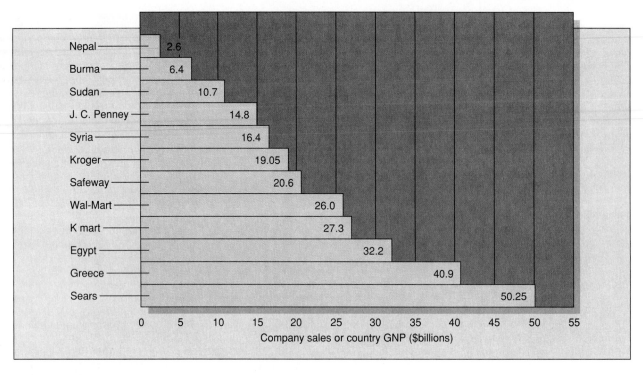

FIGURE 16–3
Republic of K mart?

1 When an Amway sales representative brings products into a potential buyer's home, what utility is provided?

2 Two measures of the importance of retailing in the American economy are _____ and _____ .

CLASSIFYING RETAIL OUTLETS

For manufacturers, consumers, and the economy, retailing is an important component of marketing that has several variations. Because of the wide number of alternative forms of retailing, it is easier to understand the differences among retail institutions by recognizing that outlets can be classified in several ways:

- **Form of ownership:** Who owns the outlet.
- **Level of service:** The degree of service provided to the customer.
- **Merchandise line:** How many different types of products a store carries and in what assortment.
- **Method of operation:** The manner in which services are provided—how and where the customer purchases products.

Within each method of classification there are several alternative types of outlets, as shown in Figure 16–4 and explained in the following pages.

METHOD OF CLASSIFICATION	DESCRIPTION OF RETAIL OUTLET
Form of ownership	Independent retailer
	Corporate chain
	Contractual system
	Retailer-sponsored cooperative
	Wholesaler-sponsored voluntary chain
	Franchise
Level of service	Self-service
	Limited service
	Full service
Merchandise line	Depth
	Single line
	Limited line
	Breadth
	General merchandise
	Scrambled merchandising
Method of operation	Store retailing
	Nonstore
	Direct marketing
	In-home retailing

FIGURE 16–4
Classifying retail outlets

FORM OF OWNERSHIP

Independent Retailer   One of the most common forms of retail ownership is the independent business, owned by an individual. The neighborhood dry cleaner or florist is often an independent retailer. The advantage of this form of ownership for the owner is that he or she can be his or her own boss. For customers the independent store often provides a high level of personal service.

Corporate Chain   A second form of ownership, the corporate chain, involves multiple outlets under common ownership. If you've ever shopped at Marshall's, Meldisco, CVS, Freddy's, Kay-Bee Toys, or Linens 'n Things, you've shopped at a chain outlet owned by the Melville Corporation.

In a chain operation, centralization in decision making and purchasing is common. Chain stores have advantages in dealing with manufacturers, particularly as the size of the chain grows. A large chain can bargain with a manufacturer to obtain good service or volume discounts on orders. Sears's large volume makes it a strong negotiator with manufacturers of most products. The power of chains is seen in the retailing of computers: small independents buy at 75 percent of list price, but large chains such as ComputerLand pay only 60 to 65 percent of list price.[3] Consumers also benefit in dealing with chains because there are consistent merchandise and policies, as well as multiple outlets.

During the 1980s many corporate chains restructured (as discussed in Chapter 3), and the financial health of many of these retailers is now in doubt. Federated-Allied and R. H. Macy are two chains struggling for survival, and Sears has laid off over 20,000 workers in an attempt to keep its chain alive.[4]

Contractual System Contractual systems involve independently owned stores that band together to act like a chain. The three kinds described in Chapter 14 are retailer-sponsored cooperatives, wholesaler-sponsored voluntary chains, and franchises. One retailer-sponsored cooperative is the Associated Grocers, which consists of neighborhood grocers that all agree with several other independent grocers to buy their meat from the same wholesaler. In this way, members can take advantage of volume discounts commonly available to chains and also give the impression of being a large chain, which may be viewed more favorably by some consumers. Wholesaler-sponsored voluntary chains such as Western Auto and Independent Grocers' Alliance (IGA) try to achieve similar benefits.

As noted in Chapter 14, in a franchise system an individual or firm (the franchisee) contracts with a parent company (the franchisor) to set up a business or retail outlet. McDonald's, Car-X, and Holiday Inn all involve some level of franchising. The franchisor usually assists in setting up the store, selecting the store location, advertising, and training personnel. The franchisee pays a yearly fee, usually tied to the store's sales. Although this might be seen as a relatively new phenomenon, this ownership approach has been used with gas stations since the early 1900s. Franchising is attractive because of the opportunity for people to enter a well-known, established business where managerial advice is provided. Also, the franchise fee may be less than the cost of setting up an independent business.

License fees paid to the franchisor can range from as little as $7,000 for a "Five-Minute Oil Change" business to $750,000 for an A&W fast-food restaurant.[5] Figure 16–5 shows some of the businesses that can be entered through a franchise, along with the costs of becoming a franchisee.

For the organization deciding to franchise, the trade-off is the advantage of reduced expenses to expand but the loss of some control. A good franchisor

FIGURE 16–5
The possibilities and costs of franchising

FRANCHISE	LINE OF BUSINESS	TOTAL START-UP COST
Almost Heaven Hot Tubs	Makers of hot tubs, saunas, and whirlpools	$5,000
Merry Maids, Inc.	Home cleaning service	$28,500–$33,500
ChemLawn Services	Lawn maintenance	$30,000
White Hen Pantry, Inc.	Neighborhood convenience stores	$41,300–$48,000
TCBY—The Country's Best Yogurt	Retail yogurt/desserts shops	$90,000
Putt-Putt Golf Courses of America	Miniature golf courses	$25,000–$125,000
Days Inn of America	Hotels/motels	$600,000
Benihana of Tokyo, Inc.	Japanese steak house	$1,000,000
Jazzercise	Fitness	$2,000–$3,000

Source: "10 Top Franchises for the 1990s," *Money Magazine* (Fall 1990), p. 40; Bill Kelley, "The Franchise Option," *Sales & Marketing Management* (January 1990), pp. 38–42; and *1989 Directory of Franchising Organizations* (Babylon, N.Y.: Pilot Books, 1989).

has strong control of the outlets in terms of delivery and presentation of merchandise.

There are three trends evident in franchising today. One trend involves the tightening of franchise contracts. This occurs because franchising has existed for several years. Older franchise organizations like Kentucky Fried Chicken, Marriott, and Holiday Inn initially grew via attracting franchisees by offering relatively loose constraints. As these chains have matured the companies are trying to tighten their control, which is leading to channel conflict and often lawsuits between the franchisors and their franchisees. Also, many franchisees are now suing their franchisors for changing policies during the period of the contract or for lack of sufficient franchisor support.[6] A second trend is called **piggyback franchising,** where stores operated by one chain sell the products of another franchised firm. For example, Dairy Queens sell the products of Mr. Donut. With the changes in Europe (as discussed in Chapter 3), a third trend in franchising is occurring—more companies are looking to Eastern Europe for new franchise opportunities. Zenox Corporation in Atlanta is franchising Payless Rent-a-Car systems and Mr. Donut shops in Hungary and the Soviet Union. This possibility became obvious to many organizations after McDonald's opened its first restaurant in the Soviet Union in January 1990.[7]

LEVEL OF SERVICE

Even though most customers perceive little variation in retail outlets by form of ownership, differences among retailers are more obvious in terms of level of service. In some department stores, such as Loehman's, individual dressing room stalls are not provided. Rather, all the women try on clothes in a large, enclosed area. Some grocery stores, such as the Cub chain, have customers individually mark the price on their purchases and bag the food in sacks brought from home. Other outlets, such as Ayers in Cincinnati, provide a wide range of customer services from gift wrapping to wardrobe consultation.

Self-Service   Self-service is at the extreme end of the level of service continuum, because the customer performs many functions and little is provided by the outlet. Home building supply outlets, discount stores, and catalog showrooms

McDonald's is one of many franchising operations to take advantage of new operations in eastern Europe and the Soviet Union.

are often self-service. Warehouse stores, usually in buildings several times larger than a conventional store, are self-service with all nonessential customer services eliminated. Levitz furniture stores, Big E food stores in Indiana, and Hinky Dinky in Nebraska, Missouri, and Texas are examples of the no-frills, self-service approach.

Limited Service   Limited-service outlets provide some services, such as credit, merchandise return, and telephone ordering, but not others, such as custom making of clothes. Department stores typically are considered limited-service outlets.

Full Service   The full-service retailer provides a complete list of services to cater to its customer. Specialty stores are among the few stores in this category. Nordstrom's, a Seattle-based retail chain, has set the standard for full service among department stores. The store typically has 50 percent more salespeople on the floor than similar-sized stores. Salespeople often write customers thank-you notes, or deliver purchases to customers' homes. In most stores, customers are serenaded by the sounds of a grand piano.[8]

MERCHANDISE LINE

Retail outlets also vary by their merchandise lines, the key distinction being the breadth and depth of the items offered to customers (Figure 16–6). **Breadth of product line** refers to the variety of different items a store carries. **Depth of product line** means that the store carries a large assortment of each item, such as a shoe store that offers running shoes, dress shoes, and children's shoes.

Depth of Line   Stores that carry a considerable assortment (depth) of a related line of items are limited-line stores. Herman's sporting goods stores carry considerable depth in sports equipment ranging from weight lifting accessories to running shoes. Stores that carry tremendous depth in one primary line of merchandise are single-line stores. Victoria's Secret, a nationwide chain, carries great depth in women's lingerie. Both limited- and single-line stores are often referred to as *specialty outlets.*

FIGURE 16–6
Breadth versus depth of merchandise lines

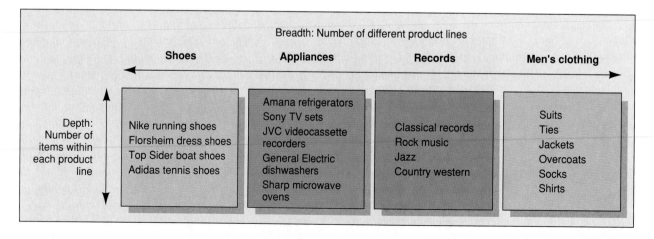

Breadth of Line   Stores that carry a broad product line, with limited depth, are referred to as *general merchandise stores.* For example, a large department store carries a wide range of different types of products, but not unusual sizes. The breadth and depth of merchandise lines are important decisions for a retailer. Traditionally, outlets carried related lines of goods. Today, however, **scrambled merchandising,** offering several unrelated product lines in a single store, is common. The modern drugstore carries food, camera equipment, magazines, paper products, toys, small hardware items, and pharmaceuticals. Department stores repair automobiles, provide travel planning services, and sell insurance.

A major new form of scrambled merchandising in the United States opened in Dallas, Texas, on December 28, 1987, when the Wal-Mart chain opened its first Hypermarket U.S.A. Showing strong sales, the company quickly followed with a second in January 1988, in Topeka, Kansas, and a third in Washington, Missouri, not far from St. Louis. A French firm, Carrefour, operates 115 of these stores in France, Spain, Brazil, and Argentina. In February 1988, they opened their first store in the United States, in Philadelphia. Salesclerks roller skate down 12-foot wide aisles to help customers, and they direct buyers to one of 61 checkout lanes.[9]

Such **hypermarkets** are defined as large stores (over 100,000 square feet), offering a mix of 40 percent food products, and 60 percent general merchandise. Prices are typically 5 to 20 percent below discount stores. Most stores are so large that they could contain a baseball field, a basketball court, an Olympic-sized swimming pool, three tennis courts, and a par three golf course. Stores typically stock up to 50,000 items.[10] Figure 16–7 shows the layout of Hypermarket U.S.A., which has 50 checkout lanes within 220,000 square feet of selling space. The size of this store has caused problems for both companies and consumers. Parent companies, like Wal-Mart, have had problems finding land big enough to build such a facility in some metropolitan areas, and consumers often report that the size of the store makes shopping difficult. As a result, Wal-Mart has decided future hypermarkets will be 150,000 square feet.[11]

Scrambled merchandising is convenient for consumers because it eliminates the number of stops required in a shopping trip. However, for the retailer this merchandising policy means there is competition between very dissimilar types of retail outlets, or **intertype competition.** A local bakery may compete with a department store, discount outlet, or even a local gas station. Scrambled merchandising and intertype competition make it more difficult to be a retailer.

Counter to the trend of scrambled merchandising is the **specialty discount outlet** which focuses on one area of product, like electronics (Highland stores), business supplies (Staples), or party goods (Streamers). These outlets are referred to in the trade as *category killers.* They offer large selections in a narrow range of products at very competitive prices.[12]

METHOD OF OPERATION

Retail outlets have begun to vary widely in the way their services are provided, or the method of operation. Throughout this discussion, we have talked in terms of retail outlets, rather than stores. Classifying retail outlets by method of operation means dividing these outlets into store and nonstore retailing.

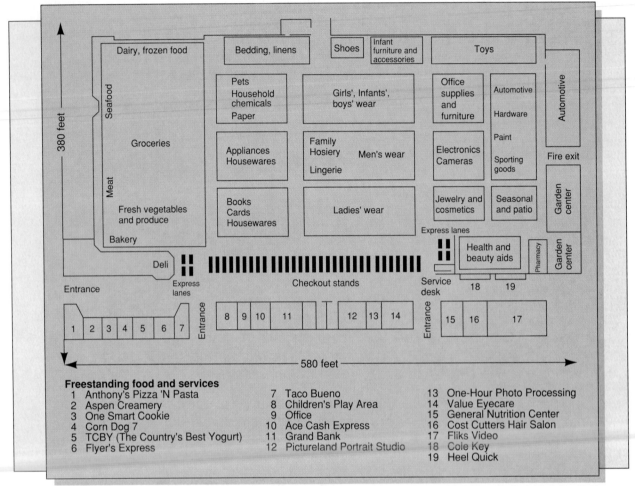

FIGURE 16–7
Layout of Hypermarket U.S.A.

Source: Redrawn from "Wal-Mart Launches Hypermarket U.S.A." By permission from *Discount Store News* (January 18, 1988), p. 11. Copyright Lebhar-Freidman, Inc.

Store Retailing   Traditionally, retailing meant the consumer went to the store and purchased a product—which is store retailing. Most of the retailing examples discussed earlier in the chapter, such as corporate chains, department stores, and limited- and single-line specialty stores, involve store retailing.

Nonstore Retailing   Viewing retailing as an activity limited to sales in a store is too narrow an approach. Nonstore retailing occurs outside a retail outlet, such as through direct marketing, described in Chapter 14 (mail order, vending machines, computer, and teleshopping), and in-home retailing.

Few areas of retailing have grown as rapidly during the past decade as mail-order retailing. During the late 1980s, catalog sales grew 10 percent per year. The number of people shopping by catalog grew by over 50 percent during the 1980s, with over 12.4 million catalogs mailed in 1988 alone.[13] Today, the average household receives about 50 catalogs per year.[14]

Mail-order retailing is attractive because it eliminates the cost of a store and clerks. American Express, which has no store, offers a 50-page Christmas cat-

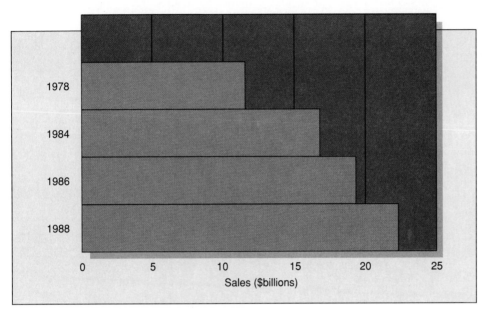

Growing vending sales

Source: Data from "Vending Industry," *Vending Times* Industry Issue (1989), p. 12.

alog with gifts ranging from fur coats to Nautilus fitness equipment. American Express is now one of the nation's largest retailers of fur coats.

As the growth in mail-order retailing slows, two trends are emerging in the industry. One approach is that of specialization or niche catalogs, which focus on a very narrow line of products. L. L. Bean, a long-standing mail-order retailer, has developed individual catalogs for fly fishing devotees and hunters. Lands' End, a very successful mail-order retailer, continually develops new approaches as it looks for new market niches. (The accompanying Marketing Action Memo profiles this company.) Art of Collecting sells paperweights, while Garnet Hills promotes mostly blankets. The second trend involves selling through or opening retail stores. The Sharper Image, a mail-order retailer of high-tech gadgets, has now opened over 60 stores in cities like San Francisco and Boston. Williams-Sonoma now sells its cookware through selected retailers.[15]

There are threats to the continued success of many mail-order retailers. One concern is market saturation—the number of new catalogs has grown by over 16 percent a year the past few years. Second, in 1991 the U.S. Postal Service rate increase raised the cost of third-class mail an average of 17 percent, which reduced the profits of this form of retailing.[16]

Direct marketing also encompasses vending machines, which make it possible to serve customers when and where stores cannot. Maintenance and operating costs are high, so product prices in vending machines tend to be higher than those in stores. Typically, small convenience products are available in vending machines. Two trends, however, signal likely continued growth for vending sales. First, improved technology will soon allow vending machines to accept credit cards. This change will permit more expensive items to be sold through this form of retailing.[17] Second, there is a movement toward smaller vending units that can be installed in the workplace. Coca-Cola has developed a small

Marketing Action Memo

NO END IN SIGHT FOR LANDS' END!

How often have you looked forward to receiving one of those fifty catalogs mentioned in the text? Often the response is one of boredom. Not so when the catalog is Lands' End. Often between the pages touting pinpoint weave shirts or soft Egyptian cotton, a browser comes across the story of Peruvian culture, or an expedition through the Sahara desert. These exotic tidbits are all part of the image of the Lands' End buyer: going to extremes to find the best garments and the highest quality.

Lands' End, of Dodgeville, Wisconsin, is one of the most successful mail-order retailers in the United States, not only by virtue of its far-flung buyers. "Everything we do is geared to the principle of customer service," says Gary Comer, founder of Lands' End. To that end, the company pioneered the use of toll-free telephone numbers and emphasizes quick response times both for its sales personnel and order fulfillment. Ninety percent of all orders are filled within 24 hours, and are backed by a customer service guarantee. In fact, in terms of convenience and response time, the company likes to think of itself as a "direct merchant," a store with no crowds.

Successful marketing involves understanding consumers, and this has been a rule of Lands' End. Each month all customer comments are printed out for managers to review. And customer requests are not taken lightly. Lands' End responded to customer demands with a new line of children's clothes that produced $15 million in sales.

While sales grew 20 percent in 1989, Lands' End is striving to stay ahead of the competition by responding to changing consumer tastes with more stylish looks and bolder prints. But the changes are

not all that keep Lands' End ahead of the pack. The company also goes to great lengths to maintain their brand identity of quality. Before offering a rugby style shirt in their catalog, they tested the product with the University of Chicago rugby team. The item was returned to the supplier twice before the quality met Lands' End standards.

The next time you need an Egyptian cloth shirt or a sweater made of 14-ounce cotton, call Lands' End. The phone will always be answered in three rings.

Sources: Francine Schwadel, "Lands' End Stumbles as Fashion Shifts Away from Retailer's Traditional Fare," *The Wall Street Journal* (April 27, 1990), pp. B1, B8; "Lands' End Looks a Bit Frayed at the Edges," *Business Week* (March 19, 1990), p. 42; "A Mail-Order Romance: Lands' End Courts Unseen Customers," *Fortune* (March 13, 1989), pp. 44–45; and Ronit Addis, "Big Picture Strategy," *Forbes* (January 9, 1989), pp. 70–72.

desk-top vending unit, called the BreakMate postmix vendor, aimed at the 2 million plus small offices market in the United States, while Pepsi-Cola has their own version, the Compact Vendor.[18]

Computer-assisted retailing allows customers to view products on their TV screen or computer monitor and then order the desired item from their terminal. Several companies have entered this form of retailing in recent years.

There's nothing new about having everything you need in one place.

With CompuServe, it's all at your fingertips.

Modems allow computer users access to many types of information and services.

The largest are CompuServe, Prodigy, and Genie. For an annual fee (such as Genie's $29.95) these companies provide customers access to a computerized databank of products. Prodigy, for example, has merchandise from stores like J. C. Penney, K mart, Lechmere, and manufacturers like Levi Strauss, Rubbermaid, and Fuji. Travel reservations, stock transactions, and encyclopedia searches can also be made via this system.[19] Prodigy charges retailers up to $25,000 to sign up on the service, and there is an ongoing fee of approximately one third of the retailer's gross margin.[20]

In early 1990, there were 1.5 million subscribers to the interactive computer shopping services. A recent study by Frost & Sullivan predicts these systems will have 8.1 million users by 1994, but success hasn't come easily. Early companies like Knight-Ridder lost $40 million in attempting to make these systems work. A major obstacle has been the equipment needed to use such shopping services. A computer, a modem for communication over telephone lines, and graphics capability for displaying items on the computer monitor are required. The continued growth in home computer ownership is making the forecast for this form of retailing more optimistic. As a result, in September 1990 Prodigy announced a nationwide rollout of its services.[21]

A fourth form of direct marketing is television home shopping (teleshopping). In 1990 television shopping sales totaled $1 billion. Unlike interactive computer shopping, the consumer sits at home and tunes into a television show on which products are displayed. This form of nonstore shopping experienced rapid growth from mid-1985 to 1987, but during 1988 it entered a more mature phase and several home shopping networks, such as the Consumer Discount Network, Shoppers University, The Home Shopping Game Show, and Value Television, went off the air.

The limitation of teleshopping is the lack of buyer–seller interaction and the fact that consumers cannot control the items they see. But with fiber optics allowing homes to be wired for interactive video to allow direct ordering, and the development of high-definition television, home shopping may grow even faster in the 1990s.[22]

CONCEPT CHECK

1 Centralized decision making and purchasing are an advantage of _____ ownership.

2 Would a shop for big men's clothes carrying size 40 to 60 pants have a broad or deep product line?

3 What are some examples of direct marketing?

RETAILING STRATEGY

This section identifies how a retail store positions itself and three areas where it can take actions to establish or alter that position: (1) retail pricing, (2) store location, or (3) image and atmosphere.

POSITIONING A RETAIL STORE

The four classification alternatives presented in the previous section help determine one store's position relative to its competitors.

Retail Positioning Matrix   The **retail positioning matrix** is a matrix developed by the MAC Group, Inc., a management consulting firm.[23] This matrix positions retail outlets on two dimensions: breadth of product line and value added. As defined previously, breadth of product line is the range of products sold through each outlet. The second dimension, *value added,* involves the service level and method of operation, which includes elements such as location (as with 7-Eleven stores), consistent product (as with Holiday Inn or McDonald's), or a prestigious image (as with Saks Fifth Avenue or Brooks Brothers).

The retail positioning map in Figure 16–8 shows four possible positions. An organization can be successful in any box, but unique strategies are required within each quadrant. Consider the four stores shown in the map:

1 Bloomingdale's has high value added and a broad product line. Retailers in this quadrant pay great attention to store design and product lines. Merchandise often has a high margin of profit and is of high quality. The stores in this position typically provide high levels of service.

2 K mart has low value added and a broad line. K mart and similar firms typically trade a higher price for increased volume in sales. Retailers in this position focus on price with low service levels and an image of being a place for good buys.

3 Tiffany's has high value added and a narrow line. Retailers of this type typically sell a very restricted range of products that are of high status quality. Customers are also provided with high levels of service.

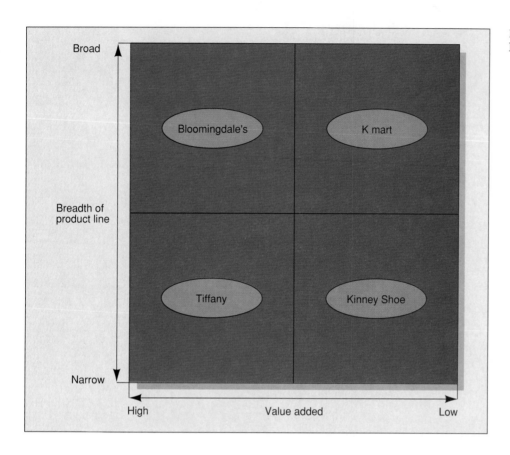

FIGURE 16–8
Retail positioning map

4 Kinney has low value added and a narrow line. Such retailers are specialty mass merchandisers. Kinney, for example, carries attractively priced shoes for the entire family. These outlets appeal to value-conscious consumers. Economies of scale are achieved through centralized advertising, merchandising, buying, and distribution. Stores are usually the same in design, layout, and merchandise; hence they are often referred to as "cookie-cutter" stores.

Keys to Positioning   To successfully position a store, it must have an identity that has some advantages over the competitors yet is recognized by consumers. A company can have outlets in several positions on the matrix, but this approach is usually done with different store names. Dayton-Hudson, for example, owns Dayton's, Diamonds, and Hudson's department stores (with high value added and a broad line) and Target and Lechemere discount stores (low value added and a broad line). Shifting from one box in the retail positioning map to another is also possible, but all elements of retailing strategy must be reexamined.

RETAILING MIX

In developing retailing strategy, managers work with the **retailing mix,** which includes the (1) goods and services, (2) physical distribution, and (3) communications tactics chosen by a store (Figure 16–9).[24] Decisions relating to the mix

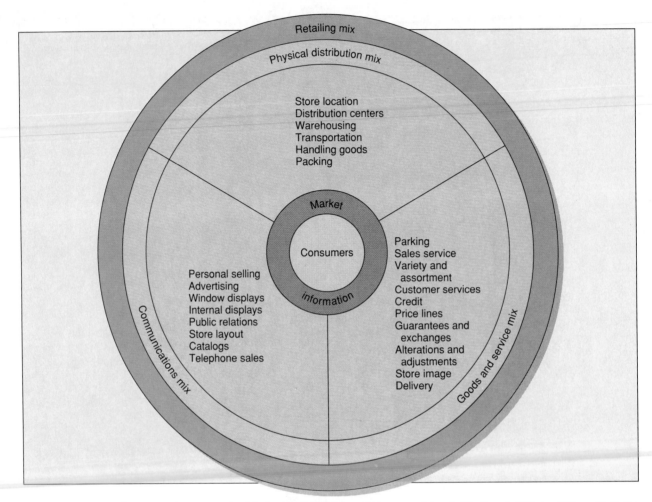

Source: Redrawn from William Lazer and Eugene J. Kelley, "The Retailing Mix: Planning and Management," *Journal of Retailing* vol. 37 (Spring 1961), pp. 34–41. By permission of The American Marketing Association.

FIGURE 16–9
The retailing mix

focus on the consumer. Each of the areas shown is important, but we will cover only three basic areas: (1) pricing, (2) store location, and (3) image and atmosphere. The communications and promotion components are discussed in Chapter 18 on advertising and Chapter 19 on personal selling.

Retail Pricing   In setting prices for merchandise, retailers must decide on the markup, markdown, and timing for markdowns. Off-price retailers are one type of outlet stressing low-price policies.

As mentioned in the appendix to Chapter 13, the *markup* refers to how much should be added to the cost the retailer paid for a product to reach the final selling price. Retailers decide on the *original markup,* but by the time the product is sold, they end up with a *maintained markup.* The original markup is the difference between retailer cost and initial selling price. When products do not sell as quickly as anticipated, their price is reduced. The difference between the final selling price and retailer cost is the maintained markup, which is also called the *gross margin.*

Discounting a product, or taking a *markdown,* occurs when the product does not sell at the original price and an adjustment is necessary. Often new models or styles force the price of existing models to be marked down. Remember the original Sony Walkman? It first sold in stores for $150. However, to meet competition, Sony developed new Walkman models. As demand for the original version dropped, retailers began to take markdowns. The original Walkman was being sold for less than $70 within eight months of its introduction.

Although most retailers plan markdowns, many retailers use price discounts as part of their regular merchandising policy. In the Northeast, Filene's basement stores are well-known outlets for out-of-season and slow-selling merchandise. Filene's has an automatic discount policy:

- Merchandise not sold after 12 selling days is reduced 25 percent.
- Merchandise not sold after 18 selling days is reduced 50 percent.
- Merchandise not sold after 24 selling days is reduced 75 percent.
- After 30 selling days merchandise is given to charity.

All items in Filene's basement stores are tagged with the initial date on which they were displayed. The automatic discount policy adjusts price as a function of demand. If you want that suit now discounted at 25 percent, will you risk waiting six more days to get it for 50 percent off?

A final issue, *timing,* involves deciding when to discount the merchandise. Many retailers take a markdown as soon as sales fall off to free up valuable selling space and cash. However, other stores delay markdowns to discourage bargain hunters and maintain an image of quality. There is no clear answer, but retailers must consider how the timing might affect future sales.

Off-Price Retailing   Off-price retailing is a growing trend in retail pricing that is most commonly found in clothing sales. **Off-price retailing** involves selling brand-name merchandise at lower than regular prices. In 1989, off-price sales accounted for 7.5 percent of all clothing sales.[25] Figure 16–10 shows the growth of off-price clothing retailers compared with other types of retail outlets.

Filene's has turned its original basement into an off-price, free-standing basement chain. Other off-price outlets familiar to women are Hit or Miss (The TJX Cos.) and Loehman's (Associated Dry Goods Corporation); men know Kuppenheimer Manufacturing Company (Hartmarx); kids have Kids "R" Us (Toys "R" Us Co.); and the general public has Marshall's (Melville Corporation) stores.

There is a difference between the off-price retailer and a discount store. Off-price merchandise is bought by the retailer at prices below wholesale prices, while the discounter buys at full wholesale price but takes less of a markup (compared with traditional department stores). Merchandise in off-price retailers turns over eight to ten times a year rather than the four times for the department store. Savings to the consumer at off-price retailers are reported as high as 70 percent off the prices of a traditional department store.

There are two growing variations of off-price retailing. One is the warehouse club (similar to hypermarkets). These large stores (over 100,000 square feet) began as rather stark outlets with no elaborate displays, customer service,

FIGURE 16–10
Retail sales trends

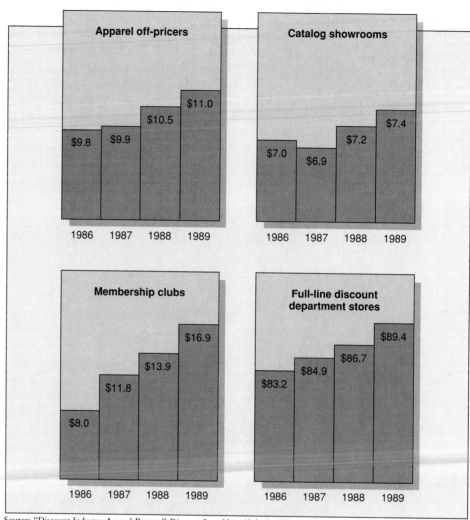

Source: "Discount Industry Annual Report," *Discount Store News* (July 3, 1989), p. 3.

or home delivery. They require a yearly membership fee (usually $25) for the privilege of shopping there. While a typical K mart stocks 100,000 items, warehouse clubs carry about 3,500 items and usually stock just one brand name of appliance or food product. Service is minimal, and customers pay by cash or check. However, the extremely competitive pricing of merchandise makes warehouse clubs attractive.[26] There are four major warehouse clubs in the United States, which account for 90 percent of the sales. These are Wal-Mart's Sam's Wholesale Clubs, K mart's Pace Membership Warehouse, Price Company's Price Club, and Costco Warehouse Club. Sales of these off-price retailers have grown dramatically, as shown in Figure 16–10, and are forecasted to rise to $28 billion in 1991 (compared to $1 billion in 1983).[27] One of the leading warehouse clubs, Sam's, has added more services to encourage more warehouse shoppers to visit the store.

A second trend is the "one-price" apparel chain. These outlets, such as Dre$$ to the Nine$ in Ft. Lauderdale or $5 Clothing Store in California and

Regional centers, or suburban malls, such as the new Mall of America, often consist of 100 or more stores anchored by one, two, or even four (as in this case) large national or regional retailers.

Nevada, sell everything in their store (usually women's apparel and accessories) for one price. These outlets have sprung up as many of the early off-price retailers have started to appeal to the more affluent shopper. The one-price outlet targets the lower- and middle-income, value-oriented consumer.[28]

Store Location   A second aspect of the retailing mix involves deciding where to locate the store and how many stores to have. Department stores, which started downtown in most cities, have followed customers to the suburbs, and in recent years more stores have been opened in large regional malls. Most stores today are near several others in one of five settings: the central business district, the regional center, the community shopping center, the strip, or the power center.

The **central business district** is the oldest retail setting, the community's downtown area. Until the regional outflow to suburbs, it was the major shopping area, but the suburban population has grown at the expense of the downtown shopping area. Detroit, experiencing a decade of population decline, lost its last major department store in 1982 when Hudson's left the central city.

Regional shopping centers are the suburban malls of today, containing up to 100 stores. The typical drawing distance of a regional center is over 5 to 10 miles from the mall. These large shopping areas often contain one or two *anchor stores,* which are well-known national or regional stores such as Sears, Saks Fifth Avenue, and Bloomingdale's. The largest variation of a regional center is the Mall of America being built in Bloomington, Minnesota. Scheduled to open in September 1992, the mall will contain four major department stores, 800 specialty stores, 100 nightclubs and restaurants, and a theme park based on the cartoon character Snoopy.[29]

A more limited approach to retail location is the **community shopping center,** which typically has one primary store (usually a department store branch) and often about 20 to 40 smaller outlets. Generally, these centers serve a population base of about 100,000.

Marketing Action Memo

ATMOSPHERE, IMAGE, MIX—YOU CAN GET IT ALL (OR RETURN IT) AT NORDSTROM'S

*T*he atmosphere and image of a store are important ingredients in its success. Many things are involved in creating the right image—personnel, return policies, and store layout are but a few. The best store in the United States for 1990 was Nordstrom's, winner of the National Retail Merchant's Association Gold Medal Award.

Nordstrom's is well known to consumers who live in the Western United States. The company was founded in 1901 by John W. Nordstrom, a Swedish immigrant who settled in Seattle. Today, Nordstrom's is a chain of over 50 stores in six states, and it has ambitious expansion plans for the 1990s. The store has been described as elevating customer service to an art form. Tales abound of the most liberal return policy in the industry. One of the more famous is of the salesperson who graciously took back a set of tires from an irate customer. Nothing unusual, you say. Possibly true, except Nordstrom's doesn't sell tires. One woman told of her recent experience in buying an expensive evening dress. When trying it on, she realized that she wasn't wearing the proper undergarment. No problem, the salesperson ran up to the store's next level to get her one. Then, the woman realized she didn't have the right color shoes. No problem, the salesperson ran down one level to get the color

needed. When the customer got the dress home, she found a flaw in it. "No problem," said the Nordstrom's salesperson, "Bring it back or take $100 off the price."

Customer service accounts for only part of Nordstrom's success. Store decor has lots of polished wood and marble rather than chrome or bright colors. Nordstrom's is also known for its great depth of merchandise. Apparel is generally available in every color and size offered by the manufacturer.

So the next time you're in Seattle or McLean, Virginia, stop in at Nordstrom's. Experience the retailer that moved Estee Lauder, the perfume and cosmetic maker, to call it ". . . the future of retailing." And don't be surprised if a few days later, you get a hand-written thank-you note from the salesperson who helped you. You, too, may soon sport a bumper sticker on your car that is commonly seen in Seattle, "I'd rather be shopping at Nordstrom's."

Sources: "Will 'The Nordstrom Way' Travel Well?" *Business Week* (September 3, 1990), pp. 82–83; Susan C. Faludi, "At Nordstrom, Customers Come First, But Sometimes at a Big Price," *The Wall Street Journal* (February 20, 1990), pp. A1, A16; Joan Bergman, "Nordstrom Gets the Gold," *Stores* (January 1990), pp. 44–67; "How Nordstrom Got There," *Stores* (January 1990), pp. 68–76; and Richard W. Stevenson, "Watch Out Macy's Here Comes Nordstrom," *New York Times Magazine* (August 27, 1989), pp. 34–40.

Not every suburban store is located in a shopping mall. Many neighborhoods have clusters of stores, referred to as a **strip location,** to serve people who are within a 5- to 10-minute drive and live in a population base of under 30,000. Gas station, hardware, laundry, and grocery outlets are commonly found in a strip location. Unlike the larger shopping centers, the composition of these stores is usually unplanned.

A new variation of the old strip shopping location is called the **power center,** which is a huge shopping strip with multiple anchor (or national) stores. Power centers are seen as having the convenient location found in many strip centers and the additional power of national stores. These large strips often have two to five anchor stores and often contain a supermarket, which brings the shopper to the power center on a weekly basis.[30]

Retail Image and Atmosphere   Deciding on the image of a retail outlet is an important retailing mix factor that has been widely recognized and studied since the late 1950s. Pierre Martineau described image as "the way in which the store is defined in the shopper's mind, partly by its functional qualities and partly by an aura of psychological attributes.[31] In this definition, *functional* refers to mix elements such as price ranges, store layouts, and breadth and depth of merchandise lines. The psychological attributes are the intangibles, such as a sense of belonging, excitement, style, or warmth. Image has been found to include a store's personnel, return policies, and cleanliness.[32] Few stores have succeeded better in terms of establishing a defined image and unique atmosphere than Nordstrom's. Read the accompanying Marketing Action Memo to learn why Nordstrom's is referred to as "the future of retailing."

In designing a store's image, retailers must consider the area in which they're located and the type of customers they attract. On Rodeo Drive in Beverly Hills, status is the image promoted by "bijan's," an exclusive men's clothing store. Entry to the store is by appointment only. The store only averages six customers a day, but the typical shopper spends several thousand dollars per visit. It's not difficult when silk ties are $175, cotton shirts $650, shoes $850, and suits start at $3,500. Price, appointments, and personal attention by Mr. Bijan give this store a distinct image.

Closely related to the concept of image is the store's atmosphere, or ambiance. Many retailers believe that sales are affected by layout, color, lighting, and music in the store, as well as by how crowded it is.

Hardware stores, for example, are attempting to shift from their earlier all-male image and meet the demands of a growing segment of female buyers. ServiStar in Virginia has redesigned its stores with bright lighting, chrome display gridwork, and wall murals.[33] In creating the right image and atmosphere, a retail store tries to identify its target audience and what the target audience seeks from the buying experience so its atmosphere will fortify the beliefs and the emotional reactions buyers are seeking.[34]

1 What are the two dimensions of the retail positioning map?

2 How does original markup differ from maintained markup?

3 An area with two anchor stores and up to 100 other stores is a _____ center.

THE CHANGING NATURE OF RETAILING

Retailing is the most dynamic aspect of the channel of distribution. Stores like bijan's or pricing approaches such as off-price retailing show that new retailers are always entering the market, searching for a new position that will attract customers. The reason for this continual change is explained by two concepts: the wheel of retailing and the retail life cycle.

THE WHEEL OF RETAILING

The **wheel of retailing** describes how new forms of retail outlets enter the market.[35] Usually they enter as low-status, low-margin stores such as a drive-in hamburger stand with no indoor seating and a limited menu (Figure 16–11, Box 1). Gradually these outlets add fixtures and more embellishments to their stores (in-store seating, plants, and chicken sandwiches as well as hamburgers)

FIGURE 16–11
The wheel of retailing

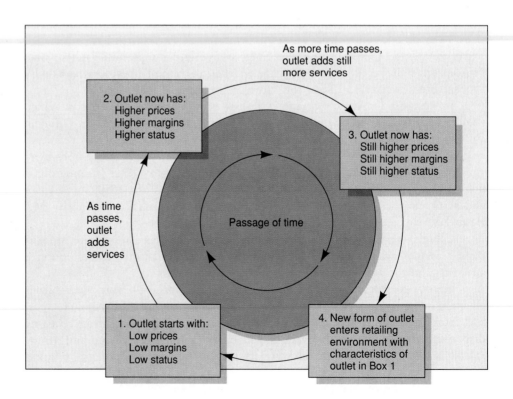

As more time passes, outlet adds still more services

2. Outlet now has:
Higher prices
Higher margins
Higher status

3. Outlet now has:
Still higher prices
Still higher margins
Still higher status

As time passes, outlet adds services

Passage of time

1. Outlet starts with:
Low prices
Low margins
Low status

4. New form of outlet enters retailing environment with characteristics of outlet in Box 1

to increase the attractiveness for customers. With these additions, prices and status rise (Box 2). As time passes, these outlets add still more services and their prices and status increase even further (Box 3). These retail outlets now face some new form of retail outlet that again appears as a low-status, low-margin operator (Box 4), and the wheel of retailing turns as the cycle starts to repeat itself.

In the 1950s, McDonald's and Burger King had very limited menus of hamburgers and french fries. Most stores had no inside seating for customers. Over time, the wheel of retailing for fast-food restaurants has turned. These chains have changed by altering their stores and expanding their menus. As the wheel turns today, McDonald's has expanded its menu into offering pizza.[36] For others, the wheel has come full circle. Hooker's Hamburgers in the South and Burger Street in Texas are very small, fast-food hamburger chains with a very limited menu. The stores can run with six employees, and only offer take-out service. The prices are about 80 cents lower than McDonald's for a burger, fries, and cola.[37]

Discount stores were a major new retailing form in the 1950s and priced their products below those of department stores. As prices in discount stores rose, in the 1970s they found themselves overpriced compared with a new form of retail outlet—the warehouse retailer.

THE RETAIL LIFE CYCLE

The process of growth and decline that retail outlets, like products, experience is described by the **retail life cycle**.[38] Figure 16–12 shows the retail life cycle and the position of various current forms of retail outlets on it. Early growth is the stage of emergence of a retail outlet, with a sharp departure from existing competition. Market share rises gradually, although profits may be low because of start-up costs. In the next stage, accelerated development, both market share and profit achieve their greatest growth rates. Usually multiple outlets are established as companies focus on the distribution element of the retailing mix. In this stage some later competitors may enter. Wendy's, for example, appeared on the hamburger chain scene almost 20 years after McDonald's had begun operation. The key goal for the retailer in this stage is to establish a dominant position in the fight for market share.

The battle for market share is usually fought before the maturity phase, and some competitors drop out of the market. In the wars among hamburger chains, Jack In The Box, Gino Marchetti's, and Burger Chef used to be more dominant outlets. New retail forms enter in the maturity phase, stores try to maintain their market share, and price discounting occurs. In the early 1990s, the major fast-food chains like Wendy's and McDonald's began to aggressively discount their prices. McDonald's began to offer a 99-cent Quarter Pounder (regularly a $1.90) in some cities, while Wendy's followed with a kid's Value Menu.[39]

The challenge facing retailers is to delay entering the decline stage in which market share and profit fall rapidly. Many retailers are looking to overseas markets for new growth opportunities to keep the life cycle alive. Tiffany's,

FIGURE 16–12
The retail life cycle

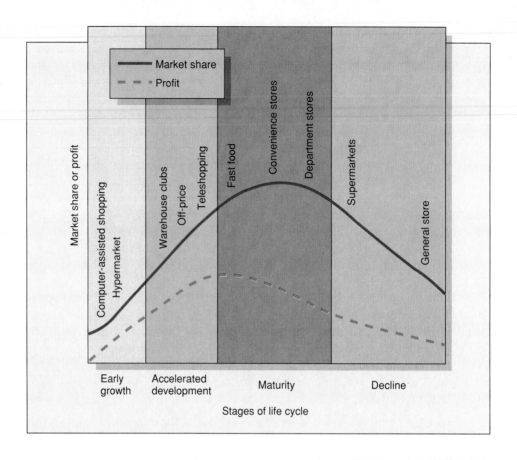

Toys "R" Us, and Barneys New York have all opened outlets in Japan to capitalize on the growing consumer boom in that country.[40]

Figure 16–13 shows how many of today's retail institutions evolved. It shows the difficult challenge facing today's retailers: the time to move from early growth to maturity is decreasing, so there is less time for a retail outlet to achieve profitability. Department stores took 100 years to reach maturity, whereas warehouse clubs are expected to reach maturity in five years. As a result, retailers must continually modify their mix to avoid early decline.

FUTURE CHALLENGES IN RETAILING

The challenges facing retailers come from many directions, including (1) the advent of computerization, (2) the cost of shrinkage, and (3) the retailing of services. Because services marketing has become a dominant trend in recent years, Chapter 23 covers this topic. The following sections address the former two issues.

COMPUTERIZATION OF THE RETAIL STORE

Computers are in use today in most medium-to-large stores in the form of computerized checkouts (or scanning systems) that read items being purchased. They are rapidly replacing traditional cash registers. One survey in 1989 found

INSTITUTIONAL TYPE	PERIOD OF FASTEST GROWTH	PERIOD FROM INCEPTION TO MATURITY (YEARS)	STAGE OF LIFE CYCLE	REPRESENTATIVE FIRMS★
General store	1800–1840	100	Declining	A local store
Single-line store	1820–1840	100	Mature	Hickory Farms
Department store	1860–1940	80	Mature	Marshall Field's
Variety store	1870–1930	50	Declining	Morgan-Lindsay
Corporate chain	1920–1930	50	Mature	Sears
Discount store	1955–1975	20	Mature	K mart
Conventional supermarket	1935–1965	35	Mature/declining	A&P
Shopping center	1950–1965	40	Mature	Paramus
Gasoline station	1930–1950	45	Mature	Texaco
Convenience store	1965–1975	20	Mature	7-Eleven
Home-improvement center	1965–1980	15	Late growth	Lowes
Super specialists	1975–1985	10	Late growth	The Limited
Warehouse clubs	1990–?	5 (projected)	Early growth	Price Club
Computer-assisted retailing	1990–?	7 (projected)	Early growth	Genie
Hypermarkets	1990–?	5 (projected)	Early growth	Wal-Mart

★These firms are representative of institutional types and are not necessarily in the stage of life cycle specified for the institutional group as a whole.

Source: Adapted from J. Barry Mason and Morris L. Mayer, *Modern Retailing: Theory and Practice,* 5th ed. (Homewood, Ill.: Business Publications/Richard D. Irwin, 1990), p. 25.

FIGURE 16–13
The evolution of today's retail institutions

that 77 percent of all medium-sized retailers ($50–$500 million in sales) and 82 percent of large retailers (over $500 million in sales) are committed to scanning technology. With the assistance of scanning technology, retailers can analyze the profitability of every shelf in the store week by week.[41]

To record the items being purchased, scanning systems use the **universal product code** (UPC), which is a number assigned to identify each product. It is represented by a series of bars with varying widths. The scanner converts this UPC symbol, identifies the product, and accesses the price stored in the firm's computer. Scanners provide retailers with savings through faster checkouts, fewer misrings, and better control of inventory.

Dillard's department stores built a centralized computer system that links 115 stores in 11 Midwestern and Southern states to track inventory. Consumers also benefit: speed, accuracy, and more courteous checkout clerks have been reported as advantages.[42] Studies have shown that the common uses for scanner data have been in five areas: monitoring current products, new product research, monitoring prices, studying the impact of coupons, and assessing advertising effectiveness.[43] Also, some supermarkets benefit by selling the scanner data on unit sales to firms manufacturing consumer products.

Technology will also affect retail operations in terms of ordering merchandise from suppliers. Two thirds of all retailers are expected to place orders and communicate with vendors through interactive computers called *electronic data interchange* (EDI) by 1991.[44] This interactive computer approach will allow retailers to make faster merchandising decisions in response to changing consumer buying preferences.

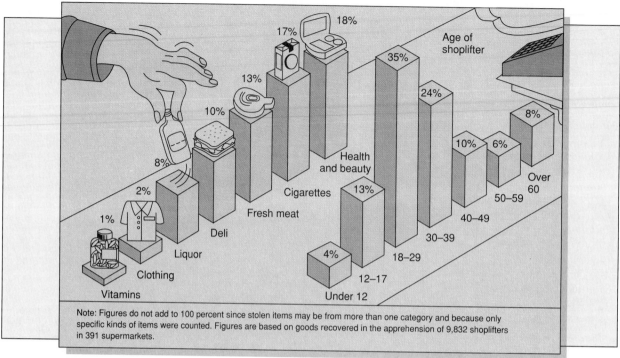

Note: Figures do not add to 100 percent since stolen items may be from more than one category and because only specific kinds of items were counted. Figures are based on goods recovered in the apprehension of 9,832 shoplifters in 391 supermarkets.

Source: *U.S. News & World Report* (March 13, 1989), p. 73.

FIGURE 16–14
Who takes what?

THE SHRINKAGE PROBLEM

A long-standing, growing problem in retailing is **shrinkage,** or theft of merchandise by customers and employees. Shrinkage now amounts to a $9 billion-a-year problem. In department stores shrinkage amounts to 2.07 percent of sales, followed by music and video stores (1.87 percent), convenience stores (1.60 percent), and college bookstores (.69 percent).[45] Figure 16–14 shows the most frequently stolen items from supermarkets and the ages of shoplifters.

Retailers have begun to use a variety of approaches to combat this problem. Locked cases, observation towers, two-way mirrors, and magnetic detectors on merchandise are a few of the approaches.[46] Lionel Kiddie City Toys, a 90-store chain, uses a complex television system to screen and track customers from entrance to exit. Some companies, like Best Products, a catalog showroom, offers cash rewards for inside tips that lead to the apprehension of a dishonest employee or shoplifter. These are but a few examples of how retailers are battling a significant problem that affects their profits and consumers' prices.

CONCEPT CHECK

1 According to the wheel of retailing, when a new retail form appears, how would you characterize its image?

2 Market share is usually fought out before the _____ stage of the retail life cycle.

3 What is shrinkage?

ETHICS AND SOCIAL RESPONSIBILITY IN THE 1990s

CONSUMER LARCENY: A NATIONAL PASTIME

Larceny, or the wrongful taking of another's goods, takes many forms—robbery, burglary, embezzlement, and shoplifting. It may surprise you to know that shoplifting is the fastest growing form of larceny. Retailers spend about $100 million each year to deter shoplifting. Nevertheless, retailer losses due to shoplifting continue to grow at a rate of 35 percent per year.

Listed below are three common kinds of shoplifting. How do you think students in a Marketing Principles course would rate each practice on a scale from 1 to 5 where 1 means never wrong and 5 means always wrong?

1 Eating food without paying for it in a supermarket: 1   2   3   4   5
2 Returning worn clothing to a store: 1   2   3   4   5
3 Taking store merchandise worth less than $20:   1   2   3   4   5

Source: Based on Francine Schwadel, "Chicago Retailers' 'Sting' Aims to Put Shoplifting Professionals Out of Business," *The Wall Street Journal* (June 5, 1990), pp. B1, B2; " 'Tis the Season for Taking," *Dallas Times Herald* (December 5, 1989), pp. B1, B9; and Catherine A. Cole, "Research Note: Deterrence and Consumer Fraud," *Journal of Retailing* (Spring 1989), pp. 107–120.

SUMMARY

1 Retailing provides a number of values to the consumer in the form of various utilities: time, place, possession, and form. Economically, retailing is important in terms of the people employed and sales represented.

2 Retailing outlets can be classified along several dimensions: the form of ownership, level of service, merchandise line, or method of operation.

3 There are several forms of ownership: independent, chain, trade cooperative, or franchise.

4 Stores vary in the level of service, being self-service, limited service, or full service.

5 In terms of method of operation, retailing includes store and direct marketing operations. Direct-mail retailers are now setting up store operations. Interactive computer buying services have had disappointing growth, whereas teleshopping has rapidly matured in the past few years.

6 Retail outlets vary in terms of the breadth and depth of their merchandise lines. Breadth refers to the number of different items carried, and depth refers to the assortment of each item offered. In assessing their competitive position, retail outlets should consider their position in terms of breadth of merchandise line and the amount of value added, which is the service level and method of operation.

7 Retailing strategy is based on the retailing mix, consisting of goods and services, physical distribution, and communications.

8 In retail pricing, retailers must decide on the markup, markdown, and timing for the markdown. A growing trend is off-price retailing, in which the retailer offers nonbrand merchandise at lower than regular prices. This retailing form is most common in the clothing industry.

9 Retail site location is an important retail mix decision. The common alternatives are the central business district, a regional shopping center, a community shopping center, or a strip location. A relatively new development is the power center, which is a strip location with multiple national anchor stores and a supermarket. These alternatives differ in terms of the distance from which they draw customers and the number and types of stores.

10 New retailing forms are explained by the wheel of retailing. Stores enter as low-status, low-margin outlets. Over time, they add services and raise margins, which allows a new form of low-status, low-margin retailing outlet to enter.

11 Like products, retail outlets have a life cycle consisting of four stages: early growth, accelerated development, maturity, and decline. Over the past 100 years the time it takes for each new retailing form to reach maturity has declined.

12 Computerized scanning systems are playing a major role in retail store operations. These scanners read the UPC symbol for each item and provide timely sales and inventory data. Computer interactive technology is also allowing for ongoing, immediate networking between retailers and their suppliers.

KEY TERMS AND CONCEPTS

retailing p. 432
form of ownership p. 436
level of service p. 436
merchandise line p. 436
method of operation p. 436
piggyback franchising p. 439
breadth of product line p. 440
depth of product line p. 440
scrambled merchandising p. 441
hypermarkets p. 441
intertype competition p. 441
specialty discount outlet p. 441

retail positioning matrix p. 446
retailing mix p. 447
off-price retailing p. 449
central business district p. 451
regional shopping centers p. 451
community shopping center p. 451
strip location p. 452
power center p. 452
wheel of retailing p. 454
retail life cycle p. 455
universal product code p. 457
shrinkage p. 458

CHAPTER PROBLEMS AND APPLICATIONS

1 In recent years in the United States, among more households both the husband and the wife are employed outside the home. Assuming that this trend continues, discuss the impact on (*a*) nonstore retailing and (*b*) the retail mix.

2 How does value added affect a store's competitive position?

3 In retail pricing, retailers often have a maintained markup. Explain how this maintained markup differs from original markup and why it is so important.

4 What are the similarities and differences between the product and retail life cycles?

5 How would you classify K mart in terms of its position on the wheel of retailing versus that of an off-price retailer?

6 Develop a chart to highlight the role of each of the three main elements of the retailing mix across the four stages of the retail life cycle.

7 In Figure 16–8 Kinney Shoes was placed on the retail positioning matrix. What strategies should Kinney follow to move itself into the same position as Tiffany?

8 Breadth and depth are two important components in distinguishing among types of retailers. Discuss the breadth and depth implications of the following retailers discussed in this chapter: (*a*) Wal-Mart, (*b*) Nordstrom's, (*c*) Lands' End, and (*d*) Staples.

9 According to the wheel of retailing and the retail life cycle, what will happen to off-price retailers?

10 The text discusses the development of teleshopping and computer-assisted retailing in the United States. How does the development of each of these retailing forms agree with the implications of the retail life cycle?

CHAPTER 17

Promotional Process, Sales Promotion, and Publicity

*A*fter reading this chapter you should be able to:

- Explain the communication process and its elements.
- Understand the promotional mix and the uniqueness of each component.
- Select the promotional approach appropriate to a product's life-cycle stage and characteristics.
- Differentiate between the advantages of push and pull strategies.
- Understand the alternative strengths and weaknesses of consumer-oriented and trade-oriented sales promotions.
- Appreciate the value of an integrated publicity approach.

Mass Marketing Isn't So Simple Anymore!

Business for mass marketers such as Procter and Gamble (P&G) used to be much simpler. Utilitarian products such as Crest, Tide, and Ivory were designed for a large, homogeneous market. Promotion techniques consisted of network television and radio advertising, as well as couponing. Distribution was through supermarkets, which had an abundance of shelf space.

Today, as the mass market fractures into smaller and smaller groups, new promotion techniques are being developed to help businesses become "micromarketers." For P&G, which spent over $1.7 billion on advertising in 1989, messages are now placed on walls in dentists' offices, on videocassettes, and on supermarket shopping carts. Other promotions include sponsoring the Pampers' Mobile Baby Care Center at state fairs, a Pepto–Bismol chili cooking contest, and the Jif peanut butter and Pringles potato chips hydroplane, which competes in summer boat-racing events.[1]

One of P&G's most exciting new efforts is a checkout system called *Visions*. To use Visions, customers insert an electronic card into the checkout register, and as each product is scanned the price and other information is shown on a color monitor. Each product purchased provides the customer with "points," which can be accumulated and exchanged for gifts and prizes—much like a frequent flyer program on an airline.[2]

As new techniques are added to P&G's promotional efforts, funds are also being redistributed among the traditional methods. Coupons are likely to receive less attention in the future, while cable television and specialized magazines are likely to be a popular alternative. These changes are part of P&G's marketing strategy, which is designed to make it a leader in each of its 39 product categories. As the pioneer of consumer marketing techniques and the current leader in 22 product categories, P&G is leading the way to a new era of marketing and promotion.[3]

Promotion represents the fourth element in the marketing mix. The promotional element comprises a mix of tools available for the marketer called the *promotional mix,* which consists of advertising, personal selling, sales promotion, and publicity. All of these elements can be used to (1) inform prospective buyers about the benefits of the product, (2) persuade them to try it, and (3) remind them later about the benefits they enjoyed by using the product. This chapter first gives an overview of the communications process and the promotional elements used in marketing and then discusses sales promotion and publicity. Chapter 18 covers advertising, and Chapter 19 discusses personal selling.

FIGURE 17–1
The communication process

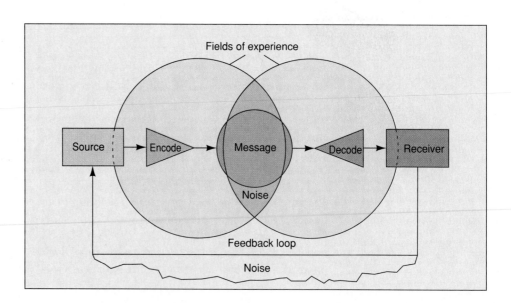

THE COMMUNICATION PROCESS

Communication is the sharing of meaning and requires five elements: a source, a message, a receiver, and the processes of encoding and decoding[4] (Figure 17–1). The **source** may be a company or person who has information to convey. The information sent by a source, such as a description of a new weight reduction drink, forms the **message.** Consumers who read, hear, or see the message are the **receivers.** The message is communicated by means of a channel—the television, radio, or a salesperson standing outside your door.

ENCODING AND DECODING

Encoding and decoding are essential to communication. **Encoding** is the process of having the sender transform an abstract idea into a set of symbols. **Decoding** is the reverse, or the process of having the receiver take a set of symbols, the message, and transform them back to an abstract idea. Look at the Alfa Romeo advertisement: who is the source, and what is the message?

Decoding is performed by the receivers according to their own frame of reference: their attitudes, values, and beliefs.[5] In the ad, Alfa Romeo is the source and the message is this advertisement, which appeared in *Forbes* magazine (the channel). How would you interpret (decode) this advertisement? The picture and text in the advertisement show that the source's intention is to introduce a new product and to position Alfa Romeo as the "marque of high performance"—a position the source believes will appeal to the upper-income readers of the magazine.

The process of communication is not always a successful one. Errors in communication can happen in several ways. The source may not adequately transform the abstract idea into an effective set of symbols, a properly encoded message may be sent through the wrong channel and never make it to the

A source and a message.

receiver, the receiver may not properly transform the set of symbols into the correct abstract idea, or finally, feedback may be so delayed or distorted that it is of no use to the sender. Although communication appears easy to perform, truly effective communication can be very difficult.

COMMUNICATING THE MESSAGE EFFECTIVELY

For the message to be communicated effectively, the sender and receiver must have a mutually shared **field of experience**—similar understanding and knowledge. Figure 17–1 shows two circles representing the fields of experience of the sender and receiver, which overlap in the message. Some of the better-known communication problems have occurred when U.S. companies have taken their messages to cultures with different fields of experience. Many misinterpretations are merely the result of bad translations. For example, General Motors made a mistake when its "Body by Fisher" claim was translated into Flemish as "Corpse by Fisher."[6]

FEEDBACK

Figure 17–1 shows a line labeled *feedback loop*. **Feedback** is the communication flow from receiver back to sender and indicates whether the message was decoded and understood as intended. Chapter 18 reviews approaches called *pretesting* that ensure that advertisements are decoded properly.

NOISE

Noise includes extraneous factors that can work against effective communication, such as distorting a message or the feedback received (Figure 17–1). Noise can be a simple error, such as a printing mistake that affects the meaning of a newspaper advertisement, or using words or pictures that fail to communicate the message clearly. Noise can also occur when a salesperson's message is misunderstood by a buyer, such as when a buyer concentrates on not liking the salesperson's smoking rather than hearing the sales message.

CONCEPT CHECK

1 What are the five elements required for communication to occur?

2 A difficulty for U.S. companies advertising overseas is that the audience does not share the same _____ .

3 A misprint in a newspaper ad is an example of _____ .

THE PROMOTIONAL MIX

To communicate to consumers, a company can use one or more of four promotional alternatives: advertising, personal selling, sales promotion, and publicity. A firm's **promotional mix** is the combination of one or more of the promotional elements it chooses to use. Figure 17–2 summarizes the distinc-

PROMOTIONAL ELEMENT	MASS VERSUS INTERPERSONAL	PAYMENT	STRENGTHS	WEAKNESSES
Advertising	Mass	Fees paid for space or time	• Efficient means for reaching large numbers of people	• High absolute costs • Difficult to receive good feedback
Personal selling	Interpersonal	Fees paid to salespeople as either salaries or commissions	• Immediate feedback • Very persuasive • Can select audience • Can give complex information	• Extremely expensive per exposure
Publicity	Mass	No direct payment to media	• Often most credible source in the consumer's mind	• Difficult to get media cooperation
Sales promotion	Mass	Wide range of fees paid, depending on promotion selected	• Effective at changing behavior in short run • Very flexible	• Easily abused • Can lead to promotion wars • Easily duplicated

FIGURE 17–2
The promotional mix

tions among these four elements. Three of these elements—advertising, sales promotion, and publicity—are often said to use *mass selling,* because they are used with groups of prospective buyers. In contrast, personal selling uses *interpersonal selling,* because the seller usually talks person-to-person with an individual who is a prospective buyer.

ADVERTISING

Advertising is any paid form of nonpersonal communication about an organization, good, service, or idea by an identified sponsor. The *paid* aspect of this definition is important, because the space for the advertising message normally must be bought. An occasional exception is the public service announcement, where the advertising time or space is donated. A full-page, four-color ad in *Time* magazine, for example, costs $128,000. The *nonpersonal* component of advertising is also important. Advertising involves mass media (such as TV, radio, and magazines), which are nonpersonal and do not have an immediate feedback loop as does personal selling. So before the message is sent, marketing research plays a valuable role; for example, it determines that the message is understood by the target market and that the target market will actually see the medium chosen.

There are several advantages to a firm using advertising in its promotional mix. It can be attention-getting—as with the Nike ad shown—and also communicate specific product benefits to prospective buyers. By paying for the

An attention-getting advertisement.

advertising space, a company can control *what* it wants to say and, to some extent, to *whom* the message is sent. If a stereo company wants college students to receive its message about CD players, advertising space is purchased in a college campus newspaper. Advertising also allows the company to decide *when* to send its message (which includes how often). The nonpersonal aspect of advertising also has its advantages. Once the message is created, the same message is sent to all receivers in a market segment. If the message is properly pretested, the company can trust that the same message will be decoded by all receivers in the market segment.

Advertising has some disadvantages. As shown in Figure 17–2 and discussed in depth in Chapter 18, the costs to produce and place a message are significant, and the lack of direct feedback makes it difficult to know how well the message was received.

PERSONAL SELLING

The second major element of the promotional mix is **personal selling,** defined as the two-way flow of communication between a buyer and seller, designed to influence a person's or group's purchase decision. Unlike advertising, personal selling is usually face-to-face communication between the sender and receiver (although, as discussed in Chapter 19, use of telephone sales is growing). Why do companies use personal selling?

There are important advantages to personal selling, as summarized in Figure 17–2. A salesperson can control to *whom* the presentation is made. Although some control is available in advertising by choosing the medium, some people may read the college newspaper, for example, who are not in the target audience for CD players. For the CD-player manufacturer, those readers outside the target audience are *wasted coverage*. Wasted coverage can be reduced with personal selling. The personal component of selling has another advantage over advertising in that the seller can see or hear the potential buyer's reaction

Face-to-face sales presentation.

to the message. If the feedback is unfavorable, the salesperson can modify the message.

The flexibility of personal selling can also be a disadvantage. Different salespeople can change the message so that no consistent communication is given to all customers. The high cost of personal selling is probably its major disadvantage. On a cost-per-contact basis, it is generally the most expensive of the four elements in the promotional mix.

PUBLICITY

A nonpersonal, indirectly paid presentation of an organization, good, or service is termed **publicity.** It can take the form of a news story, editorial, or product announcement. A difference between publicity and both advertising and personal selling is the "indirectly paid" dimension. With publicity a company does not pay for space in a mass medium (such as television or radio) but attempts to get the medium to run a favorable story on the company. In this sense there is an indirect payment for publicity in that a company must support a public relations staff.

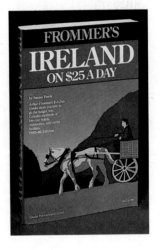

An advantage of publicity is credibility. When you read a favorable story about a company's product (such as a glowing restaurant review), there is a tendency to believe it. Travelers throughout the world have relied on Arthur Frommer's guides such as *Ireland on $25 a Day.* These books outline out-of-the-way, inexpensive restaurants, hotels, inns, and bed-and-breakfast rooms, giving invaluable publicity to these establishments. Such businesses do not (nor can they) buy a mention in the guide, which in recent years has sold millions of copies.

The disadvantages of publicity relate to the lack of the user's control over it. A company can invite a news team to preview its innovative exercise equipment and hope for a favorable mention on the 6 P.M. newscasts. But without buying advertising time, there is no guarantee of any mention of the new equipment or that it will be aired when the target audience is watching. The company representative who calls the station and asks for a replay of the story may be told, "Sorry, it's only news once." With publicity there is little control over what is said, to whom, or when. As a result, publicity is rarely the main component of a promotional mix.

Sales promotions arouse interest.

SALES PROMOTION

A fourth, and also supplemental, promotional element is **sales promotion,** a short-term inducement of value offered to arouse interest in buying a good or service. Used in conjunction with advertising or personal selling, sales promotions are offered to intermediaries as well as to ultimate consumers. Coupons, rebates, samples, and sweepstakes like that used by Consort shampoo shown here are just a few examples of sales promotions discussed later in this chapter.

The advantage of sales promotions is that the short-term nature of these programs (such as the expiration date of a coupon or sweepstakes) often stimulates sales for their duration. Offering value to the consumer in terms of a cents-off coupon or rebate provides an incentive to buy.

Sales promotions cannot be the sole basis for a campaign because gains are often temporary and sales drop off when the deal ends.[7] Advertising support is needed to convert the customer who tried the product because of a sales promotion into a long-term buyer.[8] If sales promotions are conducted continuously, they lose their effectiveness. Customers begin to delay purchase until a coupon is offered, or they question the product's value. Some aspects of sales promotions also are regulated by the federal government. These issues are reviewed in detail later in this chapter.

CONCEPT CHECK

1 Explain the difference between advertising and publicity when both use television.

2 Which promotional element should be offered only on a short-term basis?

3 Cost per contact is high with the _____ element of the promotional mix.

SELECTING PROMOTIONAL TOOLS

In putting together the promotional mix, a marketer must consider the balance of elements to use. Should advertising be emphasized more than personal selling? When should a promotional rebate be offered? Should all promotional activities be coordinated?[9] Several factors affect such decisions: the target audience for the promotion,[10] the stage of the product's life cycle, characteristics of the product, decision stage of the buyer, and even the channel of distribution.

THE TARGET AUDIENCE

Promotional programs are directed to the ultimate consumer, intermediary (retailer, wholesaler, or industrial distributor), or both. Promotional programs of consumer products to ultimate consumers use mass media. Geographical dispersion and the number of potential buyers are the primary reasons for a mass approach. Personal selling is used at the place of purchase, generally the retail store.

To industrial buyers, advertising is used more selectively, as in trade publications such as *Fence* magazine for buyers of fencing material. Because industrial buyers often have specialized needs or technical questions, personal selling is particularly important. The salesperson can provide information and the necessary support after sales.

Intermediaries are often the focus of promotional efforts. As with industrial buyers, personal selling is the major promotional ingredient. The salespeople inform retailers on future advertising efforts to ultimate users, for example, and they assist retailers in making a profit. Intermediaries' questions often pertain to the allowed markup, merchandising support, and return policies, which are best handled by a salesperson.

Related to the issue of the target audience is the composition of the *decision-making unit* (DMU), or the people in a household or a buying center in an organization involved in making the decision to buy the product. The more people in the DMU, the greater the emphasis on personal selling. A salesperson can provide a specific message for each member of the DMU to try to address his or her concerns and objections. For example, in office equipment sales, a salesperson can address more efficiently the technical concerns of the office worker, the cost concerns of the financial officer, and the service questions of the purchasing agent. Three separate messages in very different magazines would be required if advertising were used.

THE PRODUCT LIFE CYCLE

All products have a product life cycle (see Chapter 11), and the composition of the promotional mix changes over the four life-cycle stages, as shown for Purina Puppy Chow in Figure 17–3.

Introduction Stage   Informing consumers in an effort to increase their level of awareness is the primary promotional objective in the introduction stage of the product life cycle. In general, all the promotional mix elements are used at this time, although the use of specific mix elements during any stage depends on the product and situation. Stories on Purina's new nutritional food are placed in *Dog World* magazine, trial samples are sent to registered dog owners in 10 major cities, advertisements are placed during reruns of the TV show *Lassie,* and the

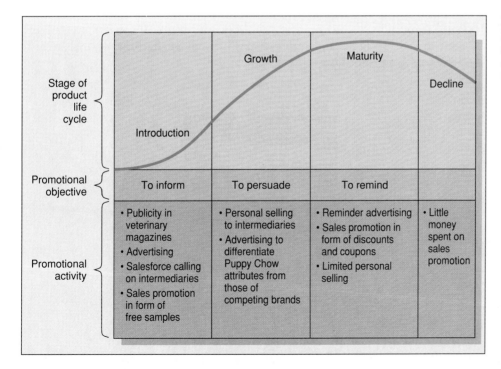

FIGURE 17–3
Promotional tools used over the product life cycle of Purina Puppy Chow

salesforce begins to approach supermarkets to get orders. Advertising is particularly important as a means of reaching as many people as possible to build up interest. Publicity may even begin slightly before the product is commercially available.

Growth Stage   The primary promotional objective of the growth stage is to persuade the consumer to buy the product—Purina Puppy Chow—rather than substitutes, so the marketing manager seeks to gain brand preference and solidify distribution. Sales promotion assumes less importance in this stage, and publicity is not a factor because it depends on novelty of the product. The primary promotional element is advertising, which stresses brand differences. Personal selling is used to solidify the channel of distribution. For consumer products such as dog food, the salesforce calls on the wholesalers and retailers in hopes of increasing inventory levels and gaining shelf space. For industrial products, the salesforce often tries to get contractual arrangements to be the sole source of supply for the buyer.

Maturity Stage   In the maturity stage the need is to maintain existing buyers, and advertising's role is to remind buyers of the product's existence. Sales promotion, in the form of discounts and coupons offered to both ultimate consumers and intermediaries, is important in maintaining loyal buyers. In a test of one mature consumer product, it was found that 80 percent of the product's sales at this stage resulted from sales promotions.[11] Price cuts and discounts can also significantly increase a mature brand's sales. The salesforce at this stage seeks to satisfy intermediaries. An unsatisfied customer who switches brands is hard to replace.

Decline Stage   The decline stage of the product life cycle is usually a period of phaseout for the product, and little money is spent in the promotional mix—especially in sales promotions.

Purina Puppy Chow: a product in the maturity stage of its life cycle.

PRODUCT CHARACTERISTICS

The proper blend of elements in the promotional mix also depends on the type of product. Three specific characteristics should be considered: complexity, risk, and ancillary services. *Complexity* refers to the technical sophistication of the product and hence the amount of understanding required to use it. It's hard to provide much information in a one-page magazine ad or 30-second television ad, so the more complex the product, the greater the emphasis on personal selling.

A second element is the degree of *risk* represented by the product's purchase. Risk for the buyer is a cost in financial terms (such as $4,000 spent for the IBM PS/2 personal computer), or social or physical terms. A hair transplant procedure might represent all three risks. Expensive, yes. But will it work? Does it hurt? Although advertising helps, the greater the risk, the more the need for personal selling.

The level of *ancillary services* required by a product also affects the promotional strategy. Ancillary services pertain to the degree of service or support required after the sale. This characteristic is common to many industrial products and consumer purchases. Who will repair your automobile or microwave oven? Advertising's role is to establish the seller's reputation. However, personal selling is essential to build buyer confidence and provide evidence of follow up.

STAGES OF THE BUYING DECISION

Knowing the customer's stage of decision making can also affect the promotional mix. Figure 17–4 shows how the importance of the three directly paid promotional elements varies with the three stages in a consumer's purchase decision.

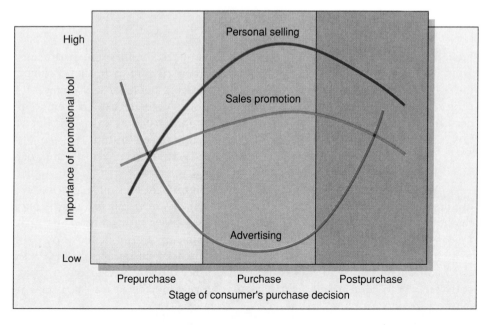

FIGURE 17–4

How the importance of three promotional elements varies during the consumer's purchase decision

Prepurchase Stage   In the prepurchase stage advertising is more helpful than personal selling, because advertising informs the potential customer of the existence of the product and the seller. Sales promotion in the form of free samples also can play an important role to gain low-risk trial. When the salesperson calls on the customer after heavy advertising, there is some recognition of what the salesperson represents. This is particularly important in industrial settings in which sampling of the product is usually not possible.

Purchase Stage   At the purchase stage the importance of personal selling is highest to close the sale, whereas the impact of advertising is lowest. Sales promotion in the form of coupons, deals, point-of-purchase displays, and rebates can be very helpful in encouraging demand. Figure 17–4 oversimplifies the importance of advertising. Although by itself it is not an active influence during the purchase stage, it is the means of delivering the coupons, deals, and rebates that are often important.

Postpurchase Stage   In the postpurchase stage the salesperson is still important. In fact, the more personal contact after the sale, the more the buyer is satisfied. Advertising is also important to assure the buyer that the right purchase was made. Advertising and personal selling help reduce the buyer's postpurchase anxiety.[12] Sales promotion in the form of coupons can help encourage repeat purchases from satisfied first-time triers.

CHANNEL STRATEGIES

Chapter 14 discussed the channel flow from producer to intermediaries to consumer. Achieving control of the channel is often difficult for the manufacturer, and promotional strategies can assist in moving a product through the channel of distribution. This is where a manufacturer has to make an important decision about whether to use a push strategy, pull strategy, or both in its channel of distribution.[13]

Push Strategy   Figure 17–5A shows how a manufacturer uses a **push strategy,** directing the promotional mix to channel members to gain their cooperation in ordering and stocking the product. In this approach, personal selling and sales promotions play major roles. Salespeople call on wholesalers to encourage orders and provide sales assistance. Sales promotions, such as case discount allowances (20 percent off the regular case price), are offered to stimulate demand. By pushing the product through the channel, the goal is to get channel members to push it to their customers.

Anheuser-Busch, for example, spends a significant amount of its marketing resources on maintaining its relationship with its distributors, and through them, with retailers. Anheuser-Busch provides a series of incentives and assistance to its distribution system to maintain its channel dominance. The company arranges group discounts on purchase of trucks, insurance, and even the IBM computers that wholesalers use to order beer. Even specialized computer software is provided to help retailers maximize the shelf space of Anheuser-Busch products.[14]

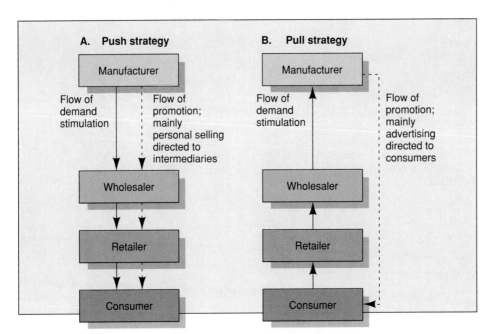

FIGURE 17–5
A comparison of push and pull promotional strategies

Pull Strategy   In some instances manufacturers face resistance from channel members who do not want to order a new product or increase inventory levels of an existing brand. As shown in Figure 17–5B, a manufacturer may then elect to implement a **pull strategy** by directing its promotional mix at ultimate consumers to encourage them to ask the retailer for the product. Seeing demand from ultimate consumers, retailers order the product from wholesalers and thus the item is pulled through the intermediaries. IBM allocated $30 million to media advertising to stimulate consumer demand for its new PS/1 personal computer. This strategy was designed to pull the product through the channel despite the 1985 failure of a similar IBM product, the PCjr, and the reluctance of some distributors who saw the product competing with the more expensive PS/2.[15] Successful advertising campaigns, such as the "IBM Brings It All Home" campaign, can have dramatic effects on the sales of a product.

The distinguishing elements in a push or pull strategy are (1) the target audience for promotional efforts and (2) the emphasis on personal selling or advertising. Companies may rely on elements of a push strategy, a pull strategy, or both, because intermediaries and consumers are crucial to the brand's success.

WHEN TO STRESS ADVERTISING AND PERSONAL SELLING

In the promotional mix, publicity and sales promotions are supportive and rarely the key elements in a firm's strategy. Often a firm must make a trade-off between emphasizing advertising or personal selling. Figure 17–6 summarizes the major factors that lead to an emphasis on either approach.

FIGURE 17–6
When to emphasize advertising or personal selling

BASIS OF COMPARISON	HEAVIER RELIANCE ON . . .	
	ADVERTISING	PERSONAL SELLING
Target audience	Ultimate consumers	Resellers and industrial buyers
Risk in purchase	Low	High
Size of decision-making unit	Small	Large
Complexity of product	Simple	Complex
Level of ancillary services	Low	High
Stage of purchase decision	Prepurchase	Purchase
Channel strategy	Pull	Push
Geographical dispersion of customers	Great	Little

CONCEPT CHECK

1 For consumer products, why is advertising emphasized more in promotion than is personal selling?

2 At what stage of the product life cycle is publicity an important promotional activity?

3 Explain a push versus a pull strategy.

SALES PROMOTION

THE IMPORTANCE OF SALES PROMOTION

Sales promotion is a supplemental ingredient of the promotional mix and is not as visible as advertising, but more than $100 billion is spent annually on it. As shown in Figure 17–7, during the 1980s there was a major shift of dollars from media advertising to trade and consumer promotion. By 1988 about 69 percent of these expenditures were for trade and consumer promotion.[16] As the use of sales promotion has increased, marketers have developed methods for selecting and assessing the impact of the various techniques. These methods require a good understanding of the advantages and disadvantages of each kind of sales promotion.[17] In addition, if the sales promotions are used in other countries, some of the issues described in the accompanying Marketing Action Memo must be considered.

CONSUMER-ORIENTED SALES PROMOTIONS

Directed to ultimate consumers, **consumer-oriented sales promotions,** or simply consumer promotions, are sales tools used to support a company's advertising and personal selling. The alternative consumer-oriented sales promotion tools are shown in Figure 17–8.

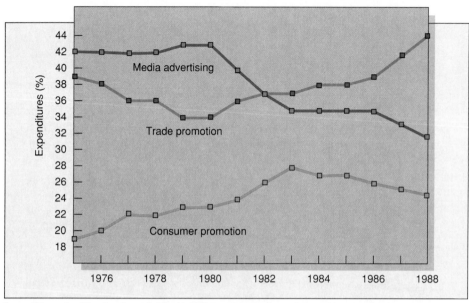

FIGURE 17–7
Trends in expenditures for media advertising, trade promotion, and consumer promotion

Source: "Promotional Practices Survey," *Adweek's Marketing Week* (March 14, 1988), pp. 10–11; and "Where the Promotion Dollar Goes," *Adweek's Marketing Week* (June 19, 1990), p. 10. Reprinted with permission of *Adweek's Marketing Week*.

FIGURE 17–8
Sales promotion alternatives

KIND OF SALES PROMOTION	OBJECTIVES	ADVANTAGES	DISADVANTAGES
Coupons	Stimulate demand	Encourage retailer support	Consumers delay purchases
Deals	Increase trial; retaliate against competitor's actions	Reduce consumer risk	Consumers delay purchases; reduce perceived product value
Premiums	Build goodwill	Consumers like free or reduced-price merchandise	Consumers buy for premium, not product
Contests	Increase consumer purchases; build business inventory	Encourage consumer involvement with product	Require creative or analytical thinking
Sweepstakes	Encourage present customers to buy more; minimize brand-switching behavior	Get customer to use product and store more often	Sales drop after sweepstakes
Samples	Encourage new product trial	Low risk for consumer to try product	High cost for company
Trading stamps	Encourage repeat purchases	Help create loyalty	High cost for company
Point-of-purchase displays	Increase product trial; provide in-store support for other promotions	Provide good product visibility	Hard to get retailer to allocate high-traffic space
Rebates	Encourage customers to purchase; stop sales decline	Effective at stimulating demand	Easily copied; steal sales from future; reduce perceived product value

Marketing Action Memo

SALES PROMOTION GOES GLOBAL

*A*round the world, the interest in sales promotion activities has increased dramatically. This is particularly true in countries with a powerful trade or limited electronic media advertising. At Nestlé, analysis of the importance of promotion in the marketing mix showed significant differences between countries. The accompanying table illustrates the promotional differences of one packaged good in five countries.

	U.S.	JAPAN	U.K.	CANADA	MEXICO
Total advertising and promotion as a percentage of sales	27%	33%	26%	27%	1%
Advertising	12	39	42	19	68
Consumer promotion	26	25	25	15	11
Trade promotion	62	36	33	66	22

Examples of some of the sales promotion differences found in other countries include:

- In the Philippines, high-value on-pack premiums are not appropriate because the final price is usually beyond the reach of consumers.
- In Japan, coupons are not redeemed because consumers are too embarrassed to be seen at a checkout with them.
- In Malaysia, contests are allowed only if they involve a game of skill rather than chance.

As international sales promotion costs increase, top management will ask how much coordination across countries is needed. The answer is that it depends on whether the brand is local, regional, or global. Global brands will require attention from an international sales promotion coordinator who will:

- Facilitate transfer of successful promotion ideas.
- Propose special events.
- Develop and present sales promotion training programs.
- Gather performance data on promotions run by a brand in multiple countries.

Local and regional brands will logically require unique sales promotion programs that address differences in economic development, market maturity, perceptions, regulations, and trade structure in each country.

Source: Kamran Kashani and John A. Quelch, "Can Sales Promotion Go Global?" *Business Horizons* (May–June 1990), pp. 37–43. Copyright 1990 by The Foundation for the School of Business at Indiana University. Used with permission.

A study of consumer-oriented sales promotions showed that the following types are most frequently used[18]:

TYPE OF PROMOTION	FREQUENCY OF USE
Coupons	66%
Price/quantity promotions	11
Refunds	10
Premiums	8
Prize promotions	4
Samples	1
Total	100%

Coupons   Coupons such as those offered by Gillette in an effort to reach basketball fans are sales promotions that usually offer a discounted price to the consumer, which encourages trial. As noted in the accompanying Marketing Research Report, approximately 190 billion coupons are distributed by mail in the United States each year. In 1989, the face value of distributed coupons was about $115 billion and the total value of redeemed coupons was $4.5 billion.[19]

Gillette coupons heavily.

For mature products, couponing may only reduce gross revenues from already loyal users. But a recent study showed that 14 percent of coupon redeemers were first-time buyers of the brand, 34 percent rarely or occasionally used the brand, and 52 percent almost always bought the brand.[20] Manufacturers are offering coupons with greater values, such as $5 coupons for pots and pans sold by Wear-Ever Cookware. Coupon use is also expanding beyond food products to drugs, toys, and appliances.[21]

Coupons are often far more expensive than the face value showing the price discount; a 20-cent coupon can cost three times that after paying for the advertisement to deliver it, handling, redemption, and so on.

Deals   Deals are short-term price reductions, commonly used to increase trial among potential customers or to retaliate against a competitor's actions. For example, if a rival manufacturer introduces a new cake mix, the company responds with a "two packages for the price of one" deal. This short-term price reduction builds up the stock on the kitchen shelves of cake mix buyers and makes the competitor's introduction more difficult.

Premiums   A promotional tool often used with consumers is the premium, which consists of merchandise offered free or at a significant savings over retail. This latter type of premium is called *self-liquidating,* because the cost charged to the consumer covers the cost of the item. Burger King, for example, has offered a Teenage Mutant Ninja Turtles videocassettte and figurines of "the Simpsons" through the Burger King Kids Club. Seagrams offers a carry-home "clamshell" package that includes all the ingredients for drinks mixed with Meyer's rum.[22] By pricing the premium at its cost, companies encourage customers to return frequently or to use more of the product.

Successful premiums must have consumer appeal, and when they are offered on a self-liquidating basis, the cost must represent a real value. The more

Marketing Research Report

DO DIRECT-MAIL COUPONS INCREASE SALES?

Approximately 190 billion coupons are distributed by mail in the United States each year. For managers who use coupons as a promotional technique, understanding the impact of coupons on sales is critical. Bawa and Shoemaker studied 5,192 households to help determine (1) if coupons lead to increases in sales, and (2) the demographic characteristics of the households most likely to respond to coupons.

The households were studied for 24 weeks before the coupons were delivered and for 12 weeks afterward. This allowed the researchers to observe the change in household purchases due to the coupons. Three coupon values—high, medium, and low—were used to determine if the face value of the coupon influenced redemption.

The results of the study suggest that coupons do influence sales. In the four-week period immediately after the coupons were mailed, market share increased by 50 percent! In addition, the most dramatic increase occurred among the households that received the high face-value coupons. The accompanying table shows that larger households whose

Average additional sales due to coupons

DEMOGRAPHIC VARIABLE	LEVEL	ADDITIONAL SALES (OUNCES)
Income	< $20,000	1.05
	≥ $20,000	2.30
Female head of household's education	Up to high school	1.29
	Beyond high school	2.12
Homeowner	No	.74
	Yes	1.94
Household size	1–2 members	1.73
	3–4 members	1.36
	5 + members	2.53

members are more educated, and homeowners have higher additional purchases due to coupons.

Hence direct-mail coupon promotions can lead to a significant increase in sales, and sales response can be increased by targeting specific demographic groups.

Source: Kapil Bawa and Robert W. Shoemaker, "Analyzing Incremental Sales from a Direct-Mail Coupon Promotion," *Journal of Marketing* (July 1989), pp. 66–78.

effective premiums have a functional or logical relationship to the product being promoted. Gatorade offered a squeeze bottle for its drink that was similar to those used by athletic teams.[23] A baby food manufacturer offers a sterling silver baby spoon for $1.

Contests A fourth sales promotion in Figure 17–8, the contest, is where consumers apply their analytical or creative thinking to try to win a prize. For example, White Horse scotch whiskey ran a contest based on information on the back of the bottle. Although not requiring purchase, it resulted in the customer going to the store, reading the label, and buying the product. More than 250,000 entries were received, and sales rose consistently during the contest.[24]

Sweepstakes *Reader's Digest* and Publisher's Clearing House are two of the better-promoted sweepstakes. These sales promotions require participants to submit some kind of entry form but are purely games of chance requiring no analytical or creative effort by the consumer. In October 1969 the Federal Trade Commission issued trade rules covering sweepstakes, contests, and games to regulate their fairness, ensure that the chance for winning is represented honestly, and guarantee that the prizes are actually awarded.[25]

Samples   Another common consumer sales promotion is sampling, which is offering the product free or at a greatly reduced price. Used for new products, sampling puts the product in the consumer's hands. A trial size is generally offered that is smaller than the regular package size. If consumers like the sample, it is hoped they will remember and buy the product. Sampling is appropriate for products that are frequently purchased, have a low unit cost, and are new. Sampling is often done in test marketing a new product. For example, P&G test marketed Cheer with Color Guard, a superconcentrated detergent, in Arizona in 1990 using samples, in-store coupons, and TV ads.[26]

Trading Stamps   Trading stamps are a sales promotion tool in which customers are given stamps in relation to the dollar size of their purchase. These stamps can be redeemed for merchandise or cash. This sales promotion was widely used by supermarkets and gas stations in the 1960s and 1970s to encourage store loyalty, but has declined recently because of the cost involved.

Point-of-Purchase Displays   In a store aisle, you often encounter a sales promotion called a *point-of-purchase display*. These product displays take the form of advertising signs, which sometimes actually hold or display the product, and are often located in high-traffic areas near the cash register or the end of an aisle. The accompanying picture shows gravity-feed bins that Nabisco uses for its animal crackers; it helps ensure product freshness, provides storage, and captures the consumer's attention as an end-aisle, point-of-purchase display.[27] A recent survey of retailers found that 87 percent plan to use more point-of-purchase materials in the future, particularly for products that can be purchased on impulse.[28]

A gravity-feed bin that doubles as a point-of-purchase display.

Some studies estimate that two thirds of a consumer's buying decisions are made in the store. This means that grocery product manufacturers want to get their message to you at the instant you are next to their brand in your supermarket aisle—perhaps through a point-of-purchase display. In the next few years this may be done through the VideOcart. Sitting on the handlebar of your supermarket shopping cart, the VideOcart's liquid-crystal screen will remind you twice per aisle about products next to your cart that you might consider buying. The displays on your screen are triggered by transmitters on the store shelves. Although the technology exists today to make it talk to you, your VideOcart will remain silent. The reason: try to imagine 100 VideOcarts in a large supermarket all talking at the same time![29]

Rebates   A final consumer sales promotion in Figure 17–8, the cash rebate, offers the return of money based on proof of purchase. This tool has been used heavily by car manufacturers facing increased competition. Computer companies like Apple have also used it effectively in selling PCs to ultimate consumers. When the rebate is offered on lower-priced items such as detergent or dog food, the time and trouble of mailing in a proof-of-purchase to get the rebate check means that many buyers—attracted by the rebate offer—never take advantage of it. However, this "slippage" is less likely to occur with those frequent users of rebate promotions.[30] In fact, a firm now offers a 900 number for consumers to call for information about rebates and for personalized rebate certificates.[31]

The VideOcart: gentle video reminders on your shopping trip through your supermarket.

TRADE-ORIENTED SALES PROMOTIONS

Trade-oriented sales promotions, or simply trade promotions, are sales tools used to support a company's advertising and personal selling directed to wholesalers, retailers, or distributors. Some of the sales promotions just reviewed are used for this purpose, but there are three other common approaches targeted uniquely to these intermediaries: (1) allowances and discounts, (2) cooperative advertising, and (3) training of distributors' salesforces.

Allowances and Discounts   Trade promotions often focus on maintaining or increasing inventory levels in the channel of distribution. An effective method for encouraging such increased purchases by intermediaries is the use of allowances and discounts. However, overuse of these "price reductions" can lead to retailers changing their ordering patterns in the expectation of such offerings. Although there are many variations that manufacturers can use with discounts and allowances, three common approaches include the merchandise allowance, the case allowance, and the finance allowance.[32]

Reimbursing a retailer for extra in-store support or special featuring of the brand is a *merchandise allowance*. Performance contracts between the manufacturer and trade member usually specify the activity to be performed, such as a picture of the product in a newspaper with a coupon good at only one store. The merchandise allowance then consists of a percentage deduction from the list case price ordered during the promotional period. Allowances are not paid by the manufacturer until it sees proof of performance (such as a copy of the ad placed by the retailer in the local newspaper).

A second common trade promotion, a *case allowance,* is a discount on each case ordered during a specific time period. These allowances are usually deducted from the invoice. A variation of the case allowance is the "free goods" approach, whereby retailers receive some amount of the product free based on the amount ordered, such as 1 case free for every 10 cases ordered.[33]

A final trade promotion, the *finance allowance,* involves paying retailers for financing costs or financial losses associated with consumer sales promotions. This trade promotion is regularly used and has several variations. One type is the floor stock protection program—manufacturers give retailers a case allowance price for products in their warehouse, which prevents shelf stock from running down during the promotional period. Also common are freight allowances, which compensate retailers that transport orders from the manufacturer's warehouse.

Cooperative Advertising   Resellers often perform the important function of promoting the manufacturer's products at the local level. One common sales promotional activity is to encourage both better quality and greater quantity in the local advertising efforts of resellers through **cooperative advertising.** These are programs by which a manufacturer pays a percentage of the retailer's local advertising expense for advertising the manufacturer's products.

Usually the manufacturer pays a percentage, often 50 percent, of the cost of advertising up to a certain dollar limit, which is based on the amount of the purchases the retailer makes of the manufacturer's products. In addition to paying for the advertising, the manufacturer often furnishes the retailer with a selection of different ad executions, sometimes suited for several different media. A manufacturer may provide, for example, several different print layouts as well as a few broadcast ads for the retailer to adapt and use.

Cooperative advertising represents a substantial investment for the manufacturer. However, it is very effective because both the manufacturer and the retailer receive benefits. The retailer receives partial payment of the local advertising expenses along with better-quality ads. The manufacturer, on the other hand, involves the retailer in local advertising and generally receives stronger support in other areas such as maintaining sufficient inventory and receiving prominent display space for their products in the retailer's store.

Training of Distributors' Salesforces   One of the many functions the intermediaries perform is customer contact and selling for the producers they represent. Both retailers and wholesalers employ and manage their own sales personnel. A manufacturer's success often rests on the ability of the reseller's salesforce to represent its products.

Thus it is in the best interest of the manufacturer to help train the reseller's salesforce. Because the reseller's salesforce is often less sophisticated and knowledgeable about the products than the manufacturer might like, training can increase their sales performance. Training activities include producing manuals and brochures to educate the reseller's salesforce. The salesforce then uses these aids in selling situations. Other activities include national sales meetings sponsored by the manufacturer and field visits to the reseller's location to inform and motivate the salesperson to sell the products. Manufacturers also develop incentive and recognition programs to motivate reseller's salespeople to sell their products.

CONCEPT CHECK

1 Which sales promotional tool is most common for new products?

2 What's the difference between a coupon and a deal?

3 Which trade promotion is used on an ongoing basis?

Chrysler-Plymouth and
Dodge rebate offer.

PUBLICITY

As noted previously, publicity is a form of promotion that is not paid for directly. The responsibility for publicity usually rests with a public relations director, who maintains or creates a favorable image of the organization and its products. The nonpaid aspect of publicity pertains only to the placement of the message. Money is required for staff and for creating opportunities to obtain media coverage of a product. Media representatives may have to be entertained in the hopes of getting a favorable story. News releases have to be prepared and sent. All these efforts result in some internal, indirect cost of publicity. In days of increasing consumerism and skepticism, many companies have begun to hire public relations directors and public relations firms to help their credibility.[34]

THE TOOLS OF PUBLICITY

In developing a campaign, several methods of obtaining nonpersonal presentation of an organization, good, or service without direct cost—**publicity tools**—are available to the public relations director. Many companies frequently use the *news release,* consisting of an announcement regarding changes in the company or the product line. The objective of a news release is to inform a newspaper, radio station, or other medium of an idea for a story. A recent study found that over 40 percent of all free mentions of a brand name occur during news programs.[35]

A second common publicity tool is the *news conference.* Representatives of the media are all invited to an informational meeting, and advance materials regarding the content are sent.

Nonprofit organizations rely heavily on *PSAs (public service announcements),* which are free space or time donated by the media. For example, the charter of the American Red Cross prohibits any local chapter from advertising, so to solicit blood donations local chapters often depend on PSAs on radio or television to announce their needs.

Finally, today many high-visibility individuals are used as publicity tools to create visibility for their companies, their products, and themselves. Lee Iacocca uses visibility to promote Chrysler, Victor Kiam uses it to sell shavers, and Madonna uses it to promote herself as a professional entertainer. These publicity efforts are coordinated with news releases, conferences, advertising, donations to charities, volunteer activities, endorsements, and any other activities that may have an impact on public perceptions.[36]

Chrysler's Lee Iacocca

ETHICAL DIMENSIONS OF PROMOTION IN TODAY'S SOCIETY

Promotional activities often reflect the values of society. Perhaps this explains why in recent years greater concern has arisen about (1) misleading sales promotions and advertisements, (2) advertising and TV programs directed toward children, and (3) more realistic portrayals of women and minorities. Although laws and court decisions have set some standards, sound ethical judgments of key marketing executives are needed in most of the areas described below.

MISLEADING SALES PROMOTIONS AND ADVERTISEMENTS

Unfortunately, over the years many consumers have been misled—or even deceived—by some sales promotions and advertisements. Examples include sweepstakes in which the gifts were not awarded, rebate offers that were a terrible hassle, and advertisements whose promises were great, until the buyer read the small print.

As noted earlier, the Federal Trade Commission stepped in to set precise guidelines on sweepstakes to protect consumers, an example of formal government regulation by an agency of the federal government. Concerning rebates, the buyer usually needs to send proof-of-purchase evidence to the manufacturer to receive a check for the offered price reduction. Suppose that the hassle of finding the proof-of-purchase rebate offer at the bottom of the giant-size package of detergent you bought—because of the rebate—discourages you from sending it in. This slippage raises ethical questions about the manufacturer perhaps deliberately making it difficult for you to take advantage of the rebate. To address some advertising abuses in airline ads, 21 states got together in 1987 to try to set standards for (1) the fine print in airline ads that said special tickets were nonrefundable and (2) sudden changes in frequent flyer programs that penalized past users.[37]

It is clearly too expensive to rely on formal regulation by federal, state, and local governments of all sales promotions and advertisements. As a result, there are increasing efforts by private organizations at *self-regulation,* ethical guidelines set by advertisers, industries, advertising agencies, and advertising associations.[38] This requires solid, continuing ethical judgments by individuals in these organizations. Two examples of self-regulation are (1) Taco Bell recently recalled 300,000 plastic sports bottles following a report that a child dismantled the bottle top and tried to swallow the mouthpiece, and (2) Hardee's recalled 2.8 million "Ghostblaster" toys after the noisemakers were found to have parts that could be swallowed.[39]

ADVERTISING AND TV PROGRAMS FOR CHILDREN

Advertising to children is a subject of great debate. Some critics have suggested prohibiting advertising on all TV programs watched by a significant proportion of children under 8 years of age. Because it has been estimated that the average 2- to 11-year-old American child watches about 26 hours of TV a week and sees between 22,000 and 25,000 TV commercials a year,[40] the concern is real. Children who watch a great amount of TV want more advertised products and ask for them more often than do children who watch less TV.

Clear policies by the government and companies remain to be developed to ensure advertising to children is responsible and ethical. Advertisers and consumers have clear differences of opinion on which TV ads and programs are appropriate for children.[41] This concern has escalated as the link between advertising, cartoons, movies, toys, and games has become stronger. A walk down the cereal aisle in the supermarket today reveals products such as *Teenage Mutant Ninja Turtles Cereal* and *Breakfast with Barbie.* In some cases toy manufacturers have helped produce cartoons featuring a toy character that they sell to children. A federal appeals court directed the Federal Communications Commission to study this problem and the related barter arrangement in which toy manufacturers exchange a TV program they offer for free advertising time from the station.[42]

REALISTIC PORTRAYALS OF MINORITIES AND WOMEN

Just two decades ago, fewer than 5 percent of all advertisements portrayed blacks, but today blacks appear far more often in TV and print advertisements. Further, they are now shown in more favorable jobs and environments than they were in the past. The same is true of other minority groups, such as Hispanics, Native Americans, and Asian Americans.

Advertisers are also presenting a more realistic view of women's roles in society. Women are now shown in advertisements as having a multifaceted role extending beyond housekeeping chores, which was still the way they were portrayed in many ads in the 1970s. In fact, showing a realistic role of today's women—more than half of whom work outside the home—not only is ethically sound but also makes good marketing sense: several studies have shown that realistic role portrayals of women strongly influence advertising effectiveness, such as the recall of major selling points in an ad and a willingness to consider buying a product.[43]

Advertisers and advertising agencies are increasingly staffed by minorities and women, both to improve the effectiveness of their communications to targeted audiences and to avoid offending these audiences.

CONCEPT CHECK

1 **What is a news release?**

2 **What is the difference between government regulation and self-regulation?**

ETHICS AND SOCIAL RESPONSIBILITY IN THE 1990s

CHILDREN: BALANCING PROMOTION AND PROTECTION

In 1990, children spent $6.2 billion for snacks, toys, clothing, movies, and video arcade games, and influenced $54 billion of purchases by their parents. Marketers have responded with promotional campaigns targeted at children. For example, Bubble Yum brand bubble gum is sponsoring a contest, the Big Bubble Yum Blowout, in 23 cities; Sampling Corporation of America gives free samples to 10 million children through 23,000 elementary schools; and Hasbro, Mattel, and other toy manufacturers are linking new product lines to TV programs and movies.

Programs such as these have led to questions about the need for restrictions on promotions to children. In the case of television advertising, the American Association of Advertising Agencies and the Federal Communications Commission have suggested restrictions to programs for children age 12 and younger. The Association of National Advertisers and the American Advertising Federation recommend restrictions for programs targeting children 7 years and younger. And the National Association of Broadcasters argues that the restrictions should apply to programs targeting children 8 years and younger.[44]

What issues should be considered to determine if restrictions are necessary? If some restrictions are needed, to what age group should they apply?

 ## SUMMARY

1 Communication is the sharing of meaning and requires a source, message, receiver, and the processes of encoding and decoding.

2 For effective communication to occur, the sender and receiver must have a shared field of experience. Feedback from receiver to sender helps determine whether decoding has occurred or noise has distorted the message.

3 The promotional mix consists of advertising, personal selling, sales promotion, and publicity. These tools vary according to whether they are personal, can be identified with a sponsor, and can be controlled with regard to whom, when, where, and how often the message is sent.

4 In selecting the appropriate promotional mix, marketers must consider the target audience, the stage of the product's life cycle, characteristics of the product, decision stage of the buyer, and the channel of distribution.

5 The target for promotional programs can be the ultimate consumer, an intermediary, or both. Ultimate consumer programs rely more on advertising, whereas personal selling is more important in reaching industrial buyers and intermediaries.

6 The emphasis on the promotional tools varies with a product's life cycle. In introduction, awareness is important. During growth, creating brand preference is essential. Advertising is more important in the former stage and personal selling in the latter. Sales promotion helps maintain buyers in the maturity stage.

7 The appropriate promotional mix depends on the complexity of the product, the degree of risk associated with its purchase, and the need for ancillary services.

8 In the prepurchase stage of a customer's purchase decision advertising is emphasized; at the purchase stage personal selling is most important; and during the postpurchase stage advertising, personal selling, and sales promotion are used to reduce postpurchase anxiety.

9 When a push strategy is used, personal selling and sales promotions directed to intermediaries play major roles. In a pull strategy, advertising and sales promotions directed to ultimate consumers are important.

10 More money is spent on sales promotion than on advertising. Selecting sales promotions requires a good understanding of the advantages and disadvantages of each option.

11 There is a wide range of consumer-oriented sales promotions: coupons, deals, premiums, contests, sweepstakes, samples, trading stamps, point-of-purchase displays, and rebates.

12 Trade-oriented promotions consist of allowances and discounts, cooperative advertising, and training of distributors' salesforces. These are used at all levels of the channel.

13 Publicity is a nonpersonal, indirectly paid presentation of an organization, good, or service conducted through news releases, news conferences, or public service announcements.

14 Special ethical concerns in today's promotional activities include misleading sales promotions and ads, ads and TV programs directed toward children, and realistic portrayals of minorities and women.

≡ KEY TERMS AND CONCEPTS

communication p. 463

source p. 465

message p. 465

receivers p. 465

encoding p. 465

decoding p. 465

field of experience p. 466

feedback p. 466

noise p. 466

promotional mix p. 466

advertising p. 467

personal selling p. 468

publicity p. 469

sales promotion p. 469

push strategy p. 474

pull strategy p. 475

consumer-oriented sales promotions p. 476

trade-oriented sales promotions p. 482

cooperative advertising p. 483

publicity tools p. 484

CHAPTER PROBLEMS AND APPLICATIONS

1 After listening to a recent sales presentation, Mary Smith signed up for membership at the local health club. On arriving at the facility, she learned there was an additional fee for racquetball court rentals. "I don't remember that in the sales talk; I thought they said all facilities were included with the membership fee," complained Mary. Describe the problem in terms of the communication process.

2 Product managers who are responsible for most of the promotional decisions for a brand are usually well-paid, well-educated marketing professionals. Consider for a minute the average consumer for Kraft Macaroni and Cheese. Are there any potential problems in terms of the fields of experience of these two groups with respect to promotional campaigns? How might any potential differences be overcome?

3 Develop a matrix to compare the four elements of the promotional mix on three criteria—to *wh*om you deliver the message, *wh*at you say, and *wh*en you say it.

4 Explain how the promotional tools used by an airline would differ if the target audience were *(a)* consumers who travel for pleasure and *(b)* corporate travel departments that select the airlines to be used by company employees.

5 Suppose you introduced a new consumer food product and invested heavily both in national advertising (pull strategy) and in training and motivating your field salesforce to sell the product to food stores (push strategy). What kinds of feedback would you receive from both the advertising and your salesforce? How could you increase both the quality and quantity of each?

6 Fisher-Price Company, long known as a manufacturer of children's toys, has introduced a line of clothing for children. Outline a promotional plan to get this product introduced in the marketplace.

7 Cray Research makes supercomputers to handle the information and computing needs of government agencies, such as the weather service, and entire countries, such as France. Unlike Apple Computer, Cray does no advertising on television. Explain why two computer companies have such different promotional strategies.

8 Many insurance companies sell health insurance plans to companies. In these companies the employees pick the plan, but the set of offered plans is determined by the company. Recently Blue Cross–Blue Shield, a health insurance company, ran a television ad stating, "If your employer doesn't offer you Blue Cross–Blue Shield coverage, ask why." Explain the promotional strategy behind the advertisement.

9 Identify the sales promotion tools that might be useful for *(a)* Tastee Yogurt—a new brand introduction, *(b)* 3M self-sticking Post-it notes, and *(c)* Wrigley's Spearmint Gum.

10 When the Gannett Corporation introduced the daily newspaper *USA Today*, free copies were distributed at airports and check-in counters of car rental companies such as Hertz and Avis. *(a)* What was the rationale behind this promotional strategy? *(b)* Who was the original target audience?

CHAPTER 18

Advertising

*A*fter reading this chapter you should be able to:

- Explain the differences between product and institutional advertising and the variations within each type.

- Understand the steps used to develop, execute, and evaluate an advertising program.

- Understand alternative ways to set an advertising budget.

- Explain the advantages and disadvantages of alternative advertising media.

Bo or Snoopy: Who Would You Choose to Represent a Product?

Bo Jackson has been pitching Nike shoes since 1988 — first in the "Just Do It" campaign, then in a series of cross-training commercials claiming that "Bo Knows," and in a "Multiple Bos" campaign that includes Sonny Bono. Snoopy has been busy also. He and Woodstock have appeared in Metropolitan Life ads for several years, and now A&W Brands has enlisted Snoopy as a "spokesdog" for their root beer and cream soda products.

Bo and Snoopy are just two of many rock stars, athletes, actors, and cartoon characters who appear in advertisements today. You may have seen Paula Abdul in a diet Coke ad, M.C. Hammer in a Pepsi ad, or the Little Mermaid in a McDonald's ad.[1] Why? Because companies want to capture potential customers' attention.

Americans today face more advertising messages than ever before, and TV viewers can "zap" TV ads by quickly switching from channel to channel to avoid the ads.[2] Advertisers believe that a spokesperson can help keep viewers watching. Alan Pottasch of the ad agency BBDO says that celebrities in "mini-dramas" entertain and sell.[3] For example, American Express Travelers Checks has created a long-running campaign with Karl Malden.

Choosing a spokesperson can be difficult, though. One reason is that special circumstances, such as Bo Jackson's injury, are almost impossible to anticipate. In addition, ratings of the most popular commercials suggest that celebrities may be losing credibility and that animated, animal, and fantasy ads are gaining popularity. Ralston's Energizer battery bunny, which interrupts fake ads for competitors' products and bursts in on real ads for other Ralston products, was one of the 10 best-recalled ads in 1990, and the claymation California Raisins claimed the number one spot for the two previous years.[4]

Successful ads like these are a challenge. The first few seconds are the key, or all that is discussed in this chapter is zapped. Movies, soap, hospitals, politicians, various causes, and even AIDS prevention are all promoted by advertising. Advertising is the most visible and highly criticized element of the marketing mix and an important aspect of promotion.

Advertising is defined as any *paid* form of *nonpersonal* communication about an organization, good, service, or idea, by an identified sponsor. Two terms are highlighted: *paid* distinguishes advertising from publicity, and *nonpersonal* separates it from personal selling.

Advertisements serve varying purposes. Which ad would be considered (1) pioneering, which is (2) competitive, and which is used as a (3) reminder?

TYPES OF ADVERTISEMENTS

As you look through any magazine, the number of advertisements and the varying themes are overwhelming. Advertisements are prepared for different purposes, but they basically consist of two types: product or institutional.

PRODUCT ADVERTISEMENTS

Focused on selling a good or service, **product advertisements** take three forms: (1) pioneering (or informational), (2) competitive (or persuasive), and (3) reminder. Look at the ads for Chrysler, Maytag, and Echelon contact lenses and guess the type and objective of each ad.

Used in the introductory stage of the life cycle, *pioneering* advertisements tell people what a product is, what it can do, and where it can be found. The key objective of a pioneering ad (such as that for Echelon bifocal contact lenses) is to inform the target market. Informative ads have been found to be interesting, convincing, and effective, according to consumer judgment.[5]

Advertising that promotes a specific brand's features and benefits is *competitive*. The objective of these messages is to persuade the target market to select the firm's brand rather than that of a competitor. An increasingly common form of competitive advertising is *comparative* advertising, which shows one brand's strengths relative to those of competitors.[6] The Chrysler ad, for example, highlights its competitive advantage over two other brands. Before the late 1970s, two of the three national TV networks would not allow comparative ads in which a competitor's brand name was used. However, the Federal Trade Commission (FTC) endorsed comparative advertising in 1979, and now over one

Dial soap uses reinforcement ads to encourage consumers to keep using the product.

fifth of network radio and television commercials are comparative ads.[7] Firms that use comparative advertising (such as Chrysler) need market research and test results to provide legal support for their claims.[8]

    Reminder advertising is used to reinforce previous knowledge of a product. The Maytag ad shown reminds consumers about the dependability associated with its product. Reminder advertising is good for products that have achieved a well-recognized position and are in the mature phase of their product life cycle. Coors tried a form of reminder advertising with its nostalgia campaign—reminding people of the 1960s and 1970s when the brand was distributed only in Western states and was often taken home by vacationers after skiing or camping trips.[9] Another type of reminder ad, reinforcement, is used to assure current users they made the right choice. One example: "Aren't you glad you use Dial? Don't you wish everybody did?"

INSTITUTIONAL ADVERTISEMENTS

The objective of **institutional advertisements** is to build goodwill or an image for an organization, rather than promote a specific product or service. Institutional advertising has been used by companies such as GTE, Beatrice, and Chevron to build confidence in the company name.[10] Often this form of ad-

An advocacy advertisement about the responsible use of alcohol.

vertising is used to support the public relations plan or counter adverse publicity. Four alternative forms of institutional advertisements are often used:

1. *Advocacy* advertisements state the position of a company on an issue. Anheuser-Busch places ads discussing its views on the responsible use of alcohol, as shown in the accompanying ad.
2. *Pioneering institutional* advertisements, like the form of pioneering ads for products discussed above, are used for a new announcement about what a company is, what it can do, or where it is located.
3. *Competitive institutional* advertisements promote the advantages of one product class over another and are used in markets where different product classes compete for the same buyers. The dairy farmers' association runs ads to that show that milk is an "every time of the day drink" and not just for kids. The goal of these ads is to increase demand for milk as it competes against other beverages.
4. *Reminder institutional* advertisements, like the product form, simply bring the company's name to the attention of the target market again.

CONCEPT CHECK

1 **What is the difference between pioneering and competitive ads?**

2 **What is the purpose of an institutional advertisement?**

DEVELOPING THE ADVERTISING PROGRAM

Because media costs are high, advertising decisions must be made carefully, using a systematic approach. Paralleling the planning, implementation, and control steps described in the strategic marketing process (Chapter 2), the advertising decision process is divided into (1) developing, (2) executing, and (3) evaluating the advertising program (Figure 18–1). Development of the advertising program focuses on the four *W*s:

- *Who* is the target audience?
- *What* are (1) the advertising objectives, (2) the amounts of money that can be budgeted for the advertising program, and (3) the kinds of copy to use?

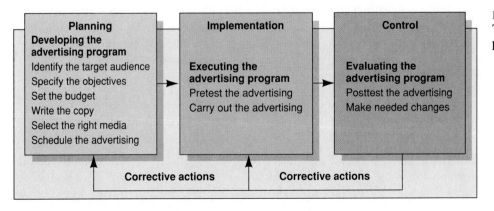

FIGURE 18–1
The advertising decision process

- *When* should the advertisements be run?
- *Where* should the advertisements be run?

IDENTIFYING THE TARGET AUDIENCE

The first decision in developing the advertising program is identifying the *target audience,* the group of prospective buyers toward which an advertising program is directed. To the extent that time and money permit, the target audience for the advertising program is the target market for the firm's product, which is identified from marketing research and market segmentation studies. The more a firm knows about its target audience's profile—including their lifestyle, attitudes, and values—the easier it is to make an advertising decision. If a firm wanted to reach you with its ad, it would need to know what TV shows you watch and what magazines you read. Companies also recognize that consumers receive communications and accept ideas and products at different times.

SPECIFYING ADVERTISING OBJECTIVES

After the target audience is identified, a decision must be reached on what the advertising campaign is to accomplish. Consumers can be said to respond in terms of a **hierarchy of effects,** which is the sequence of stages a prospective buyer goes through from initial awareness of a product to eventual action (either trial or adoption of the product).[11]

- *Awareness:* The consumer's ability to recognize and remember the product or brand name.
- *Interest:* An increase in the consumer's desire to learn about some of the features of the product or brand.
- *Evaluation:* The consumer's appraisal of how he or she feels about the product or brand.
- *Trial:* The consumer's actual first purchase and use of the product or brand.
- *Adoption:* Through a favorable experience on the first trial, the consumer's repeated purchase and use of the product or brand.

For a totally new product the sequence applies to the entire product category, but for a new brand competing in an established product category it applies to the brand itself. These steps can serve as guidelines for developing advertising objectives.

Although sometimes an objective for an advertising program involves several steps in the hierarchy of effects, it often focuses on a single stage. No matter what the specific objective might be, from building awareness to increasing repeat purchases, advertising objectives should possess three important qualities. They should (1) be designed for a well-defined target audience, (2) be measurable, and (3) cover a specified time period.

SETTING THE ADVERTISING BUDGET

You might not remember who advertised during the 1973 Super Bowl, but it cost the company $207,000 a minute. By 1991 the cost of one minute during Super Bowl XXV was $1.7 million (Figure 18–2). The reason for the escalating

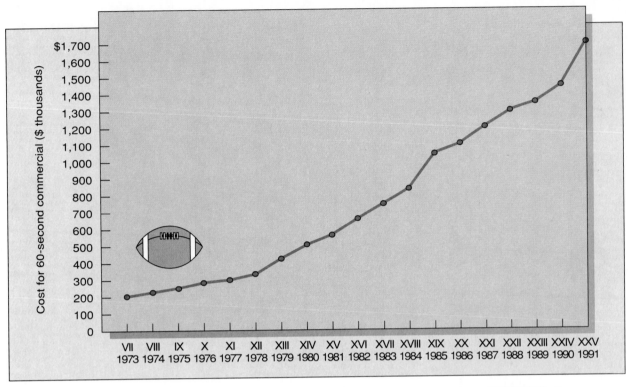

FIGURE 18–2
**Rising media costs:
Super Bowl, super
dollars**

cost is the growing numbers of viewers: an estimated 118 million people tune in for at least a few minutes of the game.[12]

From Figure 18–3 it is clear that the advertising expenditures needed to reach U.S. households are enormous. Note that four companies—Philip Morris, P&G, Sears, and General Motors—each spend more than a billion dollars annually on advertising.

After setting the advertising objectives, a company must decide on how much to spend. Determining the ideal amount for the budget is difficult because there is no precise way to measure the exact results of spending advertising dollars. However, there are several methods used to set the advertising budget.

Percentage of Sales In the **percentage of sales budgeting** approach, funds are allocated to advertising as a percentage of past or anticipated sales, in terms of either dollars or units sold. A common budgeting method,[13] this approach is often stated in terms such as, "Our ad budget for this year is 3 percent of last year's gross sales." The advantage of this approach is obvious: it's simple and provides a financial safeguard by tying the advertising budget to sales. However, there is a major fallacy in this approach, which implies that sales cause advertising. Using this method, a company may reduce its advertising budget because of a downturn in past sales or a forecast downturn in future sales—situations where it may need advertising the most.

Competitive Parity A second common approach, **competitive parity budgeting,** is matching the competitor's absolute level of spending or the proportion per point of market share. This approach has also been referred to as

FIGURE 18–3

Advertising expenditures by companies in 1989

RANK	COMPANY	ADVERTISING EXPENDITURES (Millions)
1	Philip Morris	$2,072
2	Procter & Gamble	1,779
3	Sears	1,432
4	General Motors	1,363
5	Grand Metropolitan PLC	823
6	PepsiCo	786
7	McDonald's	774
8	Eastman Kodak	718
9	RJR Nabisco	703
10	Kellogg	611
11	Nestlé	608
12	Unilever N.V.	604
13	Ford	602
14	Anheuser-Busch	591
15	Warner-Lambert	585

Source: R. Craig Endicott and Kevin Brown, "Top 100 Boost Ad Spending 6.4% to Almost $34 Billion," *Advertising Age* (September 26, 1990), p. 1.

matching competitors or *share of market*. It is important to consider the competition in budgeting.[14] Consumer responses to ads are affected by competing ads, so if a competitor runs 30 radio ads each week, it may be difficult for a firm to get its message across with only five messages.[15] The competitor's budget level, however, should not be the only determinant in setting a company's budget. The competition might have very different advertising objectives, which require a different level of advertising expenditures.

All You Can Afford   Common to many small businesses is **all you can afford budgeting,** in which money is allocated to advertising only after all other budget items are covered. As one company executive said in reference to this budgeting process, "Why, it's simple. First, I go upstairs to the controller and ask how much they can afford to give us this year. He says a million and a half. Later, the boss comes to me and asks how much we should spend, and I say 'Oh, about a million and a half.' Then we have our advertising appropriation."[16]

Fiscally conservative, this approach has little else to offer. Using this budgeting philosophy, a company acts as though it doesn't know anything about an advertising–sales relationship or what its advertising objectives are.

Objective and Task   The best approach to budgeting is **objective and task budgeting,** whereby the company (1) determines its advertising objectives, (2) outlines the tasks to accomplish these objectives, and (3) determines the advertising cost of performing these tasks.[17]

This method takes into account what the company wants to accomplish and requires that the objectives be specified.[18] Strengths of the other budgeting methods are integrated into this approach because each previous method's

---

OBJECTIVE

To increase awareness among college students for the new CD-player cleaning kit. Awareness at the end of one semester should be 20 percent of all students from the existing 0 percent today.

TASKS	COSTS
Advertisements once a week for a semester in 500 college papers	$280,000
Advertisements weekly for a semester on the nationally syndicated "Rockline" radio show	25,000
Three monthly, full-page ads in *Audio* magazine	9,000
Total budget	$314,000

FIGURE 18–4

The objective and task approach

strength is tied to the objectives. For example, if the costs are beyond what the company can afford, objectives are reworked and the tasks revised. The difficulty with this method is the judgment required to determine the tasks needed to accomplish objectives. Would two or four insertions in *Time* magazine be needed to achieve a specific awareness level? Figure 18–4 shows a sample media plan with objectives, tasks, and budget outlined. The total amount to be budgeted is $314,000. If the company can only afford $200,000, the objectives must be reworked, tasks redefined, and the total budget recalculated.

WRITING THE COPY

The central element of an advertising program is the *advertising copy,* the messages that the target audience is intended to see (as in magazines, newspapers, and TV) or hear (as in radio and TV). This usually involves identifying the key benefits of the product that are deemed important to a prospective buyer in making trial and adoption decisions.

Message Content   Every advertising message is made up of both informational and persuasional elements. These two elements, in fact, are so intertwined that it is sometimes difficult to tell them apart. For example, basic information contained in many ads such as the product name, benefits, features, and price are presented in a way that tries to attract attention and encourage purchase. On the other hand, even the most persuasive advertisements have to contain at least some basic information to be successful.

Information and persuasive content can be combined in the form of an appeal to provide a basic reason for the consumer to act. Although the marketer can use many different types of appeals, common advertising appeals include fear appeals, sex appeals, and humorous appeals.

Fear appeals suggest to the consumer that he or she can avoid some negative experience through the purchase and use of a product, or through a change in behavior. Insurance companies often try to show the negative effects of premature death on the relatives of those who don't carry enough life or mortgage

A fear appeal.

Marketing Action Memo

DESIGNING ADS THAT DEAL WITH NEGATIVE ISSUES

*H*ave you ever developed anxiety over a message you've received from an advertisement? If your answer is yes, chances are that your reaction was the result of what advertisers call a *fear appeal*. Examples you may be familiar with include fire or smoke detector ads that depict a family home burning, political candidate endorsements that warn against the rise of communism or other unpopular ideologies, or social cause ads warning of the serious consequences of drug use, alcoholism, or AIDS. This approach is based on three steps—the creation of a fearful situation, suggesting that the danger is serious enough to warrant attention, and offering a solution as a means of fear reduction.

How individuals react to fear appeals, though, varies significantly. Indeed, the varying levels of anxiety that result from the ads suggest several ethical concerns for the psychological well-being of consumers. Therefore, advertisers need to consider five guidelines when developing their ads:

1 Attempt to create positive rather than negative images.
2 Whenever possible, use low or moderate (rather than high) levels of fear.
3 Offer more than one alternative as a solution.
4 Avoid deceptive implications (e.g., that a product will completely eliminate a dangerous or fearful condition).
5 Pretest each ad to ensure an effective balance between the message and the associated level of anxiety.

Examples of fear appeal advertisements

SPONSOR	MEDIUM	THEME
American Express Travelers Checks	Television	A couple on a vacation was shown victimized by a robbery and left in a state of shock and desperation.
American Trauma Society	Television	The inside of a car with a broken windshield was shown with a voice stating, "The head that could make the decision to buckle up no longer can."
Trojan-Enz, Inc.	Print	A man with a serious facial expression showed concern about the need to use condoms. He had heard the U.S. Surgeon General's warning about the new severe threats of venereal disease.
Prudential Insurance	Television	A man was shown dying on an operating table. The message focused on who will take care of his children.
Partnership for a Drug-Free America	Print and television	Photos of an unbroken egg, a hot pan, and the egg frying in the pan are shown. The copy reads: "This is your brain on drugs."

Sources: Michael S. LaTour and Shaker A. Zahra, "Fear Appeals as Advertising Strategy: Should They Be Used?" *The Journal of Consumer Marketing* (Spring 1989), pp. 61–70; and Joshua Levine, "Don't Fry Your Brain," *Forbes* (February 4, 1991), pp. 116–17.

insurance. Food producers encourage the purchase of low-fat, high-fiber products as a means of reducing cholesterol levels and the possibility of a heart attack.[19] The famous advertising slogan of "ring around the collar" shows that others will be repelled if they observe a person with a stained collar. When using fear appeals, the advertiser must be sure that the appeal is strong enough to get the audience's attention and concern, but not so strong that it will lead them to "tune out" the message. The accompanying Marketing Action Memo suggests some guidelines for developing an ad with a fear appeal.

A creative advertisement with "warmth" for Royal Viking.

In contrast, *sex appeals* suggest to the audience that the product will increase the attractiveness of the user. Sex appeals can be found in almost any product category, from automobiles to toothpaste. Unfortunately, many commercials that use sex appeals are only successful at gaining the attention of the audience; they have little impact on how consumers think, feel, or act. Some advertising experts even argue that such appeals get in the way of successful communication by distracting the audience from the purpose of the ad.

Humorous appeals imply either directly or more subtly that the product is more fun or exciting than competitors' offerings. As with fear and sex appeals, the use of humor is widespread in advertising and can be found in many product categories. Unfortunately for the advertiser, humor tends to wear out quickly, thus boring the consumer. Bartles and Jaymes, featuring the Frank and Ed characters, frequently changes the television commercials for its wine coolers to avoid this advertising "wearout."

Creating the Actual Message   The "creative people," or copywriters, in an advertising agency have the responsibility to turn appeals and features such as quality, style, dependability, economy, and service into attention-getting, believable advertising copy. They often rely on creative use of fear, sex, humor, sound, or visual effects.

A seven-year-old advertising agency started by three creative directors, Goodby, Berlin, & Silverstein, was designated as *Advertising Age* magazine's 1989 U.S. Agency of the Year by using "freshness, wit, and warmth" in its ads. Mr. Goodby explained that their approach is to "get at things before people overthink them, to get at their initial, instinctive emotions."

Goodby's television commercials for Supercuts, a hair salon chain, never mention stylish hair but suggest the romantic possibilities it affords. For the *San Francisco Examiner,* the agency developed a campaign depicting "Wild Bill Hearst," the newspaper's publisher, recklessly driving a delivery truck over the hills of the city. And for Royal Viking Cruise Line, Goodby found an old typeface to add feeling to its claim that "A Truly Great Ship Is Something Of a Destination in Itself."[20] All of these campaigns use emotion to get the audience's attention.

Translating the copywriter's ideas into an actual advertisement is also a complex process. Performing quality artwork, layout, and production for the advertisements is costly and time consuming. High-quality TV commercials typically cost about $125,000 to produce a 30-second ad, a task done by about 2,000 small commercial production companies across the United States. High-visibility commercials can be even more expensive: two 15-second Rolaids commercials involved $500,000 and 75 people over a six-month period. About 70 "takes" are necessary, and typical, to get things "right."[21]

CONCEPT CHECK

1 What are characteristics of good advertising objectives?

2 What is the weakness of the percentage of sales budgeting approach?

SELECTING THE RIGHT MEDIA

Every advertiser must decide where to place its advertisements. The alternatives are the *advertising media,* the means by which the message is communicated to the target audience. Newspapers, magazines, radio, and TV are examples of advertising media. This "media selection" decision is related to the target audience, type of product, nature of the message, campaign objectives, available budget, and the costs of the alternative media. Figure 18–5 shows expenditures on alternative major advertising media and indicates that expenditures more than doubled from 1980 to 1989 to about $124 billion.[22]

Choosing a Medium and a Vehicle within that Medium   In deciding where to place advertisements, a company has several media to choose from and a number of alternatives, or vehicles, within each medium. Often advertisers use a mix

FIGURE 18–5
U.S. advertising expenditures, by category

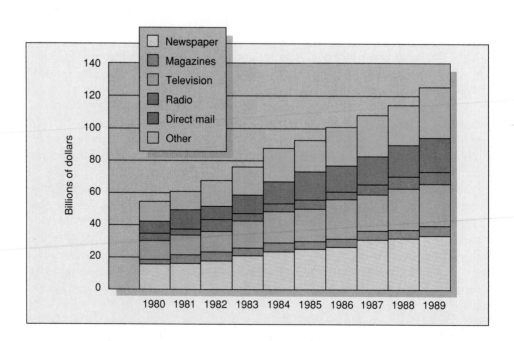

of media forms and vehicles to maximize the exposure of the message to the target audience while at the same time minimizing costs. These two conflicting goals of (1) maximizing exposure and (2) minimizing costs are of central importance to media planning.

Basic Terms   Media buyers speak a language of their own, so every advertiser involved in selecting the right media for their campaigns must be familiar with some common terms used in the advertising industry. Figure 18–6 shows the most common terms used in media decisions.

Because advertisers try to maximize the number of individuals in the target market exposed to the message, they must be concerned with reach. **Reach** is the number of different people exposed to an advertisement.

The exact definition of reach sometimes varies among alternative media. Newspapers often use reach to describe their total circulation or the number of different households that buy the paper. Television and radio stations, in contrast, describe their audience using the term **rating**—the percentage of households in a market that are tuned to a particular TV show or radio station. In general, advertisers try to maximize reach in their target market at the lowest cost.

Although reach is important, advertisers are also interested in exposing their target audience to a message more than once. This is because consumers often do not pay close attention to advertising messages, some of which contain large amounts of relatively complex information. When advertisers want to reach the same audience more than once, they are concerned with **frequency,** the average number of times a person in the target audience is exposed to a message or advertisement.

For example, if an advertiser places a full-page ad in your local newspaper on each of the five weekdays, some individuals will be exposed to none of the ads, others will see one of them, still others two, and so on. Frequency tells you the average number of times individuals in the target audience were exposed to these five ads. Like reach, greater frequency is desirable. But because of the cost, the media planner often must balance reach and frequency. **Cost per thousand** (CPM) refers to the cost of reaching 1,000 individuals or households with the advertising message in a given medium (*M* is the Roman numeral for 1,000).

TERM	WHAT IT MEANS
Reach	▪ The number of different people exposed to an advertisement.
Rating	▪ The percentage of households in a market that are tuned to a particular TV show or radio station.
Frequency	▪ The average number of times an individual is exposed to an advertisement.
Cost per thousand (CPM)	▪ The cost of advertising divided by the number of thousands of individuals or households who are exposed.

FIGURE 18–6
The language of the media buyer

DIFFERENT MEDIA ALTERNATIVES

Figure 18–7 summarizes the advantages and disadvantages of the important advertising media, which are described in more detail below.

Television   Television is a valuable medium because it communicates with both sight and sound. Print advertisements alone could never give you the sense of a sports car cornering at high speed or communicate NutraSweet's excitement about its 10th anniversary. In addition, network television is the only medium that can reach 95 percent of the homes in the United States.[23]

Television's major disadvantage is cost: the average price of a prime-time 30-second network spot is now $112,600. Because of these high charges, many advertisers have reduced the length of their commercials from 30 seconds to 15 seconds. This practice, referred to as *splitting 30s,* reduces costs but severely restricts the amount of information that can be conveyed. Although the popularity

FIGURE 18–7

Advantages and disadvantages of major advertising media

MEDIUM	ADVANTAGES	DISADVANTAGES
Television	Reaches extremely large audience; uses picture, print, sound, and motion for effect; can target specific audiences.	High cost to prepare and run ads; short exposure time and perishable message; difficult to convey complex information.
Radio	Low cost; can target specific audiences; ads can be placed quickly; can use sound, humor, and intimacy effectively.	No visual excitement; short exposure time and perishable message; difficult to convey complex information.
Magazines	Can target specific audiences; high-quality color; long life of ad; ads can be clipped and saved; can convey complex information.	Long time needed to place ad; limited control of ad position; relatively high cost; competes for attention with other magazine features.
Newspapers	Excellent coverage of local markets; ads can be placed and changed quickly; ads can be saved; quick consumer response; low cost.	Ads compete for attention with other newspaper features; can't control ad position on page; short life span; can't target specific audiences.
Direct mail	Best for targeting specific audiences; very flexible (3–D, pop-up ads); ad can be saved; measurable.	Relatively high cost; audience often sees it as "junk mail"; no competition with editorial matter.
Billboard (outdoor)	Low cost; local market focus; high visibility; opportunity for repeat exposures.	Message must be short and simple; low selectivity of audience; criticized as a traffic hazard, eyesore.

Sources: Courtland L. Bovée and William F. Arens, *Contemporary Advertising,* 2nd ed. (Homewood, Ill.: Richard D. Irwin, 1986), pp. 382–83; and William G. Nickels, *Understanding Business* (St. Louis: Times Mirror/Mosby College Publishing, 1987), p. 204.

of 15-second ads has grown from 20 percent of all ads in 1986 to 38 percent in 1989, their popularity declined in 1990 as advertisers began to recognize the limitations of the shorter time period.[24] Another problem with television is the likelihood of *wasted coverage*—having people outside the market for the product see the advertisement. In recent years the cost and wasted coverage problems of TV have been reduced through the introduction of cable TV, whose advertising time is often less expensive than the prime time on major networks. This often allows far greater control over who sees the advertisement.

Radio   There are seven times as many radio stations as television stations in the United States. The major advantage of radio is that it is a segmented medium. There are the Farm Radio Network, the Physicians' Network, all-talk shows, and punk rock stations, all listened to by different market segments. The average college student is a surprisingly heavy radio listener and spends more time during the day listening to radio than watching network television—2.2 hours versus 1.6 hours (Figure 18–8). Thus advertisers with college students as their target market must consider radio.

The disadvantage of radio is that it has limited use for products that must be seen. Another problem is the ease with which consumers can tune out a commercial by switching stations. Radio is a medium that competes for people's attention as they do other activities such as driving, working, or relaxing. Peak radio listening time is during the drive times (6 to 10 A.M. and 4 to 7 P.M.).

TV storyboards lead to commercials, which communicate with sight and sound.

FIGURE 18–8
Media usage by college students

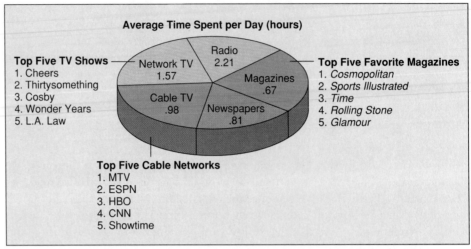

Average Time Spent per Day (hours)

Top Five TV Shows
1. Cheers
2. Thirtysomething
3. Cosby
4. Wonder Years
5. L.A. Law

Network TV 1.57
Cable TV .98
Radio 2.21
Magazines .67
Newspapers .81

Top Five Favorite Magazines
1. *Cosmopolitan*
2. *Sports Illustrated*
3. *Time*
4. *Rolling Stone*
5. *Glamour*

Top Five Cable Networks
1. MTV
2. ESPN
3. HBO
4. CNN
5. Showtime

Source: Anita M. Busch, "What Media Hold Student Interest," *Advertising Age* (February 5, 1990), pp. S-4, S-5

Magazines   Magazines were one of the fastest-growing media of the 1980s—over 2,800 new magazines were introduced during the decade.[25] The marketing advantage of this medium is the great number of special-interest publications that appeal to defined segments. Runners read *Runner's World,* sailors buy *Sail,* gardeners subscribe to *Organic Gardening,* and children peruse *Sports Illustrated for Kids.* Over 200 publications cater to the computer industry, and high-tech companies fill about one-fourth of the ad pages in *Fortune, Forbes, Business Week,* and *Dun's.*[26] Each magazine's readers often represent a unique profile. Take the *Rolling Stone* reader, who tends to travel, backpack, and ski more than most people—a manufacturer of ski equipment that places an ad in *Rolling Stone* may be reaching the desired target audience. In addition to the distinct audience profiles of magazines, good color production is an advantage that allows magazines to create strong images, such as the "Portraits" series used by American Express that won the *Advertising Age* Print Campaign of the Decade award.[27]

Rolling Stone has had a perception problem: many prospective advertisers in the magazine saw it as a magazine read only by 1960s-era hippies. To alter this misperception, it developed a series of "Perception–Reality" ads targeted at its prospective advertisers and ran them in magazines such as *Advertising Age,* which media buyers read. The advertising succeeded in increasing the number of pages of advertising sold in *Rolling Stone.*

The cost of national magazines is a disadvantage compared with radio, but many national publications publish regional and even metro editions, which reduce the absolute cost and wasted coverage. *Time* publishes well over 100 different editions, ranging from a special edition for college students to a version for the area around Austin, Texas. In addition to cost, a limitation to magazines is their infrequency. At best, magazines are printed on a weekly basis, with many specialized publications appearing only monthly or less often.

High technology is arriving in magazine ads. Cardboard pop-up ads have been used by Dodge trucks and Disney World. Revlon offered actual samples of eye shadow in fashion magazines, and if you read *Architectural Digest,* you could

Good color production increases an ad's effectiveness.

even smell a Rolls Royce leather interior using a special scent strip. What's on the horizon? Probably a music-and-blinking-light IBM PC magazine ad made possible by a computer microchip—an ad that has already run in France.[28]

Newspapers Newspapers are an important local medium with excellent reach potential. Because of the daily publication of most papers, they allow advertisements directed to immediate consumer actions such as "sale today only." Usually local retailers use newspapers as almost their sole advertising medium.

Newspapers are rarely saved by the purchaser, so companies are generally limited to ads that call for an immediate customer response (although customers

Who is the target audience? In what type of magazine should it be run? What action is it supposed to trigger? For the answers, see the text.

can clip and save ads they want). Companies also cannot depend on newspapers for color reproduction as good as that in most magazines.

National companies rarely use this medium except in conjunction with local distributors of their products. In these instances both parties often share the advertising costs using a cooperative advertising program, which was described in Chapter 17.

Direct Mail   Direct mail allows the greatest degree of audience selectivity. Direct-mail companies can provide advertisers with a mailing list of their market, such as students who live within two miles of the store, product managers in Texas, or people who own mobile homes. Direct mail has an advantage in providing complete product information, compared with that provided in 30-second or 60-second television or radio spots. In 1989, over 92 million Americans responded to direct-mail advertisements and spent over $183 billion on mail-order purchases.[29]

One disadvantage of direct mail is that rising postal costs are making it more expensive. In fact, many direct-mail advertisers are beginning to use private delivery services, which charge less than the U.S. Postal Service, for catalogs and other "flats."[30] The major limitation is that people view direct mail as junk, and the challenge is to get them to open a letter. Look at Figure 18–9 to see which envelope you think was most successful in overcoming the junk-mail hurdle.

If you picked the one with the simple word *Free,* in a white circle, pass "go," collect $200, and think about becoming a direct-mail consultant. This envelope stands out because of its size. It also gives the impression of a strong offer by prominently displaying the word *free*—a key word in direct mail. This package generated 48 percent more subscription orders than the other two pieces combined. The second-best response was obtained with the "mousetrap" appeal. The splashy graphic with the bright orange circle helped, and again the magic word *free* is displayed. The piece generated 56 percent more promotions

FIGURE 18–9
Are you an expert? Which of the three envelopes did best? The text gives the answer and the reasons.

Source: Based on Jim Powell, "The Lucrative Trade of Crafting Junk Mail," *New York Times* (June 20, 1982), p. F7.

than the third offer. No strong offer is provided with the "Preferred Subscription Invitation," and the envelope is standard size with little enticement to the reader to open it.[31] In this industry, a 1 percent to 2 percent response rate to a mailer is considered good.

Billboards   A very effective medium for reminder advertising is outdoor billboards, such as the eye-catching sign by Sunrise Preschool shown in the accompanying ad. These signs often result in good reach and frequency and have been shown to increase purchase rates.[32] The visibility of this medium is good supplemental reinforcement for well-known products, and it is a relatively low-cost, flexible alternative. A company can buy space just in the desired geographical market.

A disadvantage to billboards is that no opportunity exists for lengthy advertising copy, and thus it is restricted to well-known products. Also, a good billboard site depends on traffic patterns and sight lines. In many areas environmental laws have limited the use of this medium.

Transit   If you have ever lived in a metropolitan area, chances are you might have seen some transit advertising. This medium includes messages on the interior and exterior of buses, subway cars, and taxis. As use of mass transit grows, transit advertising may become increasingly important. Selectivity is available to advertisers, who can buy space by neighborhood or bus route. To some extent, once inside the bus, the riders are captured readers.

One disadvantage to this medium is that the heavy travel times, when the audiences are the largest, are not conducive to reading advertising copy. People are standing shoulder to shoulder on the subway, hoping not to miss their stop, and little attention is paid to the advertising. Also, the demographic profile of the transit user is heavily weighted to middle-class and lower middle-class people with average incomes and educational profiles.

Other Media   A variety of other media exist, ranging from hot air balloons to skywriting and theater advertising (where ads are shown on the screen before the movies are shown). Although you might expect to see advertisements *before*

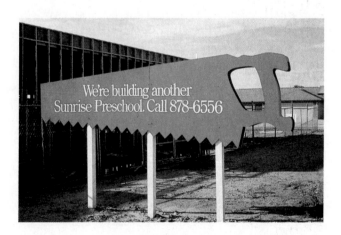

A unique billboard ad.

the movie in your local theater, do you expect to see them *in* the movie itself? Called *product placement,* the brand-name products used in a movie may be there because their manufacturer paid for the privilege. Ads are even starting to appear on the protective boxes covering rental VCR movies and at the start of the movies themselves—and would you believe?—on toilet stall doors![33]

Selection Criteria   Choosing between these alternative media is difficult and hinges on several factors. First, knowing the media habits of the target audience is essential to deciding among the alternatives. Second, occasionally product attributes necessitate that certain media be used. For example, if color is a major aspect of product appeal, radio is excluded. Newspapers allow advertising for quick actions to confront competitors, and magazines are more appropriate for complicated messages because the reader can spend more time reading the message. The final factor in selecting an alternative medium is cost. When possible, alternative media are compared using a common denominator that reflects both reach and cost—a measure such as CPM.

SCHEDULING THE ADVERTISING

There is no correct schedule to advertise a product, but three factors must be considered. First is the issue of *buyer turnover,* which is how often new buyers enter the market to buy the product. The higher the buyer turnover, the greater is the amount of advertising required. A second issue in scheduling is the *purchase frequency;* the more frequently the product is purchased, the less repetition is required. Finally, companies must consider the *forgetting rate,* the speed with which buyers forget the brand if advertising is not seen.

Setting schedules requires an understanding of how the market behaves. Most companies tend to follow one of two basic approaches:

An ad to stimulate seasonal demand.

1 *Steady ("drip") schedule:* When demand and seasonal factors are unimportant, advertising is run at a steady or regular schedule throughout the year.
2 *Pulse ("burst") schedule:* Advertising is distributed unevenly throughout the year because of seasonal demand, heavy periods of promotion, or introduction of a new product.

For example, products such as dry breakfast cereals have a stable demand throughout the year and would typically use a steady schedule of advertising. In contrast, products such as toys, snow blowers, and suntan lotions have seasonal demands and receive heavier, pulse-schedule advertising during the heavy demand season.

CONCEPT CHECK

1 You see the same ad in *Time* and *Fortune* magazines and on billboards and TV. Is this an example of reach or frequency?

2 What is the most selective medium available?

3 What factors must be considered when choosing among alternative media?

EXECUTING THE ADVERTISING PROGRAM

As shown earlier in Figure 18–1, executing the advertising program involves pretesting the advertising copy and actually carrying out the advertising program. John Wanamaker, the founder of Wanamaker's Department Store in Philadelphia, remarked, "I know half my advertising is wasted, but I don't know what half." The purpose of evaluating advertising efforts is to try to ensure that the advertising is not wasted. Evaluation is done usually at two separate times: before and after the advertisements are run in the actual campaign. Several methods used in the evaluation process at the stages of idea formulation and copy development are discussed below. Posttesting methods are reviewed in the section on evaluation.

PRETESTING ADVERTISING

To determine whether the advertisement communicates the intended message or to select among alternative versions of the advertisement, **pretests** are conducted before the advertisements are placed in any medium.

Portfolio Tests   Portfolio tests are used to test copy alternatives. The test ad is placed in a portfolio with several other ads and stories, and consumers are asked to read through the portfolio. Afterward subjects are asked for their impressions of the ads on several evaluative scales, such as from "very informative" to "not very informative."

Jury Tests   Jury tests involve showing the ad copy to a panel of consumers and having them rate how they liked it, how much it drew their attention, and how attractive they thought it was. This approach is similar to the portfolio test in that consumer reactions are obtained. However, unlike the portfolio test, a test advertisement is not hidden within other ads.

Theater Tests   Theater testing is the most sophisticated form of pretesting. Consumers are invited to view new television shows or movies in which test commercials are also shown. Viewers register their feelings about the advertisements either on hand-held electronic recording devices used during the viewing or on questionnaires afterward.

CARRYING OUT THE ADVERTISING PROGRAM

The responsibility for actually carrying out the advertising program can be handled in one of three ways, as shown in Figure 18–10. The **full-service agency** provides the most complete range of services, including market research, media selection, copy development, artwork, and production. Agencies that assist a client by both developing and placing advertisements are compensated by receiving 15 percent of media costs. **Limited-service agencies** specialize in one aspect of the advertising process such as providing creative services to develop the advertising copy or buying previously unpurchased media space. Limited-service agencies that deal in creative work are compensated by a

FIGURE 18–10
Alternative structures of advertising agencies used to carry out the advertising program

TYPE OF AGENCY	SERVICES PROVIDED
Full-service agency	Does research, selects media, develops copy, and produces artwork
Limited–service agency	Specializes in one aspect of creative process; usually provides creative production work; buys previously unpurchased media space
In-house agency	Provides range of services, depending on company needs

contractual agreement for the services performed. Finally, **in-house agencies** made up of the company's own advertising staff may provide full services or a limited range of services.

EVALUATING THE ADVERTISING PROGRAM

The advertising decision process does not stop with executing the advertising program. The advertisements must be posttested to determine whether they are achieving their intended objectives, and results may indicate necessary changes that must be made in the advertising program.

POSTTESTING ADVERTISING

An advertisement may go through **posttests** after it has been shown to the target audience to determine whether it accomplished its intended purpose. Five approaches common in posttesting are[34]:

Aided Recall (Recognition–Readership)   After being shown an ad, respondents are asked whether their previous exposure to it was through reading, viewing, or listening. The Starch test shown in the accompanying photo uses aided recall to determine the percentage (1) who remember seeing a specific magazine ad *(noted)*, (2) who saw or read any part of the ad identifying the product or brand *(seen-associated)*, and (3) who read at least half of the ad *(read most)*. Elements of the ad are then tagged with the results, as shown in the picture.

Unaided Recall   A question such as, "What ads do you remember seeing yesterday?" is asked of respondents without any prompting to determine whether they saw or heard advertising messages.

Attitude Tests   Respondents are asked questions to measure changes in their attitudes after an advertising campaign, such as whether they have a more favorable attitude toward the product advertised.[35]

Inquiry Tests   Additional product information, product samples, or premiums are offered to an ad's readers or viewers. Ads generating the most inquiries are presumed to be the most effective.

Sales Tests   Sales tests involve studies such as controlled experiments (e.g., using radio ads in one market and newspaper ads in another and comparing the results) and consumer purchase tests (measuring retail sales that result from a given advertising campaign). The most sophisticated experimental methods today allow a manufacturer, a distributor, or an advertising agency to manipulate an advertising variable (such as schedule or copy) through cable systems and observe subsequent sales effects by monitoring data collected from checkout scanners in supermarkets.[36]

MAKING NEEDED CHANGES

Results of posttesting the advertising copy are used to reach decisions about changes in the advertising program. If the posttest results show that an advertisement is doing poorly in terms of awareness or cost efficiency, it may be dropped and other ads run in its place in the future. On the other hand, sometimes an advertisement may be so successful it is run repeatedly or used as the basis of a larger advertising program, as with Diet Pepsi's "You've Got the Right One, Baby" ads, which first ran during Superbowl XXV.

CONCEPT CHECK

1 Explain the difference between pretesting and posttesting advertising copy.

2 What is the difference between aided and unaided recall posttests?

ETHICS AND SOCIAL RESPONSIBILITY IN THE 1990s

IS ELECTRONIC ADVERTISING A FREEDOM OF SPEECH OR AN INVASION OF PRIVACY?

Advances in communication technology have led to several new forms of advertising. For example, over 180,000 businesses use automatic-dialing systems to deliver prerecorded messages to 7 million telephone owners daily. In addition, many businesses use fax machines to transmit unsolicited ads to other businesses with fax machines.

Some consumers suggest that calls from "electronic salespeople" are an invasion of privacy. Fax machine owners observe that they are paying for the paper their machine uses to print a message they did not request. Several policy-makers have argued that use of an electronic medium is guaranteed by our constitutional right to free speech, while about a dozen states have passed legislation to restrict electronic advertising. The White House says the number of complaints currently does not warrant legislation.

Can this issue be resolved without a bill from Congress? As an advertiser, what would you recommend?

Source: Jill Smolowe, "Read This," *Time* (November 26, 1990), pp. 62–70.

 ## SUMMARY

1 Advertising may be classified as either product or institutional. Product advertising can be pioneering, competitive, or reminder oriented. Institutional ads are one of these three or advocacy.

2 Advertising decisions center on determining who is the target audience, what to say, when to say it, and where the message should be said. The advertising decision process involves developing, executing, and evaluating the advertising program.

3 Setting advertising objectives, the *what* component, is based on the hierarchy of effects. Objectives should be measurable, have a specified time period, and state the target audience.

4 Budgeting methods often used are percentage of sales, competitive parity, and the all you can afford approaches. The best budgeting approach is based on the objectives set and tasks required.

5 Copywriters have the responsibility of identifying the key benefits of a product and communicating them to the target audience with attention-getting advertising copy. Common appeals include fear, sex, and humor.

6 In selecting the right medium, there are distinct trade-offs among television, radio, magazines, newspapers, direct mail, billboards, transit, and other media. The decision is based on media habits of the target audience, product characteristics, message requirements, and media costs.

7 In determining advertising schedules, a balance must be made between reach and frequency. Scheduling must take into account buyer turnover, purchase frequency, and the rate at which consumers forget.

8 Advertising is evaluated before and after the ad is run. Pretesting can be done with portfolio, jury, or theater tests. Posttesting is done on the basis of aided recall, unaided recall, attitude tests, inquiry tests, and sales tests.

9 To execute an advertising program, companies can use several types of advertising agencies. These firms can provide a full range of services or specialize in creative or placement activities. Some firms use their own in-house agency.

KEY TERMS AND CONCEPTS

product advertisements p. 493
institutional advertisements p. 494
hierarchy of effects p. 496
percentage of sales budgeting p. 497
competitive parity budgeting p. 497
all you can afford budgeting p. 498
objective and task budgeting p. 498
reach p. 503

rating p. 503
frequency p. 503
cost per thousand p. 503
pretests p. 511
full-service agency p. 511
limited-service agencies p. 511
in-house agencies p. 512
posttests p. 512

CHAPTER PROBLEMS AND APPLICATIONS

1 How does competitive product advertising differ from competitive institutional advertising?

2 Suppose you are the advertising manager for a new line of children's fragrances. Which major form of media would you use for this new product?

3 You have recently been promoted to be director of advertising for the Timkin Tool Company. In your first meeting with Mr. Timkin, he says, "Advertising is a waste! We've been advertising for six months now and sales haven't increased. Tell me why we should continue." Give your answer to Mr. Timkin.

4 A large life insurance company has decided to switch from using a strong fear appeal to a humorous approach. What are the strengths and weaknesses of such a change in message strategy?

5 Some national advertisers have found that they can have more impact with their advertising by running a large number of ads for a period and then running no ads at all for a period. Why might such a pulsing strategy be more effective than a steady schedule?

6 Which medium has the lowest cost per thousand?

MEDIUM	COST	AUDIENCE
TV show	$5,000	25,000
Magazine	2,200	6,000
Newspaper	4,800	7,200
FM radio	420	1,600

7 Federated Banks has just developed two versions of an advertisement to encourage senior citizens to directly deposit their Social Security checks with the bank. Direct deposit means the government sends the funds directly to the bank, so that the consumer does not have to go and deposit the check. Suggest how the bank can determine the better ad.

8 The Toro Company has a broad product line. What timing approach would you recommend for the advertising of (1) the lawn mower line and (2) the new line of lawn and garden furniture?

9 What are two advantages and two disadvantages of the advertising posttests described in the chapter?

CHAPTER 19

Personal Selling and Sales Management

*A*fter reading this chapter you should be able to:

- Recognize different types of personal selling.
- Describe the stages in the personal selling process.
- Specify the functions and tasks in the sales management process.
- Determine whether a firm should use manufacturer's representatives or a company salesforce.
- Calculate the number of people needed in a company's sales force.
- Understand how firms recruit, select, train, motivate, compensate, and evaluate salespeople.

A New Breed of Sales Professional

What images come to mind when you hear the word *sales* mentioned as a career? Do you think of fast-talking, yarn-spinning people who travel a lot and are only interested in peddling their products or services? If you do, then you should talk with Wanda Truxillo of IBM (see opposite page). She epitomizes the new breed of sales professionals who list sincerity, customer service, attention to customer needs both before and after a sale, and good listening as the ingredients for successful selling and sales management.

Ms. Truxillo will quickly tell you that "Knowing your customer's business and the products or service you are selling should be second nature. What really sets you apart from your competition is how responsive, ethical, knowledgeable, and good-natured you are when interfacing with your customer. Customer satisfaction is at the core of any successful business."

Wanda Truxillo has been bringing solutions to IBM customers for over 14 years. Her career path illustrates many of the topics described in this chapter. Wanda joined IBM at the age of 23. After training for a year, she became a marketing representative selling office products. Her principal style of selling, emphasizing a close, trusting relationship with customers, soon made her one of the top salespersons in her area. By age 28, she was the specialist for communications products supporting the Southern U.S. region. Within a year, Ms. Truxillo was promoted to marketing manager in a major Southern city. In this capacity, she recruited, trained, motivated, and evaluated a large marketing team responsible for establishing new accounts.

In 1985, Ms. Truxillo became assistant to the president of IBM's National Marketing Division after completing a short staff assignment in strategy and plan management. She is currently manager of mid-range applications, U.S. Marketing and Services. In this position, Ms. Truxillo is responsible for 23 program managers who develop and execute marketing plans and customer programs for IBM's U.S. salesforce, which is consistently rated as one of the best in the country.

Wanda Truxillo has distinguished herself both as an IBM salesperson and a manager of the sales and customer service function. But Ms. Truxillo believes that "Even as a manager you still have to think like a salesperson and maintain constant contact with your customers."[1]

This chapter examines the scope and significance of personal selling and sales management in marketing. It highlights the many forms of personal selling and outlines the selling process. Finally, the functions of sales management are described.

SCOPE AND SIGNIFICANCE OF PERSONAL SELLING AND SALES MANAGEMENT

Chapter 17 described personal selling and management of the sales effort as being part of the firm's promotional mix. Although it is important to recognize that personal selling is a useful vehicle for communicating with present and potential buyers, it is much more. Take a moment to answer the questions in the personal selling and sales management quiz in Figure 19–1. As you read on, compare your answers with those in the text.

NATURE OF PERSONAL SELLING AND SALES MANAGEMENT

Personal selling involves the two-way flow of communication between a buyer and seller, often in a face-to-face encounter, designed to influence a person's or group's purchase decision. However, with advances in telecommunications, personal selling also takes place over the telephone, through video teleconferencing and interactive computer links between buyers and sellers. For example, customers of Haggar Apparel Company can enter purchase orders into

FIGURE 19–1
**Personal selling and
sales management quiz**

1 How attractive do you think each of the following rewards would be to the average salesperson? Rank them, with 1 being "most attractive" and 7 being "least attractive."

REWARDS	RANK
More pay	_____
Sense of accomplishment	_____
Opportunities for personal growth	_____
Promotion	_____
Liking and respect by peers	_____
Security	_____
Recognition	_____

2 "A salesperson's job is finished when a sale is made." True or false? (Circle one)

3 "The primary job of all salespeople is to sell to the user." True or false? (Circle one)

4 About how much is the average cost of making a single sales call by an industrial product salesperson? (Check one)

$100 _____ $150 _____ $200 _____
$125 _____ $175 _____ $225 _____

5 On average, sales training programs devote about what percentage of time to sales techniques? (Check one)

20% _____   40% _____   60% _____
30% _____   50% _____   70% _____

their computer, have it contact Haggar's computer, and find out when the requested products can be shipped.[2]

Personal selling remains a highly human-intensive activity despite the use of technology. Accordingly, the people involved must be managed. **Sales management** involves planning the selling program and implementing and controlling the personal selling effort of the firm. Numerous tasks are involved in managing personal selling, including setting objectives; organizing the sales force; recruiting, selecting, training, and compensating salespeople; and evaluating the performance of individual salespeople.

PERVASIVENESS OF SELLING

"Everyone lives by selling something," wrote author Robert Louis Stevenson a century ago. His observation still holds true today. The Bureau of Labor Statistics reports that about 12 million people are employed in sales positions in the United States. Included in this number are manufacturing sales personnel, real estate brokers, stockbrokers, and salesclerks who work in retail stores. In reality, however, virtually every occupation that involves customer contact has an element of personal selling. For example, attorneys, accountants, bankers, and company personnel recruiters perform sales-related activities, whether or not they acknowledge it.

Victor Kiam, president
and CEO of Remington
Products, Inc., is also
Remington's "principal
salesperson."

Many executives in major companies have held sales positions at some time in their careers. For example, the president of IBM has historically come from the sales department rather than engineering as one might expect. Victor Kiam, the flamboyant president and chief executive officer of Remington Products, Inc., previously held a sales position at Lever Brothers. It might be said that today Kiam is Remington's principal salesperson. It is no accident that these individuals rose from sales and marketing positions to top management. Almost 30 percent of the chief executive officers in the 1,000 largest U.S. corporations have significant sales and marketing experience in their work history.[3] Thus selling often serves as a stepping-stone to top management, as well as being a career path in itself.

PERSONAL SELLING IN MARKETING

Personal selling serves three major roles in a firm's overall marketing effort. First, salespeople are the critical link between the firm and its customers. This role requires that salespeople match company interests with customer needs to satisfy both parties in the exchange process. Second, salespeople *are* the company in a consumer's eyes. They represent what a company is or attempts to be and are often the only personal contact a customer has with the company. For example, IBM takes pride in the image its people like Wanda Truxillo convey to buyers. The "look" projected by salespeople for Avon Products, Inc., is an important factor in communicating the benefits of the company's cosmetic line. Third, personal selling may play a dominant role in a firm's marketing program. This situation typically arises when a firm uses a push marketing strategy, described in Chapter 17. Avon, for example, pays almost 40 percent of its total sales dollars for selling expenses.[4] Pharmaceutical firms and office and educational equipment manufacturers also rely heavily on personal selling in the marketing of their products.

CONCEPT CHECK

1 What is personal selling?

2 What is involved in sales management?

A Frito-Lay salesperson is an order taker.

THE MANY FORMS OF PERSONAL SELLING

Personal selling assumes many forms based on the amount of selling done and the amount of creativity required to perform the sales task. Broadly speaking, three types of personal selling exist: order taking, order getting, and sales support activities.[5] While some firms use only one of these types of personal selling, others use a combination of all three.

ORDER TAKING

Typically an **order taker** processes routine orders or reorders for products that were already sold by the company. The primary responsibility of order takers is to preserve an ongoing relationship with existing customers and maintain sales. Two types of order takers exist. Outside order takers visit customers and replenish inventory stocks of resellers, such as retailers or wholesalers. For example, Frito-Lay salespeople call on supermarkets, neighborhood grocery stores, and other establishments to ensure that the company's line of salty snack products (such as Doritos and Tostitos) is in adequate supply. In addition, outside order takers typically provide assistance in arranging displays. Inside order takers, also called *order* or *salesclerks*, typically answer simple questions, take orders, and complete transactions with customers. Many retail clerks are inside order takers, as are people who take orders from buyers by telephone. In industrial settings, order taking arises in straight rebuy situations. For instance, stationery supply firms have inside order takers. Order takers, for the most part, do little selling in a conventional sense and engage in little problem solving with customers. They often represent simple products that have few options, such as confectionery items, magazine subscriptions, and highly standardized industrial products.

FIGURE 19–2

Comparing order takers and order getters

BASIS OF COMPARISON	ORDER TAKERS	ORDER GETTERS
Objective	Handle routine product orders or reorders	Identify new customers and sales opportunities
Purchase situation	Focus on straight rebuy purchase situations	Focus on new buy and modified rebuy purchase situations
Activity	Perform order processing functions	Act as creative problem solvers
Training	Require significant clerical training	Require significant sales training
Source of sales	Maintain sales volume	Create new sales volume

ORDER GETTING

An **order getter** sells in a conventional sense and identifies prospective customers, provides customers with information, persuades customers to buy, closes sales, and follows up on customers' use of a product or service. Like order takers, order getters can be inside (an automobile salesperson) or outside (an IBM salesperson). Order getting involves a high degree of creativity and customer empathy and typically is required for selling complex or technical products with many options, so considerable product knowledge and sales training are necessary. In modified rebuy or new buy purchase situations in industrial selling, an order getter acts as a problem solver who identifies how a particular product may satisfy a customer's need. Similarly, in the purchase of a service, such as insurance, an insurance agent can provide a mix of plans to satisfy a buyer's needs depending on income, stage of the family's life cycle, and investment objectives. Figure 19–2 compares order getters and order takers to illustrate some important differences between them.

Order getting is an expensive process.[6] It is estimated that the median direct cost of a single sales call for an industrial product is $224.87; a consumer product, $196.26; and a service, $165.85. (What amount did you check for Question 4 in Figure 19–1?) The direct annual cost for a salesperson, including compensation and field expenses (including travel, entertainment, food, and lodging) is $90,250 for industrial products, $80,200 for consumer products, and $68,100 for services. These costs illustrate why telephone selling, with a significantly lower cost per call (in the range of $20–$25) and little or no field expenses, is so popular today.[7]

SALES SUPPORT PERSONNEL

Sales support personnel augment the selling effort of order getters by performing a variety of services. For example, **missionary salespeople** do not directly solicit orders but rather concentrate on performing promotional activities and introducing new products. They are used extensively in the pharmaceutical industry, where they persuade physicians to prescribe a firm's product. Actual

A Xerox Corporation advertisement featuring team selling.

sales are made through wholesalers or directly to pharmacists who fill prescriptions. A **sales engineer** is a salesperson who specializes in identifying, analyzing, and solving customer problems and brings know-how and technical expertise to the selling situation, but often does not actually sell products and services. Sales engineers are popular in selling industrial products such as chemicals and heavy equipment. In short, not all salespeople sell to the actual user. (What was your answer to Question 3 in the quiz?)

In many situations firms engage in **team selling,** the practice of using an entire team of professionals in selling to and servicing major customers.[8] Team selling is used when specialized knowledge is needed to satisfy the different interests of individuals in a customer's buying center. For example, a selling team might consist of a salesperson, a sales engineer, a service representative, and a financial executive, each of whom would deal with a counterpart in the customer's firm. Team selling takes different forms. In **conference selling,** a salesperson and other company resource people meet with buyers to discuss problems and opportunities. In **seminar selling,** a company team conducts an educational program for a customer's technical staff, describing state-of-the-art developments. IBM and Xerox Corporation pioneered this approach in working with prospective buyers. However, other firms have embraced this idea, as described in the accompanying Marketing Action Memo.

CONCEPT CHECK

1 What is the principal difference between an order taker and an order getter?

2 What is team selling?

Marketing Action Memo

THE AUGMENTED SALESPERSON: TEAM SELLING TODAY

*T*he day of the lone salesperson calling on a customer is rapidly becoming history. Many companies today are using teams of professionals to work with customers to improve relationships, find better ways of doing things, and, of course, sell products and services.

Xerox and IBM pioneered team selling, but other firms were quick to follow. General Electric used a team of 50 professionals to win a contract for power equipment at General Motors' new Saturn plant. Procter & Gamble recently formed teams of marketing, sales, advertising, computer systems, and distribution executives to work with its major retailers, such as Wal-Mart. Digital Equipment Corporation (DEC) has created teams composed of salespeople, programmers, and systems engineers pointed at existing and new cus-

tomer accounts. AT&T commonly uses teams composed of product specialists and technical consultants who work with prospective customers.

The popularity of team selling is expected to grow in the 1990s. Why? According to a DEC executive, "We need more resources pointed at customers." Many sellers are now realizing the importance of nurturing long-term and widespread relationships within its customer organization, made possible by team selling.

Sources: Based on Laurie Freeman, "P&G Rolls Out Retailer Sales Teams," *Advertising Age* (May 21, 1990), p. 18; Mark Blessington, "Five Ways to Make Team Selling Work (Really!)" *Business Month* (August 1989), pp. 71–72; "DEC Has One Little Word for 30,000 Employees: Sell," *Business Week* (August 14, 1989), pp. 86, 88; Kate Bertrand, "Marketers Cater to National Accounts," *Business Marketing* (May 1989), p. 37; and "Coordinated Team Effort Shows Winning Results," *The Wall Street Journal* (December 17, 1990), p. B1.

THE PERSONAL SELLING PROCESS

Selling, and particularly order getting, is a complicated activity. Although the salesperson–customer interaction is essential to personal selling, much of a salesperson's work occurs before this meeting and continues after the sale itself. The **personal selling process** consists of six stages: (1) prospecting, (2) preapproach, (3) approach, (4) presentation, (5) close, and (6) follow-up (Figure 19–3).

PROSPECTING

Personal selling begins with *prospecting*—the search for and qualification of potential customers. For some products that are one-time purchases such as encyclopedias, continual prospecting is necessary to maintain sales. There are three types of prospects. A *lead* is the name of a person who may be a possible customer. A *prospect* is a customer who wants or needs the product. If an individual wants the product, can afford to buy it, and is the decision maker, this individual is a *qualified prospect*.

Leads and prospects are generated using several sources. For example, advertising may contain a coupon or a toll-free number to generate leads, as shown in the accompanying AT&T advertisement. Some companies use exhibits at trade fairs, professional meetings, and conferences to generate leads or prospects. Staffed by salespeople, these exhibits are used to attract the attention of prospective buyers and disseminate information. Another approach for generating leads is through *cold canvassing* in person or by telephone.[9] This approach

STAGE	OBJECTIVE	COMMENTS
Prospecting	Search for and qualify prospects	Start of the selling process; prospects produced through advertising, referrals, and cold canvassing.
Preapproach	Gather information and decide how to approach the prospect	Information sources include personal observation, other customers, and own salespeople.
Approach	Gain prospect's attention, stimulate interest, and make transition to the presentation	First impression is critical; gain attention and interest through reference to common acquaintances, a referral, or product demonstration.
Presentation	Begin converting a prospect into a customer by creating a desire for the product or service	Different presentation formats are possible; however, involving the customer in the product or service through attention to particular needs is critical; important to deal professionally and ethically with prospect skepticism, indifference, or objections.
Close	Obtain a purchase commitment from the prospect and create a customer	Salesperson asks for the purchase; different approaches include the trial close and assumptive close.
Follow-up	Ensure that the customer is satisfied with the product or service	Resolve any problems faced by the customer to ensure customer satisfaction and future sales possibilities.

FIGURE 19–3
Stages and objectives of the personal selling process

simply means that a salesperson may open a telephone directory, pick a name, and visit or call that individual. Although the refusal rate is high with cold canvassing, this approach can be successful. For example, Ford Motor Company used a telephone campaign involving 20 million telephone calls, which produced enough leads to keep its 34,000 salespeople busy making presentations for 30 days.[10]

PREAPPROACH

Once a salesperson has identified a qualified prospect, preparation for the sale begins with the preapproach. The *preapproach* stage involves obtaining further information on the prospect and deciding on the best method of approach. Activities in this stage include finding information on who the prospect is, how the prospect prefers to be approached, and what the prospect is looking for in a product or service. For example, a stockbroker will need information on a

An AT&T prospecting advertisement for its direct marketing service.

prospect's discretionary income, investment objectives, and preference for discussing brokerage services over the telephone or in person. For industrial products the preapproach involves identifying the buying role of a prospect (for example, influencer or decision maker), important buying criteria, and the prospect's receptivity to a formal or informal presentation. Identifying the best time to contact a prospect is also important. For example, Northwestern Mutual Life Insurance Company suggests the best times to call on people in different occupations: dentists before 9:30 A.M., lawyers between 11:00 A.M. and 2:00 P.M., and college professors between 7:00 and 8:00 P.M.[11]

APPROACH

The *approach* stage involves the initial meeting between the salesperson and prospect, where the objectives are to gain the prospect's attention, stimulate interest, and build the foundation for the sales presentation itself. The first impression is critical at this stage, and it is common for salespeople to begin the conversation with a reference to common acquaintances, a referral, or even the product or service itself. Which tactic is taken will depend on the information obtained in the prospecting and preapproach stages.

PRESENTATION

The *presentation* is at the core of the order-getting selling process, and its objective is to convert a prospect into a customer by creating a desire for the product

A counter clerk often uses a stimulus-response presentation, whereas a door-to-door salesperson often uses a formula selling presentation.

or service. Three major presentation formats exist: (1) stimulus-response format, (2) formula selling format, and (3) need-satisfaction format.

Stimulus-Response Format   The **stimulus-response presentation** format assumes that given the appropriate stimulus by a salesperson, the prospect will buy. With this format the salesperson tries one appeal after another, hoping to "hit the right button." A counter clerk at McDonald's is using this approach when he or she asks whether you'd like an order of french fries or a dessert with your meal. The counter clerk is engaging in what is called *suggestive selling.* Although useful in this setting, the stimulus-response format is not always appropriate, and for many products a more formalized format is necessary.

Formula Selling Format   A more formalized presentation, the **formula selling presentation** format, is based on the view that a presentation consists of information that must be provided in an accurate, thorough, and step-by-step manner to persuade the prospect to buy. A popular version of this format is the *canned sales presentation,* which is a memorized, standardized message conveyed to every prospect.[12] Used frequently by firms in telephone and door-to-door selling of consumer products (for example, Fuller Brush Company and Encyclopaedia Britannica), this approach treats every prospect the same, regardless of differences in needs or preference for certain kinds of information. Canned sales presentations can be advantageous when the differences between prospects are unknown or with novice salespeople who are less knowledgeable about the product and selling process than experienced salespeople. Although it guarantees a comprehensive presentation, it often lacks flexibility and spontaneity and, more important, does not provide for feedback from the prospective buyer—a critical component in the communication process.

Need-Satisfaction Format   The stimulus-response and formula selling formats share a common characteristic: the salesperson dominates the conversation. By comparison, the **need-satisfaction presentation** format emphasizes probing

Marketing Action Memo

SELLING BY LISTENING—IT WORKS!

Listening, not talking, is a key ingredient in making successful sales presentations. According to Curtis R. Berrien, an executive with Forum Corporation (a major Boston-based sales training firm), a bad salesperson has "an inability to listen, to care, to get off his [or her] agenda and onto the customer's agenda, to be patient. He's [she's] pushy, talks all the time, goes in with preconceived notions, shoots down objectives, drops a client after he [she] makes a sale." A good salesperson is the opposite of this description.

There is good reason why contemporary sales training emphasizes that a salesperson be a good listener and questioner, sensitive to the needs of prospective customers, and a knowledgeable advisor on products and services. Research shows that corporate buyers are impressed most by salespeople who really listen, understand client needs, and answer questions in an honest and forthright manner. On the other hand, corporate buyers are turned off by the hard sell and overly talkative salespeople.

The effective salesperson's primary tools are the probing question and a keen ear, not the quick sales pitch. Probing and listening allows the salesperson to uncover a sales opportunity. Further questions convert the sales opportunity into a need for a product and ultimately the prospect into a customer.

Does this approach work? Firms consistently rated as having the best salespeople, such as IBM, Caterpillar, Scott Paper, Xerox, and Merck, all teach and implement this approach.

Sources: Based on "Talk, Talk, Talk, Talk: Try a Little Listening," *The Wall Street Journal* (March 22, 1990), p. B1; Sharyn Hunt and Ernest F. Cooke, "It's Basic but Necessary: Listen to the Customer," *Marketing News* (March 5, 1990), p. 22; "What Sales Skills Do Your Sales Representatives Lack?" *Inc.* (March 1990), p. 90; Jeremy Main, "How to Sell by Listening," *Fortune* (February 4, 1985), pp. 52–54; and "The Best Salesforce Survey," *Sales & Marketing Management* (June 1989), pp. 32–48.

and listening by the salesperson to identify needs and interests of prospective buyers.[13] Once these are identified, the salesperson tailors the presentation to the prospect and highlights product benefits that satisfy the prospect. The need-satisfaction format, which emphasizes problem solving, is the most consistent with the marketing concept, so many firms have adopted this approach, as described in the accompanying Marketing Action Memo. Two selling styles are associated with this format. **Adaptive selling** involves adjusting the presentation to fit the selling situation, such as knowing when to offer solutions and when to ask for more information. **Consultative selling** focuses on problem identification, where the salesperson serves as an expert on problem recognition and resolution.[14] Both styles are used for industrial products such as computers and heavy equipment. Many consumer service firms such as brokerage and insurance firms and consumer product firms like AT&T and Gillette also subscribe to these selling styles.

Handling Objections   A critical concern in the presentation stage is handling objections. *Objections* are excuses for not making a purchase commitment or decision. Some objections are valid and are based on the characteristics of the product or service or price. However, many objections reflect prospect skepticism or indifference. Whether valid or not, experienced salespeople know that objections do not put an end to the presentation. Rather, techniques can be used to deal with objections in a courteous, ethical, and professional manner. The following six techniques are the most common[15]:

1 *Acknowledge and convert the objection:* This technique involves using the objection as a reason for buying. For example, a prospect might say, "The price is too high." The reply: "Yes, the price is high because we use the finest materials. Let me show you. . . ."

2 *Postpone:* The postpone technique is used when the objection will be dealt with later in the presentation: "I'm going to address that point shortly. I think my answer would make better sense then."

3 *Agree and neutralize:* Here a salesperson agrees with the objection, then shows that it is unimportant. A salesperson would say: "That's true and others have said the same. However, they concluded that issue was outweighed by the other benefits."

4 *Accept the objection:* Sometimes the objection is valid. Let the prospect express such views, probe for the reason behind it, and attempt to stimulate further discussion on the objection.

5 *Denial:* When a prospect's objection is based on misinformation and clearly untrue, it is wise to meet the objection head on with a firm denial.

6 *Ignore the objection:* This technique is used when it appears that the objection is a stalling mechanism or is clearly not important to the prospect.

Each of these techniques requires a calm, professional interaction with the prospect, and is most effective when objections are anticipated in the preapproach stage. Handling objections is a skill requiring a sense of timing, appreciation for the prospect's state of mind, and adeptness in communication. Objections also should be handled ethically. Lying or misrepresenting product or service features are grossly unethical practices.

CLOSE

The *closing* stage in the selling process involves obtaining a purchase commitment from the prospect. This stage is the most important and the most difficult because the salesperson must determine when the prospect is ready to buy. Telltale signals indicating a readiness to buy include body language (prospect reexamines the product or contract closely), statements ("This equipment should reduce our maintenance costs"), and questions ("When could we expect delivery?"). The close itself can take several forms. Three closing techniques are used when a salesperson believes a buyer is about ready to make a purchase: (1) trial close, (2) assumptive close, and (3) urgency close. A *trial close* involves asking the prospect to make a decision on some aspect of the purchase: "Would you prefer the blue or gray model?" An *assumptive close* entails asking the prospect to make choices concerning delivery, warranty, or financing terms under the assumption that a sale has been finalized. An *urgency close* is used to commit the prospect quickly by making reference to the timeliness of the purchase: "The low interest financing ends next week," or, "That is the last model we have in stock." Of course, these statements should be used only if they accurately reflect the situation; otherwise, such claims would be unethical. When a prospect is clearly ready to buy, the final close is used and a salesperson asks for the order.[16]

FOLLOW-UP

The selling process does not end with the closing of a sale. Rather, professional selling requires customer follow-up. One marketing authority equated the follow-up with courtship and marriage,[17] by observing, " . . . the sale merely consummates the courtship. Then the marriage begins. How good the marriage is depends on how well the relationship is managed." The *follow-up* stage includes making certain the customer's purchase has been properly delivered and installed and difficulties experienced with the use of the item are addressed. Attention to this stage of the selling process solidifies the buyer–seller relationship. Moreover, research shows that the cost and effort to obtain repeat sales from a satisfied customer is roughly half of that necessary to gain a sale from a new customer.[18] In short, today's satisfied customers become tomorrow's qualified prospects or referrals. (What was your answer to Question 2 in the quiz?)

CONCEPT CHECK

1 What are the six stages in the personal selling process?

2 What is the distinction between a lead and a qualified prospect?

3 Which presentation format is most consistent with the marketing concept? Why?

THE SALES MANAGEMENT PROCESS

Selling must be managed if it is going to contribute to a firm's overall objectives. Although firms differ in the specifics of how salespeople and the selling effort are managed, the sales management process is similar across firms. Sales management consists of three interrelated functions: (1) sales plan formulation, (2) sales plan implementation, and (3) evaluation of the sales force (Figure 19–4).

SALES PLAN FORMULATION

Formulating the sales plan is the most basic of the three sales management functions. According to the vice president of the Harris Corporation, a manufacturer of electronics products, "If a company hopes to implement its marketing strategy, it really needs a detailed sales planning process."[19] The **sales plan** is a statement describing what is to be achieved and where and how the selling effort of salespeople is to be deployed. Formulating the sales plan involves three tasks: (1) setting objectives, (2) organizing the salesforce, and (3) developing account management policies.

Setting Objectives   Setting objectives is central to sales management because this task specifies what is to be achieved. In practice, objectives are set for the total salesforce and for each salesperson. Selling objectives can be output related and focus on dollar or unit sales volume, number of new customers added, and profit. Alternatively, they can be input related and emphasize the number of sales calls and selling expenses. Output- and input-related objectives are used for the salesforce as a whole and for each salesperson. A third type of objective that

Source: Based on Gilbert A. Churchill, Jr., Neil M. Ford, and Orville C. Walker, Jr., *Sales Force Management,* 3rd ed. (Homewood, Ill.: Richard D. Irwin, 1990), pp. 20–29.

FIGURE 19–4
The sales management process

is behaviorally related is typically specific for each salesperson and includes his or her product knowledge, customer service, and selling and communication skills. Increasingly, firms are also emphasizing knowledge of competition as an objective, since salespeople are calling on customers and should see what competitors are doing.[20]

Whatever objectives are set, they should be precise and measurable and specify the time period over which they are to be achieved. Once established, these objectives serve as performance standards for the evaluation of the salesforce—the third function of sales management.

Organizing the Salesforce   Establishing a selling organization is the second task in formulating the sales plan. Three questions are related to organization. First, should the company use its own salesforce, or should it use independent agents such as manufacturer's representatives? Second, if the decision is made to employ company salespeople, then should they be organized according to geography, customer type, or product or service? Third, how many company salespeople should be employed?

The decision to use company salespeople or independent agents is made infrequently.[21] However, Apple Computer recently switched from using agents to its own salesforce, and Coca-Cola's Food Division replaced its salesforce with independent agents (food brokers). The Optoelectronics Division of Honeywell, Inc., has switched back and forth between agents and its own salesforce over the last 25 years. The decision is based on an analysis of economic and behavioral factors. An economic analysis examines the costs of using both types of salespeople and is a form of break-even analysis.

Consider a situation in which independent agents would receive a 5 percent commission on sales, and company salespeople would receive a 3 percent commission, salaries, and benefits. In addition, with company salespeople, sales administration costs would be incurred for a total fixed cost of $500,000 per year. At what sales level would independent or company salespeople be less costly? This question can be answered by setting the costs of the two options equal to each other and solving for the sales level amount, as shown in the equation below:

$$\underset{0.03(X) + \$500{,}000}{\underline{\text{Total cost of company salespeople}}} = \underset{0.05(X)}{\underline{\text{Total cost of independent agents}}}$$

where X = sales volume. Solving for X, sales volume equals $25 million,

FIGURE 19–5
The case for using company salespeople versus independent agents

CRITERIA	CASE FOR COMPANY SALESFORCE	CASE FOR INDEPENDENT AGENTS
Control	Company selects, trains, supervises, and can use multiple rewards to direct salespeople.	Agents are equally well selected, trained, and supervised by the representative organization.
Flexibility	Company can transfer salespeople, change customer selling practices, and otherwise direct its own salesforce.	Little fixed cost is present with agents; mostly there are variable costs; therefore firm is not burdened with overhead.
Effort	Sales effort is enhanced because salespeople represent one firm, not several; firm loyalty is present; there is better customer service because salespeople receive salary as well as commission.	Agents might work harder than salespeople because compensation is based solely on commissions; customer service is good, since it builds repeat business.
Availability	Knowledgeable agents might not be available where and when needed.	Entrepreneurial spirit of agents will make them available where a marketing opportunity exists.

indicating that below $25 million in sales independent agents would be cheaper, but above $25 million a company salesforce would be cheaper.[22]

Economics alone does not answer this question, however. A behavioral analysis is also necessary and should focus on issues related to the control, flexibility, effort, and availability of independent and company salespeople.[23] Figure 19–5 shows the common behavioral arguments for independent agents versus a company salesforce. An individual firm must weigh the pros and cons of the economic and behavioral considerations before making this decision.

If a company elects to employ its own salespeople, then it must choose an organizational structure based on (1) geography, (2) customer, or (3) product (Figure 19–6). A geographical structure is the simplest organization, where the United States, or indeed the globe, is first divided into regions and each region is divided into districts or territories. Salespeople are assigned to each district with defined geographical boundaries and call on all customers and represent all products sold by the company. The principal advantage of this structure is that it can minimize travel time, expenses, and duplication of selling effort. However, if a firm's products or customers require specialized knowledge, then a geographical structure is not suitable.

When different types of buyers have different needs, a customer sales organizational structure is used. In practice this means that a different salesforce calls on each separate type of buyer. For example, Firestone Tire & Rubber has one salesforce that calls on its own dealers and another that calls on independent dealers, such as gasoline stations. The rationale for this approach is that more effective, specialized customer support and knowledge is provided to buyers. However, this structure often leads to higher administrative costs and some

FIGURE 19–6 **Organizing the salesforce by customer, product, and geography**

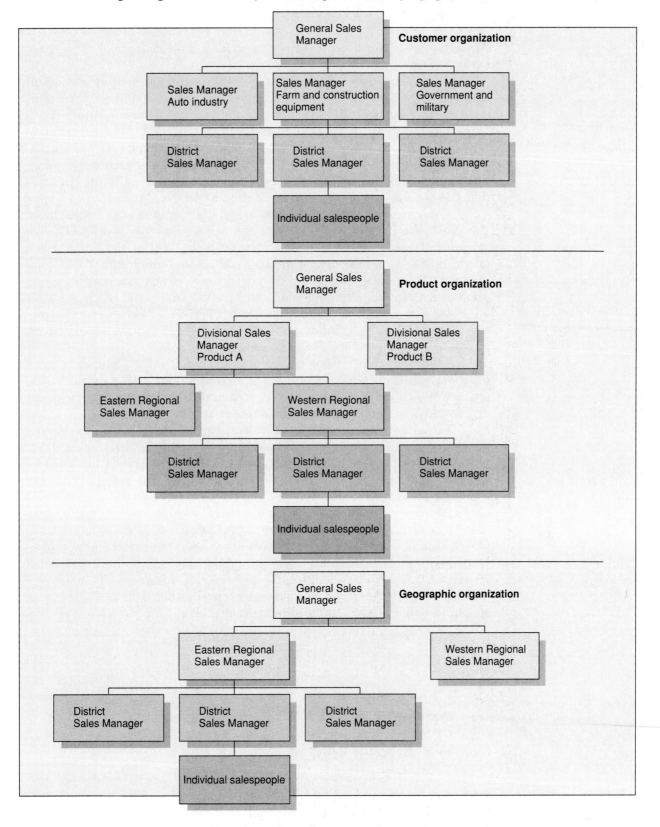

duplication of selling effort, since two separate salesforces are used to represent the same products.

A variation of the customer organizational structure is **major account management,** the practice of using team selling to focus on important customers so as to build mutually beneficial, long-term, cooperative relationships.[24] Major account management involves teams of sales, service, and often technical personnel who work with purchasing, manufacturing, engineering, logistics, and financial executives in customer organizations. This recent innovation, which often assigns company personnel to a customer account, results in "customer specialists" who can provide exceptional service. At the same time, it suffers from the same disadvantages of the typical customer sales organization.

When specific knowledge is required to sell certain types of products, then a product sales organization is used. For example, Procter & Gamble has a salesforce that sells household cleaning products and another that sells food products. The primary advantage of this structure is that salespeople can develop expertise with technical characteristics, applications, and selling methods associated with a particular product or family of products. However, this structure also produces high administrative costs and duplication of selling effort, since two company salespeople call on the same customer.

In short, there is no one best sales organization for all companies in all situations. Rather, the organization of the salesforce should reflect the marketing strategy of the firm. Each year about 10 percent of U.S. firms change their sales organizations to implement new marketing strategies.[25]

The third question related to salesforce organization involves determining the size of the salesforce. For example, why does Keebler have about 1,300 salespeople who call on supermarkets and grocery stores to sell snack foods, whereas Frito-Lay, Inc., has about 10,000 salespeople? The answer lies in the difference between these firms in terms of the number of accounts (customers) served, the frequency of calls on accounts, the length of an average call, and the amount of time a salesperson can devote to selling.

A common approach for determining the size of a sales force is the **workload method.**[26] This formula-based method integrates the number of customers served, call frequency, call length, and available selling time to arrive at a figure for the salesforce size. For example, Frito-Lay needs about 10,000 salespeople according to the workload method formula:

$$NS = \frac{NC \times CF \times CL}{AST}$$

where:

NS = number of salespeople

NC = number of customers

CF = call frequency necessary to service a customer each year

CL = length of an average call

AST = average amount of selling time available per year

Frito-Lay sells its products to 315,000 supermarkets, grocery stores, and other establishments. Salespeople should call on these accounts at least once a week, or 52 times a year. The average sales call lasts 54 minutes (0.90 hour). An average salesperson works 2,000 hours a year (50 weeks × 40 hours a week), but 10 hours a week are devoted to nonselling activities such as travel, leaving 1,500 hours a year. Using these guidelines, Frito-Lay would need:

$$NS = \frac{315,000 \times 52 \times 0.90}{1,500} = 9,828 \text{ salespeople}$$

The value of this formula is apparent in its flexibility, since a change in any one of the variables will affect the number of salespeople needed. Changes are determined, in part, by the firm's account management policies.

Developing Account Management Policies   The third task in formulating a sales plan involves developing **account management policies** specifying whom salespeople should contact, what kinds of selling and customer service activities should be engaged in, and how these activities should be carried out.[27] These policies might state which individuals in a buying organization should be contacted, the amount of sales and service effort that different customers should receive, and the kinds of information salespeople should collect before or during a sales call.

An example of an account management policy in Figure 19–7 shows how different accounts or customers can be grouped according to level of opportunity and the firm's competitive sales position. When specific account names are placed in each cell, salespeople clearly see which accounts should be contacted,

FIGURE 19–7

Account management policy grid

		COMPETITIVE POSITION OF SALES ORGANIZATION	
		High	Low
ACCOUNT OPPORTUNITY	High	1 *Attractiveness:* Accounts offer good opportunity, since they have high potential and sales organization has a strong position. *Account management policy:* Accounts should receive high level of sales calls and service to retain and possibly build accounts.	3 *Attractiveness:* Accounts may offer good opportunity if sales organization can overcome its weak position. *Account management policy:* It should emphasize a heavy sales and service effort to build sales organization position or shift resources to other accounts if stronger sales organization position impossible.
	Low	2 *Attractiveness:* Accounts are somewhat attractive, since sales organization has a strong position, but future opportunity is limited. *Account management policy:* Accounts should receive moderate level of sales and service to maintain current position of sales organization.	4 *Attractiveness:* Accounts offer little or no opportunity, and sales organization position is weak. *Account management policy:* Accounts should receive minimal level of sales and service effort by replacing personal calls with telephone sales or direct mail. Consider dropping account.

Sources: Adapted from Gilbert A. Churchill, Jr., Neil M. Ford, and Orville C. Walker, Jr., *Sales Force Management*, 3rd ed. (Homewood, Ill.: Richard D. Irwin, 1990), p. 232; David W. Cravens and Raymond W. LaForge, "Sales Force Deployment," in Arch G. Woodside, ed., *Advances in Business Marketing* (Greenwich, Conn.: JAI Press, Inc., 1986), pp. 67–112; Raymond W. LaForge and Clifford E. Young, "A Portfolio Model for Planning Sales Call Coverage of Accounts," *Business*, vol. 35 (1985), pp. 10–16; and Alan Dubinsky and Thomas Ingram, "A Portfolio Approach to Account Profitability," *Industrial Marketing Management*, vol. 13 (1984), pp. 33–41.

with what level of selling and service activity, and how to deal with them. For example, accounts in Cells 1 and 2 might have high frequencies of sales calls and increased time spent on a call. Cell 3 accounts will have lower call frequencies, and Cell 4 accounts might be contacted by telephone rather than in person.

SALES PLAN IMPLEMENTATION

The sales plan is put into practice through the tasks associated with sales plan implementation. Whereas sales plan formulation focuses on "doing the right things," implementation emphasizes "doing things right." The three major tasks involved in implementing a sales plan are (1) salesforce recruitment and selection, (2) salesforce training, and (3) salesforce motivation and compensation.

Salesforce Recruitment and Selection   Effective recruitment and selection of salespeople is one of the most crucial tasks of sales management.[28] It entails finding people who match the type of sales position required by a firm. Re-

FIGURE 19–8
Job analysis for an order-getting salesperson

JOB FACTOR	ACTIVITIES
Assisting and working with district management	Assisting district sales management in market surveys, new product evaluations, etc.
	Preparing reports on territorial sales expenses
	Managing a sales territory within the sales expense budget
	Using district management to make joint sales calls on customers
Customer service	Arranging credit adjustments on incorrect invoicing, shipping, and order shortages
	Informing customers of supply conditions on company products
	Assisting customers and prospects in providing credit information to the company
Personal integrity and selling ethics	Representing company products at their true value
	Working within the merchandising plans and policies established by the company
	Investigating and reporting customer complaints
Direct selling	Knowing correct applications and installations of company products
	Making sales presentations that communicate product benefits
	Handling sales presentations
Developing relationships with customers	Maintaining a friendly, personal relationship with customers
	Using equipment to strengthen the business relationship with customers
	Providing customers with technical information on company products
Keeping abreast of market conditions	Keeping customers informed of market conditions that affect their businesses
	Keeping the company informed of market conditions
Meeting sales objectives	Identifying the person with authority to make the purchasing decision
	Closing the sale and obtaining the order
	Selling company products at a volume that meets or exceeds expectations
Maintaining complete customer records	Maintaining customer records that are complete and up to date
	Checking customers' inventory and recommending orders

Source: Lawrence M. Lamont and William J. Lundstrom, "Defining Industrial Sales Behavior: A Factor Analytic Study," *1974 Combined Proceedings* (Chicago: American Marketing Association, 1974), pp. 493–98; by permission of the American Marketing Association.

cruitment and selection practices would differ greatly between order-taking and order-getting sales positions, given the differences in the demands of these two jobs. Therefore recruitment and selection begin with a carefully crafted job analysis.

A **job analysis** is a written description of what a salesperson is expected to do, and therefore it differs among firms.[29] Figure 19–8 shows a job analysis for building material salespeople—an order-getting sales position. This analysis identifies eight major job factors and describes important activities associated with each. Note particularly the frequent mention of customer service functions and the specific reference to personal integrity and selling ethics.

Determining what makes a good salesperson is tricky, and the list of characteristics is endless. However, a study that asked sales executives to differentiate between successful and unsuccessful salespeople concerning 24 personal characteristics identified the profiles shown in Figure 19–9. Clearly, a pattern emerges that is consistent with the description of successful selling behaviors discussed in the beginning of this chapter.

Firms use a variety of methods for evaluating prospective salespeople. Personal interviews, reference checks, and background information provided on

FIGURE 19–9
Characteristics of successful and unsuccessful salespeople

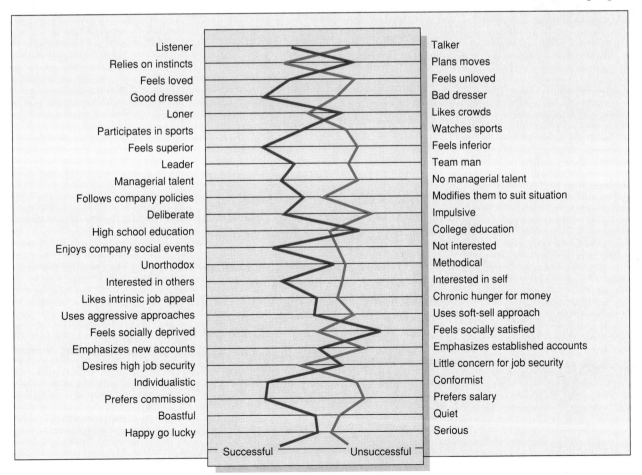

Source: Redrawn from Bradley D. Lockman and John H. Hallaq, "Who Are Your Successful Salespeople?" *Journal of the Academy of Marketing Science* (Fall 1982), p. 466.

Marketing Research Report

PROBING THE PSYCHE OF THE SUCCESSFUL SALESPERSON

How would you answer the following two questions?

1 If performing the following activities paid the same compensation and carried equal status, which would you choose? (*a*) Representing clients in court, (*b*) performing as a concert pianist, (*c*) commanding a ship, or (*d*) advising clients on electronic problems.

2 Among these statements, which best describes you? (*a*) I don't need to be the focus of attention at parties, (*b*) I have a better understanding of what politicians are up to than most of my associates, or (*c*) I don't delay making decisions that are unpleasant.

Your answers, when considered with answers to 179 other questions, could offer insight into your potential as a salesperson, according to Herbert Greenberg, president of Personality Dynamics, Inc. (PDI), a management consulting and testing firm. Greenberg, along with other behavioral scientists, believes that personality may have more to do with successful selling than a person's experience, age, education, or sex.

Although training is important, behavioral scientists point out that the basic raw material must be there to work with. Testing allows sales managers to look beyond the employment interview and résumé and examine fundamental behavioral characteristics, including personal drive, a desire to persuade others, resiliency, and empathy for others.

Are such tests useful? One company gave the PDI test to 20 salespeople, including a group of top performers and those who were soon to be fired. The test identified both groups perfectly.

However, the value of psychological testing remains a hotly debated issue. About 25 percent of U.S. companies use these tests in the salesperson selection process, but almost 50 percent of multinational firms use them in salesperson selection.

Sources: Based on "Latest Psychological-Testing Craze Aims to Look Ahead to the Way We'll Work," *The Wall Street Journal* (February 7, 1990), pp. B1, B6; John S. Hill and Meg Birdseye, "Salesperson Selection in Multinational Corporations: An Empirical Study," *Journal of Personal Selling & Sales Management* (Summer 1989), pp. 39–47; Richard Nelson, "Maybe It's Time to Take Another Look at Tests as a Sales Selection Tool?" *Journal of Personal Selling & Sales Management* (August 1987), pp. 33–38; and Sara Delano, "Improving the Odds for Hiring Success," reprinted with permission, *Inc.* magazine (June 1983). Copyright 1983 by *Inc.* Publishing Company, 38 Commercial Wharf, Boston, MA 02110.

application blanks are the most frequently used methods.[30] However, a number of firms use psychological tests to complement these methods, as described in the accompanying Marketing Research Report.

Salesforce Training Whereas recruitment and selection of salespeople is a one-time event, salesforce training is an ongoing process that affects both new and seasoned salespeople. For example, new IBM salespeople train for two years, and experienced IBM salespeople are expected to spend 15 percent of their time each year in additional training. Sales training covers much more than selling practices. On average, training programs devote 35 percent of time to product information, 30 percent to sales techniques, 25 percent to market and company information, and 10 percent to other topics, including ethical practices.[31] (What was your answer to Question 5 on the quiz?)

Training salespeople is an expensive and time-consuming process.[32] The direct cost of training a new industrial product salesperson (excluding salary) is $22,236, and takes eight months. Training a new consumer product salesperson costs $11,616, and takes five months, and training new salespeople in service industries costs $14,501, and takes seven months. On-the-job training is the most popular type of training, followed by individual instruction taught by experienced salespeople. Formal classes and seminars taught by sales trainers are also growing in popularity.[33]

Salesforce Motivation and Compensation   A sales plan cannot be successfully implemented without motivated salespeople. Research on salesperson motivation suggests that (1) a clear job description, (2) effective sales management practices, (3) a sense of achievement, and (4) proper incentives or rewards will produce a motivated salesperson.[34] A study on the attractiveness of different rewards given to salespeople by companies indicates that more pay was most preferred, followed in order by opportunities for personal growth, a personal sense of accomplishment, promotion, liking and respect for peers, job security, and recognition.[35] (How did you answer Question 1 on the quiz?)

The importance of more pay as a motivating factor means that close attention must be given to how salespeople are financially rewarded for their efforts. Salespeople are paid using one of three plans: (1) straight salary, (2) straight commission, or (3) a combination of salary and commission. Under a **straight salary compensation plan** a salesperson is paid a fixed fee per week, month, or year. With a **straight commission compensation plan** a salesperson's earnings are directly tied to the sales or profit generated. For example, an insurance agent might receive a 2 percent commission of $2,000 for selling a $100,000 life insurance policy. A **combination compensation plan** contains a specified salary plus a commission on sales or profit generated. Obviously each plan has its advantages and disadvantages and is particularly suited to certain situations (Figure 19–10).

Of course, nonmonetary rewards are also given to salespeople for meeting or exceeding objectives. These rewards include trips, honor societies (such as the Xerox President's Club), distinguished salesperson awards, and letters of commendation.[36] Some unconventional rewards include the new pink Cadillacs, fur coats, and jewelry given by Mary Kay Cosmetics to outstanding salespeople.

Mary Kay recognizes a top salesperson.

Effective recruitment, selection, training, motivation, and compensation programs combine to create a productive salesforce. Ineffective practices often lead to costly salesforce turnover. U.S. and Canadian firms experience an annual 27 percent turnover rate, which means that about one of every four salespeople are replaced each year. The expense of replacing and training a new salesperson, including the cost of lost sales, can be as high as $75,000.[37] Moreover, new recruits are often less productive than established salespeople.

SALESFORCE EVALUATION

The final function in the sales management process involves evaluating the salesforce. It is at this point that salespeople are assessed as to whether sales objectives were met and account management policies were followed. Both quantitative and behavioral measures are used.

Quantitative Assessments   Quantitative assessments are based on input- and output-related objectives set forth in the sales plan. Input-related measures focus on the actual activities performed by salespeople such as those involving sales

	STRAIGHT SALARY	STRAIGHT COMMISSION	COMBINATION
Frequency of use	12%	5%	83%
Especially useful	When compensating new salespersons; when a firm moves into new sales territories that require developmental work; when salespersons need to perform many nonselling activities	When highly aggressive selling is required; when nonselling tasks are minimized; when company cannot closely control salesforce activities	When sales territories have relatively similar sales potentials; when firm wishes to provide incentive but still control salesforce activities
Advantages	Provides salesperson with maximum amount of security; gives sales manager large amount of control over salespersons; easy to administer; yields more predictable selling expenses	Provides maximum amount of incentive; by increasing commission rate, sales managers can encourage salespersons to sell certain items; selling expenses relate directly to sales resources	Provides certain level of financial security; provides some incentive; selling expenses fluctuate with sales revenue; sales manager has some control over salesperson's nonselling activities
Disadvantages	Provides no incentive; necessitates closer supervision of salespersons' activities; during sales declines, selling expenses remain at same level	Salespersons have little financial security; sales manager has minimum control over salesforce; may cause salespeople to provide inadequate service to smaller accounts; selling costs less predictable	Selling expenses less predictable; may be difficult to administer

Source: Gilbert A. Churchill, Jr., Neil M. Ford, and Orville C. Walker, Jr., *Sales Force Management: Planning, Implementation, and Control*, 3rd ed. (Homewood, Ill.: Richard D. Irwin, 1990), p. 543.

FIGURE 19–10
Comparison of different compensation plans

calls, selling expenses, and account management policies. The number of sales calls made, selling expense related to sales made, and the number of reports submitted to superiors are the most frequently used input measures.

Output measures focus on the results obtained and include sales produced, accounts generated, profit achieved, and orders produced compared with calls made. Dollar sales volume, last year/current year sales ratio, the number of new accounts, and sales of specific products are the most frequently used measures when evaluating salesperson output.[38]

Behavioral Evaluation   Less-quantitative behavioral measures are also used to evaluate salespeople. These include subjective and often informal assessments of a salesperson's attitude, product knowledge, selling and communication skills, appearance, and demeanor. Even though these assessments are highly subjective, they are frequently considered, and in fact inevitable, in salesperson evaluation.[39] Moreover, these factors are often important determinants of quantitative outcomes.

CONCEPT CHECK

1 What are the three types of selling objectives?

2 What three factors are used to structure sales organizations?

3 Sales training typically focuses on what two sales-related issues?

ETHICS AND SOCIAL RESPONSIBILITY IN THE 1990s

THE ETHICS OF GIFT GIVING

Gift giving is a nice gesture. However, when salespeople give a gift to a customer, ethical issues arise in the form of bribery.

A recent survey of purchasing professionals indicated that only 3 percent said they would not accept favors from sellers. This finding is surprising since most company codes of ethics specifically address the unethical nature of accepting gifts, including the value of the gift. Nevertheless, ethical judgement often must be exercised.

Listed below are three situations involving the receiving of a Christmas gift in the amount of $10, $25, and $50. What percentage of purchasing professionals do you think would view each gift as ethical or unethical?

A SALESPERSON	PERCENT SAYING GIFT WAS	
	ETHICAL	UNETHICAL
Gives a customer a $10 Christmas present	_____	_____
Gives a customer a $25 Christmas present	_____	_____
Gives a customer a $50 Christmas present	_____	_____

Source: Based on Peter Bradley, "Purchasing Ethics? The Rest of Business Should Be So Strict," *Purchasing* (May 4, 1989), pp. 24–25; "Vendors' Gifts Pose Problems for Purchasers," *The Wall Street Journal* (June 26, 1989), pp. B1, B4; and I. Fredrick Trawick and John E. Swan, "How Salespeople Err with Purchasers: Overstepping Ethical Bounds," *The Journal of Business and Industrial Marketing* (Summer 1988), pp. 5–11.

SUMMARY

1 Personal selling involves the two-way flow of communication between a buyer and a seller, often in a face-to-face encounter, designed to influence a person's or group's purchase decision. Sales management involves planning the sales program and implementing and controlling the personal selling effort of the firm.

2 Personal selling is pervasive in the U.S. economy, since virtually every occupation that involves customer contact has an element of selling attached to it.

3 Personal selling plays a major role in a firm's marketing effort. Salespeople occupy a boundary position between buyers and sellers; they *are* the company to many buyers and account for a major cost of marketing in a variety of industries.

4 Three types of personal selling exist: order-taking, order-getting, and sales support activities. Each type differs from the others in terms of actual selling done and the amount of creativity required to perform the job.

5 The personal selling process, particularly for order getters, is a complex activity involving six stages: (1) prospecting, (2) preapproach, (3) approach, (4) presentation, (5) close, and (6) follow-up.

6 The sales management process consists of three interrelated functions: (1) sales plan formulation, (2) sales plan implementations and (3) evaluation of the salesforce.

7 A sales plan is a statement describing what is to be achieved and where and how the selling effort of salespeople is to be deployed. Sales planning involves setting objectives, organizing the salesforce, and developing account management policies.

8 Effective salesforce recruitment and selection efforts, sales training that emphasizes selling skills and product knowledge, and motivation and compensation practices are necessary to successfully implement a sales plan.

9 Salespeople are evaluated using quantitative and behavioral measures that are linked to selling objectives and account management policies.

KEY TERMS AND CONCEPTS

personal selling p. 518
sales management p. 519
order taker p. 521
order getter p. 522
missionary salespeople p. 522
sales engineer p. 523
team selling p. 523
conference selling p. 523
seminar selling p. 523
personal selling process p. 524
stimulus-response presentation p. 527
formula selling presentation p. 527
need-satisfaction presentation p. 527
adaptive selling p. 528

consultative selling p. 528
sales plan p. 530
major account management p. 534
workload method p. 534
account management policies p. 535
job analysis p. 537
straight salary compensation plan p. 539
straight commission compensation plan p. 539
combination compensation plan p. 539

CHAPTER PROBLEMS AND APPLICATIONS

1 Jane Dawson is a new sales representative for Charles Schwab brokerage firm. In searching for clients, Jane purchased a mailing list of subscribers to *The Wall Street Journal* and called them all regarding their interest in discount brokerage services. She asked if they have any stocks and if they have a regular broker. Those people without a regular broker were asked their investment needs. Two days later Jane called back with investment advice and asked if they would like to open an account. Identify each of Jane Dawson's actions in terms of the steps of selling.

2 For the first 50 years of business the Johnson Carpet Company produced carpets for residential use. The salesforce was structured geographically. In the past five years a large percentage of carpet sales has been to industrial users, hospitals, schools, and architects. The company also has broadened its product line to include area rugs, Oriental carpets, and wall-to-wall carpeting. Is the present salesforce structure appropriate, or would you recommend an alternative?

3 Where would you place each of the following sales jobs on the order taker/order getter continuum shown below? *(a)* Burger King counter clerk, *(b)* automobile insurance salesperson, *(c)* IBM computer salesperson, *(d)* life insurance salesperson, and *(e)* shoe salesperson.

Order taker   **Order getter**

4 Listed below are three different firms. Which compensation plan would you recommend for each firm, and what reasons would you give for your recommendations? (*a*) A newly formed company that sells lawn care equipment on a door-to-door basis directly to consumers, (*b*) the Nabisco Company, which sells heavily advertised products in supermarkets by having the salesforce call on these stores and arrange shelves, set up displays, and make presentations to store buying committees, and (*c*) the Wang word processing division, which makes word processing system presentations to company buying committees consisting of purchasing agents and future users.

5 The TDK tape company services 1,000 audio stores throughout the United States. Each store is called on 12 times a year, and the average sales call lasts 30 minutes. Assuming a salesperson works 40 hours a week, 50 weeks a year, and devotes 75 percent of the time to actual selling, how many salespeople does TDK need?

6 A furniture manufacturer is currently using manufacturer's representatives to sell its line of living room furniture. These representatives receive an 8 percent commission. The company is considering hiring its own salespeople and has estimated that the fixed cost of managing and paying their salaries would be $1 million annually. The salespeople would also receive a 4 percent commission on sales. The company has sales of $25 million dollars, and sales are expected to grow by 15 percent next year. Would you recommend that the company switch to its own salesforce? Why or why not?

7 Suppose someone said to you, "The only real measure of a salesperson is the amount of sales produced." How might you respond?

8 Which input and output salesperson evaluation measures might be best suited for the order-getting salesperson described in the job analysis in Figure 19–8?

9 Which type of personal selling—order getting, order taking, or support—is the most likely to be taken over by interactive computer links between buyers and sellers? Why?

10 How might a company personnel recruiter use the six-stage selling process when recruiting you during a campus interview?

Managing the Marketing Process

Part V explains how marketing executives search for and maintain sustainable competitive advantage through planning, implementation, and control. In Chapter 20 three key aspects of planning—situation analysis, goal setting, and the marketing program—are described. In Chapter 21 the incredible success of Thomas S. Monaghan, founder of Domino's Pizza, illustrates implementation and control. Both chapters utilize a case description of how Steven Rothschild, president of General Mills's Convenience and International Food Group, planned, implemented, and controlled the marketing of Yoplait yogurt.

CHAPTER 20

The Strategic Marketing Process: The Planning Phase

After reading this chapter you should be able to:

■ Describe how the three key aspects of planning—situation analysis, goal setting, and the marketing program—relate to the strategic marketing process.

■ Explain how sales response functions help a marketing manager allocate the firm's marketing effort.

■ List the generic strategies available to increase profit.

■ Describe the characteristics of a good marketing plan.

■ Explain how marketing managers can use the growth-share matrix and the market-product grid to help plan strategy.

Swiss Chocolate and Cereal: The Latest Breakfast Combination

When General Mills decided to enter the European market with its consumer package goods, it faced a formidable task—obtaining distribution of its products. Although the European market for ready-to-eat cereal was worth $1.6 billion, General Mills had no sales outside North America. The solution: a joint venture with Nestlé, the largest food company in the world, which had an extensive distribution system in Europe.

The decision to move overseas followed market research that showed the cereal business was growing at a rate of more than 20 percent in France and Italy, and at about 10 percent in West Germany. As one analyst explained, however, "General

547

Mills would not have been able to make much progress on its own." The arrangement with Nestlé represents an efficient way to quickly become a competitive force in the European market. In addition, the strategy is consistent with General Mills's commitment to finding new investment opportunities and serving attractive consumer segments. From 1990 through 1992, General Mills will invest over $1.35 billion in its businesses.[1]

The company's investments have led to dramatic changes during the past two decades. During the 1970s and 1980s, General Mills moved out of some businesses, such as specialty retailing, while increasing its offerings in two core businesses—consumer foods and restaurants. The consumer foods include well-known grocery products such as Wheaties, Cheerios, and Total cereals; Betty Crocker cake, brownie, and muffin mixes; Pudding Roll-Ups; and Yoplait yogurt. The restaurant lines include the Red Lobster chain and over 210 Olive Garden restaurants. These businesses have helped General Mills increase sales by more than 10 percent per year, to over 6 billion dollars.[2] To continue this growth through the 1990s, the company faces some critical decisions in applying its strategic marketing process to adding new products, serving new markets, and allocating resources to current businesses.

This chapter covers planning, the first phase in the strategic marketing process introduced in Chapter 2. Implementation and control, the second and third phases, are discussed in Chapter 21.

STRATEGIC MARKETING'S GOAL: EFFECTIVE RESOURCE ALLOCATION

Marketing executives search continuously to find **sustainable competitive advantage**—a strength such as reputation for quality, customer service, or low-cost production—in the markets they serve and the products they offer. Having identified this sustainable competitive advantage, they must allocate their firm's resources to exploit it.[3]

ALLOCATING MARKETING RESOURCES USING SALES RESPONSE FUNCTIONS

A **sales response function** relates the expense of marketing effort to the marketing results obtained. For simplicity in the examples that follow, only the effects of annual marketing effort on annual sales revenue will be analyzed, but the concept applies to other measures of marketing success—such as profit, units sold, or level of awareness—as well.

Maximizing Incremental Revenue Minus Incremental Cost   Economists give managers a specific guideline for optimal resource allocation: allocate the firm's marketing, production, and financial resources to the markets and products where the excess of incremental revenues over incremental costs is greatest. This parallels the marginal revenue–marginal cost analysis of Chapter 12.

Figure 20–1 illustrates this resource allocation principle. The firm's annual marketing effort, such as sales and advertising expenses, is plotted on the horizontal axis. As this annual marketing effort increases, so does the resulting

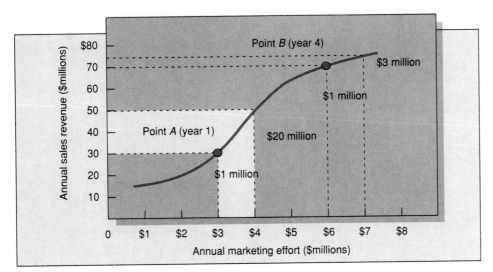

FIGURE 20–1
Sales response function showing the situation for two different years

annual sales revenue. The relationship is assumed to be S-shaped, showing that an additional $1 million of marketing effort results in far greater increases of sales revenue in the mid-range (such as $4 million) than at either end (such as $2 million or $7 million).

A Numerical Example of Resource Allocation   Suppose Figure 20–1 shows the situation for a new General Mills product such as Yoplait Light yogurt. Also assume the sales revenue response function doesn't change through time. Point *A* shows the position of the firm in year 1, and point *B* shows it three years later in year 4. Marketing effort in the form of advertising and other promotions has increased from $3 million to $6 million a year, while sales revenue has increased from $30 million to $70 million a year.

Let's look at the major resource allocation question: what are the probable increases in sales revenue in years 1 and 4 for an extra $1 million of marketing effort? As Figure 20–1 reveals:

Year 1
   Increase in marketing effort from $3 million to $4 million = $1 million
   Increase in sales revenue from $30 million to $50 million = $20 million
   Ratio of incremental sales revenue to effort = $20,000,000:$1,000,000 = 20:1
Year 4
   Increase in marketing effort from $6 million to $7 million = $1 million
   Increase in sales revenue from $70 million to $73 million = $3 million
   Ratio of incremental sales revenue to effort = $3,000,000:$1,000,000 = 3:1

Thus in year 1 a dollar of extra marketing effort returned $20 in sales revenue, whereas in year 4 it returned only $3. If no other expenses are incurred, it might make sense to spend $1 million in year 4 to gain $3 million in incremental sales revenue. However, it may be far wiser for General Mills to invest the money in one of its other businesses, such as additional promotion for Olive Garden restaurants. The essence of resource allocation is simple: put incremental resources where the incremental returns are greatest over the foreseeable future.

ALLOCATING MARKETING RESOURCES IN PRACTICE

General Mills, like many firms in these businesses, does extensive analysis using **share points**, or percentage points of market share, as the common basis of comparison to allocate marketing resources effectively. This allows it to seek answers to the question "How much is it worth to us to try to increase our market share by another 1 [or 2, or 5, or 10] percentage point?"

This also enables higher-level managers to make resource allocation trade-offs among different kinds of businesses owned by the company, such as between Oatmeal Swirlers hot cereal, Red Lobster restaurants, and Gold Medal flour. To make these resource allocation decisions, marketing managers must estimate (1) the market share for the product, (2) the revenues associated with each point of market share (it may be $50 million for hot cereals, $10 million for seafood restaurants, and $5 million for flour), and (3) the contribution to overhead and profit (or gross margin) of each share point.

The resource allocation process has helped General Mills to focus on its core businesses and select from among many investment opportunities. Here are some of the decisions it made in 1989 and 1990:

- *Consumer foods:* Introduce two Cheerios brand line extensions—Apple Cinnamon Cheerios and Honey Nut Cheerios; a new popcorn product—Pop Secret Light; a new fruit snack product—Surfs Up!; and several new flour products. Expand production capacity of Squeezit fruit drink, and expand distribution of two new fruit snacks—Berry Bears and Shark Bites.
- *Restaurants:* Acquire 26 Seafood Broiler restaurants in Southern California and convert them to Red Lobster restaurants. Begin to use nationwide network television advertising. Continue to add new Olive Garden restaurants in North America, and move toward a goal of 350 units within five years.

These decisions reflect General Mills's assessment of what actions will best prepare it for the 1990s. Given the many product and market options and a constantly changing environment, the company must continually evaluate which alternatives are most likely to meet company growth and profit targets. For example, less than two years ago it decided against expanding its cereal business into Europe because the expected returns would not justify the investment risk. Today, the new venture with Nestlé represents an acceptable investment.[4]

CONCEPT CHECK

  1   **What is the significance of the S-shape of the sales response function in Figure 20–1?**

  2   **What is the purpose of resource allocation in an organization?**

THE PLANNING PHASE OF THE STRATEGIC MARKETING PROCESS

After clarifying some basic terms, we will analyze the three steps of the planning phase of the strategic marketing process: situation analysis, goal setting, and marketing program.

ROLE OF THE STRATEGIC MARKETING PROCESS

To understand the role of the strategic marketing process in a firm, it is important to recognize some key terms, distinguish between annual and long-range marketing plans, and understand the activities and information present in the process.

Key Terms   The strategic marketing process varies from organization to organization, and so do the terms used to describe various aspects of this process. However, the purpose of the strategic marketing process and all planning activities is very clear: to allocate the organization's resources most efficiently. For clarity, let's summarize pertinent terms, some of which are defined in Chapter 2:

- **Strategic marketing process**: The steps taken at the product and market levels to allocate marketing resources to viable marketing positions and programs; involves phases of (1) planning, (2) implementation, and (3) control.
- **Goals** (or objectives): Precise statement of results sought, quantified in time and magnitude, where possible.
- **Marketing strategies** (or marketing actions): Means by which the marketing goals are to be achieved.
- **Marketing program** (or marketing plan): Written statement identifying the target market, specific marketing goals, the budget, and timing for the marketing program.
- **Industry**: Group of firms offering products that are close substitutes for each other.

Annual and Long-Range Marketing Plans   A marketing plan is the heart of a firm's business plan. Stated broadly, marketing plans, or marketing programs, fall into two categories. **Annual marketing plans** deal with the marketing goals and strategies for a product, product line, or entire firm for a single year, whereas **long-range marketing plans** cover from two to five years into the future. Except for firms in industries like autos, steel, or forest products, marketing plans rarely go beyond five years into the future because the tremendous number of uncertainties present make the benefits of planning less than the effort expended. To allow adjustments to the increasing uncertainties in the marketplace, many firms today are trying to develop a process that allows strategic thinking more frequently than just once a year.[5]

The steps a consumer package goods firm (such as food, health, and beauty products) takes in developing its annual marketing plan are shown in Figure 20–2. This annual planning cycle starts with a detailed marketing research study of present users and ends after 48 weeks with the approval of the plan by the division general manager—10 weeks before the fiscal year starts. Between these points there are continuing efforts to uncover new ideas through brainstorming and key-issues sessions with specialists both inside and outside the firm. The plan is fine tuned through a series of often excruciating reviews by several levels of management, which leaves few surprises and little to chance.

Actions and Information   Figure 20–3 summarizes the strategic marketing process introduced in Chapter 2, along with the actions and information that compose it. The upper half of each box highlights the actions involved in that

FIGURE 20–2
Steps a large consumer package goods firm takes in developing its annual marketing plan

STEPS IN ANNUAL MARKETING, PLANNING PROCESS	WEEKS BEFORE APPROVAL OF PLAN 50	40	30	20	10	0
1 Obtain up-to-date marketing information from marketing research study of product users.	▲					
2 Brainstorm alternatives to consider in next year's plan with own marketing research and outside advertising agency personnel.	▲					
3 Meet with internal media specialists to set long-run guidelines in purchase of media.			▲			
4 Obtain sales and profit results from last fiscal year, which ended 16 weeks earlier.			▲			
5 Identify key issues (problems and opportunities) to address in next year's plan by talks with marketing researchers, advertising agency, and other personnel.				▲		
6 Hold key issues meeting with marketing director; form task force of line managers if significant product, package, or size change is considered.						
7 Write and circulate key issues memo; initiate necessary marketing research to reduce uncertainty.				▱▲		
8 Review marketing mix elements and competitors' behavior with key managers, keeping marketing director informed.				▱▱▲		
9 Draft marketing plan, review with marketing director, and revise as necessary.					▱▲	
10 Present plan to marketing director, advertising agency, division controller, and heads of responsible line departments (product, packaging, sales, etc.) and make necessary changes.					▲	
11 Present marketing plan to division general manager for approval, 10 weeks before start of fiscal year.						▲

KEY: ▲ Planned period of work, ▲ Planned completion date

Source: Adapted from Stanley F. Stasch and Patricia Langtree, "Can Your Marketing Planning Procedures Be Improved?" *Journal of Marketing* (Summer 1980), p. 82; by permission of the American Marketing Association.

part of the strategic marketing process, and the lower half summarizes the information and reports used. Note that each phase has an output report:

PHASE	OUTPUT REPORT
Planning	Plans (or programs) that define goals and the marketing mix strategies to achieve them
Implementation	Results (memos or computer outputs) that describe the outcomes of implementing the plans
Control	Corrective action memos, triggered by comparing results with plans, that (1) suggest solutions to problems, and (2) take advantage of opportunities

STEP 1 IN PLANNING: SITUATION ANALYSIS

To find out where a firm has been, is now, and is headed with present plans requires very detailed information. This includes past, current, and projected information about revenues, expenses, and profits for the entire industry and the

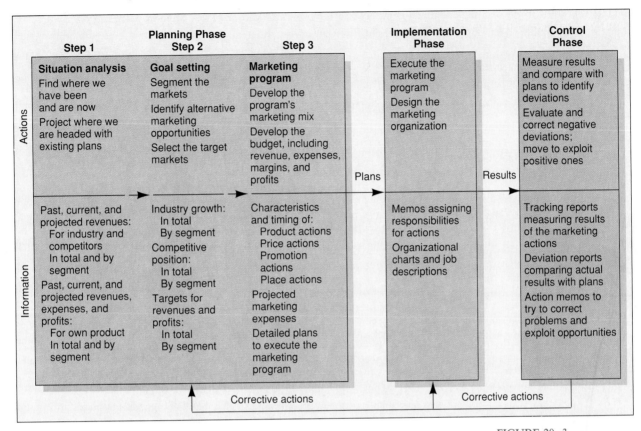

	Planning Phase			**Implementation Phase**	**Control Phase**
	Step 1	**Step 2**	**Step 3**		
Actions	**Situation analysis** Find where we have been and are now Project where we are headed with existing plans	**Goal setting** Segment the markets Identify alternative marketing opportunities Select the target markets	**Marketing program** Develop the program's marketing mix Develop the budget, including revenue, expenses, margins, and profits	Execute the marketing program Design the marketing organization	Measure results and compare with plans to identify deviations Evaluate and correct negative deviations; move to exploit positive ones

Information	Past, current, and projected revenues:
	  For industry and competitors
	  In total and by segment
	Past, current, and projected revenues, expenses, and profits:
	  For own product
	  In total and by segment
		Industry growth:
		  In total
		  By segment
		Competitive position:
		  In total
		  By segment
		Targets for revenues and profits:
		  In total
		  By segment
			Characteristics and timing of:
			  Product actions
			  Price actions
			  Promotion actions
			  Place actions
			Projected marketing expenses
			Detailed plans to execute the marketing program
				Memos assigning responsibilities for actions
				Organizational charts and job descriptions
					Tracking reports measuring results of the marketing actions
					Deviation reports comparing actual results with plans
					Action memos to try to correct problems and exploit opportunities

Plans   Results

Corrective actions   Corrective actions

FIGURE 20–3
The strategic marketing process; actions and information

firm's own products (and ideally competitors' products), in total and by individual segments. This is a big order, but it makes possible goal setting, the second step in the planning phase of the strategic marketing process. Additional information is needed to develop the marketing mix actions, timing, and budgets for the marketing program to complete the planning phase. Finally, the results must be measured during the marketing implementation phase so that corrective actions can be taken in the control phase.

The survey of 176 product managers summarized in Figure 20–4 shows the actual information they use in developing their marketing plans. At least 70 percent of the product managers made forecasts of their own product's sales, direct costs, and direct contribution (gross margin). At least half also used forecasts of industry sales, projections of their own product's market share, and projected profitability statements for their own product. Shaded rows in Figure 20–4 show data used by more than half of those surveyed.

Of these six kinds of information, only one deals with something other than the product manager's own product: forecasts of industry sales. In most situation analyses two principal ingredients are the size of the industry market now and its growth rate in the near future. This tells the product manager what the size of the total pie is and the amount by which it is growing annually, and it enables the manager to assess the size of the slice of pie (the product's market share) obtained now and likely to be obtained in the future. For example, key factors for General Mills in starting its Olive Garden restaurant chain were the

FIGURE 20–4 **Information that product managers use for their marketing plans. Shaded planning data were used by more than half of the product managers surveyed**

KIND OF DATA	PLANNING ACTIVITY	PLANNING DATA	PERCENTAGE USING
Basic forecast data	Sales forecasts	Three-year forecasts of "own" product sales	72%
		Three-year forecasts of industry sales	59
		"Own" product sales forecasts by segments	39
		Industry sales forecasts by segments	22
	Market share forecasts	Three-year projections of "own" product's share	52
		Projections of "own" product's share by segments	44
		Three-year projections of competing products' shares	34
		Projections of competing products' shares by segments	30
	Product contribution forecasts	Estimate of product's direct costs	71
		Three-year projection of product's direct contribution	70
		Estimates of product's direct contribution by segments	17
Strategy analysis data	Relative market share forecasts	Absolute market share converted to relative share★	49
		Three-year projections of product's relative share	38
		Estimates of product's relative share by segments	33
	Value of market share forecasts	Value of market share computed	28
		Three-year projections of product's relative share	15
		Estimates of market share by segments	11
Financial data	Profit and financial forecasts	Product profitability statements for three or more years	52
		Present value of income streams for market share alternatives	25

★Relative market share, defined later in the chapter for strategic business units, in this case is sales of the firm's product divided by sales of the leading product in the industry.

Source: Adapted from Thomas J. Cosse and John E. Swan, "Strategic Marketing Planning by Product Managers—Room for Improvement?" *Journal of Marketing* (Summer 1983, pp. 92–102; by permission of the American Marketing Association.

limited supply of Italian restaurants, the fact that Italian food is the top-ranked ethnic cuisine in the United States, and the growing trend toward "eating out." Although the United States has 17,000 Oriental restaurants and 14,000 Mexican restaurants, it has only 4,800 Italian restaurants. Further, there is an increasing trend in the United States toward eating out—$4 of every $10 of food expenditures today compared with $2.50 two decades ago.[6]

STEP 2 IN PLANNING: GOAL SETTING

Marketing goals tie directly to corporate goals and should be quantified both in terms of how much—such as "an increase in unit sales from 375,000 to 500,000"—and when—such as "by the end of fiscal 1992." General Mills has specified a goal for its European cereal business of $1 billion in sales by the year 2000. Arriving at these goals requires the involvement not only of the product managers but also of senior management and other personnel inside and outside the firm. Involving senior management is essential throughout the planning process so the company can alter objectives and strategies if they are too far off the mark. Involvement of middle-level and lower-level personnel inside and outside the firm is needed for the creative ideas they bring to the planning and goal-setting process. It also gives them personal "ownership" in the goals when

Inside one of the Olive Garden restaurants.

they are called on to carry out the plans or even to discover new ideas that may lead to new businesses.[7] As shown in the accompanying Marketing Action Memo, 3M publicizes its corporate goals to its employees and encourages them to convert their ideas into products that can lead to the start of entirely new divisions. This is probably the ultimate success in tying personal and corporate goals together to the benefit of both employee and employer.

STEP 3 IN PLANNING: THE MARKETING PROGRAM

Step 3 in the planning phase of the strategic marketing process involves designing a marketing program—the specific marketing plan—to achieve the goals set by the firm and product manager. Elements of the marketing mix most likely to be singled out for specific strategy statements in a firm's marketing plan include pricing policy, sales promotion, advertising themes, and new product development.[8]

A **generic marketing strategy** is one that can be adopted by any firm, regardless of the product or industry involved, to achieve a sustainable competitive advantage. Research suggests that two broad general strategies of successful firms are differentiation from competitors in terms of products offered or markets served (often combined with a focus on a market niche) and becoming the most efficient, low-cost producer in the industry.[9] Some specific generic marketing strategies for accomplishing these broader strategies are shown in Figure 20–5. So if a business wants to increase its profits, it can attempt to (1) increase revenues, (2) decrease expenses, or (3) do both.

Generic Strategies to Increase Revenues   The generic strategy of increasing revenues can only be achieved by using one or a combination of four ways to address present or new markets and products (Figure 20–5): (1) market pene-

How do 3M's Post-it notes reflect the company's corporate goals? See the following Marketing Action Memo for the answer.

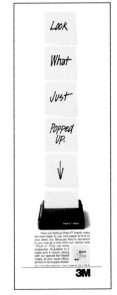

Marketing Action Memo

3M's "DIVIDE AND GROW" PROCESS: ACHIEVING PERSONAL OWNERSHIP OF CORPORATE GOALS

Someone has estimated that each day close to half the *world's* population benefits in some way from 3M products. Whether the estimate is correct or not, each day billions of people are exposed to some of 3M's 60,000 products, including:

- Scotch brand anti-static videotape.
- Scotchlite reflective road signs.
- Translucent dental braces.
- Synthetic ligaments for damaged knees.
- Waterproof sandpaper.

The bonds that tie together 45 major product lines utilizing 85 distinct technologies in more than 50 3M international companies are four specific corporate goals:

- 10 percent or better annual growth in earnings per share.
- 27 percent return on capital employed.
- 20 to 25 percent return on equity.
- 25 percent of a division's sales coming from products or services introduced within the past five years.

3M has succeeded in building what it calls "a company of entrepreneurs" through a process of "divide and grow." This means that 3M employees are encouraged to take an idea—even when others lose faith in it—and run with it. If the idea succeeds, the employee has a chance to manage the product as though it were his or her own business. That single product may spin off enough related products to become an entire 3M division. This is one reason 3M encourages its technical researchers to "bootleg" 15 percent of their time pursuing whatever they think is best for 3M.

This divide and grow process gives employees a personal stake in the four 3M corporate goals. It has given the world thousands of products—from exotic medical devices to everyday ones such as Scotch tape and Post-it notes—and is producing more than 200 new products annually.

Sources: Russell Mitchell, "Masters of Innovation: How 3M Keeps Its New Products Coming," *Business Week* (April 10, 1989), pp. 58–63; "Financial Objectives Restated by Company," *3M Today* (October/November, 1985), pp. 12–13; *3M: Getting to Know Us* (St. Paul: 3M Company, 1987), pp. 1–12; Christopher Knowlton, "What America Makes Best," *Fortune* (March 28, 1988), p. 45; and Susan Feyder, "3M Changes Some Elements of Its Style," *Star Tribune* (May 23, 1988), pp. 1D, 9D.

---

tration, (2) product development, (3) market development, and (4) diversification (which are described in Chapter 2).

Procter & Gamble has followed a successful strategy of market penetration (present markets, present products) by concentrating its effort on becoming the market leader in each of its 39 product categories. It is currently first in 22 categories, up from 17 several years ago.[10]

In contrast, Hershey Food Corporation has succeeded with a product development strategy—finding new products for its present markets—to complement Hershey bars and Reese's Peanut Butter Cups, its best seller. To compete with Mars, the number two producer in the domestic candy business, Hershey developed Hershey Bar None, a peanut and chocolate wafer; Symphony, a creamy-tasting chocolate bar; and ChipAway, chocolate balls with cookie centers.[11]

Walt Disney Co. has pursued a market development strategy (new market, present product) since the success of the original Disneyland in Anaheim, California. The first market expansion, of course, was to Orlando, Florida, and

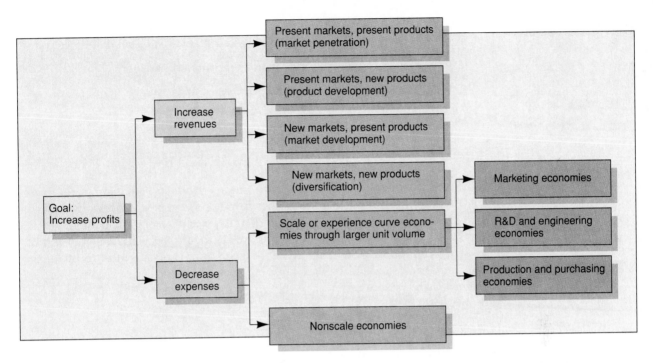

FIGURE 20–5
**Generic marketing
strategies for increasing
a firm's profits**

more recently Disney has built theme parks in Tokyo and Paris.[12] Finally, Philip Morris, which depended on Marlboro cigarettes for 60 percent of its profits in 1988, has used a diversification strategy (new market, new product) to reduce its dependence on a single brand. In recent years Philip Morris has purchased Seven-Up, Miller Brewing, General Foods, and Kraft to create a portfolio of consumer products.[13]

Generic Strategies to Decrease Expenses   Generic strategies for decreasing expenses fall into two broad categories (Figure 20–5). One is relying on scale economies or experience curve benefits from an increased volume of production to drive unit costs down and gross margins up. In the kitchen disposal business, In-Sink-Erator has used statistical process control, just-in-time inventory, and make-it-right-the-first-time tactics to lower costs by 25 percent and increase market share from 30 percent to 70 percent.[14] Scale economies may occur in marketing, as well as in research and development (R&D), engineering, production, and purchasing.

The other generic strategy to decrease expenses is simply finding other ways to reduce costs, such as cutting the number of managers, increasing the effectiveness of the salesforce through more training, or reducing the product rejects by inspectors. Stephen Wolf, chairman of United Airlines, has been trying to lower the company's labor costs to allow it to better compete with American Airlines. In meeting with employees he argues, "We want to get 100 people doing what 110 would do now."[15] Georgia-Pacific Corporation sawmills now produce more railcars of lumber each year because of stronger saw blades only half as thick as the old ones. The thinner saw blades added 800 railcars of lumber that otherwise would have been sawdust.[16]

CONCEPT CHECK

1 What is the difference between a marketing goal and a marketing strategy?

2 Why is industry growth important to a product manager?

3 What are four generic marketing strategies to increase revenue?

FRAMEWORKS TO IMPROVE MARKETING PLANNING

Marketing planning for a firm with many products competing in many markets—a multiproduct, multimarket firm—is a complex process. Two techniques that are useful in helping marketing executives in such a firm make important resource allocation decisions are (1) the growth-share matrix and (2) the market-product grid. Each of these techniques is discussed in terms of the information needed for its use, how it is used in marketing planning, and its strengths and weaknesses.

BCG'S GROWTH-SHARE MATRIX

Many large firms address their complex resource allocation decisions by breaking their organization into decentralized profit centers, often called **strategic business units** (SBUs), each of which is treated as though it were a separate, independent business. Ideally, an SBU has several distinct characteristics: it (1) is a single business that can be planned independently of other businesses, (2) has its own competitors, and (3) has one manager with profit responsibility.[17] Planning is done first at the SBU level, then SBUs are combined into groups, and finally groups are combined into a complete picture of the entire company.

Information Needed A nationally known management consulting firm, the Boston Consulting Group (BCG), has developed one of the most recognized approaches to **business portfolio analysis**, analyzing a firm's SBUs as though they were a collection of separate investments. BCG advises its clients to locate the position of each of its SBUs on a growth-share matrix (Figure 20–6). The vertical axis is the **market growth rate**, which is the annual rate of growth of the specific market or industry in which a given SBU is competing. This axis in the figure runs from 0 to 20 percent, although in practice it might run even higher. The axis has arbitrarily been divided at 10 percent into high-growth and low-growth areas.

The horizontal axis is the **relative market share**, defined as the sales of the SBU divided by the sales of the largest firm in the industry. A relative market share of 10× (at the left end of the scale) means that the SBU has 10 times the share of its largest competitor, whereas a share 0.1× (at the right end of the scale) means it has only 10 percent of the sales of its largest competitor. The scale is logarithmic and is arbitrarily divided into high and low relative market shares at a value of 1×.

BCG has given specific names and descriptions to the four resulting quadrants in its growth-share matrix based on the amount of cash they generate for or require from the firm:

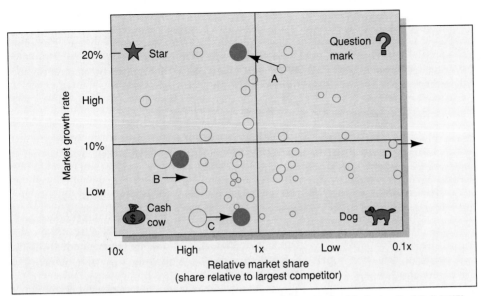

FIGURE 20–6
Boston Consulting Group growth-share matrix for a strong, diversified firm showing some strategic plans

Source: Adapted from "The Experience Curve Reviewed, IV. The Growth Share Matrix of the Product Portfolio," © 1973, The Boston Consulting Group.

- Cash cows (lower-left quadrant) are SBUs that typically generate large amounts of cash, far more than they can invest profitably in their own product line. They have a dominant share of a slow-growth market and provide cash to pay large amounts of company overhead and to invest in other SBUs.

- Stars (upper-left quadrant) are SBUs with a high share of high-growth markets that may not generate enough cash to support their own demanding needs for future growth. When their growth slows, they are likely to become cash cows.

- Question marks or problem children (upper-right quadrant) are SBUs with a low share of high-growth markets. They require large injections of cash just to maintain their market share, much less increase it. Their name implies management's dilemma for these SBUs: choosing the right ones to invest in and phasing out the rest.

- Dogs (lower-right quadrant) are SBUs with a low share of low-growth markets. Although they may generate enough cash to sustain themselves, they do not hold the promise of ever becoming real winners for the firm. Dropping SBUs in this quadrant from a business portfolio is generally advocated except when relationships with other SBUs or competitive considerations exist.[18]

The hollow circles in Figure 20–6 show the location of the SBUs in a strong, diversified firm. The area of each hollow circle is proportional to that SBU's annual sales revenue.

Use in Marketing Planning   The portfolio in Figure 20–6 is a strong and diversified one because over half the SBUs have high relative market shares, there are many stars, the cash cows are strong and numerous enough to feed the needs of the question marks, and even most of the question marks and dogs have high market shares. Most firms are unable to influence the market growth rate—the factor shown on the vertical axis; an exception is a firm whose product is strong enough to stimulate primary demand for the entire product class. If a firm cannot affect market growth, its main planning alternative using business portfolio analysis is to try to change the relative market share, the factor on the horizontal axis. This is done mainly through a conscious management decision to either inject or withdraw cash from a specific SBU.

A firm must determine what role to assign each SBU in trying to assemble its ideal future portfolio.[19] BCG identifies four alternative objectives for an SBU. Ranked from most to least cash infused into an SBU, these four alternatives are described below and pictured in Figure 20–6.

1 **Build:** Increase the SBU's market share through injections of cash, even foregoing short-term profits to do so. This is often an appropriate strategy for question marks that need large amounts of cash to become stars. By injecting cash into SBU A in Figure 20–6, a firm hopes to move it from its present question mark position to a star (solid circle). In 1986 Motorola was almost driven from the semiconductor business by competitors' low-cost chips. In response, it poured billions of dollars into R&D—$1.8 billion in 1989 alone—and focused on increasing market share. Today Motorola is the largest producer of semiconductors in the United States and the fourth largest producer in the world.[20]

2 **Hold:** Maintain the SBU's market share, without appreciably altering the cash it uses. SBU B is typical of a holding strategy often applied to cash cows that are generating large amounts of cash and are intended to retain that same position in the future. The Dayton Hudson retail chain is using a holding strategy for its department stores that are in a slow-growth segment of the retail market.

3 **Harvest:** Increase the SBU's short-term cash output, even if this results in a loss of market share. This strategy can be used with question marks, dogs, or cash cows; an example of the latter is shown as SBU C. The resulting cash can then be pumped into stars or question marks. When General Mills marketing research showed that the decor and menu in Red Lobster restaurants were losing customer appeal, it diverted cash from its profitable consumer food divisions to cover the refurbishing cost of $200,000 per restaurant.

4 **Divest:** Sell the SBU to put its cash, physical, and human resources to use elsewhere in the firm. Question marks and dogs (such as SBU D) that require too much cash are candidates for divestiture. Westinghouse recently sold its elevator unit because it competed entirely in the mature North American market, and to become a dominant global competitor would have required a substantial investment of capital.[21] Similarly, General Electric sold its small appliance division to Black & Decker to raise cash for other GE businesses.

Just as most products have life cycles, so do most SBUs. An SBU often starts out as a question mark and then moves counterclockwise around the growth-share matrix—question mark to star to cash cow to dog—as industry competition increases. This means a firm's portfolio of SBUs and their positions are changing continuously, and the firm must always be on the lookout for new products and business opportunities to become the stars and cash cows in its future portfolio.

GE's "divest" strategy was the start of Black & Decker's small appliance line.

Strengths and Weaknesses   Primary strengths of business portfolio analysis include (1) forcing a firm to assess each of its SBUs in terms of its relative market share and industry market growth rate, which in turn (2) requires the firm to forecast which SBUs will be cash producers and cash needers in the future. Weaknesses are that (1) it is often difficult to get the information needed to locate each SBU on the growth–share matrix, (2) there are other important factors missing from the analysis such as possible synergies among the SBUs when they use the same salesforce or research and development facilities, and (3) there are problems in motivating people in an SBU that has been labeled a dog or even a cash cow and is unlikely to get new resources from the firm to grow and provide opportunities for promotion.[22]

Underlying the BCG analysis is the assumption about the importance of the firm's absolute market share and, in turn, relative market share. Many early analyses suggested that if a firm could gain an increase in market share, then a sizeable increase in ROI would automatically follow, a conclusion about which there is increasing debate.[23]

MARKET-PRODUCT GRID

A marketing manager responsible for an individual SBU can use the market-product grid to identify specific product opportunities or market niches that might be pursued.

Information Needed   As summarized in Chapter 8, the process of segmenting a market first necessitates finding characteristics to form market segments and then product clusters. Displaying these in a table forms a market-product grid. The use of this grid in the strategic marketing process is based on the kind of detailed information shown in Figure 20–3: (1) past, current, and projected information, (2) about revenues, expenses, and profits, (3) for the entire industry and the firm's own products, (4) in total and by individual market segments and product clusters.

Use in Marketing Planning   The market-product grid facilitates trade-offs in the strategic marketing process. Suppose you are a product manager for Great States Corporation's line of nonpowered lawn mowers sold to the consumer market. You are looking for new product and new market opportunities to increase your revenues and profits.

You conduct a market segmentation study and develop a market-product grid to analyze future opportunities. You identify three major segments in the consumer market based on geography: (1) city, (2) suburban, and (3) rural areas. These segments relate to the size of lawn a consumer must mow. The product clusters are (1) nonpowered, (2) powered walking, and (3) powered riding mowers.

Five alternative marketing strategies are shown in market-product grids in Figure 20–7[24]:

- *Market-product concentration:* Great States's initial strategy focused its efforts on one market segment (city households with small lawns) with a single product line (nonpowered mowers). Most large markets evolve from initial product-market concentration strategies.[25]
- *Market specialization:* This entails retaining the focus on a single market segment (city households) but adding two new product lines (powered walking and powered riding mowers). The strategic problem is developing and manufacturing two product lines new to Great States.
- *Product specialization:* This involves retaining Great States's focus on a single product line (nonpowered mowers) but marketing it to two unknown markets (suburban and rural households). The potential danger is entering two markets in which a producer may have no marketing experience or distribution outlets.

FIGURE 20–7
Market-product grid of alternative strategies for a lawn mower manufacturer

	P_1 NONPOWERED	P_2 POWERED, WALK	P_3 POWERED, RIDE		P_1 NONPOWERED	P_2 POWERED, WALK	P_3 POWERED, RIDE		P_1 NONPOWERED	P_2 POWERED, WALK	P_3 POWERED, RIDE		P_1 NONPOWERED	P_2 POWERED, WALK	P_3 POWERED, RIDE		P_1 NONPOWERED	P_2 POWERED, WALK	P_3 POWERED, RIDE
CITY MARKET M_1	1	2	3	M_1				M_1				M_1				M_1			
SUBURBAN MARKET M_2	4	5	6	M_2				M_2				M_2				M_2			
RURAL MARKET M_3	7	8	9	M_3				M_3				M_3				M_3			

Market-product concentration   Market specialization   Product specialization   Selective specialization   Full coverage

- *Selective specialization:* This involves targeting separate product lines for separate segments: nonpowered mowers for city households and powered walking mowers for suburban dwellers. The difficulty is the lack of scale economies available in the two previous strategies.
- *Full coverage:* With this strategy Great States will offer all three product lines in all three market segments.

The five grids in Figure 20–7 highlight some trade-offs that marketing managers face in designing strategies. For example, marketing economies of scale run horizontally across the rows: adding new products for a given market segment represents few new marketing expenses but sizeable new R&D and production expenses. The reverse is true for R&D and production economies of scale: these run vertically down a column. This often means balancing marketing economies of scale available from expanding across the rows against R&D and production economies available by expanding vertically down the columns.

As a firm expands under a product specialization strategy, it usually gains additional revenue by entering new markets with its existing line of products. Thus Great States can expect new revenues by selling nonpowered mowers to suburban and rural households. However, often this is not the case in expanding by selling new products to an existing market segment under a market specialization strategy. Great States, which now offers only nonpowered mowers, may gain new sales revenue by offering powered mowers to city households but with the potential danger of merely stealing the new sales from city customers formerly buying nonpowered mowers. This product cannibalism can present real revenue problems for a firm. For example, when General Foods introduced its freeze-dried Maxim brand, it stole sales from the company's Maxwell House brand.[26]

The market-product grid also clarifies trade-offs available in the diversification matrix described in Chapter 2. For example, the first grid in Figure 20–7 suggests four opportunities to a Great States lawn mower product manager:

- *Increase market penetration (present markets, present products):* Gain more sales in Cell 1.
- *Undertake market development (new markets, present products):* Take the nonpowered mower into the new markets in Cells 4 and 7.
- *Undertake product development (present markets, new products):* Produce new powered walking and riding mowers for the existing market, which means obtaining revenues from Cells 2 and 3.
- *Undertake diversification (new markets, new products):* Produce new powered walking and riding mowers for new suburban and rural markets, which means obtaining revenues from Cells 5, 6, 8, and 9.

Market development or product development strategies pose fewer dangers for Great States than diversification because each involves solving only one new unknown—either new market challenges for the marketing department or new product challenges for the R&D and manufacturing departments. Diversification causes difficulties for the firm in *both* marketing and R&D and manufacturing. A diversification strategy can be dangerous because it may result in a firm acquiring a business it can't run, a violation of the dictum "Stick to your knitting."[27] In undertaking moves into new markets or new products, a firm must be aware of barriers or gateways to entry such as technology, patents, and strong existing production or distribution systems.[28]

Strengths and Weaknesses   The market-product grid benefits marketing managers in the strategic marketing process by (1) identifying potential opportunities to fill market niches or product gaps for the firm, (2) highlighting potential economies of scale in either marketing or R&D and manufacturing that result from entering new markets or offering new products, and (3) showing potential revenue losses caused by product cannibalism. The disadvantages include the time and effort needed (1) to form meaningful market segments, (2) to form useful product clusters, and (3) to develop revenue and profit estimates for the cells in the grid.

CONCEPT CHECK

1   What's the difference between a star and a cash cow in BCG's growth-share matrix?

2   If Great States chose to take its nonpowered mower into suburban and rural markets, would the economies of scale accrue to marketing or R&D and production?

SOME PLANNING AND STRATEGY LESSONS

Applying these frameworks is not automatic but requires a great deal of managerial judgment. Commonsense requirements of an effective marketing plan are discussed below, followed by problems that can arise.

REQUIREMENTS OF AN EFFECTIVE MARKETING PLAN

President Dwight D. Eisenhower, when he commanded Allied armies in World War II, made his classic observation, "Plans are nothing; planning is everything." It is the process of careful planning that focuses an organization's efforts and leads to success. The plans themselves, which change with events, are often secondary. Effective planning and plans are inevitably characterized by identifiable objectives, specific strategies or courses of action, and the means to execute them.

Measurable, Achievable Goals   Ideally, objectives should be measurable in terms of *what* is to be accomplished and by *when*. This means, where possible, goals should be quantified: "Increase market share from 18 percent to 22 percent by December 31, 1995" is preferable to "Maximize market share given our available resources." As noted previously, these measurable goals also provide a benchmark with which to compare results to determine when corrective action is required.

To motivate the people in an organization whose job it is to reach the goals, the goals must be achievable. Unrealistically difficult goals will not motivate marketing personnel.

A Base of Facts and Valid Assumptions   The more a marketing plan is based on facts and valid assumptions, rather than guesses, the less uncertainty and risk are associated with executing it. Using marketing research to verify some assumptions increases the chance of successfully implementing a plan.

Simple but Clear and Specific Plans   Effective execution of plans requires that the doers understand what, when, and how they are to accomplish their tasks. Superfluous elements in a plan should be dropped so that the remaining ones are as straightforward as possible, thereby preventing misunderstandings.

Complete and Feasible Plans   Marketing plans must be complete in the sense that a marketing program has been designed that has considered all the marketing mix factors and incorporated the key ones in the marketing plan. Marketing resources must be adequate to make the plan feasible.

Controllable and Flexible Plans   Few plans are carried to completion without a hitch. Results of marketing actions are compared with the measurable, targeted goals to discern problem areas and trigger new, corrective actions. Marketing plans must provide for this control, which in turn allows replanning—the flexibility to update the original plans.

PROBLEMS IN MARKETING PLANNING AND STRATEGY

From postmortems on company plans that did work and also on those that did not work, a picture emerges as to where problems occur in the planning phase of a firm's strategic marketing process. The following list explores these problems:

1 Corporate plans may be based on very poor assumptions about environmental factors, especially changing economic conditions and competitors' actions. As shown in Figure 20–8, Western Union's plan failed because it didn't reflect the impact of deregulation and competitors' actions on business.

2 Planners and their plans may have lost sight of their customers' needs. BusinessLand failed to realize that high-cost customer service would not appeal to business customers who had PC experts in their offices. But Figure 20–8 shows that Liz Claiborne and Merck had marketing strategies that succeeded because of customer-oriented products.

3 Too much time and effort may be spent on collection and analysis of data required for the plans. The result is that line managers have their focus diverted from developing and implementing creative strategies. Westinghouse has cut its planning instructions for operating units "that looked like an auto repair manual" to five or six pages.

4 Responsibility for planning and strategy development may be assigned to the planners so that line operating managers feel no sense of ownership in

FIRM	STRATEGY	RESULT
PLANS THAT DID WORK		
General Foods	Invest $50 million in Jell-O, a no-growth cash cow for over 20 years, by introducing Jigglers—a new form of Jell-O you can hold in your hand.	Sales increased by 40 percent and profits moved upward.
Liz Claiborne	Create a line of attractive, colorful clothing for working women; provide retailers prompt delivery and quality control.	The company has become the second-largest apparel company on the *Fortune* 500 list; the 10-year return on equity is 40 percent.
Merck	Develop important drugs (such as cholesterol-reducing Mevacor, and a powerful antibiotic, Primaxin); hire research scientists with world-class reputations.	Ranked number one on the *Fortune* 1991 list of most admired corporations for the fifth straight year.
PLANS THAT DIDN'T WORK		
Oldsmobile	Create a new image for Oldsmobile that makes it distinct from other GM lines (such as Buick) with the "This is not your father's Oldsmobile" campaign.	Although the campaign drew a lot of attention, it did not explain what an Oldsmobile is supposed to be. Sales declined from 1.1 million cars in 1986 to 560,000 cars in 1990.
Western Union	Go beyond the telegraph business to become full-service in telecommunications after that industry was deregulated.	Failed to recognize intensity of competition and time needed to become profitable, and ran out of money.
BusinessLand	Sell sophisticated personal computers backed by high-margin services from technical personnel.	Failed to recognize that large businesses only wanted low price and prompt delivery because they had their own PC experts. BusinessLand lost $2.9 million in six months.

Sources: Brian Dumaine, "The New Turnaround Champs," *Fortune* (July 16, 1990), pp. 36–44; Walter Guzzardi, "The National Business Hall of Fame," *Fortune* (March 12, 1990), pp. 118–26; James B. Treece, "They're Still Groping," *Business Week* (July 9, 1990), p. 31; "The Sad Saga of Western Union's Decline," *Business Week* (December 14, 1987), pp. 108–14; Barbara Buell, "BusinessLand Seems Stuck in No-Man's Land," *Business Week* (July 2, 1990), pp. 34–35; and Alison L. Sprout, "America's Most Admired Corporations," *Fortune* (February 11, 1991), pp. 52–82.

FIGURE 20–8
Results of strategic marketing plans

implementing the plans. This is the refrain running throughout today's blue-ribbon American firms, including General Electric, General Motors, U.S. Steel, and Rockwell International. The solution is to assign more planning activities to line operating managers.

WHERE PLANNING AND STRATEGY ARE HEADED

The focus of this chapter is on using the strategic marketing process to compete with products offered by other businesses. However, in today's corporate environment, the head of a corporation competes in another market as well: the market for corporate control. His or her goal is to run the various divisions and strategic business units so that they are more valuable together than standing alone. If this is not possible, the corporation may be purchased by outsiders, who sell off the divisions one by one with the goal of receiving a bigger collective amount for the pieces than they paid to buy the entire corporation.

In this form of planning, a firm's value is the value of its future cash flows discounted back to their present value. *Value-based planning* combines marketing planning ideas discussed in this chapter and financial planning techniques to assess how much a division or SBU contributes to the price of a company's stock (or shareholder wealth).[29] Although the topic is beyond the main focus of this book, it promises to influence marketing planning and strategy significantly.

CONCEPT CHECK

1 **What is a measurable goal?**

2 **Why is it important to include line operating managers in the planning process?**

YOPLAIT YOGURT: THE PLANNING PHASE OF THE STRATEGIC MARKETING PROCESS

To illustrate these planning concepts, let's follow the strategic marketing process of an actual new product introduction and describe how Yoplait USA, a subsidiary of General Mills, introduced its yogurt.[30] In the next chapter we'll see the implementation and control phases of Yoplait.

CORPORATE MISSION STATEMENT OF GENERAL MILLS

General Mills has a stated mission: "To be competitively excellent in everything it decides to undertake." Its corporate goal is one of consistent growth in sales and earnings, which General Mills defines as achieving a return on equity in the upper 25 percent of larger American companies—about 15 percent to 19 percent in a typical year. To achieve this, it has set some broad corporate strategies[31]:

- Balance its diversification in the industry groups in which it competes.
- Undertake aggressive consumer marketing that can lead to strong brands that outperform competitive brands, ideally becoming first or second in market share in their product category.
- Enter industry growth segments early, starting with small commitments and then investing heavily in opportunities that promise substantial growth.
- Achieve the internal financial goal of 25 percent ROI.

These strategies guide General Mills's business units in developing their strategic marketing plans.

SITUATION ANALYSIS

In 1977 a General Mills team including Steven Rothschild investigated the yogurt business—a dairy business that was new to General Mills, whose experience was in its traditional grocery products such as breakfast cereals and cake mixes. The team conducted a detailed situation analysis that revealed information on yogurt's history, current types of yogurt, consumer use and preferences, and the industry and competition.

History Yogurt, a cultured milk product, has been around for centuries. It is widely consumed in the Middle East and parts of Europe. Yogurt first came to the United States in the 1930s but didn't have much consumer appeal until the 1960s. Then, in the late 1970s, yogurt became one of the fastest-growing food products in the country.

Types of Yogurt Rothschild and the team discovered that about 95 percent of the yogurt consumed in the United States is mixed with fruit or flavoring and about 5 percent is plain. About 95 percent is consumed in 8-ounce cups. The team also found that there are four basic types of yogurt available in the United States today in addition to plain yogurt:

- Sundae style, with fruit on bottom of cup.
- Swiss style, with fruit blended throughout using stabilizers to keep it from settling.
- Western style, with fruit on bottom and flavored syrup on top.
- Frozen style, in ice cream or soft custard form.

Other research showed that yogurt is available in 20 different flavors and a wide range of textures. When refrigerated, it has a shelf life of 21 to 60 days, depending on whether preservatives are added.

Consumer Preferences and Use Rothschild found the U.S. annual per capita consumption of yogurt was low (five cups per person) compared with consumption in European countries (27 cups per person a year in France). Research data showed that 25 percent of U.S. households had eaten yogurt in the past month; 30 percent had eaten it but less frequently; and 45 percent had never bought or eaten it.

When asked why they eat yogurt, about 48 percent of yogurt consumers said, "It tastes good," and another 18 percent said, "For weight watching." Almost two thirds ate it as a between-meal snack. The heaviest monthly consumption was from April to September.

Indexes were developed to identify where yogurt consumption was concentrated, using an index of 100 as average. These indexes showed heavy use by households with over $20,000 annual income (index 166), 18- to 34-year-old women (index 121), and 12- to 17-year-old girls (index 118). In geographic consumption West Coast households consumed the most yogurt (index 162), followed by those in New England (index 156) and the Middle Atlantic states (index 139).

Yoplait's products face off against competitive products.

Industry and Competition   Steven Rothschild estimated that industry sales of yogurt in the United States for 1978 would be about $350 million, with unit sales of 80 million 12-pack cases of single-serving cups. Unit sales of yogurt averaged 18 percent annual growth from 1970 to 1977. Strong continued growth was anticipated.

There was no national brand of yogurt, but there were about a half dozen premium-quality regional brands, including Dannon in the East and Midwest and Knudsen on the West Coast. About three fourths of U.S. dairies offered private label, local brands to customers.

GOAL SETTING

Rothschild and the team recommended that General Mills enter the yogurt market. In doing so, it committed the yogurt venture to the following goals set for new products at General Mills:

1 Fit with General Mills's strengths: "high value-added products distributed through supermarkets."
2 Achieve 20 percent share of the yogurt market in five years.
3 Achieve $100 million in sales in five years—double the minimum required by General Mills.
4 Meet internal financial goals of 25 percent ROI in five years.
5 Become a multiproduct business.

A yogurt product also met some other brand goals for a new product at General Mills: (1) a high-turnover branded item that allows a significant profit margin, (2) a product for which the firm's skills in positioning, advertising, packaging, and promotion will provide an advantage over competition, and (3) a business that will capitalize on trends resulting from long-term changes in consumer behavior.

MARKETING PROGRAM

Rothschild was convinced that General Mills must move quickly and decisively into the yogurt market if it was to succeed. He concluded the company didn't have time to develop its own yogurt in its own laboratories, so he moved to acquire a high-quality yogurt and then devise a marketing mix strategy.

Yogurt Acquisition   In October 1977 General Mills acquired the right to market Yoplait yogurt in the United States from Sodima, a large French cooperative. It named Steven Rothschild to head the team of people in its new subsidiary, Yoplait USA. At that time Yoplait was the best-selling yogurt in France and was being distributed in less than 10 percent of the United States. Rothschild estimated the acquisition would save General Mills three years compared with developing and marketing its own brand from scratch.

Positioning Strategy   Rothschild and his team decided to try to position Yoplait as a French yogurt that would appeal to the typical American consumer.

Product Strategy   The team saw some significant product benefits in Yoplait yogurt:

- One hundred percent natural yogurt with active yogurt cultures without artificial sweeteners and preservatives.
- Creamy French-style yogurt with real fruit mixed throughout.
- Outstanding taste as measured by marketing research.

The team decided to market Yoplait in a convenient, attention-getting package.

Pricing Strategy   Their strategy was to set a price that would provide margins for retailers comparable to those of major regional brands. This margin should provide enough profit in this high-velocity consumer product (at 2.6 stockturns per week) for retailers to advertise and promote Yoplait in their local market.

Promotional Strategy   The advertising would be designed to inform consumers about Yoplait's outstanding taste and unique texture while reminding them of its French heritage. Television, print media, and sampling would be used to introduce consumers to Yoplait.

Place Strategy   National distribution was needed as soon as possible. Because of fast turnover, a plan was made to avoid running out of stock by a carefully scheduled inventory program tied to delivery frequency and sales level of the store. Because Yoplait is best when consumed within 30 days of manufacture, each package would be marked with a 30-day "use by" date. Inventory on the shelf beyond that date would be destroyed, the reasons investigated, and recurrence prevented.

How Steven Rothschild has implemented and controlled Yoplait's strategy is described at the end of Chapter 21.

ETHICS AND SOCIAL RESPONSIBILITY IN THE 1990s

**PATRIOTISM VERSUS PROFITEERING:
CAN YOU ADJUST YOUR PLAN FOR A WAR?**

The strategic marketing process discussed in this chapter encourages marketing managers to monitor changes in the environment to identify specific product-market opportunities. During and following the Persian Gulf War, many organizations observed an increase in consumers' patriotism and modified their marketing plans to take advantage of the change. Boeing, for example, ran an ad showing military people at work that said, "We'd like to take this opportunity to say thanks to each of them." Bulova Corp. created a new line of watches called The Patriot and donated the profits to the USO. Baseball cardmaker Topps Co. began selling a series of Desert Storm collectors cards featuring such leaders as General Colin Powell and General Norman Schwarzkopf. And the U.S. Army developed a new recruiting ad campaign titled "Count on Me" to reinforce the new confidence that the American people were feeling in the Army.

Critics of these firms suggested that they would be perceived as war profiteers by running ads or offering products that take advantage of the emotions created by the war. What is your reaction? Should marketing plans try to anticipate, and take advantage of, changes such as war, disease, political unrest, or other emotional issues?

Source: "War-Related Products Face 'Profiteering' Tag," *Marketing News* (March 18, 1991), pp. 1, 2; and Steven W. Colford, "Military Launches Ads," *Advertising Age* (March 4, 1991), pp. 1, 47.

SUMMARY

1 Marketing managers using the strategic marketing process search continuously for sustainable competitive advantages in the markets they serve and the products they offer.

2 They exploit these competitive advantages by allocating their resources as effectively as possible. Sales response functions help them assess what the market's response to additional marketing effort will be.

3 With so much at risk from bad decisions, the strategic marketing process often requires an enormous amount of detailed information that includes (*a*) past, current, and projected information (*b*) about revenues, expenses, and profits (*c*) for the entire industry, the firm, and competitors (*d*) in total and by individual segments.

4 Generic strategies for a firm to increase its profits are (*a*) increasing revenues, (*b*) decreasing expenses, and (*c*) a combination of both.

5 BCG's growth-share matrix enables a firm to position its strategic business units (SBUs) on a two-dimensional graph whose axes are (*a*) annual market (industry) growth rate and (*b*) the SBU's relative market share (firm's sales divided by those of the largest competitor).

6 The market-product grid displays an SBU's market segments and product clusters in a table to identify opportunities to fill market niches; assess economies of scale in marketing, R&D, and production; and project possible lost revenues if new products steal sales from existing products.

7 An effective marketing plan has measurable, achievable objectives; uses facts and valid assumptions; is simple, clear, and specific; is complete and feasible; and is controllable and flexible.

KEY TERMS AND CONCEPTS

sustainable competitive
  advantage p. 548
sales response function p. 548
share points p. 550
strategic marketing process p. 551
goals p. 551
marketing strategies p. 551
marketing program p. 551

industry p. 551
annual marketing plans p. 551
long-range marketing plans p. 551
generic marketing strategy p. 555
strategic business units p. 558
business portfolio analysis p. 558
market growth rate p. 558
relative market share p. 558

CHAPTER PROBLEMS AND APPLICATIONS

1 Assume a firm faces an S-shaped sales response function. What happens to the ratio of incremental sales revenue to incremental marketing effort at the (*a*) bottom, (*b*) middle, and (*c*) top of this curve?

2 What happens to the ratio of incremental sales revenue to incremental marketing effort when the sales response function is an upward-sloping straight line?

3 Does the S-shaped (Question 1) or upward-sloping straight line (Question 2) sales response function best describe the typical situation facing a firm?

4 From 1991 to 1993 General Mills plans to invest $1.65 billion in expanding its cereal and restaurant businesses. In deciding how to allocate this money between these two businesses, what information would General Mills like to have?

5 Campbell Soup now has 60 percent of the canned soup business. Write a specific marketing goal for Campbell Soup.

6 In early 1985 General Mills's product portfolio included Bisquick, Wheaties, Red Lobster restaurants, Eddie Bauer retail stores, Izod sportswear, and Parker Brothers video games. From the chapter and what you know, categorize these products in terms of the BCG matrix. What does this tell you about why General Mills got out of the sportswear and video game businesses?

7 Explain why a product often starts as a question mark and then moves counterclockwise around BCG's growth-share matrix.

8 Suppose Apple Computer wants to increase its profits by increasing its revenues. Use its market-product grid shown in the Marketing Action Memo in Chapter 8 to identify an action it might take for each of the four generic strategies for increasing revenues.

9 In Figure 20–8, which generic strategies for increasing revenues seem to have been followed by (*a*) General Foods, (*b*) Oldsmobile, and (*c*) Western Union?

The Strategic Marketing Process: Implementation and Control Phases

After reading this chapter you should be able to:

- Relate the implementation and control phases to the strategic marketing process.

- Describe the alternatives for organizing marketing activities and the role of a product manager in a marketing department.

- List the key activities needed to ensure that a marketing program is implemented effectively.

- Schedule a series of tasks to meet a deadline using a Gantt chart.

- Understand how sales and profitability analyses and marketing audits are used to evaluate and control marketing programs.

Eleven Years to Get It Right: Tasty, Hot, Home-Delivered Pizzas in 30 Minutes

Thomas S. Monaghan tried to succeed in two parts of the pizza business: sit-down and delivery. He finally realized that doing both was one too many things to implement and control. So he focused on delivery, which resulted in the most successful home-delivered meal business in the United States.

The focus for his better idea: delivering tasty, hot, custom-made pizzas to consumers' homes within 30 minutes of receiving their telephone order. What could be simpler? It only took Monaghan 11 years and a near bankruptcy to implement and control that one idea.[1]

In 1960 Monaghan scraped together $500 to buy a tiny Italian restaurant near Eastern Michigan

University, hoping to make enough money to finance his architecture degree. On the theory that tasteless dormitory food generates demand for pizza near college campuses, less than one year later he opened outlets near the University of Michigan and Central Michigan University. By 1965 he was thousands of dollars in debt, so he crossed out every entrée on the menu except pizza, threw out the tables and chairs, and concentrated on pizza delivery.

Searching for the Better Idea   Monaghan started franchising the outlets, found he couldn't fulfill the promises he made to the franchisees, and saw his headquarters burn down. "We just went too far, too fast, without being ready," he reflects. Finding himself $1 million in debt when franchisees and creditors filed 150 lawsuits, Monaghan watched a bank take over his restaurants.

Monaghan went back to working in his restaurants, paid off his debts, and regained control of the business in 1971. He observes, "I began rebuilding by staking out a business niche—free delivery—and doing it better and faster than anyone else." In fact, his stores also offer carry-out service but target the delivery segment, which explains why 90 percent of sales are home delivery. He called his firm Domino's Pizza, Inc., and by 1980 it had 398 outlets, mostly franchised, and $98 million in sales.[2]

Precise Implementation: One Key to Success   Monaghan decided he had to reduce his dependence on colleges and try to penetrate the lucrative residential market. Research showed that taste and prompt delivery are the key buying criteria for both the main (ages 18 to 34) and secondary (age 35 and over) target markets of Domino's. This helped him select and emphasize Domino's unique appeal: delivery of a hot pizza to a customer's home within 30 minutes from the phone order, or a $3 discount for the customer. In addition, the company has a product guarantee.

Monaghan's actions are a textbook example of the precise, effective implementation and control phases of a marketing program. In 1989, Domino's average delivery time was 23 minutes. His strategy also includes an acute attention to quality and detail (see the accompanying Marketing Action Memo). For example, the cheese is half the cost of a pizza. Unlike competitors who have cut quality, Monaghan insists on using an expensive, 100 percent real cheese.[3]

Employee motivation is also critical. The big carrot for good performance as a driver and in the store is—surprise!—a Domino's Pizza franchise. With no franchises available on the open market, the only way to get one is to earn it by starting out in the store, often as a driver, then working on the "make-line," and successfully completing the manager-in-training program. After accomplishing this, the employee has the opportunity to franchise. This ensures quality of the product and of store operations.

Future Goals   By 1990 Domino's had more than 5,000 outlets. Tom Monaghan has announced his new goal: 10,000 outlets by 1992.

Domino's success is testimony to the notion that great marketing ideas are usually clear, simple, and workable. Also, they must be capable of being implemented and controlled—the phases of the strategic marketing process covered in this chapter—by ordinary people, not geniuses (Figure 21–1).

Marketing Action Memo

WHAT IMPLEMENTATION INVOLVES AT DOMINO'S PIZZA

*T*he implementation actions at Domino's Pizza involve an acute level of detail.

SIMPLE, FLEXIBLE MENU

Domino's offers only two sizes of thin-crust pizza (medium and large), one size of deep dish pan pizza (medium), 10–14 toppings, and one beverage (cola).

PRECISE ORDERING INSTRUCTIONS FOR CUSTOMERS

Domino's puts five instructions on its menu to facilitate prompt delivery:

1 Know what you want before ordering (size of pizza, toppings, beverages).
2 Know the phone number and address of the residence from which you are calling.
3 When placing an order, let us know if you have large-denomination bills.
4 Remain by the phone after ordering. We may call back to confirm the order.
5 Turn on your porch light.

On this list Item 3 is intended to protect the driver, and Item 4 discourages crank calls.

DETAILED ORDER-PROCESSING AND DELIVERY PROCEDURES

When a customer phones in an order, a dispatcher records it and locates the customer's house on a blown-up map of the surrounding community. Employees on the make-line assemble the pizza by adding ingredients in order from the bottom up: dough, sauce, cheese, and toppings. Ideally, after seven minutes (one to make and six to bake) the hot pizzas are put in rigid corrugated boxes in racks earmarked for specific delivery routes.

CONTINUING CUSTOMER FEEDBACK

A questionnaire often accompanies each pizza delivered asking about factors such as the courteousness of telephone and delivery personnel, pizza quality, and delivery time. Survey results are turned over to regional offices, which then correct problems in individual stores.

This concern for effective implementation should help Domino's fend off new types of competition including Pizza Hut's takeout business and Little Ceasar's Pizza Stations, which are about to open in 400 Kmart stores.

Sources: John P. Cortez, "Pizza Chains Hungry for New Venues," *Advertising Age* (June 24, 1991), p. 51. Bradley A. Stertz, "Domino's Beefs Up Menu to Keep Pace with Rivals," *The Wall Street Journal* (April 21, 1989), pp. B1, B6; Bernie Whalen, "'People-Oriented' Marketing Delivers a Lot of Dough for Domino's," *Marketing News* (March 15, 1984), pp. 4ff.; and Kevin T. Higgins, "Home Delivery Is Helping Pizza to Battle Burgers," *Marketing News* (August 1, 1986), pp. 1, 6.

THE IMPLEMENTATION PHASE OF THE STRATEGIC MARKETING PROCESS

The Monday morning diagnosis of a losing football coach often runs something like "We had an excellent game plan: we just didn't execute it."

IS PLANNING OR IMPLEMENTATION THE PROBLEM?

The planning-versus-execution issue applies to the strategic marketing process as well: a difficulty when a marketing plan fails is determining whether the failure is due to a poor plan or poor implementation. Figure 21–2 shows the outcomes of (1) good and bad marketing planning and (2) good and bad marketing implementation. Good planning and good implementation in Cell 1 spell

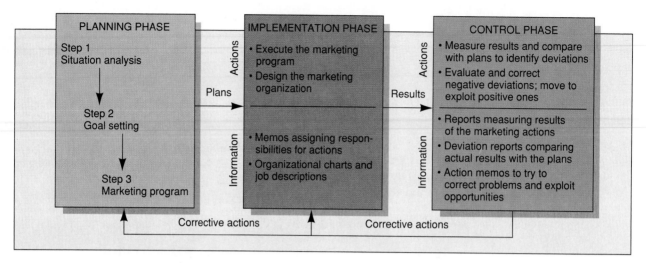

FIGURE 21–1

The strategic marketing process: actions and information in the implementation and control phases

success, as with IBM's entry into the PC business with a strong product coupled with excellent advertising, distribution, and pricing. Xerox fell into the "bad-bad" Cell 4 when it developed a personal computer without direct knowledge of customer needs and then failed to integrate the product's introduction with other Xerox marketing efforts.[4]

Cells 2 and 3 indicate trouble because either the marketing planning *or* marketing implementation—not both—is bad. A firm or product does not stay permanently in Cell 2 or 3. If the problem is solved, the result can be success (Cell 1); if not, it is failure (Cell 4).[5]

American Express used good implementation on a bad marketing strategy (Cell 2) when it applied the superior mass-marketing skills it had developed selling credit cards to a variety of financial services. Consumer demand never

FIGURE 21–2

Results of good and bad market planning and implementation

MARKETING IMPLEMENTATION	MARKETING PLANNING AND STRATEGY	
	Good (appropriate)	Bad (inappropriate)
Good (effective)	1 *Success:* Marketing program achieves its objectives.	2 *Trouble:* Solution lies in recognizing that only the strategy is at fault and correcting it.
Bad (ineffective)	3 *Trouble:* Solution lies in recognizing that only implementation is at fault and correcting it.	4 *Failure:* Marketing program flounders and fails to achieve its objectives.

Source: Reprinted by permission of the *Harvard Business Review*. An exhibit from "Making Your Marketing Strategy Work" by Thomas V. Bonoma (March/April 1984). Copyright © 1984 by the President and Fellows of Harvard College; all rights reserved.

materialized and American Express is now considering selling some of the services and focusing on credit cards.[6] Goodyear Tire and Rubber Co. found itself in Cell 3 after it successfully developed all-season radial tires but created problems with the 640 dealer distribution network by raising wholesale prices. The poor implementation led to a 2 point decline in market share—a drop of 3 million tires.[7]

INCREASING EMPHASIS ON MARKETING IMPLEMENTATION

In the 1990s, the great importance of the role of the implementation phase of the strategic marketing process has emerged in American corporations. What often happened in the past was that the firm's strategic planners from its corporate staff designed plans that were imposed on the firm's line managers and personnel to implement. The predictable result was near disaster for many firms in the "us versus them" confrontations—staff planners versus line operating personnel.

Like many restructured and downsized American corporations, GE has done away with hundreds of planning jobs. Although planners had some successes at GE, chairman John F. Welch, Jr., is trying to make line managers both planners and doers (see the accompanying Marketing Action Memo). In fact, the head of GE's aircraft engine business says that the quick development of a more powerful fan to upgrade a midsize jet engine was possible only because of a reduction in the number of staff planners, which eliminated multiple layers of review; this enabled GE to beat out an international consortium led by Pratt & Whitney and win $1 billion in new orders, including those for the Airbus 340 wide-body commercial jet.[8]

IMPROVING IMPLEMENTATION OF MARKETING PROGRAMS

No magic formula exists to guarantee effective implementation of marketing plans. In fact, the answer seems to be equal parts of good management skills and practices. Managerial skills that contribute to successful implementation include an ability to interact with people inside and outside the company; a capacity to budget time, people, and money; an ability to track or monitor marketing activities; and an affinity for creating communication networks within the organizational structure.[9] Important management practices include moving decisions as far down the organization as possible, setting deadlines, and rewarding individuals for successful implementation. Combining these skills and practices suggest some guidelines for improving program implementation.

Communicate Goals and the Means of Achieving Them to the Doers   Those called on to implement plans need to understand both the goals sought and how they are to be accomplished. Everyone in Domino's Pizza—from Tom Monaghan to telephone order takers, make-line people, and drivers—is clear on what the firm's goal is: to deliver tasty, hot pizzas within 30 minutes to homes of customers who order them by telephone. All Domino's personnel are trained in detail to perform their respective jobs to help achieve that goal. The goals must be consistent with organizational capabilities and they should be modified as capabilities change.[10]

Marketing Action Memo

GENERAL ELECTRIC'S MANAGER OF THE 1990s: IMPLEMENT A VISION IN A LEAN ORGANIZATION

*B*ecause GE is the most diversified company in America, it has a significant effect on American management style. In fact, when GE's management techniques change, so do those in corporate America.

GE decentralized into profit centers in the 1950s and installed a huge staff of corporate strategic planners in the early 1970s. Thousands of American companies followed suit.

GE Appliance Group planners correctly predicted the large-scale entry of Japanese appliances into U.S. markets in the 1980s. But GE planners misread the 1970s' energy crunch and sent GE into a crash program to improve refrigerator insulation when it should have redesigned its refrigerator compressors—a far better way than insulation to improve energy efficiency.

When John F. Welch, Jr., was named chairman of GE, he drastically reduced the size of the corporate strategic planning staff from 350 to approximately 20 because they were too costly, spent too much time "meddling" and "nitpicking," and demanded reports that didn't lead to making and marketing better products. Today, fewer managers have a greater stake in the outcome of their business, which is one reason sales per employee have risen 46 percent since 1984.

What about the future? Welch is moving decision making and authority lower in the organization by making line managers both planners and doers. In addition, he is promoting teamwork to create a "boundaryless organization" in which technology, information, managers, and management practices are continually shared. According to *Business Week* magazine, Welch knows what he wants in a future GE manager. He or she must be able to develop a vision of what their unit is to become, gain an acceptance of the vision through effective communication, and then "relentlessly drive implementation of that vision to a successful conclusion."

Many experts think this GE strategy, which emphasizes implementation, will become standard in American companies in the 1990s.

Sources: Monica Roman, "Big Changes Are Galvanizing General Electric," *Business Week* (December 18, 1989), pp. 100–102; Ronald Henkoff, "How to Plan for 1995," *Fortune* (December 31, 1990), pp. 70–79; "Jack Welch: How Good a Manager?" *Business Week* (December 14, 1987), pp. 92–103; Thomas Moore, "Goodbye, Corporate Staff," *Fortune* (December 21, 1987), pp. 65–76; and "The New Breed of Strategic Planner," *Business Week* (September 17, 1984), pp. 62–68.

Have a Responsible Program Champion Willing to Act   Successful high-technology programs, such as the programs for IBM's PC and Cray Research's supercomputers, almost always have a **product or program champion** who is able and willing to cut red tape and move the program forward. Such people often have the uncanny ability to move back and forth between big-picture strategy questions and specific details when the situation calls for it. This program champion idea applies to the successful implementation of marketing plans, but the title varies with the firm and position. For Domino's Pizza this person in day-to-day operations is the franchise owner who is running the restaurant, whereas for Sara Lee Corporation it might be the product manager responsible for Chef Pierre pies. Diffused responsibility in marketing programs at best can mean important delays and at worst can result in disaster when team members don't know who is responsible for decisions.

GE's approach to strategic planning helped it put its engine in this commercial jet.

Have Doers Benefit Personally from Successful Program Implementation
People work best when they have a clear goal. When the organization's goal and their own personal goal are consistent or the same, they have maximum incentive to see a program implemented successfully because they have personal ownership and a stake in that success. This also means employees are more willing to jump into critical situations and perform tasks that are "below" them or not in their job descriptions. Drivers delivering Domino's pizza take their job seriously—because it may lead directly to their owning a franchise in a few years.

Take Action and Avoid "Paralysis by Analysis"   In their book *In Search of Excellence,* Thomas J. Peters and Robert H. Waterman, Jr., warn against paralysis by analysis, the tendency to excessively analyze a problem instead of taking action. To overcome this pitfall, they call for a "bias for action" and recommend a "do it, fix it, try it" approach.[11] They conclude that perfectionists finish last, so getting 90 percent perfection and letting the marketplace help in the fine tuning makes good sense in implementation.

Lockheed Aircraft's Skunk Works got its name from the comic strip *L'il Abner* and its legendary reputation from achieving superhuman technical feats with a low budget, ridiculously short deadlines, and only 7 percent to 25 percent of the people used on comparable aircraft industry programs. Under the leadership of Kelly Johnson, in 35 years the Skunk Works has turned out the first American jet airplane (the P-80), the highest flying reconnaissance plane (the U-2), and one of aviation's fastest jets (the SR-71). Called out of retirement to work on the nation's most untrackable aircraft (the Stealth), Johnson restated two of his basic tenets: (1) make decisions promptly and (2) avoid paralysis by analysis. In fact, one U.S. Air Force audit showed that Johnson's Skunk Works could carry out a program on schedule with 126 people, whereas a competitor on a comparable program was behind schedule with 3,750 people.[12]

Program champions are notoriously brash in overcoming organizational hurdles. The U.S. Navy's Admiral Grace Murray Hopper not only gave the world the COBOL computer language but also the word *bug*—meaning any glitch in a computer or computer program. Probably more important is this program champion's famous advice for moving decisions to actions by cutting through an organization's red tape: "Better to ask forgiveness than permission." Using this strategy, 3M's Art Fry championed Post-it notes to success, an idea he got while looking for a simple way to mark his hymnal while singing in his church choir.

Foster Open Communication to Surface the Problems   Bugs and glitches aren't limited to computer programs—both technical and marketing programs have them too, but success often lies in fostering a work environment that is open enough so doers are willing to speak out when they see problems without fear of recrimination. The focus is placed on trying to solve the problem as a group rather than finding someone to blame. Solutions are solicited from anyone who has a creative idea to suggest—from the janitor to the president—without regard to status or rank in the organization.

Two more Kelly Johnson axioms from Lockheed's Skunk Works apply here: (1) when trouble develops, surface the problem immediately, and (2) get help; don't keep the problem to yourself. This latter point is important even if it means getting ideas from competitors.

Saturn is GM's attempt to create a new company where participatory management and improved communications lead to a successful product. The goal is to sell 80 percent of its cars to drivers who otherwise would have purchased a Honda or a Toyota. To accomplish this GM has invested $3.5 billion in the project, and has tried to avoid some of the common communication problems of large organizations. To encourage discussion of possible cost reductions each employee receives 100 to 750 hours of training, including balance sheet analysis. As a result, even a $30 error in a telephone bill was detected by

For the unusual way GM developed its Saturn, see the text.

employees. To avoid the "NIH syndrome"—the reluctance to accept ideas "not invented here" or not originated inside one's own firm—Saturn engineers bought 70 import cars to study for product design ideas, and selected options that would most appeal to their target market. Finally, to create a management–labor partnership all decisions are reached by consensus, including the selection of suppliers, the advertising agency, and dealers.[13]

Schedule Precise Tasks, Responsibilities, and Deadlines   Successful implementation requires that people know the tasks for which they are responsible and the deadline for completing them. With Domino's Pizza's drivers, their task (deliver a hot pizza) and deadline (within 30 minutes from the telephone order) are very clear.

To implement the thousands of tasks on an orbiting satellite, GE's Aerospace Group typically holds weekly program meetings. The outcome of each of these meetings is an **action item list** that has three columns: (1) the task, (2) the name of the person responsible for accomplishing that task, and (3) the date by which the task is to be finished. Within hours of completing a program meeting, the action item list is circulated to those attending. This then serves as the starting agenda for the next meeting. Meeting minutes are viewed as secondary and backward looking. Action item lists are forward looking, clarify the targets, and put strong pressure on people to achieve their designated tasks by the deadline.

Related to the action item lists are formal *program schedules,* which show the relationships through time of the various program tasks. Starting with the design of the Polaris submarines in the 1950s, computer-based scheduling techniques such as PERT (Program Evaluation and Review Technique) developed in defense programs became very complex. However, simplified software programs based on these techniques are now available for PCs.

FIGURE 21–3
Tasks in completing a term project

Shown below are the tasks you might face as a member of a student team to complete a marketing research study using a mail questionnaire. Elapsed time to complete all the tasks is 15 weeks. How do you finish the project in an 11-week quarter? For an answer, see the text.

TASK	TIME (WEEKS)
1 Construct and test a rough-draft questionnaire for clarity (in person, not by mail) on friends.	2
2 Type and mimeograph a final questionnaire.	2
3 Randomly select the names of 200 students from the school directory.	1
4 Address and stamp envelopes; mail questionnaires.	1
5 Collect returned questionnaires.	3
6 Tabulate and analyze data from returned questionnaires.	2
7 Write final report.	3
8 Type and submit final report.	1
Total time necessary to complete all activities	15

Source: Adapted from William Rudelius and W. Bruce Erickson, *An Introduction to Contemporary Business,* 4th ed. (New York: Harcourt Brace Jovanovich, 1985), p. 94. Copyright © 1985 by Harcourt Brace Jovanovich, Inc. Reprinted by permission of the publisher.

Scheduling an action program involves (1) identifying the main tasks, (2) determining the time required to complete each, (3) arranging the activities to meet the deadline, and (4) assigning responsibilities to complete each task.

Suppose, for example, that you and two friends are asked to do a term project on the problem, "How can the college increase attendance at its performing arts concerts?"[14] And suppose further that the instructor limits the project in the following ways:

1 The project must involve a mail survey of the attitudes of a sample of students.
2 The term paper with the survey results must be submitted by the end of the 11-week quarter.

To begin the assignment, you need to identify all the project tasks and then estimate the time you can reasonably allocate to each one. As shown in Figure 21–3, it would take 15 weeks to complete the project if you did all the tasks sequentially; so to complete it in 11 weeks, your team must work on different parts at the same time, and some activities must be independent enough to overlap. This requires specialization and cooperation. Suppose that of the three of you (A, B, and C), only Student C can type. Then you (Student A) might assume the task of constructing the questionnaire and selecting samples, and Student B might tabulate the data. This division of labor allows each student to concentrate on and become expert in one area, but you should also cooperate. Student C might help A and B in the beginning, and A and B might help C later on.

You must also figure out which activities can be done concurrently to save time. In Figure 21–3 you can see that Task 2 must be completed before Task 4.

TASK DESCRIPTION	STUDENTS INVOLVED IN TASK	WEEK OF QUARTER 1 2 3 4 5 6 7 8 9 10 11
1 Construct and test a rough-draft questionnaire for clarity (in person, not by mail) on friends.	A	
2 Type and photocopy the final questionnaire.	C	
3 Randomly select the names of 200 students from the school directory.	A	
4 Address and stamp envelopes; mail questionnaires.	C	
5 Collect returned questionnaires.	B	
6 Tabulate and analyze data from returned questionnaires.	B	
7 Write final report.	A, B, C	
8 Type and submit final report.	C	

KEY: ▲ Planned completion date   ▢ Planned period of work   Current date
◣ Actual completion date   ◼ Actual period of work

FIGURE 21–4
Gantt chart for scheduling the term project

Source: Adapted from William Rudelius and W. Bruce Erickson, *An Introduction to Contemporary Business*, 4th ed. (New York: Harcourt Brace Jovanovich, 1985), p. 95.

However, Task 3 might easily be done before, at the same time as, or after Task 2. Task 3 is independent of Task 2.

Scheduling production and marketing activities—from a term project to a new product rollout to a space shuttle launch—can be done efficiently with Gantt charts. Figure 21–4 shows one variation of a Gantt chart used to schedule the class project, demonstrating how the concurrent work on several tasks enables the students to finish the project on time. Developed by Henry L. Gantt, this method is the basis for the scheduling techniques used today, including elaborate computerized methods. The key to all scheduling techniques is to distinguish tasks that *must* be done sequentially from those that *can* be done concurrently. As in the case of the term project, scheduling tasks concurrently often reduces the total time required for a project.

Scheduling any action program (1) translates plans into specific, understandable tasks, (2) forces planners to distinguish sequential from concurrent tasks, reducing the time to implement the program, and (3) forces people to take responsibility for specific tasks and allot time to them. Otherwise, they tend to concentrate on the tasks they prefer and neglect the others.

CONCEPT CHECK

1 Why does GE want the "doers" to be responsible for planning?

2 What is the meaning and importance of a program champion?

3 Explain the difference between sequential and concurrent tasks in a Gantt chart.

ORGANIZING FOR MARKETING

A marketing organization is needed to implement the firm's marketing plans. Basic issues in today's marketing organizations include understanding (1) how line versus staff positions and divisional groupings interrelate to form a cohesive marketing organization and (2) the role of the product manager.

Line versus Staff and Divisional Groupings Although simplified, Figure 21–5 shows the organization of Pillsbury's Prepared Dough Products Business Unit in detail and highlights the distinction between line and staff positions in marketing. People in **line positions,** such as group marketing managers, have the authority and responsibility to issue orders to the people who report to them, such as marketing managers. In this organizational chart, line positions are connected with solid lines. Those in **staff positions** (shown by dotted lines) have the authority and responsibility to advise people in line positions but cannot issue direct orders to them. For example, the directors of R&D, marketing research, and sales advise the vice president/general manager of the Prepared Dough Products Business Unit but do not report directly to him or her. Instead, they report directly to other vice presidents (not shown in this organizational chart) who issue them orders.

Most marketing organizations use divisional groupings—such as product line, functional, and geographical—to implement plans and achieve their organizational objectives (discussed in Chapter 19). All appear in some form in Pillsbury's organizational chart in Figure 21–5. At the top of its organization,

FIGURE 21–5
Organization of the Pillsbury Company's U.S. Foods Division

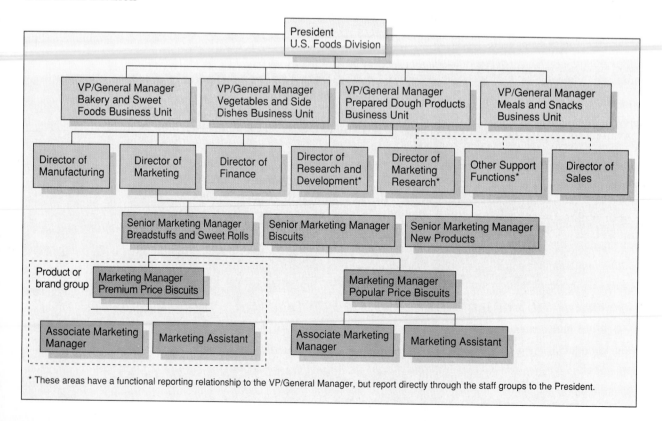

* These areas have a functional reporting relationship to the VP/General Manager, but report directly through the staff groups to the President.

Pillsbury organizes by **product line groupings,** in which a unit is subdivided according to product offerings for which it is responsible. For example, the entire company is first divided into four broad product line groupings. In addition to the U.S. Foods Division shown in Figure 21–5 are three other divisions not shown: Restaurant (including Burger King, Bennigan's, and Steak & Ale), International, and Growth and Technology. Heads of these four divisions, which are divided by product line groupings, report to Pillsbury's chief executive officer (not shown in Figure 21–5).

The U.S. Foods Division in turn has four main product lines: Bakery & Sweet Foods, Vegetables & Side Dishes, Prepared Dough Products, and Meals & Snacks. These product line groupings reflect a 1985 Pillsbury reorganization that grouped products by the way consumers think about them, rather than by the previously used sales-oriented distribution systems (Dry Grocery, Frozen, and Refrigerated Foods).

The Prepared Dough Products Business Unit is organized by **functional groupings** such as manufacturing, marketing, and finance, which are the different business activities within a firm.

Pillsbury uses **geographical groupings** for its more than 500 field sales representatives throughout the United States. Each director of sales has several regional sales managers reporting to him or her, such as Western, Southern, and so on. These, in turn, have district managers reporting to them (although for simplicity these are not shown in the chart).

A relatively new position in consumer products firms is the *category manager* (senior marketing manager in Figure 21–5). Category managers have profit-and-loss responsibility for an entire product line—all biscuit brands, for example. They attempt to reduce the possibility of one brand's actions hurting another brand in the same category. In addition, category managers have authority to approve decisions that otherwise would need approval by senior management.[15]

Products from Pillsbury's line of prepared dough products.

Role of the Product Manager   The key person in the product or brand group shown in Figure 21–5 is the manager who heads it. As mentioned in Chapter 11, this person is often called the *product manager* or *brand manager,* but in Pillsbury he or she carries the title *marketing manager.* This person and the assistants in the product group are the basic building blocks in the marketing department of most consumer and industrial product firms. The function of a product manager is to plan, implement, and control the annual and long-range plans for the products for which he or she is responsible. This responsibility includes six primary tasks:[16]

1 Developing long-range competitive strategies for the product that will achieve target sales, profit, and market share objectives.
2 Preparing annual marketing plans, sales forecasts, and budgets.
3 Working with advertising agencies to develop advertising appeals, copy, and campaigns.
4 Developing support for the product from the firm's salesforce and distributors.
5 Gathering continuous marketing research information on customers, non-customers, dealers, competitors, the product's performance, and new opportunities and problems.
6 Finding ways to improve the existing products and create new ones.

Although these six functions are common to both consumer product and industrial product managers, some important differences exist. Consumer product managers are typically responsible for fewer products and spend more time working with marketing people inside their firm (marketing research, packaging design, and sales) and outside it (advertising agencies and distributors). In contrast, industrial product managers like those in Intel who are responsible for integrated circuit chips usually have more products and spend more time working with technical personnel in the firm's engineering, production, and R&D departments and in talking directly to sales representatives and important customers.[17]

There are both benefits and dangers to the product manager system used by many consumer product and industrial product companies. On the positive side, product managers become strong advocates for the assigned products. This means they (1) can react quickly to problems or changes in the marketplace and cut red tape to work with people in various functions both inside and outside the organization (Figure 21–6); (2) can orchestrate and balance both marketing and nonmarketing activities; and (3) can assume profit-and-loss responsibility for the performance of the product line.

Balanced against these benefits are some potential dangers that all relate to one factor: even though product managers have major responsibilities, they have relatively little direct authority. Product managers, responsible for one or more products, typically have two people reporting to them at most—often less in industrial product manager positions. However, all the other groups and functions shown in Figure 21–6 must be coordinated and used to meet the product's goals.[18] To successfully coordinate the many functions, managers must use persuasion rather than orders. Further, because promotions or transfers to other

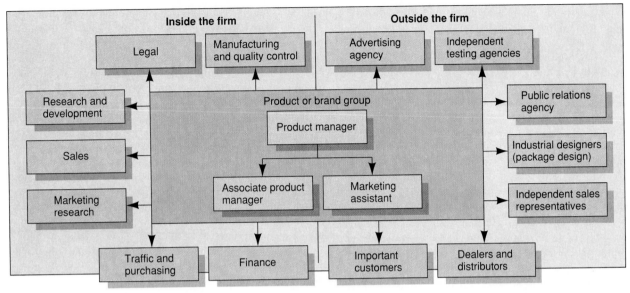

FIGURE 21–6
Units with which the product manager and product group work

products may take place after only a few years on the job, product managers often become concerned with immediate results rather than long-term performance of their products.[19]

CONCEPT CHECK

1 **What is the difference between a line and a staff position in a marketing organization?**

2 **What are three groupings used within a typical marketing organization?**

THE CONTROL PHASE OF THE STRATEGIC MARKETING PROCESS

The essence of control, the final phase of the strategic marketing process, is comparing results with planned goals for the marketing program and taking necessary actions.

THE MARKETING CONTROL PROCESS

Ideally, quantified goals from the marketing plans developed in the planning phase have been accomplished by the marketing actions taken in the implementation phase (Figure 21–7) and measured as results in the control phase. A marketing manager then uses *management by exception,* which means identifying results that deviate from plans to diagnose their causes and take new actions. Often results fall short of plans, and a corrective action is needed. For example, after 50 years of profits Caterpillar accumulated losses of $1 billion. To correct the problem, Caterpillar focused its marketing efforts on core products and

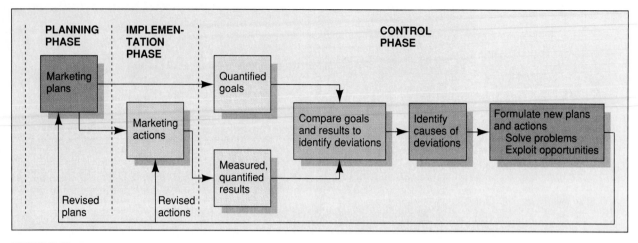

FIGURE 21–7
The control phase of the strategic marketing process

reduced its manufacturing costs.[20] At other times the comparison shows that performance is far better than anticipated, in which case the marketing manager tries to identify the reason and move quickly to exploit the unexpected opportunity.

Marketing control is an especially difficult and important problem in today's corporations, with many divisions carrying diverse products and services among which scarce resources must be deployed. John Sculley, chairman of Apple Computer, faced such a situation when he evaluated the company and decided that "there was little possibility that we could afford all the projects it was working on." Through a control process the company began to concentrate its efforts on the introduction of a new low-cost model of the Macintosh, and on a few projects such as publishing, communications and electronic mail, and software programming.[21]

Measuring Results   Without some quantitative goal, no benchmark exists with which to compare actual results. Manufacturers of both consumer and industrial products are increasingly trying to develop marketing programs that have not only specific action programs but also specific procedures for monitoring and measuring them. For example, computer analysis of scanner data from UPC markings now enables a retailer to quickly recognize "hot" sales items.[22]

Taking Marketing Actions   When results deviate significantly from plans, some kind of action is essential. Deviations can be the result of the process used to specify goals, or can be due to changes in the marketplace.[23] Levi Strauss discovered that consumer tastes in the 1980s shifted from jeans to more fashionable clothes. As a result, it took decisive actions: it increased its local advertising budgets dramatically, offered retailers volume discounts for the first time in history, sold through Sears and J. C. Penney (thereby alienating some of its smaller retailers, who dropped the Levi's line), and closed nine plants. To stay in touch with retail trends, Levi Strauss affixes UPC bar-code labels to each product at its factory, which enable it to spot new sales trends quickly.[24]

SALES ANALYSIS

For controlling marketing programs, **sales analysis**—using the firm's sales records to compare actual results with sales goals and identify areas of strength and weakness—is critical. All the variables that might be used in market segmentation may be used in **sales component analysis** (also called microsales analysis), which traces sales revenues to their sources, such as specific products, sales territories, or customers. Common breakdowns include:

- Customer characteristics: demographics. Standard Industrial Classification, size, reason for purchase, and type of reseller (retailer or wholesaler).
- Product characteristics: model, package size, and color.
- Geographical region: sales territory, city, state, and region.
- Order size.
- Price or discount class.
- Commission to the sales representative.

Today's computers can easily produce these breakdowns, provided the input data contain these classifications. Therefore it is critical that marketing managers request the breakdowns they require from accounting and information systems departments.

The danger is that marketing managers or chief executive officers are so overwhelmed by the volume of computerized reports that they can't spot the key performance numbers in the report needed for control and subsequent action. Each Tuesday, Ken Iverson, sitting in a small town in South Carolina, carefully inputs into the computer numbers on the tons of steel each of Nucor's divisions produced the previous week. What makes the situation unique is that Iverson is chief executive officer of Nucor, whose efficient "minimills" have revolutionized American steel production and distribution. Although Nucor's "no frills" operation is lean (17 people, counting secretaries, in the corporate headquarters of an $800-million-a-year company), saving money is *not* the reason he does his own computer inputting. His explanation, "By keying in the numbers, you're forced to look at every figure for every week. That's the value."[25]

PROFITABILITY ANALYSIS

To their surprise, marketing managers often discover the 80/20 principle (see Chapter 15) the hard way, on the job. **Profitability analysis** enables the manager to measure the profitability of the firm's products, customer groups, sales territories, channels of distribution, and even order sizes. This leads to decisions to expand, maintain, reduce, or eliminate specific products, customer groups, or channels.[26]

For example, following the 80/20 principle, a marketing manager will try to find the common characteristics among the 20 percent of the customers (or products, brands, sales districts, salespeople, or kinds of orders) that are generating

80 percent (or the bulk) of revenues and profits to find more like them to exploit competitive advantages. Conversely, the 80 percent of customers, products, brands, and so on that are generating few revenues and profits may need to be reduced or even dropped entirely unless a way is found to make them profitable.

Profitability analysis provides the basis for such decisions. The type of profitability analysis discussed here is **contribution margin analysis,** which monitors controllable costs and indicates the contribution to profit of specific marketing factors. To obtain cost information for this type of analysis, companies like Hewlett-Packard are developing new accounting systems based on input from marketing, manufacturing, product design, and accounting.[27]

Figure 21–8 is an example of a contribution margin analysis of the sales performance of three sales representatives who make up a sales district. The report, provided by a spreadsheet program, breaks the sales revenue, contribution margin, and personal selling costs down by sales territory to show the net contribution of each sales representative.

FIGURE 21–8

Comparative income statement for three sales representatives and the total sales district

The specific costs for each sales representative are expressed as a percentage of sales revenue, or an **expense-to-sales ratio.** This ratio reveals important deviations from the average for the total district. For example, sales represen-

	E. MARTIN		J. TAYLOR		W. JONES		DISTRICT TOTALS	
	DOLLARS (thousands)	PER-CENTAGE	DOLLARS (thousands)	PER-CENTAGE	DOLLARS (thousands)	PER-CENTAGE	DOLLARS (thousands)	PER-CENTAGE
Sales	$2,200	100.00%	$2,500	100.00%	$2,000	100.00%	$6,700	100.00%
Cost of goods sold	1,721	78.23	1,887	75.48	1,543	77.15	5,151	76.88
Contribution margin	479	21.77	613	24.52	457	22.85	1,549	23.12
Account costs								
Freight	63	2.86	65	2.60	60	3.00	188	2.80
Inventory	44	2.00	30	1.20	39	1.95	113	1.69
Accounts receivable	64	2.91	75	3.00	59	2.95	198	2.96
Technical services	18	0.82	18	0.72	17	0.85	53	0.79
Advertising and promotion	21	0.96	35	1.40	18	0.90	74	1.10
Total customer costs	$210	9.55%	$223	8.92%	$193	9.65%	$626	9.34%
Personal selling costs								
Compensation	$31.50	1.43%	$33.00	1.32%	$29.90	1.50%	$94.40	1.41%
Transportation	6.00	0.27	5.00	0.20	7.00	0.35	18.00	0.27
Lodging, meals	3.50	0.16	3.50	0.14	4.00	0.20	11.00	0.16
Telephone	1.35	0.06	1.70	0.07	1.20	0.06	4.25	0.06
Entertainment	3.00	0.14	1.00	0.04	2.50	0.12	6.50	0.10
Samples, brochures	2.00	0.09	2.00	0.08	1.50	0.07	5.50	0.08
Miscellaneous	0.50	0.02	0.50	0.02	0.30	0.02	1.30	0.02
Total personal selling costs	$47.85	2.17%	$46.70	1.87%	$46.40	2.32%	$140.95	2.10%
Net territory contribution	$221.15	10.05%	$343.30	13.73%	$217.60	10.88%	$782.05	11.67%

tative Taylor's personal selling costs are 1.87% of sales revenues, while the district average is 2.10 percent, because costs such as transportation, lodging, and entertainment are lower than those of the other representatives.[28]

THE MARKETING AUDIT

Both sales and profitability analyses like those just discussed have great value in the control phase of the strategic marketing process, but the focus of such analyses is usually quite narrow, such as monthly, quarterly, or annual deviations that address a specific product, customer segment, sales territory, or order size.

Often a broader marketing perspective is needed, one that covers a longer time horizon and relates the marketing mix factors to environmental, consumer, competitive, and industry variables. This is the role of a **marketing audit,** which is a comprehensive, unbiased, periodic review of the strategic marketing process of a firm or strategic business unit (SBU). The purpose of the marketing audit, which serves as both a planning and control technique, is to identify new problems and opportunities that warrant an action plan to improve performance.[29]

Most firms undertaking a marketing audit use a checklist such as that shown in Figure 21–9. Before deciding where the firm or SBU should go (the goal-setting step in the planning phase), the firm must determine where it is now through a situation analysis. The checklist used covers factors ranging from the marketing mix factors and customer profiles to markets and competitors.

For a meaningful, comprehensive marketing audit, the individual or team conducting the audit must have a free rein to talk to managers, employees, salespeople, distributors, and customers, as well as have access to all pertinent internal and external reports and memoranda. They need to involve top management and the doers in the process to ensure that resulting action recommendations have their support.

CONCEPT CHECK

1 What two components of the strategic marketing process are compared to control a marketing program?

2 What is the difference between a sales analysis and a profitability analysis?

3 What is a marketing audit?

YOPLAIT YOGURT: IMPLEMENTATION AND CONTROL PHASES OF THE STRATEGIC MARKETING PROCESS

Having seen the planning phase of Yoplait yogurt in Chapter 20, let's now look at its implementation and control phases.[30]

PRODUCTS/SERVICES: THE REASON FOR EXISTENCE

1 Is the product/service free from deadwood?
2 What is the life-cycle stage?
3 How will user demands or trends affect you?
4 Are you a leader in new product innovation?
5 Are inexpensive methods used to estimate new product potentials before considerable amounts are spent on R&D and market introduction?
6 Do you have different quality levels for different markets?
7 Are packages/brochures effective salespeople for the products/services they present?
8 Do you present products/services in the most appealing colors (formats) for markets being served?
9 Are there features or benefits to exploit?
10 Is the level of customer service adequate?
11 How are quality and reliability viewed by customers?

CUSTOMER: USER PROFILES

1 Who is the current and potential customer?
2 Are there geographic aspects of use: regional, rural, urban?
3 Why do people buy the product/service; what motivates their preferences?
4 Who makes buying decisions; when, where?
5 What is the frequency and quantity of use?

MARKETS: WHERE PRODUCTS/SERVICES ARE SOLD

1 Have you identified and measured major segments?
2 Are small, potential market segments overlooked in trying to satisfy the majority?
3 Are the markets for the products/services expanding or declining?
4 Should different segments be developed; are there gaps in penetration?

COMPETITORS: THEIR INFLUENCE

1 Who are the principal competitors, how are they positioned, and where are they headed?
2 What are their market shares?
3 What features of competitors' products/services stand out?
4 Is the market easily entered or dominated?

PRICING: PROFITABILITY PLANNING

1 What are the objectives of current pricing policy: acquiring, defending, or expanding?
2 Are price policies set to produce volume or profit?
3 How does pricing compare with competition in similar levels of quality?
4 Does cost information show profitability of each item?
5 What is the history of price deals, discounts, and promotions?

FIGURE 21–9
Marketing audit questions

IMPLEMENTATION PHASE

After developing the marketing plans and strategies described in Chapter 20, Yoplait USA then had to implement them in detail. These details ranged from fine-tuning the target market and positioning to devising production capacity to mesh with the execution of marketing mix strategies.

Target Market   Present and prospective yogurt eaters tend to be urban, upscale, and better educated. The Yoplait product manager went one step beyond these demographics to cover psychographic segmentation as well, targeting early adopters who try new products and influence others.

Product Positioning   The product team built on Yoplait's personality and its French origin to stress its differences and position it as a unique, high-quality product with fresh fruit. The team tried to generate consumer awareness and trial by differentiating Yoplait from its American competitors, which are mainly sundae style with fruit preserves on the bottom that have to be stirred up.

6 Are intermediaries making money from the line?

7 Can the product/service support advertising or promotion programs?

8 Will the manufacturing process require more volume?

MARKETING CHANNELS: SELLING PATHS

1 Does the system offer the best access to all target markets?

2 Do product/service characteristics require specials?

3 What is the most profitable type of presentation for each market: direct vs. reps, master distributors or dealers, etc.?

4 What are the trends in distribution methods?

SALES ADMINISTRATION: SELLING EFFICIENCY

1 Are customers getting coverage in proportion to their potential?

2 Are sales costs planned and controlled?

3 Does the compensation plan provide optimum incentive and security to reasonable cost?

4 Is performance measured against potential?

5 Are selling expenses proportionate to results and potentials within markets or territories?

6 Are there deficiencies in recruitment, selection, training, motivation, supervision, performance, promotion, or compensation?

7 Are effective selling aids and sales tools provided?

ADVERTISING: MEDIA PROGRAM

1 Are media objectives and strategies linked to the marketing plan?

2 What are the objectives of the ad program?

3 How is media effectiveness measured?

4 Is advertising integrated with promotion and sales activity?

5 Is the ad agency's effectiveness periodically evaluated?

6 Do you dictate copy theme and content to the agency?

7 Are you spending realistically, in relation to budget?

SALES PROMOTION: SALES INDUCEMENT

1 Does the sales promotion support a marketing objective?

2 Is it integrated with advertising and selling activity?

3 How is it measured for results?

4 Are slogans, trademarks, logos, and brands being used effectively?

5 Is point-of-sale material cost effective?

6 Are you effectively using couponing, tie-ins, incentives, sampling, stuffers, combination offers?

7 How do you evaluate trade shows for effectiveness?

Source: Adapted from Hal W. Goetsch, "Conduct a Comprehensive Marketing Audit to Improve Marketing Planning," *Marketing News* (March 18, 1983), p. 14; by permission of the American Marketing Association.

FIGURE 21–9 *(concluded)*

Manufacturing   There was no sense promoting Yoplait if manufacturing couldn't produce enough to fill the distribution channels and get the product on supermarket shelves. General Mills has no other refrigerated products, so it had no applicable experience in producing and distributing a product such as yogurt. It started initial production in two plants.

Product Actions   The team took maximum advantage of Yoplait's unique creamy texture, its popular taste, the fruit spread throughout the yogurt, and its "100 percent natural" ingredients with no artificial sweeteners or preservatives. The team wanted to maintain its unique package shape and use 6-ounce containers (compared with 8 ounces from competitors) because research showed that 6 ounces is a good amount to eat at one sitting. It also used image-reinforcing packaging that stressed the product's origin with some French words.

Pricing Actions   It was decided to set distributor margins to achieve a price for Yoplait similar to competitors' prices at the retail level.

Promotional Actions   The Yoplait team developed advertising to enhance the image-building copy on its package. It positioned Yoplait as the yogurt of France, with the copy execution using Americans as presenters: TV personalities Jack Klugman and Loretta Swit and Los Angeles Dodgers manager Tommy Lasorda.

The media plan—directed at upscale early adopters—relied on nighttime television plus unconventional print vehicles: city magazines, *The Dial* (the Public Broadcasting System publication), *Psychology Today,* and *Cosmopolitan.* The print campaign included pictures of the TV campaign celebrities.

The Yoplait team was convinced that if it could get people to try Yoplait once, the product would sell itself. The team hired a fleet of refrigerated vans, dressed the servers in French outfits, and gave away free Yoplait packages downtown at noon on weekdays and at the beach on weekends. It had a French balloonist take reporters on a free balloon ride and give them free Yoplait samples, which resulted in tremendous amounts of publicity. The brand group devised the "50-kilometer bicycle challenge" and gave a semitrailer full of Yoplait away at the finish line to both participants and spectators.

Place Actions   The salesforce worked closely with distributors to ensure that Yoplait was profitable for them. To achieve a stock turnover in supermarkets of 2.6 times a week, the salesforce sought 4 feet in the dairy sections (25 percent of that normally allotted to yogurt), the second or third shelf in horizontal sections, and a position near other premium brands.

Marketing Organization   The initial marketing organization was a bare-bones product management team containing only five people: President Steven Rothschild, a marketing vice president, and a brand group consisting of a product manager, an assistant product manager, and a marketing assistant.

CONTROL PHASE

Implementation activity is one thing and market performance another. Did the execution work?

Measured Results   After only three years, Yoplait was in national distribution, had a 13.2 percent market share, and was the second best-selling yogurt, behind Dannon. After six years it had a 21.7 percent market share of retail sales and $135 million in annual sales—exceeding its original goals. Yoplait also achieved its 25 percent ROI target.

Resulting Actions   The Yoplait team concluded that after three years it had attracted new consumers to yogurt and had contributed substantially to growth of the entire product class. The creamy French style of yogurt was now an entirely new yogurt segment. To continue growth, General Mills introduced new Yoplait flavors and an 18-ounce package.

One of the original objectives was to become a multiproduct business. Soon after Yoplait was acquired, the team set up a new business group that screened over 100 new product ideas. Looking at the market segments, the group realized that although it had created the creamy segment, four fifths of the market was still devoted to thick yogurt—sundae and Swiss style. To attract this group, Yoplait carefully developed new products using two other bases of segmentation:

1 *Texture segmentation:* Yoplait introduced custard-style yogurt to compete with thick yogurts.
2 *Texture and usage segmentation:* Yoplait added its Breakfast Yogurt, creamy yogurt with nuts, fruit, and grains.

In the process Yoplait grew rapidly to four brand groups.

Yoplait Yogurt Today   Buoyed by Yoplait's success, new people added to the team apparently watched as national brands (such as Dannon and Kraft) and regional brands attacked. Although number 2 nationally, Yoplait's market share and profit fell. Its Fruit-on-the-Bottom line failed. Steven Rothschild, promoted now to president of General Mills's Convenience and International Food Group, commented, "Our offering wasn't unique enough, and implementation wasn't up to standards." In response to extensive marketing research studies, a revitalized Yoplait has taken important corrective actions[31]:

1 Reformulated the entire Original Yoplait yogurt line to give it a thicker, creamier texture.
2 Introduced new Yoplait Light, a low-calorie fruit yogurt targeted at the health-conscious and weight-conscious segments, and Yoplait snack-size packs, targeted at convenience and lunchbox segments.
3 Developed a bold new advertising campaign ("Yoplait—taste how good yogurt should be") that featured TV personalities like Allyce Beasley (*Moonlighting*) and Phylicia Rashad (*The Cosby Show*).

Although the yogurt industry today is extremely competitive, Yoplait has maintained its number 2 market share through expert use of its marketing control procedures.

Yoplait yogurt's product line, including the recently introduced Yoplait Light and snack packs.

ETHICS AND SOCIAL RESPONSIBILITY IN THE 1990s

NOT ALL RESULTS LOOK GOOD

The control phase of the strategic marketing process requires that results of marketing actions be measured and quantified. Popular measures include sales revenue, market share, return on investment, return on sales, number of distribution outlets, and customer satisfaction, among others. Unfortunately, the conclusion a manager may come to about the effectiveness of a marketing program may depend on which measures are given highest priority. At IBM, for example, sales increased by 9 percent to reach $69 billion in 1990, while return on sales declined from 16 percent in 1984 to 9 percent in 1990. At the product level, Prodigy—an on-line information service offered through a joint venture between IBM and Sears—has been a success in terms of number of subscribers, but has not been profitable since its introduction in 1984.

How should managers present positive and negative control phase information? How should qualitative information such as "impact on the environment" be incorporated into the control process?

Sources: Eugene F. Bryan, "The World Turned Upside Down? IBM in the 1990s," *Business Horizons* (November–December 1990), pp. 39–47; "The Fortune 500 Largest U.S. Industrial Corporations," *Fortune* (April 23, 1990), pp. 346–47; and Jeffrey Rothfeder and Mark Lewyn, "How Long Will Prodigy Be a Problem Child?" *Business Week* (September 10, 1990), p. 75; and "The Fortune 500," *Fortune*, April 22, 1991, pp. 286–87.

 ## SUMMARY

1 The implementation phase of the strategic marketing process is concerned with executing the marketing program developed in the planning phase. Successful marketing programs require both effective planning and effective implementation.

2 Today successful marketing implementation has high priority in many firms. Keys to this include communicating both goals and means to doers: finding a program champion; having doers benefit from success; acting rather than overanalyzing; fostering open communications to surface problems; and scheduling precise tasks, responsibilities, and deadlines.

3 Essential to good scheduling is separating tasks that can be done concurrently from those that must be done sequentially. Gantt charts are a simple, effective means of scheduling.

4 Organizing marketing activities necessitates recognition of two different aspects of an organization: (1) line and staff positions and (2) product line, functional, and geographical groupings.

5 The product manager performs a vital marketing role in both consumer and industrial product firms, interacting with numerous people and groups both inside and outside the firm.

6 In many consumer product organizations the product manager heads up a product or brand group. A product manager has important responsibilities in being an advocate for the product line but often suffers from a lack of direct authority to get things done.

7 The control phase of the strategic marketing process involves measuring the results of the actions from the implementation phase and comparing them with goals set in the planning phase. Deviations are identified, and actions are taken to correct deficiencies and exploit opportunities.

8 Sales analyses, profitability analyses, and marketing audits are used to control marketing programs.

KEY TERMS AND CONCEPTS

product or program champion p. 580
action item list p. 583
line positions p. 586
staff positions p. 586
product line groupings p. 587
functional groupings p. 587
geographical groupings p. 587

sales analysis p. 591
sales component analysis p. 591
profitability analysis p. 591
contribution margin analysis p. 592
expense-to-sales ratio p. 592
marketing audit p. 593

CHAPTER PROBLEMS AND APPLICATIONS

1 After first selecting sites for his Domino's Pizza restaurants near college campuses, Tom Monaghan also located them near military bases. Why? What implementation problems are (*a*) similar and (*b*) different for restaurants near a college campus versus a military base?

2 What is the "offering" to a Domino's Pizza customer? What needs to be measured to determine if the offering is satisfactory to customers?

3 A common theme among managers who succeed repeatedly in program implementation is fostering open communication. Why is this so important?

4 Parts of Tasks 6 and 7 in Figure 21–4 are done *both* concurrently and sequentially. How can this be? How does it help the students meet the term paper deadline?

5 In Pillsbury's organizational chart in Figure 21–5, where do product line, functional, and geographical groupings occur?

6 In what way can a product manager in a grocery products firm have *both* (*a*) significant responsibility and (*b*) limited authority?

7 Why are quantified goals in the planning phase of the strategic marketing process important for the control phase?

8 In Figure 21–8, which sales representative makes the least net territory contribution to the sales district? Why?

9 Before Pillsbury's reorganization (shown in Figure 21–5), the four units headed by vice presidents/general managers were vegetables, refrigerated business, entrées business, and frozen vegetables business. Where would Totino's Pizza, Green Giant canned corn, Green Giant frozen peas, and Van de Kamp's frozen dinners fit in the old and new organizations? What are the advantages and disadvantages of the old and new organizations?

Expanding Marketing Settings

Marketing has become an important activity in many new settings. The traditional focus on mature products in domestic markets has now expanded to include goods and services in a global marketplace. Chapter 22 introduces the concept of international marketing and explains how the marketing concepts discussed in previous chapters must be adapted to compete in an international arena. In Chapter 23 Michael Eisner, CEO of Walt Disney Company, provides insight about the role of marketing as our economy becomes increasingly service-based. Part VI emphasizes that applying marketing to international markets and services represent some of today's most exciting opportunities for marketing managers and for consumers.

CHAPTER 22

International Marketing

*A*fter reading this chapter you should be able to:

- Describe why U.S. firms are undertaking international marketing.

- Contrast global and customized approaches to international marketing.

- Understand the importance of environmental factors (political and legal, economic and cultural) in successful international marketing.

- Identify alternative modes of entering international marketing operations.

- Explain how and why U.S. firms may have to adapt their marketing mix when entering the international arena.

Kellogg's Global Challenge: Marketing Cold Cereals against Wurst, Cheese, and Croissants

Germans often eat wurst for breakfast, Swedes prefer cheese on brown bread, and the French have their croissants. Therein lies the Kellogg Company's global challenge: getting its Corn Flakes and other cold cereals onto breakfast tables of consumers around the world.

Take French consumers as an example. Kellogg's French subsidiary, Kellogg's P.A., is working hard to overcome its citizens' long-time breakfast habits. In marketing Kellogg's Corn Flakes to the French, three problems are especially severe: (1) over 30 percent of French adults skip breakfast entirely, (2) most of the rest have a cup of café au lait and bread at home or a croissant and coffee standing up at a bar on the way to work, and (3) many French adults still view corn, which first arrived on French farms after World War II, as only fit for chickens and pigs to eat.

Kellogg's P.A.'s marketing strategy for selling breakfast cereals in France is similar to that of many American firms taking a familiar domestic product abroad that is exotic to foreign tastes—and for foreign firms selling their products in the United States. This strategy involves great patience, advertising budgets far out of line with sales, and a thorough understanding of what local consumers want. For example, marketing research revealed that 40 percent of French consumers eating cereal for breakfast pour on *warm* milk. So Kellogg's TV ads carefully show milk poured on its corn flakes from a transparent glass pitcher—traditionally used in France for cold milk—and not the opaque porcelain one that holds the hot milk used for café au lait.

Kellogg's efforts generally have been rewarded in Europe, where it has about 50 percent of the cold cereals market. But progress in France has been painfully slow where French consumers—still loyal to their croissants—average only 1.1 pounds of cold cereals annually, compared to an American consumer's 9.8 pounds.[1]

After defining exactly what international marketing is and why firms such as Kellogg assume great risks to do it, this chapter discusses the importance of environmental factors in successful international marketing, describes alternative means of entering the international market, and explains how successful marketing programs in the United States often have to be modified for use abroad.

THE SCOPE OF INTERNATIONAL MARKETING

Why would a successful U.S. company like Kellogg want to enter the international market when domestic marketing seems so much easier? Indeed, with the potential problems of foreign languages, different currencies, volatile political and legal arenas, and different consumer needs and expectations, why get involved in international marketing at all? Let us try to answer these questions.

WHAT INTERNATIONAL MARKETING IS

Stated simply, **international marketing** is marketing across national boundaries. Since the end of World War II, improved travel, communications, and technology have fostered a tenfold increase in trade among nations.

The General Agreement on Tariffs and Trade (GATT) is an international agreement established in 1948 that seeks to "liberalize world trade and place it on a secure basis, thereby contributing to economic growth and development and to the welfare of the world's peoples." It assists in reducing trade barriers around the world and in creating more favorable conditions for world trade. Since GATT was established, this agreement has helped build world trade from $60 billion to $6 trillion annually. However, GATT negotiations "to liberalize world trade" can bog down and extend for years because of the desire of countries to protect jobs in their domestic industries. Four years of trade talks broke up in 1990 because Western Europeans sought protection for their agricultural industry and the United States for its textile industry.[2]

BENEFITS AND DIFFICULTIES OF INTERNATIONAL MARKETING

A company choosing to enter international markets can achieve many benefits, but it can also encounter many difficulties.

Benefits of International Marketing   The main reason for companies to do international marketing is to exploit a better business opportunity in terms of increased sales and profits. Either firms are limited in their home country or their opportunities are great in the foreign countries.

Many companies find themselves with little room for growth in their domestic market. Competition may increase and leave a smaller portion of the pie to enjoy, or demand may shift to a newer, better product. The economic environment in the home country may be undesirable because of higher taxes or a recession. It would seem logical to turn to other markets in any of these cases, as Japan's Honda has done.

So foreign markets may offer an opportunity for growth. A product that is mature and facing dwindling sales at home may be new and exciting in other countries. For example, France's Sodima, whose Yoplait yogurt was in a mature phase of its product life cycle at home, was happy to license its product to General Mills for sale in the United States, where yogurt sales were growing rapidly (see Chapters 20 and 21). Similarly, Kellogg hopes that its Corn Flakes will catch hold in France, where the product is at an early stage in its product life cycle and competition in the ready-to-eat cereal market is less intense than in the United States. Volvo cannot sell enough cars in its own domestic Swedish market, so it must achieve global sales to achieve necessary production and marketing economies of scale. Figure 22–1 summarizes the main reasons why U.S. companies consider entering international markets.

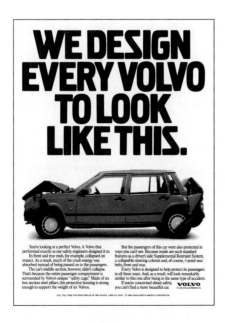

Why do firms "go international" and why must Volvo seek markets outside its domestic Swedish market? For the answers, see the text.

FIGURE 22–1
Key reasons U.S. firms "go international"

1 To counter adverse economic factors in the home market.
2 To extend a product's life cycle.
3 To reduce or avoid competition.
4 To enhance economies of scale in production and marketing.
5 To spread fixed costs over more units sold.
6 To dispose of inventories.
7 To export (and import) new technology.
8 To increase profits/shareholder economic well-being.

Difficulties of International Marketing   Is international marketing easy? Not in the least. For U.S. firms anxious to enter the Japanese market and make profits quickly, strategy consultant Kenichi Ohmae reminds them it took perhaps 50 years to build their U.S. firm and 15 years to develop their European business. So he asks these firms to recognize that in entering the Japanese market—one of the toughest markets in the world—it may take at least 25 years to achieve the same success it found in the United States or Europe.[3] Although international marketing involves the same principles of domestic marketing discussed throughout this book, those principles must be applied with care.

Campbell Soup, the company with a 60 percent market share in the U.S. wet soups category, lost $30 million in Great Britain. The problem was that Campbell's didn't clearly communicate that the soup was condensed, and consumers saw it as a poor value compared with the larger cans stocked next to it.

Americans recognize the brand names of foreign products that have been introduced successfully here: Honda and BMW cars, Sony TV sets, Nestlé candy bars, and Shell gasoline products. Although this chapter will describe foreign successes in the United States, it will also identify how American firms can overcome difficulties in marketing their products abroad.

THE IMPORTANCE OF INTERNATIONAL MARKETING

The dollar volume of U.S. exports and imports indicates the importance of international marketing and why it affects virtually every American today. The **balance of trade** is the difference between the monetary value of a nation's exports and imports. When its exports exceed its imports, it has incurred a *surplus* in its balance of trade. When imports exceed exports, a *deficit* has occurred. In the 25 years after World War II ended in 1945, European countries and Japan were rebuilding their shattered economies. They had limited money to import products, and what money they had was often used to import U.S. construction equipment and machine tools to rebuild their cities and factories. So, as shown in Figure 22–2, because of the long-range economic effects of World War II, the United States ran a surplus in its balance of trade until 1970.

Figure 22–2 also shows that since 1970 two important things have happened in U.S. exports and imports. First, with a few exceptions, imports have significantly exceeded exports each year, indicating that the United States is running a continuing balance of trade deficit. Second, the volume of both exports and imports is about 15 to 20 times what it was in 1965—showing why

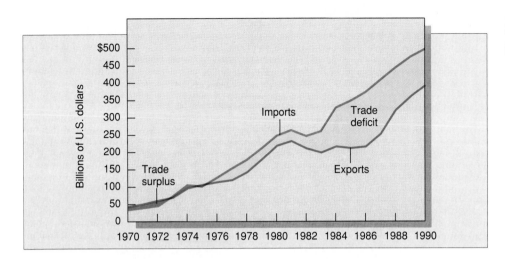

FIGURE 22–2
**Trends in the U.S.
balance of trade**

almost every American is significantly affected. The effect varies from the products they buy (TV sets from Japan, wool suits from Great Britain, wine from France) to those they sell (GM's cars to Europe, Du Pont's chemicals to the Far East) and the additional jobs and improved standard of living that result.

HOW TRANSNATIONALS SUCCEED IN INTERNATIONAL MARKETING

A **transnational corporation** is a business firm that looks at the entire world as one market and conducts research and development, manufacturing, financing, and marketing activities wherever they can best be done. National boundaries and regulations are largely irrelevant, and the best people available are placed in key positions regardless of national origin.[4]

The phrase *transnational corporation* is replacing *multinational corporation* because the latter has developed an unpleasant, predatory connotation. A transnational corporation runs its business and makes its decisions based on all the possible choices in the world, not simply favoring domestic options because they are convenient.

As American transnationals in many industries find themselves losing ground against foreign competitors, policymakers are increasingly asking why some companies and some industries in a nation succeed internationally while others lose ground or fail. As summarized in Figure 22–3, Professor Michael Porter suggests a "diamond" to explain a nation's competitive advantage and why some industries and firms become world leaders. He sees four key elements, which appear in Figure 22–3:

1 *Factor conditions*: These reflect a nation's ability to turn its natural resources, education, and infrastructure into a competitive advantage. The Dutch lead the world in the cut-flower industry because of their research in flower cultivation, packaging, and shipping—not because of their weather.

2 *Demand conditions*: These include both the number and sophistication of domestic customers for an industry's product. Japan's sophisticated consumers demand quality in their TVs and radios, thereby making Japan's producers the world leaders in the electronics industry.

FIGURE 22–3
Porter's "diamond" of national competitive advantage

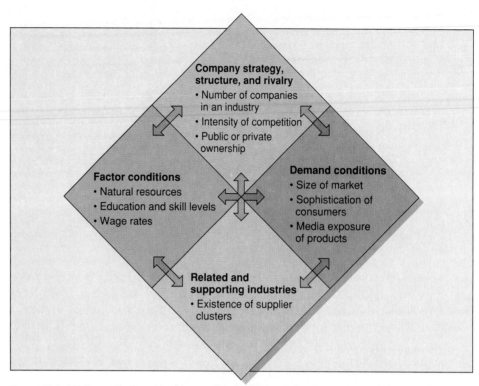

Sources: Michael E. Porter, *The Competitive Advantage of Nations* (New York: Free Press, 1990); and Michael E. Porter, "Why Nations Triumph," *Fortune* (March 12, 1990), pp. 94–108.

3 *Related and supporting industries:* Firms and industries seeking leadership in international markets need clusters of world-class suppliers that accelerate innovation. The German leadership in printing relates directly to the cluster of supporting German suppliers.

4 *Company strategy, structure, and rivalry:* These factors include the conditions governing the way a nation's businesses are organized and managed, along with the intensity of domestic competition. The Italian shoe industry has become the world leader because of intense domestic competition that enhances quality and innovation.

In his study, Porter analyzed the case histories of firms in over 100 industries. While he found that strategies employed by the most successful transnationals were different in many respects, a common theme emerged—a firm that succeeds in international markets has first succeeded in intense domestic competition. Hence competitive advantage for transnational firms grows out of relentless, continuing improvement, innovation, and change.[5]

It is important to note, however, that it is not essential to be a giant transnational to gain benefits in international markets. Numerous small firms succeed in foreign niche markets or by utilizing unique information, licenses, or technology. In fact, in one unusual respect a small regional American firm has an advantage over its huge transnational rivals in the international arena. That is when it can trade product technology and marketing ideas with foreign firms with whom it does not compete directly. Minnesota Color Envelopes is a small firm that produces a variety of specialized packaging for photofinishers (shown in the accompanying picture). By exchanging information with regional European printers, it is able to obtain information on new printing equipment, inks, running speeds, and printing plates that give high-quality printing—thereby gaining an advantage over its American competitors. It, in turn, provides ideas to the European printers, so the exchange benefits both parties.[6]

GLOBAL VERSUS CUSTOMIZED PRODUCTS

As international marketing grows, firms selling both consumer and industrial products in foreign countries face a dilemma: should they use a global or customized strategy in the products they sell, or a strategy in between?

A **global approach** is an international marketing strategy that assumes that the way the product is used and the needs it satisfies are universal. Therefore, the marketing mix need not be adjusted for each country. In contrast, a **customized approach** (or *local approach*) is an international marketing strategy that assumes that the way the product is used and the needs it satisfies are unique to each country. This then requires a marketing mix tailored to the needs, values, customs, languages, and purchasing power of the target country. The global approach is less common but has been successful for some firms.

U.S. firms, as discussed later, have often encountered problems when they simply took American products and marketing programs into foreign countries with almost no change (a global approach). Other U.S. firms watched these errors and shifted to a customized strategy. An example is Kodak's European launch of its Ektaprint copier-duplication line. It had watched Xerox take a successful U.S. copier into Great Britain only to discover that the equipment didn't fit through narrower British doorways. When Kodak introduced its European copier into Europe, the design included language keys on the control panel that are tailored to individual countries and a variable reduction capability

For the way a small U.S. envelope firm exchanges ideas with foreign companies to be more competitive, see the text.

for different page sizes, since there is no standard paper size in Europe comparable to the American 8½ × 11 inch.

Professor Theodore Levitt, however, argues that a firm can overreact and carry customized marketing too far in trying to respond to wants of consumers, and that a global strategy is needed.[7] When a global strategy succeeds, huge savings are possible in manufacturing, packaging, and advertising costs. For example, when Colgate-Palmolive introduced its Colgate tartar-control toothpaste in over 40 countries, its marketing executives in these countries received only two TV ads from which to choose. The ads were translated to the local language and were a success. Colgate-Palmolive estimates that it saves up to $2 million in TV production costs for each country that runs the same TV ad.[8]

But when a globalization strategy doesn't work, it can be a disaster. Parker Pen, Ltd., is an example. In 1982, it was making about 500 styles of pens and letting local marketing managers in about 150 countries create their own ads and packaging. Using a globalization strategy, by 1984 it had reduced the number of styles of pens to about 100 and offered only a single ad campaign—one that could be translated into local languages. The strategy backfired because local marketing managers resented the standardization of ads and advertising agencies. The company almost went bankrupt until it returned to its customized strategy and let each country develop its own ads.[9]

McDonald's—the undisputed world hamburger ruler—seems to have achieved the ideal hybrid between a global and a customized strategy. Although it has standardized much of its menu, it gives a degree of flexibility to franchisees to allow for local customer preferences in their countries. Experts have coined the term **glocalization** to describe the McDonald's approach, which is an in-

McDonald's: use a global or customized strategy overseas—or something in between? For McDonald's very successful strategy, see the text.

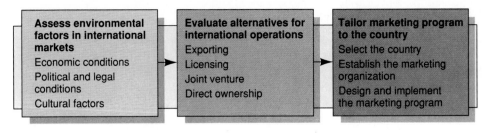

FIGURE 22–4
Sequence of decisions in entering international markets

ternational marketing strategy that seeks to combine the best features of both the global and customized (local) approaches by encouraging local managers to modify the global strategy, where appropriate, to the needs of customers in their country.

McDonald's in Germany and France has beer on its menu, and its restaurants in Japan offer saki. In the Philippines, where noodle houses are popular, its customers can find—what else?—McSpaghetti! After 14 years of negotiations, McDonald's first Moscow restaurant opened in February 1990 with an awesome size: 700 seats, 27 cash registers, and a capacity of 15,000 customers per day. McDonald's even had to train these customers how to eat their Russian "Big Mak," because Soviets aren't used to eating finger food and initial customers disassembled their Big Maks and ate them one layer at a time.[10]

Companies such as Kodak, Colgate-Palmolive, and McDonald's had to make a series of decisions when they entered international markets. These decisions, outlined in Figure 22–4, are discussed in more detail throughout the remainder of the chapter.

CONCEPT CHECK

1 Given the risks involved, what are several reasons a firm might undertake international marketing?

2 What is a transnational corporation?

3 How does glocalization combine two international marketing strategies?

ASSESSING ENVIRONMENTAL FACTORS

The uncontrollable environmental variables—including economic factors, political and legal concerns, and cultural differences—that affect international marketing are strikingly different from those in domestic markets. This is why many transnational firms considering marketing efforts in a new country undertake serious marketing research—ranging from using published data to interviews with end users and distributors in the country.[11]

Traditional marketing research methods used in the United States often need to be modified in surveying foreign consumers. For example, telephone surveys in the Soviet Union would not give a representative sample of consumers, because only 28 percent of city families and 9 percent of farm families have their own telephone.[12]

ECONOMIC CONDITIONS

There are several important rules to international marketing in light of a country's economic conditions: the product must fit the needs of the country's consumers and the product must be sold where there is the income to buy it and effective means of distributing, using, and servicing it. Five aspects of these considerations are (1) the country's stage of economic development, (2) multination trade groups, (3) the country's economic infrastructure, (4) consumer income, and (5) currency exchange rates.

Stage of Economic Development   There are over 200 countries in the world today, each of which is at a slightly different point in terms of its stage of economic development. However, they can be classified into two major groupings that will help the international marketer better understand their needs:

- *Developed* countries have somewhat mixed economies. Private enterprise dominates, although they have substantial public sectors as well. The United States, Canada, Japan, and most of Western Europe can be considered developed.
- *Developing* countries are in the process of moving from an agricultural to an industrial economy. There are two subgroups within the developing category: (1) those that have already made the move and (2) those that remain locked in the preindustrial economy. Countries such as Poland, Hungary, Australia, Israel, Venezuela, and South Africa fall into the first group. In the second group are Pakistan, Sri Lanka, Tanzania, and Chad, where living standards are low and show little promise of improvement. One third of the world's population is in this second group.

The stage of economic development significantly affects other economic factors, as discussed below.

Multination Trade Groups   In recent years a number of countries with similar economic goals have formed multination trade groups to enhance their economies. The best-known of these is what has been called in the past the *Common Market* or the *European Economic Community,* and is now known as the *European Community,* or simply the *EC.*

On December 31, 1992, 12 European countries will reduce most—if not all—of the barriers to the free flow of goods, services, capital, and labor across their national borders. These European Community countries hope this will be a first step to a giant economic leap forward for their peoples and businesses. The 12 countries are the United Kingdom, Ireland, Denmark, Belgium, the Netherlands, Luxembourg, Germany, France, Italy, Greece, Portugal, and Spain.

As shown in Figure 22–5, the collective economic size of the 12 nations that comprise the European Community give it great international significance. For example, its 342 million consumers give it 93 million more than the United States, and its gross national product is only slightly less than that of the United States. The size of such new markets is one reason many transnational firms are increasing their activity in EC countries. A second reason is that even huge corporations in large countries can no longer survive competing only in their

FIGURE 22–5
**Where the markets are:
Countries and
multination trade groups
of major economic
importance**

RANK BY GROSS NATIONAL PRODUCT	COUNTRY OR GROUP OF COUNTRIES	1987–1989 GROSS NATIONAL PRODUCT (in billions) of U.S. dollars)	1989 POPULATION ESTIMATE (in millions)
1	United States	$5,232	249
2	12 European Community countries[a]	4,527	342
3	Japan	2,839	123
4	Soviet Union	2,460	289
5	6 European Free Trade Agreement countries[b]	648	32
6	Canada	493	26
7	China	471	1,112
8	6 Eastern European countries[c]	322	120
9	4 Asian "Little Dragons"[d]	294	72
10	India	281	812
11	5 Largest Latin American countries[e]	243	293

[a]Includes the United Kingdom, Ireland, Portugal, Spain, Denmark, Belgium, the Netherlands, Luxembourg, France, Germany, Italy, and Greece.
[b]Includes Norway, Sweden, Finland, Iceland, Austria, and Switzerland.
[c]Includes Poland, Hungary, Czechoslovakia, Yugoslavia, Romania, and Bulgaria.
[d]Includes Hong Kong, Singapore, South Korea, and Taiwan.
[e]Includes Mexico, Venezuela, Argentina, Brazil, and Chile.

Sources: *Statistical Abstract of the United States*, 110th ed. (Washington, D.C.: U.S. Department of Commerce, 1990); and *International Financial Statistics Yearbook*, vol. 43 (New York: International Monetary Fund, 1990).

domestic market if they are in global industries. They must be not only in North America but in Europe and Asia, too.[13] For example, a British pharmaceutical expert estimates that in the 1970s it took 4 or 5 years and $16 million to develop a new drug. Today it takes up to 12 years and $250 million—a price that is only possible for a global product in a global market.

Figure 22–5 also contains information on other multination trade groups (both formal and informal) and on individual countries that represent important markets of the 1990s. The six European Free Trade Agreement (EFTA) countries (Austria, Switzerland, Norway, Sweden, Finland, and Iceland) have tariff-free trade with the EC, but none of the political commitments.[14]

When Russian General Secretary Mikhail S. Gorbachev proposed his *perestroika* (economic restructuring) policy to encourage more free-market incentives in the Soviet Union, even he never dreamed of the economic and political revolutions that followed: tearing down the Berlin Wall, a united Germany, and open elections and free-market economies in most of Eastern Europe. The six Eastern European countries mentioned in Figure 22–5 have no formal economic agreements among themselves, but several have talked to the six EFTA countries about joining. These Eastern European countries have a population the size of Japan's and a huge potential for the future. The transition period into free-market economies will be traumatic for these countries, which face soaring prices and unemployment as they redirect their resources.[15]

Almost lost in the excitement of "EC 1992" and the changes in Eastern Europe is the United States–Canada Free Trade Agreement enacted in late 1988. Its goal is to phase out all tariffs over the next decade and smooth the flow of business activities and the process of settling trade disputes. About 70 percent of Canadian exports are to the United States, while about 22 percent of U.S. exports go to Canada. Under consideration is the possibility of adding Mexico to the United States–Canada agreement, to establish a three-country North American free-trade bloc and even a hemispheric free-trade bloc.[16]

Economic Infrastructure   The **economic infrastructure**—a country's communication, transportation, financial, and distribution systems—is a critical consideration in determining whether to try to market to a country's consumers and organizations. This is why American appliance makers have generally avoided China. But sales of industrial products is a different matter. GE has sold its locomotives, and Boeing its 747 commercial jet aircraft, to China in conjunction with programs to train Chinese engineers and technicians to maintain and service these products. Two-lane roads with horse-drawn carts that limit average speeds to 35 or 40 miles per hour are commonplace in Eastern Europe and the Soviet Union—and a nightmare for new firms requiring fast trucking services. About 75 percent of the potato crop in the Soviet Union never reaches stores because of damage in handling, lack of transportation, poor storage facilities, and theft.[17]

Consumer Income   An international marketer selling consumer goods also must consider what the average per capita income is among a nation's consumers and how the income is distributed. Per capita income is less than $200 annually in some of the developing countries. However, a country's distribution of income is important, too. India, for example, has a per capita income of about $300, but some researchers estimate that by the end of the 1990s India will have 300 million upper- and middle-class consumers that will represent a huge market for transnational companies.[18]

Currency Exchange Rates   Fluctuations in exchange rates among the world's currencies are of critical importance in international marketing. Such fluctuations affect everyone—from international vacationers to transnational corporations.

The strength of the U.S. dollar against foreign currencies in 1985 and 1986 was a stroke of good fortune to Americans traveling abroad. Some luxury goods, such as Zeiss binoculars and Gucci handbags, were priced 30 percent to 70 percent less in Europe than in the United States. By early 1988, the value of the dollar against foreign currencies had plummeted. For example, in mid-1985, one American dollar could be exchanged for 10.7 French francs, but in mid-1990 a dollar only bought 5.55 francs—barely half its value five years earlier.

Figure 22–6 shows the impact of these swings in the dollar–franc exchange rate on the prices in a French McDonald's restaurant. The highlighted rows show that in mid-1990 a Big Mac, french fries, and medium Coke would cost $7.21 in France—about twice its cost in dollars in mid-1985. Figure 22–6 also shows the identical names used on the French menu for many of McDonald's items (a global strategy), although tap beer or "biere" also appears (a degree of customized strategy). As mentioned earlier in the chapter, McDonald's glocalization strategy is what many international marketers are seeking. Although McDonald's extensive procedures manual (19 steps to cook the perfect french

MCDONALD'S MENU ITEM		PRICE IN FRANCS, MID-1990	PRICE IN DOLLARS	
IN FRANCE	IN THE UNITED STATES		MID-1990*	MID-1985†
Hamburger	Hamburger	7.60*f*	$1.37	$ .71
Big Mac	Big Mac	18.00	3.24	1.68
Chicken McNuggets (6 morceaux)	6 Chicken McNuggets	17.50	3.15	1.64
Chocolate shake	Chocolate shake	8.70	1.57	.81
Biere	Beer on tap	9.10	1.64	.85
Frites (grand)	French fries (large)	12.70	2.29	1.19
Coca-Cola (moyen)	Coca-Cola (medium)	9.30	1.68	.87

*At $1.00 = 5.55 French francs
† At $1.00 = 10.70 French francs

FIGURE 22–6
Price variations in a French McDonald's restaurant caused by currency exchange fluctuations

fries, as described in the Marketing Action Memo) is legendary and enables tight controls on things like cleanliness and the quality of its french fries, it allows flexibility to let outlets in foreign countries adapt to local conditions.[19]

In seeking to protect their investments, transnational corporations face even more frantic currency exchange problems than individual tourists. Many transnational corporations have foreign currency traders whose job goes on 24 hours a day. Currency fluctuations can wipe out a firm's profits from regular operations, so decisions on when to buy and sell foreign currencies are critical. For example, in one four-year period in the 1980s, Kodak lost about $500 million because the strong dollar made its foreign receivables less valuable when converted to dollars.[20]

POLITICAL AND LEGAL CONDITIONS

The difficulties in assessing the political and legal condition of a country lie not only in identifying the current condition but also in estimating exactly how long that condition will last. Some transnational companies use analyses ranging from computer projections to intuition and lost-horse forecasts (see Chapter 8) to assess a country's condition. The dimensions being evaluated include the government attitude toward foreign marketers, the stability and financial policies of the country, and government bureaucracy.

Government Attitude Some countries invite foreign investment through offering investment incentives, helping in site location, and providing other services. Hungary is currently offering a five-year "tax holiday"—a period during which no corporate taxes will be assessed—to encourage foreign firms to develop manufacturing capabilities there. In addition, a country or group of countries can establish equitable standards to enable foreign products to compete fairly in their domestic markets. The European Community has a huge staff in Brussels, Belgium, developing directives to establish such standards for products marketed in the EC after 1992.[21]

Marketing Action Memo

HOMEWORK IN INTERNATIONAL MARKETING: MCDONALD'S SEARCH FOR THE PERFECT—POLISH—FRENCH FRIES

*T*hose french-fried potatoes that we wolf down at our local McDonald's restaurant aren't made from just any potato. McDonald's has spent thousands of dollars finding the *right* potato, slicing it into the *right* thickness, and dipping it in the *right* cooking oil for the *right* length of time.

McDonald's potatoes illustrate the special problems in international marketing. Only one potato meets McDonald's exacting standards: the Russet Burbank that is grown mainly in Idaho. The company uses millions of pounds of french fries in Western European restaurants but they aren't quite up to McDonald's standards because they aren't Russet Burbank, which aren't grown in Europe and are too costly to ship from Idaho.

Enter Poland. The job of growing the right potatoes was entrusted to Mr. Marian Dobrowolski, who was born in Poland but now works in Illinois at McDonald's headquarters and the site of its Hamburger University. Poles produce more than 36 million tons of potatoes annually, but Dobrowolski discovered that these potatoes didn't meet McDonald's taste standards. He asked Polish

farmers to grow the Russet Burbank potatoes he had shipped in from Idaho. The problem: the Polish farmers weren't about to pamper these potatoes to the degree needed, and they didn't grow.

So Dobrowolski asked Polish food scientists at the Guzow Vegetable Experiment Station to grow 15 acres of the needed potatoes. In 1986 a sample of these potatoes was harvested, cut to shape, french fried, and served to Dobrowolski for the critical taste test. Dobrowolski pronounced them "OK" and he and the food scientists toasted each other.

"To the golden orchards," toasted one scientist.

"Arches," said Dobrowolski. And raising his glass, he toasted, "To Poland."

So after six years of work, Polish-grown Russet Burbank potatoes cross international borders to McDonald's Golden Arches restaurants across Western Europe.

Source: Barry Newman, "Its Eye on Fries, Poland Pursues Potato Parity," *The Wall Street Journal* (October 9, 1986), pp. 1, 28. Reprinted by permission of *The Wall Street Journal*, © 1986 Dow Jones & Company, Inc. All rights reserved worldwide.

Stability and Financial Policies   Millions of dollars have been lost in the Middle East as a result of war and changes in governments. Holiday Inn has been badly hurt during the war in Lebanon. Oil drilling firms have lost vast sums throughout the Iran–Iraq and Gulf Wars. Losses like these encourage careful selection of stable countries not likely to be suddenly at war.

When instability is suspected, companies do everything they can to protect themselves against losses. Companies will limit their trade to exporting products into the country, minimizing investments in new plants in the foreign economy. Currency will be converted as soon as possible. Many transnationals are now reluctant to expand operations in Hong Kong, currently a British crown colony, because of uncertainties about what will happen after 1997, when it reverts to China.

Even friendly countries can change their policies toward international marketing. Quotas can be revised or set, currency can be blocked, duties can be imposed, and in extreme cases companies can be expropriated. A **quota** is a legal limit placed on the amount of a product allowed to enter or leave a country. **Blocked currency** means that a government will not allow its currency to be converted into other currencies. A **duty** is a special tax on imports or exports. **Expropriation** is the situation when a foreign company or its assets are taken over by the host country.

Bureaucracy Even though having a law degree isn't essential, it certainly is advantageous when engaging in international trade. Governments can bog down any business transaction with restrictions in a number of forms: tariffs, quotas, boycotts, barriers to entry, and state ownership. These restrictions can apply to an industry, a company, or even a specific product. A **tariff** is an official schedule of the duties imposed by a government on imports or exports. A **boycott** is the refusal by the government of one country to have dealings with another country, often to express disapproval for past actions.

One way to measure a country's attitude toward active encouragement of international trade is to examine the restraints put on it. If tariffs and quotas are plentiful and restrictive, chances are the country is not very receptive to foreign involvement in its economy. But even the United States has its share of quotas and tariffs. For example, the United States sets a quota of 48 million synthetic-fiber sweaters a year to be imported from Taiwan. It puts a 34.2 percent tariff on each sweater imported. Designed to protect U.S. textile firms and jobs, experts estimate that this protectionism adds $20 billion annually to the prices U.S. consumers pay for clothing.[22]

CULTURAL FACTORS

Understanding a foreign nation's society and its culture is of vital importance. The culture of a country will influence what needs consumers have and how they go about satisfying them.

Language An international marketer not only should know the native tongue of a country but also the nuances and idioms of a language. This can spell the difference between success and failure in a marketing program. Not doing so may trigger classic mistakes like these:

- Those who speak Spanish might wonder why Chevrolet sells a car with the name *Nova*—which to them means "It won't go."
- 3M seemed a little silly to the Japanese when it said its Scotch tape "sticks like crazy," which to the Japanese means it sticks foolishly.
- In Taiwan the ad slogan "Come Alive with Pepsi" was translated too literally and read in Chinese "Pepsi brings your ancestors back from the grave."

International marketers should test and retest their communications in a foreign country to verify that they are saying, in fact, what they want to be saying. Often this is very difficult. Mars Candy has successfully introduced its M&M's across Europe. But it had a special problem in France making the name pronounceable because neither the ampersand nor the apostrophe *s* plural exists. The solution: explain to the French that M&M's should be pronounced "aim-ainaimze!"[23]

" THEY'RE MADE IN ITALY. "

Customs   **Customs** are the norms and expectations about the way people do things in a specific country. Clearly customs can vary significantly from country to country. Did you know that mothers in Tanzania don't serve their children eggs? They believe that eggs cause both baldness and impotence. General Mills designed a cake mix especially for preparation in the rice cookers used by Japanese consumers. It failed because of a lack of understanding of Japanese cultural values and customers: Japanese take pride in the purity of their rice, which they thought would be contaminated if the cooker were used to prepare another food. The 3M Company's Scotch-Brite floor-cleaning product got lukewarm sales in the Philippines. When a Filipino employee explained that consumers there often clean floors by pushing coconut shells around with their feet, 3M changed the shape of the pad to a foot and sales soared.[24] Some other customs unusual to Americans include:

- In France, men wear more than twice the number of cosmetics that women do.
- Unlike American managers who tend to jump in and express opinions early in a meeting, Japanese managers prefer to wait and listen—and the higher their position, the more they listen.[25]
- Businesspeople in South America prefer to negotiate within inches of their colleagues; Americans who find this difficult can offend their potential associates and ruin a possible agreement.

New firms are springing up to counsel expatriates-to-be on the business practices, social customs, and lifestyles they will encounter in their new country of residence.

Values A nation's values reflect the religious or moral beliefs of its people. Understanding and working with these aspects of a society are also factors in successful international marketing. For example:

- A door-to-door salesman would find selling in Italy impossible, because it is improper for a man to call on a woman if she is home alone.
- McDonald's and other hamburger restaurants would not have a chance in India, where the cow is considered sacred.
- The British don't believe marketing is quite respectable, a factor contributing to their loss of markets in which they had the technological lead.

German exporters such as BMW (cars) and Stihl (chain saws) probably are the most sophisticated in understanding the values of the customers of the nation's to which they sell products. In 1986 Germany (*not* Japan) passed the United States as the world's largest exporter through a strategy that stresses high-quality products sold to specific market segments by a strong network of dealers.[26]

CONCEPT CHECK

1 Why is analysis of the international marketing environment so important?

2 When a firm is considering another country as a potential market, why is that country's per capita income important?

3 How might the religious beliefs of a nation affect international marketing to that country?

EVALUATING ALTERNATIVES FOR INTERNATIONAL OPERATIONS

Once a company has decided to enter the international marketplace, it must select a means of entry. The option chosen depends on its willingness and ability to commit financial, physical, and managerial resources. As Figure 22–7 demonstrates, the amount of financial commitment, risk, and profit potential increases as the firm moves from exporting to direct ownership. Host countries not only seek the benefits of additional products available for sale but are often even more interested in the number of good jobs available for local workers. Figure 22–7 shows that local employment increases significantly as a firm's financial commitment increases.

EXPORTING

Exporting is producing goods in one country and selling them in another country. This entry option allows a company to make the least number of changes in terms of its product, its organization, and even its corporate goals. Host countries usually do not like this practice, because it provides less local employment than under alternative means of entry.

FIGURE 22–7
Alternative methods for entering international markets

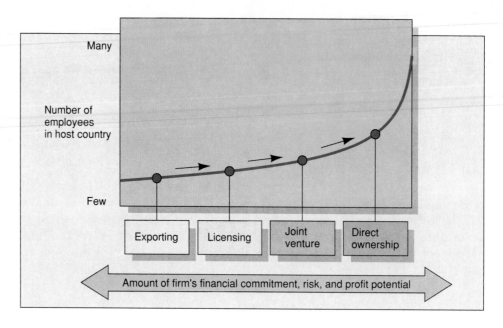

Indirect exporting** is when a firm sells its domestically produced goods in a foreign country through an intermediary. It involves the least amount of commitment and risk, but will probably return the least profit. This kind of exporting is ideal for the company that has no overseas contacts but wants to market abroad. The intermediary is often a broker or agent that has the international marketing know-how and the resources necessary for the effort to succeed.

Direct exporting is when a firm sells its domestically produced goods in a foreign country without intermediaries. Most companies become involved in direct exporting when they believe their volume of sales will be sufficiently large and easy to obtain that they do not require intermediaries. For example, the exporter may be approached by foreign buyers that are willing to contract for a large volume of purchases. Direct exporting involves more risk than indirect exporting for the company, but also opens the door to increased profits.

LICENSING

Under licensing a company offers the right to a trademark, patent, trade secret, or other similarly valued items of intellectual property, in return for a royalty or a fee. In international marketing the advantages to the company granting the license are low risk and a capital-free entry into a foreign country. The licensee gains information that allows it to start with a competitive advantage, and the foreign country gains employment by having the product manufactured locally. Yoplait yogurt is licensed from Sodima, a French cooperative, by General Mills for sales in the United States.

There are some serious drawbacks to this mode of entry, however. The licensor foregoes control of its product and reduces the potential profits gained from it. In addition, while the relationship lasts, the licensor may be creating its own competition. Some licensees are able to modify the product somehow and enter the market with product and marketing knowledge gained at the expense of the company that got them started. To offset this disadvantage, many companies strive to stay innovative so that the licensee remains dependent on them for improvements and successful operation. Finally, should the licensee prove to be a poor choice, the name or reputation of the company may be harmed.

Two variations of licensing, local manufacturing and local assembly, represent alternative ways to produce a product within the foreign country. With local manufacturing, a U.S. company may contract with a foreign firm to manufacture products according to stated specifications. The product is then sold in the foreign country or exported back to the United States. With local assembly, the U.S. company may contract with a foreign firm to assemble (not manufacture) parts and components that have been shipped to that country. In both cases, advantage to the foreign country is the employment of its people and the U.S. firm benefits from the lower wage rates in the foreign country.

JOINT VENTURE

When a foreign company and a local firm invest together to create a local business, it is called a **joint venture.** These two companies share ownership, control, and profits of the new company. Investment may be made by having either of the companies buy shares in the other or by creating a third and separate entity.

The advantages of this option are twofold. First, one company may not have the necessary financial, physical, or managerial resources to enter a foreign market alone. The joint venture between Ericsson, a Swedish telecommunications firm, and CGCT, an ailing French switch maker, enabled them together to beat out AT&T for a $100 million French contract. Ericsson's money and technology combined with CGCT's knowledge of the French market helped them to win the contract that neither of them could have won alone. Second, a government may require or strongly encourage a joint venture before it allows a foreign company to enter its market. This was exactly the condition set down by the French government in the award of its large contract to Ericsson.[27]

The disadvantages arise when the two companies disagree about policies or courses of action for their joint venture. For example, U.S. firms often prefer to reinvest earnings gained, whereas some foreign companies may want to spend those earnings. Or a U.S. firm may want to return profits earned to the United States, while the local firm or its government may oppose this—the problem now faced by many potential joint ventures in Russia and Eastern Europe.

DIRECT OWNERSHIP

The biggest commitment a company can make when entering the international market is **direct ownership,** which entails a domestic firm actually investing in and owning a foreign subsidiary or division. Examples of direct ownership are Honda's Marysville, Ohio, plant that produces Civics and Accords, and Nissan's Smyrna, Tennessee, plant that produces pickup trucks. Many U.S. transnational corporations are also switching to this mode of entry. McDonald's chose this alternative in Great Britain and built a plant to produce 2 million buns a week when no local bakers would make them to McDonald's specifications.[28]

To understand how Ericsson used a joint venture to beat AT&T and win a large French contract, see the text.

The advantages to direct ownership include cost savings, better understanding of local market conditions, and fewer local restrictions. Firms entering foreign markets using direct ownership believe that these advantages outweigh the financial commitments and risks involved.

CONCEPT CHECK

1 What mode of entry could a company follow if it has no previous experience in international marketing?

2 How does licensing differ from joint venture?

TAILORING MARKETING PROGRAMS TO THE COUNTRY

Marketing programs must be adapted to the international scene, not simply be duplicates of those at home. Three basic steps in adapting a marketing program for foreign marketing are (1) selecting a country for entry, (2) establishing the most effective organization for marketing on an international level, and (3) designing the marketing program to fit the market's needs.

SELECTING A COUNTRY FOR ENTRY

In choosing a country for its international marketing efforts, a company must evaluate many factors, following these steps.

Specify the marketing objectives. These objectives should be achievable yet challenging. Profit levels, return on investment (ROI), sales, and competitive positions are all areas for which objectives are delineated.

Choose a single- or multiple-country strategy. Choosing to enter a single country or several countries in a region is based on the product or products being sold and the sales potential. If several adjacent countries all want the same size or style of product, the marketing and production economies of scale may suggest a multiple-country strategy. The accompanying Marketing Action Memo gives some key guidelines for U.S. firms using a multiple-country strategy to enter the European Community market.

Specify the candidate countries or regions to consider. Alternative countries or regions that meet both the stated objectives for international marketing and the economic profile needed for success should be listed as potential candidates.

Estimate the ROI for each of the candidates. To estimate the ROI, a company must project the size of the market, the expected revenues, the expenses, and the profits for each candidate country or region.

Select the one or more countries or regions to enter. The preceding analysis screens the candidates to provide a list of the one or more countries or regions that appear most likely to achieve the firm's objectives for its international marketing program.

Granted, these are all estimates and include some room for error. However, they will provide the necessary framework to enable the firm to make a knowledgeable choice between countries and regions.

Avon targets Latin American markets.

Marketing Action Memo

RULES U.S. FIRMS NEED FOR THE "EC 1992 GAME"

*H*ere are some rules that are emerging for U.S. firms that want access to European Community (EC) markets after 1992:

1 Get behind the EC wall now. Exporting products to the EC after 1992 will be difficult, so U.S. companies should have their own production plants—often through joint ventures or strategic alliances with European firms.
2 Reduce overcapacity, centralize production, and standardize products where possible. 3M's plant in Wales now makes videotapes and videocassettes for all of Europe, with only the language on the package being different.
3 Read the fine print about the products your firm plans to sell. EC's 10,000-person office in Brussels is writing 408 directives that set standards on products, ranging from forklift trucks to beef, that will be sold in the EC. For some products these sales rules are incredibly complex.
4 Open top jobs to foreign employees. When General Electric acquired a French medical electronics business, it merged it with its own U.S. operations and named a French executive to run the whole business—in its Wisconsin plant.

Finally, stay alert to the constant changes that will be coming in global markets.

Sources: Eric G. Friberg, "1992: Moves Europeans Are Making," *Harvard Business Review* (May–June 1989), pp. 85–89; Walter S. Mossberg, "As EC Markets Unite, U.S. Exporters Face New Trade Barriers," *The Wall Street Journal* (January 19, 1989), pp. A1, A4; and Jeremy Main, "How to Go Global—and Why," *Fortune* (August 28, 1989), pp. 70–76.

ESTABLISHING A MARKETING ORGANIZATION

After selecting a country for entry, an appropriate marketing organization must be established. Its goal is to respond to the different needs of international marketing, yet take advantage of the experience and knowledge of domestic marketers. Some alternative marketing organizations are discussed below.

Export Department   When a company is simply exporting its goods, this is typically done through an export department. Made up of a manager and perhaps several assistants, this group handles the necessary paperwork.

Foreign Subsidiary   A wholly owned foreign subsidiary commonly has its own head of operations, who reports directly to the company president. Sales of Apple's Macintosh computer in Japan were slow until it established a subsidiary there. Sales started rising when the subsidiary developed a Japanese-language operating system for the Macintosh and announced that much of its software would use the new system.[29]

International Division   When international sales become substantial or when modes of entry other than simple exporting are added, a company usually expands to include an international division. This division can be either geographically based or product based. All international marketing—the movement of products and also their marketing—is then handled by this group.

Worldwide Products Division   A worldwide products division is used when a company decides that it is no longer a company conducting international marketing, but a transnational firm marketing throughout the world. Like an international division, this structure can be divided by regions, with each division responsible for all products within a region, or it can be divided by products, with each division responsible for all markets where its product is sold. Most likely this structure is accompanied by a management base recruited from around the world.

DESIGNING A MARKETING PROGRAM

An international marketer goes through the same steps in designing a marketing program as a domestic marketer. However, the international marketer must decide whether to use a global or customized approach. Gillette is seeking ways to develop some global brands in its marketing strategy that includes 800 products. To do this the firm moved to a global advertising strategy, to reach consumers in all Western European countries with exactly the same video part of its TV ads. Its razor became simply "Blue II" across Europe. Dubbed in 10 languages, the audio part of the TV ads invited consumers to "step into the blue" and buy Blue II.

    As mentioned earlier, careful marketing research must be done to help the international marketer decide whether to modify or maintain domestic product, price, place, and promotion strategies.

Product   The product may be sold internationally in one of three ways: (1) in the same form as in the domestic market, (2) with some adaptations, or (3) as a totally new product.

- *Extension:* Selling the same product in other countries is an extension strategy. It works well for products like Coca-Cola, Wrigley's gum, General Motors cars, and Levi's jeans. However, it didn't work for Jell-O (a more solid gelatin was preferred to the powder in England) or for Duncan Hines (which was seen as too moist and crumbly to eat with tea in England).
- *Adaptation:* Changing a product in some way to make it more appropriate for a country's climate or preferences is an adaptation strategy. Heinz baby food offers strained lamb brains for Australians and strained brown beans in the Netherlands. Exxon sells different gasoline blends based on each country's climate.
- *Invention:* Designing a product to serve the unmet needs of a foreign nation is an invention strategy. This is probably the strategy with the most potential, since there are so many unmet needs, yet it is actually the least used. National Cash Register has followed a reverse invention strategy by introducing crank-operated cash registers in some developing nations that have unreliable or inaccessible electric power.

In international markets—as in domestic ones—nothing succeeds like quality products that satisfy consumer needs and wants at reasonable prices. Honda motorcycles, Caterpillar construction equipment, Canon cameras, and Black & Decker power tools are examples.

Price   Most foreign countries use a cost-plus pricing strategy. For international firms this can mean their products are priced higher than the local goods. Why? International products must include not only the cost of production and selling, but also tariffs, transportation and storage costs, and higher payments to intermediaries.

Quality products: essential for entering foreign markets.

Dumping is when a firm sells a product in a foreign country below its domestic price. This is most often done to build a share of the market by pricing at a competitive level. Another reason is that the products being sold may be surplus or cannot be sold domestically, and are therefore already a burden to the company. The firm may be glad to sell them at almost any price.

Some U.S. pharmaceutical firms have sold penicillin, for example, at a lower price in foreign countries than at home. They justify this by saying that R&D costs are not included in foreign prices. Japan has been accused of following a dumping strategy for some of its products in the United States. Its response is that the volume sold here allows economies of scale, the savings of which are passed on to U.S. consumers.

An unusual pricing dimension of international marketing is **countertrade,** using barter rather than money in making international sales. Although countertrade accounts for only about 10 percent of the world trade, it is growing in importance. An example is when Boeing sold 10 747 jet aircraft to Saudi Arabia in return for crude oil valued at 10 percent below posted world prices.[30]

An unpleasant aspect of pricing is **bribery,** the practice of giving or promising something of value in return for a corrupt act. This is a common practice in many countries to reduce red tape and make sales. Although in many countries bribery is an accepted business practice in some international sales, it is officially illegal in all countries. Under the Foreign Corrupt Practices Act of 1977 such a practice is illegal for U.S. companies. Even if a U.S. firm labels the bribe a sales commission and includes it on its books, in the United States this is now a federal offense punishable by fines for the company and prison terms for the individuals responsible.

Place   An international marketer must establish a channel of distribution to meet the goals it has set. Figure 22–8 outlines the channel through which a product manufactured in one country must travel to reach its destination in a foreign country. The first step involves the seller; its headquarters is the starting point and is responsible for the successful distribution to the ultimate consumer.

The next step is the channel between the two nations, moving the product from the domestic market to the foreign market. Intermediaries that can handle this responsibility include resident buyers in the foreign country, independent merchant wholesalers who buy and sell the product or agents who bring buyers and sellers together.

Once the product is in the foreign nation, that country's distribution channels take over. Foreign channels can be very long or surprisingly short, depending on the product line. In Japan fresh fish go through three intermediaries before getting to a retail outlet. Conversely, shoes only go through one intermediary. In other cases the channel does not even involve the host country. P&G

FIGURE 22–8
International marketing channel of distribution

After the tourists leave, New Zealand is a sight!

Imagine a fresh green gem of a world tucked into a crystal blue corner of the South Pacific.

With warm, wide beaches nestled at the foot of soaring snowy peaks. Primeval fern forests, alpine flower meadows, Polynesian canoe races, the Old West revisited, Olde England revered, and rolling green hills dotted with fluffy white lambs everywhere.

New Zealand, the one and only original!

It's not just a trip to a special place in the South Pacific, it's like a trip to a special place in time. A time when people still held to certain values.

A world much like the world we thought we'd lost. When people remembered to say "please" and "thank you," and held doors. When

tips were unexpected, triple locks unneeded, smog alerts unheard of, and the land un-littered. A world where you felt cared-about, listened-to, a bit more yourself.

Find that world again. In New Zealand.

It's not just what's missing in your vacation. It may just be what's missing in your life.

For your free brochure, clip and send to: New Zealand Tourism Office, 501 Santa Monica Blvd., Suite 500, Santa Monica, CA 90401. Or ring us up at: 1-800-456-3170

Name:
Address:
City/State/Zip:

New Zealand
The things that shouldn't change...haven't.

A common language helps New Zealand market itself to U.S. tourists.

sells its soap door to door in the Philippines because there are no other alternatives in many parts of that country. The sophistication of the distribution channel increases with the economic development of the country. Supermarkets facilitate selling products in many nations, but they are not popular or available in many others where low incomes, culture, and lack of refrigeration dictates shopping on a daily rather than weekly basis.

A joint venture can simplify distribution problems. For example, General Mills recently formed a joint venture with Switzerland's Nestlé to manufacture and distribute its breakfast cereals in Europe. Called "Cereal Partners Worldwide," the joint venture provides access to the European market for General Mills—where it has almost no sales—through Nestlé's strong distribution system.[31]

Promotion   Various aspects of promotion may have to be changed to reflect the differences in foreign markets. Advertising programs provide examples. Because values differ substantially from country to country, a product that is a luxury in one country may be a necessity in another. Creative messages in advertisements must then be designed to directly address the peculiarities within each market.

Western Europeans, however, are becoming more like Americans in the TV programs they watch and the products they can buy. In 1987, massive changes in TV came to Western Europe, significantly affecting the TV programs these millions of consumers watch and the TV ads they see. For example,

Spanish and Italian consumers can now see private and cable TV rather than only state-run TV. The effect has been a tremendous increase in advertising, now making possible global brands that can be advertised across Europe.

Where there is a common language, many TV and print ads can be used both domestically and in a common-language country. For example, New Zealand markets vacations to the United States while America markets winter trips to New Zealanders—both often using domestic ad campaigns in the other country as well.

CONCEPT CHECK

1 **What steps should a company follow to select appropriate international markets to enter?**

2 **What are the three international marketing product strategies, and when might each be used?**

3 **What is countertrade?**

ETHICS AND SOCIAL RESPONSIBILITY IN THE 1990s

WHAT SHOULD THE U.S. GOVERNMENT DO?

Business Week magazine says that some foreign-owned transnationals avoid $13 billion to $30 billion of U.S. taxes annually by a clever use of transfer pricing. It works like this:

1 A foreign manufacturer builds a VCR in a factory in its country for $50.
2 It sells the VCR to a captive U.S. distributor that it owns for a price of $150, making $100 in home-country profit on the sale.
3 The U.S. distributor spends $50 per unit on advertising and sells the product to U.S. consumers at a price of $200. Since it paid $150 for the VCR and had proportional costs of $50 for it, the distributor makes $0 of profit and pays no U.S. taxes.[32]

What should the U.S. government policy be on this situation?

SUMMARY

1 International marketing, or trade between nations, is filled with risks and problems but promises profits to those who undertake it. The size of international marketing is large and growing—over 12 percent of the U.S. GNP.

2 Although international and domestic marketing are based on the same marketing principles, many underlying assumptions must be reevaluated when a firm moves into international operations. Environmental variables

such as economic conditions, political and legal conditions, and cultural factors must be carefully assessed to achieve successful operations.

3 International markets should be selected on the basis of their size, consumer income, potential market growth, cost of doing business in that country, competitive advantage that would be realized, and risk involved in entering them.

4 Four basic modes of entry into international marketing are exporting, licensing, joint ventures, and direct ownership. The relative difficulty of international marketing, as well as the amount of commitment, risk, and profit potential increase in moving from exporting to direct ownership.

5 An organizational structure for international marketing should respond to the unique needs of international marketing, while still taking advantage of the experience and know-how of the domestic marketers.

6 Because foreign countries have different languages, customs, values, purchasing power, needs, and levels of economic development, a firm must take great care in deciding whether to use a global or customized strategy.

7 Product, price, promotion, and place strategies can all be modified or adapted to reflect these differences and improve the chances of success in international markets.

 ## KEY TERMS AND CONCEPTS

international marketing p. 604	**tariff** p. 617
balance of trade p. 606	**boycott** p. 617
transnational corporation p. 607	**customs** p. 618
global approach p. 609	**exporting** p. 619
customized approach p. 609	**indirect exporting** p. 620
glocalization p. 610	**direct exporting** p. 620
economic infrastructure p. 614	**joint venture** p. 621
quota p. 616	**direct ownership** p. 621
blocked currency p. 616	**dumping** p. 627
duty p. 617	**countertrade** p. 627
expropriation p. 617	**bribery** p. 627

 ## CHAPTER PROBLEMS AND APPLICATIONS

1 Campbell Soup Company introduced its products in England to considerably less than rave reviews because it used a global approach in their introduction. What are the advantages and disadvantages of the global approach? If Campbell had pursued a customized approach, what dimensions, in addition to the size of the can, might it have explored?

2 In 1991 the British pound was worth $1.78 in exchange for American dollars; in 1985 it was worth about $1.05. In which year would you choose to travel to Great Britain? In which year should a U.S. firm market internationally? Why?

3 A manufacturer of shoes has decided to enter the international market. As a point of entry, she has selected India. Her assumption is that with such a large population, a lot of shoes can be sold. Why might India be a good or bad market opportunity? What steps should the manufacturer follow to select the appropriate market?

4 What steps do some countries take to discourage trade? Why might they do this?

5 As a novice in international marketing, which type of operations would you select to get you feet wet? Why? What other alternatives do you have for market entry?

6 What are the three product strategies a marketer can use in foreign market introductions? Which strategy has the most potential? Why? Can you think of any reverse inventions that might be successful?

7 Knowing that owning Western goods is a status symbol in the Soviet Union, what goods might you want to sell to that market? How would the current economic system in the U.S.S.R. affect your decision to enter this market?

8 Develop a SWOT analysis (see Chapter 2) for a U.S. company considering building a plant to produce consumer products in Eastern Europe to reach consumers living there.

9 Because English is the official language in Australia, many U.S. companies might select this market as an easy one to expand to internationally. Others, however, believe that this similarity in language could make it even harder to successfully engage in foreign trade. Who's right? Why?

10 Coca-Cola is sold worldwide. In some countries Coca-Cola owns the manufacturing facilities: in others it has signed contracts with licensees. When selecting a licensee in each country, what factors should Coca-Cola consider?

CHAPTER 23

Marketing of Services

- Describe four unique elements of services.
- Recognize how various services differ and how they can be classified.
- Understand the way in which consumers view and judge services.
- Develop a customer contact audit to identify service advantages.
- Understand the important role of internal marketing in service organizations.
- Explain the role of the four Ps in the services marketing mix.

How Do You Make a Service Company Successful? Be an Imagineer!

Walt Disney often encouraged his employees to be creative thinkers and cheerleaders for new ideas—what he called "Imagineers." The approach led to many childhood favorites such as Mickey Mouse, Thumper, Pinocchio, Dumbo, Bambi, and Snow White, and two theme parks in California and Florida. Now, 25 years after Walt Disney's death, the company he founded is still producing new entertainment ideas for children and adults.

For example, company CEO Michael Eisner—shown in the accompanying photo with a Disney friend—hatched the idea of making a movie about a Beverly Hills policeman. *Beverly Hills Cop* eventually became one of the most successful comedies ever produced. Another recent success is the 135-acre Disney–MGM Studios Theme Park at Walt

Disney World. At the park, visitors discover the craft of moviemaking by being a guest star on the *Ed Sullivan Show,* providing sound effects in the *Monster Sound Show,* or visiting a scene from *Casablanca* or *Aliens*. On television, Eisner has become one of the most easily recognized CEOs in America as the host of *The Magical World of Disney*.

In the future Disney hopes to follow its successful movies *Dick Tracy, Dead Poets Society,* and *Who Framed Roger Rabbit?* with sequels to films like *Good Morning Vietnam*. Euro Disneyland—a $2.6 billion theme park under construction near Paris—will also debut in the near future.

How does Disney ensure the success of its ideas? It employs several general principles:

- *Stay ahead technologically:* New technologies such as lasers, fiber optics, and robotics are continually used in Disney productions.
- *Control costs:* Disney's average cost of producing a film is about $14.5 million, versus the $18 million industry average.
- *Stretch the marketing budget:* The costs of exhibits or attractions are often shared with corporations through "participant campaigns." Delta Airlines, for example, paid $40 million to be the official airline of Disney World.

These principles and imagineering have even led Eisner and the Walt Disney Company to success in China, where the most popular children's TV program (seen by almost 200 million viewers each Sunday night) is the *Mickey and Donald Show*.[1]

As the Walt Disney Company illustrates, the marketing of services offers great challenges. In this chapter we discuss how services differ from traditional physical products (goods), how consumers make service purchase decisions, and the ways in which the marketing mix is used.

THE UNIQUENESS OF SERVICES

As noted in Chapter 1, **services** are intangible items such as airline trips, financial advice, or telephone calls that an organization provides to consumers. To obtain these services, consumers exchange money or something else of value, such as their own time.

Services are quickly becoming one of the most important components of the U.S. economy. About 90 percent of 36 million new jobs created in the past two decades were in the services sector. In addition, over half of the gross national product now comes from services. As shown in Figure 23–1, services accounted for an estimated $2.845 trillion in 1990, which was an increase of 125 percent since 1980. Services also represent a large export business—the $131 billion of services exports in 1990 is expected to grow 5 percent per year (after inflation) throughout the 1990s.[2]

The growth in this sector is the result of increased demand for services that have been available in the past, and the increasing interest in new services. Personalized Services in Chicago, for example, will do just about anything that is legal, including walking the dog, picking up the kids, or waiting in line for tickets. Founder Lois Barnet says, "We'll find it, we'll do it, we'll wait for it."[3]

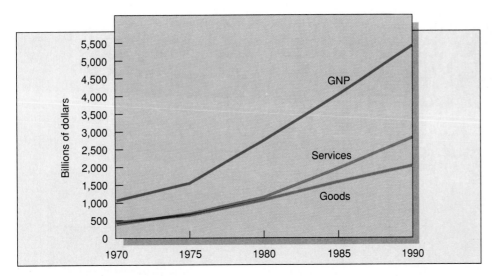

FIGURE 23–1
Importance of services in the U.S. Gross National Product (GNP)

Other new service firms include Prodigy, an electronic catalog shopping service; Molly Maid, Inc., a home-cleaning service with franchises in 25 states; and Jiffy Lube, the franchiser of fast oil-change and lube shops. In California, Oasis Laundries, Inc., offers laundromats with big screen TVs, video games, snack bars, and attendants.[4] These firms and many others like them are examples of the groundbreaking and imaginative services that will play a role in our economy in the future.

THE FOUR I'S OF SERVICES

There are four unique elements to services: intangibility, inconsistency, inseparability, and inventory. These four elements are referred to as the **four I's of services**.

Intangibility   Services are intangible; that is, they can't be held, touched, or seen before the purchase decision. In contrast, before purchasing a traditional product, a consumer can touch a box of laundry detergent, kick the tire of an automobile, or sample a new breakfast cereal. A major marketing need for services is to make them tangible or show the benefits of using the service.[5] A Norwegian Cruise Line advertisement shows happy vacationers enjoying themselves on an island beach, American Express emphasizes the year-end summary of charges they send you, and a leading insurance company says, "You're in Good Hands with Allstate."

Inconsistency   Marketing services is challenging because the quality of a service is often inconsistent. Since services depend on the people who provide them, their quality varies with each person's capabilities and day-to-day job performance. Inconsistency is much more of a problem in services than it is with tangible goods. Tangible products can be good or bad in terms of quality, but with modern production lines the quality will at least be consistent. On the

Services must emphasize their benefits.

other hand, one day the Philadelphia Phillies baseball team may have great hitting and pitching and look like a pennant winner, and the next day lose by 10 runs. Or a soprano at New York's Metropolitan Opera may have a bad cold and give a less-than-perfect performance. Whether the service involves tax assistance at Arthur Andersen or guest relations at the Hyatt Regency, organizations attempt to reduce inconsistency through standardization and training.[6]

Inseparability A third difference between services and goods, related to problems of consistency, is inseparability. In most cases the consumer cannot (and does not) separate the service from the deliverer of the service or the setting in which the service occurs. For example, to receive an education, a person may attend a university. The quality of the education may be high, but if the student has difficulty parking, finds counseling services poor, or sees little opportunity for extracurricular activity, he or she may not be satisfied with the educational experience.

Inventory Inventory of services is different from that of goods. Inventory problems exist with goods because many items are perishable and, as noted in Chapter 15, there are costs associated with handling inventory. With services, inventory carrying costs are more subjective and are related to **idle production capacity**, which is when the service provider is available but there is no demand. The inventory cost of a service is the cost of reimbursing the person used

Services are people.

to provide the service along with any needed equipment. If a physician is paid to see patients but no one schedules an appointment, the fixed cost of the idle physician's salary is a high inventory carrying cost. In some service businesses, however, the provider of the service is on commission (the Merrill Lynch stockbroker) or is a part-time employee (a counterperson at McDonald's). Inventory carrying costs can be significantly lower or nonexistent because the idle production capacity can be cut back by reducing hours or having no salary to pay because of the commission compensation system. Figure 23–2 shows a sliding scale of inventory carrying costs represented on the high side by airlines and hospitals and on the low end by real estate agents and hair stylists. The inventory carrying costs of airlines is high because of high-salaried pilots and very expensive equipment. In contrast, real estate agents and hair stylists work on commission and need little expensive equipment to conduct business.

FIGURE 23–2
Inventory carrying costs in services

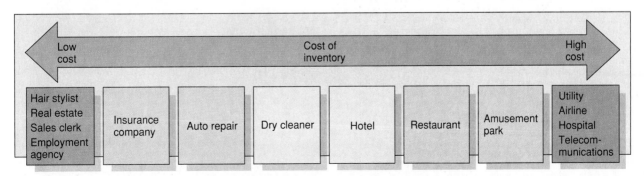

THE SERVICE CONTINUUM

The four I's differentiate services from goods in most cases, but many companies are not clearly service-based or good-based organizations. Is Wang a computer company or service business? Does Dow Jones provide only goods in the sense of publishing *The Wall Street Journal,* or does it consider itself a service in terms of up-to-date business information? As companies look at what they bring to the market, there is a range from the tangible to the intangible or good-dominant to service-dominant offerings referred to as the **service continuum** (Figure 23–3).

Teaching, nursing, and the theater are intangible, service-dominant activities, and intangibility, inconsistency, inseparability, and inventory are major concerns in their marketing. Salt, neckties, and dog food are tangible goods, and the problems represented by the four I's are not relevant in their marketing. However, some businesses are a mix of intangible service and tangible good factors. A clothing tailor provides a service but also a good, the finished suit. How pleasant, courteous, and attentive the tailor is to the customer is an important component of the service, and how well the clothes fit is an important part of the product. As shown in Figure 23–3, a fast-food restaurant is about half tangible goods (the food) and half intangible services (courtesy, cleanliness, speed, convenience).

CLASSIFYING SERVICES

Throughout this book, marketing organizations, techniques, and concepts have been classified to show the differences and similarities in an organized framework. Services can also be classified in several ways, according to (1) whether

FIGURE 23–3
Service continuum

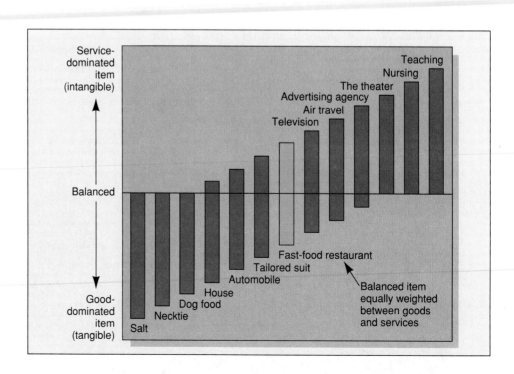

they are delivered by people or equipment, (2) whether they are profit or non-profit, or (3) whether or not they are government sponsored.

Delivery by People or Equipment   As seen in Figure 23–4, companies offering services provided by people include management consulting firms such as Booz, Allen & Hamilton, and executive recruitment companies such as the Physicians Executive Management Center in Tampa. Unskilled labor such as that used by Brinks store-security forces is also a service provided by people.

Equipment-based services do not have the marketing concerns of inconsistency because people are removed from provision of the service. Electric utilities, for example, can provide service without frequent personal contact with customers. To keep in touch with their customers, many utilities such as the Public Service Company of New Mexico now conduct frequent marketing research efforts.[7]

Profit or Nonprofit Organizations   Many organizations involved in services also distinguish themselves by their tax status as profit or nonprofit organizations. In contrast to *profit organizations, nonprofit organizations'* excesses in revenue over expenses are not taxed or distributed to shareholders. When excess revenue exists, the money goes back into the organization's treasury to allow continuation of the service. Based on the corporate structure of the nonprofit organization, it may pay tax on revenue-generating holdings not directly related to its core mission.

The American Red Cross, United Way, Greenpeace, St. Mary's Health Center in St. Louis, and the University of Florida are nonprofit organizations. Such organizations historically have not used marketing tactics in the belief that they were inappropriate. In recent years, however, competitive pressures have

FIGURE 23–4
Service classifications

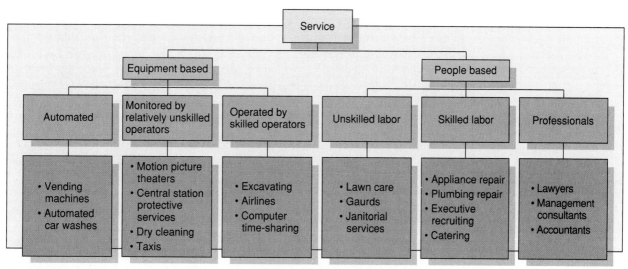

Source: Reprinted by permission of the *Harvard Business Review*. An exhibit from "Strategy Is Different in Service Businesses" by Dan R. E. Thomas (July/August 1978). Copyright © 1978 by the President and Fellows of Harvard College; all rights reserved.

Nonprofit and
government services
often advertise.

forced these organizations to reevaluate their strategies. The accompanying
Marketing Action Memo describes some of the changes nonprofit organizations
have undertaken. Some nonprofit agencies have formed useful alliances with
business firms. In the spring of 1991, Midway airlines distributed 2,000 boxes of
Girl Scout cookies on over 100 flights, generating favorable publicity for both
organizations.

Government Sponsored or Not   A third way to classify services is based on
whether they are government sponsored. Although there is no direct ownership and they are nonprofit organizations, governments at the federal, state,
and local levels provide a broad range of services. The U.S. Army, for
example, has adopted many marketing activities. Their "Be All You Can Be"
campaign has succeeded at emphasizing adventure and opportunity. In addition, education benefits provide up to $27,000 for college as an incentive for
Army enlistment.

CONCEPT CHECK

1 What are the four I's of services?

2 Would inventory carrying costs for an accounting firm with certified public
   accountants be (*a*) high, (*b*) low, or (*c*) nonexistent?

3 To eliminate service inconsistencies, companies rely on _____
   and _____ .

Marketing Action Memo

THE GIRL SCOUTS TAKE A MARKETING COURSE

*F*or many years, nonprofit agencies avoided the word *marketing*. They were concerned that marketing activities were inappropriate for organizations not motivated by profit. Today, that attitude is changing. As John Garrison, president of the National Easter Seal Society, explains, "Almost everyone now realizes that commitment isn't enough anymore. You also have to have professionalism or you're going to go out of business."

The Girl Scouts of the U.S.A. is a good example. Faced with eight straight years of falling membership, the organization began asking questions such as "What is our business?" "Who is the customer?" and "What does the customer value?" Market studies showed that girls had changed— they were now more interested in areas such as science, the environment, and business—but the Girl Scouts had not. By focusing on contemporary issues, encouraging equal access to all types of girls, and becoming customer-oriented, the Girl Scouts reversed its membership trend and served over 2 million young girls in 1990.

Other nonprofit organizations are also utilizing marketing techniques:

- The United Way used focus groups to discover that people didn't know how United Way worked. In response, United Way launched a national TV ad campaign describing how individuals received assistance.

- The American Red Cross raised $300,000 using cause-related marketing techniques in conjunction with MasterCard International.

- The YMCA reorganized to include three divisions: corporate communications, public relations, and marketing.

As the number of nonprofit organizations with interest in marketing grows, so does the need for marketing education. Planned Parenthood's headquarters has developed a marketing training program available to members of the 178 affiliate chapters. J. Carter Brown, director of the National Gallery of Art, got an MBA degree. Many other organizations send their managers to marketing seminars and executive training programs. Because so many nonprofit organizations rely on volunteers, management expert Peter Drucker has observed that the training of volunteers to create unpaid professionals "may be the most important development in American society today."

Sources: John A. Byrne, "Profiting from the Nonprofits," *Business Week* (March 26, 1990), pp. 66–74; Kathleen Vyn, "Nonprofits Learn How-to's of Marketing," *Marketing News* (August 14, 1989), pp. 1, 2; and Peter Drucker, "What Businesses Can Learn from Nonprofits," *Harvard Business Review* (July–August 1989), pp. 88–93.

HOW CONSUMERS PURCHASE SERVICES

Colleges, hospitals, hotels, and even charities are facing an increasingly competitive environment. Successful service organizations, like successful product-oriented firms, must understand how the consumer views a service and in what ways a company can present a differential advantage relative to competing offerings.

THE PURCHASE PROCESS

The intangible and inseparable aspects of services affect the consumer's evaluation of the purchase. Because services cannot be displayed, demonstrated, or illustrated, consumers cannot make a prepurchase evaluation of all the charac-

FIGURE 23–5
How consumers evaluate goods and services

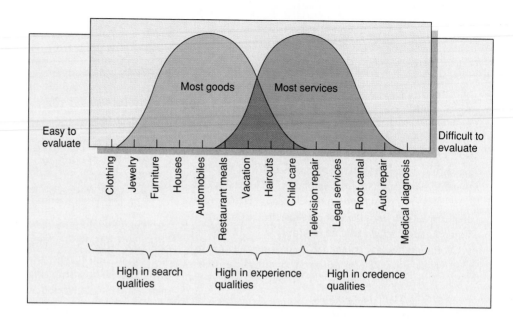

teristics of services.[8] Similarly, because services are produced and consumed simultaneously, the buyer must participate in producing the service and that participation can affect the evaluation of the service. Figure 23–5 portrays how different types of goods and services are evaluated by consumers. Tangible goods such as clothing, jewelry, and furniture have *search* qualities, such as color, size, and style, which can be determined before purchase. Services such as restaurants and child care have *experience* qualities, which can only be discerned after purchase or during consumption. Finally, services provided by specialized professionals such as medical diagnoses and legal services have *credence* qualities, or characteristics that the consumer may find impossible to evaluate even after purchase and consumption.[9] Some services, such as those of the banks described in the accompanying Marketing Research Report, may have all three qualities!

PURCHASE EVALUATION

Once a consumer tries a service, how is it evaluated? Primarily by comparing expectations about a particular service to the actual experience a consumer has with the service. Differences between the consumer's expectations and experience are identified through **gap analysis**. This type of analysis asks consumers to assess their expectations and experiences on dimensions of service quality such as those described in Figure 23–6 on page 644. Expectations are influenced by word-of-mouth communications, personal needs, past experiences, and promotional activities, while actual experiences are determined by the way an organization delivers its service.[10] In the fast-food industry, Burger King is an example of a firm trying to implement gap analysis. According to Barry Gibbons, Burger King's CEO, the company is "measuring our performance against their [customer's] expectations" by using a 24-hour hot line to receive 4,000 customer calls per day.[11]

Marketing Research Report

HOW DO YOU SELECT A BANK?

Selecting a bank requires potential customers to evaluate many aspects of the service. Bank managers, faced with the issue of attracting and retaining customers, have attempted to understand how people make the decision to use one bank instead of another.

A study of consumer bank selection was designed to help understand this decision. In the first phase, focus groups discussed the attributes they evaluated when selecting a bank. In the second phase, 1,300 questionnaires were mailed from three types of banks (city, college, and rural) to persons who had opened a new account during the past six months. Respondents (307) rated the importance of 12 characteristics of financial institutions. The results are shown at right.

There are significant differences in the characteristics used to select a bank that depend on the type of community in which it is located. City people ranked pricing, reputation, and location convenience highest. The customers of the college community bank ranked time convenience, ownership, and employee expertise highest. And the rural community placed pricing, employee attitudes, and return on investment highest. So bank

Rank order of bank characteristics

CHARACTERISTIC	TYPE OF BANK		
	CITY	COLLEGE	RURAL
Pricing of services	1	6	1
Reputation	2	8	7
Services offered	5	4.5	9
Time convenience	2	1	10
Location convenience	3	10	6
Employee expertise	7	3	4
Employee attitudes	6	4.5	2
Ownership of institution	9	2	5
Return on investments	10	7	3
Security of deposits	12	11	8
Physical appearance	8	9	12
Promotion efforts	11	12	11

service marketers must be sensitive not only to the various characteristics that may be evaluated but also to the unique needs of potential customers in different communities.

Source: Based on Gene W. Murdock and Robert G. Roe, "Consumer Bank Selection: Attributes of Choice," in Terence A. Shimp et al., eds., *AMA Educator's Proceedings* (Chicago: American Marketing Association, 1986), pp. 12–17.

CUSTOMER CONTACT AUDIT

Consumers judge services on the tangible aspects of their experience and on their interaction with the service provider. To focus on these experiences or "service encounters," a firm can develop a **customer contact audit**—a flowchart of the points of interaction between consumer and service provider.[12] This is particularly important in high-contact services such as hotels, educational institutions, and automobile rental agencies.[13] Figure 23–7 is a consumer contact audit for renting a car from Hertz. Look carefully at the sequence.

A Customer's Car Rental Activities A customer decides to rent a car and (1) makes a telephone reservation (see Figure 23–7). An operator answers and receives the information (2) and checks the availability of the car at the desired location (3). When the customer arrives at the rental site (4) the reservation system is again accessed, and the customer provides information regarding payment, address, and driver's license (5). A car is assigned to the customer (6),

FIGURE 23–6
Dimensions of service quality

DIMENSION AND DEFINITION	EXAMPLES OF SPECIFIC QUESTIONS RAISED BY STOCK BROKERAGE CUSTOMERS
Tangibles: Appearance of physical facilities, equipment, personnel, and communication materials	▪ Is my stockbroker dressed appropriately?
Reliability: Ability to perform the promised service dependably and accurately	▪ Does the stockbroker follow exact instructions to buy or sell?
Responsiveness: Willingness to help customers and provide prompt service	▪ Is my stockbroker willing to answer my questions?
Competence: Possession of the required skills and knowledge to perform the service	▪ Does my brokerage firm have the research capabilities to accurately track market developments?
Courtesy: Politeness, respect, consideration, and friendliness of contact personnel	▪ Does my broker refrain from acting busy or being rude when I ask questions?
Credibility: Trustworthiness, believability, and honesty of the service provider	▪ Does my broker refrain from pressuring me to buy?
Security: Freedom from danger, risk, or doubt	▪ Does my brokerage firm know where my stock certificate is?
Access: Approachability and ease of contact	▪ Is it easy to get through to my broker over the telephone?
Communication: Keeping customers informed in language they can understand, and listening to them	▪ Does my broker avoid using technical jargon?
Understanding the customer: Making the effort to know customers and their needs	▪ Does my broker try to determine what my specific financial objectives are?

Source: Adapted from Valarie A. Zeithaml, A. Parasuraman, and Leonard L. Berry, *Delivering Quality Service* (New York: Free Press, 1990), pp. 21–22. Copyright © 1990 by The Free Press, a division of Macmillan, Inc.

who proceeds by bus to the car pickup (7). On return to the rental location (8), the car is parked and the customer checks in, providing information on mileage, gas consumption, and damages (9). A bill is subsequently prepared (10).

Each of the steps numbered 1 to 10 is a customer contact point where the tangible aspects of Hertz service are seen by the customer. Figure 23–7, however, also shows a series of steps lettered A to E that involve two levels of inspections on the automobile. These steps are essential in providing a car that runs, but they are not points of customer interaction. To create a service advantage, Hertz must create a competitive advantage in the sequence of interactions with the customer.

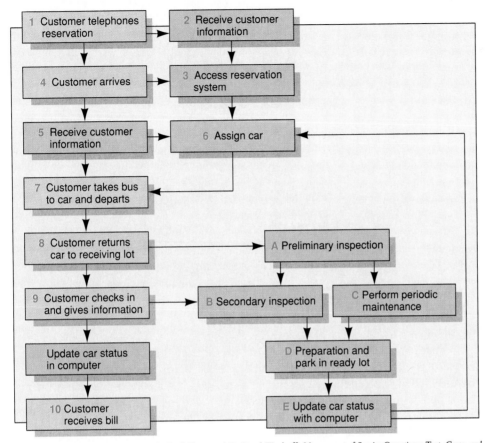

FIGURE 23–7
Customer contact in car rental (shaded boxes indicate customer activity)

Source: Adapted from W. Earl Sasser, R. Paul Olsen, and D. Daryl Wyckoff, *Management of Service Operations: Text, Cases, and Readings* (Boston: Allyn & Bacon, 1978).

CONCEPT CHECK

1 What are the differences between search, experience, and credence qualities?

2 Hertz created its differential advantage at the points of _____ in their customer contact audit.

MANAGING THE MARKETING OF SERVICES

Just as the unique aspects of services necessitate changes in the consumer's purchase process, the marketing management process requires special adaptation. As emphasized earlier in the chapter, in services marketing the employee plays a central role in attracting, building, and maintaining relationships with customers.[14] This aspect of services marketing has led to a new concept—internal marketing.[15]

At Hertz, "You don't just rent a car. You rent a company."

Internal marketing is based on the notion that a service organization must focus on its employees, or internal market, before successful programs can be directed at customers.[16] The internal marketing concept holds that an organization's employees (its "internal market") will be influenced to develop a market orientation if marketing-like activities are directed at them. This idea suggests that employees and employee development through recruitment, training, communication, and administration are critical to the success of service organizations.[17]

Let's use the four Ps framework of the text for discussing the marketing mix for services.

PRODUCT (SERVICE)

To a large extent, the concepts of the product component of the marketing mix discussed in Chapters 10 and 11 apply equally well to Cheerios (a good) and to American Express (a service). Yet there are three aspects of the product/service element of the mix that warrant special attention: exclusivity, brand name, and capacity management.

Exclusivity   Chapter 10 pointed out that one favorable dimension in a new product is its ability to be patented. Remember that a patent gives the manufacturer of a product exclusive rights to its production for 17 years. A major difference between products and services is that services cannot be patented. Hence the creator of a successful fast-food hamburger chain could quickly discover the concept being copied by others. Domino's Pizza now sees competitors copy its quick delivery advantage, which has propelled the company to the success discussed in Chapter 21.

Logos create service identities.

Branding   An important aspect in marketing goods is the branding strategy used. However, because services are intangible, the brand name or identifying logo of the organization is particularly important in consumer decisions because it is more difficult to describe what is being provided.[18] Allegis, for example, failed at an attempt to create an umbrella organization for well-known brands United Airlines, Hertz, Hilton, and Westin Hotels, in part because consumers didn't understand what it meant or how it should be pronounced. Federal Express, however, is a strong service brand name because it suggests the possibility that it is government sanctioned, and it describes the nature and benefit (speed) of the service.[19] Take a look at the figures in the accompanying photo to determine how successful some companies have been in branding their service by name, logo, or symbol.

Capacity Management   A key distinction between goods and services is the inseparability of services. To buy and simultaneously use the service, the customer must be present at the service delivery site. For example, a patient must be in a hospital to "buy" an appendectomy, and a guest must be in a hotel to "buy" an accommodation. So the product/service component of the mix must be made available to the consumer by managing demand. This is referred to as **capacity management**.

   Service organizations must manage the availability of the offering to (1) smooth demand over time so that demand matches capacity and (2) ensure that the organization's assets are used in ways that will maximize the return on investment (ROI).[20] Figure 23–8 shows how a hotel tries to manage its capacity during the high and low seasons. Differing price structures are assigned to each segment of consumers to help moderate or adjust demand for the service. Airline contracts fill a fixed number of rooms throughout the year. In the low season, when more rooms are available, tour packages at appealing prices are used to attract groups or conventions, such as an offer for seven nights in Orlando at a reduced price. Weekend packages are also offered to buyers. In the high-demand season, groups are less desirable because guests who will pay high prices travel to Florida on their own.

PRICING

In the service industries, *price* is often referred to in various ways. Hospitals refer to charges; consultants, lawyers, physicians, and accountants to fees; airlines to fares; and hotels to rates.

FIGURE 23–8
Balancing capacity management

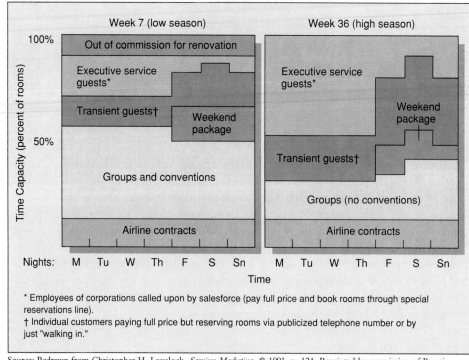

Source: Redrawn from Christopher H. Lovelock, *Services Marketing,* © 1991, p. 124. Reprinted by permission of Prentice Hall, Englewood Cliffs, New Jersey.

Setting Prices Two common methods of pricing services are cost plus percentage-of-cost and target ROI pricing.

Cost plus percentage-of-cost pricing, discussed in Chapter 13, entails charging a customer for the cost of providing the service plus an additional fixed percentage. Professional service organizations such as accounting firms charge a fee based on a billable rate. The billable rate is the cost of the accountant (salary, benefits, training, and overhead) plus a markup. This pricing is common to most professional service organizations such as law, medicine, and consulting.

In *target ROI pricing,* the price for the service is based on a targeted ROI. This method of setting price is common in capital-intensive services such as airlines or public utilities.

Role of Pricing Pricing services plays two essential roles: (1) to affect consumer perceptions and (2) to be used in capacity management. Because of the intangible nature of services, price can indicate the quality of the service. Would you be willing to risk a $100 surgery? Or a $50 divorce lawyer? Studies have shown that when there are few well-known cues by which to judge a product, consumers use price.[21] Look at the accompanying ad. Would you have concerns about a $795 delivery or think it's a good value for the money?

The capacity management role of price is also important to movie theaters, hair stylists, restaurants, and hotels. Many service businesses use **off-peak pricing,** which consists of charging different prices during different times of the day

ONE MAGNIFICENT HOLIDAY
- Guest room accommodations for two nights
- Continental Breakfast each morning
- Chilled bottle of champagne
- Complimentary valet parking
- Exclusive Michigan Avenue gift certificates
- Fresh rose for the lady
- Available for a Friday or Saturday arrival
- Upgrade to suite for $100 extra per night
- Taxes and gratuities included
- $269 per couple

FIVE DIAMOND HOLIDAY
- Penthouse suite accommodations for two nights
- Limousine service from your residence (greater Chicago area) or from airport to hotel
- Chilled bottle of Taittinger Blanc de Blanc and beluga caviar served during the trip to the hotel
- Two dozen fresh roses for the lady
- Dinner served in the privacy of the penthouse suite from a special menu
- Breakfast in bed Saturday morning
- Limousine tour of galleries, shops and other sights during the day on Saturday
- Exclusive Michigan Avenue gift certificates
- Gourmet picnic lunch served from the limousine anywhere in Chicago
- Dinner at Cricket's

- A "special event" chosen personally by our concierge
- A very special gift before retiring: a crystal decanter of one of the world's best brandies and imported chocolates
- Brunch Sunday morning at Cricket's
- Limousine service to residence or airport
- Taxes and gratuities included
- $2,500 per couple—this weekend is so personalized, only one will be sold per weekend, per hotel

THE WHITEHALL
312-944-6300 800-621-8295
THE TREMONT
312-944-6300 800-621-8295

John B. Coleman Hotels/Chicago

or days of the week to reflect variations in demand for the service. Restaurants offer luncheon specials, and movie theaters offer matinee prices. Sunrise Hospital in Las Vegas offered a 5¼ percent rebate on the total hospital bill to patients admitted on a Friday or Saturday so it could level out the demand for surgical suites.[22]

PLACE (DISTRIBUTION)

Place or distribution is a major factor in developing service marketing strategy because of the inseparability of services from the producer. Rarely are intermediaries involved in the distribution of a service; the distribution site and service deliverer are the tangible components of the service.

Historically in professional services marketing, little attention was paid to distribution. But as competition grows, the value of convenient distribution is being recognized. Hairstyling chains such as Fantastic Sam's Family Haircutters, legal firms such as the Hyatt chain, and accounting firms such as Arthur Young all use multiple locations for the distribution of services. For several years banks have offered automatic teller services to their customers. Today customers of participating banks using the Cirrus system can access any one of thousands of automatic teller systems throughout the United States.

Price influences
perceptions of services.

PROMOTION

The value of promotion, specifically advertising, for many services is to show the benefits of purchasing the service, such as the outcome of using United Airlines. It is valuable to stress availability, location, consistent quality, and efficient, courteous service.[23] In addition, services must be concerned with their image. Promotional efforts such as the American Express super-premium "platinum" card campaign, or Merrill Lynch's use of the bull in its ads, contribute to image and positioning strategies.[24] In most cases promotional concerns of services are similar to those of products. For example, sales promotions such as the all-expenses-paid trip to Jamaica described in the accompanying Marketing Action Memo can be used to encourage trial. However, publicity is a more common tool in the promotion of services.[25]

Publicity Publicity has played a major role in the promotional strategy of nonprofit services and some professional organizations. Nonprofit organizations such as public school districts, the Chicago Symphony Orchestra, religious organizations, and hospitals have used publicity to disseminate their messages. Because of the heavy reliance on publicity, many services use public service announcements (PSAs). Because PSAs are free, nonprofit groups have tended to rely on them as the foundation of their media plan.[26] However, as

Marketing Action Memo

THE NEW COLLEGIANS: A TARGET FOR CABLE TV

*D*oes an all-expenses-paid trip to Jamaica or 24 hours with the Rolling Stones sound appealing to you? If you are a college student, programming service Music Television (MTV) hopes they will. According to vice president of marketing Bob Friedman, "We want our promotions to be unlike anything else. They must be something fantasy-like, a dream we can give away." The dreams are those of students like you, who represent $20 billion in annual discretionary purchasing power. The promotion is intended to capture your entertainment interest.

Cable TV is considered a "mature" industry where success requires that programming meet the needs of a well-defined market segment. New services such as The Fashion Channel, Gospel Music Network, Movietime, and The Travel Channel are products designed to fill special needs. MTV and New York-based Campus Network's National College Television (NCTV) are targeted specifically to the 12.5 million college students in the United States.

College life is changing. Several years ago, a TV and a stereo were luxuries at college; today, students may have stereo systems, VCRs, PCs, CD players, and cable-ready color TVs. To purchase and maintain these entertainment centers, students spend more than 80 percent of their disposable income. They also have primary interest in music, movies, and comedy—three types of entertainment that cable TV can provide.

For example, in response to the findings of studies of their viewing audience, NCTV offers two hours of video music called *Audiophila,* a 60-minute concert, and a progressive video program called *New Grooves.* Bradley I. Siegel of NCTV explains, "We found that the college student does not always want to watch what the networks and independent stations offer during prime time." Another system, Video Center Events (VCE), will offer live concerts, political/social issue debates, and Broadway shows to college auditoriums via satellite. Also, Home Box Office (HBO) and MTV are joining forces to bring you the Comedy Network (CTV), which will provide comedy 24 hours a day. So the alternatives for college student TV watchers are increasing dramatically, as is the competition for your time.

See you in Jamaica!

Sources: Based on Susan Duffy, "Will a Little Less Rock Get MTV Rolling Faster?" *Business Week* (April 30, 1990), pp. 62, 66; David Lieberman, "Take My Comedy Programming Please," *Business Week* (December 18, 1989), p. 73; Christopher Colletti, "Dormitories Wired for Success," *Advertising Age* (February 2, 1987), pp. S1, S16; Marilyn Adler and Geralyn Wiener, "Student Buying Rates High Interest," *Advertising Age* (February 2, 1987), p. S1; and Wayne Walley, "New Services Need to Channel Resources," *Advertising Age* (December 7, 1987), pp. 514–15.

discussed in Chapter 17 on promotion, the timing and location of a PSA are under the control of the medium, not the organization. So the nonprofit service group cannot control who sees the message or when the message is given.

Negative Attitudes   In the past, advertising has been viewed negatively by many nonprofit and professional service organizations. In fact, professional groups such as law, dentistry, and medicine had previously barred their members from advertising by their respective professional codes of conduct. A Supreme Court case in 1976, however, struck down this constraint on professional services advertising.[27] In recent years these associations have set up ethical guidelines on the use of promotion.

Services need
promotional programs.

Although opposition to advertising remains strong in some professional groups, the barriers to promotion are being broken down. In recent years, advertising has been used by religious groups; legal, medical, and dental services; educational institutions; and many other service organizations.

SERVICES IN THE FUTURE

What can we expect from the services industry in the future? Two factors that will have a major effect are the deregulation of the services industries and technological development.[28]

As Figure 23–9 illustrates, one by one, transportation, communications, financial institutions, professional services, and other services have gone through some kind of regulatory changes. The changes have generally led to greater variety of services and the recognition that services require management of all functions, including marketing. Technological changes in services have radically changed how they conduct business. For example, the computer support system at Toronto Dominion Bank is designed to allow the employees who interface with customers to deliver the full capabilities of the bank, while Merrill Lynch's 480 domestic brokerage offices are linked to a central office to allow constant, up-to-date information management.[29]

Other changes in services are being driven by changes in consumer interests. According to Barbara Feigin of Grey Advertising's Strategic Services, "time will be the currency of the 1990s." Consumers will search for new services

FIGURE 23–9
**Key events in
deregulating the services
industries**

YEAR	DEVELOPMENT
1969	The Federal Communications Commission gives MCI the right to hook its long-distance network into local phone systems.
1970	The Federal Reserve Board frees interest rates on bank deposits over $100,000 with maturities of less than six months.
1975	The Securities and Exchange Commission orders brokers to cease fixing commissions on stock sales.
1977	Congress passes the "Federal Express" bill, deregulating the air freight industry.
1977	Merrill Lynch offers the Cash Management Account, competing more closely with commercial banks.
1978	Congress deregulates the passenger airline industry.
1979	The Federal Communications Commission allows AT&T to sell nonregulated services, such as data processing.
1980	The Federal Reserve System allows banks to pay interest on checking accounts.
1980	Congress deregulates the trucking and railroad industries.
1981	Sears becomes the first one-stop financial supermarket, offering insurance, banking, brokerage, and real estate services.
1982	Congress deregulates the intercity bus industry.
1984	AT&T agrees to divest its local phone companies; receives permission to compete in other computing and communications activities.
1988	The Supreme Court rules that states cannot prohibit lawyers from using direct-mail advertising.
1990	The Court of Appeals allows hospitals to enter into exclusive contracts for medical services.

Source: Adapted from James L. Heskett, *Managing in the Service Economy* (Boston: Harvard Business School Press, 1986), p. 156.

that reduce the time needed to go to the post office, bank, or supermarket or to prepare food, clean clothes, or maintain their homes. In addition, experts say the 1990s will be the Earth Decade, and services such as the low-environmental-impact travel service offered by the Audubon Society will be in increasing demand.[30]

CONCEPT CHECK

1 How does a movie theater use off-peak pricing?

2 Smoothing demand is the focus of _____ management.

3 Does a lawyer use cost plus percentage-of-cost or target return on investment pricing?

ETHICS AND SOCIAL RESPONSIBILITY IN THE 1990s

WHY ARE 900 NUMBERS A CONTROVERSIAL SERVICE?

There are approximately 7,000 telephone lines with a 900 prefix currently in operation. They are provided by AT&T, US Sprint, MCI, and Telesphere, and they offer services ranging from the Dow-Jones Journalphone, which gives stock quotes, to a number that plays recordings of obscene jokes. Regardless of their purpose, however, 900 numbers have caused considerable controversy.

Many marketers view 900 numbers as a cost-effective way to target specific customers. For example, customers who want warranty information about a technical product would be directed to an 800 number, but those who want to be walked through a computer program would use a 900 number. Some carriers, such as US Sprint, have started to review the content of their 900 services and strictly prohibit applications that are indecent, obscene, pornographic, illegal, or misleading. Businesses that use 900 numbers have created the National Association of Information Services (NAIS) to provide standards covering programming content, services targeted to children, ad guidelines, fraud, and complaint handling. Also, some newspapers have refused to run ads for 900 services.

Why are services that utilize 900 numbers so controversial? Are legitimate businesses suffering because of a poor image created by a few questionable 900 offerings? Is federal regulation needed?

Source: Cyndee Miller, "It's Not Just for Sleaze Anymore: Serious Marketers Want Consumers to Dial 1-900," *Marketing News* (October 15, 1990), pp. 1–2. By permission of The American Marketing Association.

 ## SUMMARY

1. Services have four unique elements: intangibility, inconsistency, inseparability, and inventory.

2. Intangible means advertising is needed to present the service benefits. Inconsistency refers to the difficulty of providing the same level of quality each time a service is purchased. Inseparable means that service deliverers represent the service quality. Inventory costs for services are related to the cost of maintaining production capacity.

3. Services can be classified in several ways. The primary distinction is whether they are provided by people or equipment. Other distinctions of services are in terms of tax status (profit versus nonprofit) or whether the service is provided by a government agency.

4. Consumers can evaluate three aspects of goods or services: search qualities, experience qualities, and credence qualities.

5. A gap analysis determines if consumers' expectations are different from their actual experiences.

6. A customer contact audit is a flowchart of the points of interaction between a service provider and its customers, where competitive differential advantages should be created.

7. Internal marketing, which focuses on an organization's employees, is critical to the success of a service organization.

8 In new service development a difficulty for organizations is that patent rights protecting the developer's exclusivity are not awarded. Therefore brands and logos (which can be protected) are particularly important to help distinguish among competing service providers.

9 Because of the inseparability of production and consumption of services, capacity management is important in the service element of the mix. This process involves smoothing demand to meet capacity.

10 The intangible nature of services makes price an important cue to indicate service quality to the consumer.

11 Inseparability of production and consumption in services eliminates intermediaries in most service marketing. Distribution is important as a tangible component of a service offering.

12 Historically, promotion has not been viewed favorably by many nonprofit and professional service organizations. In recent years this attitude has changed, and traditional reliance on publicity is waning. Service organizations are seeking greater control of their promotional programs.

KEY TERMS AND CONCEPTS

services p. 634
four I's of services p. 635
idle production capacity p. 636
service continuum p. 638
gap analysis p. 642

customer contact audit p. 643
internal marketing p. 646
capacity management p. 647
off-peak pricing p. 648

CHAPTER PROBLEMS AND APPLICATIONS

1 Explain how the four I's of services would apply to a Marriott Hotel.

2 Idle production capacity may be related to inventory or capacity management. How would the pricing component of the marketing mix reduce idle production capacity for (*a*) a car wash, (*b*) a stage theater group, and (*c*) a university?

3 What are the search, experience, and credence qualities of an airline for the business traveler and pleasure traveler? What qualities are most important to each group?

4 Outline the customer contact audit for the typical deposit you make at your neighborhood bank.

5 The text suggests that internal marketing is necessary before a successful marketing program can be directed at consumers. Why is this particularly true for service organizations?

6 Outline the capacity management strategies that an airline must consider.

7 Draw the channel of distribution for the following services: (*a*) a restaurant, (*b*) a hospital, and (*c*) a hotel.

8 How does off-peak pricing differ from the target return on investment or cost plus percentage-of-cost approach?

9 In recent years, many service businesses have begun to provide their employees with uniforms. Explain the rationale behind this strategy in terms of the concepts discussed in this chapter.

10 Look back at the service continuum in Figure 23–3. Explain how the following points in the continuum differ in terms of consistency: (*a*) salt, (*b*) automobile, (*c*) advertising agency, and (*d*) teaching.

Career Planning in Marketing

Getting a Job: The Process of Marketing Yourself

Getting a job is usually a lengthy process, and it is exactly that—a *process* that involves careful planning, implementation, and control. You may have everything going for you: a respectable grade point average (GPA), relevant work experience, several extracurricular activities, superior interpersonal and communication skills, and demonstrated leadership qualities. Despite these, you still need to market yourself systematically and aggressively; after all, even the best products lie dormant on the retailer's shelves unless marketed effectively.

The process of getting a job involves the same activities marketing managers use to develop and introduce products into the marketplace. The only difference is that you are marketing yourself, not a new product. You need to conduct marketing research by analyzing your personal qualities (performing a self-audit) and by identifying job opportunities. Based on your research results, select a target market—those job opportunities that are compatible with your interests, goals, skills, and abilities—and design a marketing mix around that target market. *You* are the "product"; you must decide how to "position" yourself in the job market. The price component of the marketing mix is the salary range and job benefits (such as health and life insurance, vacation time, and retirement benefits) that you hope to receive. Promotion involves communicating your product message to prospective employers through written correspondence (advertising) and job interviews (personal selling). The place element focuses on how to reach prospective employers, such as job interviews at the campus placement center or direct contact by letters or in person.

This appendix will assist you in career planning by (1) providing information about careers in marketing and (2) outlining a job search process.

CAREERS IN MARKETING

The diversity of marketing opportunities is reflected in the many types of marketing jobs, ranging from purchasing to marketing research to public relations to product management. The growing interest in marketing by nontraditional organizations—such as hospitals, financial institutions, the performing arts, and government—has added to the numerous opportunities offered by traditional employers such as manufacturers, retailers, consulting firms, and advertising agencies. Examples of companies with opportunities for graduates with degrees in marketing in 1990 and 1991 include AT&T, Eastman Kodak, Hallmark Cards, Mellon Bank, Microsoft Corporation, Nabisco Brands, and the U.S. Coast Guard.[1] Most of these career opportunities offer the chance to work with interesting people on stimulating and rewarding problems. Comments one product manager, "I love marketing as a career because there are different challenges every day."[2]

Recent studies of career paths and salaries suggest that marketing careers can also provide an excellent opportunity for advancement and substantial pay. For example, a survey of chief executive officers (CEOs) of the nation's 500 largest industrial corporations and 500 largest service corporations revealed that CEOs were more likely to have backgrounds in marketing than in any other field.[3] Similarly, reports of average starting salaries of college graduates indicate that salaries in marketing compare favorably with those in many other fields. The average annual starting salary of new marketing undergraduates in 1990–91 was $24,273, compared with $19,516 for journalism majors, $21,483 for advertising majors, and $21,655 for students with degrees in liberal arts.[4] The future is likely to be even better. *Business Week's Guide to Careers* suggests that 3 of the top 12 entry-level positions (in terms of ultimate salary potential and number of openings expected) in business in the 1990s will be in marketing and sales.[5] Two of these positions—retail buying and international marketing—will have the highest salaries of the 12.

Figure B–1 describes marketing occupations in six major categories: product management and physical distribution, advertising, retailing, sales, marketing research, and nonprofit marketing. One of these may be right for you! (Additional sources of marketing career information are provided at the end of this appendix.)

PRODUCT MANAGEMENT AND PHYSICAL DISTRIBUTION

Many organizations assign one manager the responsibility for a particular product or group of products. For example, P&G has separate managers for Tide, Cheer, Gain, and Bold. Product or brand managers are involved in all aspects of

FIGURE B–1 **Twenty-six marketing occupations**

PRODUCT MANAGEMENT AND PHYSICAL DISTRIBUTION

Product manager for consumer goods develops new products that can cost millions of dollars, with advice and consent of management—a job with great responsibility.

Administrative manager oversees the organization within a company that transports products to consumers and handles customer service.

Operations manager supervises warehousing and other physical distribution functions and often is directly involved in moving goods on the warehouse floor.

Traffic and transportation manager evaluates the costs and benefits of different types of transportation.

Inventory control manager forecasts demand for stockpiled goods, coordinates production with plant managers, and keeps track of current levels of shipments to keep customers supplied.

Administrative analyst performs cost analyses of physical distribution systems.

Customer service manager maintains good relations with customers by coordinating sales staffs, marketing management, and physical distribution management.

Physical distribution consultant is an expert in the transportation and distribution of goods.

SALES

Direct salesperson (door-to-door) calls on consumers in their homes to make sales.

Trade salesperson calls on retailers or wholesalers to sell products for manufacturers.

Industrial or semitechnical salesperson sells supplies and services to businesses.

Complex or professional salesperson sells complicated or custom-designed products to business. This requires understanding of the technology of a product.

NONPROFIT MARKETING

Marketing manager for nonprofit organizations develops and directs mail campaigns, fundraising, and public relations.

ADVERTISING

Account executive maintains contact with clients while coordinating the creative work among artists and copywriters. In full-service ad agencies, account executives are considered partners with the client in promoting the product and helping to develop marketing strategy.

Media buyer deals with media sales representatives in selecting advertising media and analyzes the value of media being purchased.

Copywriter works with art director in conceptualizing advertisements and writes the text of print or radio ads or the storyboards of television ads.

Art director handles the visual component of advertisements.

Sales promotion manager designs promotions for consumer products and works at an ad agency or a sales promotion agency.

Public relations manager develops written or filmed messages for the public and handles contacts with the press.

Specialty advertising manager develops advertising for the sales staff and customers or distributors.

RETAILING

Buyer selects products a store sells, surveys consumer trends, and evaluates the past performance of products and suppliers.

Store manager oversees the staff and services at a store.

MARKETING RESEARCH

Project manager for the supplier coordinates and oversees the market studies for a client.

Account executive for the supplier serves as a liaison between client and market research firm, like an advertising agency account executive.

In-house project director acts as project manager (see above) for the market studies conducted by the firm for which he or she works.

Marketing research specialist for an advertising agency performs or contracts for market studies for agency clients.

Source: David W. Rosenthal and Michael A. Powell, *Careers in Marketing*, © 1984, pp. 352–54. Adapted by permission of Prentice Hall, Englewood Cliffs, N.J.

a product's marketing program, such as marketing research, sales, sales promotion, advertising, and pricing, as well as manufacturing.[6]

College graduates with bachelor's and master's degrees—often in marketing and business—enter P&G as brand assistants, the only starting position in its product or brand group. Each year over 1,000 students from 200 campuses accept positions with P&G.[7] As brand assistants, their responsibilities consist primarily of selling and sales training.

After one to two years of good performance, the brand assistant is promoted to assistant brand manager and after about the same period to brand (product) manager. These promotions often involve several brand groups. For example, a new employee might start as brand assistant for P&G's soap products, be promoted to assistant brand manager for Crest toothpaste, and subsequently become brand manager for Folger's coffee, Charmin, or Pampers. The reason, as recruiter Henry de Montebello explains, is that "in the future everybody will have strategic alliances with everybody else, and the executives who thrive will be well-rounded."[8]

Several other jobs related to product management (Figure B–1) deal with physical distribution issues such as storing the manufactured product (inventory), moving the product from the firm to the customers (transportation), maintaining good relations with customers (customer service), and engaging in many other aspects of the manufacture and sale of goods. Prospects for these jobs are likely to increase dramatically in the 1990s as more firms adopt a marketing orientation and attempt to become more adept at meeting customers' needs.

ADVERTISING

Although we may see hundreds of advertisements in a day, what we can't see easily is the fascinating and complex advertising profession. The 1,500 to 3,000 starting positions filled every year include jobs with a variety of firms.[9] Advertising professionals often remark that they find their jobs appealing because the days are not routine and involve creative activities with many interesting people.

Advertising positions are available in three kinds of organizations: advertisers, media, and agencies. Advertisers include manufacturers, retail stores, service firms, and many other types of companies. Often they have an advertising department responsible for preparing and placing their own ads. Advertising careers are also possible with the media: television, radio stations, magazines, and newspapers. Finally, advertising agencies offer job opportunities through their use of account management, research, media, and creative services.

Most starting positions in advertising are as a media buyer—the person who chooses and buys the media that will carry the ad—or as a copywriter—the person responsible for the message, or copy, in an ad. From these positions, promotion to assistant account executive, who acts as a liaison between the client and the agency's creative department, may come quickly. Because the next position, account executive, requires a mind for business and an affinity for spotting an effective advertising idea, many of the large ad agencies now encourage employees who are advancing toward the position to pursue an MBA.[10]

Students interested in advertising should develop good communications skills and try to gain advertising experience through summer employment or internships.

RETAILING

There are two separate career paths in retailing: merchandise management and store management (Figure B–2). The key position in merchandising is that of a buyer, who is responsible for selecting merchandise, guiding the promotion of the merchandise, setting prices, bargaining with wholesalers, training the salesforce, and monitoring the competitive environment. The buyer must also be able to organize and coordinate many critical activities under severe time constraints. In contrast, store management involves the supervision of personnel in all departments and the general management of all facilities, equipment, and merchandise displays. In addition, store managers are responsible for the financial performance of each department and for the store as a whole.

Most starting jobs in retailing are trainee positions. A trainee is usually placed in a management training program and then given a position as an assistant buyer or assistant department manager. Advancement and responsibility can be achieved quickly because there is a shortage of qualified personnel in retailing and because superior performance of an individual is quickly reflected in sales and profits—two visible measures of success.

SALES

College graduates from many disciplines are attracted to sales positions because of the increasingly professional nature of selling jobs and the many opportunities they can provide. A selling career offers benefits that are hard to match in any other field: (1) the opportunity for rapid advancement (into management or to new territories and accounts), (2) the potential for extremely attractive compensation, (3) the development of personal satisfaction, feelings of accomplishment, and increased self-confidence, and (4) independence—salespeople often have almost complete control over their time and activities. Many companies such as National Semiconductor now offer two sales career paths—one for people who want to go into management, and another for those who want to remain in sales for their entire career.[11]

FIGURE B–2
Typical retailing career paths

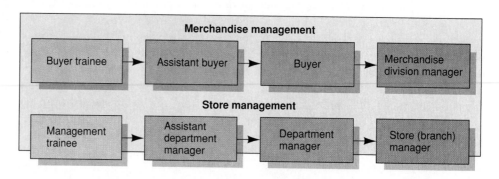

Employment opportunities in sales occupations are found in a wide variety of organizations, including insurance agencies, retailers, and financial service firms (Figure B–3). Activities in sales jobs include *selling duties,* such as prospecting for customers, demonstrating the product, or quoting prices; *sales-support duties,* such as handling complaints and helping solve technical problems; and *nonselling duties,* such as preparing reports, attending sales meetings, and monitoring competitive activities. Salespeople who can deal with these varying activities are critical to a company's success. According to RJR Nabisco, one of six companies on *Sales and Marketing Management* magazine's list of America's Best Salesforces, their recruiting priority is "finding quality people who can analyze data from customers, see things from the consumer's eyes, use available sales tools like laptops and syndicated data, and interface with the marketing people at headquarters."[12]

MARKETING RESEARCH

Marketing researchers play important roles in many organizations today. They are responsible for obtaining, analyzing, and interpreting data to facilitate making marketing decisions. This means marketing researchers are basically problem solvers. Success in the area requires not only an understanding of statistics and computers but also knowledge of consumer behavior and an ability to communicate with management. Individuals who are inquisitive, methodical, analytical, and solution oriented find the field particularly rewarding.

More than 30,000 men and women are currently working in the market research industry.[13] Their responsibilities include defining the marketing problem, designing the questionnaire, selecting the sample, collecting and analyzing the data, and, finally, reporting the results of the research. These jobs are available in three kinds of organizations. *Marketing research consulting firms* contract with large companies to provide research about their products or services. *Advertising agencies* may provide research services to help clients with questions related to advertising and promotional problems. Finally, some companies have an *in-house research staff* to design and execute their research projects.

Although marketing researchers may start as assistants performing routine tasks, they quickly advance to broader responsibilities. Survey design, interviewing, report writing, and all aspects of the research process create a challenging career. In addition, research projects typically deal with such diverse

FIGURE B–3

Employment opportunities in selected sales occupations (1988 to 2000)

OCCUPATION	1988 EMPLOYMENT	2000 EMPLOYMENT	PERCENTAGE CHANGE 1988–2000	AVERAGE ANNUAL GROWTH
Insurance sales workers	423,000	481,000	+14%	4,833
Retail sales workers	3,834,000	4,564,000	+19	60,833
Securities and financial services sales workers	200,000	309,000	+55	9,083
Real estate agents and brokers	381,000	445,000	+18	5,333
Travel agents	142,000	219,000	+54	6,417

Source: *Monthly Labor Review* (Washington, D.C.: U.S. Department of Labor, Bureau of Labor Statistics, November 1989), p. 53.

problems as consumer motivation, pricing, forecasting, and competition. A recent survey of research organizations suggested that to be successful in marketing research positions students should develop skills in written, oral, and interpersonal communication, statistics and analysis, research design, and logic. The survey also suggested that practical work experience (e.g., internships) provides a useful supplement to classroom education.[14]

THE JOB SEARCH PROCESS

Activities you should consider during your job search process include assessing yourself,[15] identifying job opportunities, preparing your résumé and related correspondence, and going on job interviews.

ASSESSING YOURSELF

You must know your product—you—so that you can market yourself effectively to prospective employers. Consequently a critical first step in your job search is conducting a self-analysis, which involves critically examining yourself on the following dimensions: interests, abilities, education, experience, personality, desired job environment, and personal goals.[16] The importance of performing this assessment was stressed by a management consultant[17]:

> Many graduates enter the world of work without even understanding the fact that they are specific somebodies, much less knowing the kinds of competencies and motivations with which they have been endowed. . . . The tragedy of not knowing is awesome. Ignorant of who they are, most graduates are doomed to spend too much of their lives in work for which they are poorly suited. . . . Self-knowledge is critical to effectively managing your career.

Asking Key Questions   A self-analysis, in part, entails asking yourself some very important and difficult questions (Figure B–4). It is critical that you respond to the questions honestly, because your answers ultimately will be used as a guide in your job selection. A less-than-candid appraisal of yourself might result in a job mismatch.

Identifying Strengths and Weaknesses   After you have addressed the questions posed in Figure B–4, you are ready to identify your strengths and weaknesses. To do so, draw a vertical line down the middle of a sheet of paper and label one side of the paper "strengths" and the other side "weaknesses." Based on your answers to the questions, record your strong and weak points in their respective column. Ideally this cataloging should be done over a few days to give you adequate time to reflect on your attributes. In addition, you might seek input from others who know you well (such as parents, close relatives, friends, professors, or employers) and can offer more objective views. They might even evaluate you on the questions in Figure B–4, and you can compare the results with your own evaluation. A hypothetical list of strengths and weaknesses is shown in Figure B–5.

INTERESTS

How do I like to spend my time?
Do I enjoy being with people?
Do I like working with mechanical things?
Do I enjoy working with numbers?
Am I a member of many organizations?
Do I enjoy physical activities?
Do I like to read?

ABILITIES

Am I adept at working with numbers?
Am I adept at working with mechanical things?
Do I have good verbal and written communication skills?
What special talents do I have?
At which abilities do I wish I were more adept?

EDUCATION

How have my courses and extracurricular activities prepared me for a specific job?
Which were my best subjects? My worst? The most fun? The least?
Is my GPA an accurate picture of my academic ability? Why?
Do I aspire to a graduate degree? Before beginning my job?
Why did I choose my major?

EXPERIENCE

What previous jobs have I held? What were my responsibilities in each?
Were any of my jobs applicable to positions I may be seeking? How?
What did I like the most about my previous jobs? Like the least?

Why did I work in the jobs I did?
If I had it to do over again, would I work in these jobs? Why?

PERSONALITY

What are my good and bad traits?
Am I competitive?
Do I work well with others?
Am I outspoken?
Am I a leader or a follower?
Do I work well under pressure?
Do I work quickly, or am I methodical?
Do I get along well with others?
Am I ambitious?
Do I work well independently of others?

DESIRED JOB ENVIRONMENT

Am I willing to relocate? Why?
Do I have a geographical preference? Why?
Would I mind traveling in my job?
Do I have to work for a large, nationally known firm to be satisfied?
Must the job I assume offer rapid promotion opportunities?
If I could design my own job, what characteristics would it have?
How important is high initial salary to me?

PERSONAL GOALS

What are my short-term and long-term goals? Why?
Am I career oriented, or do I have broader interests?
What are my career goals?
What jobs are likely to help me achieve my goals?
What do I hope to be doing in 5 years? In 10 years?
What do I want out of life?

FIGURE B–4
Questions to ask in your self-analysis

Additional information about yourself can be obtained by developing a list of the five experiences or activities you most enjoy and analyzing what they have in common. Don't be surprised if the common characteristics are related to your strengths and weaknesses!

Taking Job-Related Tests   Personality and vocational interest tests, provided by many colleges and universities, can give you other ideas about yourself. After tests have been administered and scored, test takers meet with testing service

FIGURE B–5
Hypothetical list of job candidate's strengths and weaknesses

STRENGTHS	WEAKNESSES
Enjoy being with people	Am not adept at working with computers
Am an avid reader	Have minimal work experience
Have good communication skills	Have a mediocre GPA
Am involved in many extracurricular activities	Am sometimes impatient
Work well with others	Resent close supervision
Work well independently	Work methodically (slowly)
Am honest and dependable	Will not relocate
Am willing to travel in the job	Anger easily sometimes
Am a good problem solver	
Have a good sense of humor	
Am a self-starter, have drive	

counselors to discuss the results. Test results generally suggest jobs for which students have an inclination. If you have not already done so, you may wish to see whether your school offers such testing services.[18]

IDENTIFYING YOUR JOB OPPORTUNITIES

To identify and analyze the job market, you must conduct some marketing research to determine what industries *and* companies offer promising job opportunities that relate to the results of your self-analysis. Several sources that can help in your search are discussed below.

College Placement Office   Your college placement office is an excellent source of job information. Personnel in that office can (1) inform you about which companies will be recruiting on campus, (2) alert you to unexpected job openings, (3) advise you about short-term and long-term career prospects, (4) offer advice on résumé construction, (5) assess your interviewing strengths and weaknesses, and (6) help you evaluate a job offer. In addition, the office usually contains a variety of written materials focusing on different industries and companies and tips on job hunting. One major publication available in most campus placement offices is the *Campus Placement Annual,* which contains a list of employers, kinds of job openings for college graduates, and whom to contact about jobs in those firms.

Library   The public or college library can provide you with reference material that, among other things, describes successful firms and their operations, defines the content of various jobs, and forecasts job opportunities. For example, *Fortune* publishes lists of the 1,000 largest U.S. manufacturers and their respective sales and profits; Dun & Bradstreet publishes directories of all companies in the United States with a net worth of at least $500,000. *Careers in Marketing,* a publication of the American Marketing Association, presents career opportunities in marketing. The *Occupational Outlook Handbook* is an annual publication of the U.S. Department of Labor that provides projections for specific job prospects, as well as information pertaining to those jobs. A librarian can indicate reference materials that will be most pertinent to *your* job search.

Advertisements Help-wanted advertisements provide an overview of what is happening in the job market. Local (particularly Sunday editions) and college newspapers, trade press (such as *Marketing News* or *Advertising Age*), and business magazines (such as *Sales and Marketing Management*) contain classified advertisement sections that generally have job opening announcements, often for entry-level positions. Reviewing the want ads can help you identify what kinds of positions are available and their requirements and job titles, which firms offer certain kinds of jobs, and levels of compensation.

Employment Agencies An employment agency can make you aware of several job opportunities very quickly because of its large number of job listings available through computer data bases. Many agencies specialize in a particular field (such as sales and marketing). The advantages of using an agency include that it (1) reduces the cost of a job search by bringing applicants and employers together, (2) often has exclusive job listings available only by working through the agency, (3) performs much of the job search for you, and (4) tries to find a job that is compatible with your qualifications and interests.[19] Employment agencies are much maligned because some engage in questionable business practices, so check with the Better Business Bureau or your business contacts to determine the quality of the various agencies.

Personal Contacts An important source of job information that students often overlook is their personal contacts. People you know often may know of job opportunities, so you should advise them that you're looking for a job. Relatives and friends might aid your job search. Instructors you know well and business contacts can provide a wealth of information about potential jobs and even help arrange an interview with a prospective employer. They may also help arrange "informational interviews" with employers who do not have immediate openings. These interviews allow you to collect information about an industry or an employer and give you an advantage if a position does become available. It is a good idea to leave your résumé with all your personal contacts so they can pass it along to those who might be in need of your services. Student organizations (such as the student chapter of the American Marketing Association and Pi Sigma Epsilon, the professional sales fraternity) may be sources of job opportunities, particularly if they are involved with the business community. Local chapters of professional business organizations (such as the American Marketing Association and Sales and Marketing Executives International) also can provide job information; contacting their chapter president is a first step in seeking assistance from these organizations.

State Employment Office State employment offices have listings of job opportunities in their state and counselors to help arrange a job interview for you. Although state employment offices perform functions similar to employment agencies, they differ in listing only job opportunities in their state and providing their services free.

Direct Contact   Another means of obtaining job information is direct contact—personally communicating to prospective employers (either by mail or in person) that you would be interested in pursuing job opportunities with them. Often you may not even know whether jobs are available in these firms. If you correspond with the companies in writing, a letter of introduction and an attached résumé should serve as your initial form of communication. Your major goal in direct contact is ultimately to arrange a job interview.

WRITING YOUR RÉSUMÉ

A résumé is a document that communicates to prospective employers who you are. An employer reading a résumé focuses on two key questions: (1) What is the candidate like? and (2) What can the candidate do for me?[20] It is imperative that you design a résumé that addresses these two questions and presents you in a favorable light. Personnel in your campus placement office can provide assistance in designing résumés.

The Résumé Itself   A well-constructed résumé generally contains up to nine major sections: (1) identification (name, address, and telephone number), (2) job or career objective, (3) educational background, (4) extracurricular activities, (5) work experience or history, (6) skills or capabilities (that pertain to a particular kind of job for which you may be interviewing), (7) accomplishments or achievements, (8) personal interests, and (9) personal references.[21] There is no universally accepted format for a résumé, but three are more frequently used: chronological, functional, and targeted. A *chronological* format presents your work experience and education according to the time sequence in which they occurred (i.e., in chronological order). If you have had several jobs or attended several schools, this approach is useful to highlight what you have done. With a *functional* format, you group your experience into skill categories that emphasize your strengths. This option is particularly appropriate if you have no experience or only minimal experience related to your chosen field. A *targeted* format focuses on the capabilities you have for a specific job. This alternative is desirable if you know what job you want and are qualified for it.[22] In any of the formats, if possible, you should include quantitative information about your accomplishments and experience, such as "increased sales revenue by 20 percent" for the year you managed a retail clothing store. A résumé that illustrates the chronological format is shown in Figure B–6.

Letter Accompanying a Résumé   The letter accompanying a résumé, or cover letter, serves as the job candidate's introduction. As a result, it must gain the attention and interest of the reader or it will fail to give the incentive to examine the résumé carefully. In designing a letter to accompany your résumé, address the following issues:

- Identify the position for which you are applying and how you heard of it.
- Indicate why you are applying for the position.
- Summarize your main qualifications.
- Refer the reader to the enclosed résumé.
- Request a personal interview.

SALLY WINTER

Campus address (until 6/1/92):   Home address:
Elm Street Apartments #2B   123 Front Street
College Town, Ohio 44042   Teaneck, NJ 07666
Phone: (614) 424-1648   Phone: (201) 836-4995

Education

B.S. in Business Administration, Ohio State University, 1992, Cum laude—3.3 overall GPA—3.6 GPA in major

Work Experience

Paid for 70 percent of my college expenses through the following part-time and summer jobs:

Legal Secretary, Smith, Lee & Jones, Attorneys at Law, New York, NY—summer 1990

- Took dictation and transcribed tapes of legal proceedings
- Typed contracts and other legal documents
- Reorganized client files for easier access
- Answered the phone and screened calls for the partners

Salesclerk, College Varsity Shop, College Town, Ohio—1989–1991 academic years

- Helped customers with buying decisions
- Arranged stock and helped with window displays
- Assisted in year-end inventories
- Took over responsibilities of store manager when she was on vacation or ill

Assistant Manager, Treasure Place Gift Shop, Teaneck, NJ—summers and Christmas vacations—1988–1991

- Supervised two salesclerks
- Helped select merchandise at trade shows
- Handled daily accounting
- Worked comfortably under pressure during busy seasons

Campus Activities

- Elected captain of the women's varsity tennis team for two years
- Worked as a reporter and night editor on campus newspaper for two years
- Elected historian for Mortar Board chapter, a senior women's honorary society

Personal Interests

- Collecting antique clocks, listening to jazz, swimming

References Available on Request

Source: Adapted from C. Randall Powell, "Secrets of Selling a Resume," in Peggy Schmidt, ed., *The Honda How to Get a Job Guide* (New York: McGraw-Hill, 1985), pp. 4–9.

A sample letter comprising these five factors is presented in Figure B–7. Some students have tried creative approaches to making their letter stand out—sending a gift with their letter or using creative packaging, for example. Although these tactics may gain a recruiter's attention, most hiring managers say that a frivolous approach makes for a frivolous employee. As a general rule, nothing works better than an impressive cover letter and good academic credentials.[23]

FIGURE B–7
**Sample letter
accompanying a résumé**

Sally Winter
Elm Street Apartments #2B
College Town, Ohio 44042
January 31, 1992

Mr. J. B. Jones
Sales Manager
Hilltop Manufacturing Company
Minneapolis, MN 55406

Dear Mr. Jones:

Dr. William Johnson, Professor of Business Administration at the Ohio State University, recently suggested that I write to you concerning your opening and my interest in a sales position. With a B.S. degree in business administration and courses in personal selling and sales management, I am confident that I could make a positive contribution to your firm.

During the past four years I have been a salesclerk in a clothing store and an assistant manager in a gift shop. These two positions required my performing a variety of duties including selling, purchasing, stocking, and supervising. As a result, I have developed an appreciation for the viewpoints of the customer, salesperson, and management. Given my background and high energy level, I feel that I am particularly well qualified to assume a sales position in your company.

My enclosed résumé better highlights my education and experience. My extracurricular activities should strengthen and support my abilities to serve as a sales representative.

I am eager to talk with you because I feel I can demonstrate to you why I am a strong candidate for the position. I have friends in Minneapolis with whom I could stay on weekends, so Fridays or Mondays would be ideal for an appointment. I will call you in a week to see if we can arrange a mutually convenient time for a meeting. I am hopeful that your schedule will allow this.

Thank you for your kind consideration. If you would like some additional information, please feel free to contact me. I look forward to talking with you.

Sincerely,

Sally Winter

enclosure

INTERVIEWING FOR YOUR JOB

The job interview is a conversation between a prospective employer and a job candidate that focuses on determining whether the employer's needs can be satisfied by the candidate's qualifications. The interview is a "make or break" situation: if the interview goes well, you have increased your chances of receiving a job offer; if it goes poorly, you probably will be eliminated from further consideration.

Preparing for a Job Interview   To be successful in a job interview, you must prepare for it so you can exhibit professionalism and indicate to a prospective employer that you are serious about the job. When preparing for the interview, several critical activities need to be performed.

Before the interview, gather facts about the industry, the prospective employer, and the job. Relevant information might include the general description for the occupation; the firm's products or services; the firm's size, number of employees, and financial and competitive position; the requirements of the position; and the name and personality of the interviewer.[24] Obtaining this information will provide you with additional insight into the firm and help you formulate questions to ask the interviewer. The above information might be gleaned, for example, from corporate annual reports, *The Wall Street Journal,* Moody's manuals, Standard and Poor's *Register of Corporations, Directors, and Executives,* selected issues of *Business Week,* or trade publications. If information is not readily available, you could call the company and indicate that you wish to obtain some information about the firm before your interview.

Preparation for the job interview should also involve role playing, or pretending that you are in the "hot seat" being interviewed. Before role playing, anticipate questions interviewers may pose and how you might address them (Figure B–8). Do not memorize your answers, though, because you want to appear spontaneous, yet logical and intelligent. Nonetheless it is helpful to practice how you might respond to the questions. In addition, develop questions you might ask the interviewer that are important and of concern to you (Figure B–9).

FIGURE B–8
Questions frequently asked by interviewers

INTERVIEWER QUESTIONS
1 What can you tell me about yourself?
2 What are your strengths? Weaknesses?
3 What do you consider to be your most significant accomplishment to date?
4 What do you see yourself doing in five years? In 10 years?
5 Are you a leader? Explain.
6 What do you really want out of life?
7 How would you describe yourself?
8 Why did you choose your college major?
9 In which extracurricular activities did you participate? Why?
10 What jobs have you enjoyed the most? The least? Why?
11 How has your previous work experience prepared you for a job?
12 Why do you want to work for our company?
13 What qualifications do you think a person needs to be successful in a company like ours?
14 What do you know about our company?
15 What criteria are you using to evaluate the company for which you hope to work?
16 In what kind of city would you prefer to live?
17 What can I tell you about our company?
18 Are you willing to relocate?
19 Are you willing to spend at least six months as a trainee? Why?
20 Why should we hire you?

FIGURE B–9
Questions frequently asked by interviewees

INTERVIEWEE QUESTIONS

1 Why would a job candidate want to work for your firm?
2 What makes your firm different from competitors?
3 What is the company's promotion policy?
4 Describe the typical first-year assignment for this job.
5 How is an employee evaluated?
6 What are the opportunities for personal growth?
7 Do you have a training program?
8 What are the company's plans for future growth?
9 What is the retention rate of people in the position for which I am interviewing?
10 How can you use my skills?
11 Does the company have development programs?
12 What kind of image does the firm have in the community?
13 Why do you enjoy working for your firm?
14 How much responsibility would I have in this job?
15 What is the corporate culture in your firm?

When role playing, you and someone with whom you feel comfortable should engage in a mock interview. Afterward ask the stand-in interviewer to candidly appraise your interview content and style. You may wish to videotape the mock interview; ask the personnel in your campus placement office where videotaping equipment can be obtained for this purpose.

Before the job interview you should attend to several details. Know the exact time and place of the interview; write them down—do not rely on your memory. Get the full company name straight. Find out what the interviewer's name is and how to pronounce it. Bring a notepad and pen along on the interview, in case you need to record anything. Make certain that your appearance is clean, neat, professional, and conservative. And be punctual; arriving tardy to a job interview gives you an appearance of being unreliable.

Succeeding in Your Job Interview   You have done your homework, and at last the moment arrives and it is time for the interview. Although you may experience some apprehension, view the interview as a conversation between the prospective employer and you. Both of you are in the interview to look over the other party, to see whether there might be a good match. You know your subject matter (you); furthermore, because you did not have a job with the firm when you walked into the interview, you really have nothing to lose if you don't get it—so relax.[25]

When you meet the interviewer, greet him or her by name, be cheerful, smile, and maintain good eye contact. Take your lead from the interviewer at the outset. Sit down after the interviewer has offered you a seat. Do not smoke. Sit up straight in your chair and look alert and interested at all times. Appear relaxed, not tense. Be enthusiastic.

During the interview, be yourself. If you try to behave in a manner that is different from the "real" you, your attempt may be transparent to the interviewer or you may ultimately get the job but discover that you aren't suited for it. In addition to assessing how well your skills match those of the job, the interviewer will probably try to assess your long-term interest in the firm. William Kucker, a recruiter for General Electric, explains, "We're looking for people to make a commitment."[26]

As the interview comes to a close, leave it on a positive note. Thank the interviewer for his or her time and the opportunity to discuss employment opportunities. If you are still interested in the job, express this to the interviewer. The interviewer will normally tell you what the employer's next step is. Rarely will a job offer be made at the end of the initial interview. If it is and you want the job, accept the offer; if there is any doubt in your mind about the job, however, ask for time to consider the offer.

Following Up on Your Job Interview   After your interview, send a thank-you note to the interviewer and indicate whether you are still interested in the job. If you want to continue pursuing the job, "polite persistence" may help you get it. According to one expert, "Many job hunters make the mistake of thinking that their career fate is totally in the hands of the interviewer once the job interview is finished."[27] You *can* have an impact on the interviewer *after* the interview is over.

The thank-you note is a gesture of appreciation and a way of maintaining visibility with the interviewer. (Remember the adage, "Out of sight, out of mind.") Even if the interview did not go well, the thank-you note may impress the interviewer so much that his or her opinion of you changes. After you have sent your thank-you note, you may wish to call the prospective employer to determine the status of the hiring decision. If the interviewer told you when you would hear from the employer, make your telephone call *after* this date (assuming, of course, that you have not yet heard from the employer); if the interviewer did not tell you when you would be contacted, make your telephone call a week or so after you have sent your thank-you note.

As you conduct your follow-up, be persistent but polite. If you are too eager, one of two things could happen to prevent you from getting the job. The employer might feel that you are a nuisance and would exhibit such behavior on the job, or the employer may perceive that you are desperate for the job and thus are not a viable candidate.

Handling Rejection   You have put your best efforts into your job search. You developed a well-designed résumé and prepared carefully for the job interview. Even the interview appears to have gone well. Nevertheless, a prospective employer may send you a rejection letter. ("We are sorry that our needs and your superb qualifications don't match.") Although you will probably be disappointed, not all interviews lead to a job offer because there normally are more candidates than there are positions available.

If you receive a rejection letter, you should think back through the interview. What appeared to go right? What went wrong? Perhaps personnel from your campus placement office can shed light on the problem, particularly if they are in the custom of having interviewers rate each interviewee. Try to learn lessons to apply in future interviews. Keep interviewing and gaining interview experience; your persistence will eventually pay off.

SELECTED SOURCES OF MARKETING CAREER INFORMATION

The following is a selected list of marketing information sources that you should find useful during your academic studies and professional career.

BUSINESS AND MARKETING REFERENCE PUBLICATIONS

Stewart H. Britt and Norman F. Guess, eds., *The Dartnell Marketing Manager's Handbook,* 2nd ed. (Chicago: Dartnell Corporation, 1983). This handbook contains 76 chapters on many important marketing topics, including organization and staffing, establishing objectives, marketing research, developing a marketing plan, putting the plan into action, promoting products and services, international marketing, and program appraisal.

Victor P. Buell, ed., *Handbook of Modern Marketing,* 2nd ed. (New York: McGraw-Hill, 1986). This handbook was designed to provide a single authoritative source of information on marketing and marketing-related subjects. Sections and chapters contain conceptual background material to aid the reader in overall understanding followed by "how-to" information.

Business Periodicals Index (BPI) (New York; H. W. Wilson Company). This is a monthly (except July) index of almost 300 periodicals from all fields of business and management.

Chase Cochrane and Kenneth L. Barasch, *Marketing Problem Solver,* 3rd ed. (Radnor, Penn.: Chilton Book Company, 1989). A good reference for "how to" problems, this handbook contains chapters on marketing research, marketing planning, product planning, pricing, advertising, trade shows, sales promotion, legal aspects of marketing, and other topics.

Lorna M. Daniells, *Business Information Sources,* rev. ed. (Berkeley, Calif.: University of California Press, 1985). This comprehensive guide to selected business books and reference sources is useful for business students, as well as the practicing businessperson.

Doran Howitt and Marvin I. Weinberger, *Databasics: Your Guide to Online Business Information* (New York: Garland Publishing, 1984). Databasics is a comprehensive reference for finding and using information contained in online data bases.

Jerry M. Rosenberg, *Dictionary of Business and Management,* 2nd ed. (New York: John Wiley & Sons, 1983). This dictionary contains over 10,000 concise definitions of business and management terms.

Jean L. Sears, *Using Government Publications* (Phoenix: Oryx Press, 1985). An easy-to-use manual arranged by topics such as consumer expenditures, business and industry statistics, economic indicators, and projections. Each chapter contains a search strategy, a checklist of sources, and a narrative description of the sources. Volume 1: Searching by Subjects and Agencies; Volume 2: Finding Statistics and Using Special Techniques.

Irving J. Shapiro, *Dictionary of Marketing Terms,* 4th ed. (Totowa, N.J.: Littlefield, Adams & Company, 1981). This dictionary contains definitions of over 5,000 marketing terms.

Richard H. Stansfield, *The Dartnell Advertising Manager's Handbook,* 3rd ed. (Chicago: Dartnell, 1982). This handbook provides a practical review of advertising planning and practice. Topics include advertising department organization, campaign planning, agency selection, copywriting, media, and research.

CAREER PLANNING PUBLICATIONS

J. I. Biegeleisen, *Make Your Job Interview a Success,* 3rd ed. (New York: Prentice Hall, 1991).

Richard N. Bolles, *What Color Is Your Parachute? A Practical Manual for Job Hunters and Career Changers* (Berkeley, Calif.: Ten Speed Press, 1991).

Ronald W. Fry, ed., *Advertising Career Directory,* 3rd ed. (Hawthorne, N.J.: The Career Press, 1988).

Ronald W. Fry, ed., *Marketing and Sales Career Directory,* 2nd ed. (Hawthorne, N.J.: The Career Press, 1988).

Tom Jackson, *The Perfect Résumé* (New York: Doubleday, 1990).

Ronald L. Krannich and Caryl R. Krannich, *The Complete Guide to International Jobs and Careers* (Woodbridge, Va.: Impact Publications, 1990).

Dorothy Leeds, *Marketing Yourself* (New York: HarperCollins, 1991).

Adele Lewis, *How to Write Better Resumés,* 3rd ed. (Hauppauge, N.Y.: Barron's Educational Services, 1989).

Robert H. Luke, *Business Careers* (Boston: Houghton Mifflin, 1989).

Sue C. Marsh, ed., *Harvard Business School Career Guide: Marketing* 1991–92 (Boston: Harvard Business School Press, 1990).

David W. Rosenthal and Michael A. Powell, *Careers in Marketing* (Englewood Cliffs, N.J.: Prentice Hall, 1984).

Peggy J. Schmidt, *Making It on Your First Job: When You're Young, Inexperienced, and Ambitious,* rev. ed. (Princeton, N.J.: Peterson's Guides, 1991).

SELECTED PERIODICALS

Advertising Age, Crain Communications, Inc. (semiweekly). Write to 965 E. Jefferson Ave., Detroit, MI, 48207-9966 (subscription rate: $55).

Business Horizons, Indiana University (bimonthly). Write to Indiana University, School of Business, Bloomington, IN, 47405 (subscription rate: $39.95).

Business Week, McGraw-Hill (weekly). Write to 1221 Avenue of the Americas, New York, NY, 10020 (subscription rate: $39.95).

Fortune, Time, Inc. (biweekly). Write to Time, Inc., 541 N. Fairbanks Court, Chicago, IL, 60611 (subscription rate: $47.97).

Harvard Business Review, Harvard University (bimonthly). Write to Harvard University, Graduate School of Business Administration, Soldiers Field Road, Boston, MA, 02163 (subscription rate: $30).

Industrial Marketing Management, Elsevier Science Publishing Co., Inc. (quarterly). Write to 655 Avenue of the Americas, New York, NY, 10010 (subscription rate: $125).

Journal of the Academy of Marketing Science, The Academy of Marketing Science (quarterly). Write to University of Miami, School of Business Administration, P.O. Box 248505, Coral Gables, FL, 33124 (subscription rate: $75).

Journal of Advertising Research, Advertising Research Foundation (bimonthly). Write to 3 E. 54th St., New York, NY, 10022 (subscription rate: $75).

Journal of Business and Industrial Marketing, Marketing Journal Publishing Co. (quarterly). Write to 108 Loma Media Rd., Santa Barbara, CA, 93103-2152 (subscription rate: $60).

Journal of Consumer Marketing, Marketing Journal Publishing Co. (quarterly). Write to 108 Loma Media Rd., Santa Barbara, CA, 93103-2152 (subscription rate: $60).

Journal of Consumer Research, Journal of Consumer Research, Inc. (quarterly). Write to University of Florida, College of Business Administration, Gainesville, FL, 32611 (subscription rate: $66 for nonmembers, $33 for members).

Journal of Health Care Marketing, American Marketing Association (quarterly). Write to 250 S. Wacker Dr., Suite 200, Chicago, IL, 60606 (subscription rate: $47 for nonmembers, $35 for members).

Journal of Marketing, American Marketing Association (quarterly). Write to 250 S. Wacker Dr., Suite 200, Chicago, IL, 60606 (subscription rate: $56 for nonmembers, $28 for members).

Journal of Marketing Education, University of Colorado (three per year). Write to University of Colorado, Graduate School of Business Administration, Campus Box 420, Boulder, CO, 80309 (subscription rate: $30).

Journal of Marketing Research, American Marketing Association (quarterly). Write to 250 S. Wacker Dr., Suite 200, Chicago, IL 60606 (subscription rate: $56 for nonmembers, $28 for members).

Journal of Personal Selling and Sales Management, Pi Sigma Epsilon (tri-annually). Write to 155 E. Capitol Drive, Hartland, WI, 53209 (subscription rate: $30).

Journal of Retailing, Institute of Retail Management (quarterly). Write to New York University, 202 Tisch Bldg., Washington Square, New York, NY, 10003 (subscription rate: $27).

Marketing and Media Decisions, Decisions Publications, Inc. (monthly). Write to Act Three Communications, 19 W. 44th St., New York, NY, 10036 (subscription rate: $40).

Marketing Communications, Media Horizons, Inc. (monthly). Write to 50 W. 23rd St., New York, NY, 10010 (subscription rate: $50).

Marketing News, American Marketing Association (bi-weekly). Write to 250 S. Wacker Dr., Suite 200, Chicago, IL, 60606 (subscription rate: $50 for nonmembers, $25 for members).

Sales and Marketing Management, Bill Communications, Inc. (16 per year). Write to 633 Third Ave., New York, NY, 10017 (subscription rate: $35).

Stores, National Retail Merchants Association (monthly). Write to 100 W. 31st St., New York, NY, 10001 (subscription rate: $9).

PROFESSIONAL AND TRADE ASSOCIATIONS

American Advertising Federation
1400 K St. N.W., Suite 1000
Washington, DC 20005
(202) 898-0089

American Marketing Association
250 S. Wacker Dr., Suite 200
Chicago, IL 60606
(312) 648-0536

American Society of Transportation and
  Logistics
P.O. Box 33095
Louisville, KY 40232-3095
(502) 451-8150

Bank Marketing Association
309 W. Washington St.
Chicago, IL 60606
(312) 782-1442

Business/Professional Advertising
  Association
Metroplex Corporate Center
1006 Metroplex Dr.
Edison, NJ 08817
(201) 985-4441

Direct Marketing Association
11 W. 42nd St.
New York, NY 10036-8096
(212) 768-7277

International Franchise Association
1350 New York Ave., NW, Suite 900
Washington, DC 20005
(202) 628-8000

Life Insurance Marketing and Research
  Association
8 Farm Springs
Farmington, CT 06032
(203) 677-0033

Marketing Research Association
111 E. Wacker Dr., Suite 600
Chicago, IL 60601
(312) 644-6610

Marketing Science Institute
1000 Massachusetts Ave.
Cambridge, MA 02138
(617) 491-2060

National Association for Professional
  Saleswomen
P.O. Box 2606
Novato, CA 94948
(415) 898-2606

National Association of Purchasing
  Management
P.O. Box 418
496 Kinderamack Rd.
Oradell, NJ 07649
(201) 967-8585

National Association of
  Wholesaler-Distributors
1725 K St. N.W.
Washington, DC 20006
(202) 872-0885

National Retail Merchants Association
100 W. 31st St.
New York, NY 10001
(212) 244-8780

Public Relations Society of America
33 Irving Place
New York, NY 10003
(212) 995-2230

Sales and Marketing Executives
  International
Statler Office Tower, #458
Cleveland, OH 44115
(216) 771-6650

Women in Advertising and Marketing
4200 Wisconsin Ave., N.W.,
  Suite 106-238
Washington, DC 20016
(301) 369-7400

Cases

SORZAL LTD.

Sorzal Ltd. is an importer and distributor of a wide variety of South American and African artifacts. It is also a major source of authentic Southwestern Indian—especially Hopi and Navajo—jewelry and pottery. The firm's headquarters are in Phoenix, and currently there are branch offices in Los Angeles, Miami, and Boston.

Sorzal (named after the national bird of Honduras) originated as a trading post near Tucson in the early 1900s. Through a series of judicious decisions, the firm established itself as one of the more reputable dealers in authentic Southwestern jewelry and pottery. Over the years, Sorzal gradually expanded its product line to include pre-Columbian artifacts from Peru and Venezuela and tribal and burial artifacts from Africa. By carefully inspecting these artifacts for authenticity, the company developed a national reputation as one of the most respected importers of South American and African artifacts.

In the late 1980s Sorzal further expanded its product line to include replicas of authentic artifacts. For example, African fertility gods and masks were made by craftspeople who took great pains so that only the truly knowledgeable buyer—a collector—would know the difference. At present Sorzal has native craftspeople in Central and South America, Africa, and the Southwestern United States who provide these items. Replicas accounted for a small portion of total Sorzal sales, and it only agreed to enter this business at the prodding of the firm's clients, who desired an expanded line. These items found most favor among buyers of gifts and novelty items.

Sorzal's gross sales were about $12 million and had increased at a constant rate of 20 percent per year over the last decade. Myron Rangard, the firm's national sales manager, attributed the sales increase to the popularity of its product line and the expanded distribution of South American and African artifacts:

> For some reason, our South American and African artifacts have been gaining greater acceptance. Two of our department store customers featured examples of our African line in their Christmas catalogs last year. I personally think consumer tastes are changing from the modern and abstract to the more concrete, like our products.

Sorzal distributes its products exclusively through specialty shops (including interior decorators), firm-sponsored showings, and a few very exclusive department stores. Often the company is the sole supplier to its clients. The reasons for this highly limited distribution were recently expressed by Rangard:

> Our limited distribution has been dictated to us because of the nature of our product line. As acceptance grew, we expanded our distribution to specialty shops and some exclusive department stores. Previously, we had to push our products through our own showings. Furthermore, we just didn't have the product. These South American artifacts aren't always easy to get and the political situation in Africa is limiting our supply. Our perennial supply problem has become even more critical in recent years for several reasons. Not only must we search harder for new products, but the competition for authentic artifacts has increased tenfold. On top of this, we must now contend with governments not allowing exportation of certain artifacts because of their "national significance." Increasingly, our people are feeling like Indiana Jones in the movie *Indiana Jones and the Last Crusade.*

The problem of supply has forced Sorzal to add three new buyers in the last two years. Whereas Sorzal identified five major competitors a decade ago, there are 11 today. "Our bargaining position has eroded," noted David Olsen, director of procurement. "We have watched our gross margin slip in recent years due to aggressive competitive bidding by others."

"And competition at the retail level has increased also," interjected Rangard. "Not only are some of our specialty and exclusive department store customers sending out their own buyers to deal directly with some of our Hopi and Navajo suppliers, but we are often faced with amateurs or fly-by-night competitors. These people move into a city and dump a bunch of inauthentic junk on the public at exorbitant prices. Such antics give the industry a bad name."

In recent years several mass-merchandise department store chains and a number of upscale discount operations have begun to sell merchandise similar to that offered by Sorzal. Even though product quality was often mixed and most items were replicas, occasionally an authentic group of items was found in these stores, according to company sales representatives. Subsequent inquiries by both Rangard and Olsen revealed that other competing distributors had signed purchase contracts with these outlets. Moreover, the items were typically being sold at retail prices below those charged by Sorzal's dealers.

Late one spring morning Rangard was contacted by a mass-merchandise department store chain concerning the possibility of carrying a complete line of Sorzal products. The chain was currently selling a competitor's items but wished to move to a more exclusive product line. A tentative contract submitted by the chain stated that it would buy at 10 percent below Sorzal's existing prices and that the initial purchase would be for no less than $250,000. Depending on consumer acceptance, purchases were estimated to be at least $1 million annually. An important clause in the contract dealt with the supply of replicas. Inspection of this clause revealed that Sorzal would have to triple its replica production to satisfy the contractual obligation. Soon after executives of Sorzal began discussing the contract, the president mentioned that accepting the contract could have a dramatic effect on how Sorzal defined its business.

QUESTIONS

1 What might the product-market grid for Sorzal's products look like?
2 What is Sorzal's business definition? How might the contractual arrangement with the mass-merchandise department store chain change it?
3 What is Sorzal's distinctive competency?
4 Under what marketing conditions should Sorzal accept the contract?

CASE 2

GIRL SCOUTS OF AMERICA*

BE PREPARED. The motto of the Girl Scouts of America (GSA) has been the same since Mrs. Juliette Gordon Low founded the organization in 1912 with money from an inheritance and a divorce settlement. However, Girl Scout membership has declined from an all-time high of 3.9 million in 1969 to 2.3 million in the mid-1980s. Had the principles underlying GSA become obsolete, or were there other forces operating that could explain declining membership? Furthermore, would the changes adopted by GSA in the mid-1980s lead to success?

When Low founded the GSA, she wanted young girls to be self-reliant and independent and to uphold the highest standards of citizenship and moral character. The many activities of the GSA focused on young girls developing into wives and mothers, and merit badges were awarded for accomplishments such as dressmaking, homemaking, and being a hostess. The GSA also had focused on traditional family life and increasingly found itself following population migration to the suburbs and away from the cities. This meant that the GSA recruited many scouts from white, middle-class families.

However, the environment has changed in recent years. Divorce has fractured the traditional family, opportunities for women to work outside the home have expanded, more married women are working, fewer children are being born, and the technology affecting everyday living has become more complex. The racial and ethnic composition in the United States also has changed, with a growing number of African-Americans and Hispanics.

In addition to fewer girls becoming scouts, the GSA observed that girls who had become Girl Scouts as youngsters did not continue as they grew older. Many girls who had progressed from Brownies (the youngest group of 6- to 8-year-olds) to Juniors (ages 9 to 11) had dropped out before attaining the rank of Cadette at age 12, and thus never achieved the highest rank of Senior (ages 14 to 17). It seemed that the scout troop organizational structure had contributed to

*Sources: Based on "Girl Scout Campaign Pushes Active Image," *Advertising Age* (September 4, 1989), p. 28; "Profiting from the Nonprofits," *Business Week* (March 26, 1990), pp. 66ff; and Maria Shao, "The Girl Scouts Make Many Changes to Stay Viable in the 1980s," *The Wall Street Journal* (June 15, 1982), pp. 1, 22.

the loss of scouts as they grew older. The troop format required frequent meetings and was believed to be too confining as teenagers became involved in a wider range of activities. Another disadvantage of the troop format was that it demanded considerable time from the adult troop leader.

To counteract the forces in the environment, the GSA has adopted different approaches for attracting and retaining young people. For example, the GSA has focused attention on recruiting young girls, particularly African-Americans and Hispanics, in cities as well as the suburbs. Emphasis has been placed on recruiting lower-income and delinquent girls as well. The GSA has reached out to pregnant teenagers with a program dealing with career opportunities. GSA activities also have changed, as evidenced by the new merit badges. Today they are awarded in categories such as "Aerospace," "Business-Wise," "Computer Fun," and "Ms. Fix-it," which recognizes skill in home repairs. An increasing emphasis on careers is also evident. The troop concept and requirement has been relaxed. Girls can now become scouts without joining a troop, provided they attend one official event per year. Once members, they are invited to participate in special-interest projects that include field trips, guest speakers, and conferences.

These efforts were detailed in a print, radio, and television public service campaign titled "Brainstorm," aimed at encouraging girls to become scouts and stay in the program even after they entered high school. The campaign included a 30-second TV message that covered sights and sounds related to ocean liners and travel, tap dancing, piano playing, airplanes, filmmaking, a space capsule taking off, and meeting young men.

QUESTIONS

1 Did the business definition of GSA change in the 1980s?
2 How did the product-market grid for the GSA change, given environmental trends?
3 What is your prognosis for the GSA, given its response to the environment?

CASE 3

BURROUGHS WELLCOME: RETROVIR*

For a person suffering from acquired immune deficiency syndrome (AIDS), the drug azidothymidine (AZT) can mean the difference between death and a few more months of hope. Therefore, it is not surprising that the pricing of AZT

*Sources: Based on Brian O'Reilly, "The Inside Story of the AIDS Drug," *Fortune* (November 5, 1990), pp. 112–29; Joann Luklin, "Wellcome Seeks the Approval to Sell AZT to All Those Infected with AIDS Virus," *The Wall Street Journal* (November 17, 1989), p. B4; Christine Gorman, "How Much for a Reprieve from AIDS?" *Time* (October 2, 1989), pp. 81–82; "AZT Maker Expected to Reap Big Gain," *New York Times* (August 19, 1989), p. 8; Tim Kingston, "The Unhealthy Profits of AZT," *The Nation* (October 17, 1987), pp. 407–9; "The Cost of New Drugs Raises the Roof," *U.S. News & World Report* (April 6, 1987), p. 47; "Cost of AZT Could Keep It from Patients," *American Medical News* (April 17, 1987), pp. 1, 2, 3; and "A Quiet Drugmaker Takes a Big Swing at AIDS," *Business Week* (October 6, 1986), p. 32.

(sold under the trade name Retrovir by Burroughs Wellcome, a subsidiary of Britain's Wellcome P.L.C.) has sparked one of the most passionate controversies of the AIDS era. Critics of Burroughs Wellcome have accused the company of taking advantage of AIDS patients by charging a price of $1.20 per capsule to drug wholesalers, who in turn sell the drug to pharmacies for $1.30 to $1.50 per capsule. The estimated manufacturer's cost per capsule ranges from 30¢ to 50¢, according to industry sources. The cost of the drug to a person who must take 12 capsules per day can run as high as $8,000 per year, based on an average price to consumers of $1.83 per capsule. This cost prompted the U.S. House of Representatives Subcommittee on Health and the Environment in 1989 to launch an investigation into the pricing practices employed by Burroughs Wellcome.

DEVELOPMENT OF AZT

The controversy surrounding the pricing of AZT can be traced to its initial development in 1964. AZT was first synthesized by a government-sponsored scientist in Michigan who was searching for a cancer treatment. Although AZT was not found to be an effective cancer treatment, investigators at the National Cancer Institute and Burroughs Wellcome discovered in 1984 that AZT blocked the AIDS virus from reproducing. The joint effort by government scientists and Burroughs Wellcome researchers over 20 years resulted in an estimated development cost to Burroughs Wellcome of between $80 million and $100 million. While high, these development expenses were less than the typical $125 million cost of developing a new drug. In 1984, no drug manufacturer produced AZT, in part because of the expense to manufacture it. It was also believed that the drug would be helpful to only a small group of people and that more effective AIDS drugs would soon be developed. Accordingly, on behalf of AIDS patients, the FDA invoked the Orphan Drug Act of 1983, which provided drug manufacturers with financial incentives to develop treatments for rare diseases. This act also allowed the government to give Burroughs Wellcome an exclusive seven-year license to sell the drug, which would commence upon the drug's introduction to the market.

During this period, Burroughs Wellcome designed a six-step manufacturing process to convert a key ingredient, thymidine (a biological chemical first harvested from herring sperm), into AZT. The process takes seven months to produce the drug. Chemical trials of the drug were conducted and by early 1987 the FDA gave approval for its commercial distribution. AZT became publicly available for prescription sales under the name Retrovir on March 19, 1987.

CRITICISM OF RETROVIR PRICING

The introduction of Retrovir by Burroughs Wellcome was almost immediately met by criticism related to its price. One source of criticism emerged from individuals afflicted with the AIDS virus and advocates for them. The criticism stemmed from published reports, not substantiated by Burroughs Wellcome officials, that Retrovir sales volume would be $230 million in 1989 and would rise to $880 million in 1992. Estimates of profit on the drug ranged from a low of $25 million to a high of $100 million. AIDS activists expressed the view that the price should be reduced. According to the executive director of the National Gay and Lesbian Task Force, "To make AZT accessible to everyone who should be on it, Burroughs Wellcome has an obligation to give up a significant amount of money to allow people to get access." The cofounder of Project Inform, an AIDS-treatment information agency, was quoted as saying, "I think Burroughs Wellcome is very interested in getting all their money back as soon as possible, because the sun won't shine forever."

Federal and state government officials have also voiced concerns about the cost of the drug. While forecasts vary, it is estimated that Retrovir will cost the Medicaid program upwards of $150 million (and consider only 40 percent of AIDS patients are on Medicaid). Federal and state governments will spend an additional $400 million to $800 million to treat AIDS patients. These cost concerns have prompted a member of the U.S. Senate to investigate the possibility of nationalizing AZT in the interest of national security. Such action would revoke any exclusive patents and licenses for the drug. A subcommittee of the U.S. House of Representatives launched an investigation into possible inappropriate pricing of Retrovir.

RESPONSE BY BURROUGHS WELLCOME

Officials of Burroughs Wellcome have responded to the criticism in numerous ways. For example, they note that the company has distributed $10 million worth of AZT free, and cannot afford to do this any longer. Company executives also point to the market uncertainties. According to T. E. Haigler, president of Burroughs Wellcome, the high price is due to the "uncertain market for the drug, the possible advent of new therapies, and profit margins customarily generated by significant new medicines." Industry sources cite recent efforts at Bristol-Myers Company and F. Hoffmann LaRoche indicating that both companies are engaged in developing substitutes for AZT. Company officials also point to the $80 to $100 million development cost incurred. According to a company spokesperson, "We're the ones who turned this useless chemical into useful medicine." Finally, the company has on two occasions reduced the price of Retrovir, once in 1987 soon after its introduction and again in September 1989. The latter price reduction was influenced by a government study that concluded that AZT would postpone the appearance of AIDS in people who are infected by the virus but are not yet ill. This latest price reduction prompted one U.S. Congressman to note that this was "a good first step . . . but I think the company can do better." In November 1989, a Burroughs Wellcome official responded, "There's no plan to make another price cut."

QUESTIONS

1 What pricing objectives and strategies do you believe Burroughs Wellcome applied when setting the price level for Retrovir?
2 What rationale can you provide for the company's pricing objectives and strategies you identified in question 1?
3 In your view, are these pricing objectives and strategies appropriate under the circumstances? Why or why not?

CASE 4
_____

THE JOHNSONS BUY A FOOD PROCESSOR*

At 4:52 P.M. on Friday, January 19, 1990, Brock and Alisha Johnson bought a food processor. There was no doubt about it. Any observer would agree that the purchase took place at precisely that time. Or did it?

When questioned after the transaction, neither Brock nor Alisha could remember which of them at first noticed or suggested the idea of getting a food processor. They do recall that in the summer of 1988 they attended a dinner party given by a friend who specialized in French and Chinese cooking. The meal was delicious, and their friend Brad was very proud of the Cuisinart food processor he had used to make many of the dishes. The item was expensive, however—about $200.

The following summer, Alisha noticed a comparison study of food processors in *Better Homes and Gardens*. The performance of four different brands was compared. At about the same time, Brock noticed that *Consumer Reports* also compared a number of brands of food processors. In both instances, the Cuisinart brand came out on top.

Later that fall, new models of the Cuisinart were introduced and the old standard model went on sale in department stores at $140. The Johnsons searched occasionally for Cuisinarts in discount houses or in wholesale showroom catalogs, hoping to find an even lower price for the product. They were simply not offered there.

For Christmas 1989, the Johnsons traveled from Atlanta to the family home in Michigan. While there, the Johnsons received a gift of a Sunbeam Deluxe Mixer from a grandmother. While the mixer was beautiful, Alisha immediately thought how much more versatile a food processor would be. One private sentence to that effect brought immediate agreement from Brock. The box was (discreetly) not opened, although many thanks were expressed. The box remained unopened the entire time the Johnsons kept the item.

Back home in Atlanta in January, Alisha again saw the $140 Cuisinart advertised by Rich's, one of the two major full-service department stores in Atlanta. Brock and Alisha visited a branch location on a Saturday afternoon and saw the item. The salesperson, however, was not knowledgeable about its features and not very helpful in explaining its attributes. The Johnsons left, disappointed.

Two days later, Alisha called the downtown location, where she talked to Ms. Evans, a seemingly knowledgeable salesperson who claimed to own and love exactly the model the Johnsons had in mind. Furthermore, Ms. Evans said that they did carry Sunbeam mixers and would make an exchange of the mixer, which had been received as a gift and for which no receipt was available.

On the following Friday morning, Brock put the mixer in his car trunk when he left for work downtown. That afternoon, Alisha and 6-month-old Brock, Jr., rode the bus downtown to meet Brock and make the transaction.

_____

*Source: This case was written by Roy D. Adler, Professor of Marketing at Pepperdine University/Malibu, as a basis for class discussion. Copyright © by Roy D. Adler. Reproduced by permission.

After meeting downtown, they drove through heavy rainy-day traffic to Rich's to meet Ms. Evans, whom they liked as much in person as they did on the telephone. After a brief, dry-run demonstration of the use and operation of the attachments for all of the models, the Johnsons confirmed their initial decision to take the $140 basic item. They then asked about exchanging the Sunbeam mixer that they had brought with them. "No problem," said Ms. Evans.

After making a quick phone call, Ms. Evans returned with bad news. Rich's had not carried that particular model of mixer. This model mixer (i.e., I-73) was a single-color model that is usually carried at discount houses, catalog sales houses, and jewelry stores. The one carried by the better department stores, such as Rich's, was a two-tone model. Ms. Evans was sorry she could not make the exchange, but suggested that other stores such as Davison's, Richway Discount, or American Jewelers might carry the item. She even offered to allow the Johnsons to use her phone to verify the availability of the item. The Johnsons did exactly that.

Alisha dialed several of the suggested stores, looking for a retailer who carried both the Cuisinart and the Sunbeam Model I-73, but she quickly learned that they were distributed through different types of retail stores. The young man who answered the phone at American Jewelers, however, seemed friendly and helpful, and Alisha was able to obtain his agreement to take the item as a return if she could get there that afternoon.

American Jewelers was about ½ mile away. Brock volunteered to babysit for Brock, Jr., at Rich's while Alisha returned the mixer. She took the downtown shoppers' bus to American Jewelers with the still unopened mixer box under her arm.

About an hour later, Alisha returned, cold and wet, with a $57 refund. Brock, having run out of ways to entertain a 6-month-old, was very happy to see her. Together they bought the Cuisinart at 4:52 P.M. and proudly took it home.

QUESTIONS

1 Which of the Johnsons decided to buy a food processor? The Cuisinart?
2 When was the decision to buy made?
3 What were the important attributes in the evaluation of the Cuisinart brand?
4 Would you characterize the Johnsons's purchase decision process as routine problem solving, limited problem solving, or extended problem solving? Why?

CASE 5

HASBRO, INC.*

How does a toy company become number 1 in an industry marked by fads? Just ask the executives at Hasbro, Inc., a market leader with worldwide sales of $1.4

*Sources: Based on "Hasbro's Hopes for Maxie Model Come to an End," *The Wall Street Journal* (February 12, 1990), p. B4; "For Video Games, Now It's a Battle of Bits," *The Wall Street Journal* (January 9, 1990), pp. B1, B4; "Barbie Is on the Front Line for Marketing Ethnic Dolls," *Dallas Times Herald* (August 30, 1990), pp. D1, D4; "It's Kid Brother's Turn to Keep Hasbro Hot," *Business Week*

billion and $100 million in profits. Recognizing that toy companies must replace 60 percent of their toy volume each year with new products, and that 80 percent of new toys introduced each year are failures, Hasbro executives know that the secret lies in deft product development.

HASBRO PRODUCT DEVELOPMENT AND MARKETING

Hasbro, Inc., looks for three qualities in new products: (1) lasting play value, (2) the ability to be shared with other children, and (3) the ability to stimulate a child's imagination. In addition, the company provides different toys for the various stages of a child's development. Beginning with items for infants and preschool children, it also has toys and games for pre-adolescents of both sexes, and some adults (e.g., the game Scruples).

For example, preschool toys include Glo Worm and Teach Me Reader, young boys' toys include action figures like Transformers and G.I. Joe, and young girls have items such as My Little Pony. In addition, Hasbro markets stuffed toys like Yakity Yaks and Watchimals and games and puzzles including Candyland and Bed Bugs. An element of the company's marketing strategy includes reaching mothers at the time of the child's birth, for infant toys. As the child develops, toys such as G.I. Joe are promoted through Saturday morning cartoon shows where complementary toys (aircraft carriers) are advertised.

However, even Hasbro had found it difficult to compete against Mattel, Inc.'s Barbie doll for young girls. Two entries, Jem and Maxie, were both dropped after disappointing sales. Similarly, Hasbro's investment of $20 million in its Nemo videogame, designed to compete against Nintendo, proved to be a failure.

TOY INDUSTRY

The toy industry produces an estimated $13 billion in sales annually. This figure has remained largely unchanged in recent years. A percentage breakdown of volume by toy category, excluding videogames and children's books, is shown below.

CATEGORY	PERCENTAGE OF MARKET
Dolls and action figures	31.6
Games and puzzles	11.6
Preschool and infant toys	10.1
Activity toys	9.5
Toy vehicles	9.0

(June 26, 1989), pp. 152–53; "Toyland Turnaround," *Forbes* (January 9, 1989), pp. 168–69; Andrea Stone, "Toy Fair No Picnic for Toy Industry," *USA Today* (February 8, 1988), pp. B1–B2; Ann Hagedorn, "Toy Firms Search for Next Blockbuster," *Business Week* (September 22, 1986), pp. 90–92; Steve Weiner, "If a Toy Flops, It Can Be Tough Explaining Why," *The Wall Street Journal* (September 12, 1986), p. 23; Linda M. Watkins, "Tapping Hot Markets: Toys Aimed at Minority Children," *The Wall Street Journal* (September 12, 1986), p. 23; and "Marketing," *The New Yorker* (February 23, 1987), pp. 28–29.

CATEGORY	PERCENTAGE OF MARKET
Riding toys	8.6
Stuffed toys	7.6
Arts and crafts	4.2
Other	7.8
	100.0

According to the editor of *Toy & Hobby World,* a trade publication, the toy industry is a "hit-driven business." Recent hits include Cabbage Patch Kids by Coleco, which produced estimated sales $600 million in 1985 but fell to an estimated $115 million in 1987. Teddy Ruxpin, made by Worlds of Wonder, Inc., was the hit of 1986 and 1987. However, hits can quickly become disasters. For example, videogames and software produced sales of $3.1 billion in 1982; 1985 sales were nearly zero. Videogames rebounded again to $3.5 million in 1989, with the popularity of Nintendo.

The search for hit products has resulted in the production of technologically advanced toys in recent years. These include Teddy Ruxpin-like talking toys and Lazer Tag (also produced by Worlds of Wonder, Inc.), where opponents shoot at one another with infrared light-emitting guns. Creating a hit also involves making large marketing expenditures. It is estimated that a full-scale introduction of a major toy requires $5 million to $10 million in advertising, plus $12 million to $15 million to produce a cartoon show featuring the toy or character.

In recent years, some toy companies have focused on specific children. For example, some firms have recently produced African-American, Hispanic, and Asian dolls and action figures to reach previously untapped buyers. Over 54 million (10 percent of the dolls' total volume) African-American Cabbage Patch Kids have been sold since 1983. Other firms have produced dolls for disabled children. Mattel, for example, markets the Hal's Pals line, which includes a girl with leg braces and a cane, and a boy in a wheelchair. The company donates the proceeds from Hal's Pals sales to disabled-children groups.

QUESTIONS

1 How do toy marketers, including Hasbro, apply concepts from consumer behavior in the marketing of toys?
2 What variables might be used to segment the toy market?
3 What might a product-market grid for Hasbro look like, and where are new product-market opportunities for the company?
4 What are your thoughts on the subject of marketing Lazer Tag, ethnic dolls and action figures, and dolls of disabled children?

CASE 6

HONEYWELL, INC., OPTOELECTRONICS DIVISION

After several years of developing fiber optic technology for Department of Defense projects, executives in the Optoelectronics Division of Honeywell, Inc., decided to pursue commercial applications for their products and technology. The task would not be easy because fiber optics was a new technology that many firms would find unfamiliar. Fiber optics is the technology of transmitting light through long, thin, flexible fibers of glass, plastic, or other transparent materials. When it is used in a commercial application, a light source emits infrared light flashes corresponding to data. Millions of light flashes per second send streams through a transparent fiber. A light sensor at the other end of the fiber "reads" the data transmitted. It is estimated that sales of fiber optic technology could exceed $2 billion in 1992. Almost half the dollar sales volume would come from telecommunications, about 25 percent from government or military purchases, and about 25 percent from commercial applications in computers, robotics, cable TV, and other products.

Interest in adapting fiber optic technology and products for commercial applications had prompted Honeywell executives to carefully review buying behavior associated with the adoption of a new technology. The buying process appeared to contain at least six phases: (1) need recognition, (2) identification of available products, (3) comparison with existing technology, (4) vendor or seller evaluation, (5) the decision itself, and (6) follow-up on technology performance. Moreover, there appeared to be several people within the buying organization who would play a role in the adoption of a new technology. For example, top management (such as the president and executive vice presidents) would certainly be involved. Engineering and operations management (e.g., vice presidents of engineering and manufacturing) and design engineers (e.g., persons who develop specifications for new products) would also play a major role. Purchasing personnel would have a say in such a decision and particularly in the vendor-evaluation process. The role played by each person in the buying organization was still unclear to Honeywell. It seemed that engineering management personnel could slow the adoption of fiber optics if they did not feel it was appropriate for the products made by the company. Design engineers, who would actually apply fiber optics in product design, might be favorably or unfavorably disposed to the technology depending on whether they knew how to use it. Top management personnel would participate in any final decisions to use fiber optics and could generate interest in the technology if stimulated to do so.

This review of buying behavior led to questions about how to penetrate a company's buying organization and have fiber optics used in the company's products. Although Honeywell was a large, well-known company with annual sales exceeding $5 billion, its fiber optic technology capability was much less familiar. Therefore the executives thought it was necessary to establish Honeywell's credibility in fiber optics. This was done, in part, through an advertising image campaign that featured Honeywell Optoelectronics as a leader in fiber optics.

QUESTIONS

1 What type of buying situation is involved in the purchase of fiber optics, and what will be important buying criteria used by companies considering using fiber optics in their products?

2 Describe the purchase decision process for adopting fiber optics, and state how members in the buying center for this technology might play a part in this process.

3 What effect will perceived risk have on a company's decision of whether to use fiber optics in its products?
4 What role does the image advertising campaign play in Honeywell Optoelectronics's efforts to market fiber optics?

CASE 7

BOOKWORMS, INC.*

Late one August morning, Nancy Klein, coowner of Bookworms, Inc., sat at her desk near the back wall of a cluttered office. With some irritation, she had just concluded that her nearby calculator could help no more. "What we still need," she thought to herself, "are estimates of demand and market share . . . but at least we have two weeks to get them."

Klein's office was located in the rear of Bookworms, Inc., an 1800-square-foot bookstore specializing in quality paperbacks. The store carried over 10,000 titles and sold more than $520,000 worth of books in 1983. Titles were stocked in 18 categories, ranging from art, biography, and cooking to religion, sports, and travel.

Bookworms, Inc., was located in a small business district across the street from the boundary of Verdoon University (VU). VU currently enrolled about 12,000 undergraduate and graduate students majoring in the liberal arts, the sciences, and the professions. Despite national trends in enrollment, the VU admissions office had predicted that the number of entering students would grow at about 1 percent per year through the 1980s. The surrounding community, a city of about 350,000, was projected to grow at about twice that rate.

Bookworms, Inc., carried no texts, even though many of its customers were VU students. Both Klein and her partner, Susan Berman, felt that the VU bookstore had simply too firm a grip on the textbook market in terms of price, location, and reputation. Bookworms also carried no classical records, as of two months ago. Klein recalled with discomfort the $15,000 or so they had lost on the venture. "Another mistake like that and the bank will be running Bookworms," she thought. "And, despite what Susan thinks, the copy service could just be that final mistake."

The idea for a copy service had come from Susan Berman. She had seen the candy store next door to Bookworms (under the same roof) go out of business in July. She had immediately asked the building's owner, Ed Anderson, about the future of the 800-square-foot space. Upon learning it was available, she had met with Klein to discuss her idea for the copy service. She had spoken excitedly about the opportunity: "It can't help but make money. I could work there part-time and the rest of the time we could hire students. We could call it 'Copycats' and even use a sign with the same kind of letters as we do in 'Bookworms.' I'm sure we could get Ed to knock the wall out between the two stores, if you think it would be a good idea. Probably we could rent most of the copying equipment, so there's not much risk."

*Source: This case was written by Professor James E. Nelson, University of Colorado at Boulder. Used with permission.

Klein was not so sure. A conversation yesterday with Anderson had disclosed his desire for a five-year lease (with an option to renew) at $1,000 per month. He had promised to hold the offer open for two weeks before attempting to lease the space to anyone else. Representatives from copying-equipment firms had estimated that charges would run between $200 and $2,000 per month, depending on equipment, service, and whether the equipment was bought or leased. The copy service would also have other fixed costs in terms of utility expenses, interest, insurance, and the inventory (and perhaps equipment). Klein concluded that the service would begin to make a profit at about 20,000 copies per month under the best-case assumptions, and at about 60,000 copies per month under the worst-case assumptions.

Further informal investigation had identified two major competitors. One was the copy center located in the Krismann Library on the west side of the campus, a mile away. The other was a private firm, Kinko's, located on the south side of the campus, also one mile away. Both offered service while you wait, on several machines. The library's price was about ½ cent per copy higher than Kinko's. Both offered collating, binding, color copying, and other services, all on a seven-days-a-week schedule.

Actually, investigation had discovered that a third major "competitor" consisted of the VU departmental machines scattered throughout the campus. Most faculty and administrative copying was done on these machines, but students were allowed the use of some, at cost. In addition, at least 20 self-service machines could be found in the library and in nearby drugstores, grocery stores, and banks.

Moving aside a stack of books on her desk, Nancy Klein picked up the telephone and dialed her partner. When Berman answered, Klein asked, "Susan, have you any idea how many copies a student might make in a semester? I mean, according to my figures, we would break even somewhere between 20,000 and 60,000 copies per month. I don't know if this is half the market or what."

"You know, I have no idea," Berman answered. "I suppose when I was going to school I probably made 10 copies a month—for articles, class notes, old tests, and so on."

"Same here," Klein said. "But some graduate students must have done that many each week. You know, I think we ought to do some marketing research before we go much further on this. What do you think?"

"Sure. Only it can't take much time or money. What do you have in mind, Nancy?"

"Well, we could easily interview our customers as they leave the store and ask them how many copies they've made in the past week or so. Of course, we'd have to make sure they were students."

"What about a telephone survey?" Berman asked. "That way we can have a random sample. We would still ask about the number of copies, but now we would know for sure they would be students."

"Or what about interviewing students in the union cafeteria? There's always a good-sized line there around noon, as I remember, and this might be even quicker."

"Boy, I just don't know. Why don't I come in this afternoon and we can talk about it some more?"

"Good idea," Klein responded. "Between the two of us, we should be able to come up with something."

QUESTIONS

1 What sources of information should Klein and Berman use?
2 How should Klein and Berman gather data?
3 What questions should they ask?
4 How should they sample?

CASE 8

GENERAL MOTORS CORPORATION*

A beleaguered General Motors Corporation (GM) launched its 1990 model cars with great hopes, and GM Chairman Roger Smith announced that 1990 would be the "Year of the General." Net profit on car sales had fallen in each of the past four years and the company's market share had approached post-World War II lows. Efforts to bolster sales, increase market share, and reduce car inventories through low-interest financing in recent years had placed further downward pressure on profits. Other efforts to launch the Saturn project with state-of-the-art manufacturing and car styling had been slowed. Against this backdrop, GM had restructured itself and planned a new positioning strategy for its five divisions: Buick, Cadillac, Chevrolet, Oldsmobile, and Pontiac. These actions and plans, which were developed in 1984, were the basis for the high hopes for the 1990 model year. However, GM had its critics. In particular, GM was criticized for not differentiating its cars from competitors and among its five divisions. According to one critic: "It appears to me that GM doesn't have a long-term strategy to make its cars appealing to the market. They offer squarish, boxy cars, while the rest of the market is going to individual-looking autos. It smacks of not staying close to what the market wants."

GM STRATEGY

GM executives do not agree that the company lacks a long-term strategy to overcome its present car sales and profit problems. Rather, these executives point out that efforts over the past four years have laid the foundation for the future growth and prosperity of GM.

A central element of the GM strategy was the massive reorganization of the company, which began in 1984. The company divided itself into two groups—

*Sources: Based on "Exclusive Company," *Advertising Age* (July 23, 1990), p. S4; "Here Comes GM's Saturn," *Business Week* (April 9, 1990), pp. 56ff; "With Its Market Share Sliding, GM Scrambles to Avoid a Calamity," *The Wall Street Journal* (December 14, 1989), pp. A1, A14; "GM's Cadillac Cuts Top, and Thus Price of Allanté," *The Wall Street Journal* (September 1, 1989), p. B2; "GM Seeks Revival of Buick and Olds," *The Wall Street Journal* (October 15, 1988), pp. A1, A12; Alex Taylor III, "Detroit vs. New Upscale Imports," *Fortune* (April 27, 1987), pp. 69–78; Bryan S. Moskal, "Is GM Getting a Bum Rap?" *Industry Week* (January 12, 1987), pp. 41–44; Jesse Snyder, "4 GM Car Divisions Are Repositioned in Effort to Help Sales," *Automotive News* (September 15, 1986), pp. 1, 49; "General Motors: What Went Wrong," *Business Week* (March 16, 1987), pp. 102–10; "How Pontiac Pulled Away from the Pack," *Business Week* (August 25, 1986), pp. 56–57; John Koten, "Car Makers Use 'Image' Map as Tool to Position Products," *The Wall Street Journal* (March 22, 1984), p. 35; John Holuska, "G.M.'s Overhaul: A Return to Basics," *New York Times* (January 15, 1984), p. F1; and "GM Is Offering New Incentives for Auto Sales," *The Wall Street Journal* (August 6, 1987), pp. 1, 17.

FIGURE C8-1
Perceptual map of U.S. and foreign automakers

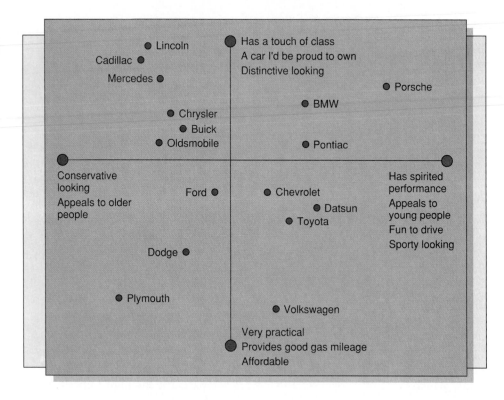

one for large cars and one for small cars (see Chapter 2). The large-car group would be responsible for manufacturing and marketing Oldsmobile, Buick, and Cadillac. The small-car group would be responsible for Chevrolet and Pontiac. This reorganization affected 300,000 of GM's 800,000 employees. These structural changes were deemed necessary to make GM more responsive to the market.

A second element of the GM strategy was the plan for positioning its divisions. Positioning the divisions, as reflected in how GM wished to project the image of each, had been of concern since the early 1980s. Moreover, GM competitors were also looking to position themselves in ways that would differentiate their automobiles from domestic and foreign car manufacturers. One example of such an effort was the research conducted by the Chrysler Corporation (Figure C8–1). The technique used by Chrysler produced a *perceptual map,* which is a variation of positioning by attributes or benefits sought by consumers. In practice, the technique involves asking owners of different brands to rate cars on a scale of 1 to 10 for qualities such as "youthfulness" and "luxury," and whether the car is "for older people" or "for younger people." For example, scales might look like those shown below:

	Plymouth is . . .	
For younger people	1 2 3 4 5 6 7 8 9 10	For older people
Sporty looking	1 2 3 4 5 6 7 8 9 10	Conservative looking

Responses indicated on each scale are then worked into a score for each car model and plotted on a graph called a perceptual map that shows which models are similar and which are different from each other. The location of each model on the map and the distance between models has strategic significance. For example, models clustered together probably will compete head–on against each other. Also, failure to have a model in a particular location on the map suggests a need for repositioning that model through changes in styling, price, or advertising.

GM's plans for positioning its divisions were drafted in 1984 (see Chapter 8). The company had traditionally positioned its divisions on price only. The lowest-price cars were sold by Chevrolet with Pontiac, Oldsmobile, Buick, and Cadillac representing higher-priced cars in ascending order. For example, a Chevrolet Caprice Classic was priced at $14,000 while the Cadillac Allanté was priced at $56,500, with the models in other divisions priced between these price levels. However, GM departed from this one-dimensional positioning approach during planning efforts in 1984. At that time, GM developed a two-dimensional positioning approach featuring price on one dimension and a family-conservative/personal-expressive orientation on the other dimension. Figure C8–2 shows the evolution of GM's plans and actual positions in 1982 and 1986.

Figure C8–2 illustrates the repositioning evident in GM's strategy. Buick and Oldsmobile were to switch positions from the 1984 plan to the 1990 plan. Oldsmobile would become more personal-expressive while Buick would become more family-conservative. Pontiac and Saturn also changed positions. The Saturn, scheduled for introduction in 1990, was initially (1985) positioned as more expensive and less personal or expressive than Pontiac. However, GM's revised 1990 plan called for Saturn to be less expensive and more personal or expressive than Pontiac, at a price between $10,000 and $12,000. Also, GM's Adam Opel subsidiary in West Germany was added to the positioning map as a higher-priced, personal-expressive car.

STRATEGY EXECUTION

Implementation of the GM planning effort was not expected to produce immediate results. However, early signals indicated that GM's efforts had an effect on the marketplace. The Pontiac Division had shown significant sales gains from repositioning. Styling changes coupled with its "We Build Excitement" advertising theme made Pontiac the fastest-growing GM division. On the other hand, Cadillac, Oldsmobile, and Buick were the three slowest-growing divisions. Chevrolet fell in the mid-range of sales gains for all GM divisions.

QUESTIONS

1 How might the "positions" of GM cars in Figures C8–1 and C8–2A be interpreted? What are the implications of these positions for GM?

2 What is your assessment of GM's 1984 repositioning goals shown in Figure C8–2B given 1984 consumer perceptions shown in Figure C8–1?

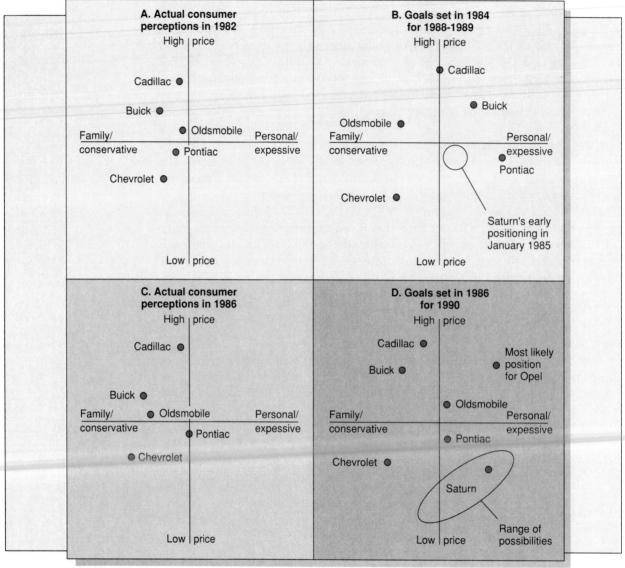

Source: Jesse Snyder, "4 GM Car Divisions Are Repositioned in Effort to Help Sales," *Automotive News* (September 15, 1986), pp. 1, 49.

FIGURE C8–2
**GM's actual and
planned positioning of
its car divisions**

3 What are your thoughts on GM's 1984 positioning (Figure C8–2B) and its changed strategy for 1988–89 (Figure C8–2D)?

4 If you were to assign GM's divisions to a location on Figure C8–2, would you make any changes? If so, what changes would you make and why?

CASE 9
_____

UPJOHN COMPANY: ROGAINE*

Rogaine, the brand name for a hair-growing drug called *minoxidil,* was expected to reap worldwide sales of $500 million a year when it was approved by the Food and Drug Administration in August 1988. However, by the end of 1989, estimated sales for Rogaine were $130 million, and the 1990 first-quarter (January–March) sales were $32 million worldwide. What factors contributed to the shortfall in expected sales? Some industry analysts and marketing and advertising consultants have pointed toward the marketing plan and execution, while others have cited the consumer buying process as a stumbling block. Uncovering the reasons for Rogaine's sales performance to date might provide clues to its future performance.

DEVELOPMENT OF ROGAINE

The development of Rogaine can be traced to the mid-1960s, when researchers at Upjohn Company noticed that the drug minoxidil reduced the heart rate of laboratory animals. Further testing on humans for cardiac use uncovered an interesting side effect—hair growth on a person's forehead or upper chest. Then, in 1973, a bald patient using minoxidil developed new hair on his head. Subsequent testing of 2,356 men with a 2 percent minoxidil solution between 1977 and 1982 showed that hair growth was apparent for a sizable number. Upjohn claimed that 39 percent of patients achieved "moderate to dense" hair growth after a year's use—a claim approved by the FDA. Moreover, hair growth was most evident for men under 30. Some side effects existed, including itching, skin irritation, and possibly a rise in heartbeat.

The properties of minoxidil and its use as a topical ointment for hair growth meant that the solution had to be applied twice every day. When not applied daily, hair loss would result. In other words, minoxidil was a lifetime treatment if its effects of hair growth and retention were to be permanent.

Upjohn began selling its minoxidil solution in other countries in 1986, under the trade name Regaine. However, more stringent and time-consuming review procedures by the FDA slowed approval for use in the United States until late 1988. The name Regaine was replaced with Rogaine, because an FDA official believed that the name Regaine suggested that the solution would result in complete hair growth. During this time, minoxidil had received considerable publicity in the media as a miracle cure for baldness.

---

*Sources: Based on "For Rogaine, No Miracle Cure—Yet," *Business Week* (June 4, 1990), p. 100; "Britain Approves Upjohn Hair Drug," *New York Times* (April 6, 1990), p. D4; Laurie Freeman, "Can Rogaine Make Gains via Ads," *Advertising Age* (September 11, 1989), p. 12; Stephen W. Quickel, "Bald Spot," *Business Month* (November 1989), pp. 36–37ff; Laurie Freeman, "Upjohn Takes a Shine to Balding Women," *Advertising Age* (February 27, 1989), p. S1; "Minoxidil," *Vogue* (September 1989), p. 56; and "Hair Today: Rogaine's Growing Pains," *New York* (October 30, 1990), p. 20.

MARKETING OF ROGAINE

Introductory marketing plans for Rogaine in the United States were developed concurrently with the FDA approval process. Since Rogaine had FDA approval as a prescription drug, Upjohn's initial attention was placed on educating its salesforce, which called on physicians. In October 1988, Rogaine was introduced to physicians by its salesforce and through advertisements in medical journals. According to an Upjohn spokesperson, "We couldn't begin marketing Rogaine to consumers until we felt the awareness level was adequate in the medical community."

The pricing of Rogaine was such that a user would spend between $700 and $900 per year for the solution and periodic visits to a physician to monitor progress. This cost would continue as long as a person used the solution.

Consumer advertising for Rogaine began in November 1988, two months ahead of the originally planned program. Slow prescription sales prompted this action. Television and print advertising emphasized a soft sell, which urged consumers to "see your doctor . . . if you're concerned about hair loss." The ads contained no mention of Rogaine, since federal regulations prohibit the use of brand names in prescription-drug advertising to consumers. With a sales rate of $4 million per month for the first quarter of 1989, a decision was made to revamp the advertising campaign. The new campaign featured a bald man standing before his bathroom mirror. Like the earlier message, viewers were urged to see their doctor. While sales improved, they remained below expected levels. Accordingly, a third advertising campaign was developed and launched in February 1990. Print advertisements featured the Rogaine name for the first time, with FDA approval, and emphasized that Rogaine was the only FDA-approved product for hair growth with the headline: "The good news is there's only one product that's proven to grow hair . . . Rogaine." Companion television advertising, however, did not mention Rogaine.

Upjohn invested heavily in advertising for Rogaine. It is estimated that $50 million was spent for advertising in 1989, and another $50 million was planned for 1990.

A variety of sales promotion activities have been implemented to complement consumer advertising. For instance, Upjohn offered rebates to people who got a Rogaine prescription from their physician. The patient would either get a certificate worth $10 toward the purchase of the first bottle of Rogaine, or $20 for sending in the box tops from the first four bottles used. Selected barbershops and salons have been provided with information packets to be given to customers worried about hair loss.

NEW INITIATIVES AND DEVELOPMENTS

As early as 1987, Upjohn researchers began studying the effect of Rogaine on women. Positive results led the company to seek FDA approval for Rogaine's use by women, even though some physicians had been already prescribing the solution for them. (Physicians can legally prescribe drugs for uses not approved by the FDA.) Company officials believe women represent an opportunity for future sales growth. For example, consumer research suggests that women might be more receptive to a hair growth product than men. This research indicates that 13.3 percent of surveyed women losing their hair have sought treatment, while 9.9 percent of men have done so. Furthermore, 38.6 percent of women say they would seek treatment if they were losing hair, compared to 30.4 percent of men who say they would seek treatment. While estimates vary, it is believed that about 30 million men and 7 million women are balding, of which an estimated 35 percent are under 30 years old.

In early 1989, Upjohn introduced Progaine Shampoo, a hair-thickener product, for use by men and women. This product does not promote hair growth, but serves as a treatment for thinning hair. It is believed the shampoo will benefit from the sound-alike name and be considered a companion to Rogaine. In April 1990, Upjohn received approval to market Rogaine in Great Britain, which opened yet another market for the product.

QUESTIONS

1 How might the buying process for a product like Rogaine be described?
2 Which psychological and sociocultural variables affect the buying process for Rogaine?
3 How would you assess the effectiveness of the overall marketing program for Rogaine to date?
4 What marketing program changes, if any, would you recommend for Rogaine?

CASE 10

LEXIS VERSUS LEXUS*

In August 1987, Toyota announced that a new line of luxury cars would be introduced at the start of the 1990 model-year, and marketed through a new Lexus division. On October 8, 1987, Mead Data General sent Toyota a letter of protest indicating that a conflict existed between the Lexus name and Lexis, Mead's computerized legal research system. Attempts to resolve the dispute were unsuccessful, even though Toyota agreed to compensate Mead for any dilution of the Lexis name that might arise from the planned multimillion dollar promotional campaign for Lexus. According to a Toyota spokesperson, they believed that no conflict existed because of the different spelling and the fact that the two companies were in noncompeting industries.

On April 22, 1988, Mead filed a suit in the U.S. District Court for the Southern District of New York, claiming Toyota's dilution of its Lexis trademark under the New York antidilution statute and unfair competition under the Federal Lanham Act. Mead sought to stop Toyota from using the Lexus name.

*Sources: Based on "Toyota's War of Words over Lexus Nameplate," *The Wall Street Journal* (March 27, 1989), p. B6; "Oops, That Name's Taken," *Time* (January 16, 1989), p. 47; "Vowels Cost More," *U.S. News and World Report* (January 16, 1989), p. 52; "Toyota Wins Lexus Name—for Now," *Automotive News* (January 9, 1989), p. 1ff; and "U.S. Appeals Court Rules Toyota Can Use Lexus Name for New Line," *The Wall Street Journal* (March 9, 1989), p. B6. Background: *Mead vs. Toyota—Lexis vs. Lexus,* Publicity Release (New York: Dorf & Stanton Communications, Inc., June 1989).

The U.S. District Court rendered its opinion on December 30, 1989. The judge ruled in favor of Toyota's assertion that the Lexus name would not be confused with Mead's Lexis legal research system. However, he also ruled that the Lexus name would dilute Mead's Lexis trademark under New York's anti-dilution statute. In doing so, the court rejected Toyota's contention that when products are so different, "only the most famous and well-known are protected from dilution." The judge noted further that the multimillion dollar advertising campaign for Lexus would "dwarf the Lexis mark." He offered to let Toyota use the name on its auto products, but set restrictions on Lexus advertising. In addition, compensation would be made to Mead for lessening the impact of the Lexis trademark in advertising. Two days later, Toyota informed the court of its intention to appeal the ruling, and requested a hearing by a three-judge panel of the U.S. Court of Appeals.

On March 3, 1989, the U.S. Court of Appeals reversed the U.S. District Court's ruling. In doing so, the U.S. Court of Appeals agreed with Toyota that when products are very different, the trademark dilution law does not apply. Furthermore, when two trademarks are used on very different products, the original trademark must be known by the general public for dilution to occur. Since Lexis was known only by a narrow market of attorneys and accountants, it was not entitled to trademark protection against Toyota. Only world-famous names such as Tiffany, Rolls Royce, or Kodak are protected by the trademark dilution law. Finally, with regard to advertising, the court held that television and radio announcers "usually are more careful and precise in their diction than is the man on the street," thereby reducing the possible confusion between Lexus and Lexis.

QUESTIONS

1 In your own words, how would you evaluate the U.S. District Court's original decision and the subsequent ruling by the U.S. Court of Appeals based on your knowledge of the Lanham Act (discussed in Chapters 3 and 11)?
2 Which behavioral concepts in Chapter 5 are present in this case?
3 List five automobile brands and nonautomobile products and services that have identical names.

CASE 11

CIRCLE K CORPORATION*

Circle K Corporation filed for bankruptcy in May 1990, after almost a decade of extraordinary growth in the convenience store industry. However, this growth had been costly, including $1.1 billion in debt used to buy and open new stores.

*Sources: Sonia L. Nazario, "Circle K Squares Off with Its Creditors," *The Wall Street Journal* (May 17, 1990), p. A4; *Circle K Corporation 10-K Report* (April 30, 1989); "Circle K Files for Chapter 11," *Dallas Times Herald* (May 16, 1990), pp. B1, B7; "Karl Eller's Big Thirst for Convenience Stores," *Business Week* (June 13, 1988), pp. 86–89; *Circle K Corporation 1989 Annual Report*; and "Troubled Circle K Is Turning This Way and That," *Business Week* (November 20, 1989), pp. 78, 80.

Efforts to generate adequate profit to pay this debt also alienated customers. According to Robert A. Dearth, Jr., the company's president, Circle K charged its customers prices well above the competition and stocked its shelves with high profit-margin products that customers did not want, while cutting back on the more popular items that attracted customers.

Soon after Circle K sought protection from its creditors under the federal bankruptcy laws, it announced plans to revamp its corporate culture, product mix, and pricing strategies to lure back former customers and attract new ones. The new initiatives and strategies would be implemented in the summer of 1990.

THE COMPANY

Circle K Corporation is the second largest operator of convenience stores in the United States. Its 4,685 stores are located in 32 states, but most are concentrated in Arizona, California, Florida, and Texas. Circle K sells over 3,800 different consumer products, including fast food, tobacco items, beverages, groceries, magazines, health and beauty aids, and numerous nonfood products. It provides such services as movie rentals, money orders, lottery tickets (where available), and banking services through automatic teller machines and debit card programs. In addition, the company sells gasoline at 3,600 of its stores through self-service dispensing equipment.

Circle K recorded sales of $3.441 billion in 1989; net earnings after taxes were $15.4 million. Sales in 1988 had been $2.61 billion and net earnings were $60.4 million. The decline in net earnings between 1988 and 1989 was due to (1) a decrease in merchandise gross profit margins, which reduced gross profit by $30 million, and (2) a $39.3 million increase in debt and interest expense.

Gross profit margin (sales less cost of goods sold) varied by the two major categories of products sold by Circle K. The gross profit margin for merchandise (food and nonfood items), which accounted for 57 percent of sales, was 36.0 percent. The gross profit margin for gasoline, which accounted for 43 percent of sales, was 10.5 percent. The company's gross profit margin on total sales was 25 percent.

MARKETING ENVIRONMENT

The convenience store industry produces annual sales of about $75 billion through 83,000 outlets. The five largest convenience store chain retailers are, in order, 7-Eleven, Circle K, Convenient Food Mart, Dairy Mart, and Cumberland Farms. On average, a convenience store is visited by 654 customers each day. Based on these data, the average sale per customer per visit is about $3.79.

Convenience store chains have distinguished themselves with the wide assortment of merchandise and services they provide. At the same time, broadened assortments have brought convenience stores into competition with a variety of other retailers. Convenience stores now compete for customers with gasoline stations, fast-food outlets, grocery stores, and video rental businesses. Even with the broadened product assortments, about 50 percent of nongasoline sales made by convenience stores are for tobacco products, beverages (beer, wine, and soft drinks), and various types of dairy items.

The convenience store customer is typically a blue-collar, white male. For example, approximately 57 percent of customers are men and 83 percent are white. The median annual household income of convenience store patrons is $20,000. However, with two-income and single-parent families becoming more common, women have been identified as an important but underdeveloped customer segment for convenience stores. The reason for this growing interest in attracting women is the lack of time to shop grocery stores. While convenience stores have historically sold time savings for higher prices on merchandise, women have still not patronized convenience stores as frequently as men. Still, as time becomes an even more scarce commodity, convenience store operators believe women will find it necessary to become frequent customers.

Industry analysts believe that the convenience store industry is maturing and there are too many stores. They note that annual sales growth has slowed in recent years to 5 percent, compared with double-digit growth rates in the late 1970s and early 1980s. Also, there were twice as many stores in 1989 as there were in 1979, and most of these new outlets have been located in Florida, California, and Texas. Slowed growth, coupled with the increasing number of stores and the lack of differentiation among convenience stores has prompted price competition in many local and regional markets. Aggressive pricing has depressed industry profit margins.

CIRCLE K MARKETING STRATEGY

The marketing strategy outlined by Circle K to deal with its financial situation contained three initiatives. First, the company planned to tailor its product assortments to the particular ethnic or socioeconomic climate of each store, and allow store managers greater latitude in merchandising. According to Mr. Dearth, "Before, if it wasn't in the order book, you couldn't order it. That was the simple rule." Second, the company would institute a 10 percent across-the-board cut in prices. "Before, we had the attitude of gouging the customer for what we could get," said Mr. Dearth. In 1989, Circle K raised its prices 6 to 7 percent, only to see companywide sales decline 8 to 10 percent. In February 1990 the company rolled back its prices to where they are now, about 5 percent more than the competition, according to an industry analyst. The third initiative focused on more aggressive promotion, including frequent-buyer incentives and a give-away program with more than $100 million in prizes, aimed at attracting customers. Both promotional approaches have been used by Circle K's competitors with mixed success.

The company planned to launch its marketing program during the summer of 1990. However, the announced marketing initiatives have met with conflicting responses. One of Circle K's bank creditors said, "We would encourage any plan that generates income. We believe this plan probably will." However, industry analysts are not so hopeful, citing the company's financial condition and the market and competitive environment in the convenience store industry.

QUESTIONS

1 How would you assess the marketing environment for convenience stores?
2 What effect do you think the 10 percent across-the-board cut in Circle K prices will have on the company's sales volume and profitability? Why?
3 What effect do you think the aggressive promotion program will have on Circle K sales volume and profitability? Why?

CASE 12

HEALTH CRUISES, INC.*

Health Cruises, Inc., packages cruises to Caribbean islands such as Martinique and the Bahamas. Like conventional cruises, the packages are designed to be fun. But the cruise is structured to help participants become healthier by breaking old habits, such as smoking or overeating. The Miami-based firm was conceived by Susan Isom, 30, a self-styled innovator and entrepreneur. Prior to this venture, she had spent several years in North Carolina promoting a behavior-modification clinic.

Isom determined that many people were very concerned about developing good health habits, yet they seemed unable to break away from their old habits because of the pressures of day-to-day living. She reasoned that they might have a chance for much greater success in a pleasant and socially supportive environment, where good health habits were fostered. Accordingly, she established Health Cruises, Inc., hired 10 consulting psychologists and health specialists to develop a program, and chartered a ship. DeForrest Young, a Miami management consultant, became the chairperson of Health Cruises. Seven of Isom's business associates contributed an initial capital outlay totaling more than $250,000. Of this amount, $65,000 went for the initial advertising budget, $10,000 for other administrative expenses, and $220,000 for the ship rental and crew.

Mary Porter, an overweight Denver schoolteacher, has signed up to sail on a two-week cruise to Nassau, departing December 19. She and her shipmates will be paying an average of $1,500 for the voyage. The most desirable staterooms cost $2,200.

Mary learned of the cruise by reading the travel section of her Sunday newspaper on October 16. On that date, the Pittsford and LaRue Advertising Agency placed promotional notices for the cruise in several major metropolitan newspapers. Mary was fascinated by the idea of combining therapy sessions with swimming, movies, and an elegant atmosphere.

Pittsford and LaRue account executive Carolyn Sukhan originally estimated that 300 people would sign up for the cruise after reading the October 16

*Source: Maurice Mandell and Larry J. Rosenberg, *Marketing,* 2nd ed., © 1981, pp. 365–66. Reprinted by permission of Prentice Hall, Englewood Cliffs, N.J.

ads. But as of November 14, only 200 had done so. Isom and Health Cruises, Inc., faced an important decision.

"Here's the situation as I see it," explained a disturbed Ms. Isom at the Health Cruises board meeting. "We've already paid out more than a quarter of a million to get this cruise rolling. It's going to cost us roughly $200 per passenger for the two weeks, mostly for food. Pittsford and LaRue predicted that 300 people would respond to the advertising campaign, but we've only got 200.

"I see three basic options: (1) we cancel the cruise and take our losses; (2) we run the cruise with the 200 and a few more that will trickle in over the next month; or (3) we shell out some more money on advertising and hope that we can pull in more people.

"My recommendation to this board is that we try to recruit more passengers. There are simply too many empty rooms on that ship. Each one costs us a bundle."

At this point, Carolyn Sukhan addressed the board: "I've worked out two possible advertising campaigns for the November 20 papers. The first, the limited campaign, will cost $6,000. I estimate that it will bring in some 20 passengers. The more ambitious campaign, which I personally recommend, would cost $15,000. I believe this campaign will bring in a minimum of 40 passengers.

"I realize that our first attempt was somewhat disappointing. But we're dealing here with a new concept, and a follow-up ad might work with many newspaper readers who were curious and interested when they read our first notice.

"One thing is absolutely certain," Sukhan emphasized. "We must act immediately if there's any hope of getting more people on board. The deadline for the Sunday papers is in less than 48 hours. And if our ads don't appear by this weekend, you can forget it. No one signs up in early December for a December 18 sailing date."

Isom interrupted, shaking her head. "I just don't know what to say. I've looked over Carolyn's proposals, and they're excellent. Absolutely first-rate. But our problem, to be blunt, is money. Our funds are tight, and our investors are already nervous. I get more calls each day, asking me where the 300 passengers are. It won't be easy to squeeze another $6,000 out of these people. And to ask them for $15,000 — well, I just don't know how we're going to be able to justify it."

QUESTIONS

1 What is the minimum number of passengers that Health Cruises must sign up by November 20 to break even with the cruise? (Show your calculations.)

2 Should Health Cruises go ahead with the cruise, since 200 passengers had signed up as of November 14?

3 Would it be worthwhile for Health Cruises to spend either $6,000 or $15,000 for advertising on November 20? If so, which figure would you recommend?

4 How realistic are Carolyn Sukhan's estimates of 20 more passengers for the $6,000 advertising campaign and 40 more passengers for the $15,000 campaign?

5 Should Health Cruises consider cutting its prices for this maiden voyage health cruise?

CASE 13
_____

HEART RATE INCORPORATED: THE VERSA-CLIMBER*

Ms. Kimberly Dubois, director of Advertising and Promotion for Heart Rate Incorporated (HRI), was assigned responsibility for preparing a marketing plan for the introduction of the 108H Versa-Climber (see Figure C13–1), the home version of the institutional models sold by the company. Mr. Dick Charnitski, president and founder of HRI and inventor of the Versa-Climber, was enthusiastic about the new introduction. Institutional Versa-Climber models had been successful in the health club and physical therapy markets, and users persuaded Mr. Charnitski to develop a more economical model for home use. While institutional models were occasionally sold to individuals, the 108H Versa-Climber would be HRI's first targeted entry into the aerobic home-fitness market.

THE COMPANY

HRI designs, develops, and markets a variety of products for use in health clubs, hospitals, and rehabilitation clinics. Company sales have grown from $9,433 in 1981, when HRI was founded, to over $3 million in 1990. The Versa-Climber is a full-body, aerobic, and strength exercise machine that simulates the physical motion of climbing a ladder. It is HRI's principal product and accounts for the great majority of company sales. Figure C13–1 shows the Versa-Climber in use.

FIGURE C13–1
The Versa-Climber—home model 108H

*The cooperation of Heart Rate Incorporated in the preparation of this case is gratefully acknowledged. This case was prepared by Steve O'Brien and Kris Sirchio, graduate students at Southern Methodist University. Some information is disguised, while other information is illustrative and not useful for research purposes. Used with permission.

The Versa-Climber utilizes one of the most intensive and rigorous activities to which the body can be subjected—continuous vertical climbing. All major muscles of the arms, shoulders, chest, back, hips, buttocks, and legs are engaged while climbing. This combined upper- and lower-body muscle contraction maximizes peripheral blood flow, resulting in higher energy expenditure and calorie consumption. The workout is effective and efficient because it takes less time and perceived effort to burn more calories, and achieves better results than other exercise activities. The rhythmic and continuous nature of the climbing exercise provides the benefits of aerobic training as well.

The machine itself consists of a column that houses the mechanical operations, pedals and handles, and a digital display module. To exercise, the user stands on two stirrup-style foot pedals and holds on to the two hand grips. All of the movement is powered by the user. The climbing motion is achieved by alternately stepping and pulling down on the handles with the left and right arms and legs. The left pedal and handle move vertically downward while the right move upward, and then alternate cyclically. This action simulates the motions of climbing a ladder.

The Versa-Climber has been endorsed and is routinely used by many professional athletes, teams, celebrities, and fitness experts. A partial list of well-known people who either own or have used the Versa-Climber includes Ivan Lendl, John McEnroe, Martina Navratilova, Madonna, Don Johnson, Sylvester Stallone, and former President and First Lady Ronald and Nancy Reagan.

HRI sells the Versa-Climber primarily in California, through a network of manufacturer's representatives and dealers who sell to institutional buyers. HRI spends little money on advertising. However, the Versa-Climber is displayed at trade shows and conventions.

The institutional Versa-Climber sells in the price range of $1,995 to $3,450, depending on the model. The 108H Versa-Climber for home use would be priced at $1,295. The price level was set after interviews with prospective buyers and a design and manufacturing cost analysis, which indicated that certain features could be eliminated for home use. The variable production cost per machine was estimated to be $430.

THE HOME-FITNESS MARKET

The home-fitness market is composed of weight-lifting equipment, exercise bicycles, rowers, treadmills, and cross-country skiing simulators. While estimates vary, it is believed that present retail sales of these products exceed $1.4 billion. The average annual sales dollar growth is 16 percent.

Exercise bicycles are the most popular home-fitness product, with 3.1 million units sold annually. Weight-lifting equipment is the second-most popular product category, with 1.8 million units sold each year.

Home-fitness products are sold through sporting goods stores, catalogs, and direct marketing, including television, magazines, and direct mail. The home-fitness product buyer is typically between the ages of 30 and 50 and has an annual income over $60,000. The buyer usually owns two or more types of home-fitness equipment and engages in athletic activities outside the home. Industry research indicates that buyers prefer equipment that is easy and fun to use and provides the benefits promised when used properly. This research also indicated the exercise equipment purchased for home use was first used at a health club or similar facility and that buyers preferred to operate the equipment before making a purchase.

MARKETING OPTIONS FOR THE 108H VERSA-CLIMBER

HRI considered two broad options for marketing the 108H Versa-Climber: (1) direct marketing and (2) marketing through retail stores. Alternative approaches within each option were also possible. However, HRI was prepared to spend no more than $300,000 annually to market the 108H Versa-Climber for home use. The manufacturer's suggested retail price to the customer would be $1,295, regardless of the option considered.

Direct Marketing Two direct-marketing approaches were identified: (1) direct-response media advertising with promotional literature to supplement inquiries, and (2) catalog houses, which assume nearly all direct-marketing functions and costs. Direct-response media advertising involved three main costs: media expenditures, brochure costs, and video costs. Because of the high cost of spot television advertising and the firm's limited resources, media expenditures would be limited to print advertising.

The direct-response strategy involved soliciting inquiries and orders through print media advertising. When inquiries were made, the company would follow up by mailing out a brochure and video and ideally making a subsequent phone call to solicit the sale. Costs associated with the direct-response channel strategy included advertising, video, brochure, telephone, and postage. The total expenditure on promotional materials sent to inquiries would be about $5.50. Shipping units individually through UPS would be $29 per unit.

Media placement costs would vary by magazine and the number of insertions. For example, a full-page color advertisement in *Men's Fitness,* a monthly magazine, would cost $4,350 for a single insertion, $22,968 for an ad run six times, and $40,428 if an ad ran in all 12 issues of a year. The advertising cost for a single full-page color insertion in *National Body & Fitness,* a monthly magazine, would be $1,700, $9,000, and $15,840 for 1, 6, and 12 insertions respectively.

Distribution through special-interest, enthusiasts', and unique product catalogs was a second approach. Some catalogs, such as *The Sharper Image,* also had showrooms where products were displayed and purchased. In placing the product in a catalog, HRI would have to design and produce the print ads, and, depending on the catalog, pay a placement fee to the catalog house per mailing or edition. These costs would be about $12,000. Catalog houses obtained a 100 percent price markup on the product and required large minimum starting inventory levels. Catalog companies stock inventory in their own warehouses, which would reduce shipping costs to bulk rates, or $15 per unit.

Retail Stores The second option involved selling through sporting goods and fitness equipment retailers. Several approaches were possible. First, HRI could sell direct to retailers, who would be recruited at trade shows and conventions. HRI believed that the sales effort, including providing service to retailers, would require at least one dedicated company salesperson. This person would be paid

$55,000 a year, including travel expenses and fringe benefits. In addition, point-of-purchase displays, brochures, and related promotional materials would cost about $12,000 per year. HRI also felt that a minimum of $50,000 should be budgeted for annual cooperative advertising allowances for retailers to promote the product in their local market. Retailers would expect a gross profit of 54 percent per unit sold. Therefore, HRI would sell the Versa-Climber to retailers at a price of $842. Shipping costs would still be $29 per unit.

A second approach involved using manufacturer's representatives rather than a company salesperson to recruit and call on retailers. Manufacturer's reps would receive a commission of 15 percent on the Versa-Climber selling price to retailers ($842) for performing the sales function. HRI would provide the same promotional support to retailers as the direct-to-retailer alternative and incur the same unit shipping expense.

A third approach considered was using athletic supply and sporting goods equipment wholesalers to stock and sell equipment to retailers. HRI would sell the Versa-Climber to these wholesalers who would then sell to retailers. Wholesalers would expect a 20 percent profit margin on each unit sold to retailers, or $168. It was believed that a half-time salesperson would be needed to work with the wholesalers and retailers. This person would also work half-time in the institutional market. The annual fixed cost of the person assigned to the home-fitness marketing program would be $27,000. The same promotional support would be provided to retailers as was planned with the two previous alternatives. In addition, sales literature for wholesalers would be prepared at an annual cost of $5,000. The shipping expense per unit would be $12, due to cost savings from bulk shipments.

QUESTIONS

1 What market-product strategy is HRI considering with the introduction of the 108H Versa-Climber to the home-fitness market?
2 What are the pros and cons of each of the five marketing options under consideration?
3 What will be HRI's contribution per unit for each 108H Versa-Climber sold for each of the five marketing options?
4 Calculate the number of units HRI must sell for each of the five marketing options to break even.
5 Which marketing option would you select? Why?

CASE 14

FIELD FURNITURE ENTERPRISES

Edward Meadows, president of Field Furniture Enterprises, met with representatives of Kelly, Astor, & Peters Advertising (KAP) and Andrew Reed, Field's vice president of marketing and sales, to discuss the company's advertising program for 1992. The KAP representatives recommended that Field Furniture increase its advertising in shelter magazines (such as *Good Housekeeping* and *Better Homes and Gardens,* which feature home improvement ideas and new ideas in home decorating) by $250,000 and maintain the expenditures for other promotional efforts at a constant level during 1992. The rationale given for the increase in advertising was that Field Furniture had low name recognition among prospective buyers of furniture and it intended to introduce new styles of living and dining room furniture. Reed, however, had a different opinion as to how Field Furniture should spend the $250,000. He thought it was necessary to (1) hire additional salespeople to call on the 30 new retail stores to be added by the company in 1992, (2) increase the funds devoted to cooperative advertising, and (3) improve the selling aids given to retail stores and salespeople.

THE COMPANY

Field Furniture is a medium-size manufacturer of medium- to high-priced living and dining room furniture. Sales in 1991 were $50 million. The company sells its furniture through 1,000 furniture specialty stores nationwide, but not all stores carry the company's entire line. This fact bothered Meadows because, in his words, "If they ain't got it, they can't sell it!" The company employs 10 full-time salespeople, who receive a $40,000 base salary annually and a small commission on sales. A company salesforce is atypical in the furniture industry, since most furniture manufacturers use selling agents or manufacturer's representatives who carry a wide assortment of noncompeting furniture lines and receive a commission on sales. "Having our own sales group is a policy my father established 30 years ago," noted Meadows, "and we've been quite successful having people who are committed to our company. Our people don't just take furniture orders. They are expected to motivate retail salespeople to sell our line, assist in setting up displays in stores, coordinate cooperative advertising plans, and give advice on a variety of matters to our retailers and their salespeople."

In 1991, Field spent $2.45 million for total promotional expenditures, excluding the salary of the vice president of marketing and sales. Promotional expenditures were categorized into four groups: (1) sales expense and administration, (2) cooperative advertising programs with retailers, (3) trade promotions, and (4) consumer advertising. Cooperative advertising allowances are usually spent on newspaper advertising in a retailer's city and are matched by the retailer's funds on a dollar-for-dollar basis. Trade promotion is directed toward retailers and takes the form of catalogs, trade magazine advertisements, booklets for consumers, and point-of-purchase materials such as displays for use in retail stores. Also included in this category is the expense of trade shows. Field Furniture is represented at two trade shows a year. Consumer advertising is directed to potential consumers through shelter magazines. The typical format used in consumer advertising is to highlight new furniture and different living and dining room arrangements. Dollar allocation for each program in 1991 was as follows:

PROMOTIONAL PROGRAM	EXPENDITURE
Sales expense and administration	$ 612,500
Cooperative advertising	1,102,500
Trade advertising	306,250
Consumer advertising	428,750
TOTAL	$2,450,000

THE INDUSTRY

The household wooden furniture industry is composed of over 5,000 firms. Industry sales at manufacturers' prices were $10 billion. California, North Carolina, Virginia, New York, Tennessee, Pennsylvania, Illinois, and Indiana are the major U.S. furniture-producing areas. Although Ethan Allen, Bassett, Henredon, and Kroehler are the major furniture manufacturers, no one firm captured over 3 percent of the total household wooden furniture market.

The buying and selling of furniture to retail outlets centers around manufacturers' expositions at selected times and places around the country. At these marts, as they are called in the furniture industry, retail buyers view manufacturers' lines and often make buying commitments for their stores. However, Field's experience has shown that sales efforts in the retail store by company representatives account for as much as half the company's sales in a given year. The major manufacturer expositions are held in High Point, North Carolina, in October and April. Regional expositions are also scheduled in June through August in locations such as Dallas, Los Angeles, New York, and Boston.

Company research on consumer furniture-buying behavior indicated that people visit several stores when shopping for furniture and the final decision is made jointly by a husband and wife in about 90 percent of furniture purchases. Other noteworthy findings are:

- Eighty-four percent of buyers believe "the higher the price, the higher the quality" when buying home furnishings.
- Seventy-two percent of buyers browse or window shop in furniture stores even if they don't need furniture.
- Eighty-five percent read furniture ads before they actually need furniture.
- Ninety-nine percent agreed with the statement, "When shopping for furniture and home furnishings, I like the salesperson to show me what alternatives are available, answer my questions, and let me alone so I can think about it and maybe browse around."
- Ninety-five percent get redecorating ideas from shelter magazines.
- Forty-one percent have written off for a manufacturer's booklet.
- Sixty-three percent feel they need decorating advice for "putting it all together."

BUDGETARY ISSUES

After the KAP Advertising representatives made their presentation, Reed again emphasized that the incremental $250,000 should not be spent for consumer advertising. He noted that Field Furniture had set as an objective that each salesperson would make six calls per year at each store and spend at least four hours at each store on every call. "Given that our salespeople work a 40-hour week, 48 weeks per year, and devote only 80 percent of their time to selling due to travel time between stores, we already aren't doing the sales job," Reed added. Meadows agreed but reminded Reed that the $250,000 increment in the promotional budget was a maximum the company could spend, given other cost increases.

QUESTIONS

1 How might you describe furniture buying using the purchase decision process described in Chapter 5?
2 How might each of the elements of the promotional program influence each stage in the purchase decision process?
3 What should Field's promotional objectives be?
4 How many salespeople does Field need to adequately service its accounts?
5 Should Field Furniture emphasize a push or pull promotional strategy? Why?

CASE 15

WILKINSON SWORD USA★

Norman R. Proulx, president, and Ronald E. Mineo, vice president of sales for Wilkinson Sword USA, were faced with a decision of strategic importance. They had to decide whether or not Wilkinson Sword USA should establish its own salesforce or continue to use manufacturer's representatives, brokers, and/or the salesforces of other companies to represent the Wilkinson Sword's line of razors and blades. If they decided to form a dedicated salesforce for Wilkinson Sword USA, they would reverse a policy that had existed for 30 years, dating back to the creation of the U.S. arm of the London-based Wilkinson Sword Ltd.

WET-SHAVE MARKET

The shaving market broadly divides into two segments: (1) the dry-shave (electric) market, and (2) the wet-shave (razor) market. The wet-shave market accounts for the majority of sales volume. The wet-shave market for razors and blades is variously estimated at $450 million to $500 million at manufacturer's

★Sources: Based on "Wilkinson Sword Limited (A) and (B)" in T. J. McNichols, *Policy-Making and Executive Action,* 5th ed. (New York: McGraw-Hill, 1977); R. Skolnik, "The Birth of a Sales Force," *Sales & Marketing Management* (March 10, 1986), pp. 42–44; Donald B. Thompson, "Can Close Shaves Cut Off Slump for Allegheny Unit?" *Industry Week* (September 16, 1985), p. 24; "Gillette: When Being No. 1 Just Isn't Enough," *Business Week* (August 13, 1984), pp. 126, 131; "100 Leaders Advertising as a Percent of Sales," *Advertising Age* (September 8, 1983), p. 166; "Daisy (A): The Women's Shaving Marketing," HBS #9-582-152; Allegheny International 10-K Reports; and Kevin Higgins, "Japanese Buyout Fuels Scripto's Campaign for Dominance in Lighter, Writing Instrument Markets," *Marketing News* (February 15, 1985), pp. 1, 15.

prices. The Gillette Company is the worldwide leader in the production and marketing of razors and blades. Furthermore, it is estimated that six out of ten American men and women who shave use Gillette products.

Four other companies are major competitors in the wet-shave market. They are Schick, American Safety Razor, Wilkinson Sword, and BIC, which is the leader in the disposable razor segment. These four competitors, coupled with private (store) brand sales, capture 40 percent of the wet-shave market.

Razors and blades are sold primarily through supermarkets, drugstores, and mass (discount) merchandisers. Although the dollar volume sold through each type of retail outlet varies over time, it is estimated that supermarkets account for 45 percent of sales, drugstores account for 30 percent of sales, and mass merchandisers account for 25 percent of sales of razors and blades. Catalogs and department stores also account for a small percentage of razor and blade sales in any given year.

Advertising and consumer promotions play an important role in the marketing of razors and blades. For example, Gillette spends over $200 millon for advertising. While this amount was for all company products, since razor and blade sales account for almost 80 percent of Gillette total sales, a sizeable percentage was presumably earmarked for these products. Consumer promotions typically take the form of premium offers, coupons, cents-off deals, and on-package premiums such as a free razor with a cartridge of blades.

Similarly, personal selling is important in the marketing of razors and blades. Salespeople typically call on retail buyers responsible for purchasing items for the health and beauty aid sections of supermarket, drug, and mass merchandise stores. Their job is to introduce new products and special promotions and generally work with buyers to gain shelf space and display, including advertising. In addition, some firms, like Gillette, also employ retail merchandisers who make sure store displays are adequately stocked. How the selling function is performed differs among firms. For example, Gillette, American Safety Razor, BIC, and Schick have their own salesforces; Wilkinson Sword has relied upon manufacturer's agents, brokers, and salesforces of other companies.

THE COMPANY

The Wilkinson Sword Company, Limited, traces its origins to 1772. At that time, the company was a major producer of guns and bayonets. In 1820, the company began manufacturing swords. At the close of the 19th century, Wilkinson Sword production of cavalry swords was between 30,000 and 60,000 annually.

The company produced its first straight-edged razor in 1890 and the first safety razor in 1898. In 1956, Wilkinson Sword introduced its first stainless steel razor blade. Then, in 1961, the company introduced its Teflon-coated Wilkinson Sword Blade. Consumer response to this innovation was phenomenal. The company's market share in Great Britain increased from 20 percent in 1962 to 45 percent in 1966. During the same period in the United States, Wilkinson Sword's market share increased from 2 to 3 percent to 15 percent.

Wilkinson Sword's competitive position in the United States during the late 1960s and 1970s was continually buffeted by product innovation and aggressive marketing efforts by Gillette, American Safety Razor, Schick, and BIC.

Nevertheless, Wilkinson's market share in the United States remained at a respectable percentage. However, by the 1980s, Wilkinson Sword's market share had fallen to 0.7 percent. Three factors contributed to this decline. First, Wilkinson Sword elected to stop advertising in the United States and focus promotional efforts on European markets. Second, product innovation had not kept pace with U.S.-based competitors. A third factor was the lack of a company salesforce. In the late 1960s and early 1970s, Wilkinson Sword's product line was sold by the Colgate-Palmolive salesforce, a large Fortune 500 manufacturer and marketer of personal care products. Wilkinson Sword parted with Colgate-Palmolive in the mid-1970s. In its place, Wilkinson Sword used manufacturer's agents to call on and service drugstores and brokers for supermarkets.

In the 1980s, Wilkinson Sword was acquired by Allegheny International Holdings, Inc., a wholly-owned subsidiary of Allegheny International, a Pittsburgh, Pennsylvania-based conglomerate. Allegheny International also owned or had major equity positions in such well-known consumer products firms as Scripto, Inc., and Sunbeam Appliance Company. Scripto, Inc., was engaged in the production and marketing of writing instruments and components and the marketing of disposable lighters. Sunbeam Appliance Company manufactured and marketed a broad line of portable electric products. Sunbeam Personal Products Company manufactured and marketed a wide line of products including hair dryers, curling irons, and electric razors, among other items.

In the 1980s, Wilkinson Sword's sales, marketing, and administrative functions in the United States were integrated into Scripto, Inc. This action, however, failed to arrest the decline in Wilkinson Sword's market share in the United States. Then, Allegheny International sold Scripto, Inc., to Tokai Seiki Company, Ltd., a Japanese lighter manufacturer. This action left Wilkinson Sword without the sales, marketing, and administrative support it had benefited from with Scripto, Inc.

At the time of the Scripto, Inc., acquisition by Tokai Seiki Company, Ltd., Norman R. Proulx was vice president and general manager of Scripto, Inc. When it became apparent that he was not going to stay with Scripto, Inc., top management at Allegheny International offered him the presidency of Wilkinson Sword USA. He accepted and offered Ronald E. Mineo, vice president of Sales for Scripto, Inc., the same position at Wilkinson Sword USA.

SALESFORCE DECISION

One of the major issues facing Proulx and Mineo was whether or not Wilkinson Sword should change its sales program in the United States. Wilkinson Sword had relied upon manufacturer's agents, brokers, or the salesforces of other companies to represent its product line in the United States for 30 years. To recruit, train, organize, and manage its own salesforce would be a major undertaking. Furthermore, the decision had a time dimension to it. The Scripto, Inc., salesforce would continue to represent Wilkinson Sword for two months following the acquisition, for a fee. After that, Wilkinson Sword USA would assume the responsibility for its own sales and marketing functions.

If Proulx and Mineo decided to create a Wilkinson Sword USA salesforce, then a sales plan would be necessary. This plan would include the policies and procedures for staffing, training, organizing, and managing a salesforce. The first step in the process would involve account identification. Mineo identified 25 key accounts from among the supermarkets, drug stores, and mass merchandisers that carried razors and blades. In addition, 400 other accounts were identified. The 25 key accounts would be managed from its Atlanta, Georgia, headquarters. The other accounts would be handled by the salesforce, including sales managers.

The sales organization would include two key account managers to handle the 25 key accounts. Three field sales managers would be needed, or one for each of the three sales divisions: West, Central, and East. Geographical sales territories would be identified within each division.

Alternatively, Proulx and Mineo could seek out manufacturer's agents, brokers, and/or another company's salesforce to represent the Wilkinson Sword USA product line. This approach would be consistent with past policies.

QUESTIONS

1 What are the advantages and disadvantages to Wilkinson Sword USA's using agents, brokers, and/or other company salesforces to represent its product line?
2 What are the advantages and disadvantages to Wilkinson Sword USA's creating its own dedicated salesforce?
3 Given the following assumptions and information provided in the case, how many salespeople will Wilkinson Sword USA need to hire, not including the two key account managers and sales managers?
   Assumptions
   a. Average amount of selling time available per year = 1,500 hours
   b. Length of an average call = 1 hour
   c. Call frequency necessary to service a customer each year = 52 times
4 Given the following assumptions, your answer to Question 3 above, and information provided in the case, should Wilkinson Sword USA use independent agents and/or brokers, or its own salesforce? What other factors should be considered?
   Assumptions
   a. Experienced salesperson salary = $35,000
   b. Agent/broker commission on sales = 10 percent
   c. Experienced sales manager salary = $50,000
   d. Salesperson commission = 5 percent
   e. Key account manager salary = $35,000
   f. Key account manager commission on sales = 5 percent

CASE 16

MEMORIAL HOSPITAL MEDICAL EMERGENCY CLINIC

"We've been open for 11 months and have yet to break even in any one month," mulled Heather Waite as she scanned last month's revenue and expense summary for the Medical Emergency Clinic (MEC) operated by Memorial Hospital. As the administrator for MEC, Waite knew that something had to change. Even though Memorial was a nonprofit hospital, the charter for MEC stipulated that it had to be self-supporting in its second year of operation.

MEC was established to serve the health care needs of people who work in the central business district. The specific services offered by MEC included (1) preventive health care (such as physical examinations), (2) minor emergencies, (3) specialized employer services (such as preemployment examinations and workers' compensation injuries), and (4) primary health care services (for personal illnesses). A breakdown of average monthly service usage and the average charge for each service was as follows:

SERVICE	PERCENTAGE OF VISITS	AVERAGE CHARGE
Personal illness	39%	$25
Physical examinations	14	25
Workers' compensation	25	39
Employment or insurance examinations	19	47
Emergency	3	67

The weighted average charge per visit was $33.94, and the weighted average variable cost per visit was $5.67. Fixed costs per month averaged $17,500. The average number of visits per month was 590.

Since its opening, MEC had surveyed patients to find out how it might better serve their needs. Patient concerns fell into two categories: service hours and waiting time. To date, MEC had been open from 8 A.M. to 5 P.M., Monday through Friday. However, patients had requested extended hours with an opening time of 7 A.M. and a closing time at 7 P.M. A second concern was waiting time, particularly during lunch hours (11 A.M. to 2 P.M.). A check of MEC records indicated that 70 percent of patient visits occurred during this period, and most of these visits were for personal illnesses and examinations for various reasons. Further checking revealed that people actually left MEC because of congestion and did not return at a later date. Waite believed these concerns could be dealt with if MEC increased its personnel. Her plan was to add another physician and support personnel to create two staffs. One staff could work from 7 A.M. to 3 P.M., and a second staff could work from 11 A.M. to 7 P.M. By using paramedical personnel and part-time medical assistants, she estimated that average monthly fixed costs would increase by only 25 percent, even with a raise in personnel salaries next year. The staff overlap at lunchtime would alleviate some of the congestion.

Still, Waite felt that something had to be done about the uneven demand for MEC's services during operating hours. She knew that personal physical examinations and employment and insurance examinations could be handled by appointment. Moreover, these services might be provided before or after normal working hours (before 8 A.M. or after 5 P.M.). Her interviews with employers and insurance companies revealed that they would schedule employment and insurance examinations during this period. Based on her interviews, she estimated that MEC could significantly modify its visit mix and number of patients in an average month. Specifically, she believed MEC would have an average of 749 patient visits per month if the hours were expanded. Almost all the additional visits would be for employment and insurance examinations. In addition,

Waite had received approval to increase the prices of MEC's major services. The new prices, which would become effective at the beginning of the second year of operation, and the forecast mix of patient visits were as follows:

SERVICE	PERCENTAGE OF VISITS	AVERAGE CHARGE
Personal illness	31%	$27
Physical examinations	11	37
Workers' compensation	20	41
Employment or insurance examinations	36	50
Emergency	2	70

Waite believed that the average variable cost per patient visit would be $6 next year, regardless of the mix of patient visits.

As she prepared her recommendation to the Memorial Hospital administrator, she identified at least two options to enable MEC to break even. She could simply institute the price increase, or she could increase prices and expand hours and incur higher fixed costs. Whatever she recommended, she knew she would have to support her argument from both a profit and service perspective.

QUESTIONS

1 How many visits below the break-even point is MEC at the present time?
2 Can MEC break even when the price increases are put into effect, assuming fixed costs remain unchanged, the visit mix is the same, but variable costs become $6 per visit?
3 Can MEC expand its hours, thereby increasing fixed cost, and break even given a price increase, the increased variable cost per visit, and the new patient visit mix expected by Waite?

CASE 17

INTERNATIONAL PLAYTEX, INC.*

Will a single advertising campaign work in 12 separate countries? Executives at International Playtex, Inc., believe it will, at least for the Playtex WOW-brand brassiere.

International Playtex, Inc., is one of the world's largest manufacturers of women's intimate apparel and personal care products. Company sales were $1.2 billion, of which intimate apparel accounted for $375 million. It is estimated that the company captures between 16 and 17 percent of the brassiere segment of the

*Sources: Based on "Maintaining Modesty in Bra Commercials Is a Snap," *Ad Week* (May 4, 1987), p. 23; "Playtex Kicks Off a One-Ad-Fits-All Campaign," *Business Week* (December 16, 1985), pp. 48–49; and Pat Sloan, "Smilow Moves to Keep Playtex in Top Position," *Advertising Age* (March 30, 1987), pp. 3ff.

intimate apparel–undergarment category of women's clothing. Fully one half of the company's sales of intimate apparel came from overseas markets.

Playtex is the leading advertiser of brassieres in the world. It accounts for 40 percent of the total media expenditures spent in the brassiere segment of the intimate apparel–undergarment category.

Coordinating an international advertising program for Playtex is not an easy task. In the past, Playtex managers and advertising agencies developed and executed advertising campaigns for individual countries. At one point, Playtex had 43 separate and distinct advertising campaigns running throughout the world at the same time. This practice proved to be costly. Moreover, as Playtex moved to streamline its international operations, it consolidated it advertising agency roster and awarded its worldwide advertising account to Grey Advertising, Inc., one of the world's largest advertising agencies. The WOW-brand brassiere campaign would be the first global campaign assigned to Grey Advertising.

The WOW-brand was the product of three years of research and development. The brand contained a new plastic that replaced wires that were used for support and shape. This feature would become the centerpiece of the global campaign because comfort, support, and shape had universal appeal to all women, according to one Grey Advertising executive.

The first step in developing the global campaign was selecting female models with universal appeal. After viewing dozens of models, three were selected—one blonde and two brunettes. These three models would be featured in commercials shown around the world.

Campaign implementation would involve dealing with a variety of specific circumstances. First, Playtex would have to overcome language differences. For example, the WOW-brand would be called *Traumbügel* (dream wire) in German and *Alas* (wings) in Spanish. Addressing unique preferences of women would also have to be considered in presenting the brand. French women prefer lacy brassieres; American women prefer plain opaque styles. Adapting to governmental regulations and TV commercial standards in different countries would be a third hurdle. For instance, the commercial for Australia had to be produced in Australia since Australian TV would show only locally produced commercials. In South Africa, TV standards precluded women from modeling bras; therefore fully clothed models would have to simply hold the item. Production constraints would be present as well. Again as a result of country differences, some commercials could be 30 seconds while others would be limited to 20 seconds. In addition, some countries required one second of no sound at the beginning of a commercial while others did not.

QUESTIONS

1 Where would you place the WOW-brand marketing strategy on a continuum from a pure globalization approach to a pure customized approach? Why?
2 Which environmental factors described in Chapter 22 would help or hinder a global marketing strategy for women's intimate apparel like that sold by Playtex?
3 What is the likelihood for success of the WOW-brand marketing strategy? Why?

CASE 18

GENERAL MILLS, INC.

General Mills, Inc., a diversified Fortune 500 company with corporate headquarters in Minneapolis, is constantly seeking new product concepts to add to its line of consumer products. One such product concept was a fruit-flavored concentrate that could be sprayed into a glass of water to produce a fruit-flavored beverage. This product concept had emerged from a study of the beverage market indicating that tremendous potential existed for a new product entry. However, a major unresolved question was how to make the product—tentatively named Jet 24—a commercial success. The product manager in charge of Jet 24 had commissioned extensive research to address this broad question.

PRODUCT DEVELOPMENT AND MARKETING RESEARCH

Product development efforts had produced a pressurized can that would contain enough concentrate to provide 24 8-ounce drinks, or the equivalent of one case of soft drinks. The pressurization, which would squirt the concentrate, coupled with the 24-drink capability in each can led to the name Jet 24. Preliminary work on flavors indicated that five or six flavors were possible: orange, grape, cherry, lemon-lime, strawberry or raspberry, and punch. Furthermore, Jet 24 would have a "light carbonated" feel in the mouth even though no carbonation was added.

Marketing research on the product concept had focused on the inherent characteristics of Jet 24 and its position in the marketplace. Several different studies were conducted. In one study focus group interviews were held with female heads of households and their children in New Orleans. The results of this study were summarized by the researcher as follows:

- Jet 24 is perceived first as a kid's drink, but also secondarily as a drink for the whole family because of its excellent quality.
- After mixing their drinks and before tasting, about half the respondents said they would buy Jet 24 and half would not. Those who had said they would buy the product were even more favorably disposed toward Jet 24 after tasting the product than before tasting it.
- Jet 24 appears to be perceived as a high-grade Kool-Aid for day-to-day use, especially in the summer, rather than as a soft drink.
- Consumers believe the can may cause problems because it may clog up, kids may make a mess with it, and parents won't know how much is left.
- The present flavors of Jet 24 concentrate taste excellent with little aftertaste. Further taste testing will be required to optimize the quality of the drinks.
- Consumers recognize that the drink produced from the Jet 24 concentrate feels slightly carbonated.
- The need for a vitamin C additive in fruit-based drinks, and thus in Jet 24, is recognized by all consumers.
- Users, especially children, enjoy squirting Jet 24 into a glass of water.

- Although 24 servings for 69 cents is considered a fair price, there is some doubt about whether the can would actually produce 24 servings.
- The possible use of Jet 24 for Popsicles, ice cream toppings, and other cooking needs should be pursued.

In a second study, four focus group interviews were held with female heads of households with at least one child between 3 and 14 years of age. This study's findings reported by the researchers were:

- Two groups had negative reaction to Jet 24, and two groups offered a positive response. The latter two said they would buy it for their children as a special treat, but not necessarily as a regular item.
- The operation of the can was a mildly pleasant surprise to the respondents. It had a "fun element" for many. However, continued use indicated that Jet 24 was a children's product, one that would likely be bought only with children in mind.
- With initial trial of this product, there would be tremendous variations in the amount of concentrate used, use of ice, and the need to stir. The wide range of colors in the final beverage indicates that consumers will be drinking very different drinks, depending on concentrate usage.
- From the interviews, three distinct categories of beverages are evident: juices, carbonated pops, and Kool-Aid. Jet 24 falls into the Kool-Aid category. In comparison to Kool-Aid, Jet 24 wins on two points—more fun to use and a tastier drink—and loses on three points—expense (24 servings is not believed), lack of food value, and messiness.
- The addition of vitamin C is almost expected today in a fruit drink. If the product is a fruit drink, it should have nutritive value; if it's a pop, this isn't expected.
- There are two areas of concern regarding the concept of Jet 24.
    a. The emphasis on the "presweetened" nature of Jet 24 produced an image of "aftertaste" and "too sweet." A large percentage of people who drink diet pop are drinking it in spite of this image, however. The term *presweetened* certainly grabs many women today because of its low-calorie implications, but simultaneously it tends to raise questions about flavor and also about "stickiness," which is a bad word in connection with any fruity beverage.
    b. The claim of 24 servings arouses skepticism.

A third study involving in-home tests under actual usage conditions indicated that Jet 24 was favored over Kool-Aid for orange, grape, and lemon-lime flavors. However, the punch flavor did not compare favorably with Hawaiian Punch. Jet 24 lost on features such as taste, color, and aftertaste. This research also revealed that most consumers (60 percent) thought Jet 24 was most similar to carbonated soft drinks, while 21 percent said it was more like a fruit drink and 19 percent thought it was like a powdered (Kool-Aid) drink.

At about this time research was also under way to determine the potential sales volume for Jet 24. According to an independent research firm retained by General Mills, the pattern of acceptance for similar products indicated that 15 percent to 20 percent of the 58 million households with children in the United

States would try the product at least once. Of those households that tried the product, 25 percent to 40 percent would make a repeat purchase. The firm estimated the average consumption of each trier to be one can and additional sales for each repeat buyer household to be three cans. The trial rate would depend, in part, on amount of funds devoted to advertising and quality of the advertising copy.

INTRODUCTORY PROGRAM CONSIDERATIONS

The Jet 24 product manager was also considering how the product would be introduced. Discussions with the firm's advertising agency had resulted in two options. One option was that advertising for Jet 24 would focus on children and feature commercials on Saturday morning cartoon shows and advertisements in Sunday comic strips. This annual expenditure level was $3,855,000. A second option was to focus on the family, including adults, and feature TV commercials during prime-time evening hours. The annual expenditure level for this option was $7,862,000. In addition, coupons applied to the purchase of Jet 24 would be inserted into "Big G" cereals and in Sunday comic strips under both options.

Distribution would be through over 50,000 food stores where General Mills had well-established working relationships. The company would sell Jet 24 to supermarkets for $12 per case of 24 cans, or 50 cents per can. Consumers would pay 69 cents per can, or 2.9 cents per 8-ounce drink. This figure for an 8-ounce serving was slightly lower than the price of powdered drinks and significantly lower than the price of soft drinks and fruit drinks.

Since General Mills had contracted with another firm to produce the cans and the concentrate, the company would have no investment in equipment. The cost of a case of Jet 24 provided a gross profit of $4.75 per case to General Mills. Other estimated variable costs were 25 cents per case.

QUESTIONS

1 How would you describe the roles of mothers and children in a purchase of this type?
2 Should Jet 24 be positioned as a powdered (Kool-Aid), carbonated, or fruit drink? Why?
3 How would you describe Jet 24's proposed distribution intensity, new product pricing strategy, and promotional strategy given its emphasis on heavy consumer advertising?
4 What would be your forecast of revenue for Jet 24?
5 What estimate(s) of profitability is (are) possible, given the data provided?
6 Would you recommend introducing Jet 24? Why or why not?

Glossary

80/20 rule The principle that 80 percent of sales (and costs) are generated by 20 percent of the items or customers, and vice versa, thus suggesting priorities.

above-, at-, or below-market pricing Pricing based on what the market price is.

accelerated development The second stage of the retail life cycle, characterized by rapid increases in market share and profitability.

accessory equipment A type of support good that includes tools and office equipment; usually purchased in small order sizes by many buyers.

account management policies Policies that specify whom salespeople should contact, what kinds of selling and customer service activities should be engaged in, and how these activities should be carried out; in advertising agency, refers to policies used by an account executive in dealing with clients.

action item list An aid to implementing a market plan, consisting of three columns: (1) the task, (2) the name of the person responsible for completing the task, and (3) the date by which the task is to be finished.

adaptive selling A need-satisfaction sales presentation involving adjusting the presentation to fit the selling situation.

advertising Any paid form of nonpersonal communication about an organization, good, service, or idea by an identified sponsor.

advocacy advertisements Institutional advertisements that state the position of a company on an issue.

all you can afford budgeting Allocating funds to advertising only after all other budget items are covered.

alternatives The factors over which the decision maker has control.

anchor stores Well-known national or regional stores that are located in regional shopping centers.

annual marketing plans Plans that deal with the marketing goals and strategies for a product, product line, or entire firm for a single year.

approach stage In the personal selling process, the initial meeting between the salesperson and prospect where the objectives are to gain the prospect's attention, stimulate interest, and build the foundation for the sales presentation.

aseptic packaging Germfree packaging which allows products to be sealed in paper containers and stored for extended periods of time without refrigeration.

assumptions Conjectures about factors or situations that simplify the problem enough to allow it to be solved within the existing constraints.

atmosphere A store's ambiance or setting.

attitudes Learned predispositions to respond to an object or class of objects in a consistent manner.

average revenue The average amount of money received for selling one unit of a product.

baby boomers The generation of children born between 1946 and 1964.

bait-and-switch advertising An advertising practice in which a company shows a product that it has no intention of selling to lure the customer into the store and sell him a higher-priced item.

balance of trade The difference between the monetary value of a nation's exports and imports.

barriers to entry Business practices or conditions that make it difficult for a new firm to enter the market.

barter The practice of exchanging goods and services for other goods and services rather than for money.

basing-point pricing Selecting one or more geographic locations (basing point) from which the list price for products plus freight expenses are charged to buyers.

beliefs A consumer's subjective perception of how well a product or brand performs on different attributes; these are based on personal experience, advertising, and discussions with other people.

bidder's list A list of firms believed to be qualified to supply a given item.

blended family Two families from prior marriages merged into a single household as spouses remarry.

blocked currency Currency that a government will not allow to be converted into other currencies.

boycott In international trade, the refusal by the government of one country to have dealings with another country, often to express disapproval for past actions.

brand equity The added value a given brand name provides a product.

brand extension A strategy of applying the same brand name to related product categories.

brand loyalty A favorable attitude toward and consistent purchase of a single brand over time.

brand manager (see product manager)

brand name Any word or device (design, shape, sound, or color) that is used to distinguish one company's products from a competitor's.

branding Activity in which an organization uses a name, phrase, design, or symbol, or a combination of these, to identify its products and distinguish them from those of a competitor.

breadth of product line The relative variety of different items a store, wholesaler, or manufacturer carries.

break-even analysis An analysis of the relationship between total revenue and total cost to determine profitability at various levels of output.

break-even chart A graphic presentation of a break-even analysis.

break-even point (BEP) Quantity at which total revenue and total cost are equal and beyond which profit occurs.

bribery The practice of giving or promising something of value in return for a corrupt act.

brokers Channel intermediaries that do not take title to merchandise and make their profits from commissions and fees by negotiating contracts or deals between buyers and sellers.

buildup forecast Summing the sales forecasts of each of the components to arrive at a total forecast.

bundle pricing The marketing of two or more products in a single "package" price.

business (see mission)

business analysis Involves specifying the features of the product and the marketing strategy needed to commercialize it and making necessary financial projections.

business analysis stage Step 4 of the new product process which involves specifying the product features and marketing strategy and making necessary financial projections to commercialize a product.

business culture Comprises the effective rules of the game, the boundaries between competitive and unethical behavior, and the codes of conduct in business dealings.

business firm A privately owned organization that serves its customers in order to earn a profit.

business portfolio analysis Analysis of a firm's strategic business units (SBUs) as though they were a collection of separate investments.

buy classes Groups of three specific buying situations organizations face: new buy, straight rebuy, and modified rebuy.

buyer turnover The frequency with which new buyers enter the market to buy a product.

buying center The group of persons within an organization who participate in the buying process and share common goals, risks, and knowledge important to that process.

buying criteria The factors buying organizations use when evaluating a potential supplier and what it wants to sell.

capacity management Managing the demand for a service so that it is available to consumers.

case allowance A trade-oriented sales promotion in which retailers receive a discount on each case ordered during a specific time period.

cash and carry wholesaler A limited-service merchant wholesaler that takes title to merchandise but sells only to buyers who call on it and pay cash for and transport their own merchandise.

category killers Specialty discount outlets which focus on one product category (large selection–narrow range) such as electronics or business supplies.

cause-related marketing Tying the charitable contributions of a firm directly to the customer revenues produced through the promotion of one of its products.

caveat emptor A Latin term that means "let the buyer beware."

cease and desist order An action by the Federal Trade Commission (FTC) ordering a company to stop practices it considers unfair.

cells Boxes in a table or cross tabulation.

central business district The oldest retail setting; the community's downtown area.

channel captain A marketing channel member that coordinates, directs, and supports other channel members; may be a manufacturer, wholesaler, or retailer.

Clayton Act (1914) A law that forbids certain actions that lessen competition, like tie-in sales, exclusive dealing arrangements, and acquisitions whose effect might be to lessen competition or help create a monopoly.

closed-end question (see fixed alternative question)

closing stage The stage in the personal selling process that involves getting a purchase commitment from a prospect.

code of ethics A formal statement of ethical principles and rules of conduct.

cognitive dissonance The feeling of postpurchase psychological tension or anxiety a consumer often experiences.

combination compensation plan A compensation plan whereby a salesperson is paid a specified salary plus a commission based on sales or profit.

commercialization The final phase of the new product process in which the product is positioned and launched into full-scale production and sale.

communication The sharing of meaning. Five elements—source, message, receiver, and the process of encoding and decoding—are required for communication to occur.

community shopping center A retail site location that typically has one primary store and a relatively large number of smaller outlets and serves a population base of about 100,000.

company forecast (see sales forecast)

comparative advertisements Advertisements that show one brand's strengths relative to those of competitors.

competition The set of alternative firms that could provide a product to satisfy a specific market's needs.

competitive advertisements Advertisements that promote a specific brand's features and benefits.

competitive institutional advertising Institutional advertising that promotes the advantages of one product class over another and are used in markets where different product classes compete for the same buyer.

competitive parity budgeting Matching the competitors' absolute level of spending or the proportion per point of market share.

computer–assisted retailing A retailing method whereby customers order products over computer linkups from their home after viewing items on the TV or on their computer monitor.

concept tests External evaluations of a product idea that consist of preliminary testing of the new product idea (rather than the actual product) with consumers.

conference selling A form of team selling where a salesperson and other company resource people meet with buyers to discuss problems and opportunities.

consolidated metropolitan statistical area (CMSA) The largest designation in terms of geographical area and market size, made up of several primary metropolitan statistical areas (PMSAs).

constraints The restrictions, such as time and money, placed on potential solutions by the nature and importance of the problem.

consultative selling A need-satisfaction sales presentation where the salesperson focuses on problem definition and serves as an expert on problem recognition.

consumer behavior Actions of a person to purchase and use products and services, including the mental and social processes that precede and follow these actions.

Consumer Bill of Rights The rights of consumers in the exchange process including the right to safety, to be informed, to choose, and to be heard.

consumer goods Products purchased by the ultimate consumer.

Consumer Product Safety Act (1972) A law that established the Consumer Product Safety Commission to monitor product safety and establish uniform product safety standards.

consumer socialization The process by which people acquire the skills, knowledge, and attitudes necessary to function as consumers.

consumer-oriented sales promotion Sales tools used to support a company's advertising and personal selling efforts directed to ultimate consumers; examples include coupons, sweepstakes, and trading stamps.

consumerism A movement to increase the influence, power, and rights of consumers in dealing with institutions.

contest A sales promotion in which consumers apply their analytical or creative thinking to win a prize.

continuous innovations New products that require no new learning to use.

contracting A strategy used during the decline stage of the product life cycle in which a company contracts the manufacturing or marketing of a product to another firm.

contractual vertical marketing system A channel arrangement whereby independent production and distribution firms integrate their efforts on a contractual basis to obtain greater economies and marketing impact.

contribution margin analysis A form of profitability analysis that monitors controllable costs and indicates the contribution to profit of specific marketing factors.

control group A group not exposed to the experimental variable in an experiment.

controlled distribution minimarkets Test markets run in smaller test areas that electronically monitor product purchases at checkout counters for more careful testing at reduced costs.

convenience goods Items that the consumer purchases frequently and with a minimum of shopping effort.

cooperative advertising Advertising programs in which a manufacturer pays a percentage of the retailer's local advertising expense for advertising the manufacturer's products.

corporate chain A type of retail ownership in which a single firm owns multiple outlets.

corporate culture The shared values, beliefs, and purpose of employees that affect individual and group behavior.

corporate takeover The purchase of a firm by outsiders.

corporate vertical marketing system A channel arrangement whereby successive stages of production and distribution are combined under a single owner.

corrective advertising FTC action requiring a company to spend money on advertising to correct prior misleading ads.

cost of goods sold Total value of the products sold during a specified time period.

cost per thousand (CPM) The cost of reaching 1,000 individuals or households with an advertising message in a given medium. (M is the Roman numeral for 1,000.)

cost plus fixed-fee pricing A pricing method where a supplier is reimbursed for all costs, regardless of what they may be, plus a fixed percentage of the production or construction costs.

cost plus percentage-of-cost pricing Settling the price of a product or service by adding a fixed percentage to the production or construction costs.

countertrade Using barter rather than money in making international sales.

coupons Sales promotions that usually offer a discounted price to consumers.

cross tabulation Method of presenting and relating data on two or more variables to display summary data and discover relationships in the data.

cue A stimulus or symbol perceived by the consumer.

culture The sets of values, ideas, and attitudes of a homogeneous group of people that are transmitted from one generation to the next.

cumulative quantity discounts The discount given to a buyer based on the accumulation of purchases of a product over a given time period, typically a year.

customary pricing A method of pricing based on a product's tradition, standardized channel of distribution, or other competitive factors.

customer contact audit A flow chart of the points of interaction between a consumer and a service provider.

customer service The ability of a logistics system to satisfy users in terms of time, dependability, communications, and convenience.

customized approach An international marketing strategy which assumes that the way the product is used and the needs it satisfies are unique to each country.

customs Norms and expectations about the way people do things in a specific country.

data The facts and figures pertinent to the problem, composed of primary and secondary data.

data base marketing (see micromarketing)

deal A sales promotion that offers a short-term price reduction.

deceptive pricing A practice by which prices are artificially inflated and then marked down under the guise of a sale.

decision A conscious choice from among two or more alternatives.

decision factors The different sets of variables—the alternatives and uncertainties—that combine to give the outcome of a decision.

decision making The act of consciously choosing from alternatives.

decision-making unit (DMU) The people in a household or an organization's buying center who are involved in the decision to buy a product.

decline stage The fourth and last stage of the product life cycle when sales and profitability decline.

decoding The process of having the receiver take a set of symbols, the message, and transform them back to an abstract idea.

deletion A strategy of dropping a product from the product line, usually in the decline stage of the product life cycle.

delivered pricing A pricing method where the price the seller quotes include all transportation costs.

Delphi forecast Polling people knowledgeable about the forecast topic to obtain a sequence of anonymous estimates.

demand curve The summation of points representing the maximum quantity of a product consumers will buy at different price levels.

demand factors Factors that determine the strength of consumers' willingness and ability to pay for goods and services.

demand-backward pricing Setting a price by estimating the price consumers would be willing to pay for goods and services.

demographics Distribution of a population on selected characteristics such as where people live, their numbers, and who they are in terms of age, sex, income, or occupation.

dependent variables The change in the behavior of what is studied.

depth of product line The assortment of each item a store, wholesaler, or retailer carries.

derived demand Sales of a product (typically industrial) which result from the sales of another item (often consumer).

desk jobber (see drop shipper)

development Phase of the new product process in which the idea on paper is turned into a prototype; includes manufacturing and laboratory and consumer tests.

dichotomous question A fixed alternative question that allows only a "yes" or "no" response.

differentiation positioning Positioning a product in a smaller market niche that is less competitive.

diffusion of innovation The process by which people receive new information and accept new ideas and products.

direct channel A marketing channel where a producer and ultimate consumer interact directly with each other.

direct exporting A firm selling its domestically-produced goods in a foreign country without intermediaries.

direct forecast An estimate of the value to be forecast without the use of intervening steps.

direct marketing Selling products by having consumers interact with various advertising media without a face-to-face meeting with a salesperson.

direct ownership In international trade, a domestic firm actually investing in and owning a foreign subsidiary or division.

discontinuous innovations New products that require totally new consumption patterns.

discounts Reductions from list price that a seller gives a buyer as a reward for some buyer activity favorable to the seller.

discretionary income The money that remains after taxes and necessities have been paid for.

disposable income The money a consumer has left after taxes to use for food, shelter, and clothing.

distinctive competency An organization's principal competitive strengths and advantages in terms of marketing, technological, and financial resources.

distribution center Warehouses that emphasize speed and efficient product flow to hold goods for short periods of time and move them out as soon as possible.

diversification A strategy of developing new products and selling them in new markets.

drive A stimulus that moves an individual to action.

drop shipper A merchant wholesaler that owns the merchandise it sells but does not physically handle, stock, or deliver; also called a desk jobber.

dual distribution An arrangement by which a firm reaches buyers by employing two or more different types of channels for the same basic product.

dumping When a firm sells a product in a foreign country below its domestic price.

durable good An item that lasts over an extended number of uses.

duty Special tax on imports or exports.

dynamically continuous innovations Products that disrupt the consumer's normal routine but do not require learning totally new behaviors.

early adopters The 13.5 percent of the population who are leaders in their social setting and act as an information source on new products for other people.

early growth The first stage of the retail life cycle, when a new outlet emerges as a sharp departure from competitive forms.

early majority The 34 percent of the population who are deliberate and rely on personal sources for information on new products.

ecology The relationship of physical resources in the environment.

economic infrastructure A country's communication, transportation, financial, and distribution systems.

economy The income, expenditures, and resources that affect the cost of running a business and household.

elastic demand A situation where a percentage decrease in price produces a larger percentage increase in quantity demanded, thereby actually increasing sales revenue.

electronic data interchange (EDI) Interactive computer systems allowing the transfer of information between retailers and suppliers.

elements of the marketing mix (see marketing mix)

encoding The process of having the sender transform an abstract idea into a set of symbols.

environmental factors The uncontrollable factors involving social, economic, technological, competitive, and regulatory forces.

environmental scanning Acquiring information on events occurring outside the company and interpreting potential trends.

ethics The moral principles and values that govern the actions and decisions of an individual or group.

Eurostyle A no frills, monochrome, geometric look to product design.

evaluative criteria Both the objective and subjective attributes of a brand important to consumers when evaluating different brands or products.

evoked set The group of brands a consumer would consider acceptable out of the set of brands in the product class of which he or she is aware.

exchange The trade of things of value between buyer and seller so that each is better off after the trade.

exclusive dealing An arrangement a manufacturer makes with a reseller to handle only its products and not those of competitors.

exclusive distribution A distribution strategy whereby a producer sells its products or services in only one retail outlet in a specific geographical area.

exclusive territorial distributorship A manufacturer grants a reseller sole rights to sell a product in a specific geographic area.

expense-to-sales ratio A form of ratio analysis in which a specific cost or expense is expressed as a percentage of sales revenue.

experience curve pricing A method of pricing where price often falls following the reduction of costs associated with the firm's experience in producing or selling a product.

experiment Obtaining data by manipulating factors under tightly controlled conditions to test cause and effect.

experimental group A group exposed to the experimental variable in an experiment.

experimental independent variable The causal condition manipulated or controlled by the experimenter.

exporting Producing goods in one country and selling them in another country.

express warranties Written statements of a manufacturer's liabilities for product deficiencies.

expropriation The situation where a foreign country or its assets are take over by the host country.

external secondary data Published data from outside the firm or organization.

extraneous independent variable The causal condition that is the result of outside factors that the experimenter cannot control.

facilitators Intermediaries that assist in the physical distribution channel by moving, storing, financing, or insuring products.

fad A product whose life cycle has two stages consisting of rapid introduction and equally quick decline.

failure fees A penalty payment made to retailers by manufacturers if a new product does not reach predetermined sales levels.

Fair Packaging and Labeling Act (1966) A law that requires manufacturers to state on the package the ingredients, volume, and identity of the manufacturer.

family branding (see multiproduct branding)

family life cycle The concept that each family progresses through a number of distinct phases, each of which is associated with identifiable purchasing behaviors.

Farm Bill (1990) Legislation which sets the standards for organic foods and products which use the term "organic."

fashion product A product whose life cycle curve may decline, then return through another life cycle.

feedback The communication flow from receiver back to sender; indicates whether the message was decoded and understood as intended.

field experiment A test of marketing variables in actual store or buying settings.

field of experience A person's understanding and knowledge; to communicate effectively, a sender and a receiver must have a mutually shared field of experience.

field warehouse A specialized public warehouse that takes possession of a firm's goods and issues a receipt that can be used as collateral for a loan.

finance allowance A trade-oriented sales promotion in which retailers are paid for financing costs or financial losses associated with consumer sales promotions.

fixed alternative question A question in which the respondent merely checks an answer from predetermined choices.

fixed cost An expense of the firm that is stable and does not change with the quantity of product that is produced and sold.

flexible-price policy Offering the same product and quantities to similar customers, but at different prices.

FOB (free on board) Refers to the point at which the seller stops paying transportation costs.

FOB origin pricing A method of pricing where the title of goods passes to the buyer at the point of loading.

FOB with freight-allowed pricing A method of pricing that allows the buyer to deduct freight expenses from the list price of the product sold; also called freight absorption pricing.

focus group An informal session of six to ten current or potential users of a product in which a discussion leader seeks their opinions on the firm's or a competitor's products.

follow-up stage The phase of the personal selling process that entails making certain that the customer's purchase has been properly delivered and installed and that any difficulties in using the product are promptly and satisfactorily addressed.

Food, Drug, and Cosmetic Act (1938) A law that prevents the adulteration or misbranding of these three categories of products.

forced distribution markets (see selected controlled markets)

Foreign Corrupt Practices Act A law which makes it a crime for U.S. corporations to bribe an official of a foreign government or political party to obtain or retain business in a foreign country.

forgetting rate The speed with which buyers forget a brand if advertising is not seen.

form of ownership Who owns a retail outlet. Alternatives are independent, corporate chain, cooperative, or franchise.

form utility The value to consumers that comes from production or alteration of a good or service.

formula selling presentation The selling format that consists of providing information in an accurate, thorough, and step-by-step manner to persuade the prospect to buy.

four I's of services Four unique elements to services: intangibility, inconsistency, inseparability, and inventory.

four P's (see marketing mix)

franchising The contractual agreement between a parent company and an individual or firm that allows the franchisee to operate a certain type of business under an established name and according to specific rules.

freight consolidators (see freight forwarders)

freight forwarders Firms that accumulate small shipments into larger lots and then hire a carrier to move them, usually at reduced rates.

frequency The average number of times a person in the target audience is exposed to a message or advertisement.

FTC Act (1914) A law that established the Federal Trade Commission (FTC) to monitor deceptive or misleading advertising and unfair business practices.

full warranty A statement of liability by a manufacturer that has no limits of noncoverage.

full-service agency An advertising agency providing a complete range of services, including market research, media selection, copy development, artwork, and production.

full-service retailer A retailer that provides a complete list of services to cater to its customers.

functional groupings Organizational divisions in which a unit is subdivided according to the different business activities, such as manufacturing, marketing, and finance.

gap analysis An evaluation tool which compares expectations about a particular service to the actual experience a consumer has with the service.

general merchandise stores General merchandise stores carry a broad product line with limited depth.

general merchandise wholesaler A full-service merchant wholesaler that carries a broad assortment of merchandise and performs all channel functions.

generic brand A branding strategy which lists no product name, only a description of contents.

generic marketing strategy A strategy that can be adopted by any firm, regardless of the product or industry involved, to achieve a sustainable competitive advantage.

geographic information systems (GIS) Technology which represents different layers of data on one map.

geographical groupings Organizational divisions in which a unit is subdivided according to geographical location.

global approach An international marketing strategy which assumes that the way a product is used and the needs it satisfies are universal.

glocalization An international marketing strategy that seeks to combine the best features of both the global and customized (local) approaches by encouraging local managers to modify the global strategy, where appropriate, to the needs of customers in their country.

goal setting Setting measurable marketing objectives to be achieved.

goals (or objectives) Precise statement of results sought, quantified in time and magnitude, where possible.

government units The federal, state, and local agencies that buy goods and services for the constituents they serve.

green marketing Marketing efforts to produce, promote, and reclaim environmentally sensitive products.

gross income The total amount of money earned in one year by a person, family, or household.

gross margin Net sales minus cost of goods sold.

growth stage The second stage of the product life cycle characterized by rapid increases in sales and by the appearance of competitors.

harvesting A strategy used during the decline stage of the product life cycle in which a company continues to offer a product but reduces support costs.

head-to-head positioning Competing directly with competitors on similar product attributes in the same target market.

hierarchy of effects The sequence of stages a prospective buyer goes through from initial awareness of a product to eventual action (either trial or adoption of the product). The stages include awareness, interest, evaluation, trial, and adoption.

high learning product A product that has a long introductory phase to its life cycle because significant education is required for consumers to use the item or appreciate its benefits.

horizontal conflict Disagreements between intermediaries at the same level in a marketing channel.

horizontal price fixing The practice whereby two or more competitors explicitly or implicitly collaborate to set prices.

hypermarket A large store (over 100,000 square feet) offering a mix of food and general merchandise.

hypothesis A conjecture about the relationship of two or more factors or what might happen in the future.

hypothesis evaluation Research to test ideas generated earlier to assist in making recommendations for marketing actions.

hypothesis generation A search for a list of ideas (hypotheses) that can be evaluated in later research.

idea generation A phase of the new product process, in which a firm develops a pool of concepts as candidates for new products.

idle production capacity A situation where a service provider is available but there is no demand.

implied warranties Warranties assigning responsibility for product deficiencies to a manufacturer even though the item was sold by a retailer.

inconsistency A unique element of services; variation in service quality because services are delivered by people with varying capabilities.

independent retailer A retail outlet for which there is an individual owner.

indirect channel A marketing channel where intermediaries are situated between the producer and consumers.

indirect exporting A firm selling its domestically produced goods in a foreign country through an intermediary.

individual interviews A situation where a single researcher asks questions of one respondent.

industrial distributor A specific type of intermediary between producers and consumers that generally sells, stocks, and delivers a full product assortment.

industrial espionage The clandestine collection of trade secrets or proprietary information about a company's competitors.

industrial firm An organizational buyer that in some way reprocesses a good or service it buys before selling it again.

industrial goods Products used in the production of other items for ultimate consumers.

industry A group of firms offering products that are close substitutes for each other.

industry potential (see market potential)

inelastic demand A situation where a small percentage decrease in price produces a smaller percentage increase in quantity demanded.

information technology Involves designing and managing computer and communication systems to satisfy an organization's requirements for information processing and access.

in-house agency A company's own group of advertising people who are included on the company payroll.

innovators The 2.5 percent of the population who are venturesome, highly educated, use multiple information sources, and are the first to adopt a new product.

inseparability A unique element of services; the fact that a service cannot be separated from the deliverer of the service or the setting in which the service occurs.

installations A type of support good consisting of buildings and fixed equipment.

institutional advertisement Advertisements designed to build goodwill or an image for an organization, rather than promote a specific product or service.

intangibility A unique element of services; the fact that they cannot be held, touched, or seen before the purchase decision.

intensive distribution A distribution strategy whereby a producer sells products or services in as many outlets as possible in a geographic area.

intermodal transportation Coordinating or combining different transportation modes to get the best features of each, while minimizing the shortcomings.

internal marketing The notion that a service organization must focus on its employees, or internal market, before successful programs can be directed at customers.

internal secondary data Data that have already been collected and exist inside a business firm or organization.

international marketing Marketing across national boundaries.

intertype competition Competition between dissimilar retail outlets brought about by scrambled merchandising.

introductory phase The first stage of the product life cycle in which sales grow slowly and profit is low.

inventory (1) Physical material purchased from suppliers, which may or may not be reworked and is available for sale to customers. (2) A unique element of services; the need for and cost of having a service provider available.

involvement The personal, social, and economic significance of the purchase to the consumer.

job analysis A written description of what a salesperson is expected to do.

joint venture In international trade, an arrangement in which a foreign company and a local firm invest together to create a local business.

jury of executive opinion forecast Asking knowledgeable executives inside the firm about likely sales during a coming period.

jury test A pretest in which a panel of customers is shown an advertisement and asked rate its attractiveness, how much they like it, and how much it draws their attention.

just-in-time (JIT) concept Inventory-supply system that operates with very lean inventories to hold down costs and requires fast, on-time delivery.

laboratory experiment A simulation of marketing-related activity in a highly controlled setting.

laggards The 16 percent of the market who have fear of debt, use friends for information sources, and accept ideas and products only after they have been long established in the market.

Lanham Act (1946) A law that allows a company to register a trademark (symbol or word) for its exclusive use.

late majority The 34 percent of the population who are skeptical, below average in social status, and rely less on advertising and personal selling for information than do innovators or early adopters.

laws Society's values and standards that are enforceable in the courts.

lead time The lag from ordering an item until it is received in stock.

learning Those behaviors that results from (1) repeated experience and (2) thinking.

level of service The degree of service provided the customer by the retailer: self, limited, or full.

licensing A contractual agreement whereby a company allows another firm to use its brand name, patent, trade secret, or other property for a royalty or fee.

lifestyle A mode of living that is identified by how people spend their time and resources (activities), what they consider important in their environment (interests), and what they think of themselves and the world around them (opinions).

Likert scale A fixed alternative question in which the respondent indicates the extent to which he agrees or disagrees with a statement.

limited-coverage warranty A manufacturer's statement indicating the bounds of coverage and noncoverage for any product deficiencies.

limited-line store A retail outlet, such as a sporting goods store, that offers considerable assortment, or depth, of a related line of items.

limited-service agency An agency that specializes in one aspect of the advertising process such as providing creative services to develop the advertising copy or buying previously unpurchased media space.

limited-service retailer A retailer that provides selected services such as credit or merchandise return to customers.

line extensions New product lines (such as linens) which use an existing brand name from an unrelated product line (such as toys) so the new items are seen as adding on to an existing product line rather than being seen as a completely new product line.

line positions People in line positions, such as group marketing managers, have the authority and responsibility to issue orders to the people who report to them, such as marketing managers.

local approach (see customized approach)

logistics management Coordination of the movement and storage of raw materials, parts, and finished goods to achieve a given service level while minimizing the total cost of these activities.

long-range marketing plans A marketing plan that deals with the marketing goals and strategies for a product, product line, or entire firm for two to five years into the future.

loss-leader pricing Deliberately pricing a product below its customary price to attract attention to it.

lost-horse forecast Starting with the last known value of the item being forecast, listing the factors that could affect the forecast, assessing whether they have a positive or negative impact, and making the final forecast.

low-learning product A product that has an immediate gain in sales in the introductory phase because the benefits are easily observed by consumers and little education is required to use it.

macromarketing The study of the aggregate flow of a nation's goods and services to benefit society.

mail-order retailer A retailing operation in which merchandise is offered to customers by mail.

maintained markup The difference between the final selling price and retailer cost; also called gross margin.

major account management The practice of using team selling to focus on important customers to build mutually beneficial long-term, cooperative relationships.

make-buy decision An evaluation of whether a product or its parts will be purchased from outside suppliers or built by the firm.

management by exception A tool used by a marketing manager that involves identifying results that deviate from plans, diagnosing their causes, making appropriate new plans, and taking new actions.

management information systems Computerized methods of processing predefined transactions to produce fixed-format reports on schedule.

management support systems Computerized methods of providing managers with the ability to query and analyze information in on-line data bases.

Magnuson–Moss Warranty/FTC Improvement Act (1975) An act that regulates the content of consumer warranties and also has strengthened consumer rights with regard to warranties through class action suits.

manufacturer's agents Individuals or firms that work for several producers and carry noncompetitive, complimentary merchandise in an exclusive territory; also called manufacturer's representatives.

manufacturer's branch office A wholly owned extension of a producer that performs channel functions, including carrying inventory, generally performed by a full-service merchant wholesaler.

manufacturer branding A branding strategy in which the brand name for a product is designated by the producer, using either a multiproduct or multibranding approach.

marginal analysis Principle of allocation resources that balances incremental revenues of an action against incremental costs.

marginal cost The change in total cost that results from producing and marketing one additional unit.

marginal revenue The change in total revenue obtained by selling one additional unit.

markdown Reduction in retail price usually expressed as a percentage equal to the amount reduced, divided by the original price, and multiplied by 100.

market People with the desire and ability to buy a specific product.

market development Selling existing products to new markets.

market growth rate The annual rate of growth of the specific market or industry in which a firm or SBU is competing; often used as the vertical axis in business portfolio analysis.

market penetration A strategy of increasing sales of present products in their existing markets.

market potential Maximum total sales of a product by all firms to a segment under specified environmental conditions and marketing efforts of the firms (also called industry potential).

market segmentation Aggregating prospective buyers into groups, or segments, that (1) have common needs and (2) will respond similarly to a marketing action.

market segments The groups that result from the process of market segmentation; these groups ideally (1) have common needs and (2) will respond similarly to a marketing action.

market share The ratio of sales revenue of the firm to the total sales revenue of all firms in the industry, including the firm itself.

market testing A phase of the new product process, in which prospective consumers are exposed to actual products under realistic purchase conditions to see if they will buy.

market-product grid Framework for relating market segments to products offered or potential marketing actions by a firm.

marketing The process of planning and executing the conception, pricing, promotion, and distribution of ideas, goods, and services to create exchanges that satisfy individual and organizational objectives.

marketing audit A comprehensive, unbiased, periodic review of the strategic marketing process of a firm or a strategic business unit (SBU).

marketing channel People and firms involved in the process of making a product or service available for use or consumption by consumers or industrial users.

marketing concept The idea that an organization should (1) strive to satisfy the needs of consumers (2) while also trying to achieve the organization's goals.

marketing decision support system (MDSS) A computerized method of providing timely, accurate information to improve marketing decisions.

marketing mix The marketing manager's controllable factors of product, price, promotion, and place he or she can take to solve a marketing problem.

marketing modifications Attempts to increase product usage by creating new use situations, finding new customers, or altering the marketing mix.

marketing orientation When an organization has one or more departments (1) actively trying to understand customers' needs and the factors affecting them, (2) sharing this information across departments, and (3) using the information to meet these customer needs.

marketing plan A written statement identifying the target market, specific marketing goals, the budget, and timing for the marketing program.

marketing program A plan that integrates the marketing mix to provide a good, service, or idea to prospective consumers.

marketing research The process of defining a marketing problem and opportunity, systematically collecting and analyzing information, and recommending actions to improve an organization's marketing activities.

marketing strategy The means by which a marketing goal is to be achieved, characterized by (1) a specified target market and (2) a marketing program to reach it.

marketing tactics The detailed day-to-day operational decisions essential to the overall success of marketing strategies.

markup The amount added to the cost of goods sold to arrive at a selling price, expressed in dollar or percentage terms.

materials handling Moving goods over short distances into, within, and out of warehouses and manufacturing plants.

mature households Households headed by people over age 50.

maturity phase The third stage of the product or retail life cycle in which market share levels off and profitability declines.

measures of success Criteria or standards used in evaluating proposed solutions to the problem.

Meat Inspection Act (1906) An act that regulated that meat products be wholesome, unadulterated, and properly labeled.

mechanical observational data Data collected by electronic or other impersonal means, such as meters connected to television sets in viewers' homes.

merchandise allowance A trade-oriented sales promotion in which a retailer is reimbursed for extra in-store support or special featuring of the brand.

merchandise line The number of different types of products and the assortment a store carries.

message The information sent by a source to a receiver in the communication process.

method of operation How and where a retailer provides services; the alternative approaches are an in-store or nonstore format (mail, vending, computer-assisted, or teleshopping).

methods The approaches that can be used to solve all or part of a problem.

metropolitan statistical area (MSA) An area within (1) a city having a population of at least 50,000 or (2) an urbanized area with a population in excess of 50,000 with a total population of at least 100,000.

micromarketing How an individual organization directs its marketing activities and allocates its resources to benefit its customers. Combining demographic, media, and consumption profiles of households with buyer profiles of stores and products in order to target buyers in a neighborhood or for a specific product.

minitrain A short train that runs frequently, often used in implementing just-in-time inventory systems.

mission A statement about the type of customer an organization wishes to serve, the specific needs of these customers, and the means or technology by which it will serve these needs.

missionary salespeople Sales support personnel who do not directly solicit orders but rather concentrate on performing promotional activities and introducing new products.

mixed branding A branding strategy in which the company may market products under their own name and that of a reseller.

modified rebuy A buying situation in which the users, influencers, or deciders change the product specifications, price, delivery schedule, or supplier.

monopolistic competition A competitive setting in which a large number of sellers offer unique but substitutable products.

monopoly A competitive setting in which there is a single seller of a good or service.

moral idealism A personal moral philosophy that considers certain individual rights or duties as universal regardless of the outcome.

motivation Motivation is the energizing force that causes behavior that satisfies a need.

multibranding A manufacturer's branding strategy in which a distinct name is given to each of its products.

multinational corporation (see transnational corporation)

multiple-zone pricing Pricing products the same when delivered within one of several specified zones or geographical areas, but with different prices for each zone depending on demand, competition, and distance; also called zone-delivered pricing.

multiproduct branding A branding strategy in which a company uses one name for all products; also referred to blanket or family branding.

need That which occurs when a person feels deprived of food, clothing, or shelter.

need-satisfaction presentation A selling format that emphasizes probing and listening by the salesperson to identify needs and interests of perspective buyers.

new buy The first-time purchase of a product or service, characterized by greater potential risk.

new product concept A tentative description of a product or service a firm might offer for sale.

new product process The sequence of activities a firm uses to identify business opportunities and convert them to a saleable good or service. There are seven steps: new product strategy, idea generation, screening and evaluation, business analysis, development, testing, and commercialization.

new product strategy development The phase of the new product process in which a firm defines the role of new products in terms of overall corporate objectives.

news conference A publicity tool consisting of an informational meeting with representatives of the media who received advanced materials on the meeting content.

noise Extraneous factors that work against effective communication.

noncumulative quantity discounts Price reductions based on the size of an individual purchase order.

nondurable good An item consumed in one or a few uses.

nonprobability sampling Using arbitrary judgments to select the sample so that the chance of selecting a particular element may be unknown or zero.

nonprofit organization A nongovernmental organization that serves its customers but does not have profit as an organizational goal.

nonrepetitive decisions Those decisions unique to a particular time and situation.

objective and task budgeting A budgeting approach whereby the company (1) determines its advertising objectives, (2) outlines the tasks to accomplish these objectives, and (3) determines the advertising cost of performing these tasks.

objectives The goals the decision maker seeks to achieve in solving a problem.

observational data Facts and figures obtained by watching, either mechanically or in person, how people actually behave.

odd-even pricing Setting prices a few dollars or cents under an even number, such as $19.95.

off-peak pricing Charging different prices during different times of the day or days of the week to reflect variations in demand for the service.

off-price retailing Selling brand name merchandise at lower than regular prices.

oligopoly A competitive setting in which a few large companies control a large amount of an industry's sales.

one-price policy Setting the same price for similar customers who buy the same product and quantities under the same conditions.

one-price stores A form of off-price retailing in which all items in a store are sold at one low price.

open-end question A question that a respondent can answer in his or her own words.

opinion leaders Individuals who exert direct or indirect social influence over others.

order cycle time (see lead time)

order getter A salesperson who sells in a conventional sense and engages in identifying prospective customers, providing customers with information, persuading customers to buy, closing sales, and following on customer experience with product or service.

order taker A salesperson who processes routine orders and reorders for products that have already been sold by the company.

organization's business (mission) A statement about the type of customer an organization wishes to serve, the specific needs of these customers, and the means or technology by which it will serve these needs.

organization's goals Specific, measurable objectives the organization seeks to achieve and by which it can measure its performance.

organization's mission (see organization's business)

organizational buyers Units such as manufacturers, retailers, or government agencies that buy goods and services for their own use or for resale.

organizational buying behavior The decision-making process that organizations use to establish the need for products and identify, evaluate, and choose among alternative brands and suppliers.

organizational buying criteria The objective attributes of the supplier's products and services and the capabilities of the supplier itself.

organizational goals Specific objectives a business or nonprofit unit seeks to achieve and by which it can measure its performance.

original markup The difference between retailer cost and initial selling price.

outsourcing Contracting work that formerly was done in-house by employees such as those in marketing research, advertising, and public relations departments to small, outside firms.

Pacific Rim The area of the world consisting of countries in Asia and Australia.

packaging The container in which a product is offered for sale and on which information is communicated.

panel A sample of consumers or stores from which researchers take a series of measurements.

parallel development An approach to new product development which involves the simultaneous development of the product and production process.

patent Exclusive rights to the manufacture of a product or related technology granted to a company for 17 years.

penetration pricing Pricing a product low in order to discourage competition from entering the market.

per se illegality An action that by itself is illegal.

perceived risk The anxieties felt because the consumer cannot anticipate the outcome but sees that there might be negative consequences.

percent of sales budgeting Allocating funds to advertising as a percentage of past or anticipated sales, in terms of either dollars or units sold.

perception The process by which an individual selects, organizes, and interprets information to create a meaningful picture of the world.

perceptual map A graph displaying consumers' perceptions of product attributes across two or more dimensions.

personal selling The two-way flow of communication between a buyer and seller, often in a face-to-face encounter, designed to influence a person's or group's purchase decision.

personal selling process Sales activities occurring before and after the sale itself, consisting of six stages: (1) prospecting, (2) preapproach, (3) approach, (4) presentation, (5) close, and (6) followup.

personality A person's consistent behaviors or responses to recurring situations.

physical distribution management Organizing the flow of finished goods to the customer.

piggyback franchising A variation of franchising in which stores operated by one chain sell the products or services of another franchised firm.

pioneering advertisements Advertisements that tell what a product is, what it can do, and where it can be found.

pioneering institutional advertisements Institutional advertisements about what a company is or can do or where it is located.

place utility The value to consumers of having a good or service available where needed.

planning gap The difference between the projection of the path to reach a new goal and the projection of the path of the results of a plan already in place.

point-of-purchase displays Displays located in high-traffic areas in retail stores, often next to checkout counters.

population The universe of all people, stores, or salespeople about which researchers wish to generalize.

portfolio test A pretest in which a test ad is placed in a portfolio with other ads and consumers are questioned on their impressions of the test ad.

possession utility The value of making an item easy to purchase through the provision of credit cards or financial arrangements.

posttests Tests conducted after an advertisement has been shown to the target audience to determine whether it has accomplished its intended purpose.

power center Megasized strip malls with multiple anchor (or national) stores.

preapproach stage The stage of the personal selling process that involves obtaining further information about a prospect and deciding on the best method of approach.

predatory pricing Selling products at a low price to injure or eliminate a competitor.

premium A sales promotion that consists of offering merchandise free or at significant savings over retail.

presentation stage The core of the personal selling process in which the salesperson tries to convert the prospect into a customer by creating a desire for the product or service.

prestige pricing Setting a high price so that status-conscious consumers will be attracted to the product.

pretests Tests conducted before an advertisement is placed to determine whether it communicates the intended message or to select between alternative versions of an advertisement.

price The money or other considerations exchanged for the purchase or use of the product, idea, or service.

price discrimination The practice of charging different prices to different buyers for goods of like trade and quality; the Clayton Act as amended by the Robinson-Patman Act prohibits this action.

price elasticity of demand The percentage change in quantity demanded relative to a percentage change in price.

price fixing A conspiracy among firms to set prices for a product.

price lining Setting the price of a line of products at a number of different specific pricing points.

pricing constraints Factors that limit a firm's latitude in the price it may set.

pricing objectives Goals that specify the role of price in an organization's marketing and strategic plans.

primary data Facts and figures which are newly collected for the project.

primary demand Desire for a product class rather than for a specific brand.

primary metropolitan statistical area (PMSA) An area that is part of a larger consolidated statistical metropolitan area with a total population of 1 million or more.

prime rate The rate of interest banks charge their largest customers.

private branding When a company manufactures products that are sold under the name of a wholesaler or retailer.

proactive strategies New product strategies that involve an aggressive allocation of resources to identify opportunities for product development.

probability sampling Using precise rules to select the sample such that each element of the population has a specific known chance of being selected.

product A good, service, or idea consisting of a bundle of tangible and intangible attributes that satisfies consumers and is received in exchange for money or other unit of value.

product advertisements Advertisements that focus on selling a product or service and take three forms: (1) pioneering (or informational), (2) competitive (or persuasive), and (3) reminder.

product cannibalism A firm's new product gaining sales by stealing them from its other products.

product (program) champion A person who is able and willing to cut red tape and move a product or program forward.

product class An entire product category or industry.

product counterfeiting Low cost copies of a popular brand, not manufactured by the original producer.

product development A strategy of selling a new product to existing markets.

product differentiation A strategy having different but related meanings; it involves a firm's using different marketing mix activities, such as product featuring and advertising, to help consumers perceive the product as being different and better than other products.

product form Variations of a product within a product class.

product item A specific product noted by a unique brand, size, and price.

product life cycle The life of a product over four stages: introduction, growth, maturity, and decline.

product line A group of products closely related because they satisfy a class of needs, are used together, are sold to the same customer group, are distributed through the same outlets, or fall within a given price range.

product line groupings Organizational divisions in which a unit is subdivided according to the product offerings for which it is responsible.

product manager A person who plans, implements, and controls the annual and long-range plans for the products for which he or she is responsible.

product mix The number of product lines offered by a company.

product modifications Strategies of altering a product characteristic, such as quality, performance, or appearance.

product placement Advertising media alternative in which the manufacturers pay for the privilege of having their brand name product in a movie.

product positioning The place an offering occupies in a consumer's mind with regard to important attributes relative to competitive offerings.

product repositioning Changing the place an offering occupies in a consumer's mind relative to competitive products.

production goods Products used in the manufacturing of other items that become part of the final product.

profit A business firm's reward for the risk it undertakes in offering a product for sale; the money left over after a firm's total expenses are subtracted from its total revenues.

profit equation Profit = Total revenue − Total cost.

profit responsibility The view that companies have a single obligation which is to maximize profits for its owners or stockholders.

profitability analysis A means of measuring the profitability of the firm's products, customer groups, sales territories, channels of distribution, and order sizes.

program schedule A formal time-line chart showing the relationships through time of the various program tasks.

promotional allowance The cash payment or extra amount of "free goods" awarded sellers in the channel of distribution for undertaking certain advertising or selling activities to promote a product.

promotional mix The combination of one or more of the promotional elements a firm uses to communicate with consumers. The promotional elements include: advertising, personal selling, sales promotion, and publicity.

prospecting stage In the personal selling process, the search for and qualification of potential customers.

protocol In the new product development process, an early statement that identifies a well-defined target market; specifies customers' needs, wants, and preferences; and states what the product will be and do.

psychographics Characteristics represented by personality and life-style traits (activities, interests, and opinions).

public service announcement (PSA) A publicity tool that uses free space or time donated by the media.

public warehouses Space and inventory-support services provided on a rental basis.

publicity A nonpersonal, indirectly paid presentation of an organization, good, or service.

publicity tools Methods of obtaining nonpersonal presentation of an organization, good, or service without direct cost. Examples include news releases, news conferences, and public service announcements.

pull strategy Directing the promotional mix at ultimate consumers to encourage them to ask the retailer for the product.

pulse schedule Distributing advertising unevenly throughout the year because of seasonal demand, heavy periods of promotion, or introduction of a new product; sometimes called "burst" scheduling.

purchase decision process Steps or stages a buyer passes through in making choices about which products to buy.

purchase frequency The frequency of purchase of a specific product.

pure competition A competitive setting in which a large number of sellers compete with similar products.

push strategy Directing the promotional mix to channel members or intermediaries to gain their cooperation in ordering and stocking a product.

quality The totality of features and characteristics of a product or service that bear on its ability to satisfy stated or implied needs.

quantity discounts Reductions in unit costs for a larger order quantity.

questionnaire data Facts and figures obtained by asking people about their attitudes, awareness, intentions, and behaviors.

quota In international trade, a legal limit placed on the amount of a product allowed to enter or leave a country.

rack jobber A merchant wholesaler that furnishes racks or shelves to display merchandise in retail stores, performs all channel functions, and sells on consignment.

rating (TV or radio) The percentage of households in a market that are tuned to a particular TV show or radio station.

reach The number of different people exposed to an advertisement.

reactive strategies New product strategies are defensive approaches in response to competitors' new items by developing new products.

rebate A sales promotion in which money is returned to the consumer based on proof of purchase.

receivers The consumers who read, hear, or see the message sent by a source in the communication process.

reciprocity An industrial buying practice in which two organizations agree to purchase products from each other.

reference group People to whom a person turns as a standard of self appraisal or source of personal standards.

regional marketing A form of geographical segmentation which develops marketing plans to reflect specific area differences in taste preferences, perceived needs, or interests.

regional rollouts Introducing a new product sequentially into geographical areas to allow production levels and marketing activities to build up gradually.

regional shopping centers Suburban malls with up to 100 stores that typically draw customers from a 5- to 10-mile radius, usually containing one or two anchor stores.

regulation The laws placed on business with regard to the conduct of its activities.

reinforcement A reward that tends to strengthen a response.

relative market share The sales of a firm or SBU divided by the sales of the largest firm in the industry; often used as a horizontal axis in business portfolio analysis.

reminder advertisements Advertisements used to reinforce prior knowledge of a product.

repeat purchasers People who tried the product, were satisfied, and buy again.

repetitive decisions Decisions repeated at standard intervals during the work year.

replenishment time (see lead time)

requirements contract A contract that requires a buyer to meet all or part of its needs for a product from one seller for a period of time.

reseller A wholesaler or retailer that buys physical products and resells them again without any processing.

response Action taken by a person to satisfy a drive.

restructuring (downsizing or streamlining) Striving for more efficient corporations that can compete globally by selling off unsatisfactory product lines and divisions, closing down unprofitable plants, and laying off employees.

retail life cycle A concept that describes a retail operation over four stages: early growth, accelerated development, maturity, and decline.

retailer-sponsored cooperative chain A contractual system involving independently owned stores that bind together to act like a chain.

retailing All the activities that are involved in selling, renting, and providing services to ultimate consumers for personal, nonhousehold use.

retailing mix The strategic components that a retailer offers, including goods and services, physical distribution, and communication tactics.

retailing positioning matrix A framework for positioning retail outlets in terms of breadth of product line and value added.

return on investment (ROI) The ratio of after-tax net profit to the investment used to earn that profit.

returns Refunds or credit granted a customer for an item returned to the seller.

Robinson–Patman Act (1936) A regulation that makes it unlawful to discriminate in prices charged to different purchasers of the same product where the result is to substantially lessen competition or help create a monopoly.

run-through train A train that carries more than one commodity but makes no stops between the points of origin and destination.

sales analysis A tool for controlling marketing programs where sales records are used to compare actual results with sales goals and to identify strengths and weaknesses.

sales component analysis A tool for controlling marketing programs which traces sales revenues to their sources such as specific products, sales territories, or customers.

sales engineering A salesperson who specializes in identifying, analyzing, and solving customer problems and who brings technological expertise to the selling situation, but does not actually sell goods and services.

salesforce survey forecast Asking the firm's salespeople to estimate sales during a coming period.

sales forecast What one firm expects to sell under specified conditions for the uncontrollable and controllable factors that affect the forecast.

sales management Planning, implementing, and controlling the personal selling effort of the firm.

sales plan A statement describing what is to be achieved and where and how the selling effort of salespeople is to be deployed.

sales promotion A short-term inducement of value offered to arouse interest in buying a good or service.

sales response function The relationship between the expense of marketing effort and the marketing results obtained. Measures of marketing results include sales revenue, profit, units sold, and level of awareness.

samples (1) Some elements taken from the population or universe, or (2) a sales promotion consisting of offering a product free or at a greatly reduced price.

sampling (1) the process of selecting elements from a population, or (2) the process manufacturers use of giving away free samples to introduce a new product.

scrambled merchandising Offering several unrelated product lines in a single retail store.

screening and evaluation The phase of the new product process in which a firm uses internal and external evaluations to eliminate ideas that warrant no further development effort.

sealed-bid pricing A method of pricing whereby prospective firms submit price bids for a contract to the buying agency at a specific time and place with the contract awarded to the qualified bidder with the lowest price.

seasonal discounts Price reductions granted buyers for purchasing products and stocking them at a time when they are not wanted by customers.

secondary data Facts and figures which have already been recorded before the project at hand.

selected controlled markets These sites also referred to as forced distribution markets are where a market test for a new product is conducted by an outside agency and retailers are paid to display the new product.

selective comprehension Interpreting information to make it consistent with one's attitude and beliefs.

selective demand Demand for a specific brand within a product class.

selective distribution A distribution strategy whereby a producer sells its products in a few retail outlets in a specific geographical area.

selective exposure The tendency to seek out and pay attention to messages consistent with one's attitudes and beliefs and to ignore messages inconsistent with them.

selective perception The tendency for humans to filter or choose information from a complex environment so they can make sense of the world.

selective retention The tendency to remember only part of all the information one sees, hears, or reads.

self-concept The way people see themselves and the way they believe others see them.

self-liquidating premium A sales promotion offering merchandise at a significant cost savings to the customer, its price covering the cost of the premium for the company.

self-regulation An industry policing itself rather than relying on government controls.

selling agent A person or firm that represents a single producer and is responsible for all marketing functions of that producer.

semantic differential scale A seven-point scale in which the opposite ends have one- or two-word adjectives with opposite meanings.

seminar selling A form of team selling where a company team conducts an educational program for a customer's technical staff describing state-of-the-art developments.

sensitivity analysis Asking "What if . . ." questions to determine how changes in a factor like pricing or advertising affects marketing results like sales revenues or profits.

service continuum A range from the tangible to the intangible or good-dominant or service-dominant offerings available in the marketplace.

services Intangible items such as airline trips, financial advice, or telephone calls that an organization provides to consumers in exchange for money or something else of value.

share points Percentage points of market share; often used as the common basis of comparison to allocate marketing resources effectively.

shelf life The time a product can be stored before it spoils.

Sherman Anti-Trust Act (1890) A law that forbids (1) contracts, combinations, or conspiracies in restraint of trade and (2) actual monopolies or attempts to monopolize any part of trade or commerce.

shopping goods Products for which the consumer will compare several alternatives on various criteria.

shrinkage A term used by retailers to describe theft of merchandise by customers and employees.

single-line store A store that offers tremendous depth in one primary line of merchandise; for example, a running shoe store.

single-source data Information provided by a single firm on household demographics and lifestyle, purchases, TV viewing behavior, and responses to promotions like coupons and free samples.

single-zone pricing Pricing policy in which all buyers pay the same delivered product price, regardless of their distance from the seller; also known as uniform delivered pricing or postage stamp pricing.

situation analysis Taking stock of where the firm or product has been recently, where it is now, and where it is likely to end up using present plans.

situational influences A situation's effect on the nature and scope of the decision process. These include (1) the purchase task, (2) social surroundings, (3) physical surroundings, (4) temporal effects, and (5) antecedent states.

skimming pricing A high initial price attached to a product to help a company recover the cost of development.

slotting fees Payment by a manufacturer to place a new product on retailer's shelf.

social audit A systematic assessment of a firm's objectives, strategies and performance in the domain of social responsibility.

social classes The relatively permanent and homogeneous divisions in a society of people or families sharing similar values, life-styles, interests, and behavior.

social forces The characteristics of the population, its income and its values in a particular environment.

social responsibility The idea that organizations are part of a larger society and are accountable to society for their actions.

societal marketing concept The view that an organization should discover and satisfy the needs of its customers in a way that also provides for society's well-being.

societal responsibility The view that firms have obligations to preserve the ecological environment and benefit the general public.

solution The best alternative that has been identified to solve the problem.

source A company or person who has information to convey.

special merchandise wholesaler A full-service merchant wholesaler that offers a relatively narrow range of products but has an extensive assortment within the products carried.

specialty discount outlet Retailers that offer large selections in a narrow range of products at very competitive prices, sometimes called category killers.

specialty goods Products that a consumer will make a special effort to search out and buy.

splitting 30s Reducing the length of a standard commercial from 30 seconds to 15 seconds.

staff positions People in staff positions have the authority and responsibility to advise people in line positions but cannot issue direct orders to them.

stakeholder responsibility The view that an organization has an obligation only to those constituencies which can affect achievement of its objectives.

Standard Industrial Classification (SIC) system The federal government's system for classifying organizations on the basis of major activity or the major good or service provided.

standard markets Sites where companies test market a product through normal distribution channels and monitor the results.

standard markup pricing Setting prices by adding a fixed percentage to the cost of all items in a specific product class.

Starch test A posttest that assesses the extent of consumers' recognition of an advertisement appearing in a magazine they have read.

statistical inference Drawing conclusions about a population from a sample taken from that population.

steady schedule A scheduling approach in which advertising insertions are steady throughout the year; sometimes called "drip" scheduling.

stimulus discrimination The ability to perceive differences in stimuli.

stimulus generalization When a response elicited by one stimulus (cue) is generalized to another stimulus.

stimulus-response presentation A selling format that assumes the prospect will buy if given the appropriate stimulus by a salesperson.

stock keeping unit (SKU) A distinct ordering number to identify a product item.

store audits Measurements of the sales of the product in stores and the number of cases ordered by a store from the wholesaler.

straight commission compensation plan A compensation plan where the salesperson's earnings are directly tied to his sales or profit generated.

straight rebuy The reordering of an existing product or service from the list of acceptable suppliers, generally without checking with the various users or influencers.

straight salary compensation plan A compensation plan where the salesperson is paid a fixed amount per week, month, or year.

strategic business unit (SBU) A decentralized profit center of a large firm that is treated as though it were a separate, independent business.

strategic channel alliances A practice whereby one firm's marketing channel is used to sell another firm's products.

strategic information systems Computerized methods of achieving long-run advantage by querying and analyzing on-line data bases linking customers and suppliers through remote devices and telecommunications.

strategic management process The steps taken at an organization's corporate and divisional levels to develop long-run master approaches for survival and growth.

strategic marketing process The steps taken at the product and market levels to allocate marketing resources to viable marketing positions and programs; involves phases of planning, implementation, and control.

strip location A cluster of stores that serves people who live within a 5- to 10-minute drive in a population base of under 30,000.

subcultures Subgroups within the larger or national culture with unique values, ideas, and attitudes.

subliminal perception Means that a person sees or hears messages without being aware of them.

supplies A type of support good, like stationery or paper clips, that is purchased with little effort using the straight rebuy method.

support goods Items used to assist in the production of other goods.

survey of buyers' intentions forecast A method of forecasting sales that involves asking prospective customers whether they are likely to buy the product or service during some future time period.

survey of experts forecast Asking experts on a topic to make a judgment about some future event.

sustainable competitive advantage A strength, relative to competitors, in the markets served and the products offered.

sweepstakes Sales promotions consisting of a game of chance requiring no analytical or creative effort to win a prize.

target market One or more specific groups of potential consumers toward which an organization directs its marketing program.

target profit pricing Setting a price based on an annual specific dollar target volume of profit.

target return-on-investment pricing Setting a price to achieve a return-on-investment target.

target return-on-sales pricing Setting a price to achieve a profit that is a specified percentage of the sales volume.

tariff In international trade, an official schedule of the duties imposed by a government on imports or exports.

team selling Using a group of professionals in selling to and servicing major customers.

technological forecast Estimating when scientific breakthroughs will occur.

technology An environmental force that includes inventions or innovations from applied science or engineering research.

teleshopping A form of direct marketing in which the consumer views products on their television set.

television home shopping (see teleshopping)

test marketing The process of offering a product for sale on a limited basis in a defined area to gain consumer reaction to the actual product and to examine its commercial viability and the marketing program.

TIGER (Topologically Integrated Geographic Encoding and Reference) A landmark project in demography by the U.S. Census Bureau which will provide a minutely detailed computerized map of the entire United States which can be combined with a company's own data.

time utility The value to consumers of having a good or service available when needed.

timing The decision point of when to discount the price of merchandise.

top-down forecast Subdividing an aggregate forecast into its principal components.

total cost The total expense a firm incurs in producing and marketing a product, which includes fixed cost and variable cost; in physical distribution decisions, the sum of all applicable costs for logistical activities.

total logistics cost Expenses associated with transportation, materials handling and warehousing, inventory, stockouts, and order processing.

total revenue The total amount of money received from the sale of a product.

trade (functional) discounts Price reductions granted to wholesalers or retailers on the basis of future marketing functions they will perform for the manufacturer.

trade name The commercial name under which a company does business.

trade-oriented sales promotions Sales tools used to support a company's advertising and personal selling efforts directed to wholesalers, retailers, or distributors: three common approaches are the merchandise, cash, and finance allowances.

trademark Legal identification of a company's exclusive rights to use a brand name or trade name.

Trademark Law Revision Act (1988) A legislative change to the Lanham Act (see glossary) by which a company can secure the rights to a name before actual use by declaring intent to use the name.

trading down Reducing the number of features, quality, or price of a product.

trading stamps A sales promotion consisting of stamps, given in relation to the dollar size of a purchase, which may be redeemed by the consumer for merchandise or cash.

trading up Adding value to a product by including more features or higher quality materials.

transnational corporation A business firm that looks at the entire world as one market and conducts research and development, manufacturing, financing, and marketing activities wherever they can be done best.

trend extrapolation Extending a pattern observed in past data into the future.

trial The initial purchase of a product by the consumer.

truck jobber Small merchant wholesalers that usually handle limited assortments of fast-moving or perishable items that are sold directly from trucks for cash.

tying arrangement A seller's requirement that the purchaser of one product also buy another product in the line.

ultimate consumers People who use the goods and services purchased for a household; sometimes also called ultimate users.

uncertainties The uncontrollable factors that the decision maker cannot influence.

uncontrollable factors (see environmental factors)

uniform delivered pricing A geographical pricing practice where the price the seller quotes includes all transportation costs.

unit train A train that is dedicated to one commodity, is loaded and unloaded with sophisticated equipment, and runs from origin to destination at high speed.

unit variable cost Variable cost expressed on a per unit basis.

unitary demand elasticity A situation where the percentage change in price is identical to the percentage change in quantity demanded.

universal product code (UPC) A number assigned to identify each product, represented by a series of bars of varying widths for scanning by optical readers.

unsought goods Products that the consumer does not know about or knows about and does not initially want.

usage rate Refers to quantity consumed or patronage during a specific period, and varies significantly among different customer groups.

utilitarianism A personal moral philosophy that focuses on the "greatest good for the greatest number" by assessing the costs and benefits of the consequences of ethical behavior.

utility The value to consumers for using the product.

Valdez Principles Guidelines that encourage firms to focus attention on environmental concerns and corporate responsibility.

value Specifically, value can be defined as the ratio of perceived quality to price. (Value = Perceived benefits/Price)

value added In retail strategy decisions, a dimension of the retail positioning matrix that refers to the service level and method of operation of the retailer.

value analysis A systematic appraisal of the design, quality, and performance requirements of a product to reduce purchasing costs.

value pricing The practice of simultaneously increasing service and product benefits and decreasing price.

values The beliefs of a person or culture; when applied to pricing, the ratio of perceived quality to price. (Value = Perceived benefits/Price)

variable cost An expense of the firm that varies directly with the quantity of product produced and sold.

vending machines A retailing operation in which products are stored in and sold from machines.

venture teams Multidisciplinary groups of marketing, manufacturing, and R&D personnel who stay with a new product from conception to production.

vertical conflict Disagreement between different levels in a marketing channel.

vertical marketing systems Professionally managed and centrally coordinated marketing channels designed to achieve channel economies and maximum marketing impact.

vertical price fixing The practice whereby sellers are required to not sell products below a minimum retail price, sometimes called resale price maintenance.

want A need that is shaped by a person's knowledge, culture, and individual characteristics.

warehouse A location, often decentralized, that a firm uses to store, consolidate, age, or mix stock; house product-recall programs; or ease tax burdens.

warehouse clubs Large retail stores (over 100,000 square feet) that require a yearly fee to shop at the store.

warranty A statement indicating the liability of the manufacturer for product deficiencies.

wasted coverage People outside a company's target audience who see, hear, or read the company's advertisement.

weighted-point system A method of establishing screening criteria, assigning them weights, and using them to evaluate new product ideas.

wheel of retailing A concept that describes how new retail outlets enter the market and change gradually in terms of status and margin.

wholesaler-sponsored voluntary chain A contractual system involving independently owned wholesalers who band together to act like a chain.

word-of-mouth People influencing each other during their face-to-face conversations.

workload method A formula-based method for determining the size of a salesforce that integrates the number of customers served, call frequency, call length, and available selling time to arrive at a salesforce size.

Chapter Notes

CHAPTER 1

1 "Microwave Popcorn: The Heat Is On," *Business Week* (July 6, 1987), p. 52.
2 "Pop Secrets," *Twin Cities* (July 1987), pp. 40–42.
3 Sonia L. Nazario, "Microwave Packages That Add Crunch to Lunch May Also Pose Chemical Risks," *The Wall Street Journal* (March 1, 1990), pp. B1–B8.
4 Anthony Carideo, "$30 a Share Watershed Has Short Sellers on Run," *Star Tribune* (October 2, 1989), pp. 1D, 11D.
5 *Report to Shareholders, Third Quarter 1989* (Edina, Minn.: Golden Valley Microwave Foods, Inc., November 9, 1989).
6 "AMA Board Approves New Marketing Definition," *Marketing News* (March 1, 1985), p. 1.
7 Robert W. Ruekert and Orville C. Walker, Jr., "Marketing's Interaction with Other Functional Units: A Conceptual Framework and Empirical Evidence," *Journal of Marketing* (January 1987), pp. 1–19.
8 Richard P. Bagozzi, "Marketing as Exchange," *Journal of Marketing* (October 1975), pp. 32–39.
9 E. Jerome McCarthy, *Basic Marketing: A Managerial Approach* (Homewood, Ill.: Richard D. Irwin, 1960).
10 Carl P. Zeithaml and Valarie A. Zeithaml, "Environmental Management: Revising the Marketing Perspective," *Journal of Marketing* (Spring 1984), pp. 46–53.
11 Michael L. Dertouzos, Richard K. Lester, and Robert M. Solow, *Made in America* (Cambridge, Mass.: The MIT Press, 1989); and Alex Taylor III, "New Lessons from Japan's Carmakers," *Fortune* (October 22, 1990), pp. 165–68.
12 Josephine Marcotty, "True Fish Story," *Star Tribune* (December 9, 1990), pp. 1A, 8A, 9A; Jan Carlzon, *Moments of Truth* (New York: Harper & Row, 1989); and Alex Taylor III, "Why Toyota Keeps Getting Better and Better and Better," *Fortune* (November 19, 1990), pp. 66–79.
13 Peter Nulty, "How the World Will Change," *Fortune* (January 15, 1990), pp. 44–54.
14 "Golden Valley Announces New Microwave French Fry Product," *Golden Valley Microwave Foods, Inc., News* (March 10, 1988), p. 1; Josephine Marcotty, "Golden Valley's Microwave Potatoes Paying Off," *Star Tribune* (October 24, 1989), p. 2D; and personal communication from James Watkins (January 1991).
15 "Pop Secrets," (reference cited), p. 41; Richard Gibson, "Producers of Microwave Potatoes Fail to Taste Success, but Fry, Fry Again," *The Wall Street Journal* (January 6, 1991), pp. B1, B3; and Josephine Marcotty, "French Fries May Save the Day at Golden Valley," *Star Tribune* (February 13, 1991), p. 8D.
16 For a contrary view, see Ronald A. Fullerton, "How Modern Is Modern Marketing? Marketing's Evolution and the Myth of the 'Production Era'," *Journal of Marketing* (January 1988), pp. 108–25.
17 Robert F. Keith, "The Marketing Revolution," *Journal of Marketing* (January 1960), pp. 35–38.
18 *1952 Annual Report* (New York: General Electric Company, 1952), p. 21.
19 John C. Narver and Stanley F. Slater, "The Effect of Market Orientation on Business Profitability," *Journal of Marketing* (October 1990), pp. 20–35.
20 Donald P. Robin and R. Eric Reidenbach, "Social Responsibility, Ethics, and Marketing Strategy: Closing the Gap between Concept and Application," *Journal of Marketing* (January 1987), pp. 44–58.
21 Shelby D. Hunt and John J. Burnett, "The Macromarketing/Micromarketing Dichotomy: A Taxonomical Model," *Journal of Marketing* (Summer 1982), pp. 9–26.
22 Philip Kotler and Sidney I. Levy, "Broadening the Concept of Marketing," *Journal of Marketing* (January 1969), pp. 10–15.
23 Ron Winslow, "Big Hospitals' Moves into New Territories Draw Local Staffs' Ire," *The Wall Street Journal* (August 18, 1989), pp. A1, A6.

CHAPTER 2

1 "A Slimmer IBM May Still Be Overweight," *Business Week* (December 18, 1989), pp. 107–8; and Joel Dreyfuss, "Reinventing IBM," *Fortune* (August 14, 1989), pp. 30–37.
2 Bob Garfield, "IBM vs. Apple—A Visual History," *Advertising Age* (August 28, 1989), p. 5–6; and Jon Lafayette, "Double-Edged Sword Handed to Lintas, WRG," *Advertising Age* (August 28, 1989), p. 5–4.
3 Roger A. Kerin, Vijay Mahajan, and P. Rajan Varadarajan, *Contemporary Perspectives on Strategic Marketing Planning* (Boston: Allyn & Bacon, 1990), chapter 1; Harper W. Boyd, Jr., and Orville C. Walker, Jr., *Marketing Management* (Homewood, Ill.: Richard D. Irwin, 1990), chapter 2; and Philip Kotler, *Marketing Management,* 7th ed. (Englewood Cliffs, N.J.: Prentice Hall, 1991), chapters 2 and 3.
4 Theodore Levitt, "Marketing Myopia," *Harvard Business Review* (July–August 1960), pp. 45–56.
5 Kenichi Ohmae, *The Mind of the Strategist* (New York: McGraw-Hill, 1982), p. 91.
6 Kate Fitzgerald, "Sears' Plan on the Ropes," *Advertising Age* (January 8, 1990), pp. 1, 42; Janice Castro, "Mr. Sam Stuns Goliath," *Time* (February 25, 1991), pp. 62–63.
7 Kate Fitzgerald, "Sears' Cudmore Takes 'Trust' Task," *Advertising Age* (January 29, 1990), pp. 3, 60; "Can Ed Brennan Salvage the Sears He Designed?" *Business Week* (August 27, 1990), p. 34; and "At Sears, the More Things Change . . . ,"

Business Week (November 12, 1990), pp. 66–68; Kate Fitzgerald, "Why Sears' McKids Failed," *Advertising Age* (January 14, 1991), p. 8.

8 "How Long Will Prodigy Be a Problem Child?" *Business Week* (September 10, 1990), p. 75; "Mr. Sam Stuns Goliath," (reference cited), p. 63; and "Are the Lights Dimming for Ed Brennan?" *Business Week* (February 11, 1991), pp. 56–57.

9 Roger A. Kerin and Robert A. Peterson, *Strategic Marketing Problems,* 5th ed. (Boston: Allyn & Bacon, 1990), pp. 4–5; and Derek F. Abell, *Defining the Business* (Englewood Cliffs, N.J.: Prentice Hall, 1980), p. 18.

10 Arthur A. Thompson, Jr., and A. J. Strickland III, *Strategic Management* (Plano, Tex.: Business Publications, 1984), pp. 178–79.

11 "Big Changes Are Galvanizing General Electric," *Business Week* (December 18, 1989), pp. 100–102.

12 Stratford P. Sherman, "The Mind of Jack Welch," *Fortune* (March 24, 1989), pp. 38–50; and "Solid as Steel, Light as a Cushion," *Time* (November 26, 1990), pp. 94–96.

13 "To Our Shareholders," *1989 Annual Report* (Fairfield, Conn.: General Electric Co., 1990), pp. 2–3.

14 H. Igor Ansoff, "Strategies for Diversification," *Harvard Business Review* (September–October 1957), pp. 113–24.

15 "The Real Thing Is Getting Real Aggressive," *Business Week* (November 26, 1990), pp. 94–104.

16 Michael J. McCarthy, "As a Global Marketer, Coke Excels by Being Tough and Consistent," *The Wall Street Journal* (December 19, 1989), pp. A1, A8.

17 Michael J. McCarthy, "Coke Fields a Sports Drink to Challenge Gatorade's Hold," *The Wall Street Journal* (March 6, 1990), pp. B1, B6.

18 Alicia Swasy, "P&G Moves to Revamp Its Pampers," *The Wall Street Journal* (August 9, 1989), p. B1.

19 Laurie Freeman, "P&G Luvs Takes Lead in Diaper Derby," *Advertising Age* (October 30, 1989), pp. 3, 71.

20 Laurie Freeman, "New Diaper Fight," *Advertising Age* (March 5, 1990), p. 4.

21 "Taming the Wild Network," *Business Week* (October 8, 1990), pp. 142–45.

22 Joanne Lipman, "IBM, in Its New PS/2 Campaign, Tries to Lose Button-Down Image," *The Wall Street Journal* (June 29, 1989), p. B4.

23 Jesse Snyder, "4 GM Car Divisions Are Repositioned in Effort to Help Sales," *Automotive News* (September 25, 1986), pp. 1, 49.

24 Alison Fahey, "Kodak Pins Hopes on a Star," *Advertising Age* (August 20, 1990), pp. 1, 66; and "A Moment Kodak Wants to Capture," *Business Week* (August 27, 1990), pp. 52–53.

25 "What Will Polaroid Do with All That Moola?" *Business Week* (October 29, 1990), p. 38.

CHAPTER 3

1 Laurie Freeman, "Marketers Nervous over Labeling Rules," *Advertising Age* (May 7, 1990), pp. 5–8; Joanne Lipman, "Health Claims for Some Foods May Be Shelved as Doubts Grow," *The Wall Street Journal* (January 29, 1990), pp. B1, B10; Richard Gibson, "Quaker Is Starting Its Counterattack on Oat Bran Study," *The Wall Street Journal* (January 29, 1990), p. B10; David Stipp, "Negative Oat Bran Study May Crimp Marketing Efforts," *The Wall Street Journal* (January

18, 1990), pp. B1, B4; "The Great American Health Pitch," *Business Week* (October 9, 1989), pp. 114–22; and "Where Does the Health End and the Hype Begin?" *Business Week* (October 9, 1989), pp. 124–28.

2 Brian O'Reilly, "Diet Centers Are Really in Fat City," *Fortune* (June 5, 1989), pp. 132–38; Blayne Cutler, "Meet John Doe," *American Demographics* (June 1989), pp. 25–27, 62; and Barry Tarshis, *The "Average" American Book* (New York: Atheneum Publishers, 1979).

3 *U.S. Statistical Abstract,* 1989, p. 13.

4 "U.S. Companies Go for the Gray," *Business Week* (April 3, 1989), p. 66.

5 Christopher Knowlton, "Consumers: A Tough Sell," *Fortune* (September 26, 1988), pp. 65–68; and "U.S. Companies Go for the Gray," (reference cited), pp. 64–67.

6 Margaret Ambry, *The Almanac of Consumer Markets* (Chicago: Probus Publishing, 1990).

7 Kathleen Deveney, "Reality of the 90's Hits Yuppie Brands," *The Wall Street Journal* (December 20, 1990), pp. B1, B5.

8 Judith Waldrop, "A Lesson in Home Economics," *American Demographics* (August 1989), p. 8.

9 Jeff Rosenfeld, "Demographics and INTERIOR Design," *American Demographics* (February 1984), pp. 28–33.

10 Sharen Shaw Johnson, "GOP Counting on Census Results," *USA Today* (December 28, 1990), p. 3A; and Judith Waldrop, "2010," *American Demographics* (February 1989), pp. 18–21.

11 "Marketing's New Look," *Business Week* (January 26, 1987), pp. 64–69.

12 Alex M. Freedman, "National Firms Find That Selling to Local Tastes Is Costly, Complex," *The Wall Street Journal* (February 9, 1987), p. 21.

13 Ambry (see note 6).

14 Kathleen Deveney, "Grappling with Women's Evolving Roles," *The Wall Street Journal* (September 5, 1990), pp. B1, B8; and Diane Crispell, "Workers in 2000," *American Demographics* (March 1990), pp. 36–40.

15 Betsy Sharkey, "The Invisible Woman," *Adweek* (July 6, 1987), pp. wr4–wr8.

16 Basia Helwig, "How Women Have Changed America," *Working Woman* (November 1986), pp. 129–46.

17 Diane Crispell, "Women in the Workforce," *American Demographics* (September 1989), pp. 26–29.

18 Nancy Giges, "More Men Food Shopping," *Advertising Age* (February 6, 1984), p. 12.

19 Richard Gibson, "McDonald's Will Put Nutritional Data for Menu on Wall Posters and Tray Liners," *The Wall Street Journal* (June 11, 1990), p. B1.

20 Thomas G. Exter, "Where the Money Is," *American Demographics* (March 1987), pp. 26–31.

21 "How Consumers Spend," *American Demographics* (October 1983), pp. 17–21.

22 Fabian Linden, Gordon W. Green, Jr., and John F. Coder, *A Marketer's Guide to Discretionary Income* (Washington, D.C.: U.S. Government Printing Office, 1984).

23 William Lazer, "How Rising Affluence Will Reshape Markets," *American Demographics* (February 1984), pp. 17–21; and Thomas J. Stanley and George Moschis, "America's Affluent," *American Demographics* (March 1984), pp. 28–33.

24 "America 2000," *Battelle* (May 3, 1983).

25 Gilbert Fuchsberg, "Hand-Held Computers Help Staff Cut Paper Work and Harvest More Data," *The Wall Street Journal* (January 30, 1990), pp. B1, B9.

26 "BMW Puts a Backseat Driver on a Chip," *Business Week* (July 30, 1990), p. 70; and Michael Waldholz, "New Plastic Is Promoted as a Natural," *The Wall Street Journal* (January 24, 1990), pp. B1, B2.

27 Eugene Carson, "Business Maps Plans for the Use of TIGER Geographic Files," *The Wall Street Journal* (June 8, 1990), p. B2; Gene Bylinsky, "Managing with Electronic Maps," *Fortune* (April 24, 1989), pp. 237–54; and "These Maps Can Find Oil—or Sell Burgers," *Business Week* (March 13, 1989), p. 134.

28 Kevin Maney, "Companies Make Products Nicer to Nature," *USA Today* (August 23, 1989), pp. 1B, 2B.

29 "A New Sales Pitch: The Environment," *Business Week* (July 24, 1989), p. 50.

30 "The Green Marketing Revolution," *Advertising Age* (January 29, 1991), special issue.

31 Kenneth Labich, "How Airlines Will Look in the 1990's," *Fortune* (January 1, 1990), pp. 50–59.

32 Michael Porter, *Competitive Strategy* (New York: Free Press, 1980).

33 Roger Rowand, "Car–Truck Sales Smash Record in Busy Year," *Automotive News* (January 12, 1987), pp. 42–43.

34 Johnnie L. Roberts, "By Concentrating on Marketing, Stride Rite Does Well Despite Slump for Shoemakers," *The Wall Street Journal* (February 22, 1983), p. 31.

35 John A. Quelch and Robert D. Buzzell, *The Marketing Challenge of 1992* (Reading, Mass.: Addison-Wesley Publishing, 1990).

36 Ford S. Worthy, "A New Mass Market Emerges," *Fortune,* special issue (Fall 1990), pp. 51–55.

37 Myron Maguet, "Restructuring Really Works," *Fortune* (March 2, 1987), pp. 38–46; and "Rebuilding to Survive," *Time* (February 16, 1987), pp. 44–47.

38 Anne B. Fisher, "The Downside of Downsizing," *Fortune* (May 23, 1988), pp. 42–52.

39 "The Best and Worst Deals of the 80's," *Business Week* (January 15, 1990), pp. 52–62.

40 Amanda Bennett, "As Big Firms Continue to Trim Their Staffs, 2-Tier Setup Emerges," *The Wall Street Journal* (May 4, 1987), pp. 1, 14.

41 David L. Birch, "Down, But Not Out," *Inc.* (May 1988), pp. 20–21.

42 "Where Trademarks Are up for Grabs," *The Wall Street Journal* (December 5, 1989), pp. B1, B4.

43 Paul C. Van Syke, *Marketing News* (December 18, 1989), p. 2.

44 *United States* v. *Trans-Missouri Freight Association,* 166 U.S. 290 (1897).

45 This conceptual framework of distribution controls was developed by Marshall Howard, *Legal Aspects in Marketing* (New York: McGraw-Hill, 1964).

46 *International Business Machines Corporation* v. *United States,* 298 U.S. 131 (1936).

47 Joanne Lipman, "Double Standards for Kids' TV Ads," *The Wall Street Journal* (June 10, 1988), p. 21.

48 Jeffrey Tannenbaum, "Listen, Anything That Eats Mice Isn't Going to Be That Choosy," *The Wall Street Journal* (June 22, 1990), p. B1.

CHAPTER 4

1 "Selling Sobriety," *Dallas Times Herald* (March 19, 1990), p. A9; "Anheuser Boosting Public Service Ads," *The Wall Street Journal* (June 28, 1989), p. 86; and "A-B Tries to Bolster Bud, Bud Light," *Advertising Age* (February 12, 1990), p. 51.

2 For a discussion of the definition of ethics, see Gene Lazniak and Patrick E. Murphy, *The Higher Road: A Path to Ethical Marketing Decisions* (Boston: Allyn & Bacon, 1992), chapter 1.

3 Verne E. Henderson, "The Ethical Side of Enterprise," *Sloan Management Review* (Spring 1982), pp. 37–47.

4 M. Bommer, C. Gratto, J. Grauander, and M. Tuttle, "A Behavioral Model of Ethical and Unethical Decision Making," *Journal of Business Ethics,* vol. 6 (1987), pp. 265–80.

5 Ray O. Werner, "Marketing and the Supreme Court in Transition, 1982–1984," *Journal of Marketing* (Summer 1985), pp. 97–105.

6 Jane Bryant Quinn, "Computer Program Deceives Consumers," *Dallas Times Herald* (March 2, 1990), p. B3.

7 "RJR Cancels Test of 'Black' Cigarette," *Marketing News* (February 19, 1990), p. 10.

8 "Business Week/Harris Poll: Is an Antibusiness Business Backlash Building?" *Business Week* (July 20, 1987), p. 71; and "Looking to Its Roots," *Time* (May 27, 1987), pp. 26–29.

9 "What Bosses Think about Corporate Ethics," *The Wall Street Journal* (April 6, 1988), p. 21.

10 Saul W. Gellerman, "Why 'Good' Managers Make Bad Ethical Choices," in Kenneth R. Andrews, ed., *Ethics in Practice* (Boston: Harvard Business School Press, 1989), pp. 18–25; and J. N. Behrman, *Essays on Ethics in Business and the Professions* (Englewood Cliffs, N.J.: Prentice Hall, 1988).

11 "Special Report: Animal Uproar," *Advertising Age* (February 25, 1990), pp. S-1–S-11.

12 "A Nation of Liars," *U.S. News & World Report* (February 23, 1987), pp. 54–61.

13 For a comprehensive review on marketing ethics, see John Tsalikis and David J. Fritzche, "Business Ethics: A Literature Review with a Focus on Marketing Ethics," *Journal of Business Ethics,* vol. 8 (1989), pp. 695–743.

14 This framework is based on O. C. Ferrell and Larry Gresham, "A Contingency Framework for Ethical Decision Making in Marketing," *Journal of Marketing* (Summer 1985), pp. 87–96; and O. C. Ferrell, Larry Gresham, and John Fraedrich, "A Synthesis of Ethical Decision Models for Marketing," *Journal of Macromarketing,* vol. 9, nb. 2 (1989), pp. 55–64.

15 "It's All in the Cards," *Time* (November 7, 1988), p. 101.

16 "Where Trademarks Are Up for Grabs," *The Wall Street Journal* (December 5, 1989), pp. B1, B4.

17 Vern Tepstra and Kenneth David, *The Cultural Environment of International Business,* 2nd ed. (Cincinnati: South-Western Publishing Co., 1985), p. 9.

18 For an extended treatment of ethics in the exchange process, see Gregory T. Gundlack and Patrick E. Murphy, "Ethical and Legal Foundations of Business Marketing Exchanges," *AMA Winter Marketing Educators' Conference* (Chicago: American Marketing Association, 1990).

19 "Group Challenges Parts of Dalkon Shield Pact," *The Washington Post* (August 25, 1989), p. C2.

20 John R. Dorfman, "As Credit-Card Disclosure Bill Advances, Consumer Groups Assail It as Too Weak," *The Wall Street Journal* (February 17, 1988), p. 25.

21 Lois Therrion, "Want Shelf Space at Supermarkets? Ante Up," *Business Week* (August 7, 1989), pp. 60–61.

22 William L. Scammon, "Competitor Intelligence or Industrial Espionage?" in William L. Scammon, Mark A. Kurland, and Robert Spitalnic, eds., *Business Competitor Intelligence* (New York: John Wiley & Sons, 1983), p. 52.

23 This example is detailed in Scammon, pp. 41–50. See also "Corporate Spies Snoop to Conquer," *Fortune* (November 7, 1988), pp. 68–76.

24 "P&G Expected to Get about $120 Million in Settlement of Chewy-Cookie Lawsuit," *The Wall Street Journal* (September 11, 1989), p. B10.

25 "Vendors' Gifts Pose Problems for Purchasers," *The Wall Street Journal* (June 26, 1989), pp. B1, B4.

26 "Galvin Admits Bribing Pentagon Aides, Planning over $2.5 Million of Payoffs," *The Wall Street Journal* (March 29, 1990), p. A4.

27 Warren J. Keegan, *Global Marketing Management,* 4th ed. (Englewood Cliffs, N.J.: Prentice Hall, 1989), p. 201.

28 David J. Fritzche, "Ethical Issues in Multinational Marketing," in Gene R. Lazniak and Patrick E. Murphy, eds., *Marketing Ethics: Guidelines for Managers* (Lexington, Mass.: Lexington Books, 1985), pp. 85–96.

29 George C. S. Benson, "Codes of Ethics," *Journal of Business Ethics,* vol. 8 (1989), pp. 305–19.

30 Leonard J. Brooks, "Corporate Codes of Ethics," *Journal of Business Ethics,* vol. 8 (1989), pp. 117–29.

31 "Look What Ill Wind Is Blowing In," *Business Week* (April 16, 1990), p. 27.

32 "Doing the 'Right' Thing Has Its Repercussions," *The Wall Street Journal* (January 25, 1990), p. B1.

33 For an extensive discussion on these moral philosophies, see R. Eric Reidenbach and Donald P. Robin, *Ethics and Profits* (Englewood Cliffs, N.J.: Prentice Hall, 1989); Shelby D. Hunt and Scott Vitell, "A General Theory of Marketing Ethics," *Journal of Macromarketing* (Spring 1986), pp. 5–16; and Donald P. Robin and R. Eric Reidenbach, "Social Responsibility, Ethics, and Marketing Strategy: Closing the Gap between Concept and Application," *Journal of Marketing* (January 1987), pp. 44–58.

34 "Bad Apple for Baby," *Financial World* (June 27, 1989), p. 48; and "What Led Beech-Nut Down the Road to Disgrace," *Business Week* (February 22, 1988), pp. 124–27.

35 James Q. Wilson, "Adam Smith on Business Ethics," *California Management Review* (Fall 1989), pp. 59–72; and Edward W. Coker, "Smith's Concept of the Social System," *Journal of Business Ethics,* vol. 9 (1990), pp. 139–42.

36 George M. Zinkhan, Michael Bisesi, and Mary Jane Saxton, "MBAs' Changing Attitudes toward Marketing Dilemmas," *Journal of Business Ethics,* vol. 8 (1989), pp. 963–74.

37 Alix M. Freedman, "Bad Reaction: Nestlé's Bid to Crash Baby-Formula Market in the U.S. Stirs a Row," *The Wall Street Journal* (February 16, 1989), pp. A1, A6; and Alix Freedman, "Nestlé to Drop Claim on Label of Its Formula," *The Wall Street Journal* (March 13, 1989), p. B5.

38 Milton Friedman, "A Friedman Doctrine: The Social Responsibility of Business Is to Increase Profits," *New York Times Magazine* (September 13, 1970), p. 126.

39 Tim Kingston, "The Unhealthy Profits of AZT," *The Nation* (October 17, 1987), pp. 407–9.

40 "Can Perrier Purify Its Reputation?" *Business Week* (February 26, 1990), p. 45; and "Perrier Expands North American Recall to Rest of Globe," *The Wall Street Journal* (February 15, 1990), pp. B1, B4.

41 The following examples are based on "Shell Pumps Cleaner Gas in 'Dirtiest' Cities in U.S.," *The Wall Street Journal* (April 12, 1990), pp. B1, B6; "Efforts to Save Dolphins Are Set by Tuna Canners," *The Wall Street Journal* (April 13, 1990), p. B5; and "U.S. Recycles 61% of Aluminum Cans," *Dallas Times Herald* (April 14, 1990), p. B2.

42 For an extended discussion on this topic, see P. Rajan Varadarajan and Avil Menon, "Cause-Related Marketing: A Coalignment of Marketing Strategy and Corporate Philanthropy," *Journal of Marketing* (July 1988), pp. 58–74. The examples given are found in this article.

43 "The Eagles Score a Touchdown with Ronald McDonald Houses," *The Wall Street Journal* (April 26, 1990), p. B2.

44 These steps are adapted from J. J. Carson and G. A. Steiner, *Measuring Business Social Performance: The Corporate Social Audit* (New York: Committee for Economic Development, 1974); also see E. M. Epstein, "The Corporate Social Policy Process: Beyond Business Ethics, Corporate Social Responsibility, and Corporate Social Responsiveness," *California Management Review* (Spring 1987), pp. 99–114.

45 *Research Report: The Only Environment We Have: How Can We Save It?* (New York: Council on Economic Priorities, November 1989).

46 "Business's Green Revolution," *U.S. News & World Report* (February 19, 1990), pp. 45–48.

47 For a listing of unethical consumer practices, see Robert E. Wilkes, "Fraudulent Behavior by Consumers," *Journal of Marketing* (October 1978), pp. 67–75; see also Catherine A. Cole, "Research Note: Determinants and Consumer Fraud," *Journal of Retailing* (Spring 1989), pp. 107–20.

48 *Manufacturers' Guide to Coupon Redemption* (Arlington, Va.: American Society for Industrial Security, 1987). See also "Coupon Criminals, Please Cut It Out," *U.S. News & World Report* (February 12, 1990), p. 19.

49 Paul Bernstein, "Cheating—The New National Pastime?" *Business* (October–December 1985), pp. 24–33; and "Video Vice: 1 in 10 Copy Videotapes Illegally," *USA Weekend* (February 9–11, 1990), p. 18.

50 Bernstein, pp. 24–33.

51 "Americans Are Willing to Sacrifice to Reduce Pollution, They Say," *The Wall Street Journal* (April 20, 1990), pp. A1, A6.

52 Alecia Swasy, "For Consumers, Ecology Comes Second," *The Wall Street Journal* (August 23, 1989), p. B1.

53 "Keeping Hair in Place—Without Messing Up the Air," *Business Week* (January 25, 1990), p. 85.

54 "Rush to Endorse 'Environmental' Goods Sparks Worry about Shopper Confusion," *The Wall Street Journal* (April 16, 1990), pp. B1, B3; and JoAnn S. Lublin, "Environment Claims Are Sowing More Confusion, 2 Reports Say," *The Wall Street Journal* (November 8, 1990), p. B8.

CHAPTER 5

1 Frieda Curtindale, "Marketing Cars to Women," *American Demographics* (November 1988), pp. 29–31; Lawrence Som-

bke, "Super Marketing," *USA Weekend* (September 8–10, 1989), pp. 4–5; "Shoppers' Video Beaming at Initial Survey Results," *Marketing News* (December 4, 1989), p. 20; Julia Lieblich, "If You Want a Big New Market . . . ," *Fortune* (November 21, 1988), pp. 178–85; and "7-Elevens Move beyond the Majority," *Dallas Times Herald* (February 14, 1990), pp. B1, B7.

2 James F. Engel, Roger D. Blackwell, and Paul Miniard, *Consumer Behavior,* 6th ed. (Hinsdale, Ill.: Dryden Press, 1990), p. 477. See also, Gordon C. Bruner III and Richard J. Pomazal, "Problem Recognition: The Crucial First Stage of the Consumer Decision Process," *Journal of Consumer Marketing* (Winter 1988), pp. 53–63.

3 For interesting descriptions of consumer experience and expertise, see Stephen J. Hoch and John Deighton, "Managing What Consumers Learn from Experience," *Journal of Marketing* (April 1989), pp. 1–20; and Joseph W. Alba and J. Wesley Hutchinson, "Dimensions of Consumer Expertise," *Journal of Consumer Research* (March 1987), pp. 411–54.

4 For a recent study on external information search patterns, see Joel E. Urbany, Peter R. Dickson, and William L. Wilkie, "Buyer Uncertainty and Information Search," *Journal of Consumer Research* (September 1989), pp. 208–15.

5 Engel, Blackwell, and Miniard, p. 479.

6 John A. Howard, *Consumer Behavior in Marketing Strategy* (Englewood Cliffs, N.J.: Prentice Hall, 1989), pp. 176–77, 361.

7 Del Hawkins, Roger J. Best, and Kenneth J. Coney, *Consumer Behavior: Implication for Marketing Strategy,* 4th ed. (Homewood, Ill.: Richard D. Irwin, 1989), p. 630.

8 Damon Darlin, "Although U.S. Cars Are Improved, Imports Still Win Quality Survey," *The Wall Street Journal* (December 12, 1985), p. 27.

9 "For Customers, More than Lip Service?" *The Wall Street Journal* (October 6, 1989), p. B1; and Patricia Sellers, "How to Handle Customers' Gripes," *Fortune* (October 24, 1988), pp. 88–89ff.

10 John E. Swan and Richard L. Oliver, "Postpurchase Communication by Customers," *Journal of Retailing* (Winter 1989), pp. 516–33.

11 Many different definitions and perspectives on involvement exist. See, for example, Richard L. Celsi and Jerry C. Olson, "The Role of Involvement in Attention and Comprehension Processes," *Journal of Consumer Research* (September 1988), pp. 210–24; and C. W. Park and S. Mark Young, "Consumer Response to Television Commercials: The Impact of Background Music on Brand Attitude Formation," *Journal of Marketing Research* (February 1986), pp. 11–24.

12 Carolyn Costley, "Meta Analysis of Involvement Research," in Michael Houston, ed., *Advances in Consumer Research,* vol. 15 (Provo, Utah: Association for Consumer Research, 1988), pp. 554–62.

13 J. Paul Peter and Jerry C. Olson, *Consumer Behavior: Marketing Strategy Perspectives* (Homewood, Ill.: Richard D. Irwin, 1990), pp. 184–96.

14 Based on Engel, Blackwell, and Miniard, pp. 496–98; Hawkins, Best, and Coney, p. 572; and Peter and Olson, pp. 184–86.

15 Estimates of the incidence of different problem solving variations are found in Hawkins, Best, and Coney, p. 592.

16 Russell Belk, "Situational Variables and Consumer Behavior," *Journal of Consumer Research* (December 1975), pp. 157–63.

17 Representative studies on situational influences include Ronald Milliman, "The Influence of Background Music on the Behavior of Restaurant Patrons," *Journal of Consumer Research* (September 1986), pp. 286–89; Meryl Gardner, "Mood States and Consumer Behavior: A Critical Review," *Journal of Consumer Research* (December 1985), pp. 281–300; Robert Donovan and John Rossiter, "Store Atmosphere: An Environmental Psychology Approach," *Journal of Retailing* (Spring 1982), pp. 34–57; and Richard F. Yalch and Eric Spangenburg, "An Environmental Psychological Study of Foreground and Background Music as Retail Atmospheric Factors," *AMA Educators' Conference Proceedings* (Chicago: American Marketing Association, 1988), pp. 106–10.

18 This perspective on motivation and personality is based on Hawkins, Best, and Coney, p. 355.

19 K. H. Chung, *Motivational Theories and Practices* (Columbus, Ohio: Grid, 1977). See also, A. H. Maslow, *Motivation and Personality* (New York: Harper & Row, 1970).

20 Arthur Koponen, "The Personality Characteristics of Purchases," *Journal of Advertising Research* (September 1960), pp. 89–92.

21 Joel B. Cohen, "An Interpersonal Orientation to the Study of Consumer Behavior," *Journal of Marketing Research* (August 1967), pp. 270–78.

22 J. Neher, "Toro Cutting a Wide Swath in Outdoor Appliances Marketing," *Advertising Age* (February 25, 1979), p. 21.

23 For further reading on subliminal perception, see Timothy E. Moore, "Subliminal Advertising: What You See Is What You Get," *Journal of Marketing* (Spring 1982), pp. 38–47; and Joel Saegert, "Why Marketing Should Quit Giving Subliminal Advertising the Benefit of the Doubt," *Psychology and Marketing* (Summer 1987), pp. 107–20.

24 Robert Settle and Pamela Alreck, "Reducing Buyers' Sense of Risk," *Marketing Communications* (January 1989), pp. 34–40: and G. R. Dowling, "Perceived Risk: The Concept and Its Management," *Psychology and Marketing* (Fall 1986), pp. 193–210.

25 This description of learning principles is based on Hawkins, Coney, and Best, pp. 320–40; and David Loudon and Albert J. Della Bitta, *Consumer Behavior,* 3rd ed. (New York: McGraw-Hill, 1988), pp. 437–74.

26 Ronald Alsop, "Brand Loyalty Is Rarely Blind Loyalty," *The Wall Street Journal* (October 19, 1989), p. 131.

27 Gordon Allport, "Attitudes," in Martin Fishbein, ed., *Readings in Attitude Theory and Measurement* (New York: John Wiley & Sons, 1968), p. 3.

28 Milton J. Rokeach, *The Nature of Human Values* (New York: Free Press, 1973).

29 Peter and Olson, pp. 149–50. See also Richard J. Lutz, "Changing Brand Attitudes through Modification of Cognitive Structure," *Journal of Consumer Research,* vol. 2 (1975), pp. 49–59.

30 Henry Assael, *Consumer Behavior and Marketing Action,* 3rd ed. (Boston: Kent Publishing, 1990), p. 275.

31 For an extended discussion of self-concept, see M. Joseph Sirgy, "Self-Concept in Consumer Behavior: A Critical Review," *Journal of Consumer Research* (December 1982), pp. 287–300. For a broader perspective, see Russell Belk,

"Possessions and the Extended Self," *Journal of Consumer Research* (September 1988), pp. 139–68.

32 This description of the VALS Program is based on *The VALS 2 Segmentation System* (Menlo Park, Calif.: SRI International, 1989); Martha Riche, "Psychographics for the 1990s," *American Demographics* (July 1989), pp. 25–31, 53; and "SRI's New Psychographic Typology Reasserts Old Stereotypes of Aging," *Maturity Market Perspective* (September/October 1989), pp. 1, 6.

33 See, for example, Lawrence F. Feick and Linda Price, "The Market Maven: A Diffuser of Marketplace Information," *Journal of Marketing* 51 (January 1987), pp. 83–97; and Peter H. Block, "The Product Enthusiast: Implications for Marketing Strategy," *Journal of Consumer Marketing* 3 (Summer 1986), pp. 51–61.

34 Meg Cox, "Ford Pushing Thunderbird with VIP Plan," *The Wall Street Journal* (October 17, 1983), p. 37.

35 "Importance of Image," *The Wall Street Journal* (August 12, 1985), p. 19.

36 Representative work on positive and negative word of mouth can be found in Jacqueline Brown and Peter H. Reingen, "Social Ties and Word-of-Mouth Referral Behavior," *Journal of Consumer Research* (December 1987), pp. 350–62; Marc Weinberger and Jean B. Romeo, "The Impact of Negative Product News," *Business Horizons* (January–February 1989), pp. 44–50; Barry L. Bayers, "Word of Mouth: The Indirect Effects of Marketing Efforts," *Journal of Advertising Research* (June–July 1985), pp. 31–39; and Marsha L. Richins, "Negative Word of Mouth by Dissatisfied Consumers: A Pilot Study," *Journal of Marketing* (Winter 1983), pp. 68–78.

37 John C. Mowen, *Consumer Behavior,* 2nd ed. (New York: Macmillan, 1990), pp. 464–65.

38 William O. Beardon and Michael G. Etzel, "Reference Group Influence on Product and Brand Choice," *Journal of Consumer Research* (September 1982), pp. 183–94.

39 "Honda Revs Up a Hip Cycle Campaign," *The Wall Street Journal* (July 31, 1989), p. B1.

40 For an extended discussion on consumer socialization, see George P. Moschis, *Consumer Socialization* (Lexington, Mass.: Lexington Books, 1987).

41 "Time Scores with Line Extension for Kids," *The Wall Street Journal* (June 8, 1989), p. B5; and Ellen Graham, "As Kids Gain Power of Purse, Marketing Takes Aim at Them," *The Wall Street Journal* (January 19, 1988), pp. 1, 8.

42 This discussion is based on *Lifestages: A Study of Dramatic Changes in the Consumer Market* (New York: J. Walter Thompson USA, 1989); Joanne Lipman, "Thompson's New Game Plan Maps Attitudes, Not Ages," *The Wall Street Journal* (June 22, 1989), p. B6; and Patrick E. Murphy and William A. Staples, "A Modernized Family Life Cycle," *Journal of Consumer Research* (June 1979), pp. 12–22.

43 Research describing the purchasing roles and influence of husbands and wives is found in Sidney C. Bennett and Elnora W. Stuart, "In Search of Association between Personal Values and Household Decision Processes: An Exploratory Analysis," *AMA Educators' Conference Proceedings* (Chicago: American Marketing Association, 1989), pp. 259–64; and Elnora W. Stuart and Sidney C. Bennett, "Perception of Marital Roles in Decision Processes: A 1980s Update," *AMA Educators' Conference Proceedings* (Chicago: American Marketing Association, 1988), p. 77.

44 "Aisle of Man," *Dallas Times Herald* (July 10, 1990), pp. D1, D4; Scott Donaton, "Study Boosts Men's Buying Role," *Advertising Age* (December 4, 1989), p. 48; and Curtindale, p. 30.

45 Patricia Sellers, "The ABCs of Marketing to Kids," *Fortune* May 8, 1989), pp. 114–20; Joe Agnew, "Children Come of Age as Consumers," *Marketing News* (December 4, 1987), p. 8; and "Kids Give 'Channel One' Thumbs Up," *Advertising Age* (March 20, 1989), p. 64.

46 Sarah O'Brien and Rosemary Ford, "Can We at Last Say Goodbye to Social Class?" *Journal of the Market Research Society* (July 1988), pp. 289–331.

47 Donald W. Hendon, Emelda L. Williams, and Douglas E. Huffman, "Social Class System Revisited," *Journal of Business Research,* vol. 17 (1988), pp. 259–70.

48 Mowen, p. 660.

49 Judith Waldrop and Thomas Exter, "What the 1990 Census Will Show," *American Demographics* (January 1990), pp. 20–30; and Marty Westerman, "Death of the Frito Bandito," *American Demographics* (March 1989), pp. 28–32.

50 Jerome D. Williams and William J. Qualls, "Middle-Class Black Consumers and Intensity of Ethnic Identification," *Psychology & Marketing* (Winter 1989), pp. 263–86; Mowen, p. 628; and Engel, Blackwell, and Miniard, pp. 91–95. See also, "The Black Middle Class," *Business Week* (March 14, 1988), pp. 62–70.

51 Mowen, p. 626.

52 This observation is based on a series of articles in H. P. McAdoo, ed., *Black Families* (Newbury Park, Calif.: Sage Publications, 1988).

53 " 'Black Pride' Plays Role in Buying Goods," *Marketing News* (February 19, 1990), p. 11.

54 Westerman, pp. 28–32; and Waldrop and Exter, pp. 20–30.

55 Westerman, pp. 28–32; Lieblich, p. 180; "The Hispanic Market's Leading Indicators," *Hispanic Business* (December 1989), p. 16; and "How to Speak to Hispanics," *American Demographics* (February 1990), pp. 40–41.

56 Westerman, pp. 28–32.

57 Lieblich, pp. 178–85.

58 "Hot Asian-American Market Not Starting Much of a Fire Yet," *Marketing News* (January 21, 1991), p. 12; "Companies Disoriented about Asians," *Advertising Age* (July 9, 1990), pp. 52, 58; Westerman, pp. 28–32; and Waldrop and Exter, pp. 20–30.

59 *The Asian-American Market* (New York: FIND/SVP, 1990); and Bryant Robey, "America's Asians," *American Demographics* (May 1985), pp. 22–29.

60 Wendy Manning and William O'Hare, "Asian-American Business," *American Demographics* (August 1988), pp. 35–37ff.

61 "Metropolitan Life Revamps Strategy to Woo Asians," *Dallas Times Herald* (July 21, 1986), p. 12A.

62 Joe Schwartz and Thomas Exter, "All Our Children," *American Demographics* (May 1989), pp. 34–37.

CHAPTER 6

1 Interview with Bob Procsal, Honeywell, MICRO SWITCH Division, March 8, 1990. Used with permission.

2 Peter LaPlaca, "From the Editor," *Journal of Business & Industrial Marketing* (Winter 1988), p. 3.

3 "US Sprint Faces Inquiry by FBI on Phone Bid," *The Wall Street Journal* (February 20, 1990), pp. A3, A7.

4 *Standard Industrial Classification Manual* (Washington, D.C.: U.S. Government Printing Office, 1982).

5 An argument that consumer buying and organizational buying do not have important differences is found in Edward F. Fern and James R. Brown, "The Industrial/Consumer Marketing Dichotomy: A Case of Insufficient Justification," *Journal of Marketing* (Spring 1984), pp. 68–77. However, most writers on the subject do draw distinctions between the two types of buying. See, for example, Robert W. Eckles, *Business Marketing Management* (Englewood Cliffs, N.J.: Prentice Hall, 1990), p. 6.

6 Implications of derived demand for marketing management can be found in William S. Bishop, John L. Graham, and Michael H. Jones, "Volatility of Derived Demand in Industrial Markets and Its Management Implications," *Journal of Marketing* (Fall 1984), pp. 95–103.

7 For a recent study of evaluative criteria used by industrial firms, see Daniel H. McQuiston and Rockney G. Walters, "The Evaluative Criteria of Industrial Buyers: Implications for Sales Training," *Journal of Business & Industrial Marketing* (Summer/Fall 1989), pp. 65–75.

8 Gary W. Dickson, "An Analysis of Vendor Selection Systems and Decisions," *Journal of Purchasing* (February 1966), pp. 5–17.

9 For a discussion of JIT, see Gary L. Frazier, Robert E. Spekman, and Charles R. O'Neal, "Just-in-Time Exchange Relationships in Industrial Markets," *Journal of Marketing* (October 1988), pp. 52–67; and Paul A. Dion, Peter M. Banting, and Loretta M. Hasey, "The Impact of JIT on Industrial Marketers," *Industrial Marketing Management* (February 1990), pp. 41–46.

10 "Southwest's New Bird," *Dallas Times Herald* (March 1, 1990), p. B2.

11 Mary C. LaForge and Louis H. Stone, "An Analysis of the Industrial Buying Process by Means of Buying Center Communications," *Journal of Business & Industrial Marketing* (Winter/Spring 1989), pp. 29–36.

12 "Where Three Sales a Year Make You a Superstar," *Business Week* (February 17, 1986), pp. 76–77.

13 Frank G. Bingham and Barney T. Raffield III, *Business to Business Marketing Management* (Homewood, Ill.: Richard D. Irwin, 1990), p. 11.

14 "McDonnell Douglas Grabs a Piece of China's Sky," *Business Week* (August 1987), p. 35; "Boeing Co. Gets Order by China for 33 Aircraft," *The Wall Street Journal* (June 1, 1990), p. A10.

15 Thomas V. Bonoma, "Major Sales: Who Really Does the Buying?" *Harvard Business Review* (May–June 1982), pp. 111–19. For recent work on buying groups, see Ajay Kohli, "Determinants of Influence in Organizational Buying: A Contingency Approach," *Journal of Marketing* (July 1989), pp. 50–65; and John R. Ronchetto, Jr., Michael D. Hutt, and Peter H. Reingen, "Embedded Influence Patterns in Organizational Buying Systems," *Journal of Marketing* (October 1989), pp. 51–62.

16 For extended discussions on Japanese business culture, see John L. Graham and Yoshihiro Sano, "Across the Negotiating Table from the Japanese," *International Marketing Review* (Autumn 1986), pp. 58–71; and Larry J. Rosenberg and George J. Thompson, "Deciphering the Japanese Cultural Code," *International Marketing Review* (Autumn 1986), pp. 47–57.

17 Herbert E. Brown and Roger W. Brucker, "Charting the Industrial Buying Stream," *Industrial Marketing Management* (February 1990), pp. 55–61; and Melvin R. Mattson, "How to Determine the Composition and Influence of a Buying Center," *Industrial Marketing Management* 17 (1988), pp. 205–14.

18 These definitions are adapted from Frederick E. Webster, Jr., and Yoram Wind, *Organizational Buying Behavior* (Englewood Cliffs, N.J.: Prentice Hall, 1972), p. 6.

19 For an extensive description of 18 industrial purchases, see Arch G. Woodside and Nyren Vyas, *Industrial Purchasing Strategies: Recommendations for Purchasing and Marketing Managers* (Lexington, Mass.: Lexington Books, 1987).

20 For insights into buying industrial services, see James R. Stock and Paul H. Zinszer, "The Industrial Purchase Decision for Professional Services," *Journal of Business Research* (February 1987), pp. 1–16.

21 Patrick J. Robinson, Charles W. Faris, and Yoram Wind, *Industrial Buying and Creative Marketing* (Boston: Allyn & Bacon, 1967).

22 Recent studies on the buy-class framework that document its usefulness include Erin Anderson, Wujin Chu, and Barton Weitz, "Industrial Purchasing: An Empirical Exploration of the Buy-class Framework," *Journal of Marketing* (July 1987), pp. 71–86; Morry Ghingold, "Testing the 'Buy-Grid' Buying Process Model," *Journal of Purchasing and Materials Management* (Winter 1986), pp. 30–36; P. Matthyssens and W. Faes, "OEM Buying Process for New Components: Purchasing and Marketing Implications," *Industrial Marketing Management* (August 1985), pp. 145–57; and Thomas W. Leigh and Arno J. Rethans, "A Script-Theoretic Analysis of Industrial Purchasing Behavior," *Journal of Marketing* (Fall 1984), pp. 22–32. Studies not supporting the buy-class framework include Joseph A. Bellizi and Philip McVey, "How Valid Is the Buy-Grid Model?" *Industrial Marketing Management* (February 1983), pp. 57–62; and Donald W. Jackson, Jamey E. Keith, and Richard K. Burdick, "Purchasing Agents' Perceptions of Industrial Buying Center Influences: A Situational Approach," *Journal of Marketing* (Fall 1984), pp. 75–83.

23 See, for example, Gary L. Lilien and Anthony Wong, "An Exploratory Investigation of the Structure of the Buying Center in the Metal Working Industry," *Journal of Marketing Research* (February 1984), pp. 1–11; and Wesley J. Johnston and Thomas V. Bonoma, "The Buying Center: Structure and Interaction Patterns," *Journal of Marketing* (Summer 1981), pp. 143–56. See also Christopher P. Puto, Wesley E. Patton III, and Ronald H. King, "Risk Handling Strategies in Industrial Vendor Selection Decisions," *Journal of Marketing* (Winter 1985), pp. 89–98.

24 For an extended discussion on how new technology like machine vision is being employed in factories, see Roy L. Harmon and Leroy D. Peterson, *Reinventing the Factory* (New York: Free Press, 1990).

25 Interview with Ward McClure, Industrial Automation Division, Texas Instruments, March 12, 1990. Used with permission.

26 William Rudelius, "Selling to the Government," in Victor Buehl, ed., *Handbook of Modern Marketing,* 2nd ed. (New York: McGraw-Hill, 1985).

27 C. William Verity, Jr., "Unleashing America's Space Entrepreneurs," *Across the Board* (April 1988), pp. 23–27.

28 Annette Kornblum, "How to Waste $12 Million," *Inc.* (December 1981), p. 95.

29 Gregory Stricharchuk, "Smokestack Industries Adopt Sophisticated Sales Approach," *The Wall Street Journal* (March 15, 1984), p. 31.

30 Ronald Henkoff, "This Cat Is Acting Like a Tiger," *Business Week* (December 19, 1988), pp. 69–76.

31 "The Rival Japan Respects," *Business Week* (November 13, 1989), pp. 108–11ff.

32 Niren Vyas and Arch Woodside, "An Inductive Model of Industrial Supplier Choice Processes," *Journal of Marketing* (Winter 1984), pp. 30–45; see also Ronald P. LeBlanc, "Insights into Organizational Buying," *Journal of Business & Industrial Marketing* (Spring 1987), pp. 5–10; and Robert E. Krapfel, Jr., "An Advocacy Model of Organizational Buyers' Vendor Choice," *Journal of Marketing* (Fall 1985), pp. 51–54.

33 "FDA Clears Monsanto Fat Substitute, Giving It a Jump on the Competition," *The Wall Street Journal* (February 23, 1990), pp. 131, 135.

CHAPTER 7

1 Kathleen A. Hughes, "Hunt for Blockbusters Has Big Movie Studios in a Spending Frenzy," *The Wall Street Journal* (May 3, 1990), pp. A1, A5; and John Greenwald, "Shooting the Works," *Time* (May 21, 1990), pp. 64–66.

2 John Koten, "How the Marketers Perform a Vital Role in a Movie's Success," *The Wall Street Journal* (December 14, 1984), p. 1.

3 Charles Champlin, "Audience's Opinions Make Final Cut," *Dallas Times Herald* (May 12, 1986), p. 30.

4 Helene Diamond, "Lights, Camera . . . Research!" *Marketing News* (September 11, 1989), pp. 10–11; and "Killer!" *Time* (November 16, 1987), pp. 72–79.

5 "How Paramount Keeps Churning Out Winners," *Business Week* (June 11, 1984), pp. 148–51; and Laura Landro, "Frank Maruso's Marketing Savvy Paves Way for Paramount Hits," *The Wall Street Journal* (June 27, 1984), p. 27.

6 "New Marketing Research Definition Approved," *Marketing News* (January 2, 1987), pp. 1, 14.

7 Rohit Deshpande, "The Organizational Context of Market Research Use," *Journal of Marketing* (Fall 1982), pp. 91–101; and John G. Myers, Stephen A. Greyser, and William F. Massy, "The Effectiveness of Marketing's 'R&D' for Marketing Management: An Assessment," *Journal of Marketing* (January 1979), pp. 17–29.

8 "Who'll Buy a Drink in a Box?" *Marketing and Media Decisions* (April 1982), p. 74ff.

9 Kate Fitzgerald, "Fisher-Price Suffers from Turmoil in Toyland," *Advertising Age* (November 20, 1989), p. 12; and "Fisher-Price: Fighting to Reclaim the Playpen," *Business Week* (December 24, 1990), pp. 70–71.

10 The dot and match problems are from Martin Scheerer, "Problem Solving," *Scientific American* (April 1963), pp. 118–28.

11 John H. Dessauer, *My Years with Xerox* (New York: Doubleday, 1971), pp. 45–48.

12 Caleb Solomon, "How Williams Cos. Turned Oil Pipelines to Conducts of Data," *The Wall Street Journal* (July 11, 1989), pp. A1, A7.

13 The bubble gum and hair dye examples are adapted from Roger Ricklefs, "Success Comes Hard in the Tricky Business of Creating Products," *The Wall Street Journal* (August 23, 1978), p. 1.

14 For example, see Gilbert A. Churchill, Jr., *Marketing Research: Methodological Foundations,* 5th ed. (Hinsdale, Ill.: Dryden Press, 1990); and Vincent P. Barabba, "The Market Research Encyclopedia," *Harvard Business Review* (January–February 1990), pp. 105–16.

15 William J. McKenna, "People Meters: The Search for Tomorrow," *Journal of Advertising Research* (August/September 1989), pp. RC-6–RC-7.

16 Kevin Goldman, "TV Networks Ask Nielsen to Alter People Meter Use," *The Wall Street Journal* (December 14, 1989), p. B4.

17 Susan Feyder, "It Took Tinkering by Twin Cities Firms to Save Some 'Sure Bets,' " *Minneapolis Star and Tribune* (June 9, 1982), p. 11A.

18 Jeffrey A. Trachtenberg, "Listening, the Old-Fashioned Way," *Forbes* (October 5, 1987), pp. 202–4.

19 Johny K. Johansson and Ikujiro Nonaka, "Market Research the Japanese Way," *Harvard Business Review* (May–June 1987), pp. 16–22.

20 O. C. Ferrell and Steven J. Skinner, "Ethical Behavior and Bureaucratic Structure in Marketing Research Organizations," *Journal of Marketing Research* (February 1988), pp. 103–9.

21 Thomas More, "He Put the Kick Back into Coke," *Fortune* (October 26, 1987), pp. 46–56; and Betsy Morris, "Coke vs. Pepsi: Cola War Marches On," *The Wall Street Journal* (June 3, 1987), p. 29.

22 Michael J. McCarthy, "Despite Challenges, Cola Remains King," *The Wall Street Journal* (March 2, 1989), p. B1; and Michael J. McCarthy, "New Coke Gets a New Look, New Chance," *The Wall Street Journal* (March 7, 1990), pp. B1, B7.

23 Betsy D. Gelb and Gabriel M. Gelb, "New Coke's Fizzle—Lessons for the Rest of Us," *Sloan Management Review* (Fall 1986), pp. 71–76.

CHAPTER 8

1 Jean Sherman, "No Pain, No Gain," *Working Woman* (May 1987), p. 92; "Can Reebok Sprint Even Faster?" *Business Week* (October 6, 1986), pp. 74–75; and "Sneakers That Don't Specialize," *Business Week* (June 6, 1988), p. 146.

2 Edward C. Baig, "Products to Watch: Reebok Pump," *Fortune* (January 1, 1990), p. 97; "Step by Step with Nike," *Business Week* (August 13, 1990), pp. 116–17; and "Where Nike and Reebok Have Plenty of Running Room," *Business Week* (March 11, 1991), pp. 56–60.

3 Peter R. Dickson and James L. Ginter, "Market Segmentation, Product Differentiation, and Marketing Strategy," *Journal of Marketing* (April 1987), pp. 1–10.

4 Joanne Lipman, "Chiat, Reebok Are Splitting Up After 3 Years," *The Wall Street Journal* (February 1, 1990), pp. B1, B6; and "Paul Fireman Pulls on His Old Running Shoes," *Business Week* (November 6, 1989), pp. 46–47.

5 "Stalking the New Consumer," *Business Week* (August 28, 1989), pp. 54–62; and "From the Publisher," *Time* (January 14, 1991), p. 4.

6 James Cook, "Where's the Niche?" *Forbes* (September 24, 1984), pp. 54–55; John Koten, "Giving Buyers Wider Choice May Be Hurting Auto Makers," *The Wall Street Journal* (December 15, 1983), p. 33; and Jacob M. Schlesinger and Joseph B. White, "The New-Model GM Will Be More Compact But More Profitable," *The Wall Street Journal* (June 6, 1988), pp. 1, 8.

7 *1988 Ford Thunderbird* (Dearborn, Mich.: Ford Motor Company, October 1987), pp. 18–21; *1988 Model Thunderbird Ordering Guide* (Dearborn, Michigan: Ford Motor Company, February 29, 1988), pp. 1–6; and Alex Taylor III, "The Tasks Facing General Motors," *Fortune* (March 13, 1989), pp. 52–59.

8 "Segmentation: Is It Real or Just a 'Research Event'?" *Marketing News* (August 28, 1987), pp. 37–40; and "Segmentation Won't Work Until It's Strategic," *Marketing News* (August 28, 1987), pp. 40–41.

9 Issues in using market segmentation studies are described in William Rudelius, John R. Walton, and James C. Cross, "Improving the Managerial Relevance of Market Segmentation Studies," in Michael J. Houston, ed., *1987 Review of Marketing* (Chicago: American Marketing Association, 1987), pp. 385–404.

10 Larry Carpenter, "How to Market to Regions," *American Demographics* (November 1987), pp. 11–15; "Marketing's New Look," *Business Week* (January 26, 1987), pp. 64–69; "GE Is Pulling Out the Stops at Home," *Business Week* (November 2, 1987), p. 94; and "On the Verge of World War in White Goods," *Business Week* (November 2, 1987), pp. 91–98.

11 Communication from Professor Jakki Mohr, University of Colorado at Boulder, August 22, 1989.

12 James S. Hirsch, "Heinz, Pleased with Plump Earnings, Expands Weight Watchers Product Line," *The Wall Street Journal* (December 4, 1989), p. B5; and Howard Schlossberg, "No 'Me Too' for These Two," *Marketing News* (May 14, 1990), pp. 1, 10.

13 Lisa H. Towle, "What's New in Frequency Marketing," *The New York Times* (December 3, 1989), p. 13.

14 Ronald Henkoff, "Big Mac Attacks with Pizza," *Fortune* (February 26, 1990), pp. 87–89; and "A New Chef Lights a Flame under Wendy's," *Business Week* (May 8, 1989), p. 70.

15 Robert Metz, "Apple Now a Strong Investment," *Minneapolis Star and Tribune* (October 1, 1987), p. 2M.

16 "The Second Comeback of Apple,"*Business Week* (January 28, 1991); G. Pascal Zachary, "Apple's Sculley Looks for a Breakthrough," *The Wall Street Journal* (March 15, 1991), p. B1; and G. Pascal Zachary, "Apple's Sculley Indicates Plans for Portables," *The Wall Street Journal* (March 19, 1991), p. B4.

17 Anthony Ramirez, "America's Super Minority," *Fortune* (November 25, 1986), pp. 148–62.

18 Joshua Levine, "Sorrell Ridge Makes Smucker Pucker," *Forbes* (June 12, 1989), pp. 166–67.

19 Advantages and disadvantages of cross tabulations are adapted from Roseann Maguire and Terry C. Wilson, "Banners or Cross Tabs? Before Deciding, Weigh Data—Format, Pros, Cons," *Marketing News* (May 13, 1983), pp. 10–11.

20 Sue Shellenbarger, "McDonald's Low-Fat Burger to Go National," *The Wall Street Journal* (March 13, 1991), p. B1.

21 Regis McKenna, "Playing for Position," *Inc.* (April 1985), pp. 92–97.

22 Joseph B. White, "Value Pricing Is Hot as Shrewd Consumers Seek Low-Cost Quality," *The Wall Street Journal* (March 12, 1991), pp. A1, A5.

23 "Are the Planets Lining Up at Last for Saturn?" *Business Week* (April 8, 1991), pp. 32–34.

24 Alex Taylor III, "The New Drive to Revive GM," *Fortune* (April 9, 1990), pp. 52–61.

25 Joseph B. White and Paul Ingrassia, "Huge GM Write-Off Positions Auto Maker to Show New Growth," *The Wall Street Journal* (November 1, 1990), pp. A1, A13.

26 Paul Ingrassia and Joseph B. White, "GM's New Boss Runs into Many Problems—But Little Opposition," *The Wall Street Journal* (February 8, 1991), pp. A1, A4.

27 Andrew Purris, "Cheaper Can Be Better," *Time* (March 18, 1991), p. 70.

CHAPTER 9

1 Michael J. McCarthy, "What Micromarketing Taught Our Reporter about His A&P," *The Wall Street Journal* (March 18, 1991), p. B1.

2 Michael J. McCarthy, "Marketers Zero In on Their Customers," *The Wall Street Journal* (March 18, 1991), pp. B1, B5.

3 Kathleen Deveny, "Segments of One," *The Wall Street Journal* (March 22, 1991), p. B4.

4 Charles Wiseman, *Strategic Information Systems* (Homewood, Ill.: Richard D. Irwin, 1988), pp. 93–100.

5 McCarthy, "Marketers Zero In," p. B1.

6 F. Warren McFarlan, "Information Technology Changes the Way You Compete," *Harvard Business Review* (May–June 1984), pp. 98–103; James I. Cash, Jr., and Benn R. Konsynski, "IS Redraws Competitive Boundaries," *Harvard Business Review* (March–April 1985), pp. 134–42; and Michael E. Porter and Victor E. Millar, "How Information Gives You Competitive Advantage," *Harvard Business Review* (July–August 1985), pp. 149–60.

7 James A. O'Brien, *Management Information Systems* (Homewood, Ill.: Richard D. Irwin, 1990), pp. 45–51; and Benn R. Konsynski and F. Warren McFarlan, "Information Partnerships—Shared Data, Shared Scale," *Harvard Business Review* (September–October 1990), pp. 114–20.

8 Max D. Hopper, "Rattling SABRE—New Ways to Compete on Information," *Harvard Business Review* (May–June 1990), pp. 118–25; and F. Warren McFarlan and James C. Wetherbe, "SABRE Rattling and the Future of the Chief Information Officer," *Harvard Business Review* (July–August 1990), pp. 176–77.

9 "Information Users Own the Future, Keynote Says," *Conference Call, National Computer Conference* (Summer 1986).

10 Wiseman, pp. 18–24; and *American Airlines, Inc.: Revenue Management* (Boston, Mass.: HBS Case Services, Harvard Business School, 1989), pp. 3–7.

11 Faye Rice, "How to Deal with Tougher Customers," *Fortune* (December 3, 1990), pp. 39–48.

12 Frank Rose, "Now Quality Means Service Too," *Fortune* (April 22, 1991), pp. 99–100; Patricia Sellers, "What Customers Really Want," *Fortune* (June 4, 1990), pp. 58–68; and Ann B. Fisher, "What Consumers Want in the 1990s," *Fortune* (January 29, 1990), pp. 108–12.

13 Rose, p. 102.

14 Amanda Bennett, "Making the Grade with the Customers," *The Wall Street Journal* (November 12, 1990), pp. B1, B4; and Kathleen Deveny, "For Marketers, No Peeve Is Too Petty," *The Wall Street Journal* (November 14, 1990), pp. B1, B6.

15 Ross Johnson and William O. Winchell, *Marketing and Quality* (Milwaukee: American Society for Quality Control, 1989), p. 2.

16 Gilbert Fuchsberg, "Gurus of Quality Are Gaining Clout," *The Wall Street Journal* (November 27, 1990), pp. B1, B3.

17 Howard Schlossberg, "Baldridge Winner Aims at 100% Satisfaction," *Marketing News* (February 4, 1991), pp. 1, 12.

18 Dom Del Prete, "Advances in Scanner Research Yield Better Data Quicker," *Marketing News* (January 7, 1991), p. 54.

19 Jeremy Main, "Computers of the World, Unite!" *Fortune* (September 24, 1990), pp. 115–22.

20 Brenton R. Schlender, "Hot New PCs That Read Your Writing," *Fortune* (February 11, 1991), pp. 113–21.

21 Joe Schwartz, "Back to the Source," *American Demographics* (January 1989), pp. 22–26; and Felix Kessler, "High-Tech Shocks in Ad Research," *Fortune* (July 7, 1986), pp. 58–62.

22 "Everything You Always Wanted to Know—By PC," *Business Week* (October 1, 1990), pp. 176–77.

23 Alan R. Andreasen, " 'Backward' Market Research," *Harvard Business Review* (May–June 1985), pp. 176–82; and Paul B. Brown, "On the Cheap," *Inc.* (February 1988), pp. 108–10.

24 Howard Schlossberg, "Marketers Moving to Make Data Bases Actionable," *Marketing News* (February 18, 1991), p. 8.

25 Michael J. Wolfe, "90's Will See a 'Great Leap Forward' in Sales Tracking," *Marketing News* (September 3, 1990), p. 2.

26 John W. Verity, "Rethinking the Computer," *Business Week* (November 26, 1990), pp. 116–24.

27 The Dahl's Food supermarket example is adapted from Josephine Marcotty, "Check It Out: An Eye on What You Buy," *Star Tribune* (February 26, 1990), pp. 1D, 6D.

28 Michael W. Miller, "Data Mills Delve Deep to Find Information about U.S. Consumers," *The Wall Street Journal* (March 14, 1991), pp. A1, A12; Cyndee Miller, "Lotus Forced to Cancel New Software Program," *Marketing News* (February 18, 1991), p. 11; and Daniel Seligman, "The Devil in Direct Marketing," *Fortune* (March 11, 1991), pp. 123–24.

29 "Analyzing Promotions: The Free-Standing Insert Coupon," *Nielsen Researchers*, no. 4 (1982), pp. 16–20.

CHAPTER 10

1 Alex Beam, "Shave-off at the Hotel Pierre," *Boston Globe* (October 4, 1989), pp. 85–86; Alison Fahey, "International Ad Effort to Back Gillette Sensor," *Advertising Age* (October 16, 1989), p. 31; Lawrence Ingrassia, "A Recovering Gillette Hopes for Vindication in a High Tech Razor," *The Wall Street Journal* (September 29, 1989), pp. A1, A4; and Mary Sit, "Gillette's $110 Million Shave," *The Boston Globe* (January 14, 1990), pp. 73, 78.

2 Mary Sit, "Demand for Sensor Poses Hairy Problem," *The Boston Globe* (March 7, 1990), pp. 65, 72.

3 Definitions within this classification are from Committee on Definitions, *Marketing Definitions: A Glossary of Marketing Terms* (Chicago: American Marketing Association, 1960).

4 Ibid.

5 "New Product Flood Likely to Recede," *The Wall Street Journal* (January 10, 1991), p. B1; and Howard Schlossberg, "If the Product's 'New' It Really May Be 'Me Too'," *Marketing News* (November 6, 1989), p. 2.

6 David S. Hopkins, *New Product Winners and Losers,* Conference Board Study Report no. 773 (New York: Conference Board, 1980).

7 "Marketing Briefs," *Business Week* (April 22, 1967), p. 120.

8 Thomas Robertson, "The Process of Innovation and Diffusion of Innovation," *Journal of Marketing* (January 1967), p. 15.

9 Paul Zachary, "Household Games, Encyclopedias to Draw Crowds at Consumer Electronics Show," *The Wall Street Journal* (January 7, 1991), p. B1.

10 "New Product Failure: A Self-Fulfilling Prophecy?" *Marketing Communications* (April 1989), p. 27.

11 Clare Ansberry, "Eastman Kodak Is Pulling Plug on Its Ultralife," *The Wall Street Journal* (April 10, 1990), pp. B1, B2.

12 Ronald Baily, "Sweet Technology, Sour Marketing," *Forbes* (May 1, 1989), p. 140.

13 " 'Smokeless' Cigarette Test Turns to Ashes," *The Boston Globe* (March 1, 1989), p. 43.

14 "How Miller Got Dunked in Matilda Bay," *Business Week* (September 25, 1989), p. 54.

15 "Marketers Blunder Their Way through the 'Herb Decade'," *Advertising Age* (February 13, 1989), pp. 3, 66.

16 Thomas F. O'Boyle, "GE Refrigerator Woes Illustrate the Hazards in Changing a Product," *The Wall Street Journal* (May 7, 1990), pp. A1, A5; and "The 'Glitch' May Cost GE $350 Million," *Business Week* (January 30, 1989), p. 28.

17 Claire Poole, "Sweating It Out," *Forbes* (October 16, 1989), p. 274.

18 R. G. Cooper and E. J. Kleinschmidt, "New Products— What Separates Winners from Losers?" *Journal of Product Innovation Management* (September 1987), pp. 169–84.

19 "Canon Finally Challenges Minolta's Mighty Maxxum," *Business Week* (March 2, 1987), pp. 89–90.

20 *New Products Management for the 1980's* (Booz, Allen & Hamilton, Inc., 1982).

21 "Masters of Innovation: How 3M Keeps Its New Products Coming," *Business Week* (April 10, 1989), pp. 58–63.

22 "Why Hershey Is Smacking Its Lips," *Business Week* (October 30, 1989), p. 140.

23 Glen L. Urban, John R. Hauser, and Nikhilesh Dholakia, *Essentials of New Product Management* (Englewood Cliffs, N.J.: Prentice Hall, 1987), pp. 15–17.

24 Michael J. McCarthy, "U.S. Companies Shop Abroad for Product Ideas," *The Wall Street Journal* (March 14, 1990), pp. B1, B4; and Amal Kumar Naj, "GE's Latest Invention: A Way to Move Ideas from Lab to Market," *The Wall Street Journal* (June 14, 1990), pp. A1, A9.

25 "M'm! M'm! Bad! Trouble at Campbell Soup," *Business Week* (September 25, 1989), pp. 68–69.

26 Marj Charlier, "Bottled Draft Beers Head for Collision as Anheuser Readies Challenge to Miller," *The Wall Street Journal* (May 1, 1990), pp. B1, B6; and Ira Teinowitz, "Draft Beer Lookalike; A-B Brings Out Another Rival to Miller," *Advertising Age* (April 4, 1990), p. 12.

27 Patricia Sellers, "Getting Customers to Love You," *Fortune* (March 13, 1989), pp. 38–49.

28 "P&G Rewrites the Marketing Rules," *Fortune* (November 6, 1989), pp. 34–38.

29 Edward M. Tauber, "Discovering New Product Opportunities with Problem Inventory Analysis," *Journal of Marketing* (January 1975).

30 Richard Gibson, "McDonald's Seeks to Cut Fat in Fare," *The Wall Street Journal* (March 4, 1990), pp. B1, B2.

31 Jeffrey Tannebaum, "Tiny Company Elevates an Idea to a Marketable Product," *The Wall Street Journal* (July 5, 1990), p. B2.

32 "Masters of Innovation," *Business Week* (April 10, 1989), pp. 58–63; and P. Ranganath Nayak and John M. Ketteringham, *Breakthroughs!* (New York: Rawson Associates, 1986), pp. 50–73.

33 "Toray May Have Found the Formula for Luck," *Business Week Innovation 1990* (June 15, 1990), p. 110; and Richard Konig, "Rich New Products, Monsanto Must Only Get Them on Market," *The Wall Street Journal* (May 18, 1990), pp. A1, A4.

34 Brian Dumaine, "Corporate Spies Stoop to Conquer," *Fortune* (November 7, 1988), pp. 68–76.

35 Lee Adler, "Before Plunging into the Market, Try a Little Concept Testing," *Sales and Marketing Management* (January 16, 1984), pp. 98–103.

36 Susan Caminiti, "What the Scanner Knows about You," *Fortune* (December 3, 1990), pp. 51–52.

37 Sak Onkvisit and John J. Shaw, *Product Life Cycles and Product Management* (New York: Quorum Books, 1989), p. 26.

38 J. Quincy Hunsicker, "Misinnovation: How to Guard against Investing in Systems that Won't Work," *Management Review* (April 1984), pp. 16–18.

39 Paul Ingrassia, "Industry Is Shopping Abroad for Good Ideas to Apply to Products," *The Wall Street Journal* (April 29, 1985), p. 1.

40 "Step by Step with Nike," *Business Week* (August 13, 1990), pp. 116–17.

41 Michael J. Baker and Ronald McTavish, *Product Policy and Management* (London: Macmillan Press, Ltd., 1976), p. 146.

42 Jay Klopmaker, David Hughes, and R. Haley, "Test Marketing in New Product Development," *Harvard Business Review* (May–June 1976).

43 Pat Seelig, "All Over the Map," *Sales & Marketing Management* (March 1989), pp. 58–64.

44 Liz Murphy, "Beer Drinkers Put Coors to the Test!" *Sales and Marketing Management* (March 12, 1984), pp. 93–100.

45 Ronald Alsop, "Companies Get on the Fast Track to Roll Out Hot New Brands," *The Wall Street Journal* (July 10, 1986), p. 27.

46 Urban and Hauser, p. 74.

47 Ibid.

48 "Pinning Down Costs of Product Introductions," *The Wall Street Journal* (November 26, 1990), p. B1.

49 "Want Shelf at the Supermarket? Ante Up," *Business Week* (August 7, 1989), pp. 60–61.

50 "How Managers Can Succeed through Speed," *Fortune* (February 13, 1989), pp. 54–59.

51 Ibid.

52 W. Christopher Musselwhite, "Time Based Innovation: The New Competitive Advantage," *Training and Development* (January 1990), pp. 53–56.

53 Bruce Ingersoll, "FDA Finds Bunk in Bottled-Water Claims," *The Wall Street Journal* (April 10, 1991), pp. B1, B12.

CHAPTER 11

1 "Fax Machines Breaking $499 Price Barrier," *USA Today* (January 8, 1990), p. B1; "FAX's Future Fracas," *Dallas Times Herald* (August 17, 1990), pp. B1, B3; "It's a Fax, Fax, Fax World," *Business Week* (March 21, 1988), p. 136; and Frederick H. Katayama, "Who's Fueling the Fax Frenzy," *Fortune* (October 23, 1989), pp. 151–56.

2 Several early studies in marketing have reported this general curve: Robert D. Buzzell and V. Cook, *Product Life Cycles* (Cambridge, Mass.: Marketing Science Institute, 1969), pp. 29–35; F. J. Kovac and M. F. Daque, "Forecasting by Product Life Cycle Analysis," *Research Management* (July 1972); M. T. Cunningham, "The Application of Product Life Cycles to Corporate Strategy: Some Research Findings," *British Journal of Marketing* (Spring 1969), pp. 32–44; and A. Patton, "Top Management's Stake in the Product Life Cycle," *Management Review* (June 1959), pp. 9–14.

3 Katayama, pp. 151–56.

4 John J. Keller, "Cellular Phones Dial Digital for Growth," *The Wall Street Journal* (May 14, 1990), pp. B1, B7; and Julie Amparano Lopez, "Marketers Spy and Entice to Get an Edge," *The Wall Street Journal* (May 14, 1990), pp. B1, B7.

5 "Fevered Pace for Fax," *Advertising Age* (September 11, 1989), p. 32.

6 Carl R. Anderson and Carl P. Zeithaml, "Stage of the Product Life Cycle, Business Strategy, and Business Performance," *Academy of Management Journal* (March 1984), pp. 5–24.

7 "The Microwave Cooks Up a New Way of Life," *The Wall Street Journal* (September 19, 1989), p. B1.

8 George J. Avlonitis, "Ethics and Product Elimination," *Management Decision,* vol. 21, no. 2 (1983), pp. 37–45; and R. T. Hise and M. A. McGinnis, "Product Elimination: Practices, Policies, and Ethics," *Business Horizons* (June 1975), pp. 25–32.

9 David R. Rink and John E. Swan, "Product Life Cycle Research: A Literature Review," *Journal of Business Research* (September 1979), pp. 218–42; and David M. Gardner, "Product Life Cycle: A Critical Look at the Literature," in Michael Houston, ed., *Review of Marketing 1987* (Chicago: American Marketing Association, 1987), pp. 162–94.

10 David R. Rink and John E. Swan, "Fitting Marketing Strategy to Varying Product Life Cycles," *Business Horizons* (January–February 1982), pp. 72–76.

11 Michael Garry, "Pain Pays," *Marketing and Media Decisions* (March 1990), pp. 45–52; and "An Epitaph for the Epilady?" *Business Week* (September 17, 1990), p. 38.

12 The terms *high* and *low learning life cycles* were developed by Chester R. Wasson, *Dynamic Competitive Strategies and Product Life Cycles* (Austin, Tex.: Austin Press, 1978).

13 James McGregor, "If This Sells, Someone Will Start on Pebble Beach," *The Wall Street Journal* (October 23, 1990), p. B1; and "If It's Friday, It Must Be Goofy Videocassette Day," *Advertising Age* (February 22, 1988), pp. 44, 45.

14 Lester A. Neidell, "Don't Forget the Product Life Cycle for Strategic Planning," *Business* (April–June 1983), pp. 30–35.

15 Carlee R. Scott, "Car Batteries Go for New Gadget to Charge Sales," *The Wall Street Journal* (March 1, 1990), pp. B1, B6.

16 "Modified Screwdrivers May Prevent Slips," *The Wall Street Journal* (December 19, 1990), p. B1.

17 Alecia Swasy, "How Innovation at P&G Restored Luster to Washed Up Pert and Made It No. 1," *The Wall Street Journal* (December 6, 1990), pp. B1, B6.

18 Jennifer Lawrence, "Nautilus Pumps Iron in Home Gym Market," *Advertising Age* (December 1987), p. 22; Jeffrey A. Tannenbaum, "Video Games Revive—and Makers Hope This Time the Fad Will Last," *The Wall Street Journal* (March 8, 1988), p. 33; and "But I Don't Wanna Play Nintendo Anymore!" *Business Week* (November 19, 1990), pp. 52–53.

19 Michael J. McCarthy, "Coke II Survives One Test City, Heads to a Second," *The Wall Street Journal* (October 5, 1990), pp. B1, B6; and Michael J. McCarthy, "New Coke Gets a New Look," *The Wall Street Journal* (March 7, 1990), pp. B1, B8.

20 Bob Geiger, "Liquid Yogurts Pour into the U.S.," *Advertising Age* (June 1, 1987), pp. 3, 62.

21 Raymond Serafin, "BMW Races Mercedes on High End of Market," *Advertising Age* (December 7, 1987), p. 4; and Raymond Serafin, "BMW Boosts Ad Budget to Pace Mercedes Sales," *Advertising Age* (March 2, 1987), p. 24.

22 "Design Patents: How the Courts Help the Copycats," *Business Week* (November 5, 1990), p. 105; "Companies Are Knocking Off the Knockoff Outfits," *Business Week* (September 26, 1989), pp. 86–88; and Damon Darlin, "Where Trademarks Are up for Grabs," *The Wall Street Journal* (December 5, 1989), pp. B1, B5. See also Robert J. Thomas, "Patent Infringement of Innovations by Foreign Competitors: The Role of the U.S. International Trade Commission," *Journal of Marketing* (October 1989), pp. 63–75.

23 Peter H. Farquar, "Managing Brand Equity," *Marketing Insights* (Summer 1990), pp. 58–64.

24 Joshua Levine, "But in the Office, No," *Forbes* (October 16, 1989), pp. 272–73.

25 Kevin Goldman, " 'Ninja Turtle' Juggernaut Demolishes Box Office Record," *The Wall Street Journal* (April 3, 1990), pp. B1, B6.

26 Daniel L. Doden, "Selecting a Brand Name That Aids Marketing Objectives," *Advertising Age* (November 5, 1990), p. 34.

27 Wade Lambert, "If They Think They're So Smart Let's See Them Spell Yankelovich," *The Wall Street Journal* (October 2, 1989), p. B1.

28 Kim Robertson, "Strategically Desirable Brand Name Characteristics," *Journal of Consumer Marketing* (Fall 1989), pp. 61–71.

29 Cyndee Miller, "Cereal Maker to Kids: Eat Breakfast with Barbie," *Marketing News* (September 25, 1989), p. 10; Francine Schwadel, "Spiegel, Crayola Plan Kids' Clothes Line," *The Wall Street Journal* (October 3, 1990), p. B1; and Pauline Yoshihashi, "Mattel Shapes a New Future for Barbie," *The Wall Street Journal* (February 12, 1990), pp. B1, B2.

30 For a review of this literature, see David A. Aaker and Kevin Lane Keller, "Consumer Evaluations of Brand Extensions," *Journal of Marketing* (January 1990), pp. 27–41.

31 Levine, pp. 272–73.

32 Laurie Freedman, "P&G Extends Pringle's Line," *Advertising Age* (January 22, 1990), p. 42.

33 Swasy, pp. B1, B6; and Alecia Swasy, "P&G to Tout Name behind the Brands," *The Wall Street Journal* (December 19, 1990), pp. B1, B7.

34 Sak Onkvisit and John J. Shaw, "The International Dimension of Branding: Strategic Considerations and Decisions," *International Marketing Review,* vol. 6, no. 3 (1989), pp. 22–34; and Walter J. Salmon and Karen A. Cmar, "Private Labels Are Back in Fashion," *Harvard Business Review* (May–June 1987), pp. 99–106.

35 Ron Suskind, "Minolta Puts Name on Polaroid," *The Wall Street Journal* (June 29, 1990), pp. B1, B8.

36 Michael J. McCarthy, "Food Companies Fear Pressure on Prices," *The Wall Street Journal* (December 10, 1990), pp. B1, B5.

37 Martha R. McEnally and Jon M. Hawes, "The Market for Generic Brand Grocery Products: A Review and Extension," *Journal of Marketing* (Winter 1984), pp. 75–83.

38 Kathleen Day, "Designers Go for a Package Deal," *Dallas Times Herald* (March 19, 1985), p. C1.

39 Walter McQuade, "Packages Bear Up under a Bundle of Regulations," *Fortune* (May 7, 1979), p. 179.

40 Yoram S. Wind, *Product Policy* (Reading, Mass.: Addison-Wesley, 1982), pp. 355–56.

41 In recent years there has been significant debate over the value of government-required grade labeling. See John A. Miller, *Labeling Research: The State of the Art,* Report No. 78-115 (Cambridge, Mass.: Marketing Science Institute, 1978).

42 "Pop-Open Packages for a Hurried Populace," *The Wall Street Journal* (April 2, 1990), p. B1.

43 Michael Hiestand and Stephen Battaglio, "The Clothes Make the Brand," *Marketing Week* (August 17, 1987), pp. 1, 4. See also Fred W. Morgan, "Tampered Goods: Legal Developments and Marketing Guidelines," *Journal of Marketing* (April 1988), pp. 86–96.

44 Alecia Swasy, "Sales Lost Their Vim? Try Repackaging," *The Wall Street Journal* (October 11, 1989), p. B1.

45 Carl McDaniel and R. C. Baker, "Convenience Food Packaging and the Perception of Product Quality," *Journal of Marketing* (October 1977), pp. 57–58.

46 Ronald Alsop, "Color Grows More Important in Catching Consumers' Eyes," *The Wall Street Journal* (November 28, 1984), p. 37.

47 Fred Feucht, "Which Hue Is Best? Test Your Color I.Q.," *Advertising Age* (September 14, 1987), pp. 18, 20.

48 Swasy, p. B1.

49 Cyndee Miller, "Use of Environment-Friendly Packaging May Take Awhile," *Marketing News* (March 19, 1990), p. 18; Bill Paul, "Package Firms Find It's Hard Being Green," *The Wall Street Journal* (May 25, 1990), pp. B1, B5; James S. Hirsch, "Heinz to Unveil Recyclable Bottle for Its Ketchup," *The Wall Street Journal* (April 4, 1990), p. B3; and Laurie

Freedman, "P&G to Tout Recycled Packages," *Advertising Age* (April 19, 1990), p. 42.

50 "The Big Brouhaha over the Little Juice Box," *Business Week* (September 17, 1990), p. 36.

51 Sonia L. Nazario, "Microwave Packages that Add Crunch to Lunch May Also Pose Chemical Risks," *The Wall Street Journal* (March 1, 1990), pp. B1, B6.

52 Robert E. Wilkes and James B. Wilcox, "Limited versus Full Warranties: The Retail Perspective," *Journal of Retailing* (Spring 1981), pp. 65–77.

CHAPTER 12

1 Interview with Dwight R. Riskey, vice president of Marketing Research and New Business, Frito-Lay, Inc., June 6, 1990. Used with permission.

2 "Small Firms Short on Cash Turn to Barter," *The Wall Street Journal* (November 26, 1990), pp. B1, B2; Arthur Bragg, "Marketing Comes of Age,"*Sales and Marketing Management* (January 1989), pp. 61–63; and Jack G. Kaikati, "Marketing without Exchange of Money," *Harvard Business Review* (November–December 1982), pp. 72–74.

3 This example is based on "Probe Helps Ford Write Another Success Story," *Dallas Times Herald* (December 17, 1989), p. 24.

4 Adapted from Kent B. Monroe, *Pricing: Making Profitable Decisions,* 2nd ed. (New York: McGraw-Hill, 1990), Chapter 4. See also Fabian Linden, "Value of the Dolls," *Across the Board* (December 1985), pp. 54–57, 60; and David J. Curry, "Measuring Price and Quality Competition," *Journal of Marketing* (Spring 1985), pp. 106–17.

5 Joseph B. White, "Value Pricing Is Hot As Shrewd Consumers Seek Low-Cost Quality," *The Wall Street Journal* (March 12, 1991), pp. A1, A5.

6 Numerous studies have examined the price–quality–value relationship. See, for example, Jacob Jacoby and Jerry C. Olsen, eds., *Perceived Quality* (Lexington, Mass.: Lexington Books, 1985); Kent B. Monroe and William B. Dodds, "A Research Program for Establishing the Validity of the Price–Quality Relationship," *Journal of the Academy of Marketing Science* (Spring 1988), pp. 151–68; and Askay R. Rao and Kent B. Monroe, "The Effect of Price, Brand Name, and Store Name on Buyers' Perceptions of Product Quality: An Integrative Review," *Journal of Marketing Research* (August 1989), pp. 351–57. For a thorough review of the price–quality–value relationship, see Valarie A. Ziethaml, "Consumer Perceptions of Price, Quality, and Value," *Journal of Marketing* (July 1988), pp. 2–22. Also see Jerry Wind, "Getting a Read on Market-Defined 'Value'," *Journal of Pricing Management* (Winter 1990), pp. 5–14.

7 These examples are from Roger A. Kerin and Robert A. Peterson, "Shanandoah Industries," *Strategic Marketing Problems: Cases and Comments,* 5th ed. (Boston: Allyn & Bacon, 1990), p. 303; and "Software Economics 101," *Forbes* (January 28, 1985), p. 88.

8 Thomas T. Nagle, *The Strategy and Tactics of Pricing* (Englewood Cliffs, N.J.: Prentice Hall, 1987), p. 107.

9 Barbara J. Coe, "Shifts in Industrial Pricing Objectives," *AMA Educators' Conference Proceedings* (Chicago: American Marketing Association, 1988), pp. 9–14. See also Barbara

Coe, "Strategy in Retreat: Pricing Drops Out," *Journal of Business & Industrial Marketing* (Winter/Spring 1990), pp. 5–26.

10 "Rich in New Products, Monsanto Must Only Get Them on Market," *The Wall Street Journal* (May 18, 1990), pp. A1, A5.

11 "MGM Grand Air Says It Will Replace 727s with Larger DC-8s," *The Wall Street Journal* (April 25, 1990), p. C21.

12 "Monsanto's Simplese Weighs In," *USA Today* (February 23, 1990), p. B1.

13 For a review of pricing objectives, see Saeed Samiee, "Pricing in Marketing Strategies of U.S.- and Foreign-Based Companies," *Journal of Business Research* (February 1987), pp. 1–16.

14 Patricia Sellers, "Busch Fights to Have It All," *Fortune* (January 15, 1990), pp. 81ff.

15 "Eastern's Fire-Sale Fares," *Business Week* (January 15, 1990), p. 32.

16 "Made Just for Him," *Time* (April 16, 1990), p. 49.

17 "Should Water Supplies Go down the Drain?" *Business Week* (March 5, 1984), pp. 104–6.

18 Michael Garry, "Dollar Strength: Publishers Confront the New Economic Realities," *Folio: The Magazine for Magazine Management* (February 1989), pp. 88–93; Cara S. Trager, "Right Price Reflects a Magazine's Health Goals," *Advertising Age* (March 9, 1987), pp. 5–8ff; and Frank Bruni, "Price of Newsweek? It Depends," *Dallas Times Herald* (August 14, 1986), pp. S1, S20.

19 For an overview of price elasticity studies, see Ruth N. Bolton, "The Robustness of Retail-Level Price Elasticity Estimates," *Journal of Retailing* (Summer 1989), pp. 193–219; and Gerard J. Tellis, "The Price Elasticity of Selective Demand: A Meta-Analysis of Econometric Models of Sales," *Journal of Marketing Research* (November 1988), pp. 331–41.

20 See, for example, Susan L. Holak and Srinivas K. Reddy, "Effects of a Television and Radio Advertising Ban: A Study of the Cigarette Industry," *Journal of Marketing* (October 1986), pp. 219–27; and Rick Andrews and George R. Franke, "Time-Varying Elasticities of U.S. Cigarette Demand, 1933–1987," *AMA Educators' Conference Proceedings* (Chicago: American Marketing Association, 1990), p. 393.

21 Monroe, pp. 24–26. See also David W. Nylen, *Marketing Decision-Making Handbook* (Englewood Cliffs, N.J.: Prentice Hall, 1990), pp. G-237–G-239.

22 For illustrations of break-even analysis that document its use and versatility, see Thomas L. Powers, "Break-Even Analysis with Semifixed Costs," *Industrial Marketing Management* (February 1987), pp. 35–41; and "Break-Even Analysis," *Small Business Report* (August 1986), pp. 22–24.

CHAPTER 13

1 Max D. Hopper, "Rattling SABRE—New Ways to Compete on Information," *Harvard Business Review* (May–June 1990), pp. 118–25; "How Airlines Will Look in the 1990's," *Fortune* (January 1, 1990), pp. 50–56; *American Airlines, Inc.: Revenue Management* (Harvard Business School Case Services, N9-190-029); and "The 50 Largest Transportation Companies," *Fortune* (June 4, 1990), p. 328.

2 "U.S. Invents, Japan Profits (Again)," *Fortune* (March 12, 1990), pp. 14–15.

3 "IBM Introduces Line of Workstations; Industry Analysts Impressed by Prices," *The Wall Street Journal* (February 16, 1990), p. B3.

4 For an extended treatment of skimming and penetration pricing, see Joel Dean, "Pricing Policies for New Products," *Harvard Business Review* (November–December 1976), pp. 141–53.

5 Jeffrey H. Birnbaum, "Pricing of Products Is Still an Art, Often Having Little Link to Costs," *The Wall Street Journal* (November 25, 1981), p. 25.

6 See, for example, V. Kumar and Robert P. Leone, "Measuring the Effect of Retail Store Promotions on Brand and Store Substitution," *Journal of Marketing Research* (May 1988), pp. 178–85.

7 For an excellent review of bundle pricing, see Joseph P. Guiltinan, "The Price Bundling of Services: A Normative Framework," *Journal of Marketing* (April 1987), pp. 74–85; and Thomas T. Nagle, *The Strategy and Tactics of Pricing* (Englewood Cliffs, N.J.: Prentice Hall, 1987), pp. 170–72.

8 For a recent discussion on the experience curve, see William W. Alberts, "The Experience Doctrine Reconsidered," *Journal of Marketing* (July 1989), pp. 36–49.

9 "Fax Machines Breaking $499 Price Barrier," *USA Today* (January 8, 1990), p. B1; *Consumer Reports* 1990 Buying Guide Issue (Mt. Vernon, N.Y.: Consumer Union of the United States), pp. 106–7; and "Calling All Cars," *Dallas Times Herald* (July 14, 1990), pp. E1, E6.

10 "Who Wins with Price-Matching Plans?" *The Wall Street Journal* (March 16, 1989), p. B1.

11 "One Word for One Price: Success," *Business Week* (May 23, 1988), p. 123.

12 "Pechin's Mart Breaks Many Rules, but not the One on Pricing," *The Wall Street Journal* (March 5, 1984), p. A1.

13 "GM's Cadillac Cuts Top, and Thus Price, of Allante," *The Wall Street Journal* (August 1, 1989), p. B2; and "Here Comes GM's Saturn," *Business Week* (April 9, 1990), pp. 56–62.

14 "A Price That's Too Good May Be Bad," *The Wall Street Journal* (November 15, 1988), p. B1.

15 "Bob Allen Is Turning AT&T into a Live Wire," *Business Week* (November 6, 1989), pp. 140–41ff.

16 For a review of quantity discounts, see George S. Day and Adrian B. Ryans, "Using Price Discounts for a Competitive Advantage," *Industrial Marketing Management* (February 1988), pp. 1–14; and James B. Wilcox, Roy D. Howell, Paul Kuzdrall, and Robert Britney, "Price Quantity Discounts: Some Implications for Buyers and Sellers," *Journal of Marketing* (July 1987), pp. 60–70.

17 "Burger King, in Big Blow to Pepsi, Is Switching to Coke," *The Wall Street Journal* (May 2, 1990), pp. B1, B6.

18 Michael Levy and Charles Ingene, "Retailers: Head Off Credit Cards with Cash Discounts," *Harvard Business Review* (May–June 1983), pp. 18–22.

19 Rockney G. Walters, "An Empirical Investigation in Retailer Response to Manufacturer Trade Promotions," *Journal of Retailing* (Summer 1989), pp. 258–72; Ronald C. Curhan and Robert J. Kopp, "Obtaining Retailer Support for Trade Deals: Key Success Factors," *Journal of Advertising Research* (December–January 1987/1988), pp. 51–60; and Michael Levy, John Webster, and Roger A. Kerin, "Formulating Push Marketing Strategies: A Method and Application," *Journal of Marketing* (Winter 1983), pp. 25–34.

20 For an overview of the legality of various pricing practices, see Susan S. Samuelson and Thomas A. Balmer, "Antitrust Revisited: Implications for Competitive Strategy," *Sloan Management Review* (Fall 1988), pp. 79–87.

21 "Saks, I. Magnin Hit on Pricing," *Chain Store Age Executive* (June 1979), p. 4.

22 For insights into resale price maintenance, see Patrick J. Kaufmann, "Dealer Termination Agreements and Resale Price Maintenance: Implications of the Business Electronics Case and the Proposed Amendment to the Sherman Act," *Journal of Retailing* (Summer 1988), pp. 113–24; and Mary Jane Sheffet and Debra L. Scammon, "Resale Price Maintenance: Is It Safe to Suggest Retail Prices," *Journal of Marketing* (Fall 1985), pp. 82–91.

23 "*Business Electronics Corp.* v. *Sharp Electronics Corp.,*" *Journal of Marketing* (January 1989), p. 99.

24 For an overview of price discrimination practices and perspectives, see Norton E. Marks and Neely S. Inlow, "Price Discrimination and Its Impact on Small Business," *Journal of Consumer Marketing* (Winter 1988), pp. 31–38; Michael H. Morris, "Separate Prices as a Marketing Tool," *Industrial Marketing Management* (May 1987), pp. 79–86; and James C. Johnson and Kenneth C. Schneider, "Those Who Can, Do—Those Who Can't . . . Marketing Professors and the Robinson-Patman Act," *Journal of the Academy of Marketing Science,* vol. 12 (1984), pp. 123–28.

25 "Tobacco Suit Exposes Ways Cigarette Firms Keep the Profits Fat," *The Wall Street Journal* (March 5, 1990), pp. A1, A6.

CHAPTER 14

1 "Here Comes GM's Saturn," *Business Week* (April 9, 1990), pp. 56–62; "Price over Pedigree," *American Way Magazine* (December 1, 1989), pp. 18–21; "Japanese Firms Push Posh Car Showrooms," *The Wall Street Journal* (October 18, 1989), p. B1; "The Coming Traffic Jam in the Luxury Lane," *Business Week* (January 30, 1989), p. 78; and "Saturn Widens Traditional Rings of Auto Distribution," *Marketing News* (July 17, 1987), p. 1.

2 "Suddenly, The PC Juggernaut Is Stuck in the Mud," *Business Week* (December 29, 1989), p. 45; and "Computer Retailers: Things Have Gone from Bad to Worse," *Business Week* (June 8, 1987), pp. 104–5.

3 "Pepsi, Concerned about Market Share in France, Will Break with Local Bottler," *The Wall Street Journal* (November 7, 1989), p. A12.

4 For an extensive review of industrial channel and distribution systems, see E. Raymond Corey, Frank V. Cespedes, and V. Kasturi Rangan, *Going to Market: Distribution Systems for Industrial Products* (Boston: Harvard Business School Press, 1989).

5 Michael D. Hutt and Thomas W. Speh, *Business Marketing Management,* 3rd ed. (Hinsdale, Ill.: Dryden Press, 1989), pp. 314–15.

6 James D. Hlavacek and Tommy J. McCuistion, "Industrial Distributors—When, Who, and How?" *Harvard Business Review* (March–April 1983), pp. 96–101.

7 John A. Quelch, "Why Not Exploit Dual Marketing?" *Business Horizons* (January–February 1987), pp. 52–60.

8 The examples are described in "Gen'l Mills/Nestlé Joint Venture," *Advertising Age* (December 4, 1989), pp. 1, 52; "GM Says Sales Arm Plans to Distribute Saab Cars in Can-

ada," *The Wall Street Journal* (May 10, 1990), p. B2; and Rustan Kosenko and Don Rathz, "The Japanese Channels of Distribution: Difficult but Not Insurmountable," *AMA Educators' Proceedings* (Chicago: American Marketing Association, 1988), pp. 233–36.

9 For an extended treatment of direct marketing, see Mary Lou Roberts and Paul D. Berger, *Direct Marketing Management* (Englewood Cliffs, N.J.: Prentice Hall, 1989); and Herbert Katzenstein and William S. Sachs, *Direct Marketing* (Columbus, Ohio: Merrill, 1986).

10 "Food Giants Take to the Mails to Push Fancy Product Lines," *The Wall Street Journal* (February 28, 1985), p. 35.

11 "Direct Response Billings by Nine Categories," *Advertising Age* (March 28, 1990), p. 43.

12 For research on similarities and differences among agents, merchant wholesalers, and sales offices and branches, see James R. Moore, Donald W. Eckrich, and Vijay Bhasim, "Industrial Channels Design and Structure: An Empirical Investigation," *The Journal of Midwest Marketing* (Fall 1988), pp. 87–98.

13 For recent research on manufacturer's agents, see Donald M. Jackson and Michael F. d'Amico, "Products and Markets Served by Distributors and Agents," *Industrial Marketing Management* (February 1989), pp. 27–33.

14 Louis W. Stern and Adel I. El-Ansary, *Marketing Channels,* 3rd ed. (Englewood Cliffs, N.J.: Prentice Hall, 1988), p. 316.

15 "Clothing Makers Don Retailers' Garb," *The Wall Street Journal* (July 13, 1989), p. B1.

16 "Manufacturers Convert Dealers into Franchisers," *The Wall Street Journal* (March 13, 1990), pp. B1, B2; and "Franchise Firms Get Good News on the '90s," *The Wall Street Journal* (February 23, 1990), p. B1.

17 This description of franchise arrangements is adapted from J. Barry Mason, Morris L. Mayer, and Hazel F. Ezell, *Retailing,* 4th ed. (Homewood, Ill.: Richard D. Irwin, 1991), pp. 596–602.

18 "Growth Areas," *Dallas Times Herald* (May 7, 1990), p. B1.

19 Frank V. Cespedes, "Channel Management Is General Management," *California Management Review* (Fall 1988), pp. 98–120.

20 "Fuller Brush Hopes to Clean Up by Expanding to Retail Stores," *Dallas Times Herald* (September 15, 1987), pp. C1, C5.

21 "Merrill Lynch's Big Dilemma," *Business Week* (January 16, 1984), pp. 60–67.

22 Toby Levin, "Flower Power," *SKY* (February 1987), pp. 11–16.

23 "Distributors: No Endangered Species," *Industry Week* (January 24, 1983), pp. 47–52.

24 "Liquid Paper Corporation," in Roger A. Kerin and Robert A. Peterson, *Strategic Marketing Problems: Cases and Comments,* 5th ed. (Boston: Allyn & Bacon, 1990), pp. 373–91.

25 Richard Green, "A Boutique in Your Living Room," *Forbes* (May 7, 1984), pp. 86–94.

26 Carla Rapoport, "You Can Make Money in Japan," *Fortune* (February 12, 1990), pp. 85–92.

27 "Quaker State Switches into a Quick-Change Artist," *Business Week* (October 16, 1989), pp. 126–27.

28 For examples of channel conflict, see Allan J. Magrath and Kenneth G. Hardy, "Avoiding the Pitfalls in Managing Dis-

tribution Channels," *Business Horizons* (September–October 1987), pp. 29–33.

29 "Bloody, Bowed, Back Together," *Business Week* (March 19, 1990), pp. 42–43.

30 "Heinz Struggles to Stay at the Top of the Stack," *Business Week* (March 11, 1985), p. 49.

31 Studies that explore the dimensions and use of power and influence in marketing channels include: Gul Butaney and Lawrence H. Wortzel, "Distributor Power versus Manufacturer Power: The Customer Role," *Journal of Marketing* (January 1988), pp. 52–63; Kenneth A. Hunt, John T. Mentzer, and Jeffrey E. Danes, "The Effect of Power Sources on Compliance in a Channel of Distribution: A Causal Model," *Journal of Business Research* (October 1987), pp. 377–98; John F. Gaski, "Interrelations among a Channel Entity's Power Sources: Impact of the Exercise of Reward and Coercion on Expert, Referent, and Legitimate Power Sources," *Journal of Marketing Research* (February 1986), pp. 62–67; Gary Frazier and John O. Summers, "Interfirm Influence Strategies and Their Application within Distribution Channels," *Journal of Marketing* (Summer 1984), pp. 43–55; Sudhir Kale, "Dealer Perceptions of Manufacturer Power and Influence Strategies in a Developing Country," *Journal of Marketing Research* (November 1986), pp. 387–93; and George H. Lucas and Larry G. Gresham, "Power, Conflict, Control, and the Application of Contingency Theory in Channels of Distribution," *Journal of the Academy of Marketing Science* (Summer 1985), pp. 27–37.

32 Portions of this discussion are based on Susan S. Samuelson and Thomas A. Balmer, "Anti-Trust Revisited—Implications for Competitive Strategy," *Sloan Management Review* (Fall 1988), pp. 79–87; and Louis W. Stern, Adel I. El-Ansary, and James Brown, *Management in Marketing Channels* (Englewood Cliffs, N.J.: Prentice Hall, 1989), pp. 52–55, 186–87.

33 Patrick J. Kaufman, "Dealer Termination Agreements and Resale Price Maintenance: Implications of the *Business Electronics* Case and the Proposed Amendment to the Sherman Act," *Journal of Retailing* (Summer 1988), pp. 113–23.

CHAPTER 15

1 "A 'NEAT' Operation," *VIA Port of NY–NJ* (August 1990), pp. 4–6.

2 Adapted from Donald V. Harper, *Transportation in America,* 2nd ed. (Englewood Cliffs, N.J.: Prentice Hall, 1982), p. 97.

3 Dick Rawe, "Procter & Gamble, Wal-Mart Develop Delivery System," *Naples Daily News* (February 19, 1989), p. 61H; and "Stalking the New Consumer," *Business Week* (August 28, 1989), pp. 54–58.

4 Herbert W. Davis, "Physical Distribution Costs: Performance in Selected Industries, 1987," in *Proceedings of the Council of Logistics Management* (1987), pp. 371–79.

5 James C. Johnson and Donald F. Wood, *Contemporary Physical Distribution and Logistics,* 3rd ed. (New York: Macmillan, 1986), p. 3.

6 Roger Kallock, "Develop a Strategic Outlook," *Transportation and Distribution* (January 1989), pp. 16–18.

7 " 'Superwarehouses' Chomp into the Food Business," *Business Week* (April 16, 1984), p. 72.

8 John J. Coyle and Edward J. Bardi, *The Management of Business Logistics,* 3rd ed. (St. Paul, Minn.: West, 1984), pp. 96–101.

9 "Europeans Think Alike When It Comes to Customer Service," *International Ambassador* (August 1990), p. 25; and "The European Customer Service Survey: Results," *Europa* (September 1990), p. 1.

10 Coyle and Bardi, p. 95.

11 "Why Federal Express Has Overnight Anxiety," *Business Week* (November 9, 1987), pp. 62–66.

12 Martin Keller, "Changing Channels," *Express Magazine* (Winter 1990), pp. 2–4.

13 "Stalking the New Consumer," p. 62.

14 Andrew Kupfer, "An Outsider Fires Up a Railroad," *Fortune* (December 18, 1989), pp. 133–46.

15 James C. Johnson and Kenneth C. Schneider, "Private Trucking: A Dinosaur?" *Business Horizons* (January–February 1988), pp. 73–78.

16 John G. Smale and John E. Pepper, "Letter to Shareholders," (Cincinnati: Procter & Gamble Company, June 11, 1987).

17 Janice Castro, "The Sky Kings Rule the Routes," *Time* (May 15, 1989), pp. 52–54; and Kenneth Labich, "How Airlines Will Look in the 1990s," *Fortune* (January 1, 1990), pp. 50–56.

18 Hank Gilman, "Rural Retailing Chains Prosper by Combining Service, Sophistication," *The Wall Street Journal* (July 2, 1984), p. 1.

19 "Wal-Mart Credits Deep Discounts to Hub-and-Spoke Planning," *Marketing News* (June 20, 1986), p. 18.

20 A. Ansari and Jim Heckel, "JIT Purchasing: Impact of Freight and Inventory Costs," *Journal of Purchasing and Materials Management* (Summer 1987), pp. 24–28.

CHAPTER 16

1 "Retailer First for Wal-Mart: Discounter Nets over $1 Billion," *Discount Store News* (March 12, 1990), p. 7; "Wal-Mart Named Retailer of the Decade," *Discount Store News* (July 3, 1989), p. 1; Francine Schwadel, "Little Touches Spur Wal-Mart's Rise," *The Wall Street Journal* (September 22, 1989), p. B1; Steve Weiner, "Golf Balls, Motor Oil, and Tomatoes," *Forbes* (October 30, 1989), pp. 130–34; and John Huey, "Wal-Mart, Will It Take Over the World," *Fortune* (January 30, 1989), pp. 52–64.

2 *Statistical Abstract of the United States,* 109th ed. (Washington, D.C.: U.S. Department of Commerce, Bureau of Census, 1989), p. 753.

3 Joel Dryfuss, "More Power to the PC Chains," *Fortune* (May 1, 1984), pp. 83–88.

4 Eric N. Berg, "Sears Says It Will Cut 21,000 Jobs," *The New York Times* (January 4, 1991), pp. D1, D4; and "Retailing: Who Will Survive?" *Business Week* (November 26, 1990), pp. 134–44.

5 Derek T. Dingle, "Franchising's Fast Track to Freedom," *Money Magazine* (Fall 1990), pp. 35–40; and *1989 Directory of Franchising Organizations* (Babylon, N.Y.: Pilot Books, 1989).

6 Jeffrey Tannebaum, "Ice Cream Chain Adjusts Mix and Franchisee Screams," *The Wall Street Journal* (June 18, 1990), p. B2; "Flaring Tempers at the Frozen Yogurt King," *Business Week* (September 10, 1990), pp. 88, 90; and Jeffrey Tannebaum and Barbara Marsh, "Firms Trying to Tighten Grip on Franchisees," *The Wall Street Journal* (January 15, 1990), pp. B1, B2.

7 Jeffrey Tannebaum, "Franchisers See a Future in East Bloc," *The Wall Street Journal* (June 5, 1990), pp. B1, B2.

8 Richard Stevenson, "Watch Out, Macy's, Here Comes Nordstrom," *New York Times Magazine* (August 27, 1989), p. 40.

9 Diana Fong, "Cherchez La Store," *Forbes* (January 9, 1989), pp. 311–12.

10 Laura Daily, "Attention Shoppers!" *US Air* (October 1989), pp. 95–99.

11 "Wal-Mart Gets Lost in the Vegetable Aisle," *Business Week* (May 28, 1990), p. 48.

12 Joseph Pereira, "Discount Department Stores Struggle against Rivals That Strike Aisle by Aisle!" *The Wall Street Journal* (June 19, 1990), pp. B1, B7; and Richard V. Sarkissian, "Retail Trends in the 1990s," *Journal of Accountancy* (December 1989), pp. 44–55.

13 Patricia Gallagher, "On Order: Fresh Catalog Ideas," *USA Today* (September 26, 1989), p. 6B.

14 Ann Hagerdon, "'Tis Already the Season for Catalog Firms," *The New York Times* (November 24, 1987), p. 16.

15 Anita Gates, "Direct Mail Goes Upscale," *US Air* (October 1989), pp. 50–58.

16 "Lands' End Looks a Bit Frayed at the Edges," *Business Week* (March 19, 1990), p. 42.

17 "Trade Exec's 'Crystal-Ball' Outlook for the 1990s," *Vending Times* (December 1989), pp. 1, 3, 8.

18 Phil Fitzell, "Opening the Floodgates," *Beverage World* (January 1990), pp. 48–58.

19 "Computer Formats Spur Variety in ER," *Discount Store News* (July 3, 1989), p. 116.

20 Gary Robins, "On-Line Service Update," *Stores* (February 1990), pp. 24–29.

21 "How Long Will Prodigy Be a Problem Child?" *Business Week* (September 1990), p. 75; and "Retailers and Videotex," *Stores* (February 1990), pp. 30–31.

22 R. Fulton MacDonald, "Capitalizing on the Coming Revolution," *Retail Control* (January 1990), pp. 22–29.

23 The following discussion is adapted from William T. Gregor and Eileen M. Friars, "Money Merchandising: Retail Revolution in Consumer Financial Services" (Cambridge, Mass.: Management Analysis Center, Inc., 1982).

24 William Lazer and Eugene J. Kelley, "The Retailing Mix: Planning and Management," *Journal of Retailing* (Spring 1961), pp. 34–41.

25 Teri Agins, "Discount Clothing Stores, Facing Squeeze, Aim to Fashion a More Rounded Image," *The Wall Street Journal* (March 15, 1990), pp. B1, B6.

26 Gary Strauss, "Warehouse Clubs Heat Up Retail Climate," *USA Today* (September 7, 1990), pp. 1B, 2B; "Where the Buyers Are," *World* (January–February 1986), pp. 38–42; and "The Mad Rush to Join the Warehouse Club," *Fortune* (January 6, 1986), pp. 59–61.

27 "Fewer Rings on the Cash Register," *Business Week* (January 14, 1991), p. 85; Kevin Helliker, "Consolidation of Warehouse Clubs Increases," *The Wall Street Journal* (November 7, 1990), pp. B1, B6; and "Clubs Share Fruits of Rapid Growth," *Discount Store News* (July 3, 1989), p. 108.

28 Kenneth M. Chanko, "One-Price Apparel Stores Carve Niche below Off-Price Chains," *Discount Store News* (March 14, 1988), pp. 3, 32.

29 Jeffrey Trachtenberg, "Largest of All Malls in the U.S. Is a Gamble in Bloomington, Minn.," *The Wall Street Journal* (October 30, 1990), pp. A1, A14; and "The Minnesota Mallers," *U.S. News & World Report* (June 26, 1989), p. 12.

30 Eric Peterson, "Power Centers! Now!" *Stores* (March 1989), pp. 61–66; and "Power Centers Flex Their Muscle," *Chain Store Age Executive* (February 1989), pp. 3A, 4A.

31 Pierre Martineau, "The Personality of the Retail Store," *Harvard Business Review*, vol. 36 (January–February 1958), p. 47.

32 For a review of the store image literature, see Mary R. Zimmer and Linda L. Golden, "Impressions of Retail Stores: A Content Analysis of Consumer Images," *Journal of Retailing* (Fall 1988), pp. 265–93.

33 Scott Kilman, "Retailers Change Their Stores and Goods, Looking to Cash In on New Buying Habits," *The Wall Street Journal* (September 8, 1986), p. 21.

34 Philip Kotler, "Atmosphere as a Marketing Tool," *Journal of Retailing*, vol. 49 (Winter 1973–1974), p. 61.

35 The wheel of retailing theory was originally proposed by Malcolm P. McNair, "Significant Trends and Development in the Postwar Period," in A. B. Smith, ed., *Competitive Distribution in a Free, High-Level Economy and Its Implications for the University* (Pittsburgh: University of Pittsburgh Press, 1958), pp. 1–25; see also Stephen Brown, "Guest Commentary: The Wheel of Retailing—Past and Future," *Journal of Retailing* (Summer 1990), pp. 143–49; and Malcolm P. McNair and Eleanor May, "The Next Revolution of the Retailing Wheel," *Harvard Business Review* (September–October 1978), pp. 81–91.

36 Richard Gibson, "McDonald's Rolls Out Pizza for Testing, but Firms's Pies Apparently Lacking Pizazz," *The Wall Street Journal* (August 6, 1990), pp. B1, B4; and "Two Big Macs, Large Fries—and a Pepperoni Pizza, Please," *Business Week* (August 7, 1989), p. 33.

37 Stephen P. Galante, "Some Hamburger Restaurants See Their Future in the 1950s," *The Wall Street Journal* (September 8, 1986), p. 29.

38 William R. Davidson, Albert D. Bates, and Stephen J. Bass, "Retail Life Cycle," *Harvard Business Review* (November–December 1976), pp. 89–96.

39 Richard Gibson, "Discount Menu Is Coming Back to McDonald's as Chain Tries to Win Back Customers," *The Wall Street Journal* (November 20, 1990), pp. B1, B10; and "McDonald's Stoops to Conquer," *Business Week* (October 30, 1989), pp. 120–21.

40 Teri Agins and Yumiko Ono, "Japanese Market Lures, Vexes Retailers," *The Wall Street Journal* (May 29, 1990), pp. B1, B6; and Teri Agins, "Barney's Style Gets Translated into Japanese," *The Wall Street Journal* (May 29, 1990), pp. B1, B6.

41 Martin Mayer, "Scanning the Future," *Forbes* (October 15, 1990), pp. 114–17; and "Bar-Coding, EDI Interest Running High, Says Study," *Chain Store Age Executive* (March 1989), pp. 98–99.

42 J. Barry Mason and Morris J. Mayer, "Retail Merchandise Information Systems for the 1980s," *Journal of Retailing*, vol. 56 (Spring 1980), pp. 56–76; Richard K. Robinson and Frederick W. Langehr, "Consumers' Evaluation of Selected Aspects of Supermarket Scanners," in Neil Beckwith, Michael Houston, Robert Mittlestaedt, Kent B. Monroe, and Scott Ward, eds., *1979 Educator's Conference Proceedings* (Chicago: American Marketing Association, 1979), pp. 389–91:

"Scanning 1½ Years Later," *Chain Store Age Executive*, vol. 52 (February 1976), pp. 16–17; and Michael D. Pommer, Eric N. Berkowitz, and John R. Walton, "UPC Scanning: An Assessment of Shopper Response to Technological Change," *Journal of Retailing*, vol. 56 (Summer 1980), pp. 25–44.

43 James M. Sinkula, "Status of Company Usage of Scanner Based Research," *Journal of the Academy of Marketing Science* (Spring 1986), pp. 63–71.

44 "Two Thirds of Retailers to Use EDI by 1991," *Chain Store Age Executive* (January 1989), p. 110.

45 Francine Schwadel, "Chicago Retailers' 'Sting' Aims to Put Shoplifting Professionals Out of Business," *The Wall Street Journal* (June 5, 1990), pp. B1, B9; and "Who Has the Stickiest Fingers," *Chain Store Age Executive* (February 1990), p. 19.

46 "Kiddie City Beefs Up Security at Urban Store," *Chain Store Age Executive* (February 1989), p. 36; and "Employee Involvement Is Key to Store Security," *Chain Store Age Executive* (April 1989), p. 80.

CHAPTER 17

1 "Stalking the New Consumer," *Business Week* (August 28, 1989), pp. 54–62; and "100 Leading National Advertisers," *Advertising Age* (September 26, 1990), p. 1.

2 Brian Dumaine, "P&G Rewrites the Marketing Rules," *Fortune* (November 6, 1989), pp. 34–48; and Alison Fahey, "Advertising Media Crowd into Aisles," *Advertising Age* (June 18, 1990), p. 18.

3 Joanne Lipman "Procter and Gamble to Demote Promotions," *The Wall Street Journal* (July 17, 1989), p. B4; "Stalking the New Consumer," pp. 54–62; and Julie Liesse Erickson, "FSI Boom to Go Bust?" *Advertising Age* (May 1, 1989), pp. 1, 82.

4 Wilbur Schramm, "How Communication Works," in Wilbur Schramm, ed., *The Process and Effects of Mass Communication* (Urbana, Ill.: University of Illinois Press, 1955), pp. 3–26.

5 E. Cooper and M. Jahoda, "The Evasion of Propaganda," *Journal of Psychology*, vol. 22 (1947), pp. 15–25; H. Hyman and P. Sheatsley, "Some Reasons Why Information Campaigns Fail," *Public Opinion Quarterly*, vol. 11 (1947), pp. 412–23; and J. T. Klapper, *The Effects of Mass Communication* (New York: Free Press, 1960), Chapter VII.

6 David A. Ricks, Jeffrey S. Arpan, and Marilyn Y. Fu, "Pitfalls in Advertising Overseas," *Journal of Advertising Research*, vol. 14 (December 1974), pp. 47–51.

7 B. C. Cotton and Emerson M. Babb, "Consumer Response to Promotional Deals," *Journal of Marketing*, vol. 42 (July 1978), pp. 109–13.

8 Robert George Brown, "Sales Response to Promotions and Advertising," *Journal of Advertising Research*, vol. 14 (August 1974), pp. 33–40.

9 Thomas McCann, "Sales Force Involvement Critical to Promotions," *Marketing News* (March 19, 1990), p. 9; and "Coordinating Ad, Sales Promotion Has Benefits Many Firms Don't See," *Marketing News* (April 16, 1990), p. 8.

10 Siva K. Balasubramanian and V. Kumar, "Analyzing Variations in Advertising and Promotional Expenditures: Key Correlates in Consumer, Industrial, and Service Markets," *Journal of Marketing* (April 1990), pp. 57–68.

11 Dunn Sunnoo and Lynn Y. S. Lin, "Sales Effects of Promotion and Advertising," *Journal of Advertising Research*, vol. 18 (October 1978), pp. 37–42.

12 J. Ronald Carey, Stephen A. Clique, Barbara A. Leighton, and Frank Milton, "A Test of Positive Reinforcement of Customers," *Journal of Marketing*, vol. 40 (October 1976), pp. 98–100.

13 James M. Olver and Paul W. Farris, "Push and Pull: A One-Two Punch for Packaged Products," *Sloan Management Review* (Fall 1989), pp. 53–61.

14 Patricia Sellers, "How Busch Wins in a Doggy Market," *Fortune*, (June 22, 1987), pp. 99–111.

15 Jon Lafayette and Alan Redding, "IBM Sets $30M Home PC Launch," *Advertising Age* (June 18, 1990), pp. 3, 86; and Steve Weiner, "Painful Positioning," *Forbes* (September 3, 1990), pp. 41–42.

16 "Where the Promotion Dollar Goes," *Adweek's Marketing Week* (June 19, 1990), p. 10; Arthur Shapiro, "Advertising Versus Promotion: Which Is Which?" *Journal of Advertising Research*, (June/July 1990), pp. RC13–RC16.

17 Magid M. Abraham and Leonard M. Lodish, "Getting the Most Out of Advertising and Promotion," *Harvard Business Review* (May–June 1990), pp. 50–60; Steven W. Hartley and James Cross, "How Sales Promotion Can Work for and against You," *Journal of Consumer Marketing* (Summer 1988), pp. 35–42; Robert D. Buzzell, John A. Quelch, and Walter J. Salmon, "The Costly Bargain of Trade Promotion," *Harvard Business Review* (March–April 1990), pp. 141–49; and Mary L. Nicastro, "Break-even Analysis Determines Success of Sales Promotions," *Marketing News* (March 5, 1990), p. 11.

18 *Consumer Promotion Report* (monograph) (New York: Dancer, Fitzgerald, Sample, 1982).

19 Scott Hume, "Coupons Go In-Store," *Advertising Age* (May 21, 1990), p. 45.

20 Roger A. Strang, "Sales Promotion—Fast Growth, Faulty Management," *Harvard Business Review*, vol. 54 (July–August 1976), pp. 115–24; Ronald W. Ward and James E. Davis, "Coupon Redemption," *Journal of Advertising Research*, vol. 18 (August 1978), pp. 51–58; similar results on favorable mail-distributed coupons were reported by Alvin Schwartz, "The Influence of Media Characteristics on Coupon Redemption," *Journal of Marketing*, vol. 30 (January 1966), pp. 41–46.

21 Michael deCourcy Hinds, "Rebates Can Be Both a Blessing and a Curse, but Manufacturers Often Lose Business without Them," *Star and Tribune* (April 24, 1988), pp. 1E, 6E.

22 Alison Fahey, "Premium Incentive: Avoiding Price Cuts," *Advertising Age* (May 7, 1990), p. 48.

23 William A. Robinson, *Best Sales Promotions of 1977–78* (Chicago: Crain Books, 1979), p. 93.

24 Don A. Schultz and William A. Robinson, *Sales Promotion Essentials* (Chicago: Crain Books, 1982).

25 Fred C. Allvine, Richard D. Teach, and John Connelly, Jr., "The Demise of Promotional Games," *Journal of Advertising Research*, vol. 16 (October 1976), pp. 79–84.

26 Laurie Freeman, "P&G to Test New 'Compact' Tide," *Advertising Age* (February 5, 1990), pp. 3, 50.

27 "New Handy Snack Display Is Dandy," *Marketing News* (October 9, 1987), p. 15.

28 Cyndee Miller, "P-O-P Gains Followers as 'Era of Retailing' Dawns," *Marketing News* (May 14, 1990), p. 2.

29 "Coming to a Shopping Cart near You: TV Commercials," *Business Week* (May 30, 1988), p. 61; and "VideOcart Shopping Cart with Computer Screen Creates New Ad Medium that Also Gathers Data," *Marketing News* (May 9, 1988), pp. 1–2.

30 Marvin A. Jolson, Joshua L. Wiener, and Richard B. Rosecky, "Correlates of Rebate Proneness," *Journal of Advertising Research* (February–March 1987), pp. 33–43.

31 Alison Fahey, "Rebate Program Rings Wright Bell," *Advertising Age* (May 21, 1990), p. 44.

32 This discussion is drawn primarily from John A. Quelch, *Trade Promotions by Grocery Manufacturers: A Management Perspective* (Cambridge, Mass.: Marketing Science Institute, August 1982).

33 Michael Chevalier and Ronald C. Curhan, "Retail Promotions as a Function of Trade Promotions: A Descriptive Analysis," *Sloan Management Review*, vol. 18 (Fall 1976), pp. 19–32.

34 Robert S. Mason, "What's a PR Director for Anyway?" *Harvard Business Review*, vol. 52 (September–October 1974), pp. 120–26; Jack Bernstein, "Kroll, Roman Discuss Role of PR," *Advertising Age* (April 11, 1988), pp. 42–43.

35 Scott Hume, "Free 'Plugs' Supply Ad Power," *Advertising Age* (January 29, 1990), p. 6.

36 Irving Rein, Philip Kotler, and Martin Stoller, *High Visibility* (New York: Dodd, Mead & Co., 1987); Mathew Schifrin and Peter Newcomb, "A Brain for Sin and a Bod for Business," *Forbes* (October 1, 1990), pp. 162–166.

37 Jonathan Dahl, "Fare Play: States Target Airlines over Ads and Frequent-Flier Plans," *The Wall Street Journal* (August 31, 1987), p. 19.

38 Courtland L. Bovée and William F. Arens, *Contemporary Advertising*, 2nd ed. (Homewood, Ill.: Richard D. Irwin, 1986), pp. 59–66; Herbert J. Rotfeld, Avery M. Abernathy, and Patrick R. Parsons, "Self-Regulation and Television Advertising," *Journal of Advertising*, 19 (4) 1990, pp. 18–26.

39 Bradley Johnson, "Promo Recalls Mean New Sensitivity," *Advertising Age* (June 18, 1990), p. 76.

40 Rita Weisskoff, "Current Trends in Children's Advertising," *Journal of Advertising Research* (February–March 1985), pp. RC-12–14.

41 Robert E. Hite and Randy Eck, "Advertising to Children: Attitudes of Business vs. Consumers," *Journal of Advertising Research* (October–November 1987), pp. 40–53.

42 J. D. Reed, "Ah, How Sweet It Is!" *Time* (May 28, 1990), p. 79; "FCC Loses in Ruling on Children's TV Program," *Marketing News* (October 23, 1987), p. 1; and Bob Davis, "Ruling Reopens Issue of Regulation of Children's TV," *The Wall Street Journal* (June 29, 1987), p. 26.

43 Thomas W. Leigh, Arno J. Rethans, and Tamatha Reichenbach Whitney, "Role Portrayals of Women In Advertising: Cognitive Responses and Advertising Effectiveness," *Journal of Advertising Research* (October–November 1987), pp. 54–63; and John B. Ford, Michael S. Latour, and William J. Lundstrom, "Contemporary Women's Evaluation of Female Role Portrayals in Advertising," *Journal of Consumer Research*, vol. 8 (Winter 1991), pp. 15–28.

44 "Kid Stuff," *Promo*, vol. 4 (January 1991), pp. 25, 42; Steven W. Colford, "Fine-Tuning Kids' TV," *Advertising*

Age (February 11, 1991), p. 35; and Kate Fitzgerald, "Toys Star-Struck for Movie Tie-Ins," *Advertising Age* (February 18, 1991), pp. 3, 45.

CHAPTER 18

1 Marcy Magiera, "Bo Jackson × 15 = ," *Advertising Age* (June 25, 1990), p. 4; Patricia Winters, "Snoopy Gets the Job as A&W's Chief Rooter," *Advertising Age* (March 26, 1990), pp. 3, 49; Thomas R. King, "For Colas, The Fault Is in Too Many Stars," *The Wall Street Journal* (January 24, 1990), pp. B1, B6.

2 Dennis Kneale, " 'Zapping' of TV Ads Appears Pervasive," *The Wall Street Journal* (April 25, 1988), p. 21; and Richard Zoglin, "Goodbye to the Mass Audience," *Time* (November 19, 1990), pp. 122–23.

3 King, pp. B1, B6.

4 David E. Thigpen, "Bo Knows Pain—and Dismissal," *Time* (April 1, 1991), p. 80; Kate Fitzgerald, "Energizer Hops onto Top 10," *Advertising Age* (January 7, 1991), p. 39; and Joanne Lipman, "When It's Commercial Time, TV Viewers Prefer Cartoons to Celebrities Any Day," *The Wall Street Journal* (February 16, 1990), pp. B1, B4.

5 David A. Aaker and Donald Norris, "Characteristics of TV Commercials Perceived as Informative," *Journal of Advertising Research,* vol. 22, no. 2 (April–May 1982), pp. 61–70.

6 William Wilkie and Paul W. Farris, "Comparison Advertising: Problems and Potentials," *Journal of Marketing,* vol. 39, no. 4 (October 1975), pp. 7–15; and Darel D. Muehling, Jeffrey J. Stoltman, and Sanford Grossbart, "The Impact of Comparative Advertising on Levels of Message Involvement," *Journal of Advertising,* vol. 19, no. 4 (1990), pp. 41–50.

7 Bill Abrams, "Comparative Ads Are Getting More Popular, Hard Hitting," *The Wall Street Journal* (March 11, 1982), p. 25.

8 Bruce Buchanan and Doron Goldman, "Us vs. Them: The Minefield of Comparative Ads," *Harvard Business Review* (May–June 1989), pp. 38–50; Dorothy Cohen, "The FTC's Advertising Substantiation Program," *Journal of Marketing* (Winter 1980), pp. 26–35; and Michael Etger and Stephen A. Goodwin, "Planning for Comparative Advertising Requires Special Attention," *Journal of Advertising,* vol. 8, no. 1 (Winter 1979), pp. 26–32.

9 Ira Teinowitz, "Coors Tries Nostalgia," *Advertising Age* (June 18, 1990), pp. 3, 85.

10 Lewis C. Winters, "Does It Pay to Advertise to Hostile Audiences with Corporate Advertising?" *Journal of Advertising Research* (June/July 1988), pp. 11–18; and Robert Selwitz, "The Selling of an Image," *Madison Avenue* (February 1985), pp. 61–69.

11 Robert J. Lavidge and Gary A. Steiner, "A Model for Predictive Measurements of Advertising Effectiveness," *Journal of Marketing* (October 1961), p. 61.

12 John McManus, "Super Bowl Rate Up 17%," *Advertising Age* (April 16, 1990), pp. 3, 65; and Patricia Winters, "Super Bowl Ads in Late Scramble," *Advertising Age* (January 28, 1991), pp. 1, 43.

13 John Philip Jones, "Ad Spending: Maintaining Market Share," *Harvard Business Review* (January–February 1990), pp. 38–42; and Charles H. Patti and Vincent Blanko, "Budgeting Practices of Big Advertisers," *Journal of Advertising Research,* vol. 21 (December 1981), pp. 23–30.

14 James A. Schroer, "Ad Spending: Growing Market Share," *Harvard Business Review* (January–February 1990), pp. 44–48.

15 Jeffrey A. Lowenhar and John L. Stanton, "Forecasting Competitive Advertising Expenditures," *Journal of Advertising Research,* vol. 16, no. 2 (April 1976), pp. 37–44.

16 Daniel Seligman, "How Much for Advertising?" *Fortune* (December 1956), p. 123.

17 James E. Lynch and Graham J. Hooley, "Increasing Sophistication in Advertising Budget Setting," *Journal of Advertising Research,* 30 (February/March 1990), pp. 67–75.

18 Jimmy D. Barnes, Brenda J. Muscove, and Javad Rassouli, "An Objective and Task Media Selection Decision Model and Advertising Cost Formula to Determine International Advertising Budgets," *Journal of Advertising,* vol. 11, no. 4 (1982), pp. 68–75.

19 Bob Garfield, "Allstate Ads Bring Home Point about Mortgage Insurance," *Advertising Age* (September 11, 1989), p. 120; and Judana Dagnoli, " 'Buy or Die' Mentality Toned Down in Ads," *Advertising Age* (May 7, 1990), p. S-12.

20 Alice Z. Cuneo, "SF's Goodby, Berlin, & Silverstein Hailed," *Advertising Age* (March 26, 1990), pp. S-4, S-53.

21 John Pfeiffer, "Six Months and a Half a Million Dollars, All for 15 Seconds," *Smithsonian* (October 1987), pp. 134–35; and Alex Ben Block, "Where the Money Goes," *Forbes* (September 21, 1987), pp. 178–80.

22 Joanne Lipman, "Ad Industry's Health Draws Mixed Prognoses," *The Wall Street Journal* (September 23, 1987), pp. 33, 41; and Robert J. Cohen, "Total National Ad Spending by Media," *Advertising Age* (September 26, 1990), p. 8.

23 Katherine Barrett, "Taking a Closer Look," *Madison Avenue* (August 1984), pp. 106–9.

24 Gupta Udayan, "A House Divided," *Madison Avenue* (October 1984), pp. 62–64; Wayne Walley, "Popularity of 15s Falls," *Advertising Age* (January 14, 1991), pp. 3, 41; and Joshua Levine, "The Last Gasp of Mass Media?" *Forbes* (September 17, 1990), pp. 176–82.

25 Stephen Pomper, "The Big Shake-Out Begins," *Time* (July 2, 1990), p. 50.

26 "Clutter Bucks," *Fortune* (October 29, 1984), pp. 78–79.

27 Julia Collins, "Image and Advertising," *Harvard Business Review* (January–February 1989), pp. 93–97; and Judith Graham, "Amex 'Portraits' Stresses Values," *Advertising Age* (January 1, 1990), pp. 12, 38.

28 "Print Ads that Make You Stop, Look—and Listen," *Business Week* (November 23, 1987), p. 38.

29 Jill Smolowe, "Read This!" *Time* (November 26, 1990), pp. 62–70.

30 Stephen Barlas, "Cataloguers Seek Cheaper Alternative to Mail," *Marketing News* (February 18, 1991), pp. 1, 19.

31 Erik Larson, "In Direct-Mail Biz, Envelopes Are What Are Run Up Flagpole," *The Wall Street Journal* (May 5, 1986), pp. 1, 15; and Jim Powell, "The Lucrative Trade of Creating Junk Mail," *The New York Times* (June 20, 1982), p. F7.

32 Arch G. Woodside, "Outdoor Advertising as Experiments," *Journal of the Academy of Marketing Science,* 18 (Summer 1990), pp. 229–37.

33 Wayne Walley, "Ads Spread to Video Covers," *Advertising Age* (September 14, 1988), p. 21; and Dan Wascoe, Jr., "What's New on Restroom Walls? Ads, That's What," *Star and Tribune* (May 9, 1988), p. 30.

34 The discussion of posttesting is based on Courtland L. Boveé and William F. Arens, *Contemporary Advertising*, 2nd ed. (Homewood, Ill.: Richard D. Irwin, 1988), p. 209.

35 David A. Aaker and Douglas M. Stayman, "Measuring Audience Perceptions of Commercials and Relating Them to Ad Impact," *Journal of Advertising Research*, 30 (August/September 1990), pp. 7–17.

36 Dave Kruegel, "Television Advertising Effectiveness and Research Innovation," *Journal of Consumer Marketing* (Summer 1988), pp. 43–51; and Laurence N. Gold, "The Evolution of Television Advertising-Sales Measurement: Past, Present, and Future," *Journal of Advertising Research* (June/July 1988), pp. 19–24.

CHAPTER 19

1 Telephone interview with Wanda Truxillo, June 1, 1990.

2 "Haggar's Quick Response System Leads Pack," *Dallas Times Herald* (January 4, 1990), pp. B1, B7.

3 *Chief Executive Officer* (Chicago: Heidrick and Struggles, 1987), p. 7.

4 Paul S. Busch and Michael J. Houston, *Marketing: Strategic Foundations* (Homewood, Ill.: Richard D. Irwin, 1985), p. 706.

5 For representative research on the types of personal selling, see William C. Moncrief, "Five Types of Industrial Sales Jobs," *Industrial Marketing Management* vol. 17 (1988), pp. 161–67.

6 *Sales & Marketing Management's 1990 Survey of Selling Costs* (February 26, 1990), p. 8.

7 Bill Kelley, "Is There Anything That Can't Be Sold by Phone?" *Sales & Marketing Management* (April 1989), pp. 60–64; Harvard Sutton, *Rethinking the Company's Selling and Distribution Channels* (New York: The Conference Board, 1986), pp. 23–25; and "Telemarketing Takes the Top Spot," *Direct Marketing* (September 1987), p. 120.

8 Thomas N. Ingram and Raymond W. LaForge, *Sales Management* (Hinsdale, Ill.: Dryden Press, 1989), p. 177.

9 J. David Lichtenthal, Sameer Sikri, and Karl Folk, "Teleprospecting: An Approach for Qualifying Accounts," *Industrial Marketing Management* vol. 18 (1989), pp. 11–17; and Marvin A. Jolson, "Qualifying Sales Leads: The Tight and Loose Approaches," *Industrial Marketing Management* vol. 17 (1988), pp. 189–96.

10 G. Scott Osborne, *Electronic Direct Marketing* (Englewood Cliffs, N.J.: Prentice Hall, 1984), p. 120.

11 Ronald B. Marks, *Personal Selling: An Integrative Approach*, 3rd ed. (Boston: Allyn & Bacon, 1988), p. 239.

12 For a variation on the "canned presentation" see Marvin A. Jolson, "Canned Adaptiveness: A New Direction for Modern Salesmanship," *Business Horizons* (January–February 1989), pp. 7–12.

13 See "Sales Training," *Training*, special issue (February 1988); Michael Belch and Robert W. Haas, "Using Buyer's Needs to Improve Industrial Sales," *Business* (September–October 1979), pp. 8–14; and Robert Saxe and Barton A. Weitz, "The Soco Scale: A Measure of the Customer Orientation of Salespeople," *Journal of Marketing Research* (August 1983), pp. 343–51.

14 Recent research on these formats can be found in Barton A. Weitz, Harish Sujan, and Mita Sujan, "Knowledge, Motivation, and Adaptive Behavior: A Framework for Improving Selling Effectiveness," *Journal of Marketing* (October 1986), pp. 174–91; Thomas W. Leigh and Patrick F. McGraw, "Mapping the Procedural Knowledge of Industrial Sales Personnel: A Script-Theoretic Investigation," *Journal of Marketing* (January 1989), pp. 16–34; David M. Symanski, "Determinants of Selling Effectiveness: The Importance of Declarative Knowledge to the Personal Selling Concept," *Journal of Marketing* (January 1988), pp. 64–67; and Rosann L. Spiro and Barton A. Weitz, "Adaptive Selling: Conceptualization, Measurement, and Normological Validity," *Journal of Marketing Research* (February 1990), pp. 61–69.

15 Based on Ronald D. Balsley and E. Patricia Birsner, *Selling: Marketing Personified* (Hinsdale, Ill.: Dryden Press, 1987), pp. 261–63.

16 An extensive listing of closing techniques is found in Robin T. Peterson, "Sales Representative Perceptions on Various Widely Used Closing Tactics," *AMA Educators' Proceedings* (Chicago: American Marketing Association, 1988), pp. 220–24.

17 Theodore Levitt, *The Marketing Imagination* (New York: Free Press, 1983), p. 111. See also Monci Jo Williams, "America's Best Salesmen," *Fortune* (October 26, 1987), pp. 122–34; F. Robert Dwyer, Paul H. Schurr, and Sejo Oh, "Developing Buyer-Seller Relationships," *Journal of Marketing* (April 1987), pp. 11–27; and Robert E. Spekman and Wesley J. Johnston, "Relationship Management: Managing the Selling and Buying Interface," *Journal of Business Research*, vol. 14 (1986), pp. 519–31.

18 William A. O'Connell and William Keenan, Jr., "The Shape of Things to Come," *Sales & Marketing Management* (January 1990), pp. 36–41.

19 *Management Briefing: Marketing* (New York: The Conference Board, October 1986), pp. 3–4.

20 See, for example, Troy A. Festervand, Stephen J. Grove, and Eric Reidenbach, "The Sales Force as a Marketing Intelligence System," *Journal of Business & Industrial Marketing* (Winter 1988), pp. 53–60; and Douglas M. Lambert, Howard Marmorstein, and Arun Sharma, "Industrial Salespeople as a Source of Market Information," *Industrial Marketing Management*, vol. 19 (1990), pp. 141–48.

21 For a discussion on managing independent agents, see Harold J. Novick, "Yes, There Is a Perfect Rep," *Business Marketing* (February 1989), pp. 73–76; and Joseph A. Bellizzi and Christine Glacken, "Building a More Successful Rep Organization," *Industrial Marketing Management* (August 1986), pp. 207–13.

22 For an examination of agents and salespeople from the perspective of transaction costs, see Erin Anderson and Barton Weitz, "Make or Buy Decisions: Vertical Integration and Marketing Productivity," *Sloan Management Review* (Spring 1986), pp. 1–19.

23 Benson Shapiro, *Sales Program Management: Formulation and Implementation* (New York: McGraw-Hill, 1977), pp. 250–55.

24 For an extended treatment of major account management, see Jerome A. Colletti and Gary S. Turbridy, "Effective Major Account Management," *Journal of Personal Selling & Sales Management* (August 1987), pp. 1–10; Richard Cardozo and Shannon Shipp, "New Selling Methods Are Changing Industrial Sales Management," *Business Horizons* (September–

October 1987), pp. 23–28; and O'Connell and Keenan, Jr., pp. 36–41.

25 Louis A. Wallis, *Marketing Priorities* (New York: The Conference Board, 1987), p. 6.

26 Walter J. Talley, "How to Design Sales Territories," *Journal of Marketing* (January 1961), pp. 7–13.

27 Gilbert A. Churchill, Jr., Neil M. Ford, and Orville C. Walker, Jr., *Sales Force Management: Planning, Implementation, and Control,* 3rd ed. (Homewood, Ill.: Richard D. Irwin, 1990), p. 84.

28 Ingram and LaForge, p. 343. See also John S. Hill and Meg Birdseye, "Salesperson Selection in Multinational Corporations: An Empirical Study," *Journal of Personal Selling & Sales Management* (Summer 1989), pp. 39–47.

29 For research on job analyses, see William C. Montcrief III, "Selling Activity and Sales Position Taxonomies for Industrial Salesforces," *Journal of Marketing Research* (August 1986), pp. 261–70.

30 Neil M. Ford, Orville C. Walker, Jr., Gilbert A. Churchill, Jr., and Steven W. Hartley, "Selecting Successful Salespeople: A Meta-Analysis of Biographical and Psychological Selection Criteria," in Michael J. Houston, ed., *Review of Marketing 1987* (Chicago: American Marketing Association, 1988), pp. 90–131.

31 Earl D. Honeycutt, Jr., Clyde E. Harris, Jr., and Stephen B. Castleberry, "Sales Training: A Status Report," *Training and Development Journal* (May 1987), pp. 42–47.

32 *Sales & Marketing Management's 1990 Survey of Selling Costs* (February 26, 1990), p. 27.

33 "Methods Used in Sales Training," *Sales & Marketing Management's 1990 Survey of Selling Costs* (February 26, 1990), p. 82.

34 See, for example, William L. Cron, Alan J. Dubinsky, and Ronald E. Michaels, "The Influence of Career Stages on Components of Salesperson Motivation," *Journal of Marketing* (January 1988), pp. 78–92; Pradeep K. Tyagi, "Relative Importance of Key Job Dimensions and Leadership Behaviors in Motivating Salesperson Work Performance," *Journal of Marketing* (Summer 1985), pp. 76–86; Richard C. Beckerer, Fred Morgan, and Lawrence Richard, "The Job Characteristics of Industrial Salespersons: Relationship to Motivation and Satisfaction," *Journal of Marketing* (Fall 1982), pp. 125–35; and Walter Kiechel III, "How to Manage Salespeople," *Fortune* (March 14, 1988), pp. 179–80.

35 Gilbert A. Churchill, Jr., Neil M. Ford, and Orville C. Walker, Jr., "Personal Characteristics of Salespeople and the Attractiveness of Alternative Rewards," *Journal of Business Research* vol. 7 (1979), pp. 25–50; and Neil M. Ford, Orville C. Walker, Jr., and Gilbert A. Churchill, Jr., "Differences in the Attractiveness of Alternative Awards among Industrial Salespeople: Additional Evidence," *Journal of Business Research* vol. 13 (1985), pp. 123–28.

36 "Types of Employee Awards," *Sales & Marketing Management's 1990 Survey of Selling Costs* (February 26, 1990), p. 82.

37 "Sales Force Turnover Has Managers Wondering Why," *Marketing News* (December 4, 1989); George H. Lucas, Jr., A. Parasuraman, Robert A. Davis, and Ben Enis, "An Empirical Study of Salesforce Turnover," *Journal of Marketing* (July 1987), pp. 34–59; and René Y. Darmon, "Identifying Sources of Turnover Costs: A Segmental Approach," *Journal of Marketing* (April 1990), pp. 46–56. See also Edward F.

Fern, Ramon A. Avila, and Dhruv Grewal, "Salesforce Turnover: Those Who Left and Those Who Stayed," *Industrial Marketing Management,* vol. 18 (1989), pp. 1–9.

38 Donald W. Jackson, Jr., Janet E. Keith, and John Schlacter, "Evaluation of Selling Performance: A Study of Current Practice," *Journal of Personal Selling and Sales Management* (November 1983), pp. 43–51. See also Erin Anderson and Richard L. Oliver, "Perspectives on Behavior-Based versus Outcome-Based Salesforce Control Systems," *Journal of Marketing* (October 1987), pp. 76–88; and Daniel A. Sauers, James B. Hunt, and Ken Bass, "Behavioral Self-Management as a Supplement to External Sales Force Controls," *Journal of Personal Selling & Sales Management* (Summer 1990), pp. 17–28.

39 Jerry McAdams, "Rewarding Sales and Marketing Performance," *Management Review* (April 1987), pp. 33–38. See also Gilbert A. Churchill, Jr., Neil M. Ford, Steven W. Hartley, and Orville C. Walker, Jr., "The Determinants of Salesperson Performance: A Meta-Analysis," *Journal of Marketing Research* (May 1985), pp. 103–18.

CHAPTER 20

1 "Euro Ventures on the Way," *Advertising Age* (December 4, 1989), pp. 1, 52; and Josephine Marcotty, "General Mills, Nestlé Strike a Deal," *Minneapolis Star Tribune* (December 1, 1989), pp. 1D, 2D.

2 *General Mills: 1989 Annual Report,* p. 2; and *General Mills Review* (First Quarter, 1991), pp. 6, 13.

3 David A. Aaker, "Managing Assets and Skills: The Key to a Sustainable Competitive Advantage," *California Management Review* (Winter 1989), pp. 91–106; David W. Cravens, "Gaining Strategic Marketing Advantage," *Business Horizons* (September–October 1988), pp. 44–54; David W. Cravens and Shannon H. Shipp, "Market-Driven Strategies for Competitive Advantage," *Business Horizons* (January–February 1991), pp. 53–61; Victor J. Cook, Jr., "Marketing Strategy and Differential Advantage," *Journal of Marketing* (Spring 1983), pp. 68–75; Pankaj Ghemawat, "Sustainable Advantage," *Harvard Business Review* (September–October 1986), pp. 53–58; and Michael E. Porter, *Competitive Advantage* (New York: Free Press, 1985).

4 *General Mills Review* (First Quarter, 1988) pp. 4–15.

5 Ronald Henkoff, "How to Plan for 1995," *Fortune* (December 31, 1990), pp. 70–79.

6 Robert Johnson, "General Mills Risks Millions Starting Chain of Italian Restaurants," *The Wall Street Journal* (September 21, 1987), pp. 1, 15.

7 Stanley F. Stasch and Patricia Langtree, "Can Your Marketing Planning Procedures Be Improved?" *Journal of Marketing* (Summer 1980), pp. 79–90; and David S. Hopkins, *The Marketing Plan* (New York: The Conference Board, 1981), p. 24.

8 Hopkins, p. 24.

9 William E. Fulmer and Jack Goodwin, "Differentiation: Begin with the Consumer," *Business Horizons* (September–October 1988), pp. 55–63; Michael E. Porter, *Competitive Strategies: Techniques for Analyzing Industries and Competitors* (New York: Free Press, 1980); George S. Day, *Strategic Market Planning* (St. Paul: West Publishing Company, 1984), pp. 102–28; and William K. Hall, "Survival Strategies in a

Hostile Environment," *Harvard Business Review* (September–October 1980), pp. 75–85.

10 Brian Dumaine, "P&G Rewrites the Marketing Rules," *Fortune* (November 6, 1989), pp. 35–48.

11 Joseph Weber, "Why Hershey Is Smacking Its Lips," *Business Week* (October 30, 1989), p. 140; "Hershey: A Hefty Ad Budget Has Profits Flying High," *Business Week* (February 13, 1984), p. 88; and Michael E. Porter, "How to Attack the Industry Leader," *Fortune* (April 29, 1985), pp. 153–66.

12 Stewart Toy, Mark Maremont, and Ronald Grover, "An American in Paris," *Business Week* (March 12, 1990), pp. 60–64.

13 Stratford P. Sherman, "How Philip Morris Diversified Right," *Fortune* (October 23, 1989), pp. 120–30.

14 Bill Saporito, "Companies That Compete Best," *Fortune* (May 22, 1989), pp. 36–44.

15 James E. Ellis, "Will the Carrot and Stick Work at United?" *Business Week* (February 6, 1989), pp. 56–57.

16 "Culture Shock at Xerox," *Business Week* (June 22, 1987), pp. 106–10; and Maggie McComas, "Cutting Costs without Killing the Business," *Fortune* (October 13, 1986), pp. 70–78.

17 Philip Kotler, *Marketing Management,* 6th ed. (Englewood Cliffs, N.J.: Prentice Hall, 1988), pp. 38–40.

18 Roger A. Kerin, Vijay Mahajan, and P. Rajan Varadarajan, *Contemporary Perspectives on Strategic Market Planning* (Boston: Allyn & Bacon, 1990), p. 52.

19 George S. Day, "Diagnosing the Product Portfolio," *Journal of Marketing* (April 1977), pp. 29–38.

20 Lois Therrien, "The Rival Japan Respects," *Business Week* (November 13, 1989), pp. 108–18.

21 Gregory Stricharchuk, "Westinghouse Relies on Ruthlessly Rational Pruning," *The Wall Street Journal* (January 24, 1990), p. A6.

22 Strengths and weaknesses of the BCG technique are based largely on Derek F. Abell and John S. Hammond, *Strategic Market Planning: Problem and Analytic Approaches* (Englewood Cliffs, N.J.: Prentice Hall, 1979); and Yoram Wind, Vijay Mahajan and Donald Swire, "An Empirical Comparison of Standardized Portfolio Models," *Journal of Marketing* (Spring 1983), pp. 89–99.

23 Robert D. Buzzell, Bradley T. Gale, and Ralph G. M. Sultan, "Market Share—A Key to Profitability," *Harvard Business Review* (January–February 1975), pp. 97–106; Carolyn Y. Woo and Arnold C. Cooper, "The Surprising Case for Low Market Share," *Harvard Business Review* (November–December 1982), pp. 106–13; and Robert Jacobson and David A. Aaker, "Is Market Share All That It's Cracked Up to Be?" *Journal of Marketing* (Fall 1985), pp. 11–22.

24 Derek F. Abell, *Defining the Business: The Starting Point of Strategic Planning* (Englewood Cliffs, N.J.: Prentice Hall, 1980), Chapter 8.

25 Regis McKenna, "Marketing in an Age of Diversity," *Harvard Business Review* (September–October 1988), pp. 88–95.

26 Michael G. Harvey and Roger A. Kerin, "Diagnosis and Management of the Product Cannibalism Syndrome," *University of Michigan Business Review* (November 1979), pp. 18–24.

27 Thomas J. Peters and Robert H. Waterman, Jr., *In Search of Excellence: Lessons from America's Best-Run Companies* (New York: Harper & Row, 1982); and Michael E. Porter, "From Competitive Advantage to Corporate Strategy," *Harvard Business Review* (May–June 1987), pp. 43–59.

28 Gary E. Willard and Arun M. Savara, "Patterns of Entry: Pathways to New Markets," *California Management Review* (Winter 1988), pp. 57–76; Fahri Karakaya and Michael J. Stahl, "Barriers to Entry and Market Entry Decisions in Consumer and Industrial Goods Markets," *Journal of Marketing* (April 1989), pp. 80–91; and George S. Yip, "Gateways to Entry," *Harvard Business Review* (September–October 1980), pp. 85–92.

29 Mary Anne Raymond and Hiram C. Barksdale, "Corporate Strategic Planning and Corporate Marketing: Toward an Interface?" *Business Horizons* (September–October 1989), pp. 41–48; Walter Kiechel III, "Corporate Strategy for the 1990s," *Fortune* (February 29, 1988), pp. 34–42; Enrique R. Arzac, "Do Your Business Units Create Shareholder Value?" *Harvard Business Review* (January–February 1986), pp. 121–26; and Alfred Rappaport, "Selecting Strategies That Create Shareholder Value," *Harvard Business Review* (May–June 1981), pp. 139–49.

30 General Mills, "The Yogurt Market" (April 4, 1977); General Mills, "Growth through Acquisition" (1984) (company documents).

31 *General Mills: 1983 Annual Report* (August 19, 1983).

CHAPTER 21

1 J. A. Dunnigan, "Hard Work, Hot Delivery Put Domino's on the Map," *Entrepreneur* (April 1985), pp. 52–55.

2 Much of the Domino's Pizza material is taken from Bernie Whalen, " 'People-Oriented' Marketing Delivers a Lot of Dough for Domino's," *Marketing News* (March 15, 1984), pp. 4ff; by permission of the American Marketing Association.

3 Kevin T. Hoggins, "Home Delivery Is Helping Pizza to Battle Burgers," *Marketing News* (August 1, 1986), pp. 1, 6; and "A Saucy Fight for a Slice of the Pie," *Time* (April 18, 1988), p. 60.

4 Tait Elder, "New Ventures: Lessons from Xerox and IBM," *Harvard Business Review* (July–August 1989), pp. 146–54.

5 Thomas V. Bonoma, "Making Your Marketing Strategy Work," *Harvard Business Review* (March–April 1984), pp. 69–76.

6 John Meehan, Jon Friedman, and Leah J. Nathans, "The Failed Vision," *Business Week* (March 19, 1990), pp. 108–13.

7 Zachary Schiller, "After a Year of Spinning Its Wheels, Goodyear Gets a Retread," *Business Week* (March 26, 1990), pp. 56, 58.

8 "Jack Welch, How Good a Manager?" *Business Week* (December 14, 1987), p. 95.

9 Thomas V. Bonoma and Victoria L. Crittenden, "Managing Marketing Implementation," *Sloan Management Review* (Winter 1988), pp. 7–14.

10 Paul S. Alder, Henry E. Riggs, and Steven C. Wheelwright, "Product Development Know-How: Trading Tactics for Strategy," *Sloan Management Review* (Fall 1989), pp. 7–17.

11 Thomas J. Peters and Robert H. Waterman, Jr., *In Search of Excellence: Lessons from America's Best-Run Companies* (New York: Harper & Row, 1982).

12 Roy J. Harris, Jr., "The Skunk Works: Hush-Hush Projects Often Emerge There," *The Wall Street Journal* (October 13,

1980), p. 1; and Tom Peters, "Winners Do Hundreds of Percent over Norm," *Minneapolis Star and Tribune* (January 8, 1985), p. 5B.

13 James Treece, "Here Comes GM's Saturn," *Business Week* (April 9, 1990), pp. 56–62; S. C. Gwynne, "The Right Stuff," *Time* (October 29, 1990), pp. 74–84; and James B. Treece, "War, Recession, Gas Hikes . . . GM's Turnaround Will Have to Wait," *Business Week* (February 4, 1991), pp. 94–96.

14 The scheduling example is adapted from William Rudelius and W. Bruce Erickson, *An Introduction to Contemporary Business,* 4th ed. (New York: Harcourt Brace Jovanovich, 1985), pp. 94–95.

15 Brian Dumaine, "P&G Rewrites the Marketing Rules," *Fortune* (November 6, 1989), pp. 34–48; and Kevin T. Higgins, "Category Management," *Marketing News* (September 25, 1989), pp. 2, 19.

16 Philip Kotler, *Marketing Management,* 6th ed. (Englewood Cliffs, N.J.: Prentice Hall, 1988), p. 709.

17 Robert W. Ruekert and Orville W. Walker, Jr., "Marketing's Interaction with Other Functional Units: A Conceptual Framework and Empirical Evidence," *Journal of Marketing* (January 1987), pp. 1–19.

18 Steven Lysonski, Alan Singer, and David Wilemone, "Coping with Environmental Uncertainty and Boundary Spanning in the Product Manager's Role," *Journal of Consumer Marketing* (Spring 1989), pp. 33–43.

19 John A. Quelch, Paul W. Farris, and James Olver, "The Product Management Audit: Design and Survey Findings," *The Journal of Consumer Marketing* (Summer 1987), pp. 45–58.

20 Robert S. Eckley, "Caterpillar's Ordeal: Foreign Competition in Capital Goods," *Business Horizons* (March–April 1989), pp. 80–86.

21 Brian O'Reilly, "Apple Computer's Risky Revolution," *Fortune* (May 8, 1989), pp. 75–83; Barbara Buell, "Apple's New Motto: Just Wait till Next Year," *Business Week* (July 16, 1990), p. 158; and Barbara Buell, Jonathan B. Levine, and Neil Gross, "Apple: New Team, New Strategy," *Business Week* (October 15, 1990), pp. 86–96.

22 "Power Retailers," *Business Week* (December 21, 1987), pp. 86–92.

23 Thomas V. Bonoma, "Marketing Performance—What Do You Expect," *Harvard Business Review* (September–October 1989), pp. 44–48.

24 "A Kick in the Pants for Levi's," *Business Week* (June 11, 1984), p. 47; and "How Levi Strauss Is Getting the Lead Out of Its Pipeline," *Business Week* (December 21, 1987), p. 92.

25 John Grossman, "Ken Iverson: Simply the Best," *American Way* (August 1, 1987), pp. 23–25; Thomas Moore, "Goodbye, Corporate Staff," *Fortune* (December 21, 1987), pp. 65–76; and Michael Schroeder and Walecia Konrad, "Nucor: Rolling Right into Steel's Big Time," *Business Week* (November 19, 1990), pp. 76–81.

26 Stanley J. Shapiro and V. H. Kirpalani, *Marketing Effectiveness: Insights from Accounting and Finance* (Boston: Allyn & Bacon, 1984); Leland L. Biek and Stephen L. Busby, "Profitability Analysis by Market Segments," *Journal of Marketing* (July 1973), pp. 48–53; V. H. Kirpalani and Stanley J. Shapiro, "Financial Dimensions of Marketing Management," *Journal of Marketing* (July 1973), pp. 40–47; and Paul Fischer and W. J. E. Crissy, "New Approaches to Analyzing Marketing Profitability," *Journal of Marketing* (April 1974), pp. 43–48.

27 Debbie Berlant, Reese Browning, and George Foster, "How Hewlett-Packard Gets Numbers It Can Trust," *Harvard Business Review* (January–February 1990), pp. 178–83.

28 G. David Hughes, "Computerized Sales Management," *Harvard Business Review* (March–April 1983), pp. 102–12.

29 Philip Kotler, William Gregor, and William Rogers, "The Marketing Audit Comes of Age," *Sloan Management Review* (Winter 1977), pp. 25–43.

30 General Mills, "The Yogurt Market" (April 4, 1977); General Mills, "Growth through Acquisition" (1984); General Mills, *Review* (Third Quarter, 1987); General Mills, *1986 Annual Report* (1986); and General Mills, *1987 Annual Report* (1987).

31 Neal St. Anthony, "General Mills Rebounds," *Minneapolis Star and Tribune* (October 19, 1987), pp. 1M, 11M.

CHAPTER 22

1 Joann S. Lublin, "U.S. Food Firms Find Europe's Huge Market Hardly a Piece of Cake," *The Wall Street Journal* (May 15, 1990), pp. A1, A20; "Let Them Eat Wheaties," *Fortune* (January 1, 1990), p. 14; and Philip Revzin, "While Americans Take to Croissants, Kellogg Pushes Cornflakes on France," *The Wall Street Journal* (November 11, 1986), p. 36.

2 *General Agreement on Tariffs and Trade: What It Is, What It Does* (Geneva, Switzerland: GATT Information and Media Relations Division, 1990), pp. 1–3; "Trading Talk, Not Goods," *U.S. News and World Report* (December 17, 1990), p. 35; and "GATT's Gordian Knot Proves Difficult to Cut," *The Wall Street Journal* (October 8, 1990), p. A1.

3 Kenichi Ohmae, "Planting for a Global Harvest," *Harvard Business Review* (July–August 1989), pp. 136–45.

4 Jeremy Main, "How to Go Global—and Why," *Fortune* (August 28, 1989), pp. 70–76; and Christopher A. Bartlett and Sumantra Ghoshal, *Managing Across Borders: The Transnational Solution* (Boston: Harvard Business School Press, 1989), pp. 73–134.

5 Michael E. Porter, *The Competitive Advantage of Nations* (New York: Free Press, 1990), pp. 577–615; and Michael E. Porter, "Why Nations Triumph," *Fortune* (March 12, 1990), pp. 94–108.

6 Edward P. Johnson, "U.S. Firms Can Benefit from European Contacts," *Photo Marketing* (March 1987), p. 60.

7 Theodore Levitt, "The Globalization of Markets," *Harvard Business Review* (May–June 1983), pp. 92–102; and Theodore Levitt, "The Pluralization of Consumption," *Harvard Business Review* (May–June 1988), pp. 7–8.

8 Joanne Lipman, "Marketers Turn Sour on Global Sales Pitch Harvard Guru Makes," *The Wall Street Journal* (May 12, 1988), pp. 1, 10.

9 Lipman, pp. 1, 10.

10 "Moscow's Big Mak Attack," *Time* (February 5, 1990), p. 51; and Scott Hume, "How Big Mac Made It to Moscow," *Advertising Age* (January 22, 1990), pp. 16, 51.

11 S. Tamer Cavusgil, "Guidelines for Export Market Research," *Business Horizons* (November–December 1985), pp. 27–33.

12 Abel Aganbegyan, *Inside Perestroika: The Future of the Soviet Economy* (New York: Harper & Row, 1990), p. 229.

13 John F. Magee, "1992: Moves Americans Must Make," *Harvard Business Review* (May–June 1989), pp. 78–84; Eric G. Friberg, "1992: Moves Europeans Are Making," *Harvard Business Review* (May–June 1989), pp. 85–89; and John A. Quelch, Robert D. Buzzell, and Eric R. Salama, *The Marketing Challenge of 1992* (Reading, Mass.: Addison-Wesley, 1990), pp. 3–85.

14 "One Big European Economy Seems Less Like a Dream," *Business Week* (November 13, 1989), pp. 43–46.

15 Barry Newman, "Poles Find the Freeing of the Economy Lifts Supplies—and Prices," *The Wall Street Journal* (February 20, 1990), pp. A1, A10.

16 Louis Kraar, "North America's New Trade Punch," *Fortune* (May 22, 1989), pp. 123–27; "Mexico: A New Economic Era," *Business Week* (November 12, 1990), pp. 102–13; and "Turning the Hemisphere into a Free-Trade Bloc," *Business Week* (December 24, 1990), p. 37.

17 "Give Us Our Daily Bread," *Time* (December 3, 1990), p. 75.

18 "Puppies and Consumer Boomers," *Time* (November 13, 1989), pp. 53–56.

19 "McWorld," *Business Week* (October 13, 1986), pp. 78–86; and Frederick Katayama, "Japan's Big Mac," *Fortune* (September 15, 1986), pp. 114–20.

20 Michael R. Sesit, "Avoiding Losses," *The Wall Street Journal* (March 5, 1984), pp. 1, 24.

21 Walter S. Mossberg, "As EC Markets Unite, U.S. Exporters Face New Trade Barriers," *The Wall Street Journal* (January 19, 1989), pp. A1, A4.

22 Lee Smith, "What's At Stake in the Trade Talks," *Fortune* (August 27, 1990), pp. 76–77; and Shawn Tully, "Is GATT Dead?" *Fortune* (January 14, 1991), p. 16.

23 Laurel Wentz, "M&M Continues Global Roll," *Advertising Age* (September 14, 1987), p. 90.

24 Louis Kraar, "Meet 25 People You Ought to Know," *Fortune* (Pacific Rim 1989), p. 108; and Susan Feyder, "In 3M's Eyes, All the World's a Market," *Star Tribune* (April 16, 1990), pp. 1D, 7D.

25 Jeremy Main, "How 21 Men Got Global in 35 Days," *Fortune* (November 6, 1989), pp. 71–77.

26 John Marcom, Jr., "British Industry Suffers from Failure to Heed Basics of Marketing," *The Wall Street Journal* (January 14, 1987), pp. 1, 12; and Thomas F. O'Boyle, "German Firms Stress Top Quality, Niches to Keep Exports High," *The Wall Street Journal* (December 10, 1987), pp. 1, 15; and Louis S. Richman, "Lessons from German Managers," *Fortune* (April 27, 1987), pp. 267–68.

27 "The Swedes Give AT&T, and the U.S., Painful Black Eyes," *Business Week* (May 4, 1987), pp. 44–45.

28 Carla Rapoport, "Seasoning for the World's Palate," *Boston Sunday Globe* (October 21, 1984), pp. A9–A10.

29 Joel Dreyfuss, "How to Beat the Japanese at Home," *Fortune* (August 31, 1987), pp. 80–83.

30 Joseph R. Carter and James Gagne, "The Do's and Don'ts of International Countertrade," *Sloan Management Review* (Spring 1988), pp. 31–37.

31 "Let Them Eat Wheaties," *Fortune* (January 1, 1990), p. 14; and John Sterlicchi and Charlotte Klopp, "Europe Faces Invasion by U.S. Cereal Makers," *Marketing News* (June 11, 1990), pp. 2, 4.

32 "Can Uncle Sam Mend This Hole in His Pocket?" *Business Week* (September 10, 1990), pp. 48–49.

CHAPTER 23

1 Barbara Rudolf, "Monsieur Mickey," *Time* (March 25, 1991), pp. 48–49; Christopher Knowlton, "How Disney Keeps the Magic Going," *Fortune* (December 4, 1989), pp. 111–32; Stewart Toy, Mark Maremont, and Ronald Grover, "An American in Paris," *Business Week* (March 12, 1990), pp. 60–64; Richard Corliss, "You're under Arrest," *Time* (May 8, 1989), pp. 102–3; "Do You Believe in Magic?" *Time* (April 25, 1988), pp. 66–76; and "Disney's Magic," *Business Week* (March 9, 1987), pp. 62–69.

2 *Statistical Abstract of the United States,* 109th Edition, (Washington, D.C.: U.S. Department of Commerce, 1989); *Survey of Current Business* (Washington, D.C.: U.S. Department of Commerce, July 1990); James L. Hesket, "Thank Heaven for the Service Sector," *Business Week* (January 26, 1987), p. 22; and "U.S. Balance of Payments," *Business America,* (March 1991), p. 25.

3 "Presto! The Convenience Industry: Making Life a Little Simpler," *Business Week* (April 27, 1987), pp. 86–94.

4 Cyndee Miller, "An Oasis for Hip Consumers," *Marketing News* (February 19, 1990), p. 2.

5 Leonard Berry, "Big Ideas in Services Marketing," *Journal of Consumer Marketing,* vol. 3 (Spring 1986), pp. 47–51.

6 Frederick F. Reichheld and W. Earl Sasser, Jr., "Zero Defections: Quality Comes to Services," *Harvard Business Review* (September–October 1990), pp. 105–11; "Standardized Services Run Gamut from Mufflers to Wills," *Marketing News,* vol. 21 (April 10, 1987), pp. 17, 43; and Valerie A. Zeithaml, Leonard L. Berry, and A. Parasuraman, "Communication and Control in the Delivery of Service Quality," *Journal of Marketing* (April 1988), pp. 35–48.

7 Howard Schlossberg, "Electric Utilities Finally Discover Marketing," *Marketing News* (November 20, 1989), pp. 1, 2.

8 Keith B. Murray, "A Test of Services Marketing Theory: Consumer Information Acquisition Activities," *Journal of Marketing* (January 1991), pp. 10–25.

9 Valarie A. Zeithaml, "How Consumer Evaluation Processes Differ between Goods and Services," in James H. Donnelly and William R. George, eds., *Marketing of Services* (Chicago: American Marketing Association, 1981).

10 Valarie A. Zeithaml, A. Parasuraman, and Leonard L. Berry, *Delivering Quality Service* (New York: Free Press, 1990); Zeithaml, Berry, and Parasuraman, "Communication and Control Processes," pp. 35–48 (see note 6); and Stephen W. Brown and Teresa Swartz, "A Gap Analysis of Professional Service Quality," *Journal of Marketing* (April 1989), pp. 92–98.

11 "Burger King Opens Customer Hot Line," *Marketing News* (May 28, 1990), p. 7.

12 Mary Jo Bitner, Bernard H. Booms, and Mary Stanfield Tetreault, "The Service Encounter: Diagnosing Favorable and Unfavorable Incidents," *Journal of Marketing* (January 1990), pp. 71–84; Eberhard Scheuing, "Conducting Customer Service Audits," *Journal of Consumer Marketing* (Summer 1989), pp. 35–41; and W. Earl Sasser, R. Paul Olsen, and D. Daryl Wyckoff, *Management of Service Operations* (Boston: Allyn & Bacon, 1978).

13 "Services Marketers Must Balance Customer Satisfaction against Their Operational Needs," *Marketing News,* vol. 20 (October 10, 1986), pp. 1, 14.

14 Patriya Tansuhaj, Donna Randall, and Jim McCullough, "A Services Marketing Management Model: Integrating Internal and External Marketing Functions," *Journal of Services Marketing,* vol. 2 (Winter 1988), pp. 31–38.

15 Christian Gronroos, "Internal Marketing Theory and Practice," in Tim Bloch, G. D. Upah, and V. A. Zeithaml, eds., *Services Marketing in a Changing Environment* (Chicago: American Marketing Association, 1984).

16 Gronroos (see note 15).

17 Sybil F. Stershic, "Internal Marketing Campaign Reinforces Service Goals," *Marketing News* (July 31, 1989), p. 11; James L. Heskett, "Lessons in the Service Sector," *Harvard Business Review* (March/April 1987), pp. 118–26; Leonard Berry, "Big Ideas in Services Marketing," *Journal of Consumer Marketing,* vol. 3 (Spring 1986), pp. 47–51; and Ray Lewis, "Whose Job Is Service Marketing?" *Advertising Age* (August 3, 1987), pp. 18, 20.

18 Dan R. E. Thomas, "Strategy Is Different in Service Businesses," *Harvard Business Review* (July–August 1978), pp. 158–65.

19 Leonard L. Berry, Edwin F. Lefkowith, and Terry Clark, "In Services, What's in a Name?" *Harvard Business Review* (September–October 1988), pp. 28–30.

20 Christopher Lovelock, *Services Marketing* (Englewood Cliffs, N.J.: Prentice Hall, 1991), pp. 122–27.

21 Kent B. Monroe, "Buyer's Subjective Perceptions of Price," *Journal of Marketing Research* (February 1973), pp. 70–80; Jerry Olson, "Price as an Informational Cue: Effects on Product Evaluation," in A. G. Woodside, J. N. Sheth, and P. D. Bennett, eds., *Consumer and Industrial Buying Behavior* (New York: Elsevier North-Holland, 1977), pp. 267–86.

22 B. D. Colen, "Hospitals Turn to Advertising," *Washington Post* (June 25, 1979), pp. 1, 6A.

23 Robert E. Hite, Cynthia Fraser, and Joseph A. Bellizzi, "Professional Service Advertising: The Effects of Price Inclusion, Justification, and Level of Risk," *Journal of Advertising Research,* 30 (August/September 1990), pp. 23–31; William R. George and Leonard L. Berry, "Guidelines for the Advertising of Services," *Business Horizons* (July–August 1981), pp. 52–56; and Eugene M. Johnson, Eberhard E. Scheuing, and Kathleen A. Gaida, *Profitable Service Marketing* (Homewood, Ill.: Dow Jones-Irwin, 1986).

24 Sak Onkvist and John J. Shaw, "Service Marketing: Image, Branding, and Competition," *Business Horizons* (January–February 1989), pp. 13–18.

25 William A. Mindak and Seymour Fine, "A Fifth P: Public Relations," in James H. Donnelly and William R. George, eds., *Marketing of Services* (Chicago: American Marketing Association, 1981), pp. 71–73.

26 Joe Adams, "Why Public Service Advertising Doesn't Work," *Ad Week* (November 17, 1980), p. 72.

27 *Bates and O'Sheen* v. *State of Arizona,* 433 U.S. 350, 391–395 (1977); "Supreme Court Opens Way for Lawyers to Advertise Prices for Routine Services," *The Wall Street Journal* (June 28, 1977), p. 4.

28 James L. Heskett, *Managing in the Service Economy* (Boston: Harvard Business School Press, 1986), pp. 153–73; and James Brian Quinn and Christopher E. Gagnon, "Will Ser-

vices Follow Manufacturing into Decline?" *Harvard Business Review,* vol. 64 (November–December 1986), pp. 95–105.

29 James Brian Quinn and Penny C. Paquette, "Technology in Services: Creating Organizational Revolutions," *Sloan Management Review* (Winter 1990), pp. 67–78.

30 Anne B. Fisher, "What Consumers Want in the 1990s," *Fortune* (January 29, 1990), pp. 108–12.

APPENDIX B

1 Amy J. Goldstein and Donna Lee Healy, eds., *Peterson's Business and Management Jobs 1990* (Princeton, N.J.: Peterson's Guides, 1990), pp. 49–50; and *CPC Annual: A Guide to Employment Opportunities for College Graduates,* 34th ed. (Bethlehem, Penn.: College Placement Council, Inc., 1990), pp. 208–09.

2 Nicholas Basta, "The Wide World of Marketing," *Business Week's Guide to Careers* (February–March 1984), pp. 70–72.

3 Maggie McComas, "Atop the Fortune 500: A Survey of the C.E.O.'s," *Fortune* (April 28, 1986), pp. 26–31.

4 L. Patrick Scheetz, *Recruiting Trends 1990–91* (East Lansing, Mich.: Michigan State University, 1990), p. 23.

5 Steven S. Ross, "Entry-Level Jobs with a Future," *Business Week's Guide to Careers* (February–March 1984), pp. 35–37, 78.

6 Sandy Gillis, "On the Job: Product Manager," *Business Week's Guide to Careers* (April–May 1988), pp. 63–66; and Richard Koenig, "P&G Creates New Posts in Latest Step to Alter How Firm Manages Its Brands," *The Wall Street Journal* (October 12, 1987), p. 23.

7 Phil Moss, "What It's Like to Work for Procter & Gamble," *Business Week's Guide to Careers* (March–April 1987), pp. 18–20.

8 David Kirkpatrick, "Is Your Career on Track?" *Fortune* (July 2, 1990), pp. 38–48.

9 Janine Linden, "The Exciting World of Advertising," *Business Week's Guide to Careers* (Spring/Summer 1984), pp. 33–34, 36.

10 Vincent Daddiego, "Making It in Advertising," in Robert H. Luke, *Business Careers* (Boston: Houghton Mifflin, 1989), pp. 189–91.

11 Milan Moravec, Marshall Collins, and Clinton Tripoli, "Don't Want to Manage? Here's Another Path," *Sales and Marketing Management* (April 1990), pp. 70–76.

12 William Keenan, Jr., "America's Best Sales Forces: Six at the Summit," *Sales and Marketing Management* (June 1990), pp. 62–72.

13 Judith George, "Market Researcher," *Business Week's Guide to Careers* (October 1987), p. 10.

14 Joby John and Mark Needel, "Entry-Level Marketing Research Recruits: What Do Recruiters Need?" *Journal of Marketing Education* (Spring 1989), pp. 68–73.

15 Hugh E. Kramer, "Applying Marketing Strategy and Personal Value Analysis to Career Planning: An Experiential Approach," *Journal of Marketing Education* (Fall 1988), pp. 69–73.

16 Ronald B. Marks, *Personal Selling* (Boston: Allyn & Bacon, 1985), pp. 451–52; and Alan Deutschman, "What 25-Year-Olds Want," *Fortune* (August 27, 1990), pp. 42–50.

17 Arthur F. Miller, "Discover Your Design," in *1984–1985 CPC Annual,* vol. 1 (Bethlehem, Penn.: College Placement Council, Inc., 1984), p. 2.

18 For an alternative approach to conducting a self-analysis, see Miller, pp. 2–8.

19 Marks, pp. 461–62.

20 John L. Munschauer, "How to Find a Customer for Your Capabilities," in *1984–1985 CPC Annual,* vol. 1 (Bethlehem, Penn.: College Placement Council, Inc., 1984), p. 24.

21 C. Randall Powell, "Secrets of Selling a Resume," in Peggy Schmidt, ed., *The Honda How to Get a Job Guide* (New York: McGraw-Hill, 1985), pp. 4–9.

22 Powell, p. 4.

23 Perri Capell, "Unconventional Job Search Tactics," *Managing Your Career: The College Edition of the National Business Employment Weekly* (Spring 1991), pp. 31, 35.

24 Julie Griffin Levitt, *Your Career: How to Make It Happen* (Cincinnati: South-Western Publishing Co., 1985).

25 Marks, p. 469.

26 Terence P. Pare, "The Uncommitted Class of 1989," *Fortune* (June 5, 1989), pp. 199–210.

27 Bob Weinstein, "What Employers Look For," in Peggy Schmidt, ed., *The Honda How to Get a Job Guide* (New York: McGraw-Hill, 1985), p. 10.

Author Index

Company/Product Index

Subject Index

Credits

CHAPTER 1

pg. 4, Courtesy of Golden Valley Microwave Foods, Inc.; pg. 9, Courtesy of Xerox Corporation; pg. 12, Photography by Sharon Hoogstraten; pg. 13, RCA SelectaVision player, Courtesy of Thomson Consumer Electronics, Inc., for RCA; pg. 16, Red Lobster restaurant; Courtesy of Red Lobster; SAS 767, Courtesy of SAS® Scandinavian Airlines; Toyota Lexus, Courtesy of Toyota Motor Sales, U.S.A., Inc.; pg. 20, Courtesy of Golden Valley Microwave Foods, Inc.; pg. 25, Courtesy of The Cleveland Clinic Foundation.

CHAPTER 2

pg. 30, Courtesy of International Business Machines; pg. 34, Courtesy of Prodigy; pg. 35, Photography by Sharon Hoogstraten; pg. 37, Courtesy of The Media Services Group, for GE Plastics; pg. 43, Photography by Sharon Hoogstraten; pg. 45, Courtesy of The Coca-Cola Company. Fresca, Cherry Coke, and PowerAde are trademarks of The Coca-Cola Company; pg. 49, Courtesy of Lintas:New York, for International Business Machines Corporation, Photography by David Langley; pg. 53, Reprinted Courtesy of Eastman Kodak Company.

CHAPTER 3

pg. 56, Photography by Sharon Hoogstraten; pg. 58, Reprinted by permission of UFS, Inc.; pg. 64, Courtesy of John Hancock Mutual Life Insurance Company; pg. 65, Photography by Sharon Hoogstraten; pg. 66, Courtesy of Consumers United Insurance Company; pg. 67, Photography by Greg Wolff; pg. 70, Courtesy of Hyatt Hotels Corporation; pg. 71, Courtesy of Consumers Digest; pg. 72, Courtesy of Tactics

International Limited; pg. 73, Ken Kerbs/DOT, Incorporated; Courtesy GARBAGE Magazine, May/June 1991, Brooklyn, New York; pg. 74, Photography by Sharon Hoogstraten; pg. 75, Photography by Greg Wolff; pg. 80, Photography by Ray Marklin; pg. 83, Photography by Sharon Hoogstraten.

CHAPTER 4

pg. 88, Courtesy of Fleishman Hillard Inc., for Anheuser-Busch Companies, Inc., Photography by Associated Press, pg. 92, Photography by Sharon Hoogstraten; pg. 93, Wide World Photos; pg. 96, Tom & Michelle Brimm/Tony Stone Worldwide; pg. 100, Photography by Sharon Hoogstraten; pg. 102, Photography by Sharon Hoogstraten; pg. 102, Courtesy of StarKist Seafood Company; pg. 103, Neil Leifer/Time Magazine; pg. 104, Bruce McAllister/Stock Imagery Inc.

CHAPTER 5

pg. 110, Courtesy of VideOcart, Inc.; pg. 120, Michelin Tires, used with permission of Michelin Tire Corporation. All rights reserved; pg. 121, Photography by Sharon Hoogstraten; pg. 122, Good Housekeeping Seal reprinted by permission of the Hearst Corporation, publishers of Good Housekeeping; Passion Perfume counter, Courtesy of Dillard Department Stores, Inc., Photography by Greg Wolff; Duncan Hines Free Trial, Courtesy of The Procter & Gamble Company; Clairol Hair Color, Photography by Voyles; pg. 124, Photography by Ray Marklin; pg. 128, Photography by Sharon Hoogstraten; pg. 135, Brochures, Courtesy of Pacific Bell.

CHAPTER 6

pg. 138, Robert Kristofik/The Image Bank; pg. 142, Courtesy of Domtar

Gypsum; pg. 145, Courtesy of Weyerhaeuser; pg. 146, Courtesy of GTE Products Corporation; pg. 149, Courtesy of Honeywell; pg. 155, Reprinted by Permission of Texas Instruments; pg. 157, Science Source/Photo Researchers, Inc.; pg. 161, Courtesy of The NutraSweet Company.

CHAPTER 7

pg. 166, Courtesy Twentieth Century Fox; pg. 169, Photography by Voyles; pg. 171, Courtesy of Fisher-Price, Division of the Quaker Oats Company; pg. 174, Photography by Ray Marklin; pg. 176, Photography by Sharon Hoogstraten; pg. 177, Photography by Sharon Hoogstraten; pg. 179, Courtesy of Nielsen Media Research; pg. 187, Photography by Sharon Hoogstraten; pg. 190, Reprinted by permission: Tribune Media Services; pg. 190, Courtesy of The Coca-Cola Company.

CHAPTER 8

pg. 194, Reprinted by permission of Reebok International Ltd.; pg. 196, Reprinted by permission of Reebok International Ltd.; pg. 199, Courtesy of Conde Nast; pg. 202, Great Starts Breakfast, Photography by Ray Marklin; Courtesy of MicroFridge, Inc.; pg. 206, Courtesy of Xerox Corporation; pg. 209, Photography by Ray Marklin; pg. 210, Photography by Ray Marklin; pg. 213, Courtesy of Apple Computer, Inc.; pg. 217, Courtesy of Volvo Cars of North America.

CHAPTER 9

pg. 222, Mel DiGiacomo/The Image Bank; pg. 226, Courtesy of American Airlines; pg. 231, Courtesy of Arbitron; pg. 232, Computer notepad photography by David Walberg; printer photography by Steven Pumphrey;

pg. 234, Courtesy of Safeway, Inc.; pg. 238, Courtesy of Advanced Promotion Technologies; pg. 241, Photography by Ray Marklin.

CHAPTER 10

pg. 252, Courtesy of The Gillette Company; pg. 255, Courtesy of Adidas U.S.A.; pg. 257, Courtesy of Geers Gross Advertising, Inc., for G. H. Bass & Company; pg. 258, Courtesy of Wedgwood U.S.A., Inc.; pg. 261, Courtesy of Canon U.S.A., Inc.; pg. 260, Photography by Ray Marklin; pg. 262, Photography by Sharon Hoogstraten; pg. 264, Photography by Sharon Hoogstraten; pg. 267, Photography by Sharon Hoogstraten; pg. 267, Photography by Sharon Hoogstraten; pg. 269, Reprinted by Permission of Texas Instruments; pg. 271, Photography by Sharon Hoogstraten; pg. 273, Courtesy of The Procter & Gamble Company; pg. 276, Photography by Sharon Hoogstraten.

CHAPTER 11

pg. 282, Courtesy of NYNEX, Photography by Gregory Heisler; pg. 287, Photography by Sharon Hoogstraten; pg. 290, Epilady Hair Remover, Courtesy of EPI Products; Cuisinart® Food Preparation Center, model DLC-7M, Courtesy of Cuisinarts Corp., Stamford, CT 06902; Teenage Mutant Ninja Turtle dishware, Photography by Sharon Hoogstraten; pg. 292, Lawrence Migdale/Stock Boston; pg. 296, Photography by Sharon Hoogstraten; pg. 301, Photography by Sharon Hoogstraten; pg. 305, Photography by Ray Marklin; pg. 306, Photography by Sharon Hoogstraten.

CHAPTER 12

pg. 312, Reproduced with permission, © PepsiCo, Inc. 1988; pg. 314, Courtesy of Jaguar Cars, Inc.; pg. 318, Courtesy of MGM Grand Air; pg. 319, Courtesy of The Simplesse Company; pg. 320, Courtesy of General Motors Corporation; pg. 322, Photography by Sharon Hoogstraten; pg. 326, Snack aisle, Photography by Voyles; Vegetable aisle, Randy Matusow/Archive Pictures, Inc.

CHAPTER 13

pg. 336, Courtesy of American Airlines; pg. 340, Courtesy of Parker Brothers; pg. 341, Courtesy of Jean Patou, Inc.; pg. 343, Courtesy of Dayton's, Inc.; pg. 345, Photography by Andrew J. Thacker; pg. 351, Courtesy of Christian Dior Monsieur, a Hartmarx brand; pg. 357, Copyright © The Toro Company; pg. 358, Photography by Voyles; pg. 360, Courtesy of Fortune Magazine; pg. 362, Courtesy of Pearle Vision Centers.

CHAPTER 14

pg. 374, Reprinted with permission of Saturn Corporation; pg. 380, Tailoring, Courtesy of Boyd's Department Store, Photography by Voyles; Gas station, Owen Franken/Stock Boston; pg. 387, Photography by Voyles; pg. 389, Western Auto, Courtesy of Western Auto Supply Company; pg. 390, Courtesy of H&R Block; pg. 392, Courtesy of the Kroger Company; pg. 394, Jiffy Lube station, Photography by Sharon Hoogstraten; pg. 396, Ad, Courtesy of the Organization of Manufacturing Representatives.

CHAPTER 15

pg. 402, Marc Romanelli/The Image Bank; pg. 405, Photography by Alan D. Levenson; pg. 407, Courtesy of Wettereau, Inc.; pg. 409, Photography by Sharon Hoogstraten; pg. 413, Courtesy of Wal-Mart Stores, Inc.; pg. 416, Courtesy of Conrail Railways; pg. 418; Trucks, Hank Lebo/Jeroboam, Inc.; Pipeline, Courtesy of Alyeska; Barge, Courtesy of CSX Corporation; Ships, Chris Brown/Stock Boston; pg. 420, Courtesy of Federal Express Corporation. All rights reserved; pg. 421, Courtesy of Federal Express Corporation. All rights reserved; pg. 422, Courtesy of Wetterau, Inc., Photography by Voyles; pg. 424, Courtesy of Rapistan Corp.; pg. 426, Advertisement Courtesy of Leaseway Transportation Corporation.

CHAPTER 16

pg. 430, Courtesy of Wal-Mart Stores, Inc.; pg. 432, Illustration by Michael Bartolos; pg. 439, Reuters/Bettmann; pg. 444, Courtesy of Lands' End, Inc.; pg. 445, Courtesy of CompuServe; pg. 451, Courtesy of Mall of America; pg. 453, bijan, Courtesy of bijan; pg. 453, Quincy Market, Ulrike Welson/Stock Boston; pg. 457, Tom Tracy/The Stock Shop.

CHAPTER 17

pg. 462, Illustration by Michael Witte; pg. 465, © 1990, Alfa Romeo Distributors of North America. Used with permission; pg. 467, Courtesy of Nike; pg. 468, Reprinted with permission of Compaq Computer Corporation. All rights reserved; pg. 469, Photography by Voyles; pg. 469, Courtesy of Alberto-Culver; pg. 470, *Fence Industry* is published and copyrighted by Communications Channels, Inc., Atlanta, GA; pg. 472, Photography by Greg Wolff; pg. 475, Courtesy of International Business Machines Corporation; pg. 479, Courtesy of The Gillette Company; pg. 479, Photography by Sharon Hoogstraten; pg. 481, Gravity feed bin, Photography by Ray Marklin; pg. 482, VideOcart, Courtesy of VideOcart, Inc.; pg. 484, Courtesy of Chrysler Corporation, Chrysler/Plymouth Division; pg. 485, Courtesy Chrysler Corporation; pg. 486, James Keyser/Time.

CHAPTER 18

pg. 491, Bo Jackson, Wide World Photos; *Snoopy,* Courtesy of A&W Brands, Inc., © 1958–1965 UNITED FEATURE SYNDICATE, INC.; pg. 492, Chrysler ad, Courtesy of Bozell Inc., for Chrysler Corporation; Echelon® ad, Courtesy of Allergan; Maytag ad, Courtesy of Maytag Company; pg. 493, Courtesy of The Dial Corporation; pg. 494, Courtesy of Fleishman Hillard Inc., for Anheuser-Busch Companies, Inc.; pg. 499, Courtesy of Partnership for a Drug Free America; pg. 501, Courtesy of Goodby Berlin & Silverstein, for Kloster Cruise Ltd.; pg. 505 Courtesy of the NutraSweet Company; pg. 507, Courtesy of Ogilvy & Mather for American Express; From Rolling Stone Magazine By Straight Arrow Publishers, Inc. © 1986. All rights reserved.; pg. 509, Courtesy of Richardson and Richardson; pg. 510, Courtesy of Corning, Inc.; pg. 513, Courtesy of Starch INRA Hooper.

CHAPTER 19

pg. 516, Courtesy of International Business Machines Corporation; pg. 520, Courtesy of Remington Products; pg. 521, Courtesy of Frito-Lay, Inc.; pg. 523, Courtesy of DDB Needham Worldwide, for Xerox Corporation; pg. 526, Courtesy of

AT&T; pg. 527, Counter clerk, Courtesy of Naugles, Inc., Photography by Voyles; Door-to-door sales, Courtesy of The Fuller Brush Company; pg. 539, Courtesy of Mary Kay Cosmetics, Photography by Ted Munger.

CHAPTER 20

pg. 546, Courtesy of General Mills, Inc.; pg. 550, SURF'S UP! is a trademark of General Mills, Inc., used with permission; pg. 555, Courtesy of General Mills, Inc.; pg. 555, Courtesy of 3M; pg. 560, Courtesy of General Mills, Inc.; pg. 561, Courtesy of Black & Decker (U.S.) Inc.; pg. 567, Photography by Voyles.

CHAPTER 21

pg. 574, Courtesy of Domino's Pizza Print Program; pg. 576, Courtesy of Domino's Pizza Print Program; pg. 581, GE Jet Engine, Courtesy of General Electric Company, Photography by Alan Bergman; Airplane, Courtesy of Airbus Industrie of North America, Inc.; pg. 583, Reprinted with permission of Saturn

Corporation; pg. 587, Photography by Sharon Hoogstraten; pg. 597, Photography by Sharon Hoogstraten.

CHAPTER 22

pg. 601, Photography by Ray Marklin; pg. 604, Courtesy of Volvo Cars of North America; pg. 608, Courtesy of Mackay Envelope Corporation, Minnesota Colour Envelopes; pg. 609, Courtesy of McDonald's Corporation; pg. 617, Illustration by Leo Cullum; pg. 621, Courtesy of Ericsson North America, Inc.; pg. 622, Courtesy of Avon; pg. 624, Courtesy of The Coca-Cola Company; pg. 625, Courtesy of Skai Shinota; pg. 627, Courtesy of New Zealand Tourism Office.

CHAPTER 23

pg. 632, Joe McNally/SYGMA; pg. 636, Courtesy of Kloster Cruise Ltd.; pg. 637, Courtesy of FCB/Leber Katz Partners, © 1991 Marriott Corporation; pg. 640, Greenpeace ad, © Greenpeace; Army ad, Army photographs courtesy U.S. government, as represented by the

Secretary of the Army; pg. 645, Courtesy of The Hertz Corporation; pg. 647, Kmart logo, Kmart is a federally registered servicemark and is used with the permission of the Kmart Corporation, Troy, Michigan; McDonald's logo, Courtesy of McDonald's Corporation; AT&T logo, Courtesy of AT&T; United Way logo, Courtesy of United Way International; pg. 649, Courtesy of Whitehall and Tremont Hotels; pg. 650, Courtesy of Inter-County Leader, Frederic, WI; pg. 649, David W. Hamilton/The Image Bank; pg. 652, Courtesy of The New Haven Symphony Orchestra.

APPENDIX B

pg. 658, Reprinted by permission of the Boston Herald; pg. 660, Photography by Paul Elledge; pg. 660, Chuck Mason/Tony Stone Worldwide; pg. 661, Courtesy of Silo, Inc., pg. 662, Reprinted with permission of Compaq Computer Corporation. All rights reserved; pg. 662, Janet Gill/Tony Stone Worldwide; pg. 671, Julie Houck/Tony Stone Worldwide.